# The Most Offending Soul Alive

Tom in the mid-1970s.

# The Most Offending Soul Alive

*Tom Harrisson and His Remarkable Life*

Judith M. Heimann

A Latitude 20 Book

 University of Hawai'i Press
Honolulu

**Library of Congress Cataloging-in-Publication Data**
Heimann, Judith M.
The most offending soul alive : Tom Harrisson and
his remarkable life / by Judith M. Heimann.
p.  cm.
"A Latitude 20 book."
Includes bibliographical references and index.
ISBN 0–8248–2149–1 (cloth : alk. paper).
— ISBN 0–8248–2199–8 (paper : alk. paper)
1.  Harrisson, Tom, 1911–1976.
2.  Ethnolgists—Great Britain Biography.
3.  Ethnologists—Pacific Area Biography.
4.  Adventure and adventurers—Great Britain.
5.  Adventure and adventurers—Pacific Area.
6.  Great Britain—Social life and customs.
7.  Pacific Area—Social life and customs.    I.  Title.
GN21.H275H45    1999
305.8'0092—dc21            99–23535
[B]                              CIP

The quotation from a W. H. Auden poem in
*Letter from Iceland* (1937)
by W. H. Auden and Louis MacNeice. Copyright W. H. Auden,
Renewed. Reprinted by permission of Curtis Brown, Ltd.

All maps are by GeoSystems Global Corporation, Columbia, MD.

Designed by Janette Thompson (Jansom)
Printed by The Maple-Vail Book Manufacturing Group

# Contents

# Acknowledgments

To restore one's faith in humanity, all one need do is try to research a book. So many people on the following list (which is undoubtedly not complete) and on the list of Persons Interviewed and/or Corresponded With went far out of their way to help me that to tell what they did would take nearly as many pages as has this entire book. I am sure they will forgive me if I single out only one person for special thanks: the late W. E. "Will" Stober, who appeared, as if by magic, toward the beginning of my research and helped me with all the difficult bits. Will is, sadly, only one of several people who helped me who are no longer around to be thanked in person.

I would also like to recognize the eminent anthropologist Sir Raymond Firth, who figures in this book as someone my protagonist regarded as a sworn enemy. Sir Raymond was one of the pioneers in his field and is a great social scientist and a generous-spirited man. His reputation is, deservedly, far too secure to be in any way harmed by Tom Harrisson's peculiar view of him.

I wish to express my gratitude to: The Honorable Rupert Allason; Godfrey Argent of Godfrey Argent, Ltd., Kathleen Audemars; the staff of the Australian War Memorial Library, Canberra; Henry S. Barlow; Peter Bartram; Caroline Belgrave; A. Bertheux-Graatsma; BirdLife International; Borneo Research Council; Gordon Bowker; British Newspaper Library, Collingwood; Louisa Brown; *Buenos Aires Herald*; Cambridge University Library; Dr. Charles Carter; Don Coop; Ruby Corrin; Prof. Bernard Crick; Anne Crossman; Prof. Clark E. Cunningham; Dr. Brian Durrans; Dr. Ruth Dudley Edwards; Joy Eldridge; Douglas Fairbanks, Jr.; Dr. M. R. D. Foot; Jill Furlong, Archivist of the George Orwell Archive, University College London; Prof. Martin Gilbert, CBE; The Reverend John H. Gill; Victor Gollancz, Ltd.; Sir David Goodall, GCMG, and Lady Goodall; Timothy Green; Graham C. Greene, CBE; Dr. T. A. Heathcote, B.A., Ph.D.; Philip Jackson; Ed LaFontaine; Datuk Haji Arni and Datin Jill Lampam; Dympna Leonard; Library of Congress (U.S.); Malaysian National Archives; Prof. George Marcus; Ambassador Edward Marks; Donald, Michelle, and Prema Marshall; Dr. Gavan McCarthy and the staff of the Australian Science Archive Project of the University of Melbourne; Dr. Robyn McDermott; Jean Corrin Morris; Barbara Myers; Larry Naughton; OEY Giok Po; Catucha Pletinckx-Ouckow; Stuart Proffitt; Public Records Office, Kew; Sir Robert

Rhodes James; Barry Roper; Royal Geographical Society; Royal Society for the Encouragement of the Arts, Manufactures and Commerce; Royal Society for the Protection of Birds; Dato' Dr. Sanib Said; Deirdre Sharp; Archivist Dorothy Sheridan and the Mass-Observation Archive at the University of Sussex; the Southeast Asia Program, Cornell University; the Special Forces Club; the Species Survival Programme of the World Conservation Union (IUCN); Prof. George W. Stocking, Jr.; Prof. Penny Summerfield; Prof. Vinson H. Sutlive, Jr.; Helen Swank; the late Julian G. Symons; the Travellers' Club; *Vanuatu Weekly*; Josephine Weston of Granada Headquarters, London; Datuk Amar K. M. James Wong; Christine Woodland, Keeper of the Crossman Archive, University of Warwick; World Conservation Monitoring Centre; Christopher Wright, Esq.; Datin Noor Azlina Yunus; and the Zoological Society of London.

The research was the enjoyable part. Thanks are also due to those who helped me through the harder job of getting the book written, shrunk to an acceptable size, and published. Chief among these were my husband John; my agent Tom Wallace, and my editor Pam Kelley. For reading early drafts of the manuscript with a kind but critical eye and for all sorts of good advice, my thanks go to my sister Sr. Miriam du Christ-Jésus, my uncle Alvin Moscow, my neighbor John Watters, and my friends Beryl Benderly, Betsy Schell, Edward Shufro, Jean-François and Anita Baré-Hubert, George Staples, and Joan Martin. Many thanks also to my children Paul and Mary, my Aunt Louise, and the many friends who were patient with me during the long period of parturition.

For permission to reproduce illustrations, I wish to thank:

Frontispiece, Figures 28 and 36, Barbara Harrisson; 1, 2, 5, and 19, Gillian Webster; 3, ©Tunbridge Sedgwick Studios, courtesy Gilliam Webster; 4, Marjorie Merchant de Collingwood; 6, 7, and 9, Mrs. Anne Richards; 8, Prof. W. G. Solheim II; 10, 11, 12, and 14, Venice Barry née Baker; 13, Jock Marshall papers (MS 7132) in the National Library of Australia; 15, the Reverend Ian Taylor; 16, ©Harold Coster Studio, courtesy Godfrey Argent, Ltd., and the Trustees of the Mass-Observation Archive; 17, ©Humphrey Spender, courtesy the Trustees of the Mass-Observation Archive, University of Sussex, and the Bolton Metro Museum; 18, Mary Fedden Trevelyan, the Trustees of the Mass-Observation Archive, University of Sussex, and the Bolton Metro Museum; 20, R. J. Blair; 21, 30, 33, 37, 38, 39, 41, and 43, Sarawak Museum; 22, Philip Henry; 23, D. L. Horsnell; 24, the late C. F. Sanderson; 25 and 32, Robert Pringle; 26, Robert Goh; 27, James Barclay; 29, ©Albert Teo; 31, Arkib Negara Malaysia; 34, Keith Barrie; 35, Celia Harrisson; 40, Prof. Derek Freeman; 42, ©Hedda Morrison, courtesy Alastair Morrison; 44 and 45, Ludmilla Forani-Rhein; 46, Barbara Crewe.

To John, with all my love.

But if it be a sin to covet honor,
I am the most offending soul alive.

*Henry V*

# Prologue

One day in 1975, the phone rang in my office in the consular section of the American embassy in Brussels. It was the British consul asking in a harassed voice if I knew a bizarre Englishman called Tom Harrisson who claimed to know me. I cautiously admitted that we had been neighbors in Borneo, and the consul went on to explain that the man was in his outer office making an unholy fuss about the renewal of his passport. He was claiming that the birth date on it and on his birth certificate was wrong.

"Look," I said, cutting short this choleric colleague, "Do yourself a favor. Look him up in *Who's Who*."

The entry that the consul would have seen in *Who's Who 1975* began: "Harrisson, Tom. DSO 1946, OBE 1959. . . .Visiting Professor and Director of Mass-Observation Archive, University of Sussex . . . " and went on for twelve column-inches to mention, inter alia,

> left Harrow (where wrote standard book on the birds of the district) to go on Oxford Expedition to Arctic Lapland; . . . one year living among cannibal mountain tribes of Malekula. . . . Determined, instead of studying primitive people, to study the "cannibals of Britain," so started with Charles Madge new type of social research organization, called Mass-Observation . . . 1945 first white man to be dropped into Borneo to organize guerrillas in Sarawak and Dutch Borneo prior to Allied landings, . . . Government Ethnologist and Curator of Museum, Sarawak 1947–66 . . . Sr. Research Associate in Anthropology and Southeast Asia Program, Cornell University. . . .

This was followed by a long list of publications on subjects ranging from ornithology to *Primitive Erotic Art*. His chief recreation was given as "living among strange people and listening to them talk about themselves."

Tom's birth certificate, though he was unable to prove it to the consul, was indeed wrong. A badly handwritten record at the British consulate in Buenos Aires seemed to show his birth in April (26-4-11) instead of his actual birth date in September (26-9-11). Tom found this official "evidence" of a wrong birth date to be more than merely irritating. In notes for his projected autobiography, he describes his discovery of this error as "womb-traumatic." All his life, people had questioned his claims to have done various things. Now it appeared that even his birthday was being denied him.

He started making notes for an autobiography (which he had tentatively titled *Was I That Man?*) about this time, in the year before his sudden death in early 1976. He planned to write a "self-pitiless account" in which he would try "to find what such a life looks like to others, what DID I really do." Taking on his project two decades after his death, I have tried to be as pitiless as he proposed to be in drawing his portrait, in showing what his life looked like to others of his day, and what he "DID" really do. In doing so, I have kept within a value system he would recognize and eschewed attempts to judge him by 1990s standards, whether feminist, anticolonialist, or postmodernist.

I started with little knowledge and few preconceptions, having known him as a neighbor and casual friend during ten years in three countries. Beginning in 1986, I spent ten years retracing his steps, on four continents, and interviewing nearly 200 people who knew him or knew of him. My qualifications for this self-imposed task were a modest fluency in Malay, a little informal familiarity with anthropology, a few years spent in Borneo, and an ability to read difficult handwriting. After five years of desultory work on the book, I retired from the diplomatic service at the first possible moment in order to devote my full attention to the project. My motives were totally selfish: I adore doing research and had long been looking for a subject that would take in two areas of the world that fascinate me, Northwest Europe and Southeast Asia. If I have succeeded in my goal, this book will allow you, the reader, to see for yourself this extraordinary man and draw your own conclusions about his life and work.

Tom Harrisson began to make a name for himself in England in the late 1930s, first as an adventurer who had lived among cannibals and written a best-seller about his experiences that argued on behalf of cannibals' rights to their land and to their way of life. He next made news as the founder of Mass-Observation, an organization that pioneered doing social surveys in England. He often appeared in the press and on BBC radio and television (yes, television, in 1936) as a guest expert on birds, ecology, cannibals, and/or the latest popular dance craze. He had a weekly column as radio critic for *The Observer* and appeared often in periodicals as different as Tom Hopkinson's *Picture Post* and John Lehmann's avant garde *New Writing*.

He was on his way to becoming a household word in England when, in March 1945, wearing a parachutist's wings and the brand new crown of a British major, he jumped into a hidden valley in the middle of Borneo to set up an intelligence network behind Japanese lines with the help of a few dozen Australian officers and men. Not satisfied with so small or simple a task, he also raised a thousand-man army of blowpiping headhunters who killed or captured nearly 1500 Japanese, losing only 21 native fighters and no Australians. For this he won the DSO.

After the war, while the social survey techniques he had been the first to use in Britain became the tools of the new market research industry, he made his home in Borneo. There, he became, over the next two decades, an amateur expert in a bewildering number of fields, from paleontology (finding the remains of the oldest *Homo sapiens sapiens* known at the time) to founding the first orphanage for infant orangutans, to helping to pioneer the conservation of the green sea turtle, to making the Sarawak Museum, of which he became the curator, the model and inspiration for smaller Third World museums. At times he would be called away to draw on his knowledge of inland Borneo to help the Gurkhas or the Special Air Service (SAS) or local security forces with a local rebellion or a clandestine Indonesian incursion. He became the best-known person in Borneo, virtually the only one heard of by outsiders.

In England, though, he was heard of only rarely, as when one of a series of television films he did on Borneo won the Cannes *Grand Prix* for documentaries and was shown on the BBC. Thus, I cannot assume that any of Harrisson's extraordinary achievements are familiar to the reader.

Worse still, of those who remember him, many are unwilling to believe that he did what he said he did. I have yet to catch him making a bald-faced lie in print, but he was certainly devious and would sometimes tailor the truth to lead the unwary to a false conclusion. He also sometimes telescoped the facts to make a story shorter or more striking, as, for example, when he said he was "sent down from both Oxford and Cambridge." In fact, he walked out of Cambridge but would probably have been sent down had he continued his rowdy carrying on with such disreputable young men as Malcolm Lowry. Though never enrolled at Oxford, he participated with great success in four Oxford expeditions but was for a time "banned" from the zoological department's premises and perhaps from Oxford University altogether. He would tell the long version if there was time or if his audience showed interest, but the phrase "sent down from Oxford and Cambridge" was in his view close enough to the truth to serve as shorthand for the facts.

Tom's habit of not always telling the exact literal truth, combined with the unlikely variety and range of his accomplishments, his skill at self-publicity, and his lifelong penchant for making enemies means virtually no achievement he claimed, or which has been claimed for him, was or is believed by the host of his detractors. For the biographer, this meant that every "fact" about Tom had to be confirmed by at least one other source known to be honest or at least impartial. When this could not be done, I have felt obliged to say so.

It is ironic that no such standards of reliability are demanded of his detractors. During his life and after his death, entirely unsubstantiated allegations were made against him, for example, that he had absconded with treasures belonging to the Sarawak Museum. One cannot simply dismiss such unsupported allegations, however, because Tom's behavior was often so dreadful as to make many unprejudiced people ready to believe the worst about him. Indeed, although many of Tom's friends would agree with the late Lord Shackleton that Tom was "the most remarkable man of my generation," some otherwise clear-thinking people who knew him are unprepared to see any good in the life and work of such a man.

I find that view understandable but cannot share it. Tom could be dreadful, but he could also be witty, warm, exciting, engaging, encouraging, and, above all, life-enhancing. His curiosity and energy were inexhaustible. And whereas the scientists of his day sought discrete areas of study small enough to master, Tom was always looking for ways to connect information and ideas across disciplines. The narrower academicians saw him for the trespasser and marauder he was. They did not welcome him careering across their carefully fenced-in special areas and opening gates into neighboring fields—and doing so without even the license of a university degree. Yet modern scholars in a number of disciplines—archaeologists, conservationists, art historians, ornithologists, and guerrilla warfare specialists—believe Tom saw some things more clearly and widely and deeply than anyone else of his generation. Even in anthropology where he feuded actively with the establishment all his life, although his work had serious flaws, his instincts brought him very close to present thinking in some respects.

Astonishingly prolific, in addition to writing for scholarly audiences, he loved appearing in the popular press and in the media. This was not just to feed his ravenous ego but also because he felt compelled to popularize what he learned so that ordinary people—including the groups of people under study—could take advantage of his research. It is hard to know which were more offensive to the academic and scientific establishment: his vices or his virtues. He was a romantic polymath, a drunken bully, an original-thinking iconoclast, a dreadful husband and father, a fearless adventurer, a Richard Burton of his time.

In what follows, then, I shall try to show what kind of a man Tom Harrisson was, in all his complexity, and what he did that makes him worth reading about.

**PART ONE**

Early Days, 1911–1933

# Chapter 1

# The View from Mount Dulit

He stood on the peak of Mount Dulit, 5,000 feet above the Tinjar River valley of northern Borneo and looked westward toward the South China Sea (see the map of Northern Borneo on p.247). His shorts were ragged, his shirt dirty, his bare feet calloused from many treks over rough terrain on three different Oxford expeditions in as many years. With his hard lean body darkened by the tropical sun and with his thick black hair, he might have been taken for one of the native porters were it not for his pale grey-blue eyes and the unconscious arrogance of his very British carriage. His name was Tom Harrisson, the year was 1932, and the day was September 26, his twenty-first birthday.

For Tom, reaching a mountain's summit had an almost mystical effect. It was as if, in being able to see far out from on top of a high peak, he could also see deeper into his own soul. He would later write of that day that

> two of the conscious impulses running through the adult life I came of age into . . . at the top of Mount Dulit . . . were (i) to prove [to] myself (it was already too late to prove it to my father) not only that I could do my own things and keep my independence, but also that I could do his own things too" [for example, be a war hero] . . . and (ii) that I could prove . . . that coming to Borneo as an outsider was not a mere flash in the pan.

It was too late to prove it to his father because Tom had just committed the unpardonable offense of dropping out of Cambridge after little more than a year, largely spent drunk and disorderly. Having found the teaching of the natural sciences at Cambridge to be a dull repetition of material he had mastered at Harrow, he had looked for companions who were as "intellectual" and "tough" as himself. After months of solitary drinking, he had nearly despaired of finding friends at Cambridge who had both of these attributes. Then, one night when drunk, while visiting another college, he "saw a party going on over the wall" at Christ's. "So I went over the wall," he later told a journalist, "and into the party, and the first two people I met were John Davenport and Malcolm Lowry. . . ."

John Davenport was "a poet compared by his contemporaries in the early Thirties to Auden and Spender and Day Lewis," although he subsequently dried up, possibly because of alcohol. He was fat and gregarious, Falstaffian, "witty, bibulous, charming, bawdy," "blithely Rabelaisian and slanderously uninhibited" but exhibiting "a profound knowledge of the arts." Three years older than Tom, Davenport was an "unusually strong man, quite short but almost square" and "was a very good heavyweight boxer."

Tom, when he met Davenport and Lowry, was only nineteen and "a very unimpressive young man at that age, rather small and skinny" (as someone who met him then recalls), but he had soon learned to project his voice, to phrase his remarks, and to hold himself so that he could become a "large character" like Davenport.

Lowry, with blond good looks and the build of a light heavyweight, was pathologically shy in company but could converse brilliantly away from the crowd. A budding novelist, he was most interesting to Tom for what he had to say about technical problems in writing. Lowry was then puzzling out how to shift between voices "from straightforward third-person narrative to songs, newspaper headlines, street cries, bird-calls and interior monologue" in an effort to encompass both the "objective world of the senses and the subjective world that the mind creates in response." A few years later, Tom would make use of this shifting narrative voice technique in his first real book.

One reason Tom had taken up with Lowry was because, like Tom, Lowry was a doer, not just a talker. At eighteen, Lowry had sailed as a merchant sea-man to the China seas for half a year. On one occasion, Tom and Lowry invaded a marine biology lecture and Tom interrupted the distinguished speaker by shouting out that you could not say you had been to sea unless you had sailed as a stoker, like Lowry. "They were both drunk and, having delivered this broadside, left."

Tom later described the Cambridge these young men experienced together as "pseudo-hyper-male" and "sort of rough." They liked to go pub-crawling and, when they had drunk enough, would become pugnacious and get into fist fights. Brawny, brawling, brilliant young men, Tom and Davenport and Lowry recognized in one another, almost like a secret hand-shake, another shared bond in their great dislike for their respective mothers. Lowry, when he spoke of his mother did so "only with hatred." Davenport's mother was the object of vitriolic comments by her son. Tom, though angry and alienated from his father, still yearned for his respect but he felt only con-tempt for his mother. In later years he recalled that, "Mummy didn't like peo-ple"; "had no idea of kids"; "never wanted to have Christmas"; "no knitting, no cards, not even drink until later"; "she would sit for hours looking into the fire"; "she never really did anything."

Tom's mother, Marie Ellen, known as "Doll," the daughter of a Liverpool heiress and William Eagle Cole, an eccentric amateur naturalist from Norfolk, had never known what it was like to have a home. Her own mother had died when she was nine and her elder sister Violet was twelve. She and Violet had spent the next ten years cycling all over France and Italy with their father so he could indulge his passion for bird-watching and butterfly collecting. They did not really settle down until 1907, when her father bought a cottage in Otterbourne, south of the Itchen valley, near Winchester in Hampshire. That same year twenty-one-year-old Doll became engaged to twenty-five-year-old Geoffry Harrisson, back from the Boer War and on his way to make his fortune in Argentina. In 1909 she sailed out to marry him.

Tom, born in Argentina in 1911, sailed with his two year-old brother Bill and his parents to England in August 1914 so that his father, like a thousand other young Britons employed by the South American railways, could join the Army. With her husband away at the Great War, Doll read avant-garde novels while a nanny took charge of Tom and Bill. Between 1915 and 1917 they lived in nine different houses. Tom recalls that he and his brother never had a "lived in, loved place." They had no playmates but one another and no toys, so that their nanny's only way to amuse them had been to take them for walks, making them into champion walkers for the rest of their lives. On these walks, Tom would ask his nanny about the little red squirrels they saw. How do they climb, run, jump? He was fascinated by insects of all kinds and would collect them in match boxes, while Bill was always carrying handfuls of wilting wildflowers. Bill was softer and, his nanny recalls, "never one to try things," whereas Tom always said, "Let me do the doing." While Bill was quiet and thoughtful, Tom was always wanting "to get onto the next thing before he had finished that one."

Their nanny let them leaf through her books on insects and flowers until they knew them by heart. Going over and over these nature books, the boys learned to read. Tom could read well by the age of five. The boys by then were calling their father "Major," never "Daddy."

Major Harrisson was off in the battlefield, being Mentioned in Dispatches five times, receiving the DSO and the CMG, membership in the Order of the Crown of Belgium, and the Belgian Croix de Guerre. Tom was immensely proud of his officer father and once at age four led the major to Knightsbridge Barracks so that he could watch delightedly as his father received the salutes due his rank. Geoffry Harrisson himself was very offhand about his decorations. He would say that they had been "handed round on a tray." Yet, having obtained the temporary rank of brigadier-general and having been granted it as an honorary rank at the end of the war in 1918, he continued to use the title the rest of his life.

In early 1919, the General and Doll returned to Argentina, leaving Tom and Bill in England in a new (French) nanny's care. All his life, Tom remembered standing with Bill at the corner of a street in Otterbourne, his cheeks wet with tears, while he waved good-bye to the car taking his parents away. Months afterward, he would go every morning to that corner looking for his parents.

Tom's life in Otterbourne was not entirely miserable. The Itchen valley was a good place for children who loved nature. Tom and Bill explored it, sometimes with the help of their naturalist "Grampy." But then, in the autumn of 1919, they were sent off to boarding school where their ignorance of—and distaste for—organized games made them pariahs. Their holidays, spent as paying guests at down-at-the-heels vicarages, were even harder to bear. Tom recalled:

> These holidays, among assorted Danes, Swedes and grass-orphans of our own sort, were agony. The hosts were out to make the maximum profit from us and in one vicarage were really heartless and unkind. I never forgave my parents for abandoning us so carelessly. However, I added to my armoury of toughness and developed the capacity to cut-off from horrid people through these experiences in homeless, loveless living. This went on for over two years without one kiss of kinship.

In 1922, after nearly three years without the boys seeing their parents, Bill got appendicitis and the General came to collect him and Tom and bring them back to Argentina, where Bill could recover his health. Aboard the *Arlanza*, a sister ship to the one that had taken Doll to marry her fiancé in 1909, in a first-class suite with the General, the boys got to know their father for the first time. A young Englishman aboard described General Harrisson in a letter home as a "topping man: You should see him teaching the small girls and boys to skip. He is about the most popular man on the boat." He noticed that the Harrisson boys seemed to be on very easy terms with their father. After three weeks of sailing, they arrived in Buenos Aires and a few days later boarded the General's private railway coach for the trip up-country.

Out of the train window was a landscape on an entirely different scale from anything the boys had seen in England. The "interminable grassland stretched to the sky-line," with "far away in the distance, a solitary *estancia* sheltered by a group of eucalyptus trees." At several of the train's infrequent stops, English settlers came out to greet General Harrisson, General Manager of the Entre Rios and North-East Argentine Railways, with rounds of drinks in the restaurant car. Toward evening, after nearly a full day and night on the train, the boys and their father reached Concordia, on the middle reaches of the Uruguay River, in the province of Entre Rios; it was the railways' headquarters and the end of their journey. They arrived there on July 21, 1922, and began the best year of their childhood.

Their big bungalow, Chalet Patterson, was quite the grandest residence in Concordia, but the warm relationship they had enjoyed with their father aboard the *Arlanza* began to cool as the General resumed life as the local squire. The boys reverted to their dependence on each other for companionship. Concordia was the biggest English settlement in Argentina outside Buenos Aires, but there were no English schools and few English children, since most of the children were sent "home" to England. The British colony in Argentina was rich, being heavily involved in railway investment and construction, and its members did not bother to learn to speak proper Spanish. Indeed, "their shocking accent" when trying to speak "the native Spanish tongue became a symbol of status, of power." Tom always blamed his genes for his inability to learn foreign languages well, but this early colonial experience may have had an unconscious effect on him. For Tom and Bill there was, of course, no question of socializing with the Argentinians. Aside from the half-dozen native servants working at Chalet Patterson, the boys never saw any.

The Harrissons kept horses, and early every morning they would all go out riding. In November (the Argentine spring), there was golden wheat all over the plains outside Concordia, and there were fields and fields of blue flax. There were enormous sunflowers and other flowers the size of gramophone records. Brilliant-colored hummingbirds flitted about in the trees. The boys' tutor, hired by the General in London, was an athletic twenty-seven-year-old Englishman. He was the best tennis player in Concordia, and he taught the boys to play. The lack of playmates their own age did not seem to bother Tom and Bill. They were accustomed to it and—occasionally with their father and more often with their Grampy (who had come for a long visit)—they explored the natural treasures of this new world. Their father taught them to shoot and, sometimes in the cooler weather, took the boys into an area of quaking bogs to hunt snipe. In the hot weather, the General's two special railway coaches, fitted up as a mobile home, would take him and the boys to bathe in the fast running water of the Salto Grande. This was a waterfall running down a steep valley rich in vegetation, insects, birds, reptiles, and mammals not far from Concordia. The General was by then a great dry fly fisherman, a skill he passed on to Bill. In the good weather, when the General was not fishing, he would take the boys shooting, canoeing in the rapids, and climbing, during which the General betrayed a fear of heights but Tom did not. Tom remembered these days with the General in Argentina as the high point of their relationship. He was his father's "companion then, . . . just tough and uncritical."

Tom's interest in birds was not only in shooting them. He collected live birds and soon had a big aviary as well as a pair of hummingbirds living in the eucalyptus tree in the garden. He and Bill adopted a young burrowing owl they found that had wandered away from its hole. Tom recalled that the owl "was piteously lost on the plain. So we tried to pick him up, to help him. In a moment that gentle ball of fluff turned into a vicious fury of fierce beak and ready claw. He nearly took my finger off." They brought the little owl home but it refused to be tamed.

He seemed to hate all of us. We had to wear thick gloves to feed him with.

In time the owl grew ready to fly. One day he hopped off the edge of the wide veranda and fluttered away over the grasslands out of sight. Goodbye to that charming selfish beggar, we thought. But next morning he was there again on the veranda rail. From that day forth he was a friend; he gave up his old beak-and-claw tactics. He was always round the place, free to fly where he liked. On that first flight he changed his mind about us.

"Birds are often curious and complex like that," Tom found, "especially in their relations with human beings."

Tom's interest in birds—already at age eleven—was part of a broader interest he had in how humans relate and react to birds and vice versa. It is an oversimplification to say that Tom and his brother found in birds the companionship they did not have with other children, but their social isolation does help to explain why they both were so interested in birds, especially Tom. He became devoted to his new hobby and often preferred to stay home in Concordia to feed and observe his birds than to go fishing with his father and Bill.

This happy year came to an end in August 1923, during the Argentine winter, when Doll brought Tom and Bill by ship to England to return them to their Winchester preparatory school. She went back to Argentina, and the boys reverted to their dreary routine of boarding school with holidays as paying guests.

If Tom had felt like a foreigner at school before he spent that year in Argentina, the feeling was even greater when he returned from South America just before his twelfth birthday. But miserable as the experience was to him then, he would later say:

I think being born far away from the country where you identify yourself was a great advantage. I wouldn't change it for anything in the world. This "stranger" situation, the feeling of belonging to England and *not* belonging to it, . . . feeling strange in Britain makes it much more exciting to be in Britain. . . .

Most important for his future career as a "people-watcher," it gave him the ability to see his own country with the eyes of an outsider. Not only having been born abroad but having spent his childhood in the company of so few caring adults (none of them reliably present when needed) and no human playmates aside from his brother, gave him a similar feeling of belonging and not belonging to human society, as if mankind belonged to a different species from himself.

He and Bill left their preparatory school for the famous public school at Harrow-on-the-Hill in the autumn of 1925. Harrow was a considerable improvement for them, largely because they were boarders at "Newlands," the house run by Tom's godfather, the Reverend D. B. Kittermaster (who had spent the year of Tom's birth in Argentina). Kittermaster was an eloquent but unorthodox preacher. He was naturally rebellious and had a special sympathy for boys who did not fit in, boys his colleagues called "Kitter's criminals."

"Kitter," Tom recalled, "was a splendid man to whom I owe much. He put up with all kinds of stuff. I was always bloody-minded and trying to start something new or saying, 'why do we have to do this?' I hated the system of privilege where the first term boys go down stairs one way and the second term another. It annoyed me like hell."

In Tom, the urge to rebel against the establishment warred with a love of—and fascination with—hierarchy. Harrow was his first exposure to an elaborate system of privilege and status, in this case based mainly on how long one had been at the school and how good one was at games. Tom recalled: "The speed at which you could move downstairs, which waistcoat buttons could be undone, what cereals could be eaten at breakfast, where you could walk, a hundred habits, were determined entirely in this way." This attention to seemingly irrational but carefully executed sumptuary rituals as part of demonstrating one's place on a status ladder helped prepare him to notice and understand the way social rank was obtained and expressed among the tribesmen of the New Hebrides and Borneo as well as among different segments of British society.

Tom, "who was rather thin and had a perpetual drip from his nose" was one of "Kitter's criminals," as was his classmate, the future playwright Terence Rattigan, who, although he always won the English prize and was a good cricketer, was also already very obviously homosexual. Tom, for his part, recalls in notes for his autobiography "falling in love with Tim S." and other brief "homolove" encounters during his Harrow years. Once an adult, he appears never again to have indulged in homosexual sex but—perhaps thanks to Kitter's tolerant example—was always on comfortable terms with homosexuals. Three years after leaving Harrow, Tom wrote, "When you say Harrow you say perversion. It is one of the bye-monopoly products of big public schools. . . ." For himself, however, "I have never been able to get very annoyed about perversion except where normal people are influenced at an early age against their instincts. . . . As long as no one tries to pervert me, I don't care a dam [sic] if my friend keeps a goat or has a polar bear in the . . . zoo." He did not regard his brief experiments with "homolove" as having made him homosexual, though more than just sexual release had been involved.

One of his schoolmates at Harrow later admitted that "I loved him a bit and he loved me a bit. It was partly his physical looks, partly that we were just drawn to one another." The initial attraction between Tom and this friend was a mutual interest in ornithology, but, in addition, the friend thought of himself in those days as being "puny" and he had admired Tom because Tom "would have been good at sports except he had no interest in them. . . . Like him, I believed in being 'tough' for its own sake and not for games. I guess we had that in common." He still remembers Tom's "sharp little face, unlike anyone else." Later, following Tom's career from a distance, he felt confirmed in his view that Tom was "one of the most remarkable people of his generation."

At Harrow, Tom was not a brilliant student overall but got good marks in science (by the end he was specializing in natural science) and would sometimes write an arresting essay on other subjects, such as divinity. He kept his head down at the beginning, avoided mentioning his Argentine background for fear of seeming different, and observed the other boys. Just as he did for his bird notes, he would mark down on index cards his schoolmates' visible traits, such as "blond, acne, worn heels" until eventually he had the entire school in his file box.

Gradually he became known as a "climber and fairly dashing practical joker." He once got a chamber pot "onto the head of [a statue of] Queen Elizabeth before some celebratory day at Harrow. On another occasion he mounted a building and fixed some flying object—trousers? —which took a lot of getting down." (Baron Deedes, who recalled these events to me in a 1994 letter, remembered that he himself had been "a wimp at Harrow" and that Tom had struck him then "as insanely brave!") He was a strong swimmer, which got him off having to play cricket. Similarly, being a good cross-country runner, he managed to avoid having to play football or rugby. That he found ways to slip past annoying requirements rather than rebelling against them may have been due to the wise counsel of Kitter.

Most important for his future life, he managed to persuade Kitter to let him run off well beyond the normal limit of a few hundred yards past the school walls in pursuit of his hobby of bird watching. "He was allowed to go within a five-mile radius of the school but he often went ten—always on foot."

In term-time, he used bird-watching as an escape from the miseries of the school, which he later described as having been a "hideous murderous place." Another English boy from Argentina who was (also thanks to Kitter) at "Newlands" in Tom's day recalls Harrow as

> a sort of a cross between a monastery and a military barracks with a little schol-
> arship thrown in. Cold baths every morning, corporal punishment (though that
> was already on its way out), fagging, games, *mens sana in corpore sano*, a special
> code of honour (you could cheat in lessons but not in games), stiff upper lip, no
> emotion, no demonstration of affection, no female company or influence—it
> would detract from one's manliness. Those softer, human touches were left for
> home and, if he had no sisters or female cousins in the holidays, a boy might leave
> school at the age of nineteen never having spoken to any female other than his
> mother or his old nurse.

This was nearly Tom's situation. The high value he put on being a man among men, and his relegation of women to a separate and less important place in his life, may have been caused by his Harrow experience. In that sense, those who would later accuse him of "partially-arrested development" may have a point. But if he was a victim of this malady, Harrow was—at least in part—the culprit. He was nonetheless proud to have gone there and for the rest of his life boasted of being an Old Harrovian. As a 1994 article on public schools in the *Sunday Times* pointed out, "What is most telling is the way in which even those who couldn't bear their schooldays . . . [had] a sense of being part of an 'inward and invisible elite' [that] was not available to the products of state schools."

The General and Doll moved back to England in the middle of Tom's Harrow career. By then Tom was sixteen and beginning to have more inter-esting vacations of his own devising. He spent a couple of school holidays liv-ing and working in one of the pioneer hostels of the Fellowship of St. Christopher, where he watched and listened to the down-and-outers of the East End of London as if they were exotic birds of the Argentine campo. Another time he took a bicycle and rode all the way through France down to Marseilles. One holiday he spent sitting in Trafalgar Square with a notebook, writing down what the people around him did and said. He was never with-out a notebook, in which he wrote very quickly and almost illegibly.

The reappearance of his parents was a mixed blessing; his strong will clashed with that of the General. A cousin remembers that there were "air-splitting scenes between Tom and his father but he was the apple of Aunt Doll's eye." But Tom by then did not care what his mother thought of him.

He was devoting every spare moment to bird-watching. He answered an appeal in *British Birds* for volunteers to help with the first British bird cen-sus, of the grey heron, a project initiated and run by a twenty-four-year-old Oxford undergraduate named Max Nicholson, who had recently helped found the Oxford University Exploration Club. Nicholson had decided to embark on this census, his first act of conservation, because fishermen regarded herons as their enemies and so, if the birds were to be protected, more needed to be known about them. In response to Tom's note offering help to cover missing areas on the heronry census, Nicholson himself, a tall young man with the face of an eagle, appeared at Harrow-on-the-Hill to interview the volunteer. Expecting an adult, Nicholson was surprised when "a somewhat strange-looking teenager was brought out for [his] inspection." It was a fateful meeting for Tom.

Seven years Tom's senior, Max Nicholson, with his striking looks, strong voice, and powerful brain, was someone for Tom to look up to and pattern himself after. Nicholson had already published two important books on birds. He went on to become Britain's most distinguished conservationist, drafter of much of the legislation that has protected the British countryside, and one of the founders of the World Wildlife Fund.

Tom proved to be an excellent helper on the heronry census and took careful note of how it was organized. Inspired by Nicholson's example, Tom, with his brother's help on the index, pulled together the bird notes both boys had kept. These notes, augmented by observations of dozens of other bird-watchers, became what Tom would describe as his first "book": "Birds of the Harrow District (North-West Middlesex) 1925–1930." It was a forty-page report published by the *London Naturalist* (1930). While not an epoch-making event in ornithology, it was a very respectable contribution to it, and a remarkable one for a nineteen year-old.

Tom was also interested in exploration. In 1929 he and two Harrow friends, Reynold Bray and Tom Manning, eager to become explorers, founded a club called The Argonauts, aimed (as they told a reporter at *The Times*) at "encouraging adventurous and enterprising holidays, especially those involving travel and life in the open air." It was a club for doers, not just talkers. Members were elected only after they had "done something enterprising in the holidays."

In 1930, Tom's father and Doll settled down permanently at "The Chase," Weeke, Winchester, whence the General could fish the River Test and commute to London, where he was on the boards of various South American railway companies.

That year, Tom's last at Harrow, before his family's move to Winchester, he and Phil Hollom (a seventeen-year-old Surrey neighbor who would later become a leading ornithologist and editor of the journal *British Birds*) did a systematic study of Surrey's aquatic birds, an "ecological study" as Tom would describe it the following year in an ornithological journal. The boys were inspired by developments in the study of birds at the time. Bird marking, using rings, had just begun. With Charles Elton's book, *Animal Ecology and Evolution* (1930), "ecology" was beginning to be thought of as a discipline. Nicholson's *How Birds Live* (1927), following upon Oxford biologist Julian Huxley's pioneering paper "The Courtship Habits of the Great Crested Grebe" (1914), had helped to revolutionize the naturalist's way of looking at bird life.

Stimulated by this contact with the frontiers of a new science and building on their own study of aquatic birds, Tom and Phil Hollom decided to do a national census of the great crested grebe the following year, 1931. Tom knew this would have to be a much more ambitious project than the Nicholson census of heronries, which had used 300 to 400 observers. The grebe could live wherever there was a sheet of water of at least four acres. The postwar boom in construction of houses and roads throughout Britain had created many large gravel pits that, with the build-up of rainwater, had turned into ideal grebe environments. Tom and Hollom found there were over a thousand "lakes" to be examined, for which work Tom hoped to obtain volunteer observers.

He published requests for help in *British Birds*, *The Scottish Naturalist*, and *The Naturalist*; he placed appeals "in daily, evening and local newspapers, weekly and sporting papers, angling and scientific journals and a special feature in *The Times*." He "wrote personally to every well-known naturalist and ornithologist, to many local observers, taxidermists, etc.," while Hollom wrote to "a great number of land-owners with likely lakes on their property." The two boys, still at their separate public schools and obliged to do this in their spare time, collected an army of bird-watchers such as Britain had never before assembled: 1,300 of them.

"We can recommend this sort of hobby for those people who find life dull," Tom informed the readers of *British Birds*, in his introduction to the completed survey. "It has involved us in some five thousand letters from fifteen countries." This project, carried out without any funding, even for postage, was nonetheless executed on a big scale, with which Tom, young though he was, felt entirely confident. Over the next fifteen years, he would put together and run other big projects in totally different fields.

In the course of planning the crested grebe census, Tom established contact with such famous scientists as Julian Huxley and Charles Elton, strengthened his ties to Max Nicholson, and became acquainted with younger enthusiasts, creating a scientific network that he would be able to call on for the rest of his life.

Before Tom began the actual census, however, two things happened. First, he received—thanks to Charles Elton, who was then chairman of the Oxford University Exploration Club—an invitation to participate in an Oxford

University Exploration Club expedition to Arctic Lapland during the summer of 1930. And, second, he was admitted to Pembroke College, Cambridge. Of the two, the former was much more exciting to Tom and of at least equal importance to his future life.

One of Tom's early notebooks, chiefly devoted to bird-watching, has an entry for February 20, 1930 that reads:

> Had lunch with Weatherby (Lapland Expedition Organiser); B. D. Nicholson [Max's brother], C. Elton and E. M. [Max] Nicholson blew in later. Then went with the Nicholsons to see the bird-trapping station in Christchurch Meadow. Later Weatherby told me that *I was definitely O.K. for Lapland*. CHEERS! and CHEERS!!!!

His Harrow days ended that spring, a term early, and his life as an explorer began.

# Chapter 2

## Arctic Adventures

On the Oxford University Expedition to Lapland of 1930, Tom was the only schoolboy. The expedition was headed by Charles Elton and another Oxford don. The other five members of the party were undergraduates, most of them from Oxford. Ever afterward Tom would regard formal requirements, especially academic degrees, as superfluous for someone who had the appropriate knowledge or experience to do a job. Being a member of the expedition was proof—to himself, if not to his father—that he could do his "own things" his own way.

Tom's chief qualification for the expedition was that he knew a lot about birds, but he brought with him another useful skill, the knowledge of how to walk. Those who had come to Lapland with heavy hobnailed boots envied Tom, who had brought tennis shoes. He hated heavy footwear. Had the ground been less rough, he would have gone barefoot.

During a two-month trek across the Norwegian Arctic, where his job as the team's "ornithologist" was to study the food and habits of the birds of the region while the zoologist Charles Elton studied the ecology of insects and small rodents, Tom learned much. Elton, eleven years Tom's senior, was already one of the great men of British science, soon to become a fellow of the Royal Society. Much later Tom would recall that Elton "greatly helped me to organize my mind in observing nature during the months we shared a tent of continuous daylight." The other members of the party were repelled by "the atmosphere" inside Tom's and Elton's tent "after a day's dissecting of birds or lemmings" on a hot day, but the "atmosphere" did not disturb Tom; he was never bothered by bad smells.

The expedition had come woefully underfunded. The party could not afford enough pack animals to carry sufficient supplies. With no time to go fishing and virtually no game to hunt, they were seriously undernourished. The only fresh fruit they had was during the second month of their trek when they found themselves in an area where they could pick wild berries. Under these pressures, the group broke into antagonistic cliques. Halfway through the two months, three of the party, including men who had come with reputations as great rowers, left for home, demoralized, tired out, and discouraged by the "ever-present problem of finance."

Tom stayed on to the end, emerging with "a great contempt for the toughness of rowing men. . . ." He swore that when and if he took charge of an expedition, it would have sufficient funds. This experience also led him to think that exploring in the Arctic was probably an overrated adventure, less worthwhile scientifically than one to the tropics, where, he remarked, "one-fiftieth of the amount of scientific work [had] been done."

Tom got back to England in time to go to Pembroke College, Cambridge, at the start of the Michaelmas (autumn) term, but his attention was more focused on the great crested grebe census, by now of mammoth proportions, and on a similar census he was making of the great black-backed gull, the largest gull in England. With these censuses and with plans for another expedition the following summer to St. Kilda in the Outer Hebrides, he had little thought to spare for his university studies.

Pembroke was the wrong place for him. It was known at the time for being anti-intellectual and full of "hearties," in particular rowing Blues, just the sort of people Tom had come to despise the previous summer. Though he joined the Cambridge Bird Club right away, he was lonely without his brother, who would not arrive until the following year.

Tom Manning, of The Argonauts club, was the only real friend to have come with him from Harrow. Manning was a taciturn "tough," and under his influence Tom honed his skills as a swimmer and long-distance runner and cyclist, skills he maintained virtually all of his life. In November 1930, he and Manning and another Cambridge undergraduate cycled the 80 miles to Oxford in one day to attend a meeting of the Oxford University Exploration Club, which Reynold Bray, his other Argonaut friend from Harrow, had already joined.

Not liking to go home to his parents, and having few friends with whom to spend free time, he filled the empty spaces in his life with alcohol. It is not as if there were no interesting young people at Cambridge then. This was perhaps Cambridge's "richest time" (as C. P. Snow contends), with Wittgenstein and Keynes in residence and the Cavendish lab at its most productive. Unfortunately for Tom, he was not only in the wrong college but in the wrong field of study to get the best out of his years there; the teaching of the natural sciences at Cambridge in that period was decidedly poor. Though Cambridge had an impressive and convivial group of undergraduate poets and painters in those days, Tom suspected such people of being limply effete, or at least not "tough." He saw himself as both "tough" and, at least potentially, "intellectual" at a time when he perceived that to his contemporaries these "were two different things." And so, much of the time he drank alone until, toward the end of his first year, he crashed that party at Christ's and met Davenport and Lowry.

Tom's first year at Cambridge drew to an end and the summer "long vac" arrived. By then, he was more than ready to leave on his next voyage of discovery, the Oxford-Cambridge Expedition to St. Kilda.

St. Kilda is a group of islands in the Outer Hebrides. Johnny Buchan (the Second Baron Tweedsmuir and son of the author of *The Thirty-Nine Steps*), was the leader of the expedition. He describes St. Kilda as "more than a hundred miles from the mainland of Scotland" and "shrouded in the mists of the Atlantic, whose rollers pound ceaselessly against its rocky cliffs." If that did not make it forbidding enough, it had just lost the last of its inhabitants, hardy islanders who had over the centuries "turned into almost a separate race." The islands had cliffs that were "an alpine climber's nightmare, for the rock is rotten and the ledges are covered with turf, which comes away in your hand."

The expedition had been mounted to "to make a reasonably close scientific investigation of the birds, the botany and the geology" of the main island, Hirta. After crossing the open sea from Glasgow in July 1931, they could barely see their destination "looming through the veil of grey rain and spray." They dropped anchor in a bay on Hirta and, in a big row boat, reached the pebble beach. Cut off until their ship returned in three weeks, they looked about the desolate village and commandeered "the cleanest of the houses, which had a small cooking stove in one room and a fireplace in the other." It was too far north for trees, but there was driftwood and peat for fuel.

They soon found, as with the Lapland expedition the previous summer, that they had "hopelessly under-estimated the amount that six hungry young men would require to eat, in three weeks of bracing isolation." To add the finishing touch, Buchan adds, "Rain fell almost every day," "every night we returned soaking wet from our researches," and "we lived with the smell of wet moorland and the salt of the ocean blowing round us." If, by the end of the previous summer, Tom had decided that exploring in the tropics would be preferable to doing so in the far north, the St. Kilda experience must have provided conclusive support for that view.

They were a reasonably cheerful company, however. The six young men "treasured the flavour of romance, and cultivated a Robinson Crusoe-like appearance. We revelled in the freedom from shaving." The atmosphere suited Tom, the more so in that his companions, like himself, were courageous to the point of foolhardiness. Buchan later recalled that Tom was a very good climber.

> I remember his silhouette to this day. He was very slim and always walked apparently leaning forward. . . . I had the hair-raising job of holding him on the end of a rope when he went down the side of a sheer cliff to examine some gulls nests. I will never forget his slipping from his hold and dangling from the rope that I was holding over a terrible void with the sea below him.

They had harrowing adventures rowing around the islands in heavy seas in an effort to add to their stock of food by fishing. They climbed up the vertical cliffs of one of the other islands in order to throw down one of St. Kilda's unique goatlike sheep to slaughter for its meat. Yet from all this hardship and danger, the expedition achieved little. Tom's chief scientific results were a complete census of the St. Kilda wren and several papers co-authored and published in appropriate scientific journals. More important to Tom, this experience helped assure him that he was tough enough for whatever he needed or wanted to do.

Returning to Cambridge to begin his second year in the autumn of 1931, Tom became secretary of the Cambridge Bird Club. He had ornithological notes and articles in print or in press in *British Birds*, *The Journal of Ecology*, and, most prestigious of all, in Britain's leading scientific journal, *Nature*. He continued to work on the crested grebe census, which still had nearly half a year to run.

Otherwise, he was doing little of a productive nature. He was spending much of his time that autumn drinking, in the company of Davenport, Lowry, and another friend, Tom Forman, a wealthy ex-Harrovian as wild as Tom. Forman had a small plane in which he and Tom "used to go stunting," Tom later recalled, and "once . . . did a falling leaf with me in it when he was dead drunk." Even Lowry would not fly with Forman, but Tom indulged to the full his appetite for life-threatening adventures. He loved physical danger the way a gambler loves playing for high stakes. He had some of the gambler's superstitiousness. For example, he had a premonition that he would die at age thirty-six. It followed, then, that until that age nothing could kill him. Tom not only liked risking his life but felt that people who did not court danger were barely alive.

Drinking much too much appealed to him as another way of risking his life. Writing two years later, Tom stated that "I once reached that rare and privileged state when (after a fortnight's solid) a lamp post walked out into the road, with a friendly smile, and shook me warmly by the hand. I have also seen a green hedgehog." Tom's boastfulness here is not merely that of the typical undergraduate. Tom really believed, as did Lowry, that excess led to success. He insisted that "Everybody ought to get drunk once every three months, properly drunk with a party, it should be a male activity and a male party. There is nothing like drunkenness to lower the barriers. . . ." It was, he felt, the only way to know a man or to learn if you could trust him.

By the autumn of 1931, Tom could not hide his contempt for Cambridge and for the average Pembroke man, with the result that he was once "set upon by a gang of hearties and projected fully clothed into the Cam." He wrote an inflammatory article about Pembroke for a new university paper as part of a series on "What's Wrong with Our Colleges" and signed it "a Pembroke Man." Next came a Guy Fawkes rag during which he tried to get a policeman's hat and got arrested. One afternoon a few weeks later, he and Lowry and Forman got drunk in Forman's rooms near Sidney Sussex College while they played records of washboard music. "After a while Forman took out a rifle . . . (he was an excellent shot) . . . and started shooting bricks off the gate tower of Sidney Sussex. The police arrived and they were arrested." Tom quit Cambridge shortly thereafter.

The idea of leaving university without a degree did not bother him unduly. He had discussed the matter with Tom Manning, who agreed with him about the teaching of zoology at Cambridge, and with Reynold Bray, who was finding Oxford a bore. Nonetheless, the decision to leave without a degree had disastrous consequences affecting the rest of Tom's life. These began as soon as the news reached the General.

Although he himself had walked out of university to join the Boer War, the General was deeply upset by Tom abandoning his studies. He promptly set about finding his son a place at King's College, London, away from the boy's drunken friends and the scenes of his disgraceful behavior. Tom tacitly allowed his father to assume he was enrolled at King's, but when the General found out, in early 1932, that Tom was not at King's, an awful row ensued, much worse than previous ones. After that, friendly relations between father and son were never restored. Bill, who had gone up to Cambridge a year after Tom and was miserably unhappy there, stuck it out nonetheless, becoming secretary of the Cambridge Bird Club in 1934 and, in 1935, the club's president. Bill was already closer to his father than Tom had been. He and his father often shot and fished together. With Tom in disgrace, Bill became, in effect, the General's only son.

Twenty-one-year-old Tom, standing on Borneo's Mount Dulit, did not yet know the other pernicious effects of his walking out of university, but he knew that by abandoning the effort to get a university degree, he had lost what chance he had ever had of earning his father's love and respect. After the big row about King's College, Tom's mother, Doll, felt caught between loyalty to her husband and love for Tom and, having long had hypochondriac tendencies, took more and more to her bed and, eventually, to drink.

Tom went to a psychiatrist on Harley Street shortly after quitting Cambridge. Doll probably encouraged the step and obtained the money for Tom to go. She was an enthusiastic believer in the new science of psychiatry and was rarely without a therapist of her own. Tom appears to have had only one or two sessions with the analyst, but he retained throughout his life a worry that he might be insane and a suspicion, gradually hardening into fixed belief, that there was madness in his genes. The type of insanity he suspected was paranoia. In notes to himself as he got older, he often recorded times and situations in which he thought he had shown traces of it.

Nonetheless, regarding his quitting university, he felt that he had made a perfectly rational choice and that his father had had no right to interfere. Sure of his own judgment, he went to Oxford, not to enroll in any formal studies but to live with—and off of—his Harrow friend Reynold Bray.

The two young men had much in common: birds and exploration, an original and inventive intelligence, Harrow, a wild sense of fun, a love of taking risks, and a hatred of their fathers. Bray, the rebellious son of a baronet, had not changed much physically since his Harrow days; he was still a lively little gnomelike creature whose friends were devoted to him. Lord Tweedsmuir still fondly remembers how Bray and Manning had invaded his rooms at Brasenose College, Oxford, the day that "Schools" (the Oxford term for final exams) ended and, "entering the general spirit of hilarity, threw all my food and furniture out of the window."

Although Tom enjoyed boisterous Bray's company, the chief reason Tom was staying in Bray's rooms at Balliol was because, upon his return from St. Kilda, he had heard from his first scientific patron, Charles Elton, that the "White Rajah" of Sarawak had agreed to a suggestion of the Curator of the Sarawak Museum, E. Banks, to invite an expedition from Oxford to explore Sarawak's inland flora and fauna. Elton asked Tom to organize an expedition there to last at least four months, beginning in the summer of 1932.

Sarawak was a state of nearly 50,000 square miles, about the size of England, and covered most of the northwest quarter of the equatorial island of Borneo. The land that comprised Sarawak had been granted by or wrested from the Sultan of Brunei or other Borneo nobles and passed to the so-called "White Rajahs" in installments. The first grant was made in 1841 to the British baronet Sir James Brooke, who thereby became the first White Rajah. In 1932, Sarawak belonged personally to H. H. Charles Vyner Brooke, the third White Rajah, who was its absolute ruler, though it had British "protection" in matters of defense and foreign affairs.

The chance to go to such a romantic place, in the tropics, and to organize the expedition himself, was the most splendid opportunity that twenty-year-old Tom could possibly imagine. He prepared for the expedition with all the energy and enthusiasm he had used for running the grebe census and with twice the experience in what to do and what not to do when arranging for a party of young men to spend months in a strange land.

When not engaged in planning for the Sarawak expedition, during the first half of 1932 Tom, still smarting from his row with his father, was in Oxford busy doing things that he knew would shock the General, such as walking the streets of Oxford in sandals with his toenails painted red. In the Oxford of 1932, as Tom reported, "the effect [was] inconceivable." The novelist Naomi Mitchison, who first met Tom at about this time, recalls that Tom was "beginning to rebel against the accepted norms in a way that became more usual . . . years later. Nobody had yet invented the term "hippie," "dropout" and all that. Not that Tom Harrisson dropped; he jumped very hard and the bottom came out—as he intended it to. . . ." "Going about in sandals," Mitchison asserts, might be "a normal thing to do, one would think, but not in those days, not in Oxford, not for a young man who might hope to lecture and be taken seriously by academics." Mitchison, fourteen years older than Tom, knew what she was talking about. Her father was the famous Oxford scientist J. S. Haldane, and her brother, J. B. S. Haldane, was the university reader in biochemistry at Cambridge. Naomi Mitchison herself was a free spirit, with discreetly rebellious elements in her dress. (For example, in the 1930s she used to carry a small dagger in her sock.) She had advanced ideas on sex and had an open marriage to the tolerant Labour M.P. Richard Mitchison (later Sir Richard). A Scottish aristocrat, she had taste, money, and a talent for friendship and used them to promote the efforts of young people of promise, such as W. H. Auden. She was prepared to give a bit of monetary and moral support to Tom. "I tried to help this young man," she later wrote, "sometimes wondering if it was worthwhile. It was."

It took someone with vision to see that. Tom, waiting around Oxford until he could head off for Sarawak, did not look like a young man of promise. He was not a student at university and was being subsidized by friends, with occasional handouts from his mother, while his father was driven livid with rage at the stories of Tom's red toenails, drunken escapades, and sordid brawls. When Tom was out late in London with no way back to Oxford, he would sometimes put a penny in the slot for a cubicle at the public toilets and go to sleep there.

"It's the cheapest way to spend the night," he told twenty-six-year-old Solly Zuckerman (later Lord Zuckerman) during their first conversation while Tom tried unsuccessfully to recruit Zuckerman to take part as zoologist and medical officer on the Sarawak expedition. It was an unfortunate introduction of Tom to the notice of a man who would become Britain's "Mr. Science" over many decades.

Although Tom failed to interest Zuckerman in the Sarawak expedition, he managed within a few months to raise what was, for those economically depressed times, a lot of money. He got funds from the British Museum, the

Royal Geographical Society, the Percy Sladen Trust, Oxford University, Magdalen College (Oxford), and the Royal Society. Cadbury gave 350 pounds of chocolate and 20 pounds of cocoa; Fortnum and Mason provided some packaged and tinned foods; and Imperial Chemical Industries (ICI) gave free ammunition for the party's guns and tutoring on how to use it. Sir Jeremiah Colman (of the mustard fortune) gave £250 and asked the expedition to bring back orchids for his collection.

Tom shamelessly coerced the parents of his potential expedition members to help the party reach his target of £2600 (£600 more than E. Banks, acting for the Sarawak government, had recommended). During lunch at the Athenaeum Club with General Sir Harold Hartley, he bargained "as to the value of taking his son, head boy of Eton, on the expedition. The General valued him at £150, I stood for a higher figure. We closed at £250 (he to pay me) in the coffee-room amidst an interested crowd of overhearers including Dean Inge and Julian Huxley. . . ." In the end, the amount of £2679 was raised and came within £100 of the actual costs.

Tom chose the members of the expedition. They were young: the average age was twenty. They were, however, young men of promise. Eighteen-year-old Cub Hartley, for whom Tom had bargained so successfully at the Athenaeum, would go on to become Air Marshal Sir Christopher Hartley, KCB. Eddie Shackleton was the son of Sir Ernest Shackleton (1874–1922), the Antarctic explorer who had won world fame by carrying off the most heroic feat of his day.* After Sarawak, Eddie went on to have a distinguished career, first as an Arctic explorer and later as a Labour politician, becoming Leader of the House of Lords in Harold Wilson's Government. Of the others, all Oxford or Cambridge men, several went on to great academic distinction.

Tom spent ten months, when not drunk or uproarious, collecting the expedition party and assembling its funds and equipment. One might wonder how it was that such a notorious young man was given the honor of organizing a project carrying Oxford's name and, even more odd, how it was that he could succeed so well. The reason appears to be partly that Tom, however much he misbehaved, was still a member of the group from which the English establishment was drawn. An upper-middle-class southerner, Tom had been to the right schools and had the presence that comes from being a member of the rul-

---

*Sir Ernest Shackleton, having previously accompanied Robert F. Scott on an Antarctic expedition, in 1914 set out in the *Endurance* in command of a trans-Antarctic expedition. When the ship was crushed in the ice, he made a trip of 800 miles with five expedition members to the north coast of South Georgia to get help. They all survived and reached their goal, thanks (it was then felt) only to the courageous and tenacious leadership of Sir Ernest. This exploit made him the era's most admired English hero. He died during a 1922 Antarctic adventure.

ing caste. Moreover, he already had an impressive curriculum vitae. During 1930–1932, when he was most noticeably drunk and disorderly, he had also written his hundred-page report on the "Great Crested Grebe Inquiry" (which would appear in *British Birds* while Tom was in Borneo), collaborated on the national census of the great black-backed gull around the coastline, and surveyed remote islands such as North Rona and Lundy, accomplishing these tasks before turning twenty-one. His work was scientifically sound. As Nicholson, by then one of the great men of ornithology, attested in 1976: "Despite the speed and multiplicity of these operations, their results have stood the test of time and subsequent repetition." Tom's reputation fifty years later as a pioneer in the scientific study of birds is based chiefly on what he had done before he left for Borneo in 1932.

He certainly saw himself as a young man of promise. Before going to Sarawak, he paid a visit to "Newlands" to see Kittermaster and arrived dressed conventionally in grey flannel trousers, a tweed coat, and a tie but wearing a bright green shirt. When someone remarked on the shirt, he said something to the effect that "I have to advertise myself now. Later on I won't need to."

On the eve of his departure, he had one last fling. Coming back to Malcolm Lowry's rooms at Cambridge after having attended a white tie party, as a gesture of shedding the conventions of civilization, he took off his tail coat and ripped it to shreds. In *Under the Volcano*, when Lowry writes of his protagonist's friend Wilson who "so magnificently abandoned the University Expedition to disappear . . . in a pair of dress trousers, into the jungles of Darkest Oceania," he is sketching Tom, in half of a dress suit, heading off to Borneo.

Standing atop Mount Dulit the day he came to his majority, Tom was still an outsider, a stranger, as he had always been. But somehow, on this tropical island, he felt certain this trip to Borneo was not just "a flash in the pan." For the first time in his life, he felt he was where he belonged.

# Chapter 3

## Borneo, 1932

The trip to Borneo exposed Tom and his party to a world of wonders. In those days before colored film and television cameras made every corner of the globe familiar, much of what they saw, once their Blue Funnel ship passed through the Suez Canal, was new to them. On July 14, 1932, they reached Penang, their first British port in the Far East. There, the expedition's botanist Paul Richards noted in his diary, they saw "queer Chinese junks with square sails" lying in the harbor alongside "small Malay and Chinese boats with eyes painted on them." They passed large coconut plantations and rice fields. They saw colorful processions and heard music from strange instruments. It was quite different from the barren, dun-colored, underpopulated northern lands where all Tom's previous expeditions had taken place.

In Singapore, the young men learned that Malay, not English, was the lingua franca not only of Singapore but of all the towns of the Malay Peninsula and Borneo. The entire expedition party, including Tom, set out to learn some "Bazaar Malay."

At a party held at a Chinese restaurant to celebrate Eddie Shackleton's twenty-first birthday, the celebrants got rather carried away and started to tear the place apart; as a result Tom and Eddie spent that night in a Singapore police station. They were released the next morning in time to board a small turbine steamship. Two days later they reached the northwest coast of the island of Borneo (see Map 3). Finding the mouth of the Sarawak River at dawn, for the next hour or two they sailed upriver, with mangrove and nipa palm swamps on either side, until they reached the dilapidated corrugated sheds at Pending, the port for the town of Kuching, Sarawak's capital.

Waiting at the docks was E. Banks, the Rajah's appointed leader of the Oxford expedition party and the man whose idea it had originally been to have such an expedition. In his early thirties, tanned, slim, and quietly handsome, Banks, an Oxford alumnus and the Sarawak Museum curator and government ethnographer, had devoted months to preparing for the arrival of the Oxford expedition party.

This was a crucial moment in Tom's life, one he would never forget. Here he was, by then a poised young man nearly six feet tall who had been responsible for the expedition party up to this point, but now he was expected to hand over the reins to Banks. He had loved the responsibility and status that had come from being in charge of organizing the expedition and immediately saw in this man Banks—so fit, so tan, so knowledgeable—a rival power. Twenty-five years later, recalling this moment, Tom wrote:

> Mr. Banks and I, from the moment we met on the messy . . . wharf did not see eye to eye. His eyes are brightly grey and mine a dreary shade of goat:* the wonder is that all four were not regularly black, the way we went on. It must have been intolerable to him to have to work in his own country alongside a highly egocentric undergraduate, in approximate charge of more.

In trying to make poor E. Banks's job as titular leader of the expedition "intolerable," Tom had the loyal support of Eddie Shackleton, who, as the son of the most admired hero in the England of his day, was trying to emerge from under the great burden of his name.

Eddie, a modest young man, had been a bit surprised and very pleased that someone so sophisticated and original as Tom had chosen him for the expedition and made it clear in other ways that he actually liked him and enjoyed his company. Tom did indeed like Eddie and recognized in him a "tough" who could meet any physical challenge with quiet competence. He encouraged rebellious thoughts in Eddie's mind, helping him free himself of the need to live up to his image of his father. Ever after, Eddie, who went on to be a great success in a number of fields, would be grateful to Tom, claiming he had "changed my life."

Others on the expedition, especially Cub Hartley, emerged from the experience feeling rather bruised and sore, having been rubbed raw by Tom's abrasiveness. Still, as Tom would later point out,

> If you don't want a lot of enemies, don't go on a lot of expeditions. The way a fellow cleans his teeth or rubs his ear or handles your only rain-worn copy of *Wuthering Heights*—these things mean nothing in England, but after a few months of odd food, extreme cold or heat, they magnify to mania size, so that you will surely pick on at least two of your companions and hate them and hate them and hate them. . . .

---

*In fact, they were a pale gray-blue.

The expedition's goals were to examine fauna and flora and make collections of them both in the lowlands along the Tinjar River and on the upper slopes of the high mountains of the Dulit range, more than 4,500 feet above sea level. There was a lot to choose from. There was the silvery gray Argus pheasant, possibly the most elegant bird in the world. There was the Rafflesia, the world's largest flower, as much as eight feet across. Unlike in the Arctic, Sarawak had many interesting mammals: the ugly proboscis-nosed monkey; the charming little tarsier, with its huge round eyes and tiny head, long prehensile toes and tail, an animal so delicate that none had survived in captivity; and, rarest of all, the orangutan, whose name means "man of the forest," called that because of its great resemblance to *Homo sapiens*.

No matter how exotic and interesting the flora and other fauna, it was the people of inland Borneo who stole the show. This was the first time in Tom's life he would meet a whole group of people whom he liked and who liked him from the beginning. He later confessed that "I found in these people something I had been looking for without success in the West. Answers to an unhappiness which I had not yet learnt to analyse and offset on my own. . . ." Among these tribespeople, his foreignness was taken for granted and he could be himself, while every effort to conform to their standards was greeted with gratitude and respect rather than contempt.

The Oxford party, none of whom had ever been to tropical Asia, had never seen or heard of people of such beauty, gaiety, charm, exoticism, and, at the same time, accessibility. The accessibility was partly because Malay was widely understood throughout the territory and partly because the natives of the interior of Borneo lived in big multifamily dwellings, called longhouses, that were rather like a row of attached beach cabins on stilts.

In the longhouse, which might lodge anywhere from tens to hundreds of people, the inhabitants spent most of their waking hours, when not in the rice fields or hunting and gathering supplemental foods. The long veranda that ran past each household's private room functioned as both a public boardwalk and community living room. In a longhouse, seated on mats on the veranda, one saw the whole community at work and at leisure. Furthermore, longhouse etiquette demanded that visitors participate in its social life, by staying at least for a drink of *borak* (homemade rice beer) and preferably by staying on for a long drunken night of dancing, singing, games, and conversation.

The eccentric Brooke Rajahs had tried to minimize what they perceived to be negative social changes in the inland areas where the longhouse dwellers—the *orang ulu* (upriver people) and the Dayaks (subcoastal pagans)—lived, instructing newly arrived English district officers that "the natives are not inferior, but different." Tom's was the first party of explorers permitted entry in a generation. Entrepreneurs and tourists were barred outright, and the more sophisticated coastal and subcoastal peoples were kept from encroaching on land being used by the *orang ulu*. Even missionaries were not allowed to proselytize except when the local native people had invited them.

The one big exception to the White Rajahs' hands-off policy regarding the longhouse people was their determination to eliminate headhunting, which they had succeeded in doing some fifteen years before Tom and his party had arrived. Until then, among many longhouse peoples, especially the Ibans (also known as Dayaks or Sea Dayaks), Tom would accurately report:

> Bringing back your head gave you as much prestige with the girls as getting a rowing blue or being an explorer. The young man who went out and got an enemy head could marry anyone available, and often his success would cause some specially attractive girl to propose to him.

Taking an enemy head in battle was one thing. There were, however, also special occasions, such as ending the mourning period after a chief's death, when fresh heads were needed, and they did not have to be from enemies. For these occasions, the head of a little old woman from another longhouse washing clothes by the river was every bit as acceptable as the head of an enemy Goliath.

The *orang ulu*, all former headhunters, felt ambivalent about the Rajahs' ban of the practice. It made life a lot safer but it also deprived their religious and ritual life of its centerpiece. It was as if the Christian mass had to take place without the wine and bread. The headhunters now had to make do with old heads that were still around, lying on candelabralike shelves above the longhouse doors, where they were ritually "fed" with bits of meat and *borak* on sacred occasions. Headhunting aside, the *orang ulu* were grateful to the Rajah and his handful of unobtrusive, tactful white officers, stationed in market towns at the bottom edge of the upriver country, and they were well disposed to white people generally.

Tom, at the head of a group of youngsters eager to get to their destination in the interior, grew restless as weeks slipped by while the Oxford party was entertained by these same tactful white officers, first in Kuching and then, as the expedition slowly made its way north along the coast, in the oil refinery town of Miri and, up the Baram, in the market town of Marudi. By the time they got to Marudi, Tom's patience was gone and he took an immediate dislike to the district officer there, a man named Pollard, who returned the sentiment. When telling of his contretemps with Pollard, Tom added:

> It is generally said that [Somerset] Maugham's story "The Outstation," refers to Marudi and I strongly recommend anyone to read that story before continuing with this one; it gets the administrative atmosphere down to a fly-button.

Finally, in late July, nearly six weeks after they had left Liverpool, the expedition party reached the Tinjar, a tributary of the Baram. There were a few crocodiles on the banks; behind the muddy banks there was bright green secondary jungle, with olive-gray-green primary jungle beyond. Tom's notes show him beginning to enjoy himself:

> Winding slowly up the slowly narrowing river, the jungle grew closer and closer about us, casting longer shadows from high overhead. Many sorts of kingfisher, glistening blue-velvety and purple, . . . blue birds flit to and fro like dumpy butterflies; while all kinds of fruit pigeon, fifteen sorts of woodpecker, Langur monkeys, parroquets and cigar-necked clumsy darters illuminate every mile of the journey. Towards evening the cicadas make your ears tingle with sound.

They got to their first longhouse that afternoon and settled comfortably in the chief's rooms. The longhouse "was a much cleaner and pleasanter place for spending a night" than botanist Richards had expected and "compared very favourably with an alpine chalet." Over the next three days en route to their base camp, the party spent each night in a different longhouse. Underneath the longhouse veranda on the muddy ground below, "dogs, fowls, goats and pigs roamed about and kept up a good deal of noise at night, the goats disagreeing with the dogs and the fowls with the pigs."

One longhouse was having a funeral for the sister of the *penghulu* (chief) of the tribal peoples of the lower Tinjar valley. Richards writes that "Banks sat on a dais with the chief men of the house and a row of fine carved chairs had been put ready for the rest of us." The dead woman was "lying in state in a marvellous carved and painted [sarcophagus]." There were white funeral flags with a "remarkable design in black" hung all over the house. "A superb painted tomb had been put up on the other bank of the river and various pennants and flags were hung from it." There was also "an interesting collection of heads hung from the usual candelabra-like arrangement, some really wonderful gothic-like carvings of monkeys on the supports of the house, a fine shield and some beautifully made hats. We had breakfast in the head man's room, where there were several old and valuable Chinese jars." The upriver people collected ancient Chinese jars, some of them Sung or earlier, and regarded them as their most valuable possessions for use in trade (such as to settle a blood debt), for their alleged magic powers, and to brew their *borak*.

The *orang ulu* living on the Tinjar were a mixture of tribes. Related by marriage and custom and similar in appearance, they were finely made, generally slim, and golden-tan with hairless bodies and smooth blue-black head hair. The men, who usually wore only a loin cloth, had elongated earlobes, which carried such ornaments as clouded leopard teeth in the upper lobes and earrings made of scarlet and yellow hornbill ivory in the lower lobes.

The women usually had "broad noses, high cheek bones, slanting eyes and often the roundest of faces." Their lower earlobes were much longer than those of the men and held heavy brass ornaments to stretch them further. The women and girls usually wore nothing above the waist, and often their breasts were beautiful. Wrapped around their bodies from the waist down would be either a short bark-cloth or handwoven cotton skirt or a long imported cotton sarong. On their bare feet and legs and occasionally on the backs of their hands and forearms were lacy black tattoos. One of the expedition party recalls that "apart from whatever passes for beauty in women, they possessed, even the plainest of them, a grace which is lost to women of civilised nations; the grace which seems to derive from bare feet and confers its own particular dignity of carriage and smooth rhythm of movement."

The *orang ulu* were proud of their traditions and welcoming to these interesting and amusing young guests, but not overawed by them. As Tom later commented, in upriver Borneo, "the European is . . . treated as a respected friend, a 'superior equal' . . . [and] is expected to join in every sort of native activity, to drink with them, to join in all ceremonies, and so on. . . . If he can charleston [which Tom could do standing on a table] or do conjuring tricks he is bound to be a success."

The expedition had not come to entertain the local people. But Tom, once he found out how pleasant and approachable the *orang ulu* were, "quietly budgeted an extra hundred pounds for entertainment," for such items as whisky and cigarettes, especially whisky. This was quid pro quo for the vast amounts of local *borak* that the hospitable longhouse ladies sluiced down the throats of their English guests during the long boisterous evening parties on their verandas. While the host men, caparisoned in war coats backed with black and white hornbill feathers, sang and danced their war dances, "bottoms up" was constantly demanded of each honored guest. If a guest "shows signs of wilting under the ordeal," the cup full of *borak* "is held to his mouth and tilted vigorously so that he must either swallow or choke. The women delight in compelling the swallow or choke."

During the expedition's months on the Tinjar, the base camp became a center of social life. "No sooner had we arrived," recalls one of the Oxford party, "than scores of curious men, women and children came paddling down the river in little shallow canoes, eager to inspect us and, on the sixth of August, we held our 'official house-warming'" to which at least a hundred men and women from a mosaic of tribes attended, although "for all these, the return journey would be three or four days of hard paddling and scrambling over rapids of the many streams which form the headwaters of the Tinjar."

The presence of these hospitable tribespeople prevented the social claustrophobia that Tom had seen plague other expeditions. But how to discourage the usual formation of antagonistic cliques within the expedition party that might interfere with the group's work? Tom had no wish to prevent the development of that hatred, or "nucleus of fire," as he called it, that naturally heats up in an expedition situation. Instead, he wanted to channel that hatred, that heat, in such a way that it was shared by the party against a single target: himself! This is a strange thing to have done deliberately; perhaps Tom's alleged plan, as described six years later, is merely an ex post facto explanation for his unpopularity with his expedition mates. Perhaps he simply took advantage of what was bound to happen anyway. But the reason it seems credible to one who knows Tom's later history that he consciously chose to make these men dislike him in order to get them to work more effectively together is that he did the identical thing—with equal success—in 1945, during World War II.

An exception to Tom's policy of encouraging the others to hate him was made for Tom's growing friendship with Eddie Shackleton. When Tom climbed Mount Dulit on his birthday, he had Eddie with him to share this mountaintop experience, which made Tom value Eddie's friendship more than ever. And it may be why, untypically for Tom, he encouraged Eddie to go off alone for three weeks at the end of the Oxford party's stay in the interior in order to have the single most newsworthy adventure of the expedition: to be the first man known to climb Mount Mulu, which, at nearly 8,000 feet, was then believed to be the highest mountain in Sarawak.

Until they broke up for their separate three-week treks at the end of the expedition, Eddie went everywhere Tom went and, like Tom, flouted the rules that Banks and Pollard and some of the other more conventional officers of the Brooke Raj laid down to try to keep the Oxford and Cambridge boys out of danger. As Tom explained it, undoubtedly with exaggeration, Banks "wanted us to sit down at the Base Camp," but "one curator being no match for eight undergraduates, we naturally had our several ways."

This was certainly the case when, at the funerary feast for a tribal chief the group attended with Banks, the young men were invited to take part in longboat races, using hundred-foot longboats with many paddles. As Shackleton later recalled; "Banks said we weren't to go, whereupon we promptly went. We just sat in the canoe and paddled with the rest of them and got up a terrific speed and I seem to remember that Banks was very angry." Tom, who would never have agreed to row for Pembroke, was happy to do so here, where it had the double appeal of sharing an adventure with the native people and flouting authority.

Yet Tom and the others, helped by local tribesmen, were very effective in carrying out their various tasks of observation and collection of local fauna and flora. The party was also helped by some Punans, pale, shy forest-dwelling hunter-gatherers. These Punans were true nomads; their property consisted only of loin cloths, straw baskets, and the superbly made blowpipes and poisoned darts with which they killed game. On one occasion, a Punan blowpiped and killed a black and yellow snake he saw in a tree overhanging the party's path. It was a banded krait, one of the deadliest poisonous snakes in the world.

While Eddie was climbing Mulu and others of the party were engaged for three weeks in other exploration, Tom headed overland along a jungle path between the Tinjar and the Belaga, a tributary of the Rejang River. (The Rejang, like the Baram, is another of the major rivers of Borneo running from the central mountains westward to the South China Sea.) By a combination of hard walking and boating, frequently interrupted by rapids that required the boat be portaged alongside the river, Tom managed to visit all the longhouses along the Belaga, which was the headquarters area of the Kenyah tribe. At one longhouse, he attended a "three-day celebration on typical Kenyah lines," that is, with much feasting, dancing, and drinking, especially drinking.

Within the year, Tom would write that "my first heterosexual experience" was "associated with a clump of trees in a tropical jungle." It probably occurred on this trip along the Belaga. As Eddie would later attest, on the Tinjar, the women "sang drinking songs to us but we didn't make passes at them, I doubt whether Tom did either. We were boringly English about them." If Tom did have a sexual encounter with a native woman, it is much more likely to have happened when traveling alone among the Kenyah of Belaga, famed for the beauty of their women, where a tradition of hospitality to male visitors included sexual favors at the discretion of the woman.

One way or another, the expedition had been a wonderfully satisfying adventure for all its young members. Even their health had been remarkably good. After four months in the field, the Oxford party finally packed up and went back down river to "civilization." Arriving in Kuching on December 12, 1932, the young men were full of pride in their achievements and in no mood to be told how to behave by their elders and self-proclaimed betters, the officers of the Brooke Raj. The expedition party had been to places some of the Sarawak expatriates had never seen, and its members now behaved like young know-it-alls.

An Englishwoman who came to Sarawak as the bride of a Brooke officer some months after the Oxford party had come through Kuching on its way home was told that the young men had shown "absolutely no manners," and that for them "any question of research [had been] very secondary." They had arrived in Kuching dirty and smelly, and as guests of the Sarawak Club, they had "thrown their weight around as the great explorers. I didn't see it myself.

But people were still up in arms when I arrived because they really felt these puppies had been so awful and had let down the side so badly." In fact, the Oxford party had bathed regularly in the river when up-country and undoubtedly took baths in town, but they might have walked around Kuching in dirty clothes, not having much town wear. They certainly boasted of their adventures and drank heavily and probably engaged in one or more barroom brawls.

Tom would not have cared what the Maughamesque members of the Sarawak Club thought of him and his party, but Banks, in his legitimate anger at the discourtesy shown him, by Tom and Eddie especially, wrote to a number of people in England—such as Solly Zuckerman, then an officer of the London Zoo, and Tom's patron, Charles Elton, as chairman of the Oxford University Expedition Club—to complain about the expedition party. Banks repeated these complaints in his "Annual Report of the Sarawak Museum for 1932," in which he deplored the fact that the party had consisted entirely of very young men. He ended with the moral that "Every bit as important as selecting technical ability is the rejecting of men lacking normal manners, uncouth in appearance or unpleasant in personality, characters admittedly in only a small proportion, yet doing much to antagonize both European and native against the Expedition's better interest." As Tom later noted, "People like me do tend to decide, if in doubt, that the nasty crack is made at them," and it was not paranoid for Tom to have concluded that when Banks wrote of men "lacking normal manners," the curator was referring to him and Eddie.

Having devoted much effort to becoming the object of Banks' wrath, Tom could hardly complain at having succeeded. What he objected to was Banks stating that he and Eddie had also been rude to, or gained the dislike of, the native people. He and Eddie and other party members always claimed that this was a false charge, and there is every reason to believe them. As Tom later wrote, "I fell for Sarawak" and its people "in a very big way" and it seems fairly certain that the liking was mutual. The career that occupied most of Tom's working life grew out of the mutual liking developed between Tom and the *orang ulu* at this time. As to whether the party had done work of use to science, forty-eight scientific papers emerged from this expedition. There probably never was another Oxford expedition to produce anything like the quantity and variety of scientific results as did this expedition to Sarawak. Banks' version, though incorrect on these points, remained ever after the accepted truth among the whites who went to Sarawak or who heard about the Oxford Expedition of 1932 from the expatriates of Sarawak; it would help to embitter Tom's future relations with people who would be his neighbors and professional colleagues during twenty years. It seems a cruelly high price to pay for a few days of youthful excess of spirits.

After a week in Kuching, the Oxford party sailed back to Singapore. Tom spent Christmas at Port Dickson, on Malaya's southwest coast, as the guest of "some anglo-snobs," confirming his prejudice against the "typical" British expatriates in the Malay-speaking world. He arrived uninvited, having wanted to see again a fellow guest, Tim S., with whom he had "fallen in love" while they were both at Harrow. Tim, however, was now infatuated with their hosts' lovely fourteen-year-old daughter, the future actress Dulcie Gray. Without understanding the reason for it, Dulcie was struck by the strength of Tom's seething jealousy of her during the twenty-four hours that she, Tim, and Tom were together with her parents at the family's seaside holiday bungalow. For Tom, who went out of his way to insult Dulcie and her parents, his friend Tim's romantic attachment to the young girl must have seemed like a betrayal. After this, Tom never "fell in love" with another man, at least not sexually.

He left with the Oxford party from Singapore on the Blue Funnel's *Sarpedon* on December 28 and reached England three weeks later. While in Sarawak, he had received (again, thanks to Elton) an invitation to be the ornithologist on yet another Oxford expedition, this time to the New Hebrides, in the Southwest Pacific, famed as "cannibal islands." He immediately accepted the offer. Reaching England, he went straight to Oxford to write up his Sarawak research and to prepare for his next tropical adventure.

# Chapter 4

## Letter to Oxford

During Tom's absence, his friends Reynold Bray and Tom Manning had walked out of university and had crossed Arctic Lapland in a reindeer sledge and gone on into Russia, for which they had no entry visa. Ending up in a Soviet jail in Leningrad, they had become overnight a cause célèbre between Britain and the Soviet Union. Tom must have been gratified that Bray and Manning had made the same decision about their studies that he had made the year before.

Back in Oxford, staying with Bray again, he enjoyed learning of the good reception given his report on the great crested grebe that had appeared in four installments of *British Birds* that autumn. *The Times* had described the report as "one of the fullest accounts of life-history which are so far available for any wild bird in any country," underlying its significance by noting that "It was the slaughter of great crested grebes, as much as any other single factor, which contributed to the strength of the mid-Victorian movement in favour of protecting British wild birds." Anybody who cared about birds in the 1930s remembers this survey. Repeating it at regular intervals has become one of the fixtures of British bird-watching activity.

Tom now expanded his Oxford circle to include a number of interesting new people. One was John Baker, the zoologist who would lead Tom's next expedition, to the New Hebrides. A shy, humorless, decent man and a great scientist, later to become a fellow of the Royal Society, Baker had studied under Julian Huxley at Oxford and, like Huxley, had scientific interests spanning all of biology. He had been to the New Hebrides twice before. Tom spent much time with him, preparing himself for the long expedition due to begin that summer, 1933, and scheduled to last up to a year.

Tom also now met a fascinating small birdlike blonde, always elegantly dressed, and thirteen years older than he, Mary Adams. She was a friend of Baker's, from the days when she had worked on cytology while on a research scholarship at Newnham College, Cambridge. By the time Baker introduced Tom to this multitalented woman, she was running the adult education office for BBC radio, prior to becoming the first woman television producer, also for the BBC, in 1936. Like Naomi Mitchison, Mary Adams would become one of Tom's best friends and patrons. If Tom did not know Naomi Mitchison before, he would get to know her now, since she was the best friend of John Baker's wife, Zita.

This being the 1930s, most of Tom's friends were actively involved on the far Left politically. Tom, though he "rather liked the Liberal Party's ideas," paid little attention to politics. But shortly after he got back from Borneo, national politics descended upon Oxford in a way even Tom could not ignore.

In February 1933, the Oxford Union came to figure in the headlines of the national press for having voted overwhelmingly in favor of the motion "That this House will under no circumstances fight for King and Country." The nation appeared to have been stunned by this affront to the values best expressed by the Kitchener First World War recruiting poster caption, "Your country needs you," to which so many young men had responded in 1914, joining up and losing their lives in unequal battles against machine guns.

Distinguished Oxford alumni organized a drive to expunge from the record the Union's infamous vote by having the motion voted on again in March, whereupon the rebellious Oxonians confirmed their original decision by an even bigger majority. As Tom commented in print shortly afterward: "Obviously in the hot blood of war-lunacy lots of those people would fight for King and Country; obviously the voting was influenced by the determination of Oxen to show interfering little outsiders that they could not bludgeon Ox into their own shape."

This comment comes from Tom's major piece of writing of this period, other than the talk he was preparing about the expedition to Sarawak for the Royal Geographical Society's meeting that June. This piece of writing was a pamphlet, meant—in a similar way to his article on "What's Wrong with Our Colleges"—to serve as a red flag to the Oxford bull, or as he persisted in calling it in his *Letter to Oxford*, the Oxford Ox.

Unlike his earlier statements about Cambridge, Tom's complaints against Oxford (a university that he admired for its intellectual superiority) were not about university men retaining a juvenile "public school" ethos but about finding in Oxford a fear of seeming to be young, a fear so strong that it kept the typical Ox from taking risks, experimenting, or doing things that only the young can do. "Perhaps," Tom suggested, "the scarcity of thirty-fivers [killed in the Great War] makes twenty-oners try to be thirty-fivy."

In reference to the Oxford Union debate, Tom asked: If the Ox was not prepared to fight for King and Country, what *was* he prepared to fight for, die for, or even risk embarrassment for? The answer seemed to be "very little." In hortatory prose sprawled over ninety-eight printed pages, Tom accused the "Oxen" of 1933 of preferring masturbation to making love, indolence to activity, a phoney tolerance and sneering boredom to full-blooded anger or hatred. If the Oxen believed that "Me is me, there is nothing to live for, there is no point," Tom replied,

> How do they know there is no point? What do they mean? Have they ever tested it? Have they ever been hungry without any knowledge of what is going to happen next? Have they ever tested the point with their bodies? Or with their minds? Have they ever been so angry that they have wanted to kill? Or so mad with happiness that they have not cared one moment for anything and everything that anybody might think about them? If they had tested hunger they would know there was tremendous point in the richness of a full belly. If they had tested anger they would know the point of raging hate and quivering nerves; if they had tested shouting ecstatic happiness it would kill all imaginings of pointlessness for ever.

As for himself, he wrote, "I believe vaguely in life. I can live on practically nothing, but am fond of spending a great deal. I believe in action—in doing a thing as well as saying it, in seeing something wrong and trying to put it right." He admonished Oxen to "*see* and *feel* the other sorts of life. Before a man can call himself a live socialist he *must* have lived among working men, be directly conscious of poverty, have been bitten by a workhouse louse. . . ." He urged them to "Go to Alaska, go to the Gold Coast, go to Hell, anywhere different and exciting and new. . . . It is easy to escape from the bondage of money, jobs, routine; you don't need a lot of brains, only guts and determination. You can see nearly everything in life without money, and it is the only way to see most of it whole." He ended on a typically adolescent note: "I do not think that my father has any right at all to shape me more than he has already done. . . . A person of twenty-one is an unstable unit. I hope to change very much every day until I die. No doubt I shall be very ashamed of this pamphlet in five years' time; the more fool I." In fact, Tom never disavowed this essay, with its idealism and its youthful callowness.

He wrote *Letter to Oxford* while staying at the Rose Revived, a small inn ten miles outside Oxford, to which Bray had moved after returning from Russia. By May, when the pamphlet was published, Tom and Bray had moved to the Gloucestershire village of Wyck Rissington, also some ten miles from Oxford. They changed the name on the gate of the cottage Bray rented to "The Trobriands" in honor of the great anthropologist, Bronislaw Malinowski, whose book, *The Sexual Life of Savages in* NW *Melanesia* (1929) about the Trobriand islanders had made a great impression on Tom.

He dictated *Letter to Oxford* to a secretary, Zita Baker, who was, in addition to being John Baker's wife and the mother of two young children, an excellent typist and stenographer. She was also what in Oxford circles would pass for a femme fatale and, if Tom could claim to have experienced "shouting ecstatic happiness," it was in Zita's arms, beginning in the spring of 1933. Zita was the first woman Tom ever loved; he would later tell his favorite cousin that Zita was "the love of his life." She was the only woman Tom ever loved simply for herself and not because she was in some way useful to him.

Ten years older than Tom, Zita had married John Baker in 1923 when she was twenty-two. The marriage had rather surprised Oxford people, since the bride was clearly not a typical don's wife. She had had many lovers by then and continued to have affairs, out of boredom and kindness—both of which she had in plenty—with a number of other young men during her apparently happy marriage to Baker. She was slim and slight, very blonde, with a snub nose and a full mouth. She once said that her face looked like that of an albino Melanesian, but she was enormously attractive, warm, gay, and unpretentious. Adventurous not only sexually, she enjoyed taking risks. She had been with Baker on his second expedition to the New Hebrides and planned to leave her children behind to come on the third expedition in the summer. Tom found her wonderful.

She tried to get Tom's pamphlet published by Blackwell's, but no proper publisher would touch it, and eventually Reynold Bray paid for the printing of it on what he and Tom baptized the "Hate Press." Tom, in sandals with his toenails red, sold it from a barrow on the streets of Oxford. As Naomi Mitchison recalls, "it raised a considerable storm at the time," to Tom's undoubted satisfaction.

On June 12, 1933, shortly after publishing *Letter to Oxford*, Tom gave a lecture about the Oxford Expedition to Borneo, before the Royal Geographical Society (RGS). He cut his hair for the occasion, in response to a request from Mr. Hinks, the RGS's secretary, but having torn up his tailcoat on the way out to Borneo, he was not willing to indulge establishment conventions to the extent of wearing evening attire. "The principle involved," Tom wrote Hinks, "prevents me from wearing evening clothes" or even a dinner jacket, but he did promise to wear "a suit, tie, shoes, etc."

This talk, to which Eddie Shackleton and Cub Hartley contributed brief remarks at the end, also drew on papers by other members. It was well received by an audience that included many of Britain's top scientists and their financial patrons. The RGS president surely spoke for many of those present in saying, after Tom and the others finished, that he envied the young men their adventure.

The RGS lecture behind him, it was now time to sail off on his fourth expedition, to the New Hebrides. In the expedition party aboard ship would be the woman he loved. In a joyous mood, he had Naomi Mitchison paint his toenails red one last time.

**PART TWO**

In the South Pacific,
1933–1935

# Chapter 5

## Zita and Santo

The long ship voyage to the New Hebrides, via Australia, covered mostly the same route as the year before, and having Zita aboard was not the delight Tom had hoped. It was wonderful when she would come to his cabin for "dictation" but awkward when she and her husband and Tom were all together on deck or in the dining room.

The Oxford expedition party consisted of John Baker, leader; Zita Baker, photographer; Tom Harrisson, ornithologist; and a Balliol man, Terence Bird, zoologist and surveyor. John's sister Ina Baker was the expedition's botanist, but she would not join the party until October. This was the first Oxford expedition with women on it but not the first trip to the New Hebrides for Zita. Six years earlier, she had accompanied John to Espiritu Santo (also known as Santo) and to Gaua, one of the Banks Islands north of Santo.

The Oxford party paused a week in Sydney before embarking on one of the Burns Philp trading steamers that traveled to and among the Western Pacific islands. They reached their destination, Hog Harbour, on the island of Santo on September 2, 1933 (see the map of Santo and Malekula on p.46). Baker wrote in his diary that "As we steamed up the coast, we were all tremendously cheerful and the day was one of the happiest of my life." They had supper with the Reverend William Anderson and his wife, missionaries on whose estate the expedition had its camp, and then started unpacking by moonlight with the help of candle lamps.

The camp at Hog Harbour had four thatch-roofed huts, one for John and Zita and one for each of the other three team members, plus a cook house, dining shelter, and laboratory shelter, but no privacy for illicit lovers. Tom and Zita would occasionally go off together to bathe in the sea or walk inland to visit a native village. Their affair had reached the stage when any time not spent alone together seemed wasted. Tom wrote to Naomi

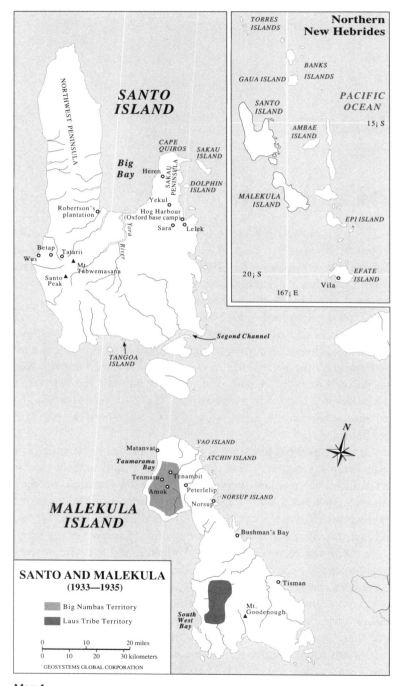

SANTO ISLAND

NORTHWEST PENINSULA

*CAPE QUIROS*

*Big Bay*    Heren

*SAKAU ISLAND*

SAKAU PENINSULA

*DOLPHIN ISLAND*

Yekul

Hog Harbour
(Oxford base camp)

Sara    Lelek

Robertson's plantation

*Yora River*

Betap    Tatarii
Wus
▲ Mt. Tabwemasana
Santo ▲
Peak

**Northern New Hebrides**

*TORRES ISLANDS*

*BANKS ISLANDS*

*GAUA ISLAND*

*SANTO ISLAND*

*PACIFIC OCEAN*

*AMBAE ISLAND*

15¡ S

*MALEKULA ISLAND*

*EPI ISLAND*

20¡ S

*EFATE ISLAND*

Vila

167¡ E

Segond Channel

*TANGOA ISLAND*

*N*

*VAO ISLAND*

Matanvat

*ATCHIN ISLAND*

*Taumarama Bay*

Tenmaru    Tenambit

Amok    Peterlelip

Norsup    *NORSUP ISLAND*

**MALEKULA ISLAND**

Bushman's Bay

Tisman

Mt. Goodenough ▲

*South West Bay*

**SANTO AND MALEKULA**
**(1933—1935)**

Big Nambas Territory

Laus Tribe Territory

| 0 | 10 | 20 miles |
| 0 | 10 | 20 | 30 kilometers |

GEOSYSTEMS GLOBAL CORPORATION

Map 1

Mitchison: "Zita in another house, Zita dear, John dear, all the time a 'couple in an expedition'. . . . Zita and I fight. This is I know due to terrific John feeling I get up, and repression and subterfuge feeling and lover-outsideness complex." Finally, on the fifth day after landing, Zita and Tom went off early to Dolphin Island and spent the night there. The official reason for this excursion was to try to get specimens of a rare grebe. But one night alone with Zita was hardly enough to satisfy Tom. Zita (writing to Naomi) seemed to be equally frustrated:

> There's John and Tom and me. We can't talk because it wouldn't be fair to the expedition but things are said and situations happen and we all talk and talk to get them better but we can't really say what is the matter. I'm much more a Tom person than a John person but I'm 12 [actually 10] years older than Tom and I've been conditioned to have little bits of everything and never one thing alone and when I have a chance of being just really Tom, I just bitch it up in some way. . . .

Baker, a very private person, would merely make terse entries in his diary, such as for September 14: "General row at dinner time."

Within two weeks of arrival, Baker left the camp with Terence Bird and a few Hog Harbour "boys" on a trip expected to last a week or two. This gave the lovers a welcome respite from John Baker's company but not from Tom's sense of rivalry with him, since Baker and Bird were embarking on an adventure that brought out all of Tom's competitive drive: a reconnaissance trip preparatory to an attempt to climb a "new" mountain.

This peak, about 6,000 feet high according to a new Admiralty map, had been, as Baker recalled, "ignored by the whites of the islands," who persisted in regarding Santo Peak, at 5,520 feet and further to the south, as the New Hebrides' highest mountain. On Baker's previous trip to Santo, uncertain whether it really existed, he had led a small party of Englishmen to where the chart placed the mountain, found it there, and climbed its lower peak. The native porters had refused to stay long enough for the explorers to figure a way up the second peak. They told the Englishmen that nobody, native or otherwise, had ever climbed the higher peak of the mountain they called Tabwemasana, or Mountain of the Double Seashell. Baker had made conquering it one of the two main objects of the present expedition. He and Bird returned to Hog Harbour in ten days, announcing to Tom and Zita that they had found a new, better route to the mountain from the north. An assault on the higher peak was scheduled for a month later.

While Baker and Bird had been away, however, Tom had bruised his shin and broken the skin. In a few days the wound had become a maggot-filled sore. Zita nursed him, pouring carbolic acid into the wound, trying to urge the maggots to exit alive rather than to die inside the wound, possibly causing an even more dangerous infection. For the next five weeks, Tom was off his feet, except during a perilous trip with Zita by native launch to the nearest hospital, along the Segond Channel on Santo's south coast, fifty miles south of Hog Harbour. The launch lost its rudder in the riptide and Tom and Zita almost drowned. Finally reaching land, Zita reembarked for Hog Harbour after having deposited Tom at the French hospital. Tom recalled that "For several days [the French doctor] injected me from every angle. . . . A nun threw alleged cocaine on my leg, and then burned the flesh for a while. Happily after a week they lost interest; it is hot in September." In those days before penicillin or sulpha drugs, it was questionable whether the wound would ever heal in that climate.

For Tom, the more serious concern was the possibility of missing the assault on the mountain. He "had sworn [to] be around the foot of that mountain somehow in three weeks, the latest date the chaps could start" before the seasonal rains made the rivers impassable. Tom placed tremendous importance on taking part in this climb. Mountains meant so much to him. Just a year earlier, in September 1932, on the peak of Sarawak's Mount Dulit, he had set himself the challenge of proving he could do his own things and keep his independence while winning the kinds of acclaim his father had won. Tom's urgent desire to be first, to be on top, and to get credit for it, was most rampant when there were new mountains to climb.

For Baker and the others back at the Hog Harbour camp, the time came for the assault on the mountain. Leaving John's sister Ina behind to tend meteorological instruments in connection with the expedition's other main task, the study of whether faunal breeding has seasons when the climate is more or less constant, John and Zita Baker and Terence Bird set off on October 24.

Tom, who was supposed to be bed-bound, sneaked out of the hospital, walking by himself for the first time in five weeks. He hired a trader's launch to take him 100 miles north from the Segond Channel along Santo's west coast. Knowing the others would be going inland from Big Bay in the north, he decided to come over the ranges from the west. "It would take them five days to reach the 4,000 foot spur where we proposed to camp for the final assault," Tom recalled. "I estimated I could just make it."

The launch got him to the west coast, seven miles due west of the "new" mountain. There, he met natives from the hill village of Betap on the coast making salt, and they agreed to take him with them into the interior. With his leg still "a mess," he followed these hill men to a village 1,000 feet up, where influenza had just killed the last man living there. Tom helped the bushmen bury the dead man and lead the surviving "daughter and wife and pigs for a day up and down over the break-back of hill and ravine" to the village of Betap. At one place, he had to cross a 200-foot-deep ravine by means of "a moss green log."

More impressive than Tom's ability to cross a ravine on a long slippery log with a wounded leg was his facility for fitting in with the local people, in this case near-naked, unwashed, woolly-haired, black-skinned Melanesians. For him, it was seemingly as effortless as joining up with a bunch of Sunday hikers in the Lake District. His attitude contrasted with that of other westerners who were utterly repelled by the looks of these New Hebrideans. A yacht that stopped off in Santo in 1935, having visited Tahiti and some of the Banks Islands as well as Malekula, carried six young American passengers who found the Sakau natives of Santo to be "the wildest, blackest, dirtiest, most ferocious savages we had ever hoped could exist." The Sakau women and children were naked but for a G-string. The men wore a simple belt, which held a small vegetal curtain in front of their genitals; a long-handled unsheathed bush knife was stuck in the belt behind. As to their faces, even Baker, although he characterized his friends among the Sakau as "nature's gentlemen," could not seemingly avoid describing these same men as "ugly, ill-developed" and "ferocious-looking."

Tom admired Captain Cook's manner of dealing with the islanders; he wrote that "Cook had a genius for native contacts. He sported absolutely no visible white man's burden. Especially he went chief-hunting. Over and over again on his voyages we find him seeking out the native aristocracy with the persistence of a gossip columnist. When there was Cook on the ship and a chief on the shore, Cook went ashore." From this expedition onward, in dealing with nonwesternized peoples, Tom followed Cook's example and courted the chiefs.

This was Tom's first extended time on his own since leaving England. Despite his sore leg and his anxiety to get to the mountain's foot by the deadline, he was elated at finding that his knack for getting on with the local people was working here, as it had in Sarawak the year before. And then, to crown his pleasure, "I saw by the path, in the low jungle, now wet and mossy, a queer little brown bird, thick like a Wryneck, alert like a Starling. It was altogether a new sort of bird and I did not mind anything any more." The bird was the mountain starling, *Aplonis santovestris*, which "is confined to the summits of a few interior peaks of Espiritu Santo and must thus be one of the world's rarest birds." Seeing a new bird or one that meant something special to him remained important to Tom all his life. Bird sightings punctuated his adventures, giving them a new turning, almost as if he saw the birds as omens, as did the inland peoples of Borneo and the New Hebrides.

Meanwhile, after three days of walking from Baker's friend "Robby" Robertson's plantation on the north coast at Big Bay, the Bakers, Bird, and their forty-one porters reached Tatarii, a deserted village that they planned to use as their base camp. Baker and Bird set some of the men to clear paths to the mountain, others to fetch water. After several hours of work, Baker "had blown the shell to recall everyone from their labours, when to my amazement a white man limped into our little clearing." Tom had got there in time.

Zita wrote to Naomi Mitchison that Tom had arrived, pale, limping, with a band of bush people, "in a terribly excited condition. . . ."

> He was very "young" and immediately poured out all his adventures in a long long Harrisson "out." He never asked what we had been doing—never thanked John for arranging about the cutter [that took Tom to the French hospital], sending his things round, paying for the hospital (£20), etc. That immediately put him wrong with John who believes almost firstly in politeness.

Zita explained to Naomi:

> It doesn't bother me at all when Tom doesn't thank or doesn't say the conventional "considerate" things any more. It used to, but I know now that he does things all the time for chaps and doesn't want to be thanked, and when there is any real considerateness needed nobody can be more "look after." I'm beginning to think it's pretty inferior of me to like being thanked and asked how the cuts on my legs are.
>
> Tom and I went down to a waterfall to bathe and there we had a long long talk in which I said that in future I was always going to keep my word to him, and if I promised to do anything with him I really would.

Two days later, Monday, October 30, was "The day!" Baker's diary notes that Tom and Terence Bird went ahead to meet the main body of carriers and to cut a path to the summit. Tom put on a bravura performance, making a vertical descent that, to Baker, "looked impossible to descend without a rope. Tom had managed it somehow, and had then been forced to climb it again in order to induce the others to follow him down." Baker records that "Harrisson worked wonders" and hacked his way with his knife to the summit of the higher peak. They all reached the summit at 11:30 A.M., after five hours of climbing.

Heavy rain started almost at once, chilling the climbers as they went about their mountaintop chores, taking barometer and temperature readings and collecting insects and plants. Tom no doubt took part in these activities, but what he remembered afterward was that he had looked at the knife that he had been given by a Kenyah swordsmith in Central Borneo the year before. He had used it to hack his way through the brush and its hornbill ivory handle had broken off from the curved blade. Holding the knife, he looked up and out at the Pacific Ocean and felt that "there was nothing else strong against one in these islands; now it was possible to do everything." It was a moment he would recall in the first sentence of his first real book, *Savage Civilisation* (1937):

> I stand for the first time on top of Mount Tabwemasana, on Espiritu Santo island . . . 6,000 feet over the sea, highest point in several thousand miles of Pacific. . . ."

On the trip back down, the rain never stopped. The party arrived in Tatarii soaked through, with torn clothes and scratched arms and hands. They had tinned steak and tinned plum pudding and whisky to celebrate, and, Baker's diary asserts, they "all felt at peace with the world," even though the ditch around their tents had flooded "and our mats, sleeping-bags and sleeping clothes were all wet." The expedition now began its scientific research, though the rain continued all during their stay near the mountain-top and they were "never dry for one moment, day or night."

The tacit battle over Zita continued. Tom, having noticed that the birds on the summit were different from those he had seen elsewhere, wanted to stay on and study them, for weeks if necessary, and wanted Zita to stay with him. Baker wanted her to come down with him and Bird and check out the route Tom had used getting to the base camp. As Zita explained to Naomi:

> I meant to stick to my promise to Tom for once and despite the most nauseating endless discussions in which nobody said what they meant, they [Baker and Bird] went down and we [Zita and Tom] stayed up. . . .
>
> We had a marvellous time at that great height with clouds and storms swirling round us and every now and then a burst of sun revealing unexpected mountain tops and long dark valleys and little bits of sea.

Tom taught her to skin birds, and she boasted to Naomi that "now I have to do all the specially important ones." They had "delightful visitors who came with their bows and arrows and shot for us and brought us presents and sat round our fire with us." After four days, however, Tom and Zita came down from the mountain and rejoined John Baker and Bird at Betap. Once again, Zita and her husband were "a couple on an expedition," sleeping in a former mission house and eating off the altar.

The tension was building to a climax, as Baker continued to plead with his wife to come back to their Hog Harbour camp with him and Bird rather than go back up the mountain again to collect birds with Tom. The next morning, with Tom present, Baker made the same points, and, as Zita wrote to Naomi,

> Tom and John began to say stinging things to each other. In the end, John could stand no more and he rushed across the room and started hitting Tom as hard as he could. Tom wasn't feeling at all angry and just didn't fight which made John soon stop.

Then I couldn't bear to see John so hurt and exasperated and I said I would go with him. . . . While we waited for guides, Tom insisted on my sitting on the mountainside with him while he said the bloodiest things to me. It was a ghastly muddle. If only one could do what one wanted to do. If only I was really tough and hadn't terrible conscience feelings. . . .

We went back to the house and all of a sudden I felt dreadfully ill. I tried to stand up and fell flat on my face. I almost fainted and then was very sick. Tom and John rallied round frantically. The natives all crowded into the house for the second time that morning—the first was the fight.

Tom and Baker filled her full of quinine and aspirin, but Zita "cried and cried." Whenever Tom caught her eye, she started all over again.

Gradually I felt better and stronger. And Tom announced that he was going to a nearby village called Nope where there was a magnificent view of Tabwemasana and was I going with him. I mentioned this to John and he said it was a matter of complete indifference to him what I did. I couldn't stand that even though I knew it was quite untrue. So after a few fierce remarks from John, [Tom and I] set off with three guides. It was a nightmare walk right over into another valley. The quinine rang in my ears and I couldn't hear and Tom knew I was having hell and bubbled and chattered, partly to make me happier, and partly because he felt exuberant with victory.

Zita could not bring herself to allow Tom's "victory" to reach its logical conclusion, as she tried to be "fair" to the two men who loved her.

It was my conscience that gave me most hell. I knew as I went along that if I didn't go down the mountain with John, the break was coming then, and it would be a hate break and a hurt break. If I went back to him at the base camp it would help a bit and keep us together but [John] wouldn't really think I was pro him unless I said I would go back to England with him. [She had originally planned to go home ahead of the others.] It seemed unfair somehow to make a break in the middle of an expedition.

So I told Tom that I would stay at Nope two nights and then return to the base camp [with Baker and Bird] and was going to give up the whole idea of coming home alone. (I'd been looking forward to that almost as much as anything else).

[Tom] felt he has been dreadfully let down. I think he has too. He is so direct and unafraid and I am a sickening mass of compromise and making the best of everything.

At Nope, Zita and Tom stayed in a little house of grass and bamboo where they talked all day and skinned birds. In the evenings they ate the pigeons the local chief had shot and cooked for them and "didn't sleep at all at night," according to Zita. But after two days and nights, Zita returned alone to

Tatarii, as she had warned Tom, and told Baker she would be coming to England with him. The Bakers and Bird left for Hog Harbour the next day.

The rain made the return to the coast for Baker, Zita, and Bird more dangerous than the outward journey. The rivers had risen, and many places they had forded easily before now had to be negotiated with rope. Zita and some of the smaller carriers "were in continual danger of being swept away and dashed against rocks." The next day they had to swim the swollen River Yora with all their clothes on. Zita wrote to Naomi that "I did really think that was going to be beyond me and said private and extravagant goodbyes to the forest and the mountains and the clouds. The current carried me a long way down but I was across. . . . Three of the Hog Harbour boys . . . were very nearly drowned there. Then there was a thirty mile walk home." After five days, Zita, Baker and Bird got back to Hog Harbour.

A day or two later Zita, quietly recovering and a bit let down after her three-week adventure, found herself feeling "utterly anti-Baker."

> He does say such frightfully mean untrue things about Tom. And anyway, Bakers are so DULL. I know exactly what they are going to say and how they are going to say it. . . . I suppose it's alright if you like it. But if one once begins to feel anti, it's shuddering. . . .
>
> Oh Naomi, don't be disapproving or elder sisterly. Tell me what makes life worth living. It isn't just work. Today I've soled a pair of shoes, dissected 41 lizards, written part of this letter, swam. It's worth a good deal loving and being loved and thinking well of oneself. Tom takes away all femaleness and unfair advantages from me and makes me gutful and self reliant. I like that, and don't want to get praise and thanks for being just a Mrs and doing Mrs things. I guess I'm a bitch. . . .
>
> No one knows how on earth Tom is going to get down off the mountains. His leg is sore still. He has no shoes or socks. . . . It annoys John a good deal that someone like Tom can get about without a lot of organisation and fuss. There's nothing spontaneous about Bakers.

Tom came back to camp in late November by a different and dryer route, further to the north, having successfully used his newly found skills at surviving alone in the interior of Espiritu Santo. This was no mean accomplishment, since the inland parts of the New Hebrides in those days contained some of the most untouched non-western people anywhere in the Pacific.

Now back at Hog Harbour under John Baker's eye, once again he had to live the way English people did in the tropics: wearing shoes and eating tinned food. The Oxford camp at Hog Harbour, located on land belonging to Anderson's sizable Presbyterian mission, had as its nearest neighbor a copra plantation. Beyond that was the "Agency," the residence of the British district agent for Santo. Mail, supplies, and occasional visitors arrived about every three weeks, on scheduled stops of interisland steamers of the Burns Philp line. A passenger on a yacht that called at Hog Harbour in the early 1930s enviously described the "pretty" house of the British district agent, Mr. J. R. Salisbury, situated on a small promontory overlooking the water with a veranda shaded by hanging baskets of orchids. Nearby was a quarter-mile crescent-shaped beach of coral sand, soft as a thick carpet. The water, placid because of an outer reef, was clear jade green. For social life (the yacht's passenger points out), there were several plantations nearby, with white planters in charge.

Mr. Salisbury's life is shown from a different angle by Tom in a letter to Naomi:

> The Government* is a fine exman. He has been here 28 years. He went back last leave to retire . . . [but] Foreign or whatever-it-is Office told him that he must go back for ten years. Being in Hog Harbour counted the same as the Civil Service in London, retire at 60. You only retire at 50 in places like Kenya and Calcutta. They refused him a pension. He had to come back. He has [had] blackwater fever twice; few white men survive one go.

Tom added that the poor man was "drinking himself systematically to heaven."

As to social life with the neighbors, Tom described those expatriates working at the plantation that lay between the Anderson mission grounds, where the base camp was, and Salisbury's residence. These were a New Zealand manager named Inskip, an Australian accountant named Reynolds, and a "half-caste" foreman named François, all of whom had gonorrhoea, which they freely shared with the eight black females who worked on the plantation alongside a host of Melanesian "boys,"that is, adult black males. Of Inskip, Reynolds, and François, Tom wrote to Naomi:

> They are all hopeless, fever struck, slightly dishonest, bullies to blacks. . . . The plantation pays its workers £1 a month (now 15/ slump). . . . All the planters are bankrupt, hopelessly in debt. Copra is being forced down by Levers. . . . Only two men have ever left these islands rich. All the rest die here. The islands have a quite impossible fascination. . . .

Zita, returned from her adventures on the new mountain, cast about for something more interesting to do than stay at the camp. She decided to reestablish herself in the nearby village of Sara, where she had first been in

---

*Tom is anglicizing the pidgin term "Guvman" or "Govman," which means district agent or district officer.

1927 during her previous time on Santo. She later told a Royal Geographical Society audience about her life in the village:

> When I first arrived at the village of Sara I saw the women just sitting in the mud doing nothing, but on seeing me they snatched up their children and fled away into the bush, shrieking. They had never seen a white woman before and they were absolutely terrified.
>
> When the women fled I wandered about the village and found the men's clubhouse, typical of Melanesia. About twenty big savages stalked out and stared at me, so I shook hands with tremendous friendliness, and they just went on staring. Then I gave them all sticks of tobacco and they pretended I had not given them anything, which is correct behaviour on receiving a present in Sara. I indicated that I would like to stay in that village, and they seemed to think that was quite all right. Therefore I proceeded to make myself at home.
>
> Gradually the women came back and peeped at me. . . . When I started eating, putting food into my mouth with implements, they were astounded. But washing really brought the house down; they themselves never wash. Later on I used to wish I had kept this washing business dark. The chief's wife got washing-conscious and wanted me to wash her very often. . . . I used to wash her and found it most interesting because of the amount of mud there was on her. . . . She looked very cross but she was not; she was really very amiable.

Her husband, the village chief, Nebv, "though he looked very ferocious, was very kind to me," Zita said, and it was "entirely due to him and his friendliness at first that the women gave me their confidence. . . ."

> He had an awful inferiority complex about his hair. He was always stroking mine [which was blond and bright] and saying "Vokovok" which means "pretty decent." I used to tell him that I thought his hair was lovely; that he had no need to wear a hat ever.

At first Zita used to sleep in Nebv's wife's house. In Sara, women and men each had their own private houses. Grown men never visited a woman's house; a married woman would go stealthily at night to her husband's house after he had come home from his clubhouse, where he socialized with other men and where he usually cooked and ate his food. Later, probably in late 1933, Nebv built a house for Zita, but it did not provide her any privacy or allow her to see Tom alone. As she recalled, "All day and most of the night my little house was absolutely full of people."

She "found it very trying doing nothing and never got used to it. . . . [On Santo] I was always waiting for things to happen and occasionally exciting things did happen; but most of the time was an alternation between days and days of nothing doing and then one day of tremendous excitement. . . . It was in my house [at Sara] that I did most of the waiting." Sometimes the villagers would take her off to watch a big pig hunt. More fun was when

> sometimes, during a rather boring day of just gossiping, they used to come and tell me that they were going out to play around the forest. I would go with the men and boys. First of all they would start to climb trees and show off with their bows and arrows. Then they would clear the ground . . . and would tie me to the end of a great liana hanging 60 feet from the tops of the trees and one would seize me and climb with me right the way up and, keeping the rope taut, let me go. It was the most wonderful swing, right up and right down.
>
> When they got tired of that, [some men] would start drumming, and all the others would start leaping and shouting, and when dusk came they took up their drums, and the drumming and shouting went on all the way back to my house.

Once, Zita wrote Naomi, she took part in the dances that accompanied a grade-taking ceremony at a village three hours' walk from Sara. The women stripped her and covered her in grease and body paint. "I joined in with all the women and all night we swayed and stamped and sang the refrains of the songs. . . ."

At the Oxford camp at Hog Harbour, Tom found that for him, too, the biggest cross he had to bear was boredom. He complained to Naomi that nothing ever happened: "The change between mosquitos that hurt a lot, and mosquitos that hurt like hell [is all that] marks the approach of dawn and of dusk. . . ." He and Zita managed to spend a week in late November alone together on Dolphin Island. The following week, Zita went back to Sara, where Tom joined her for a few days. There, she watched him have his chest scarified by Chief Nebv's wife.

But mostly Zita waited.

# Chapter 6

## Gaua

The moment Tom and Zita had waited for finally came. Baker gave his consent for his wife and Tom to spend three weeks alone together on Gaua, a small volcanic island of the Banks Islands group to the north of Santo. Sixty miles across the open sea, Gaua had fewer than 600 native inhabitants and no resident foreigners except for a Japanese who dove for trochus shell (an important source of mother-of-pearl, then the main material of shirt buttons).

Zita had been to Gaua before, in 1927, when she and Baker and another man had discovered and named the Percy Sladen Boiling Springs and had mapped Steaming Hill Lake. Zita now wanted to climb a "mountain with smoke or steam coming out" of it that she had seen in the distance then. Tom was to climb it with her and also to fill out his collection of bird skins from the region around the boiling springs and the lake.

They left for Gaua on December 16, 1933, having induced the drunken crew of the Burns Philp interisland steamer *Makambo* to deviate from their route and deposit them on Gaua. A planter from a nearby island had agreed to collect them on January 3, 1934 and sail them back to Hog Harbour. Zita later recalled that "We only had a light tent, some tarpaulin, sufficient food for about a week, a few clothes, my camera, Harrisson's equipment for skinning and stuffing birds, a gun and some cartridges, and a few books and candles. . . ." In exchange for sticks of tobacco, islanders working for the Japanese diver helped them carry these items inland to the beautiful but foul smelling boiling springs where they intended to camp for a week. Having built them a banana-leaf hut to serve as dining area and shelter for their bird skins from the daily rains, the natives trailed off, promising to return in time to help carry things back to the coast.

The next day was Christmas Eve, and so Tom and Zita went out to shoot ducks for their Christmas dinner. Zita recalled:

It was great fun paddling around the hot water . . . and hiding in the bushes. . . .

Christmas dinner next day was a triumph. We had a tinned plum pudding, and this we put into the boiling mud for hours. (We always cooked our tinned food this way.) [Tom] made a huge fire for cooking the ducks, and when it was all just hot glowing embers, we put the birds on them and toasted them. When they were pretty brown and burnt we ate them, and they were magnificent. We laughed a lot over our dirty faces when we had finished. The plum pudding we served on a banana leaf and stuck a red flower on the top. . . .

During the week at these hot springs, it rained every night, but by burrowing into the hot mud at night, they kept warm if not dry. Every day, after they had obtained their daily quota of birds, they took hot baths—their first in months—in pools from a steaming hot river flowing through the nearby forest.

A group of islanders who came by tried to discourage them from their next project, climbing the smoking mountain, telling them that it would be "bad magic." But finding the foreigners adamant, they agreed to take them by raft to the foot of the mountain and to wait all day until they came back down. Zita remembered:

> The water was boiling hot where they landed us. Then began a terrific onslaught on the vegetation by Harrisson. He had a beautiful long curved knife which he had got while exploring in Borneo, and with this, for about five hours, he slashed and hacked a way through and up and up. I followed and made extra notches on trees with my knife to guide us on the way down.

At the top, they found

> huge banks of steaming moss which we almost swam in. Most of the earth was very hot and it was difficult climbing from bank to bank. I took some photographs and we collected some specimens. We lost all sense of time, and before we realized it, it was practically dark. But after a bit, we heard shouts from the lake and it was a tremendous relief to know that our friends were waiting for us.

On the appointed day, on or about New Year's Eve, the men who had helped them make camp returned to take them back to the Japanese diver's shed, to wait to be collected by the planter's boat on January 3. But "the third of January came and went without a sign of a sail or a boat to be seen outside the reef." As the days passed, they grew gradually more worried. They had told Baker to expect them at the latest by January 10.

When that deadline passed without any word or sign of his wife and Tom, Baker began frantic attempts to rescue them: "In a few days I had covered 100 miles of walking to try to find a planter who would lend me his boat to go to the rescue, but no one would allow his boat to put to sea, as the hurricane season had now set in." He walked halfway across Santo to see if his friend Robby Robertson at Big Bay had a boat to lend him, but then the tail of a hurricane hit Santo. As he got near to Big Bay, Baker found the whole coast "littered with uprooted trees." He returned to Hog Harbour, convinced that Zita and Tom "had attempted to cross the 60 miles of open Pacific in an unsuitable boat and had been caught by the hurricane."

On Gaua, Zita and Tom tried to keep busy, while not wishing to stray from the coast for more than a night at a time in case a boat turned up. Tom did a census of the population and tried not to notice how anxious Zita was becoming as she thought of her worried husband. Their stores had given out and, not wanting to trespass indefinitely on the hospitality of their Japanese host, they went along the coast to a larger village where a deserted missionary's house had a few stores left. Zita recounted that "The natives there remembered me from a previous visit and just surpassed themselves with kindnesses. . . . Every day people would come in with bunches of bananas, oranges, coconuts, yams, chickens, fish and turtles' eggs. The last-named are just like ping-pong balls gone a bit flabby; they make awfully good scrambled eggs. . . ." Tom and Zita distributed to these friendly Gauans some of the missionaries' store of medicine but soon needed some themselves, as both of them had attacks of malaria. Zita's symptoms were "particularly alarming, as [they] had the extraordinary effect of making my head jerk backwards all the time, and we had just seen a native baby die with the same symptoms. Poor [Tom] was in an awful state, and when he wasn't busy being a good, sweet and efficient nurse, he spent the time staring at me as if waiting for the end." Next came a hurricane, causing damage to the village and confining them to their temporary home for several days. The storm also underlined the near hopelessness of expecting a boat to come for them until the hurricane season ended. "Then," Zita recalled, "miracle of miracles, six weeks after our arrival we were awakened one morning by a terrific blowing of conch shells and the stir of the whole village. I rushed out and saw everyone looking out to sea and pointing. There was a sail." The Gauans recognized the boat; it belonged to an intrepid island trader named Oliver Stephens, a well-known local "character." As Zita remarked, Stephens was "the only man in the group who defies hurricanes. He was often around collecting trochus shell . . . and he always anchored a few miles along the coast." Tom was having a bad spell of malaria, and so Zita rushed off without him to try to induce Oliver to take them back to Santo.

Back at Hog Harbour, having exhausted local possibilities, John Baker waited for the *Makambo* to turn up so he could convince the captain to take him to Gaua to look for his wife and Harrisson. The steamer was days late, having had to shelter from the hurricane. Finally, on January 29, the *Makambo* arrived late at night. Baker went on board at once and got the captain's consent.

We were just about to start when [the captain] insisted that he could see a light far out to sea to the north. Neither the other officers nor I could see anything, and we disbelieved him; but gradually a flicker became visible, and then it was clearly a light gleaming through the pouring rain. . . . In a few minutes she was alongside. My good friend, Mr. Oliver [Stephens] . . . had brought them back.

Once back at their camp, regardless of how adventurous and idyllic the lovers' time on Gaua had been, the Bakers were "a couple in an expedition" again and Tom was the third man. Zita wrote to Naomi:

The present stage in the John-Tom problem is that I realise that John and I aren't "emancipated" or "modern" enough to go quite separate ways indifferently. A big quarrel is the only way we could part and a big quarrel means bitterness and that would spoil all the grand ten years we have had. Those ten years are the most real solid good things I have and I just couldn't throw them away—especially in this insecure and changing world.

In writing of "this insecure and changing world," Zita was delicately referring to the fact that, for a woman such as herself, who had no money of her own and no moneymaking skills except shorthand and typing, things had changed very little in the hundred years since Jane Austen's heroines had had to consider a prospective husband's financial prospects as a factor outweighing all others.

On February 14, 1934, Valentine's Day, Tom (who had no financial prospects whatever) seemed unaware of the way Zita's thoughts were turning. He wrote to Naomi:

Zita & John & a third Baker are apparently going soon. . . .

I'm bleeding all over because Zita is going. I am finally indisputably (who wants to argue with me anyway?) in love with Z. . . . Zita is completely mixed in me & I cannot escape it. I am sure 6 months mosquitos & America will not reduce or obliterate it all. And I am a fearfully one person person. It has all been most awful hell for me (& Zita in her way). . . .

Now the hell is nearly over. It remains to tiptilt it finally. Sooner or later I want my money back on the bottle. (Why in the hell can't I write straight English sense. . . . Damp rot? Simile the reaction.) It just isn't any fun being a lover, is it? Is it any fun having one? . . .

As a goodbye present I have written a long poem-prose for Z, called "Coconut Moon."* There seems to be room for something rather virile & think-

---

*The poem appears in *Savage Civilisation*, pp. 387–394 and is dedicated "for Zita, 14/2/34." A revised version was published on the letter page of the *New Statesman and Nation* on January 2, 1937, with unanticipated effects on Tom's career.

making between poetry & prose. This [has] attempted it. It's about savages & god & traders & copra & depopulation & gonorrhoea & gin, mountains, maps, taboo, spears, dances, coral, coconuts, parrots, Mrs. Mitchison, Stephen Spender, *Time & Tide*, Rev. W. Anderson, . . . & God. But it's not so good as its contents.

. . . Are Clement & Sylvia [two friends of Tom's and Naomi's] still two people? Or has the before-final stage of one been reached? C & S are a symbol of security to me here, & if broken don't let me know . . . .

Tom's hope that the Baker marriage would tiptilt and that he would get his money back on the bottle and his reference to a pair of lovers about to marry suggest that he was then hoping for marriage to Zita. He was "indisputably" in love, love that had a purity and intensity he would never feel for another woman.

Strong as it was, however, his love for Zita did not fill the place in his heart that had been left empty when he lost the companionship of his brother, his only friend for all of childhood and early adolescence. Having found a woman to love, he now needed to find a man to fill the fraternal role of intimate companion and friendly rival. He would soon find such a man.

# Chapter 7

## Jock Comes to Santo

Disembarking at Hog Harbour on February 17, 1934 from the *Morinda,* which would collect the Bakers, was a young Australian: A. J. "Jock" Marshall. Tall and slim with curly blond hair, Jock Marshall appeared remarkably fit and able to deal with the ordeals of life in the bush. This was in spite of, or perhaps because of, having lost his left arm as a teenager in a shotgun accident. Jock had lost his father in another gun accident. His beloved elder brother had died when Jock was thirteen.

Full of invention and energy, Jock had been a hellion and practical joker at school until his harassed teachers asked for him to be removed at age fourteen, without his school certificate. He had then become seriously interested in zoology and had done fieldwork in the desert Outback of Australia. Baker had recruited him in Sydney on the way out to Santo to continue the sex organ sampling of five different animals and the climate data collection until September 1933, thus completing a year of study of faunal breeding in a constant climate, the main object of the expedition.

Jock hoped to make a career as a zoologist but conformed to nobody's picture of an academic scientist. Described by Australian contemporaries as "rude," "rugged," "a walking, talking caricature of the Australian character," "a literate, latter-day version of the Wild Colonial Boy," "an epic practical joker," "deflator of the pompous, irrepressible rocker of boats, and teller of wondrous tales," Jock, a half-year older than Tom, was a fair match for him in brains and pluck as well as in abrasiveness. Tom had liked the idea of Marshall joining the Oxford expedition from when he had first met him in Sydney in August 1933. He wrote the Australian from the *Morinda* en route to Santo to say, "You are *the man* for the job." He had also agreed to stay on three months after the Bakers left to introduce Marshall to the routine of recording air temperatures and breeding cycles.

Marshall arrived at Hog Harbour on his twenty-third birthday and saw Tom for the first time since the previous August in Sydney. Tom had now been in the New Hebrides nearly half a year. His appearance had altered radically. Marshall, in his light-hearted memoir of Santo, *The Black Musketeers* (1937), gave a jocular description of Tom:

> Everyone has seen the conventional portraits of Jesus Christ in the displays of ecclesiastical booksellers. So forcibly do they match the appearance of Tom Harrisson that I can think of no better method of introducing him. Dark, longhaired and bewhiskered, strangely and scantily garbed, this young Cambridge zoologist excited a lot of comment, if not admiration, wherever he went in the New Hebrides.

Jock was invited to Sara by Zita's friend Nebv, who had come to Hog Harbour to bid her farewell, and soon Jock was on almost as easy terms with Santo and its people as Tom was. Unlike so many other white men, Jock had a few good words to say about the Sakaus' looks: "They are finely-built people, these men of Sakau. Many stand almost six feet tall; a few exceed that mark. . . .The women are facially ugly, but physically very graceful. . . ." Yet, though Jock was clearly on the side of the natives against the planters, recruiters, and the Gilbertian Anglo-French Condominium government, his remarks in *The Black Musketeers* have an unconsciously patronizing tone. He noted:

> The Melanesian of mission and plantation, generally speaking, feels no desire to work hard, and a close watch must usually be kept to ensure that they do anything at all.
> "Wha' name, Peta?" [pidgin for "What's up, Peter?"] I asked severely, and fairly rocked in my chair when, with just the slightest shade of defiance, Peter [one of the native helpers] excused his late coming with the plea that he had "bin 'long church—'long *God!*"
> It was quietly and sarcastically brought home to Peter that God didn't pay him his wages or give him tobacco. . . . A planter would have given him the father of a hiding, and probably done him a lot of good. We, on the other hand, always found sarcasm as good a weapon as brutality, and never once administered corporal punishment to a native. Peter was humbly back on the doorstep a few days later, and thereafter worked like a Trojan.

Tom's account of this event in his diary has the same facts but a different attitude:

> Marshall made a good joke today. Peter had arranged to go to the cave with him at 8 am. Peter arrived at 9 am. Said he'd been to school [i.e., mission ser-

vices]. Jock said, in his elementary pidgin English: "Never mind him feller school. You work belong me. Me pay you, God he no pay you. God he no give Peter tobac. Me give you tobac."

Sedhi [the expedition's cook] and Wara [one of the part-time helpers] are still in hysterics over this joke. Jock is often very funny, funnier than this.

Tom, unlike so many people who went to the tropics before and after him, never looked upon the indigenous people there as in any way less complicated or less interesting than were people of his own race and culture. For him, it thus followed that an English observer, however well trained, could no more hope to "master" their society in a few months or years than he could that of France. The best he could do was to fill in a few of the blanks in western knowledge about them. In this respect, his attitude was closer to that of anthropologists of the 1990s than to that of his contemporaries.

His fascination with Melanesian society was superseding his interest in birds. As he announced in a February letter to Naomi:

I am now an CENSUSOLOGIST, not an "ornithologist". Human statistics are my line, Naomi. . . . I'm on to big things, so look out. . . .

One evening in March, while trying to collect census material about the villages around Hog Harbour, he gathered together in his hut the expedition's cook, Sedhi; a "half-caste" mission boy named Tommy; an "oozing and skulking" timid man named Wo, whose only virtue, as far as Tom and Jock were concerned, was that he spoke a little English as well as pidgin; and "old Tom Khor," presumably also a worker at the Anderson mission.

Tom got them to tell him of the dead children of Hog Harbour. "It was a terrible job. I had to force them to remember the *girls.*" The conversation moved on to a discussion of the villages that had been there a generation earlier and had melted away as their inhabitants were taken away by foreign "blackbirders" to work on distant plantations throughout the Pacific or succumbed to disease brought by the white man.

The sand floor of my house was turned into a map of Hog Harbour, and onto this was fingered Salisbury's, the plantation, the mission, the Blue Water. Into this pattern of whitemanism Tom Khor retraced the pattern of the past. And the pattern was an indictment more damning than any sin or sign. For between the point at the mouth of Hog Harbour and the Blue Water there were when Tom Khor was a boy (c.1890?) 24 villages. Each of these was larger than [the village of] "Lelek", averaging 50 people. Every man had a canoe. . . . And all around the Sakau coast from Big Bay to Shark Bay this packed density was. . . . They scorned my estimate of 50,000 people before. They said "more."

Then, they had fish spears and small square tents and they cultivated many plants and trees which are now forgotten or wholly lost. They ate each other.

They had dogs and cats and fowl—big red ones, not like now—before ever a white man came. . . . Then, they said, all the people were taller and larger. Now the ground is tired and the people small.

The boats from Queensland stole many and the decline was on and away before ever [District Agent] Salisbury or [the missionary] Anderson came. . . . It is impossible to realise that Tom Khor and Nialis and Iril have in their lifetime lived the destruction of a unit in humanity. How can we realise the savage mind not knowing this? What is the primitive of Sara, the dance of Sara, to the youth-days of Nialis when 2,000 people living on four miles of coast, when hundreds and hundreds of men came to one dance—bigger, taller men, and the ground not grown weary.

I must speak their epitaph. . . . In Sakau there must have been at least 500 [inhabitants] . . . or circa 10 villages to a square mile, which are now deserted.

So the map in the sand is shuffled into irregularity by my feet or my chair as I get up to light a new candle or to urinate.

Tom was thrilled at having managed—despite using the lingua franca, pidgin, rather than their mother tongue—to hold a serious conversation with these Sakau men and learn their tragic history. The idea of his "speaking their epitaph" would persist in his mind and turn into the opening section of *Savage Civilisation*, where the narrator is a traditional New Hebridean native.

While writing up notes such as these in his diary one night, Tom noticed the heads of members of the expedition camp's part-time work force popping up to listen to "Sloppy Drunk Blues" on the gramophone. Tom always liked to write with a background of noise or music, usually music hall or otherwise non-establishment music. Jock, too, "grew to love the old gramophone, whose scratched and battered records gave forth uncertain tunes. . . . Often Tom and I worked together to the music, taking turns to change the records."

During the first weeks of Jock's stay on Santo, however, Tom was irritated by the Australian's presence, especially his unrelenting competitiveness. He wrote in his diary:

> I wish I were alone here, for I find Australia wears my nerves. It can never know less, do less, see less, be worse at anything than you. It jumps right to the defensive at any suggestion that anyone outside itself is important: "Oh, but *every-one* agrees we have the finest man in the world on leeches, Kinghorn." There are only two people I would rather have here than no one—Reynold or my brother.

Bill had been Tom's companion in so many places and pursuits. Now distance and, more importantly, Tom's worsening relations with his father were pushing the two brothers apart until the gulf between them grew too wide to bridge. Reynold Bray had to some extent filled a fraternal role, but he, too, was now unreachable in the Arctic.

If Jock seemed an unsatisfactory substitute, his taking the daily temperature and humidity measurements at least freed Tom to conduct his census and collect birds. In trying to take a census of the Santo population, Tom found:

> The muddle of names here is appalling. . . . But I think I have really got them straight now, after sweating blood on it. The population here about 30 years ago was apparently terrific. These numerous and close together small villages are relics of many large ones.
>
> In the evening I returned to Vatseriati [a hamlet of Lelek] to sleep and slept in Nadha's house. . . . We had a shooting match at Lalages (I wanted skins) which I won (two hits, no miss). Everyone got very whoopee. We rushed about. Twenty rifles, bows and arrows and boys stalked one bird. It was absurd to see Nadha stalking a Lalage with the tree surrounded by people shouting that they could see the bird and here it was; he missed. . . .
>
> While we were Lalage hunting I told Timi's brother of the Tangoa superstition that a calling Lalage meant a death, for I heard one call. He said here it was the call of the Boatbill = "Mremre-withboon"—Who will win?—that meant war and death. Boatbills, as I pointed out to him, always called, but Lalage very rarely. But, he pointed out to me, people are always fighting. . . . A terrific day, very hot and on the rush from dawn till dark. Like being in London.

Tom's pleasure in this adventure among the Sakau leaps off the page. Most of all, he took pride in the fact that "I have lived for these two days entirely on what I have been given and what I have shot. I have not taken off my clothes and I have been completely native, shoeless, . . . and without property (except one sheet)."

The next day, though, brought Tom infinitely more excitement. At dawn, lying in the Lelek clubhouse he was awakened by "a sharp call. The men in the house were in a flash outside, musket plus." Tom was later told that "a man from Yekul had got past the two other villages so close . . . without awaking dogs or pigs, and sat behind a bush to shoot the first man of morning [who had walked out to urinate]. It turned out to be . . . Solru, aged about seventeen, a good person." With Solru killed, the people in the nearby villages were in "a state of ecstatic nerves. A dogbark brought everyone to the ready and creeping low."

With all the villagers frightened, Tom was "pushed ahead of a cavalcade of *braves* to go to Iurvel's [an allied clubhouse] and join up forces. Nice for me . . . Iurvel's people as near as hell shot me as I came round the corner, damn their eyes. All guns were trained through the wall." Wo (the "oozing and skulking" guide who served as Tom's interpreter) was panic struck. Tom told him no one would shoot *him* anyway and decided "the best thing, under these circumstances, was to get down to the plantation and start up the other way with a police boy." The timid Wo at first refused until Tom pointed out that "we were in greater danger of being shot here, accidentally by friends who were in an uncontrolled trigger state, than on the way home purposely by enemies."

The killing of a Lelek man meant the revival of a dormant intervillage "war" between Lelek and another village, Yekul, whence the killer was presumed to have come. The killer actually came from another village entirely, though the truth did not emerge until after the Lelek villagers had had their "revenge" by killing an innocent Yekul villager who happened to be in Hog Harbour seeing Sedhi about a pig debt. Tom and Jock got to see the body of the Yekul man: "He had been shot in at least five places, and all his guts were hanging out, a bullet in the heart, one in the chest, one in the groin, etc. I have seen no one more dead." Soon, through Sakau "logic," the Yekul man having been killed while coming to see Sedhi made Sedhi responsible in the avenging Yekul villagers' eyes, and thus he was likely to be the next target in the "Sakau war."

These "wars" were intervillage vendettas, part of a continuous rivalry, conducted more commonly by accumulating pig-debt and then calling in one's debts for a massive killing of locally bred hermaphrodite, curve-tusked pigs at an important occasion, such as a wedding or to celebrate the promotion of a village man to the next higher social grade. Neither women nor chiefs were eligible targets in these vendettas, but any other male member of the village that had offended one's own was a satisfactory victim. As Tom told the Royal Geographical Society, "These wars are not statistically serious [i.e., not in terms of reproduction], for the Sakaus have 157 adult males to every 100 females." But they made life in the Santo bush perpetually uneasy. For that reason, "the most important property of each man is his gun. These are old Tower and Snyder hammer guns of the last century. They are kept beautifully clean, rubbed daily with coconut juice and husk, so that they always shine, always look like silver. A man does not move more than five yards without his gun, for he can never know at what sudden moment he will be pointlessly ambushed." Tom, while censusing, was also collecting information on how many "kills" per gun. The oldest gun he saw dated from 1853. It was still usable and had marks on it showing it had killed seven people. "On the basis of these and previous figures, I calculate that since 1850 the kills per year have averaged 4; of course much higher earlier in period, now 1 a year?"

Tom, once back at Hog Harbour, found that "Yekul are expected to reply at once. Everyone in the mission have produced rifles from somewhere . . . and no one is doing any bush visiting *now* thank you. Sara [Nebv's village], is said to be coming into it. The best critics, including me, anticipate three more kills this month, perhaps ten." Tom then reflected in his diary on the different facets of this series of murders to be explored, such as the fact that the Lalage bird's call had indeed turned out to mean war. Tom wondered how to record the musket/kill ratio: "For eight [Lelek] guns have killed one man. Shall I add 1 to each, or 1/8th? And even worse—I don't know, nor does anyone, which Yekul gun needs re-adjusting by + 1." Full to overflowing with adrenalin from having been in the midst of dangerous and exciting events—two murders in one day—Tom could not resist a dig at Jock Marshall:

> Marshall was mightily and journalistically pleased by all this. He photoed the corpse, grave, etc. But mine was the ecstasy and understanding. . . .
>
> In the evening I felt very happy, for Marshall had taken his Australia to Reynolds and Inskip [expatriates working on the neighboring plantation], leaving Sakau with me. I felt an ecstasy of overbubbliness. The tragedy is that you need a person you love to share an ecstasy. Or, at the least, a woman.

This is the first hint in Tom's diary that he missed Zita, who had left two weeks earlier.

Tom and Jock were confined to their camp at Hog Harbour by the "Sakau war." The weather was becoming more tolerable now that the mosquitoes and flies had abated. The two young men dosed one another and their native staff and part-time helpers for dysentery and hard-to-heal skin infections. Skin infections were a terrible problem. As Jock recalled: "The only way to keep them in check was to submerge them regularly in a kerosene-bucket bath of antiseptic." Tom and Jock would eat their evening meal with their feet in buckets filled with Lysol and hot water and would examine each other's legs, pointing with fraternal glee to new potentially septic cuts the other had obtained during the day.

More worrisome was the threat of blackwater fever. At that time not yet recognized as a complication of malaria, it got its name from one of its many unattractive symptoms, that it turned urine black. It was often fatal. A brilliant young Cambridge anthropologist who worked on Malekula, Bernard Deacon, was among many white men in the New Hebrides to die of it in the late 1920s.

Although Jock had arrived in Hog Harbour a healthy man, a few weeks later he fell victim to one of Santo's fevers. On the afternoon of March 4 Tom found him

> ill and dead drowsy. Bedded him, and Aspro. No Aspirin left, Aspro useless as cf. Aspirin. Told M. this. He recovered enough to argue over it and say Aspro was the original!!

Tom dosed Jock and cared for him. The Australian was up and about in two days, by which time Sedhi was ill with malaria. That day, Jock worked as usual, but by night he was back in bed with a fever. The next day Sedhi was still ill, and Tom found "ants in the safe, dirty guns, no cheese and no water. There simply isn't time for M. and I to do everything. It is mercilessly sunny. I dreamed about the Rose Revived [where Tom had lived while writing *Letter to Oxford*] and woke up expecting Zita to have woken me." Tom noted that "A baby is crying in the village. This is unusual. I feel hard and alone, with lumps in my throat. Where is some soft and kindly?" When this self-pitying diary entry was shown to someone who had spent many years in the New Hebrides, he said, "Watch out. That is a note written by someone in the throes of a malarial attack." And, indeed, the next day's entry from Tom's diary begins: "I did not go to Sara. I let fever win for the first time since February 17 and went to bed to lie [down]. . . ." By the next day (March 10), Tom's self-pity was not malarial. The mail had come, with the *Makambo*: "I can't write because I am all knocked up by a horrible awful squabbly cross letter from Zita at Vila (18 Feb.)." This letter from Zita was written a day after leaving Santo, a week after she wrote Naomi saying she was not "modern" or "emancipated" enough to break up her marriage with Baker, "especially in this insecure and changing world." She probably now wrote something similar to Tom. As Zita wrote to Naomi another time, "God, I wish my mind was as tough as my body."

The mail that day brought Tom still other bad news, in the form of "a horrible document" from Burns Philp, announcing that "Doctor Baker advises he will be paying to the credit of the above account the sum of £35. No further funds will be available, so that, when exhausted, credit is not to be given to either Harrisson or Marshall." Furthermore, as regards fares home, "Dr. Baker states both of these gentlemen have money for this purpose." Marshall, in fact, did not have the fare. A garbled wireless message had led Baker to think Jock and Tom had more money than they had, and so he sent no more, leaving them virtually penniless from July 1934 onward. Tom complained to his diary: "If anyone is sick or any emergency arises, we are in an impossible situation. "No credit is to be given to either Harrisson or Marshall"—Not even *Mr* H and *Mr* M. I consider this disgusting. A bigger person, with less money than John [who was independently wealthy] would have placed £100 to our credit and trusted us." The letter from Zita, the worry about money, and—perhaps most serious—a relapse of malaria, dragged Tom down for a time. One evening that week he wrote in his diary:

> I need someone to talk to. I need someone to whom I can pour out my heart and find some solace. I am in a muddle coming on for lunatik. Zita's letter has destroyed my soul for a while. I just want to kill someone and hurt things. . . .
>
> Oh please Jesus be kind to your disciple and let me dream that I am at home with the comfort of my mother, and my father's great sympathy.

Although the unhappiness about Zita's letter was undoubtedly genuine, the extraordinary last sentence is so unlike anything Tom wrote in his right mind that it seems to have been the offspring of another malarial attack.

One evening soon thereafter, "a boy came from Salisbury for something to stop vomiting. I sent glucose." By the next day, the British district agent was no better. Tom noted:

> Sally [Salisbury] has been ill 4 days and it is now Blackwater Fever. If he dies I will never forgive the low swines who send him back after 30 years and make him pay income tax. Surely there is no fairness in civilisation. Rich people are bloody and governments are bloody. I must always be poor, then at least I shall be clean of one thing that stains so many people. Jock and I over and over again have been worried and upset by that £35, "the gentlemen have their fares". . . . Oh gee, if Sally dies someone will die for my Sakau revenge. This I do swear. . . .

Tom's dislike and contempt for bureaucracies run by British expatriates, activated the year before by efforts to restrain his activities by E. Banks, the Sarawak Museum curator, and by a Brooke Raj district officer, had now found much more serious grounds. Here was what looked to Tom to be criminal callousness of the colonial bureaucracy, likely to lead to the death of a good man. Tom would keep his antipathy toward the colonial service all his life, making exceptions for certain individual officers.

Tom's attitude toward money as a corrupting influence makes him sound very young, but, as with the colonial service, he did not change his view with the loss of youth. He had a strong money sense in that he was always looking for funding for scientific projects and had, from his Harrow days onward, a sharp eye out for potential sponsors. He did not, however, associate money with status and felt no need for it personally, except for what it could provide in the way of freedom to travel.

If wealth or luxury were readily available, as when married to a rich wife or when somebody else was treating, Tom would enjoy it for a time and would indulge his penchant for collecting rare and beautiful objects. He also enjoyed being generous to his friends. But the life of a wealthy man did not thrill him the way living "tough" did. He married once, probably twice, for money, but it was money for his projects and for travel, not for an easy life. He could and did live just as happily—indeed more happily—for months at a time, dressed in rags, sleeping in huts, and eating food others would have thought appallingly primitive.

Tom's malarial fever subsided and his morale and energy soon bounced back in the company of Jock. As Tom confided to his diary: "Once an hour one (usually he) of us gets hot under the collar and goes nationalist. But it is no longer tiring or nervous living together, indeed it is definitely fuN [*sic*]." As

Tom explained, "The turning point in our relations was the show down we had over Hirundo swallows nesting in rocks!!" We know no more than this about their contretemps over Hirundo swallows, but "show downs" were always a necessary element in forming and keeping friendships or even in establishing satisfactory work relationships with Tom. A young archaeologist in the 1950s going to work with Tom for the first time was well advised by an old timer "to pick a fight with Tom sometime early after you get there and win it. Then you will have no serious trouble with him thereafter." All of Tom's close friendships with men and some with women started after the other person "stood up" to Tom but was still willing to be friends with him. After such a confrontation, many people, of course, whether they stood up then or not, chose to back away from the relationship or to join the host of Tom's enemies.

Rivalry was, however, always to remain a part of Tom and Jock's fraternal friendship and gave their relationship its spice. One day after doing their usual expedition chores, they went over to the plantation and played tennis. Tom wrote in his diary:

> I beat Jock 6-5 and 2-1. He reckons he is good. We fought for it, mentally. We're a grand pair of bastards. Inskip and François were ill, Reynolds very weak. The whole atmosphere of that place is decay, unexercise of body or mind, cold fucks and half a bottle of gin. The most exciting thing ever happened there was prickly heat.

No mention is made, and probably no thought given by Tom, to Jock having only one arm.

Tom's pleasure in Jock's company made him look for ways for them to work together in the future. They made a plan for an expedition to the northwest territory of Australia to survey the Daly Creek area:

> . . . mammals, owl, parrot, plants, ecology, blacks. Only difficulty leadership. M. keen on big leader stuff—"intolerable to be under anyone else in one's own country". . . . [I] said if I came no one could lead me. Never intend to be bossed again. M. finally accepted a co-leadership. But he was not really satisfied. He has a boss mind.

Meanwhile, they decided to explore the northwestern parts of Santo together, leaving Mrs. Anderson, the missionary's wife, to mind the instruments at Hog Harbour. Just as the Bakers had done for the assault of Mt. Tabwemasana, Tom and Jock planned to use the Robertson plantation, which was halfway to their destination, as their starting point. With the Sakau "war" still on, they planned to take the mission launch to Big Bay rather than walk there.

But, before they could take off, a hurricane arrived. (Tom once commented that "a few days of hurricane blow is so trying, like living under a tram.") The wind and rain played havoc with the campgrounds and buildings. When the storm passed, they took the mission launch around Cape Quiros into Big Bay, where the destruction was clearly much worse than at Hog Harbour. A tidal wave had hit, and Robertson greeted them with the dreadful words: "I've lost everything." They abandoned their plans to explore the Northwest Peninsula in order to help Robby as best they could. Then, with several days before they had to be back at Hog Harbour, Tom and Jock split up to visit and census as many different villages as possible.

During Tom's travels without Jock, a friendly leper offered him an over-ripe wood grub to eat. Knowing that it "would never do to give offence," Tom got it down, "squeezing those squelchy purple insides through the holes of the grub's big doped eyes." His leprous host "watching, showed pleasure" and gave him and his native guide an eel to take with them. Tom had always thought he would be able to live off the land in the tropics; after this experience he *knew* he could do so.

During this trip, Tom was halfway along the Northwest Peninsula and had dinner with the great chief of a once great tribe:

> The great chief sat at one end of his great club-house. The floor was partitioned with bamboos into thirteen divisions, each with an oven, ashes and a tree-trunk stool, one for each pig grade in the rank society. You must not use another grade's partition; the visitor, such as myself, without any local pig status, has a thin time, for he may not take food or light from any fire. He must live only in the lowest partition, there make fire with the fire-sticks and cook on new stones collected fresh from the sea-shore and thrown away after each cooking.
>
> The great chief sat at one end, the high end, of his long house, perhaps thirty yards long, with its rows and rows of pigs' jaws down the rafter—the pigs that had brought this venerable old man so high, until there was no higher grade for him, every other village must have a separate tabu house for him. It was raining outside. I sat at the other end of the house, almost outside in my lowness. I shouted at him, and he quavered replies. There was nothing and no one between us but the ashes of long dead fires and this history.
>
> I had never been better put in my place.

This incident, uncomfortable and inconvenient though it was, must have also tickled Tom hugely. While he found money corrupting, he had a positive affection for social hierarchies. He liked to flaunt the names and titles of his aristocratic friends, but he did not care so much where he himself stood on a social ladder as that a ladder exist.

In late May, the two young men again handed over the meteorological instruments to Mrs. Anderson so they could explore together the Northwest Peninsula further than Tom had done alone. Jock later wrote that they brought with them "only the barest essentials. . . . Luxuries such as soap and tooth-gear would only be dreams for the next fortnight. One tin of food per night, a half-bottle of whisky, and an old play of George Bernard Shaw's, *Mrs. Warren's Profession*, were taken for psychological purposes." Their plan was to map the peninsula, find and climb the tallest peak, and collect samples of certain rare animals and plants.

Atop the highest mountain, "at last," wrote Jock, "we were alone in the clouds." They "changed into . . . dry clothing and were warm, very comfortable and happy" sitting in their tent before a smoky fire and dining "with huge enjoyment on dry bread, taro and tinned sausages." They drank lukewarm tea spiced with Scotch and took turns reading one act each of *Mrs. Warren's Profession* before making final thermometer readings and crawling into sleeping bags. The rest of the trip was less enjoyable. Tom had a relapse of malarial fever and had to stay shivering in his sleeping bag, though he managed to sit up and skin and dissect specimens and make meteorological readings while Jock hunted for food and specimens.

Having spent the entire trip in the rain, the morning they left to return to Big Bay and the Robertson plantation the weather was fine. "Annoying perhaps," wrote Jock, "but after drinking in the beauty of the sun rising over Big Bay, one felt that five minutes of such ethereal grandeur atoned for all the damp shivering hours which he had experienced."

At Big Bay, they caught the Burns Philp steamer, which providentially had just called in, on its way to Hog Harbour. On the deck of the Australian boat, these two upper-middle-class white men, bearded and barefoot, sat cross-legged, prying open tins of food and eating with their fingers.

The steamer brought a letter to Jock from John Baker, back at home on the Woodstock Road in Oxford, which provided moral—if not financial—support, ending, "I have not forgotten you would like to come to England, and I am making enquiries. . . ." There was also a letter for Jock from Zita:

> My dear Jock,
>
> It bucked us all up a tremendous lot to get your splendid letters. I think you're a grand man not to get done down by the climate and to keep on being enthusiastic even for six weeks. I'm glad you've palled up with the Sara people. Old Nebv is a gentleman. . . .
>
> Tom sounds as if he has been pretty ill. Glad you don't fight too much. I'm afraid he had a pretty tough deal over me and it probably still left him irritable and suspicious. I am very much looking forward to his return but he gave no indication whatever of when that would be. . . .

Tom, rather than brood about Zita, kept busy. When not helping Jock with the expedition work or drafting with him a paper comparing Australian birds with those of Santo, he also tried to write about non-New Hebrides matters:

> I have started on "Unhappiness and Politics." Chapter I is quite decent. I shall take my time over it and don't mind if I don't finish. I'm getting new ideas, and above all *new values*, so rapidly lately that I feel there is no hurry about anything and that I just want to LEARN and get wisdom and knowledge. So few people have knowledge of a broad useful sort about causes and unobvious things, and people's inside life. . . .

"Unhappiness and Politics" never got finished, and nothing of it survives. But the desire to "LEARN" and "get wisdom" and "knowledge of a broad useful sort about causes and unobvious things" remained with Tom always. This desire for breadth, for connections between things, was to pit him against specialists who were interested in knowledge that was deep rather than broad. In seeking to get "wisdom," he did not see universities as a likely source. In this he disagreed with Marshall, who, Tom noted in his diary "looks upon any degreed man as if he were an inhuman machine. Degrees are worth gold in Australia and . . . M. cannot get used to my accounts (cynical) of how you can snap up a BA pass degree. In Australia a BA *means* something." At the time of this note, Tom did not yet have any idea of how seriously the lack of a diploma would hamper him, both professionally and personally, in later life. After all, Reynold Bray and Tom Manning, men Tom greatly admired, had just abandoned their studies at Oxford and Cambridge, respectively, and did not seem the worse for it.

The time with Jock passed so quickly that Tom had barely noticed when the three months he had agreed to stay came to an end in May. It was now June, and Tom was considering leaving when a sore on Jock's ankle suddenly worsened. Soon it was badly inflamed, and there was fear that Jock would lose another limb.

Thus it happened that sometime in June Jock was bucketing about in an unreliable native boat on his way to the Segond Channel French hospital, in an eerie replay of what had happened to Tom nine months earlier. Jock's boat turned out to be the same one that Tom and Zita had used. Once again, it lost its rudder, which sank like a stone shortly after Jock and his Sakau crew had left Hog Harbour. After a terrifying day and night, they made their way back with a makeshift rudder.

A day or two later, Jock was taken to the Segond hospital in the mission launch. The doctors were no more effective in helping Jock than they had been with Tom. While at the hospital, Jock had another bad dose of malarial fever, and so, when he returned to Hog Harbour in mid July, Tom stayed on a couple of weeks until Jock was walking again and well enough to be left behind.

While Jock was bed-bound, all the meteorological work fell upon Tom, but, rigging a board on his bed, Jock did his share of dissecting. Tom brought Jock up to date on the various new turns the Sakau war had taken (there had been a few more murders) and the two young men talked, as only they could to one another. Writing two years later, Jock remembered:

> Those nights . . . when the little soft-winged bats fluttered through the old boat-shed and the green drifting glimmer of fireflies showed through its broken thatch—those nights we discussed every conceivable subject. We told tales, often true, of adventures in Borneo, the great deserts of Australia and idle hours among the isles of the Great Barrier Reef; of Lapland and the Lapps and Tom had been in the Old Hebrides as well as the New. Later, when the moon became suddenly obscured and a light sprinkle of rain drove us up the slope to bed, the midnight chorus of cicadas sang above the gentle patter on the leaves. Hog Harbour, or the tropics in general: how superb in reality, fragrant in retrospect, for those who love and understand.

Tom and Jock did love and understand, and in the process came to love and understand one another, after a fashion. Though Tom did not know it, this time was to be the high point of his relationship with the man who came closest to replacing his brother Bill. Tom's passionate attachment to Jock, though never expressed sexually, was the strongest he would ever feel for anyone. No woman, not even Zita, would ever matter as much to Tom as would having the right man as a loyal friend and companion; he thought he had found him in this combative, quirky Australian.

Having found him, he had to leave him. It was time to go. Writing from Hog Harbour to Mr. Hinks of the Royal Geographical Society on July 25, 1934, Tom announced that he was off for Malekula, the next big island south of Santo: "I do not plan to leave until my money is exhausted, when I shall work my way back via Tahiti and America."

# Chapter 8

## Living among Cannibals

Tom left Hog Harbour the last week of July 1934. His appearance had changed in the year since embarking on the Oxford expedition.

> I was wearing only a pair of shorts; and I had some Borneo tattoo marks on one arm and the white scars of the Santo cuts on my chest. I had a thick beard, while my hair, which had not been cut for the best part of a year, had grown nearly down to my shoulders. My legs were all scarred with coral sores and jungle bruises. My feet had got so hard from walking about without shoes that they looked like crocodile skin, and all my toenails were broken.

He was also somewhat different inside. Not yet twenty-three, he was already the man he would be thenceforward, with almost all his strengths and weaknesses.

Leaving Jock at Hog Harbour, he persuaded some native traders from Atchin Island to take him by outrigger canoe from Santo's south coast to several nearby small islands. Next they went to the northwest end of Malekula, the big island south of Santo (see Map 1), where Tom walked inland for a first glimpse of the territory of the Big Nambas, the New Hebrides' best-known cannibals. The canoers then sailed with him along the top of Malekula, leaving him on Vao, a small island off Malekula's northeast coast. From there, Tom managed to get to Norsup, a town on the Malekula mainland, where there was a French plantation and hospital.

Lacking money to hire native guides or launches and unwilling—or unable—to rely on resources provided by his fellow white men, he got about by establishing friendly relations with the islanders. Ever afterward he claimed that it was because he "had no gun or sun-helmet, or anything [that] could harm them" that he could, with surprising ease, make friends with unwesternized Melanesians. What is more, he did it in pidgin—known locally as "Bichlama"—or using interpreters who spoke the local language and Bichlama. Despite the language barrier, Tom got on better with the islanders than with the expatriates. At Norsup, the first place since Santo to have a resident white community, the French settlers tended to stay clear of this barefoot bearded young man who "might be a Bolshevik."

So instead of being taken in by one of the white settlers, he accepted the hospitality of a tall, strapping twenty-two-year-old Fijian native medical practitioner (known in the British colonies as a "dresser") named Masulome Tavela. Not only was the Fijian a kindly host and a good informant about Malekula (where he had lived for three years by then, giving thousands of injections against yaws), but he was ready to join, and might prove a useful participant in, a project that had recently begun to claim Tom's greatest attention: an expedition to New Guinea—not to Australia's Outback, as originally planned—to be led by Tom and Jock.

Back in July, while Jock was recovering, the two young men had signed a three-page typed agreement committing them both to a "Proposed Expedition to New Guinea, 1936–38." The main purpose would be to explore the western parts of the recently discovered and mostly unmapped central highlands of the great Melanesian island. Jock, the party's zoologist, would also collect various birds and mammals, while Tom would be the party's "anthropologist" and would study "Stone-Age man."

The document was typed by Jock, and he undoubtedly participated in its drafting, but it is full of practical ideas drawn from Tom's wealth of experience on expeditions. Occasional flourishes point to both signatories being in their early twenties:

> *Decisions in the field:* Where any danger or schism is involved, majority vote decides. If minority refuses, majority is justified in clubbing him into a coma and carrying him off—but not to abandon the bastard. . . .
> *Property:* To all intents and purposes, individual property becomes expedition property from the time of reaching our base camp. Though some exception may be made for those who clean their teeth.
> *Untimely death:* New Guinea is a good sort of place to meet an untimely death. Too bad. Members must clearly realize this. Though we are not afraid(?), we respect danger. It may make us stop to think, but it shouldn't make us stop. If any member dies, other members will not respect his dying wishes. His property on the expedition—clothes, notebooks, photos, etc.—become property of the survivors. If it will help them, they will barter his body to the Cannibal Heathen.
> Anyone who wishes their mother to be informed, must leave a stamped addressed envelope with T. H. H.

For weeks after he left Santo, Tom kept scribbling his thoughts on the New Guinea expedition to Jock. He also wrote to Zita, but he was not rushing back to England to be near her. As far as can be deduced from examining Tom's notes, he clearly preferred Jock's company to hers. In an August page of additions to the New Guinea proposal, on the subject of "Sex," Tom wrote:

> White women are loathsome excrescences on any expedition of young poufters.* I propose (seriously) that White Women are given no encouragement to come anywhere near our camp. Tired undergraduates who want to love a white girl for a while must go and do it far away. The only white woman we can tolerate in our camp is a straightforward (non-venereal) prostitute.
>
> Mistresses (native) are encouraged and will be paid for out of expedition funds, if not too costly. Communist principles. But nice to know your Wassermann reaction!

He added that "Buggery and Bestiality are not on the program," since such behavior would "inevitably cause native and governmental troubles."

Tom's interest in this new expedition and his desire to work out every detail of it grew obsessive. By September he was writing to Jock that, in his view, the fieldwork should last four years, not two, as had been originally envisaged. In arguing for double the time in the field, Tom asserted that nobody since Alfred Russel Wallace had "settled down to gain full knowledge in one land" and that no one had "ever made a first rate study of anything in the Pacific." He complained that "The ordinary scientist or 'explorer' leaves the explored country knowing absolutely nothing compared with the old R.C. *père* who has been there 32 years, or the officer who has patrolled 30,000 miles of bush." This desire to spend an extraordinarily long time "in the field" would stay with him for the rest of his life and make him contemptuous of professional social anthropologists who claimed to have become experts on "their" ethnic group after two years—or often less—living with the group being studied.

This attitude would make Tom attractive to a knowledgeable Australian old-timer, Ewan Corlette, a copra planter living next to the British district agent's office at Bushman's Bay, on the northeast coast of Malekula. Corlette was a cultivated, scholarly man who had spent thirty years in the New Hebrides, mostly on Malekula. Early in his stay in the islands, he had sailed to the island of Ambae, famous for the beauty of its Polynesian-looking women. He had married one, paying the traditional bride price, and brought her back to Malekula. He had learned much about the local culture and participated more than any other white man on Malekula in the ceremonial life

---

*On the theory that homosexuals would not accept being described as "poufters," one can reasonably assume that this is a joke of Tom's. From this time forward, he often addressed letters to Jock as "Dear Poufter." The humor lies in the fact that Jock, though a rather beautiful young man, was as tough a he-man as could be found in all Australia, cf. Robin Hood's Little John.

of the native people. Corlette heard of Tom and sent a note by messenger inviting him to come stay with him at Bushman's Bay.

Corlette's daughter Margaret, then a pretty twenty-one-year-old, remembers coming home from her garden "to behold this man, Tom Harrisson" who had just arrived:

> He looked like Jesus Christ! He wore a dirty looking lava-lava, (a native length of cloth around his waist), no shoes, long hair and a beard. Also a pack on his back, and to top it off, a staff! He was dirty and scruffy. He looked at me, with those amazing blue eyes, and smiled, and introduced himself. Well, what a shock!

Margaret Corlette was not the first to think that Tom looked like Jesus Christ, nor was she the last. An Australian travel writer recalls seeing Tom on a launch approaching Bushman's Bay:

> White and thin, he was young, I judged, from the springy blackness of the ragged beard that hid half his rather delicate features. A mass of black hair came almost to his shoulders and across his brow from under a cheap plaited-straw hat turned up in front. The half-sleeve singlet he wore had a hole or two, his white shorts were hardly immaculate and his feet were in soiled sand-shoes. But it was his face that held our attention.
>
> "Jesus Christ!" somebody said, then broke that spontaneous description down to "a cross between John the Baptist and a beachcomber."

It was not just the hair and the dress; there was a sense of latent energy radiating from him. There was also something almost alarming in those pale eyes that seemed to take in everything, including what one had thought hidden from view.

By this time, Tom was wearing shorts and canvas sand shoes, when in civilized company, instead of a lavalava and bare feet; this was a concession to Margaret Corlette with whom Tom was flirting, if not more. Since Tom also got on "famously" with Margaret's father, because, as Margaret recalls, "they had both attended university and could talk big," he was using the Corlette plantation as headquarters for conducting his bird sampling and population census of Malekula.

For both of these purposes, however, he also needed to return to the northwest interior of Malekula, which he had already briefly visited with the Atchin traders. The northwest had many types of birds not available elsewhere and, most important, the New Hebrides' most infamous ethnic group, the Big Nambas.

The Big Nambas were among the few people of the "bush"—as opposed to people of the coast—to volunteer for plantation labor on Malekula and elsewhere in the Pacific. (They did it mainly to buy guns at the behest of their chiefs.) Thus, they were the only Melanesian bushmen—and the only cannibals—that most outsiders ever saw, although inland there were plenty of other cannibals on Malekula. Tom reported "3,000 cannibals within 25 miles of the British Headquarters" at Bushman's Bay.

Many people nowadays accept a claim made by W. Arens in *The Man-Eating Myth: Anthropology and Anthropophagy* (1979) that cannibalism has not been practiced anywhere in modern times. Arens' basic argument is that no reliable eyewitness accounts of it exist. The chief problem in finding a "reliable" witness is that a cannibal feast would not take place in front of outsiders. Native eyewitnesses on Malekula reported it taking place in the 1920s and 1930s not only to Tom but also to such experts as John Layard (*Stone Men of Malekula*, 1942) and Bernard Deacon (*Malekula: A Vanishing People*, 1934), none of whose writing appears to have been consulted by Arens. A number of other reputable visitors to and residents of Malekula reported its existence up through the 1930s; see, for example, E. Cheesman, *Things Worth While* (1958); T. Crocker, *The Cruise of the Zaca* (1958); C. Simpson, *Pleasure Islands of the South Pacific* (1979) and *Islands of Men* (1955); and Charles Van den Broek d'Obrenan, *Voyage de la Korrigane* (1939). Darvall Wilkins, British district agent for Malekula from 1961 to 1980, claims that cannibalism lasted there until partway through World War II. The most recent account of cannibalism on Malekula from a credible source comes from a retired native policeman who had worked there in 1934. In 1994, he told Kirk Huffman, curator emeritus of the Vanuatu Cultural Centre, that cannibalism had been practiced on Malekula during Tom's stay there sixty years earlier.

In *Savage Civilisation*, Tom describes his first encounter, in the north-central Malekulan village of Peterlelip, with a group of cannibals that he calls "Middle Nambas" but whom modern experts call "Tirak": "When a native's face goes sort of grey on the flesh over the cheek-bones, that is the time to say the Lord's Prayer twice. Every face in Peterlelip went grey when I rolled in for the first time." Tom found:

> the reason for this colour performance . . . was that the first and last time they had had a white man in that area (northeast hills) was when, in 1916, they had been down to the sea near Burman Bay in the east, had cut a trader called Bridges and his half-caste children to small pieces and eaten one of the latter, in revenge for a kidnapping in which the administration failed to see that the men were returned.

A punitive expedition against these Tirak had been mounted, consisting of a British warship, a French cruiser, a hundred Australian marines, a detachment of New Guinea native police, and sections of the British and French constabulary, under the leadership of the British and French resident commissioners, the ships' captains, and the constabulary chiefs. A party of police was left to safeguard the route, but the entire police party except one British sailor had been massacred by the men of Peterlelip by the time the punitive expedition climbed back down toward the coast—after having destroyed the wrong village. "On the way down, the natives were waiting for them. They shot from prepared trenches, jumping up to fire and falling back after each shot." They captured a number of rifles and much ammunition from the punitive forces and took only one casualty.

The villagers of Peterlelip still speak of their successful escape from the 1916 punitive expedition and say that metal from the boots of the expedition forces scraping against the flinty rocks of their path made sparks, revealing the whereabouts of the oncoming forces and helping the bushman to evade them. When the punitive force started back toward the coast, the sparks helped the bushmen pick out their retreating targets in the dark. (Tom undoubtedly heard this story and he would not have forgotten it ten years later, when engaged in jungle warfare himself. It would have confirmed his prejudice against wearing shoes if one wanted to travel undetected.)

Since the 1916 victory, the people of Peterlelip had killed and eaten "six missionary teachers sent up into the bush to convert them, and on another occasion just missed a missionary doctor whom they lured inland. No mission native nor white [had] ever looked in there since. . . ." Fortunately for Tom, the Tirak, having "greyed" after they first saw him, "were so surprised that, as often with natives, they cooled off before they could decide" whether to kill him.

The murder of the Bridges family by the Tirak had occurred nearly two decades earlier, but, as Tom later reported, local "wars" on Malekula killed thirty men during the year he was there. As on Santo,

> the technique of war is ambush or stalking. Never conquest or rush. A war party may spend days out in the bush, scarcely moving, never speaking or lighting a fire, near the enemy village, waiting for a stray man to wander their way; or creep up before daylight and wait, guns trained, outside a house at the edge of the village.

After Sarawak and Santo, Malekula was the third place where Tom saw jungle ambush and stalking techniques practiced by experts and the second place where he saw them used to kill men. He would store this information away for future use.

Other man-eaters on Malekula included the Laus, a short-statured tribe that lived in the interior of southern Malekula on whom Tom paid a surprise visit in the company of guides. Tom—as always—striding ahead, walked right into the male clubhouse, and "When they saw a white leg through the door of the hut, all the men inside made one leap, burst the far end wall, and bolted. My guides bolted, too. It took days to get that mess sorted, especially as I could not talk a word of their language." By the time Tom had completed his visit among the Laus and walked the rest of the way northeast to Bushman's Bay, his embarrassed runaway guides had spread the word that Tom had been eaten by his small hosts. In fact, only his toes had been in danger: "These little folk kept their pigs tethered inside the houses, just the right distance away from the walls, for them. I was, regrettably, a foot taller. The pigs licked my feet (or sucked my toes) through the night."

Of all the cannibals of Malekula, it was the Big Nambas (known by that name because of the size of the men's distinctive penis wrapper, or *nambas*) who most interested Tom. They had what Tom thought was the "highest, purest," culture, including a "strict hereditary chieftainship, which is found nowhere else in the northern New Hebrides." A peculiar ancient feature of their culture was a tradition of homosexual relationships between adolescent boys and men two generations older. Between a particular man and "his" boy, there could be a loving relationship that would last for years, until the boy became a man after a terrifying hundred-day initiation.

The Big Nambas initiation for the making of a boy into a man, as graphically described by Tom in *Savage Civilisation*, was "a trial of character and an education in patience and determination. One got it at prep. school and public. Those who have gone through this mill together have thereafter a close community of feeling."

Tom knew the Big Nambas were the biggest ethnic group on Malekula and wanted to count them as part of his effort to census every island he visited. His censusing efforts were intended to test the then widely believed thesis that the Melanesians were gradually "vanishing" and that their high mortality rate was caused by a morbid despair, the direct result of their confrontation with western culture. The thesis, proposed by the eminent British anthropologist W. H. R. Rivers nearly two decades earlier, was that the Melanesians were dying out, not because of the virulence of the diseases to which the coming of the white man had exposed them, but because these diseases were "acting on people with so little interest left in life that they succumb at the first breath."

When the young Cambridge anthropologist, Bernard Deacon, had been on Malekula eight years before Tom, the villages Deacon visited were melting away, but Tom's census figures, covering nearly half the population of the New Hebrides, showed a surprising trend. While overall, the native population was still shrinking due to high death rates, the coastal villages had lower mortality rates than those in the bush. Those coastal villages most in contact with westerners were actually gaining population. The big death tolls were where white men had spent little or no time but where their germs had migrated.

Looking for reasons why missionized people seemed to be doing best, Tom concluded that these Melanesians received the white man's medicines that helped them combat the white man's diseases. He conceded that the missionaries "gave something" in place of old customs being lost and that what they gave also helped the missionized coastal people increase their numbers, but he differed "from current theory and many eminent authorities" in not according the psychological factor "first place." His demonstrating that the islanders were no longer "vanishing" and his finding a probable explanation as to why they were unlikely to do so was what Tom had meant when he wrote Naomi Mitchison in February 1934, that in doing his censuses, he was "on to big things": refutation of the accepted anthropological wisdom of his day. He had not yet been certain when he wrote Naomi, but nine months later when he had completed his survey of Malekula, he was. Tom resolved to publish a book about what he had learned in these cannibal islands. He looked forward to exploding not only the Rivers population decline theory but other erroneous and outworn western ideas about these so-called savages.

The largest Big Nambas village, Amok, with over a thousand inhabitants, was headed by a chief deeply hostile to whites. Tom made three trips to Amok but later said he had been warned that if he made a fourth, in order to conduct his census, the village chief would have him killed and eaten. Aside from the people of Amok, though, he found the Malekulans easy to know. He got on especially well with the Big Nambas.

His first trip to the Big Nambas area in August 1934 was to Tenmaru, a Big Nambas village about six miles inland from Taumarama Bay on the northwest coast. He went there to see the hospitable village chief, known to westerners as "Ringapat," who was accustomed to receiving white visitors. In London, Tom had heard of Ringapat from Evelyn Cheesman, an intrepid entomologist who had visited Tenmaru in 1929. In developing friendly terms with the Big Nambas, even more valuable than Ringapat's good offices were Tom's own dress and behavior. They gave the signal that the traditional white-black etiquette need not apply to dealings with him. He could, for instance, be offered the same seating place normally granted to a villager of low status, that is, someone who had no pigs or pigs owed him. Alert to every nuance of gesture and avoidance, he could also be trusted not to touch forbidden objects or otherwise break Big Nambas tabus.

Within a very short time, Tom got to learn a good deal about the Big Nambas. In an October 1934 letter to Jock, he boasted:

> I'm nearly finished census of Malekula. Done 2 long trips in Big Nambas. . . . Have been to every village in N. Malekula, mostly unvisited, and whites scared stiff to go there, even to step ashore in some places. Never carried a gun of any kind. . . . Homosexuality and cannibalism are regular and rampant. And—oh boy, hold your tits—Lesbian chums too. . . .

He went on to give many details of Big Nambas sex life, totems, descent systems, and the like.

One problem with Tom's field methods, as viewed by professional anthropologists, was that he hesitated to take out a notebook when among the people he was studying, to prevent them from behaving self-consciously. "Most of the time," he admitted, "I wrote down nothing, being too busy eating, sleeping, drinking kava, living hard and good until I became almost part of the landscape." He objected, then and later, to notes taken by an anthropologist on the site being accorded more scientific authority than the experience of living among the people being studied. He argued that recording customs had no point "until the conditions and necessities which determine them . . . are well understood." When he did take notes, he often did not consult them when writing up his reports, fearing (rightly in his case) that they would lead him to bury his narrative in excessive detail. This failure to take or consult notes led occasionally to his ascribing to one ethnic group what he had seen or heard in another community visited during the same trip.

Nonetheless, Tom came to know the people of Malekula better than any other outsider had. John Layard, still widely regarded as the New Hebrides' best ethnographer, in 1936 told the distinguished audience of the Royal Geographical Society that Tom was "the only white man, beside myself, who so far as I know, has spoken the language of these people, danced their dances, and lived in their houses with them." Layard is wrong about Tom "speaking their language." Tom only communicated through broken Bichlama and interpreters, but he certainly danced their dances and lived in their houses with them.

It was his skill as a social drinker of kava that won him the most Big Nambas friends. He is still remembered for it today by children of the men he drank with. Kava, as Tom explained in his most quoted text from *Savage Civilisation*, is a drug from the plant *Piper methysticum*, whose root is smoke-dried and then chewed and spat out by two or three men into a "palm frond trough set on four little posts at knee height by the little square crawl-in door of the great dark club house." Water is added and, when it is ready, the senior man present

> comes and kneels on the damp earth floor, puts his mouth to the kava surface . . . and sucks up as much as he can with as much noise as he can in one breath. What sort of a he-man and well-bred fellow he is, one judges, easily, by the quantity of liquid and quality of noise he can do. (I benefited enormously from being a travelled fellow. I could make nice, new, jazzy, farmyard noises while I was drinking. Thus I gained prestige.)
>
> . . . Within half an hour fellows are beginning to feel good. The effects are interesting. Kava negatives the legs. You cannot walk any more when you get enough of it on board. Your arms later get almost unliftable. But you can usually crawl over the soothing earth floor to get another suck at the dope. Your head is

affected most pleasantly. You feel like you feel when you are in your first year at Cambridge and a policeman comes up and tells you you had better go home and you talk to him like as if you weren't drunk and you think like hell I'm clever all right and do I think quick and I'm fooling the old Robert what, and he is so used to it and picked for this because he is so godarned good-natured and he just says "All right sir; the proctors are around, you'd better be pissing off, sir." You don't get drunk on kava. But it speeds up your increasing slowness. Thoughts come cleanly. You feel friendly; not beer sentimental; never cross. The world gains no new colour or rose tint; it fits in its pieces and is one (easily understandable) whole. . . . You cannot hate with kava in you.

Better still, Tom claimed, it is not addictive and leaves no hangover the next morning. "You may do the same next night and every night. It is part of the male life, the pub, with words as darts and skittles." But best of all is the way it promotes good conversation:

> Some of the most pleasant evenings of my life have been spent drinking kava, listening to the endless running flow of words, the trivial described as only the "lowest" savage and the highest genius can describe it; so that every angle, incident, word and thing appears again to conjure up a scene not simply of "He said to me, I said to him" (our way) but with the materials of reality arranged by the teller into his own pattern. I had not previously realized that talk could be more than conversation, quite probably boring if at all elaborate. Talk can be a people's highest manifestation; a fact we whites have forgotten since Dr. Johnson.

Tom, all his life, found that getting intoxicated in the company of a group of men, or merely drinking in a pub where others were drinking, gave him a wonderful sense of communion, a feeling of shared love and well-being he got no other way. His description of drinking kava, the ambience, the physical and psychic effect of it, is cited by some present-day anthropologists as the most accurate and evocative statement on the subject in print.

There is, however, serious reason to object to Tom's assertion: "I did that for a year." He did not do it for a year. If someone had asked Tom directly if he lived an entire year with the Big Nambas, he would have answered "no," but he had spent a lot of time in Big Nambas and other native Malekulan villages spread out over the course of a year. Instead, by slightly exaggerating and oversimplifying—telescoping the truth, as it were—he made his extraordinary genuine achievements open to question by many, and to denial, categorically and wrongly, by credible critics.

It is the kind of "damn fool thing" his friends would see him do over and over during the course of his life. The most egregious example—always cited by those who would deny Tom's claim to have done any of the things he said he did—is another statement made in connection with his time with the Big

Nambas in which he implies that he took part in a cannibal feast. In *Savage Civilisation*, Tom describes the dancing, the stories told, the chants sung for a cannibal feast, and how the body brought back by the successful war party is prepared for eating.

> After some hours the oven is opened. Every man must eat a portion. The taste is like that of tender pork, rather sweet. Some men are noted flesh-lovers and eat as much as a whole limb. . . . In general a small helping is enough, for this is a very filling food. The inner part of the thighs and the head are the greatest delicacies.
>
> The important feature is the communal nature of the participation. However much he dislikes the taste a member of the community must partake. . . .

Though very likely correct in its details, this is one of the most dishonest bits of prose Tom ever wrote for publication, since it makes it seem as if Tom were watching and perhaps eating, which he surely was not. Regional experts agree that it is highly improbable that a foreigner would be present at a cannibal feast. Moreover, if Tom had participated, he would have been delighted to say so. But here, instead of a clear-cut statement, the text is ambiguous, confusion being caused by the way the narrative voice switches back and forth without warning from Tom's to that of a cannibal. Having the narrator's voice shift from one person to another is a technique the novelist Malcolm Lowry had been exploring in the days when Tom had been his drinking companion at Cambridge. Tom used it repeatedly in *Savage Civilisation*. The temptation for Tom to allow the "voice" of his informants, who would have described the cannibal ceremonies to him in great detail, to merge imperceptibly into his own voice so that he seems to be there himself, must have been enormous, and he yielded to it.

Tom had a great respect for the printed word. He appears never to have told an outright lie in print, unless one considers that his comments on kava and cannibalism were lies. In letters to friends, however, or in conversation, he took pleasure in moving from fact to fantasy and letting his presumably intelligent and knowledgeable audience sort out which was which. Thus, in his letters to Jock, Tom would often boast of his sexual prowess with the wives, daughters, and servants of the white settlers:

> I am quids in with every planter and missionary in Malekula. . . . I'm the popular whitehaired boy—fifteen invites for Xmas and snazzums lying open in every direction. I just haven't enough rats to go up the bloody sewers.

According to white settlers interviewed many years later, at least some of these boasts are true. But in the same letter, Tom also boasts of having had sex with Big Nambas women living in traditional communities. These boasts are much less likely to be true. He never made them in print. The Big Nambas

did not lend women to visiting men, and to have been caught by them phi-
landering would have, at the least, closed down Tom's access to the people
he most wanted to know better. Even more than bragging about his sex life,
Tom loved writing Jock the astonishing facts he was learning on Malekula
about "human sacrifice, homosexuality, a chief pig kill in which they made
100 eunuchs, and a few other stories which are true and unbelievable. . . ."

By mid-November, he was done with his census and ready to move on: "I
hope to be in America in the New Year. In England by May. . . . Trouble is
cash." He was hoping for a windfall that would allow him to make the trip
and pay for Jock to go with him, from Tahiti via the U.S. to England,
because, as he wrote Jock, "nothing is more important as that Marshall
should meet England."

By this time, people in England were beginning to be anxious about him.
John Baker wrote to Jock in November: "I wonder where Tom is. When last
I heard of him, he was off to Malekula. I hope he hasn't been eaten." That
month the General cabled—the first word he had sent his son in two years—
to ask when was Tom coming home. Tom wired back: "As soon as you send
me seventy-five pounds." He thought he could get at least £40 from his
father, but he soon began to get an income from a much more unlikely
source, the British Colonial Service.

# Chapter 9

# On His Majesty's Service

> THH is now OHMS [On His Majesty's Service]. He is now Governor of the Northern Isles. He now receives a salute of twenty-one Tower Muskets everywhere from Epi to Santa Cruz. . . . By a mixture of graft, conceit and adultery, I bluffed Vila into giving me about £300 to do six months as Acting District Agent [for Malekula], including quelling the Big Nambas, snooping a French murderer and giving gin to the local planters.

Thus did Tom inform Jock of his December 1934 appointment as acting British district agent for Malekula and adjacent smaller islands.

Tom's travels among the Big Nambas had become known to the British district agent on Malekula, a man named Adams, whose office was next to the Corlette plantation at Bushman's Bay. Adams had made an initial visit to the Big Nambas territory guided by Tom on Tom's second trip there. He had then suggested to his superiors in Vila that Tom be used to try to pacify this bellicose tribe, and Vila had agreed. Later, when Adams was about to go on leave to try to recover from blackwater fever, he proposed that Tom temporarily take over his post. The British authorities at their Condominium headquarters at Vila assented and directed Tom "as one of his first duties again to get into contact with the warring tribes of North Malekula with a view to the continuation of our plans of pacification."

Corlette, although he enjoyed Tom's conversation enough to keep him on as his houseguest, had tried to prevent Tom's appointment. He had written hurriedly (unbeknownst to his daughter Margaret or his houseguest) to the Condominium's headquarters in Vila that Tom would be a deplorable choice and his appointment would offend all the white settlers. But, before this letter reached Vila, Tom had already been assigned the job.

The Anglo-French New Hebrides Condominium of the 1930s, with its totally separate administrations for French and British subjects, two sets of weights and measures, two currencies and two sets of postage stamps, had earned its sobriquet, the "Anglo-French Pandemonium Government," but in Tom it got a more intelligent, hardworking, and dedicated—if unconventional—colonial servant than it had bargained for. Within a month, Tom was working with characteristic energy and gusto. In a letter to Jock from Bushman's Bay, Tom wrote:

> I'm absolutely up to shit in work. I haven't a typewriter or any ink carbon, so I have to report all my activities in triplicate and copy for self. I've just copied over a 7000 word report of my just finished patrol of Big Nambas—4 times! It's like being a naughty school boy. What a life! But I'm drawing in the pelf, lad, and I can see you and I in a luxury liner off the Cocos—if I don't spend it all on gin.
>
> I'm rather short of snazz just at present. But am throwing monster whoopee for George's Jubilee and hope to have the camp bed chock-a-block then.

By the time he wrote this, in late February 1935, he had broken off his friendly relations with the Corlettes, having learned of Corlette's letter to Vila. On February 22, the day Tom wrote the letter to Jock about being "short of snazz," he had taken his revenge. Having spent the previous evening with Margaret, he left for another part of the island early in the morning, after giving orders to his household guard not to let either Margaret or her father onto the agency premises. Thereafter, Margaret refused to have anything to do with Tom. Worse still, in Ewan Corlette, Tom had made an enemy who would go out of his way for years afterward to sully Tom's reputation as a scholar and scientist.

Unworried by the slow fuse of enmity he had left burning at the Corlettes', Tom was enjoying having an official position, after having been looked upon by the other whites as a bedraggled beachcomber. He wrote to Jock, "I got a kick out of arresting my first prisoner. Turned the tables on society, so to speak. Oxford will never believe it: Harrisson OHMS (*not* Wormwood Scrubs)."

Six weeks into the job, Tom wrote a "quarterly report" in which he described briefly all the peoples living on Malekula and outlined their problems and his proposals for dealing with them. It is very much a "Tom" document, not like anything a colonial servant would write. It concludes:

> If the planters and traders had only the sense to see that what they most need is a thriving, increasing, population; that means prosperity. No. I have never met one who cared a jot either way. Most missionaries have never grasped the need for medical work on a wide scale, though their limited local efforts have been very valuable.
>
> Important in connection with the probable increase in population is the question—Where are the natives to expand to? . . . Almost all the land in the islands—

and a lot that is under the sea—is claimed by companies and individuals. Anyone who knows native custom re land tenure and sale must be appalled by the absurdity. . . . There should be, in common justice, a *real* Native Advocate to see fair play for the natives in these matters. In the near future decisions will have to be made as to what right whites have to compel natives to stay on their "own ground".

Concern for the land rights of cannibals was an entirely new idea. In the view of scholars sixty years later, Tom's report was markedly ahead of its time, especially when Tom urges that more attention be paid to indigenous property rights. It was this very question which led to the push for independence beginning in the late 1970s.

The acting resident commissioner in Vila sent Tom's report to the high commissioner for the New Hebrides, commending it to his superior as "unique of its kind and should prove most valuable when the time comes to undertake the pacification and civilisation of the tribes." In London, the secretary of state for the colonies noted on his copy that "It should provide the Colonial Office with food for thought."

Kirk Huffman, longtime curator of the Vanuatu Cultural Centre, cites this report as evidence that Tom "really kept the interests of the indigenous peoples as a priority." Tom's desire that what he learned about groups of people be used primarily by or for the benefit of the people being studied—rather than for the benefit of the colonial power or even "the advancement of science"—set him at odds, then and later, with many professional anthropologists and sociologists as well as government officials.

Tom found that getting to know the native people was not easy from the district agent's office, the "Agency," located between two large coconut plantations and cut off from access to indigenous communities. Furthermore, though the "Agency" was an attractive weatherboard house fringed with coconut palms and flowering shrubs, with a veranda looking out over the black sands of Bushman's Bay to the open sea, the land it stood on was swampy and so the house was full of anopheles mosquitoes, helping to make it "just about the hottest and bloodiest place I've ever been in," as Tom wrote Jock. In March 1935, he had a wooden house built at Matanvat, on the northwest coast, accessible to the Big Nambas villages an hour or two's walk inland. While acting district agent, Tom went back and forth between his two houses.

When on the east coast, he socialized with the other white people living there, just as he had on Santo, though, once again, he found few to his liking. To his surprise, the white men he liked best were the missionaries. He had "started by scorning and ended by admiring" them because he found them to be the outsiders who had done the least harm and most good for the islanders. Nonetheless, he saw the white man's coming as having been disastrous for the natives, causing depopulation and devastation of the indigenous culture. A British "liberal" in his thinking, Tom did not directly blame international capitalism, as exemplified by the powerful British Lever organization, which had, beginning in the 1880s, created the market for and set the buying price of New Hebrides copra. He saved his anger for the greedy and cruel planters and traders who mistreated the islanders.

While the copra trading system produced huge overseas profits for international companies, primarily Lever, Tom observed that it did not lead to the amassing of great wealth in the New Hebrides, either for whites or blacks. For most white planters, even the most unprincipled and avaricious, the chance of losing their shirts was much greater than the chance of earning a profit. When times were bad for the planters, they were worse for the other whites in the islands who lived by supplying them goods and services. In the mid 1930s, at the depth of the world depression in primary products, things were worse for these people than ever before.

Early in his stay on Malekula, when down in South West Bay for the first time, Tom met one such man, an Austrian shopkeeper named Antonio Bruno Siller, by then one of only two or three westerners left on the whole insalubrious west coast. A huge man with "sergeant's mustachios," Siller lived in a "tiny hut, perched on a high cliff looking over this lovely treacherous bay." When Tom "came panting up the cliff and up the narrow ladder to his one room, he leapt off the bed and roared at me in five languages before he found, through my mass of two-year beard, that I was an illinguistic Englishman." Gradually Tom learned that Siller, now thirty-five, had been living in "this one-ship-in-three months bay" for the previous two and a half years, during which he had contracted blackwater fever and recovered. Tom stayed a few days drinking three-day-old cold tea and listening to Siller declaim nonstop "about Europe and Dickens and poetry," this being the Austrian's first real chance to talk to an educated man in over two years. Siller's was a kind of loneliness Tom could understand and empathize with:

> For two days he talked. I wanted to go on, over the green high hills behind and into the country of the pygmy [Laus] people, unvisited. Yet I could not deny him words. . . . Sometimes he was quiet, when he entered his accounts or studied to improve his Italian. Then a native would come: threepence for a stick of tobacco from the store; or a sack of copra, worth five sticks of tobacco.

Eventually Tom left and continued his trip to the Laus area and on to the east coast and Bushman's Bay.

A few months later, "when everything was hottest and wettest," word reached Tom when he was on the west coast that Siller was having another attack of blackwater fever. Tom came "hell for leather canoeing down" to South West Bay and reached Siller's hut at sunset. "The floor was just black and teeming with the bodies of maybe forty natives, squatting there watching the big body on the bed, now vivid yellow and falling in." Tom threw out the natives but could not get rid of the thousands of bluebottle flies that settled on the carcass. "It took Siller seven days to die. I hope I shall never again see blackwater death."

Before he died in February 1935, Siller told Tom "to do something about his papers. In his loneliness he had been writing poetry and plays and stories. A suitcase full of them, in tiny German script." Tom took them away to decipher (after he left the New Hebrides) with the help of friends in Tahiti less "illinguistic" than himself and recorded some of their contents in the most poignant pages of *Savage Civilisation*. Siller had not only been writing fiction but had also been writing down his daydream about returning home fabulously rich but hiding it from his family and from the Austrian girl with whom he had quarrelled before leaving Vienna.

"In [a] black book, there were several itineraries of his return to Vienna, which he was always to reach on December 20th." Tom gave a translation of the version of three months before Siller's death. It details the elaborate hoax Siller would carry out, with the connivance of an old friend. There were dates for hiding all his luggage but one small bag. He would wear a worn-out suit and secretly buy a very large house while pretending to be out looking for a job. He would visit his ladylove, Hertha, in his newly bought elegant car, and so on. On December 23, he would confide the truth to his sister Lilly and learn what Mother needed and buy it and show Lilly the other Christmas presents: "To Father: a gold cigar box with two hundred Coronas"; to other family members yearly incomes ranging from 30,000 to 50,000 Austrian schillings; to Hertha, a Vauxhall car.

> December 24—Last purchases and preparations. In the evening I go to bring Hertha's family and the doctor and we all meet at home; we eat the famous carp with salad mayonnaise. I give the order to the chauffeur to bring the presents. While he goes to look for them, my [friend] makes a speech in which he discloses the secret. Lilly brings the sparkling drinks and everything ends in love and gaiety.

Tom goes on to say that Siller also kept accurate accounts of his real profits and losses on his various ventures, in copra, in trochus shell (for which he dived himself), and in cocoa and curios. In the most telling set of figures Tom cites, we find the results of Siller's six years in the New Hebrides: assets: £52 7s. 9d.; liabilities: £23 12s. 7d.; actual capital: £28 15s. 2d. Tom adds that "the actual capital includes some faded books valued at £1 10s" and that the ground "valued at £4 10s" did not belong to Siller. It had been "lent to him rent free by a kindly native." "By the way," Tom ends his account, Siller "did not drink or gamble."

It should be mentioned as a last ironic twist to the Siller story that Tom's removal of the Austrian's papers after his death led to a rumor (still circulating in Vila sixty years later) that Tom, attending at Siller's deathbed, had found and made off with Siller's enormous cache of savings. According to this rumor, Siller's native wife had sought and obtained a warrant for Tom's arrest in Tahiti in July 1935, Tom's first stop after leaving the New Hebrides.

In fact, Tom, on his way to Tahiti, was not able to get to Vila to hand over the few odds and ends of Siller's estate that had not been sold off to pay the Austrian's debts, nor could he deliver the remaining cash, Australian £15. The selling-off had been done by Siller's only kindly white neighbor, a beach trader who had taken over the nursing of Siller from Tom on the day the Austrian died, and there is no question of there ever having been any treasure. To clear up the estate, and to get the dead man's papers back to his family in Vienna, the British authorities in Vila had telegraphed the Colonial Office in London:

> It is alleged that Harrisson has in his possession inadvertently balance of cash and personal effects of SILLER Estate. He was due in England during September. Business address of father, G. H. Harrisson, River Plate House, Finsbury Circus. Request that Colonial Office will invite the late Agent to return cash and personal effects or offer detailed explanation as to its disposal.

One can imagine how this message was received at the office of General Harrisson.

Tom, almost as lonely as Siller had been, wrote frequent letters to Jock, nominally to discuss the preparations for the New Guinea expedition but actually to share his experiences on Malekula with the one person whom he could count on to understand them.

The correspondence between Jock and Tom shows give and take on both sides. Tom, in one of his long memoranda about the New Guinea trip, wrote:

> New Guinea: Social Life. . . . Let us MAKE NO ENEMIES IN NG. We can put up with every irritation and absurdity, for the good of our work. When we get home, we get our own back by writing them up. In the New Hebrides we made too many enemies unnecessarily.

To which Jock replied:

> When I read your little quip about not making enemies in NG I emitted boyish gurgles of amusement. My dear old BSA, do you honestly think you could go anywhere without making enemies? If so, forget it! You couldn't and one of the reasons I'm looking forward to your visit is to have a few good fights.

Still, there is a significant difference in what might best be called "heat" between the letters Tom writes to Jock and Jock's replies. Part of the difference is due to the fact that, unlike Jock who was now home in Australia, Tom was living a second year in great discomfort, danger, and isolation. Thirty Malekulans were murdered by cannibals that year, and Tom was under threat from the chief of the Big Nambas' biggest village, Amok. Malaria that year killed off a number of people Tom knew, including the Fijian dresser, Masulome Tavela, who died of blackwater fever, although he had been "a great husky fighting-fit he-man," as Tom wrote to Jock.

The isolation was greater than can now be imagined. During more than two years in the Pacific, Tom "did not read a newspaper or hear a radio." Isolation from scientists and scientific books and equipment was the worst deprivation, and he counted on Jock to help him overcome it. In one letter, Tom complained to Jock about Jock not having sent him a map of New Guinea and having told Tom to get one in Vila: "For God's sake, don't start throwing Baker tactics on me. Have you already forgotten the slowness of this place, and one's impatience for letters, instructions, literature, that never come?" Jock did remember and sent off whatever Tom asked for with remarkable promptitude, along with sympathetic comment.

Tom wrote letters to many other people during this period and, in early April, some replies came in with the *Morinda*. He announced gleefully to Jock:

> My shares are 100% in England—mail from [Julian] Huxley, Royal Geographical Society, Scottish Geographical Society, [Ernst] Mayr, British Museum, etc. asking me to come home, give lectures, write books, etc. This staying away is having good effect. Chaps begin to realise that England without Harrisson is Hell!!! Ever in haste (and booze) Tom.

Yet nothing could match the pleasure that Tom took in writing letters to and getting letters from Jock, with their ever unfolding details of Tom's holiday-cum-lecture tour in Australia, followed by a long boat trip back to England, followed by both of them writing up their New Hebrides notes and Tom showing Jock England while he orchestrated the fund-raising needed to make the New Guinea expedition possible. No wonder Tom sympathized with Siller and his dream scenarios of Vienna.

Tom's first act on becoming a salaried official was to write Jock to say he would go from Malekula direct to Sydney on the *Morinda*: "I'd give Tahiti and America the go-bye this time, and do it on the way out to New Guinea. Advantages of this scheme are (a) it will leave plenty of money for both of us to get home [to England] and (b) we can travel home together." From then on, Tom focused on this trip to Australia and their trip "home" together with tremendous intensity. He was constantly worried that Jock might go off to

England without him. He would write often to say that "WHATEVER HAP-
PENS, LADDIE, [Tom's caps] don't push off without your dearest Tom, even
if Baker sends you the cash. . . ." Even Zita, traveling in the United States
with her friend Naomi Mitchison, was now aware of how important Jock
had become to Tom. Writing Jock in April 1935 she commented:

> What a hell of a time Tom must be having on Malekula. . . . He writes pretty fre-
> quently fairly high spirited letters but he's very bitter about something. He seems
> to have given you his heart and thinks you're the grandest chap in the world. . . .

Having been "betrayed" by Zita, Tom counted on Jock to remain true to
him. Thus, a February 1935 letter from Jock would upset him more than
Jock could know. Jock wrote:

> Listen old Pachydermis, I have decided that there's a bloody lot I don't know
> about theoretical zoology that they can teach me up at the Varsity. Also would
> like a spot of chemistry—so I am saving every penny I can get and plan to start a
> course in March. . . . I haven't tried to kid myself that I wouldn't be more useful
> to the NG expedition if I had a good grounding zoological (Uni) training. So I
> start next month.

With this news, Tom had a new worry, that Jock, instead of being drawn
away from Tom's orbit by Baker, would be seduced by the prospect of getting a university degree. Not only could that interfere with the New Guinea
trip but, if Jock were to get a university degree, he would be upsides of Tom,
who was beginning to realize the disadvantages of having walked out of
Cambridge in his fourth term. Not that he put it that way to Jock. He wrote:

> I'm all for Marshall BA and Univ. boy, but NG plans come before that extra piece
> of (useless) knowledge . . . you are now gaining [and which] you will forget again
> in 2 years. . . . Compare, for example, the value of a diploma in sexology as
> against a healthy snazzum experience and a good pair of testicles.

In Tom's view, Jock's presence was crucial to the New Guinea expedition.
Tom needed to have at least two other members in the party besides himself.
Reynold Bray, Eddie Shackleton, and Tom Manning were all in the Arctic.

> If necessary, my brother can come. He will do what he is told. Is entomolo-
> gist, Cambridge biology degree, etc. Tough. Bisley shot. Good ordinary water-
> colour painter. Would learn to survey easily because good with hands and with
> pencil. Age 22. . . . My father would probably give him a few hundred for
> expenses. But would only take him (with your approval) as last pick. No fear of
> two Harrissons lining-up together against you. My brother would vote for
> Marshall every time, out of cussedness. But he's a good boy, and not a coward.
> And he is a gun man, which is useful. . . .

In searching for names, and in having to consider the possibility of getting his brother to come, Tom must have realized how few people he knew with whom he would be willing to spend eighteen months, much less four years, in a difficult and dangerous place, and Jock headed that list.

Fortunately, something bizarre and unexpected now happened that distracted Tom from anxiety about Jock's possible betrayal. This was the arrival in Bushman's Bay—on the 1930s equivalent of a magic carpet—of the 1930s equivalent of Sinbad the Sailor.

# Chapter 10

## A Hollywood Interlude

The magic carpet that wafted into Bushman's Bay came in the shape of the *Caroline*, the sumptuous hundred-foot steam yacht of—who else but the great Sinbad of the era—Douglas Fairbanks, Sr. On May 16, 1935, Tom wrote to Jock:

> I have just met Douglas Fairbanks and Lady Ashley on their yacht. They came here to see me. Doug wants to star me in a picture of Big Nambas. Is leaving an operator and is sending his yacht back from China to take me back to England.

This meant he would not go to Australia and on to England with Jock, but he would have "enough money to pay whole NG expedition off the reel if this comes off, and Doug is crazy about me (at present)—not to mention Lady A. I'd be mad if I turned them down. It's the making of NG. . . ."

Tom suggested that Fairbanks make his film of the Big Nambas at Tom's west coast headquarters of Matanvat, ten miles from the friendly Big Nambas Chief Ringapat's village of Tenmaru. Fairbanks agreed and, when he sailed off with Lady Ashley to China on the *Caroline*, he left behind at Matanvat his film man, Chuck Lewis (whom Tom describes as a "Yankee, age 33, exsoldier, degree Geology at Cornell University, Olympic runner, expert electrician, film man and film director"), along with Fairbanks's 65 horsepower racing cutter, motor launch, wireless, food (and drink) for two months, electric gramophone, furniture, and £250 cash to make a film, "Cannibal." Tom was to return with Chuck Lewis to Hollywood to complete the film "in which we tell the true and very curious story of how Doug came to meet me and how I tell him the story (true) of Big Nambas." As Tom wrote to Jock, "Doug stars as Doug, I substar as the exOx bohemian barefoot bushman among the roasted (human?) flesh!"

> Doug is of course a personal friend of people like King George, Stanley Baldwin, Theodore Roosevelt, Rockefellers, Morgans and Vanderbilts, Woolworth,

Mikado of Japan!! Any string that can be pulled can be pulled by him. . . . I think you'll agree with me that I'm doing the right thing. . . . I shall send you a hundred pounds or so to get you back to England via New Guinea, under strict condition that you reach England by January 1936. . . .

But Tom was still on his anti-university hobby horse:

> I am really upset (true) at the idea that you may be bitten by the undergrad mania and box up the whole thing as a result. . . . If we could only talk for ten minutes the whole thing would be all right. Letters get cold, out of date and dirty on the ocean.

He threw himself into preparations for making the film, including filming the wedding of Chief Ringapat's eldest daughter, which fortuitously occurred in June. He had long observed the arrangements for the wedding out of anthropological interest. He had watched the bargaining over the bride price, which, as always among the Big Nambas, was calculated in circular-tusked castrated pigs.

At the wedding, however, which had been designed by Ringapat to cement the alliance of the bride's and groom's villages against the powerful and bellicose village of Amok, the groom's village representatives arrived late with many fewer and much poorer quality pigs than had been agreed on. The Tenmaru villagers had waited, heavily armed, for the groom's family to arrive and were still fingering their weapons. It was a nasty moment. Nobody was quite sure whether intervillage war might break out.

After more than an hour of hidden deliberation in their clubhouse, the Tenmaru hosts grudgingly accepted their chief's command that the bridegroom's people be allowed to return home unharmed. Ringapat's decision not to permit violence at the wedding probably had much to do with the presence of "the guvman" in the shape of acting district agent Tom Harrisson, there to film the ceremony with Chuck Lewis.

Additional witnesses to the wedding included a handful of French tourists from the *Korrigane*, a yacht that was touring these waters at the time. To these bemused Frenchmen, Tom did not look at all as they imagined a British colonial officer should look:

> Badly shaved, dressed in rags and wearing a colonial helmet of which the green lining was hanging in ribbons, [Harrisson] carried a piece of pink flannel cloth which was apparently supposed to be the English flag. . . . Four native policemen wearing green caps with red pompons came with him. Next the dinghy returned with a handsome red-haired athletic-looking man [Chuck Lewis] with an immense blue and white umbrella. A whole train of steamer trunks and valises were lined up on the beach. We grew more and more intrigued. . . .

During the seven weeks that Tom and Lewis worked on the film, Tom found the clash of cultures between Hollywood and the New Hebrides complicated their efforts. The Hollywood film man "could not get used to people who would not be bought into doing a thing that did not amuse them." Worse, as Tom explains, the film man "always wanted people to do what were to them impossible things. . . ." Lewis wanted, for example, the women to remove the enormous purple pandanus headgear custom obliged them to wear whenever men were present.

Then there was the problem that the Big Nambas did not correspond to the Hollywood idea of cannibals. "No person in Hollywood ever having seen a cannibal, . . . they had their own cannibal dogmas." These included stone altars, crazy dances, and spears much too long to throw. Tom confessed, "I had no idea what I had let myself (or them) in for. . . ."

His hardest job was persuading the cannibals to do "retakes." Doing the same thing over and over again to please an outsider made no sense to them, and Tom got "roared hell by both sides." The film's plot also caused terrible problems. For example, Tom had once mentioned to Fairbanks that "on some islands the women often suckled the piglets. He said, 'Get that.' The trouble we had getting that!"

> The women were naturally shy about it, directly they realised it meant something different to the white. And when that was fixed, Chuck decided that a man, the evil savage husband, carrying a huge club, was to come along to his wife, the kindest-looking woman available. She was to be suckling her baby child. He was to wrench it away from her and ram a piglet into the place of honour—pigs are more than men: graphic illustration.

Lewis found a suitable pair but "they would not co-operate for a long time; and then no one would give up their baby to this unknown conspiracy; and then only in private, away from the village, secretly." After Tom had helped surmount all these objections, at the dress rehearsal, the suckling piglet bit the woman's breast hard, while "the baby misbehaved under emotional pressure, and the woman struck." The filming was finally accomplished "with a faked baby, made out of yam. The piglet had his snout securely tied."

When filming was over,* because Tom knew he would be leaving with the *Caroline* at the end of the month, he resigned from being acting district agent in mid-June, a month early. From his pay, he immediately sent Jock £80 for his fare, via New Guinea, "home" to England. He wrote to Jock that he was

---

*The footage was never made into a feature film, although it was allegedly shown many years later on Australian television.

"definitely going to America on Fairbanks['s] yacht due here end month," to Hollywood, and he would be in England well before the end of the year.

Along with the £80, Tom sent Jock "a list of suggestions for you to investigate direct in New Guinea." The list ran thirty-six pages. It covered everything from checking into paradise bird regulations, anchorage charts, maps, and portage tracks to tabus, fevers, pests, harbors, and local conditions. It instructed Jock to:

> Look out especially for special sorts of goods in demand in interior, etc. e.g., Sakau only like blue beads, Big Nambas like small white beads. . . . Natives love the chap who finds out and delivers just *the* fashionable thing for their tribe. . . .
>
> . . . Get letters of support from Australian Museum, . . . Government, Queensland, Qantas, Presbyterians, Murray, Melbourne Mus., Sydney Univ. etc. These don't mean a damn really but are in fact VERY IMPORTANT in England (and especially) America.
>
> And write up a real practical condensed 100% account of transport, travel, exploration, unentered areas, our plans, expenses NG, suitable for handing to anyone, giving a complete outline of the position up to end 1935. . . .
>
> BRING YOUR TYPEWRITER TO ENGLAND as well as your balls.

Jock accepted these suggestions with remarkably good grace, as well he might because, despite their irritating tone of command, they were full of good ideas for organizing serious fieldwork in the less developed world. He proposed leaving Sydney in November, arriving in New Guinea in December, and reaching London on March 28, 1936.

In late June, Tom left Malekula with Chuck Lewis on the *Caroline*, which had come back to take Tom and Lewis to the United States via the Panama Canal. Tom and Lewis were the only passengers, with (Tom wrote Jock) "4 stewards, 25 crew, 2 cooks, etc." and made what for Tom was a triumphal return to Santo's Hog Harbour. He had left it just a year earlier with only a few pounds in his pocket. Now he had enough cash to be sending his best friend £80, while the future seemed remarkably bright, both professionally and financially. In Hog Harbour, he and Lewis had "a damn good time, taking movies of nude tabbies and [Rev.] Bill Anderson," he informed Jock. He was enjoying being back among the Sakau, "who are the civilest, sensiblest, generousest, energeticest buggers in the world after the Malekulan bushmen. . . ."

But the letter with this euphoric sentence also contains the uncensored outpourings of Tom's ever latent rage. Throughout his life, he seemed always to need an outlet to express this rage or it would overflow. For example, once after weeks on his best behavior doing fieldwork, he found himself back in Bushman's Bay for the first night in a month. After writing all night, he went on board the *Morinda*, "got drunk, pushed 3rd officer in face, ordered all officers out of the bar (they went), etc. Result of four weeks Big Namba and yam eating. They were a lousy lot anyway—all new; not one had the guts to sock my jaw, kick my balls or break a bottle on my scalp." If he had no other way to let off steam, he did it in notes written to himself. During this period, however, he had Jock to whom he could pour out all his thoughts. Much of his correspondence to Jock contains the kind of wild fantasies of anger and revenge other people rarely write down, such as

> Do not tell any person in England or who is in touch with England that you are going there. We'll have hell's own fun walking in to the Baker home, the Harrisson home and other homes (all of which we shall ruin). I am hiding my own arrival, which will probably be in November. Christ, won't Baker be tickled! I asked my father to give me £50 to help bring a friend (= you) home. He refused, the swine. Wait till he sees you. Jock my lad, you and me is going to bullshit them bloody english plenty too much. . . .
>
> If Baker does send you any cash, hold it in reserve, don't spend it, then no obligation. Having worked hard to get you the dough I want the fun of giving socialist Baker a nasty slam in the knockers. You could walk into his Oxhouse and hand back his cash without comment, shit on the breakfast table, and go out. (No, Baker is all right, he doesn't mean it. It'll pay to exploit him rather than extirpate him). . . .

Such texts let us know some of Tom's thoughts, however fleeting. Yet are we necessarily the wiser for this knowledge? Somebody else would not write his thoughts down unless they mattered, but one cannot apply that standard safely to Tom. He wrote everything down.

He certainly was in an unstable mental condition toward the end of his two-year stint in the islands. Looking back on those final months in the New Hebrides, he later wrote, apropos of the filming interlude, that it had "snapped me out of my awful Condominium depression that was almost suicidal and merged the end of my island stay into laughter and the outside reality!"

The trip on the sumptuous *Caroline* proved less comfortable than he had expected. In the passage from the New Hebrides to Tahiti, the ocean was very rough and "there were no fans, lights, air conditioning, radiogram, running water." As the boat rocked in the swell, the loose furniture slid about the deck. The portholes below had to be kept closed, keeping out the fresh air "else the Pacific came in too." He and Lewis, forced to endure one another's exclusive company, must have had an awkward time.

Tom's malaria came back and seemed to be verging toward blackwater fever. They had been aboard for a week or more when they arrived in Papeete in time for July 14, Bastille Day, the occasion for a week's bacchanal, "when that glorious place gets even more glorious than usual." After a week on shore, either Tom was too sick or could not bear to reboard the *Caroline* or Chuck Lewis could not bear to have him aboard again. In any case, the yacht left Tom at Papeete. Tom wrote, "I stopped there for three months. The latent fever and chaos within me kept me in bed most of the time." He was physically and mentally exhausted. In addition to all the illnesses he had brought with him from Malekula, he now acquired gonorrhea, the result, he wrote to Jock, of enjoying the company of "women who washed."

Then his father got the wire from Vila that Tom had left the Condominium with Siller's cash and effects. The General cabled his son ordering him home and paying his fare. After sending the authorities in Vila the £15 cash, the papers, and other effects from the Siller estate, Tom embarked November 4, 1935, on the SS *Céphée*, a big French cargo ship that took passengers, a ship that was, to Tom's relief, "too copra-laden to move on the waves."

For the next seven weeks, he slept all day and worked all night, chiefly writing up his notes on the role of birds of prey in Pacific culture. To his abiding anger and sorrow and over his protests, one of the passengers shot down a peregrine falcon, "the finest" of birds, in Tom's opinion. Meanwhile the ship sailed eastward, along the west coast of the United States, where a penniless Tom was unable to get a visa to go ashore, through the Panama Canal, and then across the Atlantic to England. It was hardly the surprise return of the triumphant hero that Tom, like Siller, had envisaged.

**Figure 1** Geoffry Harnett Harrisson, Tom's father, at age 25 (December 1907).

**Figure 2** Marie Ellen Cole, "Doll," Tom's mother, at age 21 (December 1907).

▲ **Figure 3** Doll *(far right)* in April 1909, her bags packed for Buenos Aires and marriage, with sister Violet and servants in front of the family home at Otterbourne, south of the Itchen valley. (©Tunbridge Sedgwick Studios)

**Figure 4** Tom at age 11 *(right)*, Bill *(left)*, their English tutor, Ronald Merchant, and their dog, Foxtrot, outside Chalet Patterson, Concordia, Entre Rios, Argentina, in 1922.

**Figure 5** Tom at age 18 in 1929.

▼ **Figure 6** En route home from Borneo via Singapore aboard the *Sarpedon*, late December 1932. Paul Richards *(far left)*, Cub Hartley *(next to Richards)*, Tom Harrisson, *(fifth from left)*, Eddie Shackleton *(third from left)*.

**Figure 7** Tom at age 21 and Eddie Shackleton *(right)* wearing Bornean loincloths in Sarawak, 1932.

▼ **Figure 8** A Kayan longhouse at Long Laput on the Baram River (1959). (Wilhelm G. Solheim II)

**Figure 9** E. Banks, curator of the Sarawak Museum, in 1932.

▼ **Figure 10** Tom at the Oxford expedition camp on Santo, with a maggot-infested leg wound in 1933. (Zita Baker)

**Figure 11** Zita Baker,
circa 1937, after returning
from the New Hebrides.

**Figure 12** Zita and Nebv, chief
of the Sakau village of Sara,
standing in front of the Oxford
expedition camp building, 1933.

**Figure 13** Jock Marshall with a Sakau rifleman on Santo, 1934.

**Figure 14** Tom being scarified by Nebv's wife at Sara, 1933. (Zita Baker)

**Figure 15** Tom *(left)* and Chuck Lewis *(with solar topee)* with their Big Nambas film actors on Malekula, 1935.

**PART THREE**

People-Watching in Britain,
1936–1942

# Chapter 11

## Tom and the Thirties

"If you are not born and brought up in England it gives you a much more objective attitude to the country when you arrive," as Tom liked to remark. It was late December 1935 and he had been away from England and essentially out of touch with it for more than two years.

What kind of an England had Tom returned to? A country in the depth of an economic depression, the worst in modern times. The breakdown of the economic system had followed little more than a decade after the Great War. On the continent, fascism, Nazism, and communism were on the rise, making it nearly certain that the war to end all wars would soon be followed by another world conflagration. Old ways had failed to cope with the basic problems of modern life, and a huge proportion of the men who would have been in their mid-thirties had died in battle. As a result, the British intellectual class and the media were more receptive than ever before or since to what was new and to what iconoclastic people in their twenties were doing and thinking.

By early 1937, Tom would find a way to contribute a new idea and a new method to this age known as The Thirties. His contribution (in partnership with a young Surrealist poet, Charles Madge) would be called "Mass-Observation." Britons who were adults in the late thirties and early forties remember it.

The idea behind Mass-Observation was in Tom's mind before he reached England. The idea was to look at England's people the way he had at the cannibals of the New Hebrides. But, for the moment, there were two other matters that claimed his attention: launching the New Guinea project and seeing Zita again.

For the New Guinea project, he tried to contact Douglas Fairbanks:

Dear Doug,

Have just got back from Tahiti. . . . I am crazy to do something about that film or another, and have my pal up in Dutch New Guinea now (Stone Age Man) making ground plans for 4 year expedition. Please do let me know if I am still of interest. I couldn't get home before and couldn't get a USA visa.

He apologized that he and Lewis had not "got on frightfully well" and added,

I hope the film was OK. I did all I could. I'd very much like a lecture reel or somesuch—as usual I am utterly broke, but here there are no bananas growing by the wayside. I've written a book, "The Autobiography of a Cannibal," nearly finished.

He then went straight to Oxford to spend Christmas with the Bakers rather than with his family in Hampshire, and there he had a disappointment. Zita, who like Tom could not bear to sit still, had moved on with her life. Here is Tom's reaction, written to Naomi Mitchison from his parents' home, "The Chase," Weeke, Winchester, on New Year's Eve, 1935:

Naomi:

You asked me to write but I don't feel like it because I feel all gummed up about the muddle of everything. It is annoying. I really love Zita best and most faithfully for herself, her "mana", her, than anyone except perhaps you. But like yours, my Zitalove isn't primarily sexual or orthodox or ahead; it just is. . . .

What does annoy me, Naomi, is that either:

(a) I didn't come home earlier, quickly, so that it wouldn't have happened. But I wouldn't have been so sensible as I am, now. I am sensible now. . . . I could really enjoy my Zita now, & not spoil it all by hurling Tom-tom at her, poor darling, or

(b) That I came home at all. I was better black.

He protested:

Why didn't you or Zita have the kindness to write me one postcard saying: "Z. Baker is in love with D. Crossman, Really in love. T. Harrisson, take note." Or simply "Z. doesn't love T. any more. . . ."

Ah well. It is my fault, I am too serious & single minded to prosper in this two-edged razor-blade two ends-of-a-telephone age. I guess I'll have to change the age or something. Or just change MY age?

Love,

Tom

He was probably right in concluding he had lost his chance of keeping Zita's love by not coming home sooner. Their affair had already made Zita's marriage to Baker so fragile that it was ready to break at the next strain, and her affair with the brilliant and promising Richard Crossman had started soon after the Bakers' return to Oxford.

Four years older than Tom, Crossman was a graduate of University College, Oxford, where he had been on the fringes of the Auden, Isherwood, Spender group of predominantly homosexual poets. He had then married a German prostitute, and when she left him shortly afterward, he had divorced her. Zita became acquainted with Crossman when he was teaching philosophy at New College, Oxford, and working as a regular broadcaster on the BBC. Though he was widely acknowledged to be one of the most brilliant men of his generation, "one of the most colourful figures of modern British politics," who would achieve national fame as a broadcaster and journalist, it was in large part thanks to Zita's efforts that he was, when Tom met him in late 1935, on the bottom rung of a political career that would lead to becoming a Labour minister. (He is now best known abroad for his *Diaries of a Cabinet Minister*, first published 1975–1977.)

Naomi, who had sympathized with Tom's and Zita's love for one another, found Crossman to be a self-centered and sometimes gratuitously cruel man and did not think that he was a suitable lover for her favorite woman friend and protégée. In hopes of keeping Zita and Crossman apart, in January 1935 while Tom was in Malekula, she had taken Zita to the United States for ten weeks to learn about and show solidarity with the South's poor whites and poorer blacks. The trip was another great adventure for Zita, whose pluck, as always, was fully equal to the occasion. (It was her courage that was perhaps her most endearing trait to Tom. As with his men friends, Tom liked women who were "tough.") But if one of Naomi's purposes in taking Zita away with her had been to break up Zita's love affair with Crossman, the trip proved worse than useless. The separation strengthened the relationship. A few months before Tom returned, Zita had finally told her husband about her affair with Crossman and that it was serious. Divorce from Baker and marriage to Crossman were beginning to appear possible. She must have told Tom about Crossman within hours of his arrival on her doorstep.

Tom—a much more grown-up Tom than had entertained thoughts of marriage with her as she left Hog Harbour in February 1934—could not realistically have considered himself a possible husband for Zita now, in December 1935. He was penniless and had no academic degrees or obviously saleable skills, his only "capital" being a partly written draft of a book about the New Hebrides that might never find a publisher.

In the presence of Zita again, her charm, her courage and originality, Tom recognized what he had lost. It is easy for anyone who knew them both to feel a pang of regret that it was not possible for these two extraordinary people to build a life together. Her kindness and fundamental honesty would have been so good for him; his making no allowances for her femininity, treating her like the tough, energetic, and adventurous person she was would have been so good for her.

The start of 1936 found Tom at low ebb. Fairbanks was in Switzerland and had not replied to Tom's message. Zita was no longer in love with him. Jock was in New Guinea doing the sort of thing Tom most liked to do. Tom was back under the parental roof, weak from the cumulative effects of two and half years of malnutrition and tropical illness. He had no money except what he could get selling his diseased blood to medical students. He had a scraggly beard, hair down to his shoulders, and his clothes were almost in rags. His cousin remembers Tom lying ill at his parents' Hampshire home and his father either saying to her or making clear that he was thinking; "Here is this young man lying in bed. He went on an expedition with my money that I didn't want him to go on, and what's he ever going to amount to?" He was twenty-four years old.

His slump did not last long. The Royal Geographical Society had already asked him in December to give a talk on his Malekula experiences at its March 16, 1936, evening meeting. He got busy writing up what he would say and doing research for a new draft of his book about the New Hebrides. For help, he went to see the foremost expert on the New Hebrides, John Layard, to ask to look through Layard's enormous file of 1914–1915 field notes, and to draw on his unique expertise on things Malekulan.

Getting Layard to help him must have taken great tact on Tom's part. Ten years earlier, Layard had extended the nearly unprecedented kindness of lending Bernard Deacon all his field notes for the region of Malekula that Deacon wanted to study only to see some of his notes appear in 1934 in the galley proof of Deacon's posthumous book, unacknowledged, as if they were Deacon's own. Layard's law suit was resolved when the publishers printed a note from him at the beginning of Deacon's book pointing out which notes and ideas were his. Tom must have realized that Layard, who had still not written up virtually any of his 1914–1915 material, was likely to be hesitant to help another young person writing on Malekula.

John Willoughby Layard (1891–1974) was one of the oddest characters ever to come out of British social anthropology. Without intending to, he had spent a year, 1914–1915, alone on little Atchin Island, off Malekula's northwest coast, with only Atchin islanders for company. Except on short trips to see a Catholic priest on Vao Island—perhaps three weeks in all—he had not seen another white face. Merely to survive, he had had to learn how to behave as a young man in Atchin society, wearing native dress (a penis wrapper), learning the Atchin language, and taking part in the young men's initiation ceremonies. It was the most extreme form of cultural immersion ever practiced by a social scientist up to that time. It nearly killed him. He returned to England with a writer's block so strong that it extended to his feet. He could not walk and was, in a friend's words, "a physical and mental wreck."

Ten years later, an unorthodox psychotherapist got Layard walking again, but then the doctor died. Layard, still with a writer's block, went to Vienna and Berlin, trying different analysts and becoming suicidally depressed. By 1929 he was still in Berlin, caught up in the homosexual poetical circle of Auden and Isherwood and working-class German boys that Isherwood describes in *Christopher and His Kind*. One day while alone, Layard put a pistol in his mouth and pulled the trigger. The bullet went through the top of his mouth and lodged in his forehead but missed his brain. Waking up covered in blood, he thought he was dead and tried to walk through a wall but only banged his nose. Deeply embarrassed, cramming a hat over his head wound, he took a taxi to Auden's apartment, where he asked his friend to finish him off. Instead, Auden got him to hospital.

Layard went back to England that summer, cured of his suicidal depression but still unable to deal with his voluminous fifteen-year-old notes. He became interested in Jungian ideas and abandoned his social anthropological career for a new one as a Jungian analyst.

Then, in early 1936, in walked Tom Harrisson with his enthusiasm and energy and lifelong gift for galvanizing others into action. There was a basis for fruitful collaboration. Tom needed Layard's help to prepare his March 1936 talk on Malekula for the Royal Geographical Society and to fill in gaps in his ethnography for the book he was writing. In return, Tom offered Layard material on some of the dances he had witnessed on Malekula and other bits of ethnographic information he had acquired as well as all he had learned about bird auguries for use as an appendix to Layard's book, a book that now, with Tom to goad and encourage him, Layard was finally starting to write.

Collaboration between the two men was predictably stormy. At first, Layard handed over masses of his field notes and photographs to Tom, as he had done with Deacon. He began to regret his generosity when he learned that Tom was planning to use several of these photographs in a series of articles about the New Hebrides for the *News Chronicle*. Layard protested that this popular liberal-left daily with its circulation of a million mainly lower-middle-class readers was not the right sort of paper for such material. Tom replied that, on the contrary, its readers were precisely the kind of people to whom he wanted to speak. Similar fights went on throughout their collaboration. Layard would say that Tom was merely engaging in self-publicity, not trying to contribute to the body of scientific knowledge. Tom would retort that he was not writing for the "10,000 families" but for the man on the street, the man who needs to know but does not. Tom claimed to be trying to promote a two-way dialogue between scientists and the British people. He would tell Layard that he got more sensible comment and more intellectual stimulation from talking with a Welsh coal miner than with a fashionable academician or scientist.

Eventually Layard consented to have Tom use his photographs in the *News Chronicle*. He also agreed to give several talks with Tom on the BBC, a medium that satisfied both men's ideas of an appropriate means for dispensing information to the public. The BBC had become, in the words of a contemporary political scientist, "an invention in the sphere of social science no less remarkable than the invention of radio transmission in the sphere of natural science." Tom was a master at exploiting it.

Thanks to his friend Mary Adams, the BBC adult education officer who in 1936 became the first woman television producer for the newly established BBC television service, Tom became a frequent BBC guest. During his first year back from the New Hebrides, he appeared on radio or television a half-dozen times. He spoke about how cannibals use pigs in their climb up the social ladder, debated with Eddie Shackleton the relative merits of exploring in the tropics instead of at the poles—where Eddie was becoming the second of his name to distinguish himself—and gave a series of amusing and informative lectures on birds and their relationship to man.

On March 16, Tom gave his best lecture thus far, not on the BBC but to the Royal Geographical Society on "Living with the People of Malekula." He spoke for over an hour, describing the flora, the fauna, the geography, and especially the people of Malekula—their lives, their rituals, their values, their wars—in lively conversational prose understandable to any intelligent person but neither obvious nor patronizing.

All three Bakers were there, as was John Layard and a full house of regular RGS members, including the anthropologist Prof. H. Balfour, curator of the Pitt Rivers Museum at Oxford, who rose to congratulate Tom "on a very noteworthy success . . . in having led a purely native life and penetrated into the inner life of the people." John Baker, who seems not to have borne a grudge against Tom for his affair with Zita, came up to the platform to say:

> I think there is no possible doubt that our lecturer tonight has seen more of the savage—if I may use that word—tribes of the New Hebrides than any European has ever seen, and has also more fully entered into their life than anyone else ever has.

He ended with a plea for support for Tom's plan to study primitive man in New Guinea.

It was Layard, though, the acknowledged expert on Malekula and the greatest fieldworker of the Pacific, who did the most for Tom's professional reputation that evening, by associating himself with the talk by the younger man. At Tom's request, he showed slides of some of the Atchin dances he had photographed twenty years earlier, after saying:

> I should like to express the very great pleasure I have experienced in listening to Mr. Harrisson's account. . . . He went to the New Hebrides as an ornithologist, knowing nothing about anthropology, and he has returned knowing more about the natives than most anthropologists. I can assure you that he could supplement his brief account given to-night with many pregnant scientific observations.

Layard's endorsement in front of the great and the good of British social science is probably as close as Tom ever came to being admitted to the social anthropologists' "experts guild."

The excellent reception given Tom's talk led to many doors opening. The RGS published this lecture and asked him to write up his Santo and his general New Hebrides anthropological experiences for two other issues of the *Geographical Journal*, which Tom promptly did. Then, in June, the RGS put its seal of approval on the forthcoming New Guinea expedition by granting Tom that year's Cuthbert Peek award for use on the expedition.

The RGS prize money was only £25 but Tom, sending the cash on to Jock, who was still in New Guinea, took the award as a sign that "I am the blue eyed boy over here now." He had by then rounded up an impressive list of notables who were willing to have their names on the letterhead of the Central New Guinea Expedition as members of the committee. These included the famous writer and scientific popularizer H. G. Wells; the great zoologist Julian Huxley; and Dr. A. C. Haddon, FRS, the leading social anthropologist at Cambridge University. Still others who were, by July 1936, ready to give Tom's New Guinea expedition either moral or financial help were the present and past presidents of the RGS, Clement Attlee (Labour M.P. and leader of the Opposition), Tom's friend Naomi Mitchison (with her connections by blood and marriage to the world of science and the Labour Party), Douglas Fairbanks, Sr., and—most significant for Tom's immediate future—the publisher Victor Gollancz.

Victor Gollancz was one of the men who helped make the "The Thirties" what it was among British intellectuals: idealistic, left-leaning, anti-Nazi, and anti-Fascist. He founded the Left Book Club in May 1936. Gollancz may have attended Tom's Malekula lecture at the RGS. By late March, he had agreed to publish Tom's book, which would soon acquire its provocative title *Savage Civilisation*. He gave Tom the then surprisingly big advance for a new author of £150. People who knew both men would not have been surprised. They were much alike in their vitality, versatility, and in the total certainty each of them had that what he was doing at the moment was of the utmost importance to the world. Both men had the gift of infecting their collaborators with their own enthusiasm. Tom was grateful all his life to Gollancz for the early help the great man gave him. Years later he wrote him, "You are one of the few people in my life who genuinely, generously and *unfussily* helped me and (poor you) formed me."

Tom's book was published first by Gollancz Ltd., in January 1937, and appeared as an "additional selection" for September 1937 on the list of the Left Book Club, with its 50,000 members.

In late July 1936, having finished the manuscript, Tom wrote to Jock:

> I haven't sat in a ruddy armchair for weeks, just a good hard one and the type-writer tapping twelve hours a day but Boy, have I done a book?
>
> Tonight I am going out to meet Naomi Mitchison . . . and Attlee, leader of Government Opposition. I am going to try and arrange that a question be asked in the House of Commons about the NH [New Hebrides] just as my book is published. I doubt if I will succeed but it bloody ought to be asked and my book may raise hell against [the Condominium authorities].

As with almost all of Tom's subsequent writing, his purpose in publishing *Savage Civilisation* was threefold: first, to benefit the group being studied—in this case the "savages" of the New Hebrides; second, to educate the general public while, if possible, announcing discoveries to the world of science; and third, to satisfy his nearly unquenchable thirst for recognition. In this, his first real book, he achieved all three.

# Chapter 12

## Bolton

"It is difficult to believe that anything more fascinating will appear in 1937. . . ." trumpeted the *News Chronicle* on January 11, the day Tom's book *Savage Civilisation* came out. More praise would follow. The *Times Literary Supplement* of January 30, 1937, went on for 16 column-inches about this "important and remarkable book," proclaiming that Tom had "done a service by propounding [the Melanesians'] side of a grim and bitter story, which he has seen through their eyes." (Today it is hard to realize how new an idea it was in 1937 to view the whites as evildoers rather than as benefactors of benighted savages.)

For the serious social scientist, the review by John Layard in the August 1937 issue of *Man* gave the stamp of approval of the foremost living anthropologist to have worked in the area. Among other things, Layard noted approvingly that Tom was "remarkably free of white man's superiority complex, and freely acknowledges how much he himself learnt from the natives." In fact, Tom had done much more than that. He had claimed that the cannibal culture of Malekula was as workable and as efficient for the purposes of its participants as was western civilization for Englishmen. His description of Big Nambas' social organization as a plutocracy, with wealth based on credit and credit consisting of how many circular-tusked pigs the creditor was owed, made the system seem quite reasonable. It sounded no more absurd than a trading system in which gold was dug up in small bits around the globe, shaped into a certain form, and then buried in Fort Knox. So when reviewing a juvenile version of the book, *Living Among Cannibals* (1943), the poor ignorant *Times Literary Supplement* writer (who usually covered lawn tennis) was not sure if Tom was describing an existing society or writing an allegory.

The knowledgeable Layard, having described the book's many virtues, delicately pointed out all the book's weaknesses, only to dismiss them as minor considering what the book achieved. He noted that Tom, in his accounts of northern Malekula, with the idea of making easy reading, [is] not always too careful to state to what parts of the island or islands information culled from other sources belongs. This is a fault of quick writing, and does not worry the author, who seeks to create an impression rather than to write an exact treatise. This he certainly does, for the work is a marvel of artistry, with many-sided interest.

. . . Though his book is not arranged for anthropologists, and the author "kept no diary and made no general notes," though, in Malekula, whence come his chief native accounts, his medium was pidgin English, the work is, nevertheless, a mine of information on native life.

Layard listed a tantalizing variety of subjects that Tom explored, from cannibalism to dance to gong language to human sacrifice, adding that "Harrisson's really strong point is on the native character, which colours all his accounts."

Other reviews echoed the RGS critic who wrote "It is not possible, by way of review, to do justice to this book" and then went on for four small print pages to try to do so. Even Dick Crossman, writing Zita about his own forthcoming book on Plato, added, "I wish it was a book like Tom's. There! I am jealous."

Tom did not get off scot-free, however. The planter, Ewan Corlette, who had been one of Tom's first friends—and his first enemy—on the island of Malekula wrote a couple of irate letters to the *Pacific Island Monthly*, then the only serious regional journal read by English speakers, in which he tried to shoot down many of Tom's claims in *Savage Civilisation*. On a number of points, the old planter was right on target. But, seeking to destroy the book's credibility, Corlette shot off cannonballs where Layard, aiming at the same flaws, had merely tapped them with his lecturer's pointer. A number of Corlette's assertions are totally wrong but have been accepted by people who do not know the facts, leading to doubts in many quarters of Tom's genuine achievements.

Most present-day anthropologists who know the region share the view of Michael Young of the Research School of Pacific and Asian Studies of the Australian National University. Reading Tom's book after more than twenty-five years working on Melanesia, Dr. Young said he was "pleasantly surprised" by it, although "the scholarship leaves a bit to be desired. . . . I suspect he did not check all his sources all the time. But one can forgive him for that for the sheer exuberance of the writing. And I think he was ahead of his time in the way he bashed colonialism . . . at the time. He certainly challenged the conventional wisdom of the day—the 1930s."

The Frenchman Patrick O'Reilly, in his 1957 encyclopedic who's who in the New Hebrides wrote of *Savage Civilisation*:

One does not know quite how to define this work: a history of the New Hebrides, a story of a voyage, an essay, a study of acculturation to an alien society, . . . in any case, a work that is totally nonconformist and as exciting as it is possible to be.

A man with a bold and curious mind, a perspicacious traveller, a person who read widely and dug deep into archives, Harrisson is certainly the best informed writer on the New Hebrides and *Savage Civilisation* is the book most full of information and penetrating insights of any written about the archipelago to date. . . . A work of such dynamism could not fail to provoke reactions locally. An expatriate settler on Malekula, E. Corlette, for example, tried to pick a fight with the author in the pages of the *Pacific Islands Monthly*. But these criticisms of details in the book do not make any less true the assessment of Layard that: "Harrisson went out to the New Hebrides as an ornithologist, knowing nothing about ethnology. He comes back knowing more about the natives than many ethnologists."

Few works of scholarship in the social sciences have survived so well the sixty-odd years since Tom's book was published.

To jump back to July 1936, Tom, having given his manuscript to Gollancz, began to harry Jock, sick with malaria and alone in New Guinea, to complete his reconnaisance and come "home" to England so that they could proceed with their plans. Tom was restless. Had he not been waiting for Jock, he would have joined his friends Bray and Manning on an expedition to the Canadian Arctic. It was as well he did not go. Bray disappeared forever during that RGS-sponsored expedition, having been blown out to sea in a folboat (collapsible canoe) while exploring the upper reaches of the Hudson Bay.

Tom had arranged for Jock to drum up enthusiasm for the New Guinea expedition by lecturing about it to the RGS in August and was now trying to reschedule the talk for the winter. Jock, having agreed to reach England by March 1936, seemed to be hesitating because of money worries. Tom was sure he could help Jock earn enough to survive and wrote that he was "still as ready and eager as I ever was to share in all cash with you, and, damn it, if we are hard up we are. . . ."

> When I came home I was absolutely broke and until I gathered myself together and found that I could bullshit the whole lot of them I was nearly passing out. Now I have paid off bills, university accounts, had the best medical treatment in the country, bought all the things I want, etc. But I find cash is lousy; it is just as good to have £2 a week. When I have a lot, I just spend it all and drink and do nothing except take Imperial Airways over to the continent. . . .

While waiting for his best friend to arrive, Tom had been feeding his disappointment in love by going to see Zita and Crossman, together and separately. In the summer, Tom would sometimes appear for lunch at Crossman's Oxford house, once proudly announcing that he had been "gated" for a week for breaking up urinals.

In later life, Tom often said that he had been "banned" from Oxford. This 1936 gating may be what he was referring to, or he may have meant a later event, when the chairman of the zoology department ordered Tom be denied access to the premises after Tom and Jock followed a bibulous dinner by trying to steal a proctor's hat for Naomi.

In October, when Zita took a holiday in Hampshire, not far from Tom's parents' home, Tom came over and walked all day with her through lovely countryside. Zita noticed that he seemed to grow "gradually more depressed."

Then suddenly Tom picked himself up and moved in an entirely new direction. As he wrote Secretary Hinks of the Royal Geographical Society on November 1, 1936, "I am working in a cotton mill at present, 11 hours a day, 27/- wages. The address that will find me is The Lever's Arms, Nelson Square, Bolton." For an old Harrovian to be one of the working poor in a Lancashire mill in 1936 was almost unthinkable. But Tom, having tried in his youth to learn more about Britain—tramping holidays in Scotland and Wales and three school holidays spent in London's East End, observing the down-and-outers as if they had been exotic birds—saw now:

> with the shock of clarity that absence and return can refresh . . . that most of the things I had been studying and methods I had been using, both in ornithology and gradually in ethnology, arose just as much as problems among my "own" people. All over the world people like me were going out to study other civilizations on a scale of intimacy and detail which had not yet been applied in our "civilized" societies.

In the 1930s this was an idea just coming into its own, with the birth of a new social science, "sociology," whose practitioners sought to apply social anthropological methods to the study of "developed" societies. While waiting to head off for New Guinea, Tom decided to try out his cannibal-watching techniques on different "savages" no better known to the educated British reading public: the working-class people of the North of England. Having made his decision, the next morning he arrived at Bolton in Lancashire.

He was not the first of his class to "go native" among the lower classes in his own country. During the first half of 1936, while Tom was writing his New Hebrides book, an old Etonian, who had published a book on how it felt to be *Down and Out in Paris and London* (Gollancz, 1933) under the pen name George Orwell, was traveling through the milling and mining towns of the North to gather material for *The Road to Wigan Pier*, which would go to Gollancz in December. If Orwell's example (Tom and Orwell never seem to have met) were not goad enough to revive Tom's earlier interest in doing fieldwork among England's working poor, in the summer of 1936, just as Tom had finished the last page of his book from a two-room flat he had rented in Chelsea, the "Jarrow Crusade" of 200 unemployed men from the derelict northern town of Jarrow arrived in London.

The month-long spectacle of 200 threadbare, undernourished men marching south on behalf of their Tyneside town, where the unemployment rate was over 80 percent, drew much publicity, public interest, and support all along its route to a climactic mass meeting in Hyde Park. There, thousands of people, orchestrated by the Communist Party, were waiting to greet the marchers and wave banners. Tom may have been present; certainly half of his fashionably leftist friends were.

Given the mood among Tom's friends at the time, one is less surprised by where he did go, the North, than that, unlike George Orwell, Stephen Spender, John Cornford, and so many other bright and courageous young artists, writers, and intellectuals, Tom did not go off to Spain to help the Loyalists. Tom was not drawn to that crusade. For him, insofar as the Spanish Civil War pitted Marxists against Fascists, he would have found it hard to choose between two evils.

Unlike his Marxist friends, he had no wish for an egalitarian society. He liked hierarchy and was comfortable with inherited privilege. He felt that the privileged classes, of which he was a member, had a duty to lead. To do it well, leaders needed to be in active dialogue with the common people, to learn from them their hopes and fears, and to teach them better ways of thinking about the world and coping with its challenges.

Why choose Bolton? Tom always said afterward that it was because the founder of Unilever came from there, and that gave Bolton a link with his previous anthropological fieldwork. Lever's, by setting the world price for copra, was perhaps the single most powerful organization affecting the lives of people in the New Hebrides. He may also have been influenced by a popular BBC broadcaster, John Hilton, who came from Bolton and whom Tom had consulted in his capacity as the first British professor of industrial relations at Cambridge.

Bolton was a textile mill town that, when Tom got there, had an unemployment rate nearly double that of London and a death rate 25 percent above the national average, making it typical of the North of England during the Great Depression. The North of England, as a place to practice fieldwork techniques, had the advantage of not requiring interpreters, though Tom could hardly be said to speak the native language. He later wrote:

What excited me most of all was to find that when I took a job in a cotton-mill there was no point in my trying to disguise my "educated accent" or anything else. Unless I did something silly, none of . . . [my coworkers] would for a moment imagine that anybody came into this heat, uproar and mechanical risk unless they absolutely had to earn £3 10s 0d a week.

In Bolton, a white Englishman, unless he did something silly, like go barefoot or wear his hair long, could be inconspicuous in a way not possible in the Pacific.

Being in Bolton also gave Tom something new and positive to tell Zita. Her response was precisely what he wished. Writing in early December from rented digs in Devon, Zita announced to Crossman:

> Tom will probably be coming down [to Devon] on January 1. He has taken a job as a "feeder" in a cotton factory 7:30-7:30 compulsory overtime. He writes *marvellous* letters about it. He really is a ONE—not only exciting places for him. He has no money left and must save his fare out of what he earns. I suppose he will starve.

A week or so later, Crossman came to Devon for a long weekend, and Zita told him that she would be visiting Tom in Bolton. Upon returning home to Oxford, Crossman wrote Zita a letter sounding the alarm:

> My darling,
> . . . This weekend for the first time you really managed to hurt me and I don't think you realized it a bit.
> In the first place, suppose on Sunday evening I'd got out a time-table and begun to look up trains to Cologne in order to have two days visiting Jettie. Suppose I'd told you "Of course she is frightfully attractive and for a year she was a wonderful mistress, how because of you I don't lie with her though I'd like to. But I go as far as I can and often she gets very upset and begs me to lie with her. I must go and see her in her new job there. She writes marvellous letters about it."
> I don't think you would have liked it, and yet you expect me to stick you and Tom, which is infinitely more serious. . . .
> . . . I don't think going to Bolton matters now except as a sign of the future.
> . . . You and I both know that Tom will take all he can from you; you are having him to stay in January and yet you are going off now for another weekend to him. . . .

For Tom, however, Bolton, even with frequent visits to and from Zita, was not as much fun as the New Hebrides. In a letter to RGS Secretary Hinks in late November, he apologized for having possibly been "discourteous, or peremptory or illegible (or, all three!)" in an earlier letter, excusing himself on the grounds that he was "working physically at very high pressure and have no privacy or spare time, so that my body is tired out, and my mind too." He told Hinks of the "dreadful drab desolation of poverty, involved in my present anthropological researches, which are proving as exciting and extraordinary, as unhealthy and uncomfortable, as any in Malekula."

But it was not all drab desolate poverty, even when in Bolton. Occasionally in the evenings, "necessarily sprinkled with eau-de-cologne, I sat at the fireside of prosperous Lever relatives, feeling slightly guilty but softly elated." His elation was not just because he was given tea or sherry by a wealthy industrialist. His chief pleasure came from the fact that being there was proof that, as an Englishman, he could penetrate all classes of English society as easily as he could, as a stranger, enter into the village life of Malekulan cannibals.

> For the first discovery that I made (for myself) in Bolton, was that it came just as easy to penetrate other kinds of western society, as societies in which you are from the start in "stranger situation" (e.g., cannibal). This was in those days still a significant discovery for the sociologist. . . .

To practice penetrating different classes of this alien society, Tom soon quit the cotton mill to try being a lorry driver, an ice cream man, a shop assistant. The novelty of the work and the idea of spying on his fellow Englishmen from within the group appealed to him. Yet in spite of Bolton's many fascinations and occasional comforts, he was clearly happy to pass on to RGS Secretary Hinks in December 1936 the good news that "Marshall will be arriving in England in late February." With Jock on his way, Tom seems to have seen his days in Bolton as drawing to a close. He ends this letter to Hinks (written "as from" his parents' home, "The Chase," Weeke, Winchester): "Please do not bother to reply. I am submerged in the smoke and grime of Lancs."

# Chapter 13

## Mass-Observation

In January 1937, just before *Savage Civilisation* came out, Tom stumbled on a new career. It is the one for which he would become best known in Britain, that of co-founder of the pioneering British social survey organization Mass-Observation (M-O). It was the result of a "coincidence" that seems almost surreal.

To help launch his book, he had arranged to have "Coconut Moon," his poem dedicated to Zita, published in the *New Statesman* on January 2, 1937. Having no money to buy a copy, he went to the public library in Bolton and flipped to the page to see his poem in print. On that page, he also saw a letter entitled "Anthropology at Home," in which the author claimed to be spokesman for a group formed shortly before the abdication crisis to begin "an anthropology of our own people."

The letter was full of Surrealist jargon. The author talked of "mass wish-situations" and claimed that the group he represented used the principles of "anthropology, psycho-analysis and the sciences dealing with the behaviour of man," applying those principles to "the Crystal Palace-Abdication symbolic situation." These English Surrealists thought that there had recently occurred certain "coincidences" during which the "otherwise repressed condition of the British people materialized." One of these "coincidences" was, in their view, the burning down of the Crystal Palace in November 1936, which had been popularly regarded (according to the Surrealists) as an omen presaging Britain's involvement in a world conflagration. Another significant "coincidence" had been the political crisis culminating in the December 1936 abdication of King Edward VIII.

Before Tom could lose interest, the letter continued:

> The real observers in this case were the millions of people who were, for once, irretrievably involved in the public events. Only mass observations can create mass science. The group for whom I write is engaged in establishing observation

points on as widely extended a front as can at present be organised. We invite the co-operation of voluntary observers, and will provide detailed information to anyone who wants to take part.

It was signed "Charles Madge, 6 Grotes Buildings, Blackheath."

Surrealism aside, this was close enough to what Tom was doing in Bolton for him to be anxious to learn more about it. Immediately, he got in touch with Madge and was invited to Blackheath. Humphrey Jennings, who would become Britain's foremost documentary filmmaker; David Gascoyne, a Surrealist poet; and Kathleen Raine, a better-known poet (and a great beauty) who was now Madge's wife, were among those present that evening. Gascoyne described the occasion:

> Humphrey Jennings, who, with Charles Madge, had already . . . coined the term "Mass Observation,"* was a great talker; indeed his talent for verbal expression in conversation and talk in general was perhaps one of his greatest gifts. . . .
>
> But Tom Harrisson also turned out to have a great gift and inclination for talking and what I chiefly remember of the evening is the picture of Humphrey, with his elbow on one end of the mantelpiece, and Harrisson, with *his* elbow on the other end of the mantelpiece, both talking loudly and simultaneously to those present in general, without either of them paying the slightest attention to what the other was saying.

Nonetheless, Tom and the Madge-Jennings group found enough interest in common to want to join forces.

Tom and Madge immediately began work on a one-shilling pamphlet, *Mass-Observation*, to help recruit more mass-observers. The gloss at the back explained that Mass-Observation was a new organization aiming to do "sociological research of the first importance, and which has hitherto never been attempted." The organization would "collect a mass of data based upon practical observation, on the everyday life of all types of people" and would use the data "for the scientific study of Twentieth-Century man in all his different environments." Tom convinced his friend and patron, the eminent zoologist Julian Huxley, to write a foreword, in which he said that "the technique of Mass-Observation, here set forth by the inventors, seems to me of great value" and hoped that "out of it big things will grow."

The marriage of Tom's Bolton project to Madge, Jennings et al.'s Mass-Observation was announced January 30, 1937, in a letter to the *New Statesman*, again entitled "Anthropology at Home," but this time it was signed "Tom Harrisson, Humphrey Jennings, Charles Madge."

---

*The term soon acquired a hyphen: Mass-Observation.

The name order was presumably merely alphabetical, but it is clear that Tom had his full share of the drafting. As in Madge's earlier letter, this one had the statement that "Mass Observation develops out of anthropology, psychology and the sciences which study man—but it plans to work with a mass of observers," but the list of "problems" to be studied must surely have been mostly Tom's:

Behaviour of people at war memorials.

Shouts and gestures of motorists.

The aspidistra cult.

Anthropology of football pools.

Bathroom behaviour.

Beards, armpits, eyebrows.

Anti-semitism.

Distribution, diffusion and significance of the dirty joke.

Funerals and undertakers.

Female taboos about eating.

The private lives of midwives.

It is not just the shocking way the list draws attention to things that are never noticed or mentioned by others (except possibly by anthropologists) that stamps this list as primarily of Tom's making; it is also the emphasis on observed behavior rather than on words, written or spoken.

Discoursing on how anthropological fieldwork ought to be done, Tom often said the ideal instrument was a pair of earplugs. "*See* what people are doing. *Afterwards*, ask them what they think they are doing, if you like." Tom conceded that his approach grew out of his experience of bird-watching. "You don't ask a bird any questions. You don't try to interview it, do you?" His commitment to this technique had been strengthened by discovering in the Pacific how much you could learn by watching people whose language you did not understand.

Adapting his own ideas of anthropological fieldwork in England to "Mass-Observation," the Madge-Jennings term, Tom put the accent on "observation," while to him the "mass" meant that you looked at everybody. Madge and Jennings had a different idea of Mass-Observation. As Gascoyne explained, Madge and Jennings and their Surrealist friends had been thinking of Mass-Observation primarily as "a sounding of the English collective unconscious together with a particular attention to what was implied by [the] expression: 'Poetry ought to be made by all, not one.'"

Madge, who was working on a London newspaper but had already had two of his poems published in the W. B. Yeats edition of the *Oxford Book of Modern Verse* (1936), was in most ways the opposite of Tom, being small, neat, soft-spoken, and diffident. Like Tom, he was a scion of a privileged family and had also dropped out of Cambridge. While an undergraduate there, he had been moved to a desire to be one with the masses by seeing the Hunger Marchers (predecessors of the Jarrow Crusaders) and had promptly joined the Communist Party. He had then become interested in surrealism. As was Jennings and the other Surrealists of the era, Madge was trying to draw from the wellsprings of poetic irrationality that surrealism claimed were in our dreams in order to serve the Marxist demand that art be socially useful.

Both Jennings, with his documentary filming, and Madge, with his newspaper layout experience, were also being drawn to the so-called documentary movement, then coming into favor with filmmakers, journalists, and writers such as Orwell. The documentarists liked to juxtapose "many observed details of everyday life to build up a 'composite picture'." They tended to focus on the commonplace, turning the spotlight on the working class. So, to some degree, did the Surrealists, since they believed detailed observation with such a focus would provide clues to what was going on in the "collective unconscious." During the thirties, marxism, surrealism, and the documentary movement became linked, as many of the same people used all of them to try to break down the barriers between classes in Britain while uniting people of good will against fascism abroad and social and economic injustice at home.

Just before Tom saw Madge's *New Statesman* letter, Madge and Jennings had asked their nationwide "panel" of observers (all unpaid volunteers) to keep diaries, from February 1937 onward, of everything that happened to them and what they saw others doing on the twelfth day of the month. These diary entries were then used in Madge and Jennings's first publication for Mass-Observation (to which Tom did not contribute): a survey of what people all over the country were doing and thinking on May 12, 1937, the day of the coronation of George VI. The survey was published in the autumn of 1937 as *May the Twelfth: Mass-Observation Day-Surveys 1937 by over two hundred observers*.

*May the Twelfth*, though it sold only 800 copies, turned Mass-Observation into a subject for editorials, music hall jokes, and after-dinner speeches. "Even *Punch* [gave] the movement a full measure of its benevolent ridicule." The *New Statesman* critic, Stonier, in his review of *May the Twelfth*, projected the image of Mass-Observers under the bed, or at least observing which side of the bed you got out of in the morning. He described the typical mass-observer with "a loping walk, elephant ears," and "an eye trained to keyholes."

> Oh don't imagine you can escape. At all times, quietly, the reckoner will be at work; practising, we are told, in his spare time on the ornaments at home or the discouraged row of faces in the tube. And on field-days—the twelfth of every month is a glorious Twelfth, when he receives the "directive"* to go "hunting"— mass-observation will become frantic. . . .

He summed up the process as "a perfect subject for the Marx Brothers."

In addition to being a commercial failure, *May the Twelfth* was a disappointment to those who had looked to Mass-Observation to fulfill its promise, as understood by Julian Huxley in his foreword to the original *Mass-Observation* pamphlet, "of disclosing ourselves to ourselves by the application of scientific methods of observation and record." Tom, in 1938, privately gave his opinion that it was a "crazy idea to have it edited by a whole bunch of intellectual poets." As he watched from the sidelines as Madge and Jennings produced *May the Twelfth*, Tom thought what he could offer to the Mass-Observation "movement" was a structure built around the observation of what people really did. As Tom later explained, "what was wrong with that title," *Mass-Observation*, in the days before he arrived on the scene, was that "Humphrey and Charles really weren't going to do any observing at all. People were just going to document themselves." To Tom, an "anthropology of ourselves" would have to be primarily direct observation of ordinary Englishmen, members of the working class. Scant systematic, long-term fieldwork had been done of such Englishmen before, and virtually none of it had been conducted from inside the group, *watching* what people did when they did not realize they were being observed, as opposed to ringing their doorbells in order to read out a list of questions in an Oxbridge accent.

Tom did not oppose the Madge-Jennings idea of having panelists reply to "directives" and diarists record what went on during an average day, but, in his idea of Mass-Observation, emphasis was put on direct, objective, and to the extent possible, invisible observation, showing what people were actually doing. Replies to directives and the diaries would serve as secondary sources, recording what people *thought* they were doing. Tom also believed, as in bird-watching, that academic training was not essential to a good Mass-Observer; one only needed the will to do it, an ability to make oneself inconspicuous, and a lot of practice.

---

*Every month the Mass-Oberservation panelists were sent "directives," an M-O term meaning open-ended questions on particular topics, to which they were asked to reply in writing.

So while Madge, Jennings, and their Blackheath group tried to cope with an increasingly unwieldy avalanche of directive and diary material arriving by post every month, it was agreed that Tom should go back to Bolton (to be called "Worktown" in M-O publications to preserve anonymity). There he would collect a team to help him continue what he had been doing since the previous November, applying his bird- and cannibal-watching techniques to the observation of the North-of-England's working class.

Tom enlisted Mass-Observers who could be invisible in working-class settings. One such recruit was Walter Hood, an activist member of the Bolton Labour Party who had grown up in a northeastern mining community. A more colorful M-O recruit was a tramp preacher named "Brother Joe" Willcock. Willcock had been warden of a hostel in London's East End and was "no intellectual and no writer, and certainly no social scientist, his main asset [being] that he was able to talk to people in such a way as to gain their confidence."

Tom's enthusiasm for the Bolton project, and now for the Bolton plus Blackheath Mass-Observation movement, kept rising during early 1937. He took seriously the promise made in M-O's initial one-shilling pamphlet that he and Madge were then drafting, to try to have M-O become "the observation of everyone by everyone, including themselves." He sought to enlist participants from the working class itself, not just the left-leaning elite readership of the *New Statesman*. He got a friend from his 1933 Oxford days, Tangye Lean, by this time leader editor for the *News Chronicle* with its million readers, to give M-O's request for panelists and diarists some press play. Tom Driberg (later to be a Labour peer), whose delight in outrageous behavior and gossip had made him a friend of Tom's, was also asked to mention M-O in the much-read column of gossip and interesting happenings that he wrote for Beaverbrook's mass-circulation *Daily Express* under the pen name "William Hickey." Other papers followed suit. The number of volunteer "observers" on the M-O "panel" quickly swelled to many hundreds, including a higher proportion of working-class people.

Tom loved the publicity, both for its usefulness in informing and involving the general public and for the boost it gave his ego. Humphrey Jennings, however, uncomfortable at being onstage before an increasingly popular audience, ceased participating in M-O soon afterward, leaving the "movement" to be run by his friend Madge and the interloper, Tom Harrisson.

# Chapter 14

## Thrice Betrayed

In the midst of Tom's excitement with his new toy, Jock arrived in London on February 14, 1937, still tanned from his Australian summer and rested from his long sea voyage. At the dock to meet him, driving Zita's car, was Tom. He had spent a Lancashire winter indoors sleeping little and eating bad food. He looked pasty and stale; he also had a bad cold. It was a poor start to the long-awaited reunion.

It got worse. Tom, taking his hostly duties seriously, arranged for Jock to lecture, convinced friends at Cambridge to find work for him there, had Mary Adams interview him on television and, abetted by such friends as Naomi Mitchison, gave the Australian a privileged tour of intellectual England. Jock, perhaps embarrassed at being in debt to Tom for his trip to England and almost totally dependent on Tom's knowledge and patronage, reverted to the churlishness that had irritated Tom when the two young men had first been together three years earlier.

Jock's diary, after ten days in England, shows him looking for nits to pick: "Most people are fairly normal here, but the crowd of young intellectuals which Tom seems to lead have a curious sort of generally understandable at the moment exaggerated kind of conversation of inconsequentialities—none of which have any real logic—oh hateful word—or method." Jock complained to his diary of the overuse of catch phrases: "Catchword at the moment, "esoteric synthesis". . . . I am usually silently amused and always entertained. . . . I shall write a book about the England that I am learning to know—some day." Jock's contemptuous amusement may have been silent, but it was surely not invisible to Tom.

Tom took Jock to Harrow, where he was giving a talk on "The Anthropology of Ourselves," drawing on themes that he would use repeatedly, comparing Mass-Observation with his New Hebrides experience. Jock's diary entry for that evening reads:

Harrow School. . . . Tom at night bent on annoying people. [Giving] his oration on the anthropology of ourselves: Harrow and Bolton (slums) and Malekula and finishing "Are you so superior to these savages? And if you were put in their environment you would be stupid, ludicrous, not worth hitting on the head. You couldn't make a fire, a house, a comb, quickly cut down a tree or kill a pig. You couldn't clean your teeth with sand. What good are you?"

Tom was already much sought after as a public speaker. His voice, not unlike that of the film actor Richard Burton, was powerful without being harsh and lent authority and excitement to his words. People who were children when Tom spoke at their schools in the 1930s and 1940s still remembered fifty years later how stimulated they had been by his talk. Jock, possibly a jaundiced witness, told his diary that the Harrow boys were not impressed by Tom.

Jock was also tactless enough to surprise his host by producing his *own* manuscript for a book about his New Hebrides experience, for which he sought a publisher. Tom took him to see Gollancz, who offered him an advance of £75, but Jock signed with another publisher, Heinemann, for a respectable advance of £100. The book, *The Black Musketeers*, would come out later that year, with a foreword by Tom in which he compared Jock's book with his own *Savage Civilisation*:

> I am only writing here and now to say that this book of Marshall's is quite different from mine. In many ways, it is much better. Mine was a story of contorted history, anthropology and hate. His is adventure and humour and straightforward sense. Our accounts supplement each other, but from the point of view of the ordinary reader, this book is far the better investment.

Tom's is a generous statement of the merits of Jock's book. Read today, *The Black Musketeers* is a charming period piece that (unlike Tom's book) breaks none of the rules authors and publishers usually work by but lacks the power, the passion, and the great originality of Tom's angular prose.

Meanwhile, Zita, at a loose end from February 16 to August 16, when her divorce would become final, was forced to shunt between the houses of friends outside Oxford so as not to compromise Crossman's reputation. Tom must have realized that this was his last chance of winning her back. He pressed his suit with what Crossman felt was "alarming fervour." He got her to join the Worktown team, and she stayed in Bolton for a few days in March. He had just signed a lease on a dank, drab, sparsely furnished terraced house at 85 Davenport Street, "huddled among mills less than half a mile from the town centre." This insalubrious dwelling was now Worktown headquarters. Zita stayed there with Tom, but it was certainly clear in her mind, as Tom gradually came to realize, that she was going to marry Crossman.

In March came another heartbreak for Tom: a final row with his father, after which the General changed his will. The new will, having provided an annual sum for his wife during her lifetime, left the bulk of his considerable estate to Bill. Tom was to get £200. The General had not only disinherited his firstborn child but had provided a powerful incentive for the rift between the two brothers to widen.

Tom, already in 1932 on his twenty-first birthday on Mount Dulit, had believed that it was too late to convince his father he could live by his own efforts of "exploring, brains, birds and writing—without toeing the line of [his father's] business routine." Still, for his father to make the final brutal gesture of disinheriting him wounded Tom more deeply than anything else that was to happen in his life. He took it as proof not only that his father had never loved him but that his brother had not either.

Tom always claimed to have been toughened by being abandoned by his parents as a child, and now these three "betrayals"—by his woman, his best friend, and his family—thickened his coat of armor. He would never again let anyone get under his guard and hurt him. To judge by how he behaved thereafter, he seems to have resolved that from then on, in any relationship, he would make sure he got his thrust in first, before he was attacked, and that in a friendship or love affair, he would be the one to leave, not the one to be left. His failure to keep the love and respect of the people for whom he cared most seems also to have sharpened his obsessive need to be first, to be best, and to get recognition for his achievements.

In May, he resigned the leadership of the New Guinea expedition, and in October Jock wrote to the RGS to say the New Guinea expedition had to be postponed indefinitely because one of the participants had developed heart trouble (perhaps a sly reference to Tom's disappointment in love) and there was now no anthropologist for the trip. Jock went home to Australia at the end of the year to get an undergraduate degree, the first of a series of academic credentials that would lead him to become, eventually, the founding professor of zoology at Monash University.

It was time for Tom to discard the past and move forward. He probably did not greatly regret not going to New Guinea. Studying savages in Melanesia was something he had already done. Studying Britons as if they were savages was new, and now was the time to do it. He wrote to Naomi:

> I wish to God you could lead me to someone who would give me £1000. The
> organization is now splendid, and constantly expanding. We are on the edge of
> major results. And we are utterly bankrupt, it will be difficult for me to find the

money to reach London. To see the Labour Party spending £50,000 in propaganda, without the first bloody idea of what they are doing, keeps me awake with intellectual diarrhoea. It will be pure hell if I have to disband this show. Of course, I can easily carry on myself, working in any job and observing as I go.

It's all very worry-making. I expect it'll work out. . . .

# Chapter 15

## M-O in Bolton

Putting aside personal disappointments, Tom threw himself into the M-O project. At 85 Davenport Street, Bolton, however, money was short. He could not pay his helpers a living wage. Walter Hood recalled how "it was his job, when funds ran out, to approach Tom Harrisson for cash so that the team could buy fish and chips." Tom would occasionally get some money by giving a talk or writing a newspaper piece about his adventures among cannibals but was often not much better off than was Hood. The money problem got some temporary relief from two Bolton philanthropists, Sir Thomas Barlow and Sir Ernest Simon. Innovative and exuberant, they were just the sort of men to like Tom and be liked by him.

Whenever Tom received money, none of it went to making 85 Davenport Street more habitable. The house had a few beds and desks, an out-of-tune piano, and the services of an old crone who cooked bacon and eggs and made tea on a smoky grate. There were always three or four mass-observers in residence. The photographer Humphrey Spender (younger brother of the poet Stephen Spender and of Michael Spender, a scientist friend of Tom's) took pictures of the front room with Tom and some of his helpers finishing breakfast. These black and white photographs almost reek of bad air, damp, and cold. "It was a horrible place," Humphrey recalled, with its revolting food and endless smoking—the whole place caught fire once because of people smoking," Spender recalled. "But this kind of sordidness, Tom didn't mind at all." He may have felt about the house the way his friend, the writer J. B. Priestley, had written about Bolton in *English Journey*: "The ugliness is so complete that it is almost exhilarating."

Tom would get up late. Unwashed and unshaven, he would often go straight to work in the front room, writing letters and articles, with papers stacked all over the floor. He could work like that for sixteen hours at a time. As on Santo, he liked loud, preferably popular, music while he worked.

Woodrow Wyatt (later Lord Wyatt)—then an eighteen-year-old summer volunteer, who was recruited at a lecture Tom gave at an Oxford club that Wyatt belonged to—remembers that one of his jobs was to keep the gramophone wound and playing George Formby records to give a good Lancashire atmosphere. At night, when the M-O team ate fish and chips, often their only real meal of the day, they would sometimes take it into a pub, where "instead of being an ordinary visit to an ordinary pub, . . . it would become infused" for such enthusiastic followers as Wyatt "with the sense of significance which Tom Harrisson spread around." As one of the Mass-Observers recalled, to Tom,

> every single feature of a pub room would be significant. . . . The aspidistra, the
> obscured glass, the music on the piano, the wallpaper pattern, the style of the
> stools—whereas the ordinary person who hadn't travelled and seen primitive peoples
> would not have noticed: [Tom noticed] all the woodwork; the snob screen—which
> is a class division: saloon bar as opposed to the bar where the darts go on . . .

Alert to body language, he would discreetly eye a group of pub "regulars" and pick out who was friends with whom and who deferred to whom.

He and his recruits were observing and recording in Worktown many of the things anthropologists look at in so-called primitive societies: how leaders emerge or are chosen; religious beliefs; birth and death rites, sexual behavior; songs, dances, arts and crafts.

Though their "fieldwork" seemed to have a less scientific and academic flavor when the religious rite being described was at a Baptist revivalist meeting or a Worktown funeral parlor, when the sexual behavior being recorded took place against the walls of the back alleys of Bolton, such things were legitimate subject matter for the new social science of sociology. Yet M-O's work was very different from the sociology of its day. M-O emphasized qualitative research and descriptions of what people did; for example, M-O staffers collated answers to open-ended questions, while the academic sociologists appeared to think that only data that could be quantified was scientific. Tom argued that many of the most interesting questions about human beings were not quantifiable. He thought that by insisting on their graphs and pie charts, sociologists were neglecting many important subjects.

Tom would point out that even those things that seem amenable to quantification, such as replies to yes-no or multiple-choice questionnaires, will yield nonsensical results if nobody checks whether people's actions conform to their answers. He would note that what people will say to a stranger on the doorstep about how many baths they take a week, how much beer they drink, how many cigarettes they smoke, whom they plan to vote for, how often they go to church, or if they ever engage in extramarital sex, may prove a poor guide to what those questioned actually do.

As in the New Hebrides, Tom saw his M-O research designed not as a contribution to science only but, more importantly, as a means of benefiting the group being studied. M-O would do this by helping to bridge the gap between "us" and "them." Tom and Madge, who agreed with him on this, were like their altruistic leftist upper-class contemporaries in seeing the gap between the leaders and the led as dangerous to the functioning of British democracy. Their means of bridging the gap between classes and encouraging dialogue between leaders and led, between observer and observed, expert and amateur, specialist and generalist, was to publish their results as quickly, widely, and cheaply as possible, hoping to reach not only the book-buying establishment but also the ordinary people being studied.

If its emphasis on nonquantifiable data and its habit of publishing in the penny press were not enough to make M-O suspect to the establishment social scientist, Tom, Madge, and their mass-observers were also guilty of writing in plain, even lighthearted, English instead of employing the jargon and solemn tone of most sociological writing. Describing the mass convergence on Blackpool of Lancashire industrial workers "<u>for their single week's industrial holiday</u> [Tom's underlining] (without pay)," Tom drew on M-O interviews to claim that "Here, for one week, there are no noticeable police, no critical neighbours, no factory whistles. This, as so many people clearly state, is Life, is Paradise, is Dreamland and Heaven. . . ."

Other problems with M-O's work came from Tom's playful imagination, his unceasing search for connections between things, and his fascination with everything he saw, including all the trivia and ephemera of working-class life. These traits occasionally led him to discoveries others missed but also led him to acquire enormous stacks of unsorted pointless data.

For Tom, individual pieces of information had a magic, a meaning, that was almost sufficient in itself. John Baker once complained to Tom that some of the details of bird behavior he wrote up were unnecessary and irrelevant. "You might as well list the items on a person's mantelpiece," protested Baker. Tom's response was to make a note to have Mass-Observation investigate what people put on their mantelpieces.

With so many subjects he wanted to follow, he needed help from as many observers as he could get to work for nothing, and so he called on his friends. Michael Spender had shown Tom his brother Humphrey's photographs. Tom had been impressed enough to want Humphrey along on the New Guinea expedition and wanted him to film Worktown people at work and play. Tom had merely to ask, as Humphrey explained:

> The effect Tom had on me was absolutely magnetic, charismatic. He could reduce me to pulp or to jelly in laughter, literally. He could make me roll around on the floor and say, "Tom stop!" Anybody who has that capacity has me at his mercy.

Partly, it was because I had found my brother Michael's attitude very school-masterish and dry and puritanical and partly that Tom was breaking the scientific rules by saying such outrageous things, but with elements of truth in them. He was just an incredibly funny man.

He also had this mysterious capacity . . . that one could simply become his slave and he had only to suggest something and off you went. People said to me, "You are an absolute idiot to be doing this for nothing. One just doesn't work for nothing. There must be some money available." And Tom would say, "There isn't any money so if you are going to do it, you will do it for nothing."

Julian Trevelyan, a Surrealist painter and part of Madge's original Blackheath group, came often to Bolton too, being, like Humphrey Spender, enslaved by Tom's manner. Trevelyan remembers that Tom "was lean and serious and talked in a dead-pan voice, yet saying extremely funny things." As Trevelyan recalled:

Tom went out for his material to the pubs, to the dogs, to the dance halls. He sent a band of willing workers flying round making reports on anything from the contents of a chemist's shop window to an account of a service in a spiritualist church. "Bring back a list of the hymns and any other dope you can get hold of, and try and pinch a copy of the sermon," he would say as he sent us out on our mission.

Once, Tom instructed the noted literary critic William Empson (a friend of Madge) to report what he found in the sweet shop window. Empson, like the others, went off to do his bidding. Tom, tall and thin, with his forward-leaning purposeful stride, his thick black hair that he would toss about or rake straight back with his fingers, exposing his wild pale eyes, "had an almost hypnotic power over those who worked for him; he would ask the most impossible things of us and we would willingly do them," recalls Trevelyan. As one of his later M-O colleagues noted many years later, Tom "had this peculiar gift of getting people to work like mad for him, without them necessarily liking him overmuch."

One of the things that made people like Woodrow Wyatt and Humphrey Spender and Julian Trevelyan happy to work for Tom was that he was very encouraging. He was good at recognizing people of talent and would urge them to fulfill their potential. Seeing in Humphrey's photographs the perfect visual translation of Worktown's atmosphere, Tom pressed the photographer to come to Bolton often.

Part of what repeatedly lured Humphrey back to Bolton was the fun of carrying out Tom's outrageous commands. Tom would send him to a tea shop and ask him to see how many lumps of sugar the women customers stole or how many hat pins they wore. Poor Humphrey ran into difficulties on one occasion carrying out Tom's instructions to photograph a hotel bar.

The manager, catching him in the act, demanded that Humphrey stop taking photographs and tried to get him to destroy the film. When Humphrey loftily inquired if there were any law in England that prevented him taking photographs in public houses, the manager answered; "You needn't talk in that semi-educated way," and threatened to fetch a policeman.

It was the camera that gave Humphrey away, not his "semi-educated" speech. Although Tom brought many highly educated and well-bred helpers from Oxford and London, for the first eighteen months of the Worktown project very few Bolton people realized they were being observed. As Tom had found out early, the observer's accent did not matter so long as no one suspected his reason for being there. The invisibility of the observer and of the observing, as against the usual interview or questionnaire methods employed by other social surveyors, was in Tom's view an essential element of Mass-Observation.

Perhaps the most "invisible" of M-O observers was John Sommerfield, a staffer who came to work for Tom in 1937. Sommerfield, who had been a seaman, carpenter, stage manager, and a soldier of the International Brigade in Spain and later became known as a "proletarian novelist," in 1938 managed to get enough material on how people behaved in Bolton pubs to write the reports that formed the basis of M-O's first book for Gollancz, *The Pub and the People*, without conducting a single interview. Tom himself was rarely inconspicuous. He was a "noisy fellow," as Wyatt recalls, who enjoyed being rude to people, especially the rich and famous. He had a lot of style and liked to make a splash. For example, when in Blackpool on M-O business, he sent and received telegrams—(85 Davenport Street had no telephone)—rather than letters, which tended to impress hotelkeepers and other people standing around. He seemed at ease anywhere and could be quiet when he wanted to be. Most important, Tom was genuinely interested in what went on around him when in working-class settings. Tom's interest, being real and not patronizing, did not "get the wind up" his subjects or lead them to behave unnaturally.

Zita had some of the same gift for seeming at ease in any company and for being able, without changing dress or manner, to fit in with different surroundings. She came back up north in the summer of 1937 and, at Tom's suggestion, stood alone outside the tower in Blackpool one evening. Though she was over thirty-five, in the course of a very few minutes she received five invitations—some polite, some bolder—from five men of different social backgrounds. She was in Blackpool, her last visit to see Tom before her divorce became final, as one of many of Tom's London and Oxbridge friends he invited to the seaside resort town the summer of 1937 to help his regular M-O staffers observe the people of Bolton taking their annual vacation.

Ursula Darwin, a woman with whom Tom was in love for a year or so, beginning about two years after this time, was then married to Julian Trevelyan. She remembers Tom saying "Why don't you and Julian come up for a week and go to Blackpool?"

> It was the week when all the factories in Bolton shut down and they all go to Blackpool because everybody wants to go to Blackpool. Tom was interested in what people spent their time doing. . . . Julian and I were put in a small cheap boarding house to find out what these people did, what they dreamt about. We had to ask them about their dreams at breakfast time, and we had to trail them. There were about twenty of us friends of Tom's staying in Blackpool, from people staying in the doss house to people in the smartest hotels.

To keep a low profile, the observers were instructed to operate separately or in pairs but to cooperate when necessary.

> When we were trailing our lot, if we feared we might be noticed, we switched over with somebody else. We kept notes and we found that practically everybody spent most of their time in Woolworth's. Extraordinary, and it was very difficult not to be seen.
>
> So we switched with another couple and then we did a tremendous amount of counting of people on the sands and whether fathers or mothers looked after the children. And then, towards the end of the week, Tom was rather sorry for me because I had been having pretty dull jobs—not much fun walking around Woolworth's trying not to be seen or counting people on the sand—and Tom said, "You had a tough time, Ursula. Better give you something better. What about sex in the sand hills?"

So Tom and Ursula did "sex in the sand hills" which was "much more amusing," though, according to all reports, not much happened to have offended any but the sternest moralist.

Tom was having a wonderful time. He was ordering around the biggest group of people since his Harrow schooldays when he had coordinated the efforts of 1,300 observers of the great crested grebe. As Madge later commented accusingly, Tom loved being at the center of "a turmoil of activity."

To find out Worktown's attitudes toward contemporary art, he had Trevelyan set up his easel in the middle of the street with people looking on, while the artist made bright-colored collages of Bolton. For contrast, he had Graham Bell and William Coldstream, the two best painters of the so-called Euston Road ultra objective school of painting, put on canvas their visions of Bolton in the severe realism for which they were known. Then he had photographs of the different pictures passed around the pubs to get Boltonian reactions. Coldstream's *Bolton* (1938) now at the National Gallery of Canada, is a luminous masterpiece of "objectivity," but the Worktown people found something disturbingly dismal in this scene of smoking chimneys and empty streets. "We're dead, we are! Our people are dead!" one Bolton man said upon seeing Coldstream's picture. The Boltonians liked Trevelyan's gay collages best. A little later, Tom had M-O go to an exhibition of coal miners' paintings. To meet the painters, he brought with him such mass-observers as Madge, Spender, Trevelyan, Empson, and the Beaverbrook journalist Tom Driberg.

One of the most serious objections that professional social scientists had to M-O's methods was that M-O collected lots of data without first developing a theoretical framework and then deciding what data would be relevant. T. H. Marshall, then reader of sociology at the University of London, pointed out that the normal methods of scientific investigation "operate quite differently" and gave as an example the way a doctor diagnoses an illness, not by asking the patient to record all his sensations, but by framing questions "on the basis of his scientific medical knowledge, in order to discover, not sensations but symptoms."

In reply, Tom pointed out that M-O was collecting data of all sorts from as various a group of contributors as possible in order to record precisely those things that professional observers either never noticed or did not think worth mentioning. By recording the actions and thoughts of ordinary people, "ordinary things . . . which are . . . part of the essentials in any epoch, and are often extinct in the next," Tom claimed that M-O was filling a serious gap in information on "what was happening that was not climax, news, 'historical.'" Furthermore, Tom noted:

> Our investigations, as they go on, show an increasing discrepancy between the picture of any event that could be gained a week later by reading papers, talking to people, interviewing bigshots, etc., and what actually happened [at the time of the event itself]. . . . In this sense we are trying to write history in the present.

Though Marshall's points would still today have the support of most social scientists, Tom's argument has some merit. A biographer, trying to reconstruct what happened when, how, and why to his protagonist, knows that if one simply moves forward chronologically, without focusing too narrowly, one will often come across events not strictly related to the subject at hand that shed light on why things happened the way they did. Conversely, if you limit your field of inquiry too severely, you will often miss those seemingly extraneous, but sometimes crucial, bits of information. If this applies to the history of one man, it surely applies also to the history of a battle, a movement, a country.

The problem with this approach, one that M-O never overcame, was how to handle the flood of material that comes from not limiting in advance the types of data to be considered. Computers might have helped had they existed then, but the processes of M-O highlight the main weakness in all social research: that there is no really satisfactory way to determine what data are relevant. The narrowing in advance of the field from which data should be drawn is a form of prejudice, even when based on "scientific knowledge"; on the other hand, selection later on of what is relevant from a mountain of uncategorized data is likely to lead to the choice being mere accident or whim. To deal with this problem, Tom and Madge hoped, some-day, to have the ability to use more of the amassed material to look at an event from so many different angles that any prejudice or accidental bias would be discounted by a process of cross-checking. That day never came.

It is a sign of how uncomfortable thinking people in Britain of the late 1930s were with the way things were going that Mass-Observation was not simply dismissed as absurd by contemporary social scientists. Though it must have acted as a slap in the face to the emerging social sciences as they tried to establish their own scientific methodologies, M-O was treated seriously by some of the most prestigious authorities of the day. The leading social anthropologist in England at that time, Bronislaw Malinowski, wrote the fol-lowing in the "Anthropology" entry of the *Encyclopaedia Britannica Book of the Year for 1938*, describing how anthropological method was being applied to modern societies in various countries:

> In England the ambitious and comprehensive schemes of field-work to be effected by "Mass-Observation" under the direction of C. Madge and by a team of work-ers at Bolton, led by Tom Harrisson, whose book, *Savage Civilisation* (1937), has shown him to be, though not a trained, a highly gifted field-worker, are certainly a courageous and promising start.

In March 1938 Tom and Madge published *First Year's Work*, which includes the results of some of their first studies followed by a lengthy essay by Malinowski, describing M-O as "A Nation-wide Intelligence Service." The eminent anthropologist, then head of anthropological studies at the presti-gious London School of Economics (LSE), points out, as had T. H. Marshall, that the big problem for M-O as a scientific method is Madge-Harrisson's belief that "our first concern is to collect data, not to interpret them." He admonishes Madge-Harrisson that "the objective treatment of subjectively determined data must start at the very outset. It must be embodied in the terms of reference of every specific inquiry."

The ambivalence evident in this essay typifies the relationship between the famous professor and Tom. The two men tended to display the combi-nation of mutual respect and distrust of two large dogs circling one another. They saw each other as rivals for the public's attention, and to third parties they described each other as "crooks." Still, Tom as a younger man had christened his and Bray's Cotswold cottage "The Trobriands" in honor of Malinowski, and the latter, having heard Tom give a paper at the Institute of Sociology, after an initial irritation, had felt impelled to become better acquainted at first hand with the movement.

Malinowski's reason for lending his prestigious name to the enterprise was his belief that "the basic idea of the movement is 100 percent right. . . ." He warned the *New Statesman* critic Stonier (who had poked fun at the Mass-Observer):

> Make a parody of a scientific school and you become the godfather of its fame. Psycho-analysis has grown and thrived on jokes, . . . so has behaviorism and even relativity. One good travesty is worth stacks of reviews or volumes of pedantic criticism.

Pedantic criticism did not worry Tom or Madge unduly. By the time of this uneasy semiendorsement of M-O by the foremost anthropologist of his day, Tom had convinced Victor Gollancz to give advances for several M-O books to be written, drawing on the Worktown and Blackpool material. The advances were generous enough to keep M-O going for a couple of years.

The Bolton stable of Mass-Observers continued to expand. One new recruit was Bill Naughton, a Bolton lorry driver who learned of the Worktown project through a newspaper article featuring M-O in which a coal miner gave an account of his day. He had managed to track down M-O to its headquarters because he wanted to teach himself to write. He gradually did so, later coming to well-deserved world fame with the play and the screenplay of *Alfie*.

Tom was always seeking new subjects for Mass-Observation to study. In early 1938, having already begun M-O's investigation of the working man's response to modern painting, he decided to venture a lighthearted look at what contemporary poetry, such as the work of Auden, MacNeice, Day Lewis, and Stephen Spender, had to say to the ordinary Englishman. He produced, in the opinion of Valentine Cunningham, author of *British Writers of the Thirties*, "a sharply accurate survey . . . , a critical exercise that proved to be, on several clear counts, the '30s' best piece of structural analysis, and one so painfully right that it roused intense ire from all sides. . . ." Tom's essay, entitled "Mass-Opposition and Literature" appeared in an Oxford literary magazine that his friend Woodrow Wyatt was editing. It was meant merely to poke a bit of fun at the somberness and poverty of imagery of much of the poetry of the era. In it Tom wrote his objections to the negativism in lines such as Auden's:

The earth is an oyster with nothing in it

Not to be born is the best for man.

In voicing his objections, Tom had, in Cunningham's view, "put the finger right on the '30s' oppressed sense of being confined, enclosed, islanded, behind bars." Tom's essay produced virulent reactions in Oxbridge circles. It led to months of strongly worded letters to the *New Statesman*, in which Stonier, predictably, led the attack. Stonier got so carried away that he devoted a full-page essay to excoriating not only M-O but also anthropology and surrealism, describing their supporters as quirky faddists, comparable to "Buchmanites, Rotarians and Nudists." Thus, because of its serious work but also because of the violent reactions to it, by April 1938 it could truly be said that "Everyone has now heard of Mass-Observation."

By then, the sense of crisis, of western civilization in danger from another world war, was such that neither Tom nor his helpers could keep up much longer their enthusiasm for the kind of subject matter that had been filling M-O's file boxes during its first year. Tom was fed up with Bolton and wanted to return to London, where his interest had been drawn by a by-election in Fulham that M-O had observed in April.

Not yet having found a London base, Tom was still in Bolton that spring and summer, feeling restless and casting about for things to do. He asked his various and widely scattered Sarawak team of 1932 to contribute reminiscences of that expedition. Their uneven but exhilarating joint memoir, *Borneo Jungle,* edited by Tom, was published later that year.

Basically, though, Tom was marking time. The statistical data from his Bolton work, such as how many times people tapped which end of a cigarette, were less interesting and no easier to codify or utilize than were the long screeds from the diarists' accounts that Madge was amassing at Blackheath. There was a generalized sense of crisis in Britain, but it had not yet narrowed and become clearly defined enough to provide the structure for a major piece of mass-observing, such as the abdication crisis would have done, if Mass-Observation had been functioning at that time.

Then came Munich.

# Chapter 16

## M-O and Munich

The Munich crisis was a heaven-sent chance for Mass-Observation to track public opinion on a matter of importance. It began September 15, 1938, when Chamberlain flew to Hitler, who had already taken the Rhineland and Austria, to urge him not to move against Czechoslovakia. M-O observers found that the British prime minister had his people behind him, but they turned against him when he came home without saying "no" to Hitler—though he had not said "yes" either. A week later, Chamberlain saw Hitler again with similarly inconclusive results. The much-confused British public was (according to M-O's polls) inclined to agree to Chamberlain letting Hitler have what he wanted rather than go to war against Germany. On September 27, however, Chamberlain spoke on the radio. The message that came across to Britons was that war was imminent. The next day, M-O observers were finding people girding their loins for it: "It's now or never to stop the bastard."

That day, Chamberlain was speaking in Parliament about his frustrated efforts for peace when he was interrupted by word that Hitler wanted to see him once more. With the fervent support of the Parliament, Chamberlain flew to Munich and by the afternoon of September 30 had agreed to Hitler's demands concerning the "return" of the German-speaking parts of Czechoslovakia in exchange for a paper, signed by Hitler, renouncing any intention of going to war against Britain. This was the famous bit of paper that Chamberlain told his compatriots the next evening meant "peace in our time." The crisis was over.

There was a day or two of popular relief, encouraged by press statements describing Chamberlain as a conquering hero, even a miracle worker. But then M-O observers found that ordinary citizens had reverted to anxious bewilderment and were willing to express their earlier doubts and fears, no longer intimidated by the barrage of press and parliamentary support for appeasement.

The Munich crisis and the public's reaction to it held a moral dear to Tom: if you want to lead people in a democracy, you must inform them of the relevant facts or suffer the consequences. These consequences are that people will be misinformed by others or so confused that they retreat from reality. For there to be the dialogue between leaders and led, which is essential to a modern democracy, leaders must find out "what people do want, do get, don't get and could get to want," so that they can satisfy the people's wishes or change their minds.

Tom and Madge stressed this moral in their next book together, *Britain by Mass-Observation*, which devoted its longest chapter to the Munich crisis. *Britain* appeared in January 1939 as part of the new Penguin Special series. Alleged to have sold 100,000 copies in its first ten days, it was one of Mass-Observation's best books in terms of accomplishing what it set out to do: "provide the first comprehensive and sophisticated account of British public opinion in rapid flux." Neither Gallup polls nor TV live coverage could match it, even today, for the sense of being there, seeing, hearing, and experiencing what people were going through.

Exaggerated claims were made in *Britain* for M-O's uniqueness. M-O was not as new as Tom and Madge were saying it was. Various surveys of social conditions had been done in Britain before, including in Bolton. Scientific studies had even been done on pubs and working-class drinking habits. Public opinion polling, developed by Dr. George Gallup in the United States beginning in 1928, had been imported into England in 1936 under the name of the British Institute of Public Opinion (BIPO). BIPO had begun conducting political opinion surveys monthly for the *News Chronicle* in 1938, the same year M-O was compiling its data on the Munich crisis. Even the BBC had in place, from mid-1937 onward, a random sampling system using a panel of 2,000 listeners. Sampling techniques for market research were also beginning to be used, with many firms employing some of the same techniques as M-O.

Yet M-O did have something that these other studies and polls did not: a determination to contribute to the dialogue between leaders and led by letting both sides know what ordinary people were doing, thinking, and saying. By publishing their results promptly, in a prose accessible to all, and then publicizing them in the popular press and on the BBC, M-O tried to act as an unbiased intermediary to make the dialogue occur. Tom was impatient with the media, Whitehall, and various "experts" who claimed to know what Britain was thinking when in fact, in almost every case, they were drawing on the unsupported opinions of members of Britain's incestuous political-academic-journalistic elite.

Tom's continual efforts to establish and keep alive the "us-them" dialogue involved writing frequent articles for the *New Statesman* and for John

Lehmann's *New Writing*, appearing on BBC television, and even churning out stories for the popular tabloids, with such sensational titles as "Public Busybody No. 1."

The contemporary poetic establishment—Auden, MacNeice, Day Lewis, and others—made scathing insider references in their poems to Mass-Observation and its inventors. In 1939, Graham Greene immortalized M-O in one of his popular "entertainments," *The Confidential Agent*, in the shape of the ubiquitous Mr. Mukerji, who diligently notes down relevant and irrelevant facts in his notebook, blindly missing the significance of what are crucial clues to a murder.

> "You know how it is, Mrs. Mendrill, we mass observers are always on duty."
>
> "What do you do," the manageress said, "with all this information?"
>
> "I type it out on my little Corona and send it to the organizers. We call it Mass Observation."
>
> "And do they print it?"
>
> "They file it for reference. Perhaps one day in a big book—without my name.* We work," he said regretfully, "for science."

As Malinowski so rightly had warned, "Make a parody of a scientific school and you become the godfather of its fame." By January 1939, with *Britain* enjoying record sales, Mass-Observation had become a household word.

Then, on January 30, the social anthropology establishment struck back. Professor (later Sir) Raymond Firth, heir apparent to Malinowski's LSE seminar, and a brilliant social anthropologist whose fieldwork had taken him to the South Pacific and would take him to Malaya, gave a lecture, following an earlier one by Tom, billed as a "detached summing up of Mass-Observation" by an anthropologist.

In this lecture, Firth first acknowledged of the M-O founders that "greatly to their credit, not only did they see the problem but also invented a way of tackling it," but then he went on to cut away with the cool assurance of a surgeon at M-O's exaggerated claims to being a pioneer. He furnished salient samples from other earlier studies that had covered some of the same ground. He would not even allow that the data M-O had compiled were useful to compare with the previous material, condemning the M-O data as not clearly labeled as to source and as "not well integrated, nor linked up with the problems they have stated to be the particular subject of their investigation." Firth then cut the heart out of the statistical material of the chapter on the Munich

---

*One of the rules of the game for the M-O panel and the diarists was that their anonymity would be safeguarded forever. This rule was to assure that they did not shirk from writing the exact truth of what they said, did, and felt in their diaries or in answers to "directives."

crisis, demonstrating that a "major" opinion shift was in one case based only on a difference of five responses and that the samples were too small—and not random enough—to compete with the American straw votes or the BIPO polls of much larger groups.

Had Firth been sent as hit man from the professional social anthropologists to deal with Tom's and Madge's trespassing on their terrain, he could not have been more deadly. Tom felt deeply injured by Firth's comments and would ever after look upon social anthropology and its practitioners with a mixture of fear and loathing. As with his lack of a university degree, Tom's war with social anthropology would cause him much grief, both professional and personal, the rest of his life. The arguments Firth raised in this 1939 lecture have been repeated many times since, in denigration of the value for social science research of the vast hoards of M-O data now stored in the Mass-Observation Archive of Sussex University. In defense, social scientists using the M-O material today aver the data can be of value in providing "telling" rather than necessarily "typical" case studies and can always, at the very least, provide "apt illustrations." Furthermore, looked at with hindsight, the Munich crisis material in *Britain* does appear to have taken a pretty accurate moving picture of the British public's change of mood and opinion as information—and misinformation—filtered down to it. In the final analysis, one returns to Tom's point, with which even Firth would have agreed, that in the range and depth of what M-O was doing in the late 1930s, it had no competitor.

The publication of *Britain* was the beginning of M-O's period of greatest achievement, but it did not seem so to Tom at the time. To do the research for the Munich chapter, Tom had spent most of the autumn at Madge's Blackheath house and had perhaps contributed to the breakup of Madge's marriage to the beautiful poet Kathleen Raine. Tom was never easy to be around when writing; he liked noise and always had people coming to see him. This invasion by Tom and his helpers may have precipitated the decision of Raine to leave Madge. When she left, Madge wanted a change of scene and went along with Tom's suggestion that he and Tom trade headquarters.

So, while Madge went up to Bolton to work on a book about the economic life of Worktown, the fifth M-O book for which Gollancz had given an advance, Tom took over direction of a small team of London-based full-time staffers and became responsible for corresponding with the "panel" of nearly 1,500 volunteer observers, including 500 diarists, from Madge's Blackheath home. Tom enjoyed having a London base but soon became bored with running the panel. He felt that M-O had lost momentum. The Gollancz advances were almost gone, and the promised books were overdue. Tom could safely assume that most of them would never see print without his returning to Bolton to supervise and goad the would-be authors. But going back to that loathsome house was an unattractive prospect.

The early months of 1939 were not happy ones. The deadly criticism of M-O by Firth in late January was followed two weeks later by the death of General Harrisson at the age of fifty-seven. If Tom had ever hoped his father might change his mind, such hopes were dashed now. His mother, perhaps already alcoholic, leaned on Tom's arm during the funeral, after which the will was read.

Tom was still living in Madge's house in Blackheath and using it as the London M-O headquarters while Madge, in the Davenport Street house without a telephone, was becoming increasingly marginalized. After Tom sent out his monthly "directive" to the panel in March, he arranged for Madge to resume running the panel, from Bolton, while Tom led his London M-O team to continue "to analyse popular opinion with regard to the likelihood of war and to criticise the press for leading the public to believe that peace was assured."

Madge, however, fell in love with Inez Spender, wife of the poet Stephen Spender. She left Spender for Madge in the summer of 1939, and Madge wanted to return to London, to his home. By that time, Tom and Madge had become further estranged. This was partly the result of the distance between London and Bolton and partly the widening divergence in views and the growing mutual irritations and suspicions of the two men.

M-O was a household word and *Britain* was selling well, but with the Gollancz money spent and no new books expected to come out soon, M-O was on its way to extinction unless a new patron was found—most probably in Whitehall, if the long-anticipated European war should occur. Tom had no money except that earned from occasional articles in the press, no inheritance from his father's will, and no home now that Madge wanted his house back.

Providentially, just at this time, Tom became the lover of a fairly rich upper-class married Englishwoman who had a big handsome London house. A woman of wit, charm, and amorous propensities, she was named Betha Wolferstan (née Pellatt) Clayton, known to her friends as Biddy. Tall, very slender, with bushy dark hair, a long aristocratic nose, and a wide sexy mouth, Biddy was four years older than Tom. She was not the kind of woman that he usually found sexually appealing, but she had a lot of style and sophistication. She had the gift of making the recitation of a banal event deliciously funny. As with many witty people whose wit plays on the context in which they make their remarks, few of her hearers can remember what she said that made them laugh, but all agree that she was delightful company. She read voraciously, especially the modern novelists and poets, and was a serious collector of a fragile white Italian china known as capodimonte. She also collected Victorian furniture and furnishings, which were not fashionable then. Her large house, full of bibelots and oddities, was a meeting place of people interested in or active in the theater, journalism, the arts, and antiques. As did Tom, she liked her drink and had a notably roving eye.

It was a stormy courtship, with Tom alternately playing hard-to-get (a technique he had been using since Malekula) and being the persistent suitor. He once stood for hours in front of Biddy's door at 82 Ladbroke Road, Holland Park, ringing the bell, after one of their many quarrels. Eventually, he got her to chase out her businessman husband so he could move in. Biddy had met and married Michael Clayton, the father of her five-year old son, John, when Clayton was a teacher at the highly regarded Durnford Preparatory School in Dorset. The Durnford School, from which many boys went on to Eton, Harrow, and Rugby, had been founded and run by Biddy's father, Thomas Pellatt, an eccentric but gifted teacher, and was the main source of the family's wealth.

Biddy was the younger of Pellatt's two daughters and had been raised to think of herself as the "pretty" sister, not the "clever" one. Her father had always shown a marked preference for the clever sister, and her mother, in recompense, had spoiled Biddy. The result was that Biddy tended to chronic self-doubt and occasional grand gestures of self-indulgence. Tom (who used to boast about her wealth) encouraged Biddy's profligacy. Years later he recalled fondly how she once, simply for the pleasure of it, had hired a whole floor of a hotel and ordered up magnums of champagne.

Biddy's parents were pleased that she had managed to attract such an interesting and intelligent man as Tom. Her elder sister, already a published novelist, agreed that this time Biddy had found a man who "really was some-body." In the summer of 1939 Michael Clayton began divorce proceedings against his wife, with Tom named as corespondent.

Thus it was that when Madge returned to London to take back his Blackheath house in the autumn of 1939, Tom was already ensconced in the large house at 82 Ladbroke Road, with Biddy, her young son John, and her collection of Victorian porcelain and bric-a-brac. The M-O headquarters moved there, too, and eventually took over the ground floor.

# Chapter 17

# M-O Goes to War

In September 1939 Britain declared war on Germany. Tom, writing to Madge from his new Ladbroke Road home, gloated: "Everything is blowing into our hands. . . . We have got what no-one else has got, facts before the war." As Tom recalled in *World Within*:

> The war, which started out slowly in 1939, brought M-O into its own sort of own. Although other organizations had by now sprung up to study public opinion, we could offer a then unique service for the study of private opinion and the interpretation of broad trends: those amorphous marshlands of the mind which in war-time are dubbed "morale". Morale was meat, drink, and regular salaries for all in M-O.

Civilian morale was a field M-O was well equipped to monitor whereas, as Ian McLaine points out in his excellent book *Ministry of Morale*, Whitehall—the service ministries especially—was almost incredibly inept at doing this. McLaine cites an air ministry official describing in April 1941, almost at the end of the Blitz, as a typical "Service" attitude the idea that "The civilian's job was to ask no questions, to pay his taxes in order to keep up the Armed Forces, to take off his hat when the Colours marches past and generally to regard himself as a necessary but unfortunate adjunct to the glories of military life which, coupled with fox-hunting, really go to make up England." The services failed to realize that the nature of war had changed. Such new technologies as the long-range bomber meant that war would involve the whole people, not just soldiers. "Defeat might not flow from the collapse of armies on conventional battlefronts but from the breakdown of morale at home." The people's active support for the war effort had become crucial. But, in England at least, "the people," having gone through the Great War and the Great Depression, were less inclined than formerly to take Government's unsubstantiated word on things or to obey unquestioningly.

In early thinking about the upcoming war, the country's civilian leaders were at least aware of the need for intelligence on the public's reactions to wartime events and difficulties, both to assess popular morale and to pass on to concerned Governmental departments information on how their policies were being received by the public. This was a field that M-O had made its own. And so, the first cautious approaches to M-O were made by the embryo Ministry of Information (MoI) to see if M-O might be asked to take on projects "to obtain information . . . from typical samples of society." (The MoI would also ask the British Institute of Public Opinion.)

There was, as McLaine noted, "a good deal of nervousness attend[ing] the discussion about Mass-Observation and it was suggested that the body should be used only if the public were to believe that its inquiries had no connection with the Ministry, making it necessary therefore to finance its activities from Secret Service funds." While being paid by the Secret Service appealed to Tom's love of cloak-and-dagger adventures, it had the undesirable effect of making the Ministry of Information's entire domestic intelligence-collecting a secret rather than a transparently necessary element in the dialogue between leaders and the led. When the secret was exposed the following summer, the ensuing uproar was precisely what Government had hoped to avoid.

The primary reason for governmental caution was that officials in the new ministry feared that members of Parliament would be jealous. They knew that M.P.s were convinced they had their finger on the public pulse and could tell the Ministry of Information all it needed to know about public opinion. The press, of course, would also resent having experts check on its traditional claim to be the voice of the people. That some means of finding out what people were *really* thinking and feeling was necessary is beyond question. In those early days of World War II, the lack of any sense by those in charge of government and propaganda as to what the public might feel is impossible to exaggerate. Take, for example, the suggestions made on September 1, 1940, the day Hitler invaded Poland, by the Home Publicity Committee, meeting to discuss what immediate action should be taken to counteract panic in case of air raid. One of the committee members, Lady Grigg, suggested that a cup of tea was always comforting and provided an occasion for women to get together and talk things over. Another member, John Hilton, who, as the first professor of industrial relations at Cambridge, knew more than the others on the panel about the working class but had less political clout than the redoubtable Lady Grigg, gravely agreed that sugar was good for steadying the nerves.

With this sort of expertise about what would soothe the British public if it were bombarded from the air, the Ministry of Information mounted its first domestic propaganda campaign. The campaign's first poster, with the exception of a white emblem of the crown on top, consisted entirely of words, white letters against a red background, with some of the text underlined:

YOUR COURAGE
YOUR CHEERFULNESS
YOUR RESOLUTION
WILL BRING
US VICTORY

No clearer example of how Government saw its relation to the people it led could have been conceived. "You" do the work and make the sacrifices, allowing "us" to return to our fox hunting. Mass-Observation was hired by the Ministry of Information to report on the public response to these posters. When M-O's study for MoI showed how unsuccessful the poster campaign was proving, a key cabinet minister is alleged to have remarked: "Very good work. But if we are going to find out things as unpleasant as this, we'd better not find out anything at all." Madge, now back in London, collaborated with Tom on this study and later recalled:

> The results of this [red poster study, together] with a survey of ARP [Air Raid Precautions] volunteers in Fulham and reactions to gas masks, shelters, barrage balloons and black-outs were the basis for a book called *War Begins at Home*, for which we were . . . jointly responsible and which was published by Chatto and Windus in January 1940.

That the MoI had paid for the reports on which the book was based had clearly not influenced the authors' conclusions. In *War Begins at Home*, Tom and Madge noted the government's failure to take into account social and psychological factors in planning to cope with aerial bombardment; they held the poor quality of the dialogue between the leaders and the led responsible for this. They made the point that M-O's wartime role of providing feedback about the led to the leaders was not merely useful but essential because the traditional peacetime sources of feedback were no longer functioning at all. Because of an agreement among the major parties not to try to win parliamentary seats from one another in by-elections, the main "barometer that politicians had on public opinion" was no longer working. As Tom wrote elsewhere, the result of this political truce was that the House of Commons, elected in 1935, was "exceptionally out of touch with public opinion." Furthermore, with conscription having been instituted at the very beginning of the war, Britain's leaders were not obliged, as their fathers had been in World War I, to appeal to the patriotism of the people to recruit an army of volunteers.

In December 1939, Tom's old friend Mary Adams was appointed to the post of director of the Office of Home Intelligence of the Ministry of

Information. One of her first acts was to hire Mass-Observation to collect information she could use in a monthly report to the Ministry of Home Security, assessing domestic morale and reaction to its propaganda campaigns. This was a fortunate time for Tom to find a steady source of income. In December, the decree nisi went through for Biddy's divorce and she became pregnant with Tom's child. In January 1940, Tom wrote Madge that, "For me, M-O has become practically an obsession, and I am not really interested in anything else at the moment."

Meanwhile Madge, uncomfortable that M-O was dependent on its contract with the Ministry of Information, complained to Tom that "I see grave danger of M-O becoming propagandist." Madge, whose interests were diverging substantially from Tom's, was also tired of the strain of working with him. Not a big, sloppy brawler like Tom, Madge by early 1940 was exchanging long contentious memoranda with him, in the vain hope of resolving their disagreements. Tom had already warned Madge, in writing, in January 1937, at the very start of their collaboration: "It is useless for me to try and play down myself for long; I can't help it, and it is my up and up that makes me pamphlet, explore, work in cotton mills. It's lousy in me, I suppose. Work it out. . . ."

By mid-June 1940, Madge had decided that the best way for him to work it out was to leave.

That left Tom alone at the head of M-O, which was being kept alive chiefly by its contract with Mary Adams's Office of Home Intelligence in the Ministry of Information. That ministry had a rapid turnover of leadership. In May 1940 it had acquired its third minister in less than a year: Duff Cooper, appointed by the new Prime Minister, Winston Churchill. Luckily for Tom, Duff Cooper kept Mary Adams in place as director of the Office of Home Intelligence during the year he headed the ministry.

Ten months after the war began, with a modest income coming in from the MoI and odd bits of journalism, Tom married Biddy on June 25, 1940. The ceremony took place at St. Ethelburga's, Bishopsgate (London), but the circumstances were unpropitious. Biddy's divorce had not come through until June 17, the day that France fell to Nazi Germany. Biddy was by then six months pregnant and had been made anxious by the delay. Her divorce had been held up by the fact that in those days the Admiralty Court handled both divorces and disasters at sea, and it had been hearing a messy case concerning the accidental sinking, with almost all hands, of a new British submarine, the *Thetis*.

Tom's friends were unenthusiastic about the marriage. One of Tom's female M-O observers, hearing that Tom was marrying Biddy, had spent the day in the lavatory and would not come out. "How *could* you?" Mary Adams protested in a loud whisper, when Tom and Biddy walked down the aisle past her on their way out of the church. Tom characterized the ceremony years later as "basically false" and shudderingly recalled "those purple choirboys."

The war had officially been going on for almost a year by then. The British people were dispirited by the bad news abroad but in general were more bored than frightened. An almost criminally incompetent domestic propaganda machine was damaging morale, as M-O kept pointing out, but few bombs had fallen on British soil and British civilian casualties were in the dozens, no more.

Then in late July, the veil of secrecy that had enshrouded domestic intelligence activities being conducted for the Ministry of Information was rent when stories began to appear in the press that there were public opinion surveyors secretly hired by the Ministry of Information who were upsetting the public by asking questions about morale. The first to be uncovered were pollsters from the Wartime Social Survey, an organization that had been created by the MoI to do quantitative research as a check on M-O's qualitative work, but soon the papers were writing about M-O as well. For the next several weeks, no day went by without at least one London paper, usually several, attacking the so-called "Cooper's Snoopers" and the Ministry of Information in its entirety. There were questions in the House of Commons. It looked as if the MoI's new minister, Duff Cooper, might have to resign. On August 1, the parliamentary debate on the subject included persistent queries about connections between Mass-Observation and the Ministry. Duff Cooper tried to dodge the question the first several times. He finally decided to be extremely economical with the truth by saying the ministry had "once or twice applied to [M-O] for statistical information on certain subjects which it has been able to furnish, information which it was not worth while setting up a special inquiry to obtain." Tom, who had briefed Duff Cooper before the parliamentary debate, allegedly rode away with him after it was over to join in the celebration of the minister having beaten back those in Parliament threatening to pull him down.

Soon thereafter the fizz went out of the Cooper's Snoopers story. The allegedly reticent British public, in fact, had not objected to being questioned. Celia Fremlin, an M-O staffer, often asked Londoners for their views on various morale subjects and remembered that from this time forward people would ask, "Oh, are you one of Cooper's Snoopers?" and, on being told "yes," were more eager to be interviewed than ever. Having been mentioned in the papers and in the Commons had made the project glamorous.

M-O observers had already learned that, although British people thought they did not like to be asked questions about their private life, they actually loved it. Tom was one of the first to publicize that finding. He also discovered something that is now well known to market research organizations: women do this work better than men. The idea was not entirely new. In *Unnatural Death* (1927), Lord Peter Wimsey, Dorothy Sayers's noble fictional sleuth, set up an inquiry bureau staffed entirely by "superfluous women" to help him check out fraud and swindles. Lord Peter explained:

> People want questions asked. Whom do they send? A man with large flat feet and a notebook—the sort of man whose private life is conducted in a series of inarticulate grunts. I send a lady with a long, woolly jumper on knitting needles and jingly things round her neck. Of course she asks questions—everyone expects it. Nobody is surprised. Nobody is alarmed.

At first, not having money to pay them, Tom convinced his women observers to observe and listen while working at other jobs to earn a living. For example, Celia Fremlin was a "nippy" (waitress) at a Lyons restaurant in the summer of 1940. Tom told her to write down what the other nippies were saying. Fremlin had come down from Oxford with a classics degree and had taken on jobs as scullery maid and counter hand and waitress not only to earn her living but also to learn enough to write a book called *The Seven Chars of Chelsea* (Methuen, 1940). She was one of the first women of her class to do such a thing.

Not all of Tom's wartime observers were women. Leonard England, who had been on the M-O panel while at school and was now waiting to be called up, read an appeal from Tom for volunteers to do full-time work for M-O:

> I remember my first meeting with Tom, when I came to see him in early 1940. I was about 18 or 19 at the time. When the door of the Ladbroke Road house opened, I saw at the bottom of the stairs an enormous plaster bust of the Salvation Army founder William Booth [one of Biddy's Victorian oddities]. And behind it, dressed only in a towel, Tom Harrisson. He immediately asked me if I had seen "The Lion Has Wings," one of the first propaganda films. And I said no, so he told me to go see it right away and report on how the audience reacted to it.
>
> That was the start of my reporting on people and the movies. I reported that people booed Chamberlain and applauded Churchill. Tom's theory was that in the dark people were willing to express their real views as they might not do in public otherwise. I also covered the Music Hall and Tom loved my reports of reactions. He thought a good gauge of morale was if they laughed at jokes about Hitler. If they did, morale was good; but if the joke fell flat, morale was not. He had a genius for seeing the obvious, which others missed.

The Cooper's Snoopers scandal had been primarily a newspaper campaign that had mushroomed during the "silly season" of an uneventful British summer, with everyone waiting for the "Phoney War" to end. After the media play subsided, Mass-Observation was told to carry on with its work for the ministry, sub rosa, with morale to be M-O's special subject.

Soon there would come a powerful reason for Government to want to keep informed about citizens' morale. And Government would need M-O's help in doing so.

# Chapter 18

## Living through the Blitz

On September 9, 1940, began the Blitz, nine months of massive aerial bombardment of British population centers. Government needed desperately to know how the people were taking it. Would they panic and want to have peace at any price? Many believed that such a scenario, prophesied by Italian General Douhet after World War I, would result from high-density bombing of civilians. Now Britain was about to find out if that would, in fact, happen.

Tom and Biddy soon learned first hand what the threat of being bombed felt like when the house across the road from theirs suffered a direct hit. Tom moved his very pregnant wife, stepson, and the M-O files to Letchworth First Garden City, an early "planned community" in Hertfordshire, where there was a good day school (St. Christopher) for Biddy's six-year-old John Clayton. Leaving Ladbroke Road was a great hardship for Biddy, as most of her closest friends lived nearby, with children all attending the same neighborhood private day school. Through the school, Biddy had become a good friend of Sheila Hill Hill, wife of John Hill (no relation). Sheila's brother Heywood, owner of Hill's Book Shop in Curzon Street, was married to Lady Anne Gathorne-Hardy, Lord Cranbrook's sister. Biddy thus became part of the social circle around the talented Gathorne-Hardy family. Lord Cranbrook was a knowledgeable paleozoologist, and Tom's connection with him and his family would become important to him years later in Sarawak. Another friend Biddy had made through the school was Charles Lambe, a rising star in the British navy who was close to the Windsors, to the new king, and to "Dickie" (Lord Louis) Mountbatten. Lambe, eleven years Tom's senior, was not only well connected but unusually gifted in a number of fields and by September 1940 was assistant director of plans, a big job in the war cabinet.

Tom had been happy to get to know Biddy's intelligent and unusual upper-class friends and had taken some trouble to cultivate them. In May 1939, for example, he heard that Ming, a baby female giant panda and a star attraction at the London Zoo, was going daily, in a special car, to a film studio where a film was being made featuring her and a child actress. Tom, who positively enjoyed the company of children in their early school years and had a knack for talking to them in an unpatronizing way, arranged (probably through his friend Julian Huxley, then secretary of the Zoological Society of London) to take the older of Sheila Hill's children along with John Clayton to be photographed with the panda and to ride in the car with her. More than five decades later, those children still remembered that ride.

Tom was soon to have a child of his own. On September 29, 1940, three weeks after the London Blitz began, Maxwell Barr Harrisson was born at the Radcliffe Infirmary, Oxford. Three months later, Max was baptized at the West Stafford Church, Dorset, near Biddy's parents' home. The godparents were the Hon. Mrs. (Ruth) Gathorne-Hardy and Captain Charles Lambe, RN. Tom took a real interest in his son. He wrote comments in the baby "Log," noting that the baby sat up for the first time on March 14. "No sign of teeth at 6 months but expected, . . . lots by Jan, 10, 1942, but still more coming." He marked in the log that "Max walked at 14 months." On December 1, 1942, when Max was two and a quarter years old, Tom described his son as "very thickset and strong looking, not flabby; . . . bladder A.1—no wets for some months. Can name: bell, cup, plate, coat, hat, pants, cow, cat, horse, train, car, soldier, eye, phone, radio, shoes, fork, spoon, apple, sausage, tea, sugar, nose, butter, bomb, plane, chair, egg, sock, hankie, meat, sweet, book." By September 1943, when Max was three, Tom had counted 430 words that Max had used over a two-day period, adding that, "Every few minutes, he adds 2 or 3 words!"

Biddy adjusted quickly to her new home in Letchworth. She continued collecting Victoriana. A friend remembers that the house was "filled with bric-a-brac, dried flowers, and things in glass domes, and a particularly fascinating glass case containing china frogs playing billiards." The friend also recalled:

> Biddy took the ethnic approach, or rather the forerunner of the beatnik generation. She seemed to have little self-confidence and used to tell me how much she admired people who were skilled, adding that she herself was hopeless at everything.
>
> I think people were a bit wary of Tom, sensing that he didn't suffer fools gladly. . . . I remember him giving a talk to the children of St. Christopher School about the Borneo cannibals [presumably the Borneo headhunters and the New Hebrides cannibals] and using some colourful language that sent the headmaster's wife's eyebrows shooting up to her hairline.

The headmaster's niece, Margaret Harris Young, recalled hearing this talk when she was a child and said that it convinced her to take a degree in anthropology.

In the summer of 1941, Tom did a series of broadcasts for the BBC schools programs on learning to live like a Malekulan cannibal. He undoubtedly used the same material for talks to various groups of children, either as a way of rehearsing for the BBC or as a by-product of those broadcasts. Another by-product of the BBC talks was the charming little children's book *Living Among Cannibals* (1943).

Tom's own recollections of life at Letchworth are not so rosy. He found this middle-class housing development to be "lifeless" and "humourless" and took as a sign of its lifelessness the fact that "not one pub is permitted." His interest in Biddy was diminishing steadily, with her in Letchworth with the two children and him in London, where the Ladbroke Road house was entirely given over to Mass-Observation purposes.

M-O was busier than ever. With the Blitz in progress, nobody complained about Government using M-O to try to find out about home front morale. As Angus Calder noted, "The war saved M-O's methodological bacon. . . . And the prewar experience of observing trivia for their own sake showed its value in this and other 'war work' where the need to defeat Germany gave all observations a natural focus: what did trivia point to but morale?" With his MoI contract in hand, Tom could now pay his observers, so they threw up their other jobs and worked full-time for M-O. Celia Fremlin remembered that she and three other women would meet at the Ladbroke Road house at half past nine to get from Tom their "news quota":

> Every single morning throughout that period of the war, we had a paper with six questions and we had to go out and get twelve people anywhere on the street to answer these questions. The questions would start off, "What did you think of the news today?" And then the other five questions were relevant to the news of that day.
>
> For example, the day after Churchill gave his famous speech about "blood and tears, toil and sweat," we asked people on the street: "Did you hear Churchill's speech? What did you think of it? Can you remember any of his actual words or sentences that impressed you particularly?" And we did get the blood and tears, toil and sweat. There was an enormously favourable response to it. . . .

They each went to a different part of London and tried to choose a variety of respondents. After lunch they would each be given specific assignments:

> One of the most enjoyable assignments was simply "overheards," just to walk about the shops and on buses and simply to write down snatches of conversation relevant to the war.
>
> And sometimes there was something special. There was one time that I was concentrating on studying the queues outside the Underground shelters—because

people used to come out of the shelter at 5 a.m. and straightaway queue up for getting in the next night. There were many people who just couldn't bear the raids. And so they found it worth it waiting all day. And I would interview different people in the queues, what made it seem worthwhile and the story of how their house had been bombed, etc.

. . . And out of those interviews, which were really detailed, not like market research now, we would follow people's trains of thought about the questions—"indirect interviews," we would call them.

Tom would be given their accounts the next morning and would cut and paste them for his next report for the Ministry of Information and sometimes for a newspaper, such as *Picture Post*, in order to earn some additional income.

By the time the Blitz began, Tom had fifteen full-time investigators working for him. Although each did a share of routine investigations of opinion on events of the day, each also had a special subject to cover. "Art, sport, cinema, music hall, religion, jazz, fashion, shopping habits, astrology, and pacifism are a few of these. . . ." The human problems of evacuation from the cities were given special attention by M-0 from the time of the false alarm of September 1938 and especially after September 1940, when the Blitz was at its height.

From September 9, 1940, the day the first bombs dropped on London, until the Blitz ended the following spring, M-O staffers—and often Tom in person—were where the bombs had fallen or were falling, reporting on how people were reacting and how the government was meeting their needs. Typical of M-O's Blitz reports to Mary Adams's Office of Home Intelligence (which then were circulated to the cabinet, the Ministry of Home Security, the Ministry of Home Affairs, the service ministries, etc.), bridging the gap between "us" and "them" as only M-O could, is a description of what an ordinary person had to cope with in late April 1941 in Plymouth, after seven big raids had hit the city during the previous month:

> Take the case of a sailor's wife, her husband at sea, she keeping a small shop, which is gradually dwindling as all small shopkeepers are frozen out by new Government orders. She has two children of school age and a baby. The shop and the rooms she lives in above it received a direct hit. One of the children is killed, another slightly injured. She is naturally extremely shaken. She is living in a badly hit working class area. She finds herself homeless, moneyless, without a thing except her spirit, her morale, her common sense. What does she have to do next day?
>
> (i) She has to eat. She has to get new ration books. She goes to St. Batholomew's Hall, Milehouse.
>
> (ii) In the meanwhile, she has to find a communal feeding centre, for the children, go to the Girls' High School.

(iii) She has to try and have tinned food and other stuff in her small shop in ruins salvaged. All right, she has to go to the city's Treasurer's Office, whose last address given in an MoI leaflet is the Guildhall, but that got bombed on the previous night.

(iv) She is also supposed to report the presence of some contaminated food. Here she should contact the Medical Officer of Health, Beaumont House, Beaumont Road.

(v) She is already beginning to be faced with the problem of her surviving children as she treks around. She has to find a Rest Centre—the ones in her area are destroyed. She finally leaves them there for the time being.

(vi) But one child is dead. She has to locate the body. She has to inquire about the death certificate then, at the Information Bureau in the Technical College.

(vii) She decides she can't afford a private burial, and so applies to the War Deaths department in the Information Bureau.

(viii) Now she is faced with the problem of extra clothing, especially for the children. The address is 18, Addison Road, Sherwell.

(ix) She is advised to put in a claim for compensation for clothing, furniture, etc. So off to Mutley Baptist Church, the Assistance Board.

(x) They are able to give her a cash advance, but necessarily limited. They advise her to apply for extra help from the Mayor's relief fund, situated in Morley Chambers.

(xi) As it is obviously hopeless to get any alternative accommodation locally, she decides to apply for free travel vouchers for the homeless. The address is "Seven Trees", Lipson Road. Or a child evacuation form can be obtained from the Education Office, Cobourg Street.

(xii) Having lost the identity cards, naturally, she has to apply for new ones to 13, Thorn Park, Mannamead.

(xiii) Then to get new gas masks. Off she goes to the Corporation Surplus Stores, Mill Street.

(xiv) Of course, she has lost her "Navy book" and to get another she goes to the Pennycomequick Sorting Office in Central Park Avenue. Having got all these Plymouth matters in hand, *the problem of her billet in the country arises*—a terrible problem for the good citizen who has stayed put until actually bombed out. Here the Chief Billeting Officer, Lipson Road (no address given on MoI leaflet) appears to be involved.

(xv) Finally, being a good citizen, she decides to avail herself of the advised post-Blitz measure of typhoid inoculation. The good citizen goes to the Prince of Wales Hospital, Green Bank.

"The Blitz period, despite and even partly because of its human tragedies, was a field day for M-O," recalled Bob Willcock, one of Tom's chief collaborators at M-O's London headquarters. This was so not just for M-O but for Tom, personally, appealing as it did to his love of danger. Humphrey Spender recalled that Tom enlisted him to help do a piece for *Picture Post* about the Blitz:

> So he rang up all kinds of people, Ministry of Information people, etc., and asked "What is the town that is being the most bombed?" It turned out to be Bristol, I think.
>
> So off we go to Bristol (or wherever). And indeed it was being very heavily bombed. Tom wouldn't go to a shelter and he said "You've got to photograph me looking frightened, because I've got to pretend to be frightened." So he sticks his head out a window and tells me to lean out another window, with bombs dropping all around, and says "I'm going to look frightened" and he puts his finger in his mouth and looks like that [makes a face]. It's a terribly funny photograph.
>
> And he wouldn't let us go into a shelter at night. [He said,] "I know there will be some flares, those buggers will drop some flares and that will be enough light for us." He literally was an unfrightenable man.

He was also fast becoming unemployable by the MoI. Mary Adams left the ministry in April 1941, anticipating the departure of the unhappy Duff Cooper a month later. Brendan Bracken, a close friend of Churchill's and no friend of M-O, would take over as minister of information in June, and there would be no more MoI contracts for Tom Harrisson.

By late 1940, however, Tom had found an unlikely new patron: Admiral John Godfrey, Director of Naval Intelligence (DNI). Captain Charles Lambe, Max's godfather, introduced Tom to Admiral Godfrey over lunch at Fleming's Hotel. Godfrey was familiar with Tom's writing from his frequent contributions to the *New Statesman* and was favorably disposed toward him. The admiral was a good patron for Tom not only because working for DNI would help to keep M-O financially afloat but also because the admiral could help keep Tom out of the army. Tom had successfully delayed his conscription once, through the good offices of the Ministry of Information, and in 1941 and 1942, Godfrey himself twice quashed efforts to call Tom up by writing to the cabinet.

For someone who loved adventure and relished danger as much as Tom did, it seems strange that he was not trying hard to get into the fighting war. A possible explanation comes from David Astor. Astor, then publisher of *The Observer*, would hire Tom to write a radio column for his paper beginning in 1942. He remembers a conversation with Tom that took place in about 1940:

Tom Harrisson and I both thought the war would not last long. He decided that he would keep going with M-O and that he would not be called up. And to do this, he had to be doing something useful for the Government. And he also had to make some money. So he somehow prevailed upon the Admiralty to employ him as a Mass-Observer of opinion in the naval docks where there was quite a bit of politics, quite a bit of Left-wing politics. (You remember that at the start of the war, the Communists were not with us, because of the Hitler-Stalin pact.)

So Tom used to do this writing of the political opinions in the docks. And I remember being very amused by him saying in a mischievous way—if you knew him, you know what I mean—he said he kept the job going by making the reports rather more dramatic and alarming than he thought was strictly the case. He thought that if [DNI] were sufficiently frightened they would think they were getting valuable information on trouble in the docks, and they would keep him.

It is hard to know what weight to give this comment of Tom's, as remembered fifty years later, about exaggerating the political risk among dock workers. It is just the sort of thing he would say to a friend. He would not need to exaggerate political orientations among the dock workers to alarm Admiral Godfrey, who tended to see Reds under the bed.

Although Tom and his helpers had been instructed not to talk about M-O's work for the DNI, Tom could not resist dropping boastful hints when he had too much to drink, and this habit of indiscretion got back to Godfrey's minions. Godfrey, however, had a lot of respect for Tom's brains and abilities and found his reports "invaluable" in producing a "comprehensive review of the subject of Port Security." Recognizing that some of Tom's reports were "very verbose, . . . and at times highly coloured and dramatic," Godfrey had them shortened and some dramatic flourishes removed before passing them on to the commanders-in-chief of all the ports and flag officers at home, to the sea lords, and occasionally to the prime minister.

The admiral quickly learned not to send Tom's reports to the Minister of Home Security. This was, Godfrey explained to a colleague, because "the reaction of the Minister of Home Security when he saw [earlier] reports was extremely unfavourable and led to his trying to get them suppressed, which, of course, is all wrong." Godfrey sympathized with Tom's determination to tell the facts as he saw them without regard to how annoying they might be to people in power. They might not be flattering, but "Why should they be flattering?" Godfrey asked. Godfrey himself would lose his job as head of naval intelligence in the fall of 1942 for a similar lack of diplomacy. Among Godfrey's tactless acts was informing the air staff of the unwelcome truth he was obtaining from his sources in Germany that the bombing efforts of the Royal Air Force were not resulting in the damage being claimed by hopeful bomber crews.

M-O was not entirely dependent on Admiral Godfrey. Other Governmental departments also employed M-O, including, briefly, Herbert Morrison's Ministry of Home Security, the Ministry of Labour, and Lord Beaverbrook's Ministry of Production. M-O, of course, continued to antagonize its patrons by publicly biting the hand that fed it, pointing out genuine problems that needed solving.

M-O also published numerous war-related domestic studies in books and pamphlets, thanks to support from seven independent advertising agencies that had formed the Advertising Service Guild to demonstrate that advertising could be socially useful. There were also other clients: the owners of an armaments plant asked M-O to find out what was going wrong in the workplace. M-O sent Celia Fremlin, incognito. The results, published in M-O's *War Factory* (London: Gollancz, 1943), make fascinating reading, especially for their insights into the difference between what management valued and what the staff thought important. Tom also wrote or arranged for his staffers to write articles in *Picture Post*, the *New Statesman*, and many scholarly and popular periodicals.

In the spring of 1942, a year after the end of M-O's MoI connection and with no more DNI contracts, Mass-Observation ceased being on any special reserve list for military purposes, and M-O full-timers began to be called up. One reason suggested for the withdrawal of official protection from M-O was that Minister of Labour Ernest Bevin was said to have "sicked up his breakfast" upon reading M-O's *People in Production* (London: John Murray, 1942). Drafted quickly by Tom drawing on six months of M-O research, the book castigated working conditions for the civilian labor force.

Tom realized how offensive his book would be to Bevin and others. In his preface, he quoted Manet's dictum: "Sincerity makes a painter's work seem like a protest, though all the painter intended was to render his impression." He then applied the painter's "semi-apology" to his own work of "social science," which he described as "another less colourful but equally exacting sort of impressionism." Whether the story about Bevin is true, soon after the book came out in April 1942, all able-bodied M-O men were called up. In July 1942, Bob Willcock, who had a liver condition, was left to hold the fort at Ladbroke Road while Tom was inducted into the Army.

By mid-August Tom was a King's Royal Rifleman, based at Strensall, Yorkshire, sleeping in a barrack room inhabited by "some thirty cockneys and two public school boys [of whom Tom was one]. . . . The atmosphere pullulate[d] with nicotine, saliva and smutty language." During periods of instruction, while seeming to be taking notes on the Bren gun, he would answer the pile of mail he received daily. He missed most meals and lived on a diet of bananas and chocolate while he listened to the radio. Shortly before being called up, he had been hired to write a weekly radio column for David Astor's Sunday newspaper, *The Observer*, the first newspaper to have such a column. One or two nights a week, he walked over to the radio hut behind the canteen to write his column. He never missed a deadline, producing 122 weekly "Radio" pieces from March 1942 to June 1944. A dozen column-inches each, they are full of fresh, intelligent, and amusing comments about wartime broadcasting in Britain and show Tom's gift for picking out what is of durable interest and quality.

Tom himself had become reasonably well known through the medium of broadcasting. In October 1943, he received the Radio BBC accolade of being invited as a guest on *Desert Island Discs*. On each program, a famous person is asked to talk about his life and name and introduce eight music records he would want with him if he were a castaway on a desert island. Tom's choice of records was singularly unmusical for a man of his cultivation but provided a good foil for the script. One was a musical performance on washboards, in homage to a drunken Cambridge afternoon spent with Malcolm Lowry and Tom Forman.

Tom enjoyed his time as an ordinary soldier, living among men who did not expect him to think or act the way they did. He liked himself better in such uncompetitive surroundings. The noise and the smells never bothered him, and he had learned in Bolton when not to parade his privileged background and education. He did not mention his radio column and thus was touched and surprised to find on his bunk one night a typewriter that one of the barrack room's two professional thieves had stolen for him in nearby York. But his time as a Rifleman came to an abrupt end when he was sent "without the option" before the War Office Selection Board.

By June 1943, he was a member of the 162 Officer Cadet Training Unit at Sandhurst. Six months later, he allegedly passed out at the top of his class, with an emergency commission of 2d Lieutenant in the Reconnaissance Corps. He was posted to the 161 Reconnaissance Regiment, a unit which had until the previous August been an infantry battalion of the Green Howards. It was not a happy assignment for him. Being a new officer among a conventional bunch of "old guard" officers brought out the worst in him. Ministry of Defense records reportedly show that Tom's "views and extra-territorial activities . . . made him an object of scorn and loathing to his very regular Colonel."

Rescue came in early 1944 when he was suddenly summoned to London to the old Northumberland Avenue Hotel. There, Colonel E. Egerton Mott interviewed him, under the impression (as best Tom could deduce from the colonel's cryptic comments) that Tom was a Communist. The colonel had confused Tom with a Harrison—one "s"—who had fought for the Loyalists in Spain. Tom was inwardly amused at being thought a "Red," since at the time of the interview, he was being considered for nomination by the Liberal Party for a parliamentary seat. Gradually, it began to emerge from the colonel's convoluted conversation that his organization, Special Operations Executive, was looking, in Tom's words, for "a few men to go back into Borneo and try to save some of the face, chin-up, lost to the Japanese." Mott had already asked everybody else he could find who might have knowledge of the island of Borneo, so he was pleased when Tom "practically leapt at the offer."

Special Operations Executive (SOE) had been created by Winston Churchill in July 1940, after the fall of France "to set Europe ablaze" by encouraging resistance activities behind enemy lines. It had secret agents paid for out of the "Secret Vote" rather than by the War Office. SOE agents were inserted into the Balkans and other parts of Nazi-occupied Europe by airplane, glider, parachute, submarine, and small landing craft. They engaged in sabotage, they blew up trains and rail lines, ran escape routes for guerrillas and resistance leaders, reported back by clandestine radio, wrote in code and secret ink, and carried cyanide capsules to swallow in case of capture. To be a good SOE agent, you had to be observant, shrewd, original, independent, tough, energetic, and inured to danger and discomfort. In short, you had to be much like Tom.

He joined SOE on March 27, 1944. In April and May, he did his paramilitary training at STS 35, "The Vineyards," Hampshire ("the acquisition of so much criminal and lethal knowledge gave a kick of self-confidence," Tom later recalled), followed by a quick course in parachuting at Ringway, near Manchester. He emerged fully winged with five jumps in three days. He was now ready to go. He wrote his last radio column for *The Observer*, much to the regret of David Astor, who kept him on the payroll for the remainder of the war years in hopes of luring him back to the column later.

In early June Tom gave a farewell party at the Ladbroke Road house, which Lord Wyatt remembered long afterward: "The party was full of intellectuals, writers, jolly girls and fast-flowing and fast-consumed drink." At the end of it, a drunken Wyatt (accompanied by a drunken William Empson), at Tom's request, tried to drive an even drunker J. B. Priestley home to the Albany. Priestley, frightened by Wyatt's careering around Eros at Piccadilly Circus on the wrong side of the road, insisted on getting out at Jermyn Street and fell into the gutter. "We left him there," Wyatt recalled. "He must have got home. He went on writing, talking and complaining for years." But Tom went off to fight in a war halfway around the world.

**PART FOUR**

King of the Mountain,
1942–1946

*Chapter 19*

# Waiting for Dawn on Mindoro

At 1:00 A.M. on March 25, 1945, Tom was lying in the dark in the warm sands of the American airfield on Mindoro Island, the Philippines. Stretched out next to him was Squadron Leader Graham Pockley, an Australian pilot who had won the DSO and the Distinguished Flying Cross. The two men were waiting to board Pockley's Liberator for the third time in five days, having failed the previous times to find a hole through the thick cloud that covered the drop zone in the highlands of north-central Borneo.

Tom was keyed up. In that state, he felt he could see himself clearly. Unashamedly, in front of this kindly and quiet war hero who shared his fondness for taking risks, Tom took stock of his own strengths and weaknesses:

> What I adored in myself was an unquenchable curiosity and an apparently endless, tireless urge to record what I saw, plus a certain ability to dissociate myself from violent feelings about it. The thing which makes science tick . . . ticked in me until I wanted no other. The burning search for some sort of final satisfaction in knowledge, regardless of power.

But, he conceded, there was "the other side of Harrisson's equation—the apparently insatiable ego, the drive to do whatever I had to do or wanted to do, either *before* or *better* than anyone else (preferably both)."

It was largely that drive that had got him where he now was, a British army major in charge of seven battle-hardened special operatives with the Australian equivalent of SOE—known as "Z" Special unit—who were about to become the "first white men" to jump into Borneo behind Japanese lines.

The Allied pursuit of the war against Japan was by then divided into South West Pacific and South East Asia Commands. Borneo fell under the aegis of the Allied Theater Commander for the South West Pacific, U.S. Army General Douglas MacArthur, who had gained the agreement of the Allies that the Americans would have the chief role in attacking the Japanese mainland, while Britain, Australia, and New Zealand would weaken and destroy the Japanese garrisons to the south and east of Japan.

The Australians were to try to take the Japanese garrisons on Borneo, strategically important because Borneo bordered the two most important north-south sea routes of Southeast Asia, the South China Sea to the west and the Makassar Strait to the east. To this end, the Australian Imperial Force (AIF) would send a brigade of its Ninth Division to take Tarakan Island, off the northeast coast of Dutch Borneo. After Tarakan was secured, the remainder of the AIF's Ninth Division would seize the island of Labuan and the rest of Brunei Bay, on Borneo's northwest coast, thereby denying the enemy the oil fields of Brunei and northern Sarawak, which, during 1943 and 1944, had helped Borneo supply 40 percent of Japan's fuel oil and 25–30 percent of her crude and heavy oils.

By the time Tom got to Australia in June 1944, "Z" Special operations in Borneo were already being focused on making AIF's northern Borneo invasion easier, by going in ahead and passing intelligence to "Z" Special advance headquarters on Morotai (in the Halmaheras, 700 miles east of Borneo). The "Z" Special operatives were to report on Japanese installations and troop movements, the Bornean terrain, and the reception that the AIF landing forces could expect from the local people.

Tom's mission was to lead one of the parties of "Z" Special unit's Operation SEMUT (Malay for "ant," pronounced "smoot," rhymes with "foot") into the mountains of north-central Borneo. Arriving three months ahead, the SEMUT parties would try to gain intelligence about Japanese concentrations inland from Brunei Bay and any other information that could facilitate the AIF's Ninth Division landings in Brunei Bay in early June.

The plan had been for SEMUT to reach Borneo by submarine and go inland from the coast up the rivers that were that tropical island's only highways. Tom believed such a plan was almost certain to fail. He reasoned that any place he and his men tried to come ashore along Borneo's coast would be visible to the Japanese or to people in league with them. Even if the SEMUT operatives could get ashore there and start up one of the large rivers, they would surely be discovered. (That proved to be the fate of most of "Z" Special unit's operations arriving by sea in Japanese-occupied Malaya, Borneo, and elsewhere in insular Southeast Asia.)

The people who lived along Borneo's coast and on the banks of the rivers for as far inland as they were navigable were primarily ethnic Chinese and Malays. The Malays and Chinese had usually collaborated with the European colonizers, and now most of them did so with the Japanese. The Japanese dealt savagely with those who did not. In October 1943 local Chinese helped by Dayaks in British North Borneo carried out a well-organized rebellion and took and held Jesselton (now known as Kota Kinabalu) until driven out by Japanese forces. "This led to the execution of hundreds of Chinese by the Japanese and to harsher treatment of the civilians generally, with the result that many died of disease and malnutrition."

But inland and upriver from the last big market towns, lived (and still live) most of the non-Malay indigenous people of Borneo. These were the subcoastal Dayaks* and the *orang ulu* ("upriver people"), some of whom Tom had come to know in 1932. These people were ex-headhunters, and their way of life was entirely different from that of the coastal people.

Why not drop by parachute far inland, at the headwaters of northern Borneo's rivers, Tom wondered. "How could it fail to be both safer and easier to move from the inside outwards? *Down* the rivers, starting in areas of known toughness. . . ?" (By "toughness," Tom meant that the inland peoples, unlike the coastal Malays and Chinese, had retained their tribal vigor and had not been softened by the civilizing hand of Europeans.) "These strong energetic, warm-hearted, generous minded Borneo people possessed a *positive* affection for the symbols of power and a comparatively small regard for personal comfort or absolute safety." In 1932 Tom had been struck by the friendly feeling that the Kenyahs, Berawans and Kayans (*orang ulu* of the Tinjar, Baram, and upper Rejang) had for white men, "through the good will built up in a century of White Rajah Brooke rule." He hoped the other *orang ulu* who lived even further inland might feel similarly.

He argued that even the terrain was more suitable for guerrilla action than that further downriver. As he remembered from his 1932 travels, the means of communications were slender inside the sparsely settled uplands of Borneo where the *orang ulu* lived. Although goods were transported along the shallow rivers by dugout canoes rowed, poled, and portaged past rapids, most news and messages were passed by people walking over mountains and along narrow jungle paths to the next longhouse or to the headwaters of the next river. Tom reasoned that communications across a wide area within the far interior were possible if one had local guides. If the SEMUT operatives could win the local people (especially the local chiefs) to their side, they would find it relatively easy to control access to their camp. Furthermore,

---

*The term "Dayak" is used by outsiders for the non-Muslim indigenous peoples of Borneo. Residents of Sarawak use the term "Dayak" only for the subcoastal longhouse peoples, that is the Iban (some of whom are called "Sea Dayaks") and Bidayuh (formerly "Land Dayaks"). They use the term "*orang ulu*" for such longhouse groups as Kenyah, Kayan, Kelabit, and Lun Dayeh (formerly "Murut") and nomads, such as the Penan (and/or Punan); these groups make up under 6 percent of Sarawak's population, and they live upriver from the Dayaks. This book follows Sarawak usage.

they could keep word of the white men's presence from leaking out to the Japanese downriver and along the coast.

In making the case for being dropped from the air far inside Borneo, Tom was arguing not only against the military doctrine of Australian Special Operations at that time, which strongly favored insertion from the coast, but also against the strong aversion to parachuting of his commanding officer, Major Toby Carter. Carter, a courteous, soft-spoken, long, lean New Zealander with prewar experience in Sarawak as a Shell engineer, had been the first officer for the SEMUT operation to arrive on the scene at "Z" Special headquarters in Melbourne and thus was senior to Tom, who had arrived next. Bill Sochon, a portly middle-aged prison official in England, who also had British Borneo experience, arrived a few weeks after Tom and became the number three major of the group. But, as Tom confessed in *World Within*:

> My ego could hardly be kept out of this. . . . [When first engaged by SOE] I had been given to understand that I should be on my own. . . . The attractions of working under somebody else—especially one of a gentler and nicer character—did not seduce. I must not disguise the point, therefore: my energies were expended not only in proving the parachute approach feasible, but in claiming the privilege, if this plan were agreed, that I go in first (whoever commanded).

A bit of luck came Tom's way with the assignment to "Z" Special, to begin in February 1945, of a special flight of six B-24 Liberator long-range aircraft with Royal Australian Air Force (RAAF) crews. The Liberator had the range to get to Borneo and back to Mindoro, Philippines, which the Americans had by then liberated, or to Morotai, still further away to the east, where "Z" Special had its forward headquarters. Most important, the Liberator was a big aircraft capable of dropping parachutists and heavy supplies. For the first time, the possibility of parachuting men into north-central Borneo existed.

Still to be overcome for Tom's plan to be adopted was the lack of reliable maps. Moreover, the far interior did not seem a promising area for parachute drops. The terrain of north-central Borneo consisted of sharp mountain peaks surrounded by primary and secondary jungle. The occasional hill rice field might look like a possible drop zone from the air, but, because of the methods used in slash-and-burn rice farming, the fields were likely to have many hidden tree stumps that could act like stakes in a bear trap if parachutists were to land on them. Nonetheless, Tom won permission to look into the matter further, to see if it would in fact be possible to drop men into the middle of Borneo with some hope that they would survive the drop and be able to carry out a mission worth the risk and the resources.

Plowing into everything he could find on the subject in the Melbourne Library, he came across an article written in 1911 for the *Sarawak Museum*

*Journal (SMJ)* that gave the first clue that parachutes might be possible. An officer of the Brooke Raj named Douglas had accompanied a pacification expedition against some outlaw Kelabit tribesmen who had raided and killed Sarawak subjects. In his article, he described these Kelabits as "living right in the very centre of Borneo" in a sort of no-man's land on the border between Sarawak and Dutch territory. The area where they lived was across the Tamabo Range in a great plain, known as the Plain of Bah, between two and three thousand feet above sea level, bounded by mountain ranges on three sides, with the headwaters of the Baram River on the fourth. Coming across irrigated rice fields with crops in various stages of ripeness, Douglas was astonished that "these Kelabits, the wildest and farthest from civilization of all the tribes in Borneo, should be the only interior people to irrigate their fields and, therefore, are able to obtain two crops of rice in the year."

Finding this article was like winning the lottery. If Douglas could be believed, here was a big tableland high enough to be not too hot, protected on four sides from surprise raids of any size, with flat, open, wet rice fields ideal as drop zones. For wet rice farming, unlike for hill rice slash-and-burn farming, all the big tree stumps would have been removed. Confirmation came from no less an authority than E. Banks, the museum curator who had been Tom's rival for power on the 1932 Oxford expedition. Banks had visited the longhouse of Bario, on the Plain of Bah, in 1937 (by which time the plain belonged to Sarawak) and had written an *SMJ* article in which he described the terrain as "flat as a board, covered with long grass or scrub vegetation where not cultivated." Banks thought that he could "scarcely imagine a more ideal spot for European occupation if only more accessible."

That was all very well, Tom's "Z" Special unit bosses said, but what about the people on the Dutch side of the border, less than a day's walk from the Plain of Bah? For information about this, Tom sought the help of a Mr. Knox, the editor of a local paper, the Melbourne *Argus*. Knox had formerly been director of military intelligence of the Australian army, and Tom had come to know him in late 1944 when, finding his commando training mere repetition of what he had already learned in England, he had used some spare time to write a series of twenty-one amusing, insightful, and provocative articles for the *Argus*, giving an Englishman's view of Australians. For wartime security reasons, Tom had used a nom de plume and had chosen one that was typically self-assertive: "Lt. Col. I. M. English."

Knox had been impressed by the I. M. English articles and was happy to dig in the military intelligence files, coming up with a report to the Shell Company written just before the war by an oil geologist, Dr. W. F. Schneeberger, a Swiss with anthropological interests, who had explored precisely the area Tom was interested in. In his report to Shell, Schneeberger described a series of plains across the mountains into Dutch Borneo some twenty to fifty miles east of Sarawak's Plain of Bah. The Swiss geologist found these plains fairly densely populated by a pagan people, similar to the Kelabits, who were equally self-sufficient and who also planted wet rice on their large flat fields.

Coming on top of the earlier material, the Schneeberger report was enough to get Tom permission to go in an American Liberator to the U.S. base on the island of Morotai. Once there, he hoped to find a way to fly over northern Borneo to see what could be seen of the Plain of Bah from the air. On January 14, 1945, he got a ride from the American base on Morotai in a U.S. Navy Liberator that was looking for another Navy Liberator that had gone missing the previous day while patrolling over Brunei Bay. After the pilot had searched for the missing plane without success, he allowed Tom and an RAAF squadron leader who had accompanied him to guide the plane inland to get their first glimpse from the air of north-central Borneo. They saw the twin gleaming white rock pinnacles, like two fingers pointing upward, of a very steep mountain over 6,000 feet high, some ten or more miles north/northwest of where Banks' article had indicated they would find the village of Bario on the Plain of Bah. The mountain was not on any of their maps, so they called it Mount 200, in honor of the about-to-be-formed special "Flight 200" of Liberators for "Z" Special operations.

On their only hour of fuel over Borneo before they had to turn back toward Morotai, in the area where they had hoped to find the Kelabit country, they at first saw mountains, gorges, and heavy dark green forest canopy, but nothing worth considering as a drop zone. Tom later recalled: "We did rather uncertainly see patches of paler and brighter colour and what looked like small ponds, a few minutes' flying south-east of those twin white pinnacles." But then, "after crossing an impressive double range east again, suddenly several miles of open grassland [appeared] in a very deep, steep mountain valley." The squadron leader took a picture of this valley, a splendid-looking drop zone. He and Tom—and those to whom they showed the picture—were satisfied that this was the Plain of Bah.

The old "Z" Special plan to go in by submarine and folboat was now dropped. Tom's researches were rewarded. He was given the privilege of heading the reconnaissance party of eight operatives who would be the first to drop into Borneo, onto the Plain of Bah, near the Kelabit longhouse at Bario. Tom's party was thereafter called SEMUT 1 and its transport would be provided by two RAAF Liberators of "Z" Special's new Flight 200.

It had taken time to put all the pieces of this new plan together. It was already mid-March 1945 when Tom's dream of being the "first white man to drop into Borneo" began to seem close to fulfillment. Before he and the others left Australia, "Z" Special pulled off the coup of producing Dr. Werner Schneeberger in the flesh. The Swiss had been brought from Wyoming via San Francisco, Pearl Harbor, Canton Island, Fiji, Auckland, and Sydney, through cyclones in unpressurized B-24s, so that Tom could ask him questions about the people and terrain of inland Borneo. Much of the oil man's information proved helpful, but (according to Tom), Schneeberger also suggested that instead of bringing money to pay for the food and labor of the local people, the parachutists would be better advised to bring things the local people needed and did not make themselves, such as needles and fish hooks. "Z" Special thereupon rushed round to supply Tom and his party with 50,000 fish hooks and a quarter of a million needles.

After this final briefing on March 15, Tom and the seven others in his party left Australia, via Darwin and "Z" Special's advance headquarters on Morotai, for the American airfield at San Jose, Mindoro Island, Philippines. He and his SEMUT 1 team had then spent most of a week in a vain and dangerous attempt, flying over enemy-held land and sea, to find their drop zone under the clouds obscuring the Plain of Bah. At dawn, he would board Squadron Leader Pockley's plane and set off on a third try.

Lying in the sand during this long night of reflection before beginning a new adventure, Tom looked back on his career in England with Mass-Observation. He told Pockley, the companion of his vigil, how ashamed he felt of the way he had courted the limelight. If he ever got out of Borneo, he intended to "return to Mass-Observation and Lancashire with a new dedication." He was determined that, this time, "I must not, I must not (I said) let myself get caught up again in the whirl of ambition, publicity, money and facile prestige which had seemed to be wished upon me against my own better sense."

# Chapter 20

## SEMUT 1: Impact of Ants

A few hours later, Tom and seven other SEMUT* 1 operatives strapped into parachutes were over central Borneo waiting to jump into the Plain of Bah. Major Tom Harrisson, Commanding Officer of SEMUT 1, was in the first plane with three Australians. His second in command, Captain Eric (Ric) Edmeades, a twenty-three-year-old New Zealander, an athletic ex-paratrooper with a hundred jumps behind him, was in the other with the remaining three Australian special operatives.

Again, Mount 200's two white fingers were a visual checkpoint for the flight crew. Having identified the mountain, they flew south. As on previous flights, the clouds came quickly up over the land and started to obscure the place some 90 miles southeast of Brunei, where Bario, on the Plain of Bah, was supposed to be. Nonetheless, at 0719 local time, Tom slid from the aircraft, followed by Sergeants Fred Sanderson, Doug Bower, and Keith Barrie. The second plane dropped its four operatives, and both planes released their "storepedos," (RAAF parachute containers for up to 250 pounds of goods), and headed back to Mindoro. (Weeks later, Tom would learn that Pockley's plane had never got home. It was eventually found crashed, with its thirteen bodies aboard, in East Timor.)

"Drifting nervously down through the damp cloud," Tom recalled, "we saw below us . . . two red deer going for their lives." Tom and the three men with him landed in a soft wet bog near an area cleared for wet-rice farming. Ric Edmeades and the others from the second Liberator were nowhere to be seen, nor were the storepedos.

Sergeant Sanderson, a Eurasian, was Tom's "contact man." He had looked around as he descended and seen a longhouse some way off to the west. Upon landing, "Sandy" went ahead without waiting for orders—he sel-

---

*As has been mentioned earlier, *semut* means "ant" in Malay.

dom bothered with orders—to make a cautious reconnaissance of the long-house and, if the situation looked favorable, to introduce himself as the advance man for the SEMUT 1 party, using his Malay.

Tom and the other two men stood and waited. Soon "there appeared three tall, dark figures wearing loincloths and with leopard teeth in their ears, wading through the swamp, and waving (of all things) a white flag. . . ." They spoke no English or Malay but showed their friendliness by accepting and smoking the cigarettes the strangers proffered them. They led Tom, Bower, and Barrie through the swamp onto an open grassland plain and then to a longhouse, which, the parachutists learned from Sandy who was there to meet them, was indeed Bario, the place where they had meant to land.

The headman of the Bario longhouse in 1945 later recalled how that day he had seen "Tom Harrisson and his colleagues mysteriously floating down out of the sky. . . ." The longhouse people had been very anxious, and in the hasty conference several of them had urged killing the parachutists but had been overruled by the *penghulu* (native "chief" responsible to the Sarawak government for the non-Malay indigenous peoples of a certain area or group of longhouses). The *penghulu* had produced the white flag.

As Tom and the others approached the raised timber and bamboo long-house with their three-man escort, they saw that it would make a good SEMUT 1 headquarters, if the inhabitants were willing. The building was on a high rise, and one could see anyone approaching a long way off.

Ignoring the howls of mongrels and pig grunts coming from below, the group climbed the notched log that served as a ladder to the main floor. The light inside the longhouse, filtered through woven palm-leaf walls and glancing off the bamboo floors and woven mats, was dull gold. So too was the skin of the men's hairless well-muscled bodies, bare but for loin cloths; so too were the women's bare breasts above their thigh-length bark or woven cotton skirts.

Most of the men had elongated earlobes, as in statues of the Buddha, with ornaments such as leopard's teeth stuck in the upper lobes and heavy brass earrings extending the lower lobes almost to the shoulder. Almost all the men had a machete-like *parang* hanging from a belt at the waist. The women's faces were paler than the men's, and their lower earlobes were so stretched by heavy brass ornaments that the long loops of skin reached to their nipples. Some girls had spidery designs tattooed from their toes up to the top of their thighs that looked from a distance like black lace stockings. Against the wall were big, dark, ancient-looking, high-shouldered Chinese porcelain jars. Some of these, Tom could guess, would hold the home-brewed rice beer (*borak*) that the *orang ulu* liked to drink. In a rack hung above the veranda lay several old skeletal heads from the last head-hunting raids decades earlier.

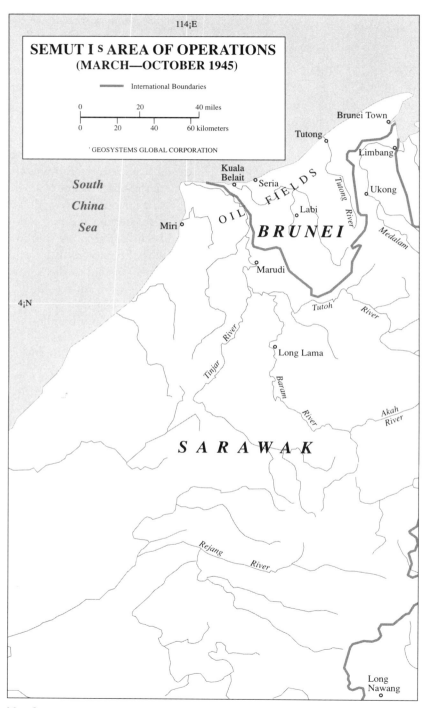

# SEMUT I S AREA OF OPERATIONS
## (MARCH—OCTOBER 1945)

——— International Boundaries

| 0 | 20 | 40 miles |
|---|----|----|
| 0 | 20 | 40 | 60 kilometers |

˙ GEOSYSTEMS GLOBAL CORPORATION

114¡E

Brunei Town

Tutong

Limbang

*South*

*China*

Ukong

Kuala
Belait

Seria

*Tutong River*

O I L   F I E L D S

*Sea*

Labi

*BRUNEI*

*Medalam*

Miri

4¡N

Marudi

*Tutoh*

*River*

*River*

Long Lama

*Tinjar*

*Baram*

*Akah
River*

*River*

*S A R A W A K*

*Rejang*

*River*

Long
Nawang

Map 2

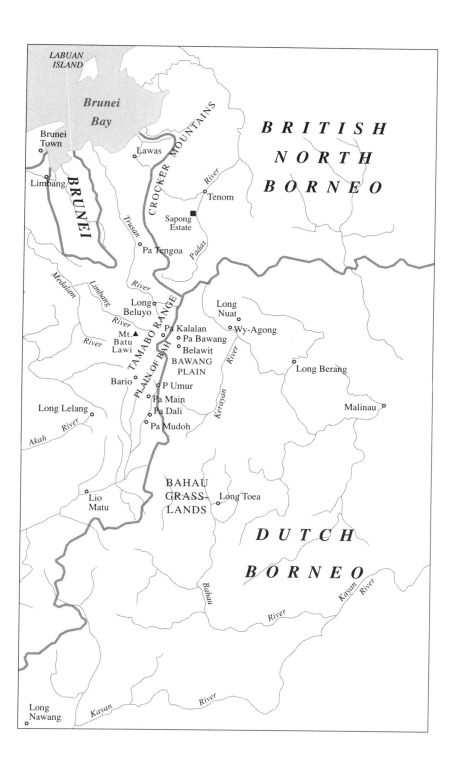

LABUAN ISLAND

Brunei Bay

Brunei Town

Limbang

BRUNEI

Lawas

CROCKER MOUNTAINS

BRITISH NORTH BORNEO

River

Tenom

Sapong Estate

Trusan

Pa Tengoa

Padas

Medalam

Limbang

River

River

Long Beluyo

Mt. Batu Lawi

Pa Kalalan

Pa Bawang

Belawit

BAWANG PLAIN

Bario

P Umur

Pa Main

Pa Dali

Pa Mudoh

Long Lelang

Akah River

River

TAMABO RANGE

PLAIN OF BAH

Long Nuat

Wy-Agong

River

Kerayan

Long Berang

Malinau

Lio Matu

BAHAU GRASS-LANDS

Long Toea

DUTCH BORNEO

Bahau

River

Kayan River

Long Nawang

Kayan

River

In all these respects, Tom was reminded of the people and longhouses he had learned to love in 1932.

The enthusiasm of his SEMUT 1 colleagues was less pronounced. Sanderson, in spite of his familiarity with Southeast Asia, was appalled at the dirt everywhere and at the toilet arrangements. As he recalls, members of both sexes came out to the edge of the veranda, "hung their backsides over the edge and let go! The instant the excreta hit the mud there was a rush of pigs" which, he found later, explained the special flavor of the local pork.

With Sandy's help, Tom was soon in conversation with the elders of the longhouse. The *penghulu*, an older mild-mannered Kelabit named Lawai Besara, who spoke some Malay, told his young men to go out and try to find the rest of the SEMUT 1 party and all the storepedos while he entertained the visitors. The young Kelabits had already brought in the contents of some of the storepedos when the parachutists from the second Liberator—Capt. Ric Edmeades, Sgt. Jack Tredrea, Sgt. Kel Hallam, and W. O. Rod Cusack—arrived at noon, after four hours spent hacking their way through jungle swamp to cover the three miles to Bario.

Tom and his deputy Ric Edmeades, with Sandy as interpreter, spent the afternoon inside the longhouse consulting with the Kelabit elders. SEMUT 1's assignment was to build an intelligence network in north-central Borneo to help the Australian Ninth Division prepare its early June invasion of the island of Labuan and the nearby coast of northwest Borneo. Tom was also supposed to try to convince the inland tribespeople to stop providing food and labor for Japanese occupation forces. But, finding an enthusiastic reception for these requests, he went beyond his instructions and told his Bario hosts he was ready to accept volunteers as guerrilla fighters against the Japanese.

While he discussed these ideas with the longhouse elders, most of the others of SEMUT 1 went out with their Kelabit helpers to locate, stow, and distribute the contents of the dropped storepedos. The two radio operators tried to put together the "Boston" wireless, which had been damaged in the drop. The *penghulu* sent runners to villages 20 miles around, and by nightfall some 500 people had come to see the arrivals.

Lian Labang, an eighteen-year-old Kelabit from a nearby longhouse, hearing that "strangers had come to Bario, had dropped into it out from the sky," came to Bario to see them:

> I was just a boy. We did not know if they were Japanese, if they were Europeans. But we went. And it was only when we reached Bario that we learned for the first time that they were white people. We met them. Tom Harrisson spoke Malay, and one of them named Sandy spoke Malay well.
>
> And the Kelabits all came to Bario to see Tom Harrisson. And he called the people from the Kelabit area together and asked what they thought about the

Japanese. He called on the Kelabits to volunteer to become guerrillas against the Japanese. So many people, including myself, decided to do it. . . .

When Tom Harrisson arrived in Bario he had with him pictures that he must have gotten from the Sarawak Museum of people and houses from the old days in the Kelabit country. He showed these pictures of Kelabit penghulus and heads of longhouses from olden times and other pictures of Kelabits. And the Kelabits quickly decided, "This is a good man, who already knows so much about the Kelabits."

The Kelabits thought they were the only people in this area like themselves. But Harrisson brought pictures of Kayans and Kenyahs and people from as far away as Papua New Guinea. And the Kelabits thought: "These are people like us—no clothes." And he showed them the pictures from New Guinea and explained that not everybody lives in this one country, that the place the Kelabits lived is Borneo and that these other people [Papuans] lived halfway to Australia and nobody of our people knew about these other places, such as Australia, at that time. They found what Harrisson said very interesting.

The Kelabits told their visitors of the Japanese attack on the north coast of Borneo in December 1941. Aside from rounding up all upcountry white missionaries and officers of the Brooke Raj, however, the tribesmen said that things in inland Sarawak had gone on as usual under the Rajah's native administrative staff until 1943. Then, the shortage of food on the coast had led the Japanese to demand rice from the *orang ulu*. The Japanese had not bothered the people living on the Plain of Bah since 1942; they were too far inland to make it worthwhile. But the war having blocked imports meant that the Kelabits could no longer get the cloth, thread, medicine, and other trade goods they wanted. Luckily, unlike many of Borneo's people at that time, the Kelabits had their own iodized salt springs and still knew how to make their own knives, bark cloth, and other necessities, so they could survive without imported goods. With their two crops a year of irrigated rice, they did not go hungry. The other *orang ulu* were not so fortunate. Unlike the Kelabits, the others grew only hill rice and had just enough to feed themselves; Japanese demands for food and labor were a real hardship to them.

Then, beginning in mid-1944, occasional American and Australian airplanes had appeared in the sky. In late 1944 and early 1945 a couple of shot-up American planes had crashed, and their occupants were found by the Lun Bawang (also called Lun Dayeh, and then also known as Murut). These tribesmen, the Kelabits' cousins over the border on the Dutch side, had helped hide most of the airmen. The Kelabits had heard that the Japanese and the local police under their orders had dealt harshly with people suspected of helping the airmen and that more than a dozen Lun Bawang had died in Japanese custody.

Yet despite the risks, and even though the Kelabits were less affected than most Sarawakians by the Japanese occupation, they expressed eagerness to work for SEMUT 1 not merely as spies but also as guerrilla fighters. During the course of discussions that day and the next, it became clear why.

These independent, self-sufficient people still had the warrior's ethic; their songs and stories told of headhunting raids that their parents and grandparents and great-grandparents had led. They had not taken heads in decades, but their religious rituals were still based on the central symbol of the outsider's head being brought back in triumph to the longhouse, to be sung and danced over, smoked and "fed," before eventually being given an honored place on the rack above the veranda. The government of the White Rajah Brooke had banned headhunting but otherwise held the Kelabits by the lightest of reins. The Brooke Raj had protected them against the depredations of other tribes, against commercial exploitation by more sophisticated peoples from the coast, and from unwanted proselytizing by missionaries, while ensuring them free access to trade goods, making the Kelabits kindly disposed to white people.

The Kelabits saw in SEMUT 1's arrival from the skies a new authority that would not only permit but would actively encourage a return to the sacred and thrilling headhunting raids of their songs and legends. As the good news spread, Kelabits and other former headhunters streamed to the SEMUT banner.

Having decided to let Tom and his colleagues stay with them, the Kelabits next had to choose appropriate names by which to address their guests. They soon dismissed the idea that Tom and his fellow parachutists might be gods or spirits, but some of the tribesmen wondered if the major's crown that Tom had put on his cap meant that he might be a "rajah," an idea that appealed to Tom. The Kelabits, however, soon learned that he was a Major and thereafter called him *Tuan Mayor*. (*Tuan*, meaning "lord," was the courtesy title used in the Malay-speaking world for any white man; *Mayor* was pronounced "my-ore.")

That first evening, Penghulu Lawai Besara and the people of Bario, along with visitors from the nearby longhouses of Pa Trap and P'Umur, welcomed the SEMUT 1 team formally with traditional singing, dancing, and drinking of copious amounts of *borak*. That night, while Sergeant Hallam slept after an exhausting day followed by a bibulous evening, the dogs ate through his left boot.

The next day, while the two radio operators continued to struggle with the wireless set, the rest of the SEMUT team, helped by dozens of Kelabits, located storepedos containing more than a ton of arms and equipment. They built several lean-tos in which they stashed spare material. Other such sheds were made into sleeping platforms, to avoid implicating the residents of

Bario if outsiders arrived and to keep the SEMUT party's things out of reach of the longhouse dogs.

Visitors came all day from other longhouses on the Plain of Bah, from Pa Main, Pa Mudoh, Pa Dali. The man appointed by the Brooke regime as chief of the southern Kelabits, Penghulu Miri, swept in from Pa Dali and took charge of the SEMUT 1 party. He produced delicious coffee sweetened with honey, had cassava flour pancakes cooked for them, and—most important—provided a torrent of good advice in fluent Malay. He suggested that, as a goodwill gesture, Sergeant Tredrea, SEMUT 1's "medic," make a tour of the longhouses of the Plain of Bah to treat illness. Tom agreed, and Tredrea, a tough, handsome, charming towhead, became the most popular person in north-central Sarawak over the next three months, giving injections for yaws, lancing boils, and treating dysentery while picking up intelligence about Japanese movements. He also recruited and trained a force of thirty Sarawak Ibans in the use of his Bren machine gun, Owen and Austin submachine guns, and .303 rifles.

That evening a great feast was held in the Bario longhouse with vast quantities of food, more music and dance, and much more *borak* than the night before. Tom, realizing it was now time for him to respond to his host, Penghulu Lawai Besara, and the chief's assembled colleagues, friends, and relations, literally rose to the occasion. Standing with folded hands, he bent his head forward and intoned a kind of prayer of thanksgiving in the style of an Anglican clergyman before leading his assorted "ants" in a sort of "conga" line while they sang in unison the only songs all eight of them knew: "Three Blind Mice," "Silent Night," "She'll Be Coming 'Round the Mountain," and, as an encore after the *borak* got to them, an Army ditty best remembered for its refrain, "Fuck 'em all, fuck 'em all, The long and the short and the tall." After the frustration of five days' preparation to drop, the terror of the fall through the clouds into the unknown, and the pleasure of being so warmly welcomed, the SEMUT 1 men were euphoric with relief and *borak*. Ric Edmeades remarked to another member of the party that evening, "What a wonderful way to go to war."

This warm reception was to color Tom's—and SEMUT 1's—view of their mission. From then on, along with the things they were being asked to do by "Z" Special unit headquarters, Tom and his men felt a special responsibility to look out for the welfare of their hosts. This attitude, applied to cannibals and the British working class, had got Tom in trouble with the social science establishment and with Whitehall in Britain and would get him in trouble with the Australian Military establishment.

The next day, their third in Borneo, the two wireless specialists tapped out their first message to the wireless relay station at Darwin telling it to notify "Z" Special headquarters in Melbourne that SEMUT 1 had arrived safely. Tom and Sandy stayed at Bario, but most of the others spread out either along the Plain of Bah or toward Long Lelang, past the headwaters of the Tutoh River catchment, where Major Carter was supposed to set up Operation SEMUT's Borneo headquarters once he arrived to take over command (see the map of SEMUT 1 on pp. 182–183).

That evening, with Sandy's help, Tom and the chiefs of longhouses for many miles in all directions met in Bario and conferred. Tom handed out some cloth and other trade goods as well as some of the gold sovereigns he had been given in Australia to help co-opt local support and devalue the Japanese paper currency. He found that the chiefs liked guns better than gold and learned from them that there was, sadly, no truth to stories of escaped Allied POWs. He told them to tell their people that the white man was coming back to Borneo but that they should not let the Japanese learn of the presence of the SEMUT 1 party. They should instruct their people no longer to supply any foodstuffs to the agents of the Japanese who came to the upriver market towns demanding them. They should spread rumors of crop failures to avoid reprisals.

Furthermore—and this was a hard idea for Tom to get across to them—they must not, MUST not, go downriver and attack the Japanese yet. That time would come later. Meanwhile, they could pick off Japanese patrols that ventured into the far interior, provided they were discreet about it.

For discreet jungle warfare, the *orang ulu* had the perfect weapon. Although in the past it had been used only on animals, it was deadly against everything from a hornbill bird to a Bornean rhino. This was the *sempit*, the bamboo blowpipe used with poisoned darts. One of SEMUT 1's irregulars described the effect of this weapon: "If a man is shot with a firearm he may not necessarily die; however if he is hit with a poisoned dart, even on a finger or toe, he is [inevitably, though not right away] . . . *sudah mati* (already dead)."

The Japanese were good soldiers and nearly tireless walkers, but the jungle and mountain trails were too narrow for anything but walking in single file. The *orang ulu* with their long knives and blowpipes could position themselves in the brush near either end of a two-to-three-mile stretch of trail that the Japanese patrol would use to move inland. Other hidden blowpipers and parang-wielding warriors, thinly scattered the length of the ambush route, would wait, as quietly as they would wait for deer, until they could pick off the patrolling Japanese, silently, one by one. By this means, *orang ulu* working for SEMUT wiped out every Japanese patrol that ventured upriver during the months before the Australian landings so that no Japanese were left to tell the story.

Spreading the word about SEMUT's presence to potential local supporters while keeping it a secret from the Japanese was not easy but was helped by the fact that the various SEMUT parties soon had downriver agents—

often Malay, Chinese, or Dayak—whose overt jobs were in positions of trust with the Japanese. When the Japanese patrols sent upriver did not return, these agents would offer plausible explanations and would secretly warn the SEMUT operatives when and where to expect Japanese search parties on follow-up missions.

On Tom's fifth day in Borneo, he left Bario accompanied by an Australian sergeant to make a tour of all the other longhouses on the Plain of Bah. He was back in Bario in three days, having incidentally established his reputation among the Kelabits as a great walker. The next day he began the same route and completed his tour in half the time. Tom's walking prowess was already known to his Australian colleagues. Once during training, he had set off with a trim twenty-one-year-old Australian corporal to cover 90 miles across the Baw Baw Range east of Melbourne in three days carrying sixty-pound packs. As the amazed corporal, the veteran of four years of hard fighting in Europe, later bore witness, Tom would jog barefoot through the snow, slush, and sleet for a hundred yards, then walk the next hundred, for the entire three days.

Back at Bario, Tom heard more reports supporting earlier rumors that some downed American airmen were being hidden by the Lun Bawang over the border. And so, on April 5, he started off eastward to cross the border mountains into Dutch territory. His diary notes that it was "hard going" even in dry weather. "Nearly all hill jungle, up and down, steep. Few bridges, many leeches. . . ." The next day he was on the Bawang Plain. He turned north toward the longhouse at Belawit, home of the senior leader of the Lun Bawang natives of the Bawang Plain, Penghulu Lasong Piri.

Walking parallel to the border mountains the length of the Bawang Plain, Tom, as he approached Belawit, came to wonder if the great flat plain he had seen from the air back in January—the photograph of which had convinced his bosses that an airdrop into the Plain of Bah was possible—was not the Plain of Bah at all but this beautiful rice-and-cattle-rich Bawang Plain Schneeberger had written about. (It was not, in fact. He would have to wait several months before finding the plain he had seen from the air and had thought was Bah.) In any case, he now realized that the plain he had seen in January had been in Dutch Borneo. He may also have realized his good fortune that nobody at "Z" Special unit headquarters had known that they were being shown a photograph of a plain in Dutch Borneo. "Z" Special headquarters would have been reluctant to ask the Dutch government-in-exile for permission to conduct this kind of intrusive operation in their part of the island.

For now, however, the border mattered not at all. The Bawang Plain looked even better than Bario as a base of operations. The potential labor supply was much bigger, since four times as many people lived on the Dutch side of Borneo's central mountains as lived on the Sarawak side. The only reasonable access to the Bawang Plain from the coast was via the upper

Trusan River, making the plain fairly easy to protect from enemy troops moving inland. There was plenty of food: in addition to ample supplies of rice and cattle, the ponds and streams of the Bawang Plain held "largish fish," as Tom noted, and all sorts of fruits and vegetables grew nearby.

These cousins to the Kelabit, the Lun Bawang—who spoke the same language as the Kelabits and grew rice in much the same way—had been successfully missionized by North American evangelicals. In 1942, they had watched with horror as the missionaries and their families had been dragged off and murdered by the Japanese. The result, to Tom's surprise, was that the Christianized Lun Bawang tribesmen were more bloodthirstily ready to attack the Japanese than were the most pagan among the Kelabits.

At Belawit, Tom was welcomed by Penghulu Lasong Piri, the most senior chief of the Lun Bawang, a squat, strong, middle-aged man with the "large head and emphatic chin" that Tom found often went with Bornean aristocracy. Although Tom would never be as comfortable with this colonized, Christianized native chief as with more untouched pagan chiefs, such as Penghulu Lawai Bisara or Penghulu Miri, he found Lasong Piri equally willing to use his prestige to endorse SEMUT 1 and to forbid his people to betray these white men to the Japanese.

On April 6, the day Tom arrived at Lasong Piri's longhouse, came the news that Tom had crossed the mountains to get: specific word about the whereabouts and condition of downed American airmen. It came in the form of a letter delivered by a Celebes-born Christianized native officer of the Dutch colonial government based at Long Berang, well to the east of the Bawang Plain. The letter, written in the round Palmer Method penmanship taught in American schools in those days and dated April 3, 1945, read:

> Dear Sir:
>
> We just received word that . . . you . . . have landed in Borneo for the purpose of organizing the natives in warfare against the Japs. There are nine of us here at Pa Silau [a day's walk from Long Berang]—seven of us from a US Army B24 which was shot down November 16 [1944] and two from a Navy B24 shot down Jan. 13 [1945].
>
> We are staying with William Makahanap [who delivered the letter]. . . . Under his supervision the natives here have killed all Japs that have come into this area. . . . Several of us are in need of medical aid and naturally we would like to get out of here as soon as possible. If there is any way that you could send word out so that we might receive some supplies or possibly be picked up some place, we would appreciate it very much. We hope to see or hear from you soon.

It was signed by 2d Lt. Philip R. Corrin and eight other American airmen.

# Chapter 21

## Moving Out

This letter was just what Tom had hoped for. It gave the whereabouts of the downed American airmen. More important, it gave solid evidence that Borneans further east in Dutch Borneo were as likely to support SEMUT 1 as were the people of the Bawang Plain. With this news, he decided to move his headquarters from Bario, Sarawak, across the border mountains into Dutch Borneo. The news also posed a new problem: how to get the Americans out of Borneo.

For the moment, all he could do was send medicine and some "comforts," such as cigarettes, chocolates, and whisky, to Corrin and the eight men with him. He also arranged for Sandy to go to see another two American airmen, U.S. Navy men too ill to be moved from Long Nuat, where they were being hidden by another man from the Celebes, a Christian missionary teacher.

While preparing to move his headquarters eastward and trying to figure out how to get the downed Americans back to the Philippines, Tom spread his own men out as far as he could. He had his deputy, Ric Edmeades, quarter the jungles of northern Borneo on foot, following a different river each time.

Everywhere Edmeades went, he recruited secret agents and guerrillas. Halfway down the Trusan, he met a tribesman who had scars on his legs from torture he received for having helped some downed U.S. Navy airmen try to escape. The man had walked up to Pa Tengoa on hearing of the white men's presence in order to join Edmeades's irregulars. He brought with him so many pineapples, bananas, and other gifts that he could hardly walk. Edmeades himself was finding the walking hard because of chafing between his legs that led him to take off his shorts and underpants and go about dressed solely in a towel wrapped around his waist, held in place by his gun belt.

Tom was pleased with Edmeades's performance thus far. Indeed, he was pleased with them all. He had tested their mettle and found it strong and supple enough for the ambitious job he had in mind. He later said that he preferred Australians to Englishmen for such work because of their physical endurance and because they could think for themselves without waiting for orders. In addition to having his operatives recruit agents and collect intelligence, he had them form the native volunteers who were flocking to their banner into a disciplined guerrilla force able to attack enemy forces when and where SEMUT 1 wanted.

The brief training that Tom and his colleagues had themselves received in "Special Operations" in Australia seemed to have little relevance to the art of living and working behind enemy lines in central Borneo. This did not bother Tom. He had his own ideas, a few simple rules that managed to infuriate most of the officers and men who worked for him or with him.

The first rule was that none of the SEMUT 1 operatives should wear regular shoes or boots in or near the longhouse, where their presence could be noticed by outsiders. The foreigners' toes were not as splayed as were the natives' toes. But the difference in footprint would only show up on close inspection, whereas the mark of an Army boot would be a dead giveaway to the Japanese or their collaborators. When SEMUT's senior medical officer, Captain "Doc" Ian McCallum, arrived with Toby Carter in mid-April, he was horrified to hear of Tom's rule against shoes. Not only was there the risk of hookworm and other tropical infections but also the dangers of tropical ulcer and snake bite. The region had a remarkable variety of poisonous snakes, from the giant king cobra to the small but equally deadly banded krait. Doc McCallum protested to Tom, who told the doctor that if he tried to countermand that order, he would have him shot. McCallum, who had expected to spend some of his time at SEMUT 1 headquarters, chose to leave Bario within two weeks to dispense his medicine to natives and SEMUT operatives out of shouting distance of "the Mad Major."

Tom's second rule was that the SEMUT 1 operatives should not be provided much, if any, food from SEMUT 1 headquarters. At various times, Tom gave different reasons for this: headquarters did not have enough to spare; there was plenty of food where the SEMUT 1 men were going; he could not ask "Z" Special headquarters to send more food because priority had to be given, when filling the storepedos, to arms, ammunition, and medicine; not carrying food meant that they could travel faster, and it liberated porters to carry arms and other essentials. All these are valid points, but the real reason seems more likely to have been based on Tom's observations of how most white Australians behaved toward nonwhite people in Australia. He knew that his SEMUT 1 operatives had no hope of surviving, much less accomplishing their mission, unless they had the wholehearted support of the local people wherever they stayed. If they could not make the local people like them well enough to feed them, they were as good as dead.

Tom's third rule was to scatter his operatives as far and as fast as possible. Within a day or so of their landing in Borneo, he would break up the SEMUT 1 parties into units of one, two, or at most three operatives, with a handful of local guides, guerrillas, and porters and send them on their way with elaborate and ambitious instructions. When they finished their task and came back to report, he would send them somewhere else. Many of his operatives he saw only twice in Borneo, when they arrived and just before they left.

This policy had several results. First, the SEMUT 1 operatives were rarely in one place long enough to be found easily should any hostile person learn of their presence. Second, because they were so few—one or two SEMUT 1 operatives staying among a group of Borneans often numbering in the hundreds—the newcomers had to learn to blend into the local community. The SEMUT 1 men grew more or less accustomed to the local food and drink; they learned local tracking, hunting, and boating skills; they learned how to walk long distances on jungle tracks and across mountains and streams; they learned to communicate through local language and gesture and how to behave courteously in a number of different tribal cultures. In short, they learned how to live and work effectively in northern Borneo.

Another result of Tom's policy of scattering his operatives thinly over a wide terrain was that it gave Tom, to whom the SEMUT 1 men reported by radio and runner, an extraordinarily complete up-to-date picture of the military and economic situation and the climate of local opinion throughout northern Borneo, from Brunei Bay to Tarakan Island. Drawing on this data, Tom sent frequent wireless messages to "Z" Special headquarters, giving detailed intelligence on enemy troops all along the coast of northern Borneo and recommending specific targets for pinpoint bombing.

The hardships the SEMUT 1 operatives suffered were appalling. They caught malaria and scrub typhus; they went without food for days at a time; some lost a third of their weight from hunger and dysentery; and their skin was often covered with sores. For leaving them without food and other comforts, for forcing them to walk all over Borneo, for never praising them directly or sympathizing with their miserable conditions, a couple of these young men seriously considered murdering Tom. One soldier went so far as to pull out his automatic and threaten Tom with it. Most of them would bear a grudge against him all their lives. But they all survived, every single one of the forty-two operatives who served under Tom in SEMUT 1. And they accomplished more than did the combined participants (with their overall 20 percent casualty rate) in the eighty other Australian Special Operations that "Z" Special unit fielded during World War II. Driver Phil Henry, looking back on his SEMUT 1 days many years later, told me,

We were not given good jungle training. . . . We were very raw. But I think Tom, telling us to go native and live off the land, in a lot of cases probably saved our lives. He said, "You've got to rough it." And when you rough it, you are alert all the time. You aren't sitting playing cards.

Another unusual element in Tom's style of command was that he paid no attention to the rank of his subordinates. To begin, he would give each of his new operatives the same size job, with some allowance made for previous experience or expressed interest. After an initial period of a few weeks, assignments grew or shrank to meet Tom's evaluation of individual performance. Sergeant Sanderson, Corporal Griffiths-Marsh, and Driver (equivalent to Private) Henry got bigger jobs with broader responsibilities than some operatives of officer rank.

Sandy, forever writing notes to Tom complaining of Tom's treatment of himself and others, would have been amazed to know how much Tom appreciated him, referring to him in a report to "Z" Special headquarters as a man "with real brains and a perfect absorption in the job in hand. Really unselfish and good. The only man in the outfit who can give his mind to detail and carry out intelligence work without aid. . . . A first class man in every respect." Others in SEMUT 1 would have been equally surprised to know of Tom's good opinion of them. He would make an instant appraisal of a subordinate but would change his mind if he got new evidence. He held his operatives by a loose rein but did not tolerate purposeless disobedience and sent one man home under "open arrest" for expressly disobeying orders. Tom's dislike of a person or his awareness of that person's animosity toward him did not enter into his appraisals for the record. For example, he could not have been unaware that Cpl. Roland Griffiths-Marsh hated him. Nonetheless, he wrote to "Z" Special unit headquarters that the corporal, though "rather self-opinionated" was "intelligent and tough. A good strong arm type." In writing, Tom had hardly a bad word to say about any of his men, or if so, it was always coupled with something positive. Of one of his men, he wrote to "Z" Special headquarters: "No brains, but plenty of guts. . . . Doing ok. Obeys orders well." Tom worked hard and effectively behind the scenes to get his men promotion and, later on, honors.

Tom knew very well how to court people, how to flatter, how to make them like him. That he deliberately avoided telling his subordinates how highly he regarded them cannot be put down to a natural reticence at praising people to their faces. It may have been Tom's policy to make himself the target of his troops' dislike as a way of molding morale. He claimed to have done that before, on the Borneo Oxford Expedition of 1932. But one is also tempted to think that Tom was trying to model himself on his own conception of how his father, the General, who *was* a diffident man, would have behaved toward his soldiers.

Tom claimed, in a report to SOE: "I have given every individual every support and encouragement for using his own initiative." This was true, if one knew how to interpret Tom's blustering manner. Like all domineering people, Tom had no respect for anyone whom he could bully into making a wrong decision, and he did not excuse the error because he had "ordered" his subordinate to do it. A subordinate was supposed to use his own judgment. If he disobeyed Tom and was proved right, Tom would admire him, though not to his face. If a subordinate used his own judgment in a difficult situation, and his action was not entirely stupid, Tom would back the man against higher authority. Tom's haughty and impatient manner, however, did not endear him to his men.

By mid-April, Tom was too worried about the future of SEMUT's mission to care about such niceties. In Bario, where he had expected to see Toby Carter and his party drop from the skies on April 14 at the latest, he, Sandy, Doug Bower, and the Kelabits waited in vain all day and the next for the sound of the Liberators carrying Carter and seven other operatives of SEMUT 2 to the drop zone on the Plain of Bah. No word had come from "Z" Special headquarters either. Tom and the others began to wonder if "Z" Special had changed its mind about the operation.

They were right to wonder. Although Tom had had his wireless men set up the radio within two days of landing, Carter and the SEMUT 2 party were not getting most of the messages, and those they got were garbled. Bower, though a good Special Operations soldier, had a poor "fist" for sending messages, and Tom was terrible at ciphers. Codes were, Tom later confessed, a "type of mental exercise which is no more my metier than crosswords, mental arithmetic, chess or bridge (all of which I abhor)." The day that Carter and the SEMUT 2 party should have taken off for Borneo from Mindoro, they received a garbled message from SEMUT 1 relayed from Darwin. Bob Long, one of the two cipher experts of the SEMUT 2 party, remembers that "only one phrase of three words was readable—'NOT COME IN'—" before the message trailed off into gibberish again. It could mean that SEMUT 1 was on the run or its radio was being operated by the enemy. Nonetheless, Major Carter in consultation with Major Sochon decided to go ahead with the mission. He told his men that if "anyone thought the mission too dangerous and wanted to drop out, there would be no adverse reflection in their Army record." No one dropped out and, on April 16, SEMUT 2 finally arrived.

Tom's diary entry for April 16 is jubilant: "[SEMUT] 2 IN!!. . . . Bill tore 14 panels. Stores all jungle. [Some] parcels found. Mostly arms. Thank God." The insertion of SEMUT 2 was notable for the sight of all 200 pounds of Maj. Bill Sochon falling through the air from 3,000 feet. After bailing out, Sochon looked up to see, first, seven panels of his parachute tear and, then, seven more panels split while he descended. It seemed miraculous that this portly middle-aged Englishman picked himself up and walked away unhurt. The real miracle was that there were no other casualties from the drop. Major Carter, who had only jumped once in his Richmond parachute course before he quit it, emerged equally unharmed. Almost as remarkable was that none of the other chutes fell apart, in spite of the ruling by the Australian military authorities that all parachutes had to have been used 100 times before being given to "Z" Special. The idea, typical of the regular AIF attitude toward the "Specials," was that giving the chutes to "Z" Special meant losing them operationally. This absurd regulation was eventually rescinded.

The arrival of Toby Carter was undoubtedly greeted by Tom with ambivalence, since Carter was, in theory, commander of all SEMUT activities in Borneo. Both in terms of personalities and logistics, this quickly proved unworkable. For one thing, SEMUT 1 was now huge, with dozens of agents and hundreds of guerrilla fighters in an ever widening circle centered on Bario, drawing in much of northern Sarawak and parts of Dutch Borneo and the colony of British North Borneo (now Sabah). Therefore, soon after Carter's arrival in Borneo, and after Tom appealed to "Z" Special headquarters over Carter's head, it was decided that each of the SEMUT commands in Borneo would be autonomous, reporting directly to "Z" Special in Morotai.

With the arrival of Carter's party came the sad news that Squadron Leader Graham Pockley's plane had disappeared three weeks earlier while coming home from the flight that had dropped Tom into Borneo. Tom vowed that some day he would do something to honor those men, especially Pockley to whom he had poured out his heart hours before landing on the Plain of Bah.

A few days after SEMUT 2's arrival, one of Tom's SEMUT 1 operatives returned to Bario with three of the American airmen: Lieutenant Corrin and Corporals Illerich and Capin. Ill and exhausted though they were, the three Americans were delighted to see Tom and SEMUT 1 headquarters. Corrin's diary entry for April 21 reads:

> Major Harrisson is a swell guy—tells us that the Australians are due to invade Tarakan in a week and the Americans [assisting the Australian 9th Division] are going to hit Brunei. We received all the latest war news and the shock that President Roosevelt is dead. The Australian doctor is giving us medicine for the itch and we've got chocolate, cigarettes, jam, cookies, peanut butter and a bottle of Scotch that the Major gave us.

At the end of April, Tom moved the main SEMUT 1 headquarters east to just across the Sarawak-Dutch border. At his new base in Dutch Borneo, he replaced his signaller Bower with the newly arrived Sgt. Bob Long, a highly competent wireless operator, who was assisted by the equally able American Cpl. Dan Illerich. The other SEMUT 1 operatives were deployed at strategic points covering all routes to the Plain of Bah and the Bawang Plain as well as manning a rear link to Carter's group on the Baram River. Major Sochon and Sergeant Barrie moved on to the Rejang valley to head up SEMUT 3, while Carter and SEMUT 2 remained on the Baram.

On May 6, 1945, Tom received a message via SOE headquarters in London that parliamentary polling day was coming up and would Tom want to come back to run as the Liberal candidate from Watford, Hertfordshire. By early 1944, Tom's M-O surveys had convinced him that Churchill's Conservatives would lose the general election of 1945. When the Liberals, seeking to field as many candidates as possible, had approached him before he left England in June 1944, he had agreed to seek nomination. But parliamentary elections seemed very far away and somewhat irrelevant and he declined the offer. Annoyed though he was that bad timing had interfered with his candidacy, there was nothing he wanted to do right then more than this Special Operations assignment. It combined all the pleasures of dealing with "primitive" people that he had enjoyed in Malekula with all the opportunities to order people about and carry out clandestine activities that he had loved while running Mass-Observation. He was in his element.

In mid-May, he moved his headquarters from further south along the Dutch border to Penghulu Lasong Piri's longhouse at Belawit. All his people—as he informed "Z" Special unit advance headquarters at Morotai— "moved further out, extending the radius of the area and getting nearer the Japanese at all points." In late May, eight new men were dropped into the Bawang Plain by Liberator as reinforcements for SEMUT 1. One of these was Driver Philip Henry. From his memoir comes a glimpse of Tom two months after his arrival in Borneo:

> [He was] . . . barefooted, wore a sarong round his waist, a shirt and an American soldier's work cap with a crown in the centre. The natives called him Tuan Besar (the Boss). He was very definite in his instructions such as: If any of us had anything to do with native women he would personally shoot us!

Tom's murderous-sounding threat was merely precautionary. Though he had initially been anxious about how his Australian "he-men" might behave toward the *orang ulu* young women, whose fine bodies were all too visible, he had learned that he need not have worried. For himself, as well, in spite of polite offers made by native chiefs to provide him a woman, he felt "no interest in the opposite sex." By the time he was addressing these SEMUT 1 reinforcements, he knew that

There was something about the tension—or excitement and satisfaction—of this for us new way of life which for a while put all the emphasis on what we conceived to be masculine attributes. Chastity and war—or to be more exact, delayed concupiscence in the smell of action—do seem to go together. . . . Fortunately for me, this phenomenon was not confined to me. . . . To the best of my belief, from the beginning to the end of the whole of our operations . . . there was no incident to cause undue disturbance of the female bosom or husband's heart.

After Tom's lecture, "within a few minutes . . . or so it seemed," as one of the party later recalled, "our party was split up," and each man was sent to a different river valley to help other SEMUT 1 operatives "report on Jap dispositions at the time of the planned 9th Division landing in the Brunei area on the 10th of June."

With the arrival of Driver Henry and other reinforcements had come news that helped answer the question that had worried Tom since first making contact with the American airmen: how to get them out. The answer would also solve another problem: how to establish a two-way transport link between SEMUT 1 and "Z" Special unit's advance headquarters on Morotai.

The AIF had only two planes with range enough to reach central Borneo from Morotai and get back home: the Liberator and the Catalina flying boat. There being no airfields in central Borneo, no Liberators could land there. A "Cat" could alight on the wide Rejang and Baram Rivers where Toby Carter and Bill Sochon were, but not in SEMUT 1's territory. A two-way air link had seemed impossible until the May 26 SEMUT 1 reinforcements brought Tom news that Tarakan's airfield, just under 200 miles away, was now in Australian hands. This distance happened to be precisely the one-way range of the AIF's short-take-off-and-landing plane, the Auster, which theoretically needed only 100 yards of runway.

The next morning Tom wired a request for an aerial reconnaissance to be done to see if an airstrip on the Bawang Plain in Dutch Borneo was practicable. Without waiting for confirmation, that same day he put Trooper Bob Griffiths in charge of building a runway. By mid-afternoon, in 110°F heat, during the "burn off" of the rice field, Trooper Griffiths started work.

The plan was ingenious. They would drain an unused portion of Belawit's wet-rice field, level its bottom and keep the outside banks intact. They would make a decking of split bamboo 30 feet wide and 100 yards long, anchored to the ground with sharp pegs. In case of a reconnaissance visit by the enemy, they could, with an hour or two's warning, quickly make a hole in the bank and flood the field to make it look like an ordinary wet-rice paddy.

After draining the area for the airstrip into lower-lying rice fields, the next task was to get the airfield leveled by filling it with soil. The soil was dug out by hand and stick and carried in reed baskets—women's work among the Lun Bawang. Bob Griffiths would sit down in his lean-to on the edge of the field with his English-Malay dictionary and work out how to write instructions, such as, "Take the earth from there and put it here," into an awkward but comprehensible Malay sentence. He would then take his Malay text to Penghulu Lasong Piri, who would read it and drill Griffiths on how to pronounce the words. Within a day or two, not only Lasong Piri's people but Dayaks, Kelabits, and other tribespeople from both sides of the Sarawak-Dutch border came to help.

On May 30, "Z" Special unit headquarters in Morotai sought to contribute to the project by dropping a load of shovels onto the Bawang Plain. These heavy metal objects falling from the sky made a spectacular show but mystified the workers, who had never seen such a tool. Out of courtesy, they tried putting the soil they had dug out by hand onto the shovel instead of carrying it in a reed basket. Griffiths started to show the women how the shovel should be used but quickly gave up when he realized that the sharp upper edges of these metal spades were unsuitable for bare feet. It was hard to imagine the work going faster than it was already, so he let his workers return to doing the job the old way.

On June 6, as Tom's men prepared to go on the warpath just ahead of the Ninth Division landings on Labuan and along Brunei Bay, there were two drops onto the Bawang Plain at Belawit, one as usual from a Liberator and the other, 100 gallons of aviation fuel, from a Catalina with two Auster pilots on board to look at the new airstrip from above.

The Auster pilots did not regard the prospect of landing on Griffiths' airstrip with enthusiasm. It was not just the fact that it was a split bamboo runway—possibly the world's first. They were also mindful that if the Bawang Plain were covered with cloud, as it often was—and *always* was by 11:00 A.M.—the Austers would have to land there anyway; they simply could not carry enough fuel to get back to Tarakan. The Auster's small load capacity meant that the pilots would have to leave behind their radios in order to carry enough fuel for the one-way trip.

June 7 was the busiest day the skies above the Bawang Plain had ever known. In addition to the Cat leading the two Austers, a Liberator from "Z" Special's Flight 200 came and dropped more storepedos. The two Auster pilots, Lieutenants Frederick Chaney and Johnny White, found Belawit, came down on the bamboo runway, ran all the way along its length, then beyond the bamboo decking, and finished up in the mud. The runway was too short. The two Austers were pulled out by the crowd of Lun Bawang, Kelabits, Ibans, and others who had come to work on the runway and had stayed to see it function.

The plan had been for the Austers to fuel up and leave, each taking one passenger, their maximum possible load. The pilot of the first Auster, Lieutenant Chaney (later Sir Frederick Chaney, KBE), was supposed to bring Tom to Tarakan so that he could catch a flight to Morotai and exchange intelligence with "Z" Special and Ninth Division people before the June 10 landings. The other Auster was supposed to bring out the sickest of the Americans, a U.S. Navy seaman.

"We were extremely doubtful," Chaney recalls, "about getting away." They had cause. After hastily getting the runway lengthened a bit more, Chaney, with Tom aboard, had just become airborne when the plane sank back onto the ground and went over onto its nose, breaking part of its back. Chaney recalls: "We dragged it back to the start and I thought that it was a complete write-off, but then Harrisson talked the Dyaks into working all night, laying further bamboo strips. We lengthened [the runway] by nearly twice as much." Aside from noting in his diary that his back hurt, Tom made no comment on how he felt during or after the crash. He sent a testy signal to "Z" Special headquarters that, not having had the "expected engineer to advise on takeoff, one pilot had tried on own initiative. Trying tomorrow. . . . Propose fly self out first. Urgent intelligence." Chaney later wrote of Tom, "We used to call him the Mad Major; . . . I don't think he knew fear."

The next morning, after the early cloud cover had dissipated and before it returned, Tom, his back still hurting, took off in Johnny White's Auster, arriving at Tarakan Island at 11:00 A.M. There he arranged for a Catalina to return to Belawit to drop fabric and dope so that Chaney could repair his plane's fuselage.

Chaney was impressed with the excellence of the "Dyaks'" craftsmanship:

> They were an amazing group of people, those Dyaks. They had irrigation laid on; water for their village came down from the mountains in bamboo pipes and then they had other little bamboos where you pulled a plug out and got a shower of water. Highly civilized, but with an uncivilized lot of people. . . . Their long house which would have done credit to any sort of building in Australia was built without one nail in it; and it was a tremendously big building. . . .

Using sign language, Chaney got the Lun Bawang to put in new struts of bamboo in his aircraft's fuselage and bind them up with thin bamboo strips, just as they did when joining wooden beams for their longhouse. Then he covered the fuselage with the new fabric and spread the dope over it. On June 10, he flew out Seaman First Class Harmes to Tarakan. The remaining ten Americans were flown out, one at a time, over the next four weeks.

# Chapter 22

## The Ants Take Heads

While Lieutenant Chaney was rebuilding his airplane in Belawit, Tom spent the day on Tarakan Island. There, he spoke at length with Brig. D. "Torpy" Whitehead, a "Desert Rat" hero from the Middle East campaign, whom he came to regard as unusual among Australian top officers in being able "to think—or any way to talk—of wider issues than the immediate; to take seriously subjects like the possible effects of present actions on the peoples of Borneo and their future behaviour in days of declared peace." That evening Tom continued his trip by Catalina to Morotai, where he noticed that the other top soldiers "appeared to be too concerned with matters of interest to the Australians only—and usually in a rather restricted way, without thinking much beyond the affairs of their own units." These consultations on Morotai with Ninth Division on the eve of their landings at Brunei Bay gave Tom his first hint that, as time went on with both Australian "regulars" and "specials" on the ground in northern Borneo, the two sets of soldiers would develop sharply different—and conflicting—war aims. For the moment, however, Tom's men were delighted that the AIF landings were imminent because, after months of preparation, they were now to go on the offensive. In fact, Sandy Sanderson and Phil Henry had already "jumped the gun."

Having been duly warned about women, Phil had been sent by Tom to meet Sgt. Fred Sanderson at the headwaters of the Limbang and go down the river with him to report on Japanese dispositions. In eight days, Sandy and Phil traveled eighty miles through mostly uninhabited jungle, northward and westward along the Limbang, to reach their destination, the area behind Brunei town. On their way downriver, they came through the subcoastal area of the Ibans, the famous "wild men of Borneo," reputedly the most enthusiastic of Borneo's headhunters.

Sandy, Phil, and their guides were welcomed courteously into their first Iban longhouse, a small one named "Rumah Bilong." When Sandy explained about having jumped into Borneo from the sky, he and Phil were questioned as to whether they were angels, of whom the Ibans had heard from missionaries. After that was cleared up, the Ibans told them the first Japanese military outpost was an hour downriver by *perahu* (dugout canoe). And, the Ibans said, from there on, the riverbanks were dotted with Japanese outposts.

Later that day, Sandy and Phil continued downriver and reached a big Iban longhouse, Rumah Kudok, where they explained that they were the vanguard of the returning British who were going to drive out the Japanese. That night, Sandy and Phil prepared themselves and the Iban men of the longhouse to enter into their first military action. They passed out their few weapons and spent the whole night teaching the men to load and cock the weapons and tried to get them to remember to put the safety catch on. Phil recorded that "Those without [guns] prepared blowpipe darts and sharpened parangs. From off the ceilings came colourful [Iban] battle jackets and feathered head-dresses." SEMUT 1 was going into battle.

On June 5, several of Sandy and Phil's Iban escort went to a five-man Japanese outpost on a tributary of the Limbang at an Iban longhouse, Rumah Brandah, where the Japanese were using forced Javanese labor to grow vegetables for the Japanese forces. Two of the Ibans hailed the Japanese on the longhouse veranda, complained of malaria, and asked the Japanese for quinine. "They reached the veranda with the pretence of collecting the medicine but instead pulled out their parangs and lopped two Japanese heads off." Sandy then shot another Japanese in the tapioca field nearby and another on the river trying to escape. One Japanese got away.

The Ibans were overcome with excitement at the first heads taken in decades and, being competitive and fiercely egalitarian (unlike the socially stratified *orang ulu*), they jostled one another like soccer players, each trying to kick toward himself one of the heads rolling on the longhouse floor. There were not enough heads. Some of the Ibans suggested, Phil wrote, that "since the Javanese had been working for the Japs, they must be enemy too, and wanted to take their heads. It took a lot of talking on Sandy's part to convince them otherwise."

At the next longhouse, the Ibans had been alerted by slit drums sounded at Rumah Brandah and had already tied up their four Japanese soldiers and were waiting for Sandy's forces to arrive. After Sandy and Phil got there, the four prisoners were taken across the river and shot. Sandy recalled: "The Ibans then took the four heads before the [bodies] had stopped kicking. The blood squirted into the river and changed the colour of the water and the women and children screeched." With a score for the day of eight Japanese killed and one escaped, Sandy wanted to go on to Ukong, a town further down the Limbang, before the escapee could give the alarm. His Iban hosts told him not to worry. The next morning upon arriving at Ukong, Sandy and Phil found the Ukong police station covered with blood from three Japanese bodies, including the escapee. In twenty-four hours, Sandy and Phil's Ibans had killed and beheaded eleven Japanese. When Sandy sent a note to Tom reporting the head-taking, Tom replied, "The civil authorities and the mission people will not like this."

The next day (June 7) Sandy and Phil and 100 Iban irregulars went on to another Iban longhouse where the Japanese had built a sawmill. Phil, whose mild expression belies his toughness, recalled:

> Again there was a confrontation with the natives . . . fighting one another for heads. This time I pointed my Owen gun at them and told them to stop what they were doing and chase an escaping Jap. For some moments there was a battle of wills but they obeyed me and from then on I had no trouble as to who was boss.

Three wartime incidents, all in Bill Sochon's SEMUT 3 Rejang area, occurred in which Ibans killed Chinese noncombatants along with Japanese soldiers and took their heads. In SEMUT 1 territory, however, with the exception of one Malay collaborator beheaded while in Phil Henry's custody, no nonenemy heads were taken throughout the war. Still, there is no denying that by June 1945 headhunting was back in vogue in northern Borneo.

On June 9 and 10, while AIF's Ninth Division got ready to land on Labuan, the remaining SEMUT forces moved to the offensive. Typical of SEMUT 1 signals to "Z" Special headquarters over the next few months is one from June 10:

> Patrol 12 men clashed with enemy party near Pa Brayon. Dead: one Kempei [Kempei Tai=Japanese police], four Jap soldiers, one Malay. Captured: four native police, one Malay coolie, six Muruts. Booty: six rifles, two swords, maps, clothes, badges, none escaped. We had no casualties.

Ninth Division, caught up in final preparations for the landings on Labuan and Brunei Bay, could understand such messages and approve them. It had a harder time when Tom let his boastfulness or journalistic style run away with him or when he yielded to an ungovernable urge to write "witty" signals. Such messages tended to discredit SEMUT 1's reporting in the eyes of its very "regular army" audience at Ninth Division. This was unfortunate, because most of what SEMUT 1 reported was accurate. Much of it provided information that Ninth Division was not getting from any other source, such as the real numbers of enemy soldiers inside northern Borneo—about 17,000—nearly twice as many as Ninth Division continued to claim were there.

On June 10, Ninth Division had its "D-Day" on northwest Borneo. As one of Australia's military historians remarked, "The 10th of June 1945 was the day when the guerrillas were no longer alone. 23,553 men of the Australian 9th Division, 6,525 men of the Royal Australian Air Force and 1,254 U.S. personnel landed in Brunei Bay, mainly on Labuan Island." While Ninth Division attacked from the coast, SEMUT 1 in the north, SEMUT 2 on the Baram, and SEMUT 3 on the Rejang "caused massive disruption of communications and put the fear of God into the Japanese, who did not know from which direction they might be attacked, particularly at night."

The regular soldiers of Ninth Division did not know of the presence of these "Z" Special unit forces and undoubtedly believed that the reason they were having such a relatively easy time advancing inland, in contrast to the high casualties suffered during the month AIF had spent conquering little Tarakan Island, was because either the Japanese were not fighting so well or the AIF was fighting better.

Ninth Division soldiers *were* aware of help they were receiving from the "Dyaks" but found their kind of help took getting used to. The "Dyaks" would sometimes bring one or more heads to brigade headquarters with the same air of triumph that a house cat would bring a dead rat to its mistress. An Iban from the Tutong River area offered to bring the heads of eighteen Japanese who had reached his village and asked for guides for travel upriver. "The Dyaks offered to deliver the heads to 'C' Company but said that they would prefer to keep them as they had a party on," the diarist of the 2/17th Battalion of the Twentieth Brigade Group recorded, before adding tersely: "Permission granted to keep heads."

Although, except at the highest level, Ninth Division was unaware of SEMUT at this time, SEMUT 1 was in a fever of activity. On June 11, Tom flew back from Morotai at dawn. He and six new men he had recruited, plus seven storepedos, dropped perfectly onto Griffiths' field at Belawit, where the bamboo runway was by now 250 yards long. Every day, there were engagements by SEMUT 1 parties in which enemy were killed and weapons and documents were captured; occasionally, prisoners were taken and escorted to Belawit.

Tom, back in Belawit, far from the fighting but carried away by war fever, tried to get a newly arrived SEMUT 1 operative, Warrant Officer I Colin McPherson, to take a small patrol to the Sapong Estate south of Tenom and locate the Japanese general headquarters reported to be there. McPherson was then supposed to either kill or capture the general officer commanding. That was General Baba, commanding the Japanese XXXVII Army, which had been in charge of northern Borneo operations since September 1944 and which by late 1944 was in charge of operations in south Borneo as well. McPherson must have blinked on reading Tom's note.

These orders to take a handful of mostly untrained men and kill the enemy commanding general were, of course, absurd, but they do show that, already by mid-June, Tom was aware—much more quickly than was anyone in Ninth Division—of a Japanese army headquarters on the edge of Borneo's far interior. Tom recognized that the Sapong Estate, a big but isolated rubber plantation in British North Borneo, strategically located near the southern end of a north-south rail line to the state's capital, would be an ideal inland garrison site for the Japanese. He realized that this headquarters could become the core around which Japanese troops from all over northern Borneo might coalesce to resist the Allies, as the Japanese had done from inside Tarakan and Labuan, causing comparatively heavy Allied casualties.

The next day, for the first time, Tom made radio contact with Special Forces (the vanguard of "Z" Special unit's advance headquarters) at Labuan as well with his commanding officer, Col. "Jumbo" Courtney, still at "Z" Special advance headquarters at Morotai. He also received messages from Sandy in the northwest (at Ukong on the Limbang) and from another SEMUT 1 operative on the Kerayan River, to the southeast. Tom's role as the spider at the center of an expanding and thickening web of guerrillas and agents, though less glamorous than that of those at the front, was essential to SEMUT 1's success.

It also involved some unpleasant chores. On June 14, Ric Edmeades came upriver to Pa Kelalan, and Tom walked down to him to consult and to bring him firearms for his Trusan forces. There the two senior SEMUT 1 leaders, assisted by two of Tom's native irregulars, took part in SEMUT 1's first execution, of an Iban policeman who had (to the best of Tom's judgment) gone beyond what was pardonable in carrying out his duties as an official of the Japanese occupation. After the execution, Tom and Ric mapped out where to place their fighting units along the north and northwest, bringing them to the coast or near it.

The leader of the longhouse at Pa Tengoa, on the middle Trusan, had accompanied Edmeades to Pa Kelalan, bringing (as a joke for Tom) the head of the Japanese chief police officer of Brunei. The head had been taken by Ibans during Ninth Division's Twentieth Brigade's fight for the town the previous day. Such treatment of the corpse of a senior Japanese policeman did not disturb either Tom or the Australians. Ninth Division had just discovered in Brunei's old British residency the rotting bodies of eight natives chained to stakes and had released others who had also been chained to stakes and were waiting to die. A few days later, the Australians liberated a prisoner-of-war camp at Kuala Belait (at the mouth of the Baram, near Seria's oil fields where thirty-seven wells had been set ablaze by the departing Japanese). A hundred Indian soldiers, captured in Singapore, had been held there. The Australians found twenty-four charred Indian bodies and evidence that others had been killed hurriedly by their Japanese captors on

June 14, just before the Japanese vacated the premises, leaving the remaining prisoners half-dead from starvation.

Although the record shows that Tom and his SEMUT 1 operatives knew what their mission was and how they should help Ninth Division take the coast of northern Borneo, it is equally clear from Ninth Division documents that "Prior to the invasion of Borneo, HQ 9 Aust Div seemed to possess little appreciation of the potentialities of SEMUT, with the result that there was little coordination of forward planning and full use of SEMUT was not made for close support of the assault." This ignorance of SEMUT activities on the part of the fighting men of the invading force was probably less the result of poor communications within Ninth Division than of the deep suspicion of and contempt for "special" forces traditionally felt by regular army forces. These were feelings SEMUT came to reciprocate as the Borneo campaign continued.

The first recorded meeting in the war zone of the two Australian forces, "regular" and "special," did not bode well for future relations. The official record of the Twentieth Brigade tells part of the story:

> On 20th and 21st June a river patrol of the 2/15th went up the Limbang River to Ukong to investigate reports that Allied prisoners were being held there. It picked up a ["Z" Special] party which had been organizing the Dyaks in that area but the report about prisoners proved false.

The "Z" Special party the patrol had "picked up" was Driver Phil Henry and his band of native guerrillas, who had been lying along the riverbank waiting to ambush the boat, which they had assumed was Japanese. They could hear its engine clearly for an hour or two as the boat snaked its way along the winding river, and they only held fire when they saw the American flag. (The Australian patrols were using American landing barges.)

One can imagine the impression Phil and his guerrillas made on the patrol. The men of the 2/15th Battalion had been in Borneo no more than ten days, and here was a Driver seemingly at home in the jungle and in charge of a band of long-eared, tattooed, naked natives armed to the teeth.

Driver Henry was indeed at home. By then he had crossed all of western Borneo from beyond the Dutch border, had cut his way for days through uninhabited mountain jungle, had swum crocodile-infested rivers, and had been guest of honor at the headhunting rites following a half-dozen bloody encounters. He had a string of native beads around his neck, his naked torso was tanned dark brown, and, all his own clothes having worn out, he was wearing a pair of brown Chinese shorts and Japanese boots. Phil recalled that the Australian patrol was "amazed to see me. I was there with about thirty irregulars, mostly Ibans, some ..iuruts. These Ibans were part of the last population expansion into Sarawak. They had been pirates and were very fierce people, very noble, proud, beautiful."

The next encounter of the Ninth Division regulars was later that day with the irrepressible Sandy. On June 21, Tom received a message from Special Forces Labuan telling him it had had a request from Sgt. Sanderson to drop him "six rifles, ammo, atebrine, salt, food, etc., direct to him in the Limbang Valley." Tom was "slightly mystified" and had asked Ric Edmeades, with whom he luckily had established wireless contact that day, to go over from the Trusan to the Limbang and "clarify." The next day, Tom got word that Ninth Division wanted to talk to both Sanderson and Henry.

Sandy who, like Tom, often went just a bit too far, had picked up word on June 16 of a large Japanese force—more than 2,000 strong—heading overland toward him and the big food cache (tons of rice and sugar) at Ukong. He had decided this information was too urgent, given the slow communications between Belawit and the field, for him not to take his message straight to Ninth Division. Therefore, when an AIF barge had came up from the coast to Ukong, where Sandy was then based, carrying a platoon of infantry—the same barge that had run into Phil—Sandy had gone back down the Limbang with the barge to the headquarters of Lt. Col. C. H. Grace's 2/15th Battalion of General Windeyer's Twentieth Brigade Group and had taken advantage of the occasion to ask for materiel.

To the end of his days, Sandy thought that his information was correct, and it may well have been. He was, however, unable to prove it. He was called into Twentieth Brigade Group headquarters at Brunei where he was told that he was "guilty of making bold and unreliable statements and was to be withdrawn from the Limbang/Brunei area." Tom, having sent Colonel Grace a signal that "Sanderson's information has always been reliable but is obviously not appreciated by 9th Division Headquarters," had then flown in to Labuan to speak up for his obstreperous but able sergeant. He missed seeing Sandy at Ukong but left a note for him bawling him out for having "disgraced us" and telling him to move over to the Padas River valley, out of Colonel Grace's district.

Sandy's report direct to brigade headquarters in Labuan had exacerbated the already strong traditional "regular" forces' prejudice against special operations. But, as SEMUT's immediate supervisor, Lt. Col. "Jumbo" Courtney later recalled, "When Sandy got into trouble with Col. Grace about that, Tom came to his support. Tom always supported his men when they got into trouble." At the time, though, Sandy did not feel supported. He had been reprimanded by Colonel Grace in person and by Tom, first in writing and then in person, when he had walked halfway across Borneo to meet him in the Bawang Valley. He then had been ordered to walk up to British North Borneo. When he had gotten partway through hostile Tagal territory, on or about July 2, he received a message from Tom telling him to turn around and go back to the Limbang; by then Ninth Division had evidence that there was, indeed, a big party of Japanese moving along the Limbang River. Colonel Grace had asked Tom to send his operative with the most knowledge and experience of the area. Sandy was the obvious choice.

As for relations between Ninth Division and SEMUT 1, they soon worsened, between a Twentieth Brigade Group patrol and Phil. Another patrol had come up the Limbang to Ukong on July 10. Phil had first hailed the barge further downriver, where he had captured a Malay collaborator he wanted to question. He got a lift for himself and his prisoner on the barge back up to Ukong. Arriving at Ukong in the late afternoon, he learned of a party of Japanese nearby. He led the Australian patrol out to engage the enemy, while the patrol's officer stayed behind, on the riverbank, to set up an ambush behind them. In accordance with regular army practice but against Phil's irregular instincts:

> We went in line abreast, with the Brenman giving covering fire. The Bren jammed at the critical moment and we had to retire as it was now dark.
>
> On the way back the Aussies said to me that to be by themselves in the jungle as I was would not be their cup of tea. I replied that their kind of fighting—advancing in line—was not my kind of fighting either.

The next day, Phil's Ibans were clearly unhappy about the disrespectful way the other Australians were treating their SEMUT leader, who had, in the grandiloquent tradition of his irregular Ibans, begun referring to himself as *Raja Limbang sungai dan Lubai sungai juga* (Rajah of the Limbang River and the Lubai River also). What was, to the Australian regulars, normal giving of orders by a subaltern to a private looked to these Ibans like an affront to the dignity of their "Tuan Pil." Perhaps for that reason, the Ibans took the opportunity, while Phil and the Australians were away checking on the Japanese casualties of the previous evening's clash, to shoot and decapitate the Malay prisoner. When Phil and the Australian officer returned to the camp, there was a headless trunk upon the ground. The Australian officer almost fainted. Phil was annoyed to lose his prisoner before he could question him but, making the best of a bad situation, offered the head to some "timid Kelabits from Kuala Madihit" who were visiting him in Ukong. "I encouraged one of them to take the head to their village," he later explained, because he needed the help of these Kelabits "as a forward watching post for a large party of Japs possibly coming their way. At that time we understood that the party was being led by officer Kamamura. He had supposedly been responsible for the death of Indian military prisoners near Tutong and had expressed his intention never to surrender." The giving of a head would be a good gesture to these potential helpers, but one can picture the effect all this made on his Ninth Division visitors.

When Phil got to Labuan in early August he walked unsuspecting into the Special Forces office to report on the continuing story of the big Japanese party coming along the Limbang, only to be "paraded before ['Z' Special unit commanding officer] Colonel [G. B. 'Jumbo'] Courtney and charged with 'murder of a British subject.'" Col. Courtney told him "to stop smiling as it was a serious charge" and that he "could end up with several years in detention. . . ." The colonel told him that if he would promise not to escape, he would be placed only under open arrest. Meanwhile, while under open arrest, Phil used his knowledge of the region to be a visual navigator on three RAAF missions.

The murder charge was later quashed. After an inquiry on Labuan in which Tom testified on Henry's behalf, Phil was flown out to Morotai and, as Phil recalls, "on direct instructions from Commander in Chief General Blamey I was exonerated from my charge. His legal advisors found that the Malay prisoner had been shot 'as he was attempting to escape.'" By then it was mid-September, a month after the war had been declared over, and Phil was flown home to Australia.

# Chapter 23

## End Game

Though Tom literally flew to the defense of his subordinates, he periodically cautioned his men to avoid showy and risky stunts, what he called the "Wingate complex." After Sandy's and Phil's awkward early contacts with Ninth Division, Tom ordered all SEMUT 1 men to avoid the regular forces and to route all communications through him.

On June 26, the advance headquarters of "Z" Special unit moved from Morotai to Labuan. The next day Tom flew to Labuan to see his bosses. By then Ninth Division knew about SEMUT and had begun to appreciate its work. The purposes for which SEMUT 1 had been created were being achieved over a much wider field and with much greater effect than its creators back in Melbourne had dared to hope.

By early July, Tom, still trying to minimize friction between his units and Ninth Division, issued orders to his men not to interfere with the local civil administration, which was then being run by the AIF in areas that Ninth Division had retaken. But this did not solve the basic problem, which was, as the Australian official military historian puts it, "the 9th Division had reached its objectives, and it was not part of its task to extend its control throughout the hinterland or to 'mop up' the broken Japanese army. The guerrilla leaders on the other hand were concerned about their Dyak friends and allies, and felt some responsibility for the protection and rehabilitation of the native peoples in their areas." By this time SEMUT 1 operatives on the Limbang, Padas, and Trusan were reporting large numbers of Japanese heading toward the Sapong Estate. Ninth Division appeared unconcerned about these forces, although SEMUT 1 was "attacking" them "constantly" with ever shrinking numbers of guns and ammunition.

Having done what he could to alert Ninth Division to this problem, Tom flew back to Belawit. He had been gone nearly three weeks. On July 15, after a night back at his mountain headquarters, he wrote in his diary: "God, cold here last night, ?after lowlands, but also definitely colder. Not feel well—tired, jaded, overwork." He nonetheless continued his long walks all over northern Borneo. These long walks added to the fatigue caused by Tom's bucketing about in unpressurized planes. By his calculations, he had spent nearly 300 hours in the air during the previous twelve months.

In late July a letter, delivered by runner, came from his old boot-wearing adversary Doc McCallum, writing from Toby Carter's SEMUT 2 headquarters on the Baram:

27 July 1945

Dear Boss No. 1,

This bloke arrived with the letter about four days after we had seen you. I have paid him for the journey here and told him you will pay him for the journey back. I see you wanted us to give him a rifle or shot guns which he said you had promised but I haven't got any spare guns with me and have told him to ask you again. Our score of Japs is going up too and will soon be near the 200 mark with any luck.

The last sentence must have bucked Tom's spirits and gratified his urge to be best, since he knew that by July 31 SEMUT 1 had a score of 728 Japanese killed and 33 taken prisoner, 218 auxiliaries killed or taken prisoner, at the cost of only 13 "Murut" and one Tagal dead or injured on the SEMUT 1 side. There were still no casualties among his "Z" Special unit operatives.

Along the Borneo coast in early August 1945, the Australian Ninth Division military actions were winding down, but Tom, far inside the island, was as busy as ever. That week, Tom walked east to Wy-Agong and Long Nuat to confer with his units there and make plans for some operatives to go ahead to the Bahau-Kayan area to prepare him a drop zone. Tom wanted to reach the Bahau-Kayan region to see if the Japanese were trying to approach the big Kenyah longhouse community of Long Nawang and from there infiltrate the center of Borneo. He planned to make the jump soon.

Walking back to Belawit, along the jungly Kerayan River and onto the Bawang Plain, Tom noted in his diary for August 9: "Never get over thrill of re-seeing this wide green open fertility and flatness." In addition to visiting his units working in the east and south, Tom was anxiously awaiting news from the two units in the north that he had assigned to watch the Sapong Estate. They reported that their informants were hearing of an estimated 2,000 Japanese at the Sapong Estate and another 2,000 to 3,000 at the interior town of Ranau, where General Baba was thought to have moved his headquarters. Nonetheless, as the Australian official military history of the period notes: "For the 9th Division, the coastal strip, with its ports, oil fields and rubber plantations was the extent of the military objective. Its occupation fulfilled the whole military purpose of the invasion of British Borneo." The official historian seems puzzled by the fact that "sometimes . . . the ["Z" Special] guerillas in the interior seemed to the 9th Division to think that, instead of their activities being in support of the main military purpose of the army, they were the advance-guard or front line and that the army was failing to support *them*."

The Hiroshima and Nagasaki atomic bombings in early August presaged an early Japanese surrender. The AIF began to plan to get all Australian forces home as quickly as possible after handing over responsibility for those areas of British Borneo under their control to the British Borneo Civil Affairs Unit of the British Military Administration. But the SEMUT operatives had different priorities. Almost to a man, they felt personally responsible for assuring that the local people they had lived and worked with were safe before they left. SEMUT 1 operatives could not understand how Ninth Division could possibly choose to pull up stakes and leave the inland Borneans to be preyed upon by a Japanese column of several hundred organized soldiers, perhaps more, that showed no intention of surrendering.

Tom made out a chart entitled "Repatriation" to figure out which of his operatives should be repatriated first as soon as peace was declared and which should stay on to deal with the Japanese and the transition to peace time. He listed his entire staff, making columns for their years of service, whether they were married, their age, and the state of their health.

The health of SEMUT 1 operatives had become a serious problem. They had paid dearly for Tom's policy of providing them almost no food. Local food, when they could get it, sometimes gave them dysentery, and many of them had sometimes gone hungry, not being as ready as Tom to eat unfamiliar food. Tom, who could remember having eaten a "high" grub from the hands of a leper in the New Hebrides, had a hard time imagining that reasonable men with no other option might still refuse to eat snake, or pork that tasted of excrement, or sago that tasted like library paste. He later joked in *World Within* about his brave Australians being able to cope with any danger or inconvenience so long as they had tinned food and something to open the tins with. Tom himself ate very well in Belawit, where local food was plentiful and where the Australian food parcels were dropped. That Tom had helped himself to food dropped in for SEMUT 1 while he made his operatives "live off the land" is undoubtedly the single biggest grievance his subordinates have held against him.

Three days after Hiroshima, Tom finally received an adjutant, RAAF Flight Lieutenant Paul Bartram, flown in by Auster from Labuan. Bartram, a tall, slender Englishman, had hoped to participate in guerrilla warfare, but the timing looked bad. The war would end officially before he had been in Belawit a week. Bartram's diary gives a picture of Belawit in those days:

> *August 10th*. Arrived in the Bawang Valley. . . . The valley's rich with rice and all sorts of fruit and livestock, water buffaloes, [other] cattle, pigs, goats, chickens, even ducks and homing-pigeons. It's an oasis of fertility in this jungle-covered land. Harrisson's HQ itself is like a holy city, surrounded by its beautiful green irrigated rice-fields which themselves are dotted with native long-houses, and banana and pineapple patches—a kind of tropic version of rural England. . . . Flying up from Labuan, I saw nothing all the way except jungle, until we came to this fine sweep of valley.
>
> As for the native people, contented, loyal, hard-working and absolutely honest, I'm told that they're like many races which have not yet had the doubtful benefits of civilisation thrust upon them. They have all they want because they know nothing more than what they see around them—and nature supplied plenty of all of that in Bawang.

On August 15, Tom received a signal from Special Forces ("Z" Special advance headquarters in Labuan) sent "to all parties":

> Japan has surrendered. Till further notice all parties will cease progress positive action against enemy forthwith. Enemy should be given no provocation justifying further armed resistance. Parties will therefore keep enemy under observation only course endeavour restrain troop practice any excesses. Further instructions follow.

That day, Tom had his wireless man, Bob Long, send fifty-four signals from Belawit, including a long message to all operatives in SEMUT 1 spelling out the implications of this surrender for the immediate future of SEMUT 1. In it, Tom told the operatives that there would be no more fighting and that firearms should be used in self-defense only, but then he added:

> As you know we . . . came into this country as first in, to get intelligence for AIF attacks by sea. It was not anticipated that we would have time to organise guerillas. And it was anticipated that the AIF would overtake and relieve us.
>
> It has not worked out like that. We have done much more—more quickly—than anyone thought possible. We provided 80% of the intelligence before D Day but since then we have provided a high percentage of the Japs killed, too. (We have done over 900).
>
> . . . So we have been given a large share in the job of cleaning up the country, rounding up stray Japs, and leaving the place in decent order. I want to get back to my wife and children and my home in London as much as anyone. But I am in a way glad that we are asked to finish the job we started. Even if it involves a few more months slogging, I would like to feel that we as a party have left everything straight, everyone happy and a good clean name for ourselves in Native history.

These people and especially the Muruts and Kelabits have done a marvellous job helping us. It is up to us to see that they get a fair deal in return and are not just left without a thank you or an aspirin. . . .

I do appreciate the A1 job you have done. I am a pommy myself but I frankly admit that after my experience here, Australians have twice the bushcraft and five times the initiative. And they don't grumble so much. . . .

. . . I know some of you want to make a career in this country either in the Government or in business of your own. Let me know about this at once and I will take it up top priority. Send me particulars of age, education. . . .

Tom told his men that, in their dealings with military and civil authorities, they should try to keep their relations friendly but "nevertheless do not let them put anything over on you." They should refer all requests on the part of First Australian Corps or Ninth Division or anyone else to take over their area to Tom at Belawit headquarters.

The next day, August 16, to Tom's surprise, an Auster arrived sent by his boss, Jumbo Courtney, with orders for Tom to ride back with him to Labuan. Two days later, he and Jumbo flew to Morotai where, Tom's diary records, the "NICA fuss starts." NICA stands for Netherlands Indies Civil Affairs, the returning Dutch colonial government of what is now Indonesia but was then the Dutch East Indies. When Tom had moved SEMUT 1 headquarters from Bario eastward across the Sarawak border to Dutch Borneo, Dutch Borneo had been Japanese-controlled territory. There being no Dutch equivalent of "Z" Special unit in that part of Borneo trying to win the territory back, Tom's bosses had "tacitly permitted us to exercise a very wide—and, as far back as Melbourne—widely known control over all the northern part of Dutch Borneo." Now overnight, with the emperor's surrender, the Dutch expressed amazement at the existence of British personnel in their territory and demanded their immediate withdrawal. Whether the Dutch amazement was real or feigned, it soon was causing political friction between the Dutch and the Australians at a high level. That was why Jumbo Courtney had sent a surprise Auster to Belawit that had collected Tom, and had flown with him to Morotai. There Tom received instructions from "Z" Special's commanding officer, Brigadier Jock Campbell, to go to Brisbane to see Colonel Spoor, head of the Dutch special operations office there, and sort things out.

When Tom finally got in to see Colonel Spoor in Brisbane in late August, the Dutchman made it clear that he disapproved of the "extent and depth" of SEMUT 1's military and civil activities in Dutch Borneo. He wanted Tom to return to Dutch Borneo subject to Dutch orders and regulations, his first duty being to disarm all his irregulars there and hand over authority to an official of the Dutch East Indies to be nominated by Spoor. Tom was unwilling to hand over to just anyone and walk back across the Sarawak border, leaving the people of the Bawang Plain vulnerable to attack by the Japanese. He wanted to continue administering the freed areas of northeast Borneo until the Dutch had enough personnel to take over administration of their territory, or at least until there was no more Japanese threat. At the end of a half-hour of argument and counterargument, Spoor exploded and Tom, to the surprise of both of them, burst into tears. The tears may have been provoked by Tom's realization that the war was now over and the high-sounding rhetoric of allies united in a crusade against a wicked enemy had given way again to the petty concerns of peacetime colonial rivalries, concerns that left no room for worries about the welfare of the natives, though the natives' welfare had been one of Tom's chief worries from the time he had landed at Bario in March.

Meanwhile, back in Belawit, letters were coming in from SEMUT 1 men in response to Tom's signal to them of August 15. A typical one read:

> I have no outstanding reason for getting out other than a natural desire to get home for Christmas. Am quite prepared to stay on till job finished. I would like to make a request that I be left in this area (Pa Tengoa) as I know it and the natives also.

Similar letters followed, many from men who had "no desire to apply for an interview for a position in the government in Borneo. . . ." Some of those asking to stay were quite sick but still did not want to abandon their felt obligations to the people of Borneo.

# Chapter 24

## SEMUT 1 and the Fujino Tai

During the latter half of August 1945, Ninth Division, responsible for surrender arrangements in British Borneo, dropped leaflets calling for an end to hostilities over "all known areas in which Japanese were concentrated" on the Limbang. But, two weeks after the emperor's surrender, Sergeant Sanderson was still actively at war with a large Japanese column.

On August 26, hearing of an enemy numbering 300 to 450, Sandy had gone with a patrol to Rumah Damo on the Medalam River, to keep this force, which had been moving up the Tutoh River, from breaking through east to the Trusan. The column was believed to be under the command of Captain "Kamamura" (more likely Kamimura), known in connection with an earlier massacre of Indian prisoners of war. Sandy made an attempt to get the column to surrender by sending five messengers to the Japanese with letters telling them that Japan had surrendered on August 12 and signed an armistice on August 14 and that they should "send one English-speaking subject to negotiate terms immediately." The next day, when Sandy's five messengers did not return, he sent a patrol to spy on the enemy, but his patrol was ambushed and fired on. Sandy's men found one messenger who had escaped downriver and who said that the other four had been taken prisoner by the Japanese. He brought solid information about the Japanese column. The enemy force was 400 strong, in good condition and with a good food supply. The commanding officer had "no intention of surrendering, disbelieves information. Three messengers reported killed at random." Sandy's medical supplies were exhausted. He was down to twenty-seven weapons. He reported that his guerrillas were "using spears against enemy force which are probably marines." He asked for Ninth Division "cooperation within next 24 hours."

Tom, unable to get anyone to drop arms to Sandy, sent a SEMUT 1 operative to visit Rumah Damo in the wake of the Japanese column. The operative reported on August 30 that an estimated enemy force of 600 to 800 had "killed all livestock and finished food. . . . Informants report four enemy high officials with red pennants, two LMGs [light machine guns], one heavy MG [machine gun]. All carry grenades. Ammo unlimited, carried by approximately thirty Javanese porters."

Given the stubbornness of this column, Tom felt frustrated at seeing his operatives being forced to leave Borneo. He tried to keep some of them, but Special Forces was unsympathetic, perhaps because the problem that SEMUT 1 was having with a tenacious enemy was exceptional. According to Toby Carter, in SEMUT 2's district, "As soon as the Japs were convinced that their orders came from the emperor, they laid down their arms, did exactly as they were told, and gave no further trouble." The enemy was behaving similarly in Bill Sochon's SEMUT 3 area. Even General Baba would soon leave the Sapong Estate and be brought to Labuan on September 19 to surrender. In Dutch Borneo, the war's official end came faster still, although it was not yet clear whether there might be Japanese in the Bahau-Kayan basin north of Long Nawang, the area Tom proposed to be dropped into.

At the beginning of September, Tom, having seen the Dutch in Brisbane, was on his way back to Belawit, which was, of course, also in Dutch Borneo. En route, he spent two days at "Z" Special headquarters in Morotai to discuss his proposed visit to the Bahau-Kayan region. He brought with him a highly unsatisfactory letter from the Dutch, a product of his tearful interview with Colonel Spoor. "Z" Special then launched a campaign to get the orders changed and went so far as to enlist the aid of Australian Commander-in-Chief General Blamey. Blamey wrote the Dutch General van Oyen what Tom accurately characterizes in his diary as "a superb letter pro me and wiping floor with Spoor." The result was a set of formal instructions on September 12 authorizing Tom to drop, along with a signaller, into the Kayan-Bahau basin where "he will operate under direct orders of [Special Forces] Labuan." Tom was to disarm those natives that SEMUT 1 had armed, turning the weapons over to the local native district officer (appointed by the Dutch before the war), leaving only enough arms as might be needed for local protection.

Tom spent the next three days in Labuan giving evidence in Phil Henry's "murder" court-martial, hearing news of General Baba's expected surrender from the Sapong Estate and learning of Sandy's latest scrape. Once again, Sandy was in trouble with Ninth Division. An impertinent signal had been sent to Colonel Grace of the 2/15th complaining of lack of cooperation from his battalion, "signed" by Sanderson, and Colonel Grace wanted Sandy court-martialed. "Oh God!" Tom wrote in his diary for September 5, "The Limbang." The next day Tom's diary records a "major row with Jumbo" as Tom sought to defend his troublesome sergeant, who had killed thirty more Japanese two days earlier.

Tom was glad to get away from all this and back "home" to Belawit on September 7. Paul Bartram had arranged a big reception for Tom's arrival by Auster, with a parade, a bamboo pipe band, and a dinner outside with the band playing. Kelabit friends from the Plain of Bah, Javanese ex-Japanese conscripts, Doc McCallum, and Paul Bartram all danced, Sgt. "Smokey" Dawson "rolled," and Sgt. Bob Long and other operatives joined in the victory celebration, drinking gin and burgundy, presumably brought in by Tom from Labuan.

Finally, on September 13, Tom looked out the window of a B-24 to see the magnificent Bahau-Kayan valley, the "miles and miles of rolling grass" he now realized was the tableland he first had seen from an American Liberator in January, when he thought he had found the Plain of Bah. The wind, however, carried him beyond the grasslands of this perfect drop zone and he and his signaller alighted near the village of Long Toea, along the Bahau River. The drop was from 6,000 feet, and Tom landed upside down in a tree, dangling seventy feet above ground, where he passed out. His chute, thanks to changes in AIF policy since the days when Bill Sochon had watched his hundred-times-used parachute fall apart above him, was still in one piece. When Tom came to, he found a Kenyah tribesman loosening the parachute from which he was hanging "crucified." Then a very long ladder appeared, and his signaller, to help him down.

Over the next week, Tom traveled through the Kenyah country. The rain continued and soon the rivers were flooded. On October 1, after much difficulty, he reached the great Kenyah settlement at Long Nawang, which he described in his diary as a "lost world." The people of Long Nawang belonged to the senior clan of the Kenyah and were the most impressive not only in numbers (thousands of people living in a series of longhouses) but also in the grandeur of their aristocracy and the glory of their art. Tom was dazzled by what he saw, such as a superb polychrome "tree of life" mural painted on the longhouse wall.

The Kenyah are a riverine people and not walkers like the Kelabit or Lun Bawang. By October 11, Tom had spent, by his own count, seventy-six hours in dugout canoes, upriver and downriver, visiting nineteen Kenyah longhouse villages. In each, he had conferred with chiefs and elders and spread the gospel of the British liberation of the area (which was in a Dutch colony) from the Japanese yoke. He warned the people to avoid the Japanese and merely to report any Japanese presence to the local district official of the Netherlands East Indies. "The expected forces of Japs had not and never did arrive in Long Nawang, as it so happened. Apparently they turned back much farther south." Tom collected superfluous arms and destroyed them. He tried to learn the people's needs to pass on to the Dutch, and was feasted and given beautiful carvings and other objects made by these Kenyah.

While Tom was in Kenyah country, the Japanese column that Sandy had been fighting had again shown signs that it planned to move from the Limbang to the Trusan. On September 22, SEMUT 1 operative Lt. Middleton, on the Limbang, warned that he expected engagement with the enemy within forty-eight hours and had almost no ammunition left. On September 23, Middleton sent another signal to Special Forces, Labuan: "Engaged enemy on three occasions yesterday. Enemy killed 55. Own troops nil. Arms still low."

Paul Bartram in Belawit, standing in for Tom, was meanwhile trying to fend off Ninth Division efforts to rid Borneo of the last of the SEMUT operatives. When Bartram got word of this to Tom, Tom signalled his adjutant:

> Stall. Must keep Chinese doctor. I am working under written orders from Morotai direct instructions General Blamey. Orders state I am to keep the necessary personnel on the Dutch side until I am satisfied it is fully cleared and a handing over report rendered for NICA. This is high policy matter and you cannot accept any countermanding orders except from high level. Dutch area is anyway not under 9 Div. You can use that tactfully if pushed around. Stand no nonsense.

But Ninth Division continued its inexorable demands for the withdrawal of all of SEMUT 1's men and equipment. As Bartram tried to carry out Tom's wishes without directly disobeying orders from Labuan, his frustration mounted. He wired Tom:

> [General] Wootten doesn't give a hoot. Cannot tell you my feelings on subject. Am powerless to carry out orders you left me and can only leave you as oldest and senior inhabitant to raise what hell you can later. All prestige built up over last six months has flopped at one stroke.

One reason why "Labuan" (in the shape of Ninth Division with the acquiescence of "Z") was ready to evacuate the SEMUT 1 operatives was that it periodically lost sight of the Japanese column and was not sure whether it really existed as an organized entity or as simply a bunch of stragglers. The stragglers, as opposed to the Japanese in the column, were a pathetic sight. They had been without food for a long time. Some had hanged themselves; others had committed inadvertent suicide by eating poisonous fern tops or, worse still, by stuffing themselves with raw unhusked rice, which expanded in their bellies causing them to rupture internally.

Now that the enemy had been conquered, with the captured troops seeming so docile and the stragglers so pathetic, the whole mood of Ninth Division had changed from fighting war to making peace. The Japanese column that Sandy and Middleton were fighting on the Limbang, a renegade force known as the Fujino Tai, was the only organized enemy unit still at war.

(*Tai* means "company of soldiers" in Japanese, and it was under the command of a Captain Fujino.) The force under Capt. "Kamamura" joined the Fujino Tai at some point, perhaps as early as July at Labi.

The Fujino Tai had stayed on the Tutoh from late July until after the cease-fire, by which time they had eaten all the local food, including the live cattle, pigs, and chickens. By late August, they had reached the Limbang, staying in the navigable part of it until October 1, when they went on to Kuala Madihit on the middle Limbang. Once the Fujino Tai had moved beyond the lower Limbang, it was no longer easily accessible to Ninth Division land forces, had Ninth Division been willing to deploy any.

Caught between the conflicting aims of Ninth Division and of those SEMUT 1 elements still facing resistance from a well-organized, reasonably well-equipped Japanese force, Jumbo Courtney, who had just turned over command of Special Forces at Labuan to Bill Jinkins, sent the following tongue-in-cheek farewell signal to SEMUT 1:

> Signal from Courtney, October 2, To all parties: To those whom it may have concerned in the past or may concern now or in the future, do not rpt not harass kill strike snub spit on or loot any Japs with whom you come in contact. Any time "Z" Special parties hurt Jap feelings in any way, Japs complain to 9 Div who then make life difficult for your poor old colonel. Let us depart in peace.

That day, orders from Labuan continued the evacuation of SEMUT 1 operatives, with a deadline of October 15. There were personal orders of the same date for "Harrisson from Courtney" and similar ones from Jinkins, telling Tom he could "submit any comment you care to make but no rpt no alteration can be made to these plans."

It took some days for these orders to reach Tom by runner; he was at Long Nawang with a transmitter that could send as far as Labuan but was too weak to receive messages. Tom's only consolation was that he had by then, with Jumbo's help, wrung the concession from Ninth Division that he be allowed to return to Belawit and collect his personal gear after his return from the Kayan, even if the British Borneo Civil Affairs Unit (BBCAU) decided not to let him stay on afterward in the highlands to work for them and help with the transition to peacetime.

Tom had assumed that there would be a long transition between the military occupation and the actual reinstallation of the governments of the four Bornean entities—Sarawak, Brunei, British North Borneo, and Dutch Borneo—in which SEMUT 1 had operated. He had decided that Bario, being in Sarawak, was the best place for him to stay, assuming he would be permitted to do so by the interim administration, the BBCAU. With that in mind, he had already arranged for the building of quarters there. BBCAU was aware of this plan and wanted to see Tom before endorsing it. That Tom had stores of food and medicine was a selling point, since it meant that BBCAU would not have to provide these supplies.

Infuriating to Tom and to his few remaining SEMUT operatives, by mid-October the Ninth Division, having almost no more SEMUT 1 units to watch for it, had again lost sight of the Fujino Tai. This was because the renegade column was much further upriver than where the RAAF was looking. Unexpectedly, the column had turned southeastward and was now heading up to the top of the Trusan in the mountains near Pa Kelalan, en route to the fertile inland plains of Bah and Bawang, in search of food. By October 12, the Fujino Tai had reached Long Beluyo, less than a day's walk from Pa Kelalan, which in turn was less than a day's walk from either Bario or Belawit. Ninth Division learned that the column had reached that point only when Paul Bartram sent a signal telling them so.

Bartram had said a tearful farewell to the hill people of the Bawang Plain and the Plain of Bah whom he felt he was now leaving in the lurch. Then he had obediently left Belawit with two SEMUT 1 operatives, en route to Labuan. They reached Pa Kelalan their first night, only to be told by native scouts that their route westward was blocked by enemy forces.

Two days later, when Tom flew into Labuan from Tarakan, the news greeted him that Paul was cut off. Bartram, unable to make his radio reach Labuan from the lower altitude of Pa Kelalan, had moved back up into his just-abandoned headquarters on the Bawang Plain and had then sent out a signal to tell Special Forces in Labuan that enemy forces were blocking his route to the coast.

With this news, Tom's patience with Ninth Division finally snapped. With Paul and the rump of SEMUT 1 plus the *orang ulu* of the inland plains under threat, Tom was not prepared to accept any more nonsense about the war being over and no more Allied casualties to be risked. If Ninth Division would not deal with this renegade column, he would do so himself.

Jumbo Courtney accompanied Tom on his rounds on Labuan: "I was quite used to accompanying Tom to GOC [General Officer, Commanding] and helping him thump on the table. And then we got permission from General Windeyer." Windeyer, by good fortune, had taken over command of Ninth Division from the much more starchy regular army General Wootten in mid-September. The result of all this table thumping was that Tom was granted permission to go all the way up the Trusan until he reached the column and try to convince Captain Fujino that the war was over and that he should surrender. Meanwhile, Bartram and Sgt. Bennett, his wireless operator in Belawit, were graciously given leave by Ninth Division to attack the column to prevent it from getting to the Plain of Bah or Bawang.

Tom, having bludgeoned Ninth Division into allowing him to try to get the Fujino Tai to surrender, now had to find out who he could get to go with him. He was able to collect a wireless operator, SEMUT 1's Sgt. Nibbs, but almost all his other operatives were gone. Even the redoubtable Sandy had been evacuated by now, as a "mental case," Tom's way of saving the sergeant from Col. Grace and a court-martial for insubordination.

Luckily, just the right man suddenly became available. This was Major Rex Blow, a "Z" Special operative whose exploits during World War II are as famous as Tom's. Blow had been with an Artillery Regiment of the AIF when Singapore fell. He had escaped from a Japanese prisoner-of-war camp on Borneo's northeast coast in 1943 with seven fellow prisoners, eventually reaching the Philippines, where he and his fellow escapees chose to stay on and help American-led native guerrillas. Blow had left for Australia in April 1945 in order to join "Z" Special so he could go back to northeast Borneo to try to rescue the 2,000 Australian and 500 British prisoners of war (POWs) who were incarcerated at Sandakan. Getting there a few days too late, he found the camp empty, the buildings burned, and the prisoners of war already embarked on the infamous march west to Ranau. On this march (it was later learned), all but 40 of the 2,500 prisoners died en route. Twelve escaped, of whom six, all Australians, survived. The remaining 28 prisoners who reached Ranau were gunned down there by their Japanese captors on August 22, 1945, a week after the war was officially over. Realizing that only a large-scale military action would have saved the POWs, Blow had returned to Australia where he prepared to lead a "Z" Special operation in eastern British North Borneo for two months, beginning in July 1945. In early September, Blow had briefly taken over civil administration of a district of British North Borneo and on October 15, his work done, he was in Labuan, waiting for a flight home. Tom met him and told him his story about the Fujino Tai.

As Blow's biographer notes:

> If Tom Harrisson had expected his listener to enthuse he was in for a disappointment. No way, Rex told him, was he going to join him. He was tired and wanted a break. . . .
>
> "But," as Rex said later, "the bastard had a bottle of whisky and by the time we'd finished it, I'd agreed to go!"

Tom must have been at his most persuasive during this visit to Labuan. In addition to convincing Blow to go with him, after having convinced Ninth Division to let him go after the Fujino Tai, he also persuaded BBCAU to take him on as a Civil Affairs Unit official after he had finished with the Fujino Tai. In that capacity, he would be allowed to reinstall himself in the Kelabit highlands after he had dealt with the Fujino Tai and reported back to Labuan.

While Tom worked out his immediate future in Borneo with BBCAU and Ninth Division, he also made an interesting discovery: the Sarawak Museum curator and government ethnographer, E. Banks, who had been Tom's adversary during the 1932 Oxford Expedition to Sarawak, had been released from the POW camp near Kuching and had gone home to England after expressing his intention not to return to his old post. Tom stored this fact away for future use.

On October 18, Tom, Blow, and Nibbs, along with an officer from Ninth Division and a captured Japanese officer with a large white flag crossed the choppy bay to the mouth of the Trusan, proceeded up the river to Lawas, where they learned that the column consisted of some 350 Japanese, and on up the Trusan. As Rex Blow recalled, "It was a bloody journey, not helped by the monsoon rains which, in that country, can cause trickling streams to become raging torrents in a matter of hours with the attendant discomfort of mud and leeches. . . . God those bloody mountains." On October 23 the Japanese were still going up the Trusan. By October 25, Tom and Rex Blow arrived at Long Beluyoh, where the Japanese had been two weeks earlier when Paul Bartram had first heard they were blocking his path. On October 27, still at Long Beluyoh, Tom got a message from Labuan that, when and if the Fujino Tai surrendered, BBCAU would not pay for its food:

> 9th Division advise they will not undertake financial responsibility purchase food Japanese POW. No rpt no expenditure can be made from BBCAU Funds. Ack[nowledge].

Tom's reply was worthy of the occasion:

> Your signal Ack. but do not understand. If meant seriously, which of three courses shall I take: (1) Death-march Japs to coast? (2) Pay from my own pocket? (3) Force natives to give remaining food free? In each case, can you assure me please: If (1) I shall not be court-martialed. If (2) I shall not be declared bankrupt. If (3), I shall not have my head cut off by infuriated Muruts. If Japs surrender, it will take weeks to get them all down. Must pass through ravaged areas. Reply immediately please.

At midday on October 27, Tom received a note sent by a SEMUT 1 guerrilla that the Japanese were at Pa Kelalan and that sounds of heavy firing were emanating from the area inland from there. A couple of hours later a signal came in from Paul Bartram dated two days earlier reporting that he was running out of ammunition. Bartram was getting his guerrilla war experience, after all.

The next afternoon, Tom, Rex Blow, and their companions were within 600 yards of the enemy and sent in envoys, including their Japanese officer.

At "1615 Fujino and Kamamura surrender," Tom wrote in his diary entry for October 28, 1945. He scribbled a note to Paul, which was delivered to Bartram the next day by one of SEMUT 1's senior native guerrillas. It was, Bartram later recalled, "rather a dirty, ordinary piece of paper, with a scribbled message in pencil. It said: 'Paul. Japs have surrendered unconditionally. I will be up tomorrow. Cease fire immediately. Tom.'" The next morning, October 29, well over two months after the war had officially ended, at 0900 the renegade column under Fujino took part in a "signing of peace."

At noon, Tom left for Belawit. By mid-afternoon he was back in his Dutch Borneo headquarters. On October 30, Blow and Nibbs went north to Pa Bawang, a few miles from Belawit, to establish a camp for the 340 prisoners—339 Japanese and 1 Chinese. The next day, Tom noted in his diary that by chance he had "read Rex's bullshit letter on *his* trip up Trusan after Japs. But he's a nice chap."

On November 1, a Beaufreighter dropped four storepedos of food at Belawit, solving the most pressing problem on Tom's agenda. Within a few days, word had spread through the inland plains that the Japanese were really conquered and that Tom was back in Belawit. Tom's first friend in Borneo, Penghulu Lawai Besara, came over from Bario to see him, and three men came all the way from Long Nawang on the Bahau-Kayan.

On November 5, a party was held at Pa Bawang, including a concert at the prison camp, where Lun Bawang and Japanese played their own and each others' songs on their own musical instruments. The next day, SEMUT 1 operatives Nibbs and Bennett left with 250 Japanese prisoners for the coast. On November 8, Tom "saw Rex off 0600 with rest of Japs bar 14 at Bawang Hospital."

By November 9, it was over. Tom, let down after all the excitement of the previous week and very conscious of his situation as the last white man in the middle of Borneo, wrote in his diary:

> Closed down W/T [wireless telegraphy]. Estimate 30,000 signals. I feel I have HAD everything. Reaction to past. Negative towards future. Paranoia very bad. But what a relief to have no W/T. . . . Think now of the crowded days, of . . . Long, Doc and . . . Paul, Bob Griffiths, flags and Jap skulls, Chaney, B24s and Cats, laughing eager natives, Malay strip workers . . . and the great march past. The busy guards and endless runners.
>
> Now that phase is over—White Borneo. We work now back into the slower, soundless rhythm of stream, wind, rain, green. . . . These have been terrific months for this seldom seen land. For Borneans, the interior has revolved on the axis of Harrisson and his numerous satellite bodies in an even hum of heavy pressure. Never again . . . ? Will it leave a vacuum effect on future government—esp. Dutch?

# Chapter 25

## Officer Administering the Interior

SEMUT 1's war was over. Tom turned his attention to carrying out his new assignment, as "officer administering the interior," serving with the British Borneo Civil Affairs Unit (BBCAU).

As soon as he moved back to Bario, Penghulu Lawai Besara provided him with a kinswoman named Bongan, a jolly Kelabit woman in her early thirties, to serve informally as a spouse. While the SEMUT 1 party had been in Sarawak as temporary war leaders, the Kelabits had acquiesced to Tom's banning of sexual relations between his men and local women. Now that he was in the highlands for what might be months or years more, the social pressure was strong on him to take a "wife." Bongan seemed a reasonable choice to Englishmen and Kelabits alike. She was not a great beauty nor in her first youth, but she was pleasant looking, gay, hard working, hard drinking, and resilient. She reminded one Englishman of a 1920s flapper.

On December 16, having completed his cleanup of Dutch Borneo matters, Tom walked back into Sarawak, reaching the Plain of Bah that afternoon: "Arrive Bario 1700. Bongan. Borak. Lovely to be home." By now, Bario was home for Tom. His sense that he was theirs and they were his became stronger as the weeks and months passed. His delight and fascination with the Kelabits and their land continued to grow. He was constantly recording observations about them: how and when they coughed and what they meant by it; how much they liked having guns and why; how they mourned a child's death.

His strong commitment to the Kelabits did not extend—at least not to the same degree—to his Kelabit "wife," Bongan. From their first days together, Tom recorded in his diary how attractive he found other local women and how irritating he found Bongan's frequent drunkenness. Heavy drinking was a big problem among the Kelabits, as well as among many other pagan longhouse people, but they also remember that Tom seemed to need a certain amount of alcohol to loosen his tongue. Without drink, he was apt to sit silent for long periods. If he had too much, though, he would become hostile and get into hot arguments and even physical fights. The next day, he would behave as if he had forgotten all about it. The Kelabits, too, would be ready to forget and did not hold grudges against him.

On December 18, he went to Pa Main to supervise the building of a schoolroom and on to P'Umur, where he had a drink and a swim and conducted a "high flirtation" with a Kelabit woman. By December 24, Tom was back in Bario, where he found his old friend Penghulu Lawai "dead drunk." Tom went to bed and had "sex with Bongan." On December 25, "At noon, realised it was Xmas day. Ate first Bario radish—huge and tasty. Felt suddenly lonely. . . . Bongan bloody drunk. Fed up. Wireless Xmas stuff, sounded odd!" The next day he spoke to Penghulu Lawai about the "hopelessness of Bongan."

Tom's greatest pleasure at this time seemed to be his vegetable garden. He recorded on December 27 that the cauliflower was up, the lettuce doing well, the radishes vast, the green peas "ok," and all of it "new to the interior."

The new year brought little change in his routine. In January, he traveled throughout the Kelabit highlands and the upper reaches of the Baram, Limbang, and Trusan Rivers, encouraging the local people to build schoolrooms and plant some of the new vegetables for which he provided the seeds. Many diary entries ended: "drink till dawn."

On February 20, he arrived at the market town of Marudi on the Baram, two-thirds of the way to the coast. There he learned that the Rajah had decided to cede Sarawak to the British Crown, and it would soon become a British Crown Colony. Signals from the British Military Administration were waiting for him when he got to Marudi, giving him travel orders to go to Labuan and Kuching. There he was given carte blanche to continue his activities.

By late March, he was back up-country, on the Trusan River, which was, according to his diary, "floodbound." He sat all day in a lean-to with fourteen other people, writing up "70 foolscap pages in [an] attempt to [draw a] picture of place, decay and hope, flies and craftsmanship. . . . Ate a lot: monkey and deer." As always, impervious to discomfort, noise, or the presence of others when his mind was engaged, he sat in that lean-to by the flooded Trusan and, having completed his seventy-page report on the situation in that valley, he planned the Batu Lawi expedition. The first anniversary was approaching of his first drop into Borneo from a Flight 200 Liberator that had never returned to base. It was time to fulfill his vow to give Squadron Leader Gordon Pockley, Jumpmaster Ben Ellis, and the Liberator's eleven-man crew a worthy memorial. He would do that by becoming the first person ever to climb Batu Lawi, the mountain they had christened "Mount 200."

During his travels through the uplands over the next several months, Tom slept with a different young woman or girl almost every time he went to a different longhouse. In a notebook entry of April 1, 1946, he wrote:

Female Kelabits very unshy of advances to you, once encouraged. Will ask to sleep with you—cf. two "*basah*" [wet] for me . . . at Main, one married, one single, urging me to try her for the one night and see if she was any good.

Women tend to be apathetic and passive in sex, but not always. Tend to lie back and take it—and show some surprise if you are very virile or long at it! Also proclaim "*sulit*" [hard, difficult] and "*mau tidor*" [want to sleep] and "*mau pulong*" [want to go home] at start and until emphatically taken. Expect to be dominated. Orgasm very hard to detect. . . . Natural attitude is on back, legs open. But are distinctly buttocks sensitive and ready also to do it other ways (tho' little idea of on top). Body conscious of male—definitely like to touch my white body.

A few weeks later, he reflected in a notebook in which he kept anthropological comments on the "Muruts" of the Trusan and the "Muruts" of Belawit that "married women are not involved but single women are free—it is up to them. They are choosy but ready to try a new person, . . . no secrecy about it as far as *I* am concerned anyway." He complained at one point that his young Kelabit male traveling companion seemed to feel that Tom must have a sex partner every evening.

By early April, he was feeling the "strain of interior life." Lack of privacy was beginning to tell on him, he had three painful cysts, and he was "generally run down." Bongan was engaged in a lawsuit with a Bario man over rights to a rice crop, and there were similar other annoying matters occupying his time, as he recorded in his notebook: "A man remarks that a lot of my time is taken up with tiny things, like some soya for a woman or steel for a boy. But it is part of local aid job, and anyway unavoidable." Even so, and despite sores on his hand and foot that caused him to "lay up in bed," Tom continued to enjoy much about his life at Bario. For one thing, he ate well: "Breakfast: rusa [deer], ground nuts, omelette, fresh peas, tomatoes, potatoes, pawpaw, banana and 'grapefruit,' honey." On April 6, a Bario sunset in which, unusually, the sky was not covered by cloud, moved him to write a poem:

As the night glides down the terrible cliffs long behind this house,

]. . .[

Many and below showy puffs below again

The evening gathered us in,

Ready to harvest the stars

So often denied to us in Bario's perfect darkness.

Meanwhile, plans were going forward to climb two mountains, not just Batu Lawi. One would commemorate SEMUT 1's March 25, 1945, drop into Borneo and the other would honor Squadron Leader Pockley and his crew. As Tom explained:

> When a hill tribesman dies, there is first of all a big party and feast a week later to celebrate his departure. For the next year, his family will be busy collecting rice, cattle and gifts to have a much bigger party. The guests may run to a couple of thousand. . . . The climax of the binge is that everyone climbs one of the local peaks and cuts a clearing or ride for 20 or 30 yards along the top of it. This is the door for the man's spirit to proceed to the after-life. The bigger the party, the more the guests feel obliged to make a bigger door on a bigger and better peak.

In mid-April, after two days of gargantuan feasting and drinking and sleeping with two more Kelabit women, Tom led a party of Kelabits to climb a mountain near Batu Lawi, where they made a clearing, or "door," and put a wooden board opposite, carved with a text commemorating the arrival in Borneo of Operation SEMUT, which had "controlled 40,000 square miles and bagged 1900 Japs." He raced up the mountain with his Kelabit friends and, having placed the commemorative board near the peak, they all ran the whole way down. Only two of the Kelabits kept up with him. That night he "slept with the beautiful Djawe" and helped the party empty fourteen jars of *borak*.

A few days later, Tom and six Kelabits set off for the twin-peaked Batu Lawi, bringing with them another carved wooden board. Neither of Batu Lawi's peaks, each about 6,600 feet high, had ever been reached before. Tom proposed to climb the lower one. (The higher peak would have to wait to be conquered by British climbers with suitable equipment many years later.) En route, he and his party passed through a mossy forest full of unusual orchids and pitcher plants of great beauty. A 1988 guidebook for mountain climbers notes:

> The mountain (which is really quite small [in diameter]) is approached from the south end of the secondary peak. At the base of the secondary peak, move cautiously along the rock side. You will notice great sheets of rock in the process of peeling off. . . . Do not touch this loose rock. One slight push could start a major rock slide. . . .
>
> The summit . . . is reached by scrambling up the ridge line. The latter is from half a meter to three meters wide with a sheer drop of hundreds of meters on both sides.

A few yards below the summit, in a rock cleft, Tom set his commemorative board:

FOR MY FRIENDS

S/LDR GRAHAM POCKLEIGH [sic] DFC

MAJ. BEN ELLIS, BRITISH ARMY AND THEIR CREW OF 200 FLIGHT RAAF.
THEY SUCCESSFULLY DROPPED US AT BAREO [*sic*] 25/3/45 BUT THEY
NEVER GOT BACK TO MOROTAI. BY BATU LAWI WE STEERED ON THIS
AND FOUR [*sic*] PREVIOUS ATTEMPTS. THEIR MAP CALLED IT MT 200.
I PLEDGED MY WORD TO CLIMB
FOR THE FIRST TIME
HERE IN LONELINESS I
REMEMBER THESE FRIENDS.
TH 20/4/46

From Batu Lawi's lower summit he could see "hundreds of miles of the whole interior of Borneo, over innumerable ranges, valleys which have never been trodden by the foot of man, and way in the far distance the faintest suggestion of the China Sea. . . ." Tom saw a peregrine falcon there, the only one he "saw in more than two years' Borneo travel."

Reaching the top of a new mountain was, as always, an exhilarating experience for him, but sighting a peregrine falcon added greatly to his pleasure, recalling the bird killed by a shipmate during that dreadful trip back to England from the Pacific in 1935. Then, Tom had been a sick and impoverished young man whose way home was being paid by an angry and disappointed father. Now, he was an army officer with exploits to his credit more impressive than those of the late General Harrisson, DSO.

The ecstasy of reaching the peak of Mt. Batu Lawi, knowing that he was part of the first group ever to do so, came a few days after he had received a letter from a friend of his and Biddy's at "home" that must have sunk his spirits. The friend had written:

I have just been in London and seen Biddy. She isn't too well, I think. She looks tired to death and thinner than ever, which can't have been easy to manage. . . .

The strain of no news has been grim. She has behaved extremely well under it, but the marks show. And now that news, a little, is coming in, she shows every sign of nervous exhaustion. Don't be shocked by it when you see her. . . . Don't mind if she cries a lot.

Max looks splendid. He's intelligent far beyond his age and I should think needs you more than most boys his age need a father, good as Biddy is with him. She took him to an ass of a doctor, recommended by someone, her sister or your mother, I forget which, who tried to frighten her about him in what seems an almost criminal way. That Max himself wasn't frightened is a tribute to her handling of him. . . .

As a postscript, the writer added, "re Biddy's £000 debts, I do not think she has given me a note of all her debts even now."

Tom copied the letter into his diary and, below it, wrote: "What a prospect!" He had not seen his wife and son in two years, and it is not certain whether he wrote to them. That Biddy was run down and nervous should have come as no surprise. She had already been very thin, nervous, drinking heavily, and making herself available to many men before Tom had even left England.

A woman friend and neighbor of Biddy's during the war often visited Biddy at "Shortlands," her Letchworth house, crammed full of Victoriana and remembers calling on her one morning and finding her sitting up in bed, with her face made up, wearing a sheer nightgown. After a cup of coffee, Biddy asked her friend to leave because she was expecting the gardener, for purposes that Biddy made no pretense of disguising.

From before their marriage, Biddy had complained to many of Tom's friends that he neglected her and did not make love to her. She had tried to entice several of his friends to fill the gap in her sex life. At least one had gone to bed with her, out of pity.

More upsetting to Tom than Biddy's infidelities may have been the hint of serious problems with Max. But then again, he may not have been surprised. When he had last seen Max, the boy had been not quite four years old. Now he was almost six. Even before Tom's departure, Max had shown signs that he was not quite normal. Sally Adams, Mary Adams' daughter, who had training in psychology, remembered:

> When Max was a baby—standing up in his cot that time at his house where I went with my mother when I was six and he was one and a half—he exhibited "hyper-reactive" behaviour that is often an early sign of schizophrenia.
>
> An ordinary child will scream and then sob and then gradually lose interest and calm down but a hyper-reactive child will scream terrifically and then it will cut off suddenly. I remember from that early time Max doing that and my finding his behaviour strange. But he was very intelligent.

Tom had paid great attention during Max's first three years, counting the number of words in his son's vocabulary and recording minute details of his progress. Then references to Max stop appearing in Tom's notes and letters. It was as if Tom had lost interest in the child. This is a strange reaction for any parent, especially for a man like Tom, who seldom lost interest in anything or anyone once his attention had been gained. An awareness that little Max was not like other children might also explain why Tom refused to father another child with Biddy, although she begged for one.

He had cause to suspect mental illness in a child of his; mental instability ran in his family. The General had spent his last years under the care of an analyst, and Doll was, by the end of the war, being treated by an Upper Brooke Street society psychotherapist named Carl Lambert for depression and alcohol and drug addiction. At Doll's suggestion, Dr. Lambert treated Biddy for similar problems. Lambert, a charismatic German with a fondness for gambling, had a clientele of well-born alcohol-addicted women who wrote large checks to him when they were under the influence of alcohol or drugs he prescribed. He may have been the doctor the letter writer complained about, who tried to frighten Biddy about Max "in what seems an almost criminal way."

Tom, perhaps dreading what he would find at "home," stayed on in the Kelabit country for a couple of months after receiving this letter. He did not find the Kelabits perfect companions. In addition to "the losing battle for privacy," he complained to his diary that "Kelabits have no *pity*. Only tears and laughter (and sadness) cf. laugh if my hand hurts—no SYMPATHY." But then he added: "I sometimes feel utterly disgusted at uproar and conflict of Kelabit life. But in ten minutes I smile into the confusion all around." However irritating the Kelabits could be, life among them seemed preferable to returning to his English wife and son.

Eventually, the choice was taken out of his hands. A signal came in May or June 1946, informing BBCAU that Harrisson's wife was in hospital for alcoholism and his son in a mental institution and that Tom was to be repatriated rapidly because his family needed him. He left Sarawak in August 1946, a year after the war had officially ended.

**Figure 16** Tom *(left)* and his partner Charles Madge, co-founder of Mass-Observation, 1937. (©Harold Coster Studio)

**Figure 17** Tom *(standing)* assigning tasks to Mass-Observation staffers at breakfast at 85 Davenport Street, Bolton, 1937. (©Humphrey Spender)

▲ **Figure 18** Tom lecturing to coal miner painters in October 1938. (©Julian Trevelyan)

**Figure 19** Captain Tom Harrisson with Max on his lap, Biddy with John Clayton on hers, in 1944, shortly before Tom left for Australia.

▲ **Figure 20** "Mount 200"
(Batu Lawi, over 6,000 feet), the
two limestone fingers that led
Tom's pilot to the drop zone in
north-central Borneo.

**Figure 21** Tom, (5 feet 11½ inches),
a major's star on his cap, wearing
a sarong, with Negri Besar, a tall
Kelabit from the Plain of Bah, 1945.

**Figure 22** Driver Phil Henry with Iban chief Penghulu Gani and his family on the Limbang River, in July 1945. A smoked head is in the foreground. Penghulu Gani was severely wounded by a Japanese bullet the following week.

**Figure 23** Punan guerrillas with blowpipes and spears, 1945.

**Figure 24** Sgt. C. F. "Fred" Sanderson, "Sandy," just after the war.

**Figure 25** Penghulu Lawai Besara *(right front)* with other Kelabit headmen, with World War II medals, 1966. (Robert Pringle)

**Figure 26** Tom, as officer administering the interior, Sarawak, 1946.

**PART FIVE**

Sarawak Museum,
1947–1956

# Chapter 26

## Back "Home" Again

Tom flew "home" from Singapore, arriving on September 2, 1946, in an England that held few attractions for him. Biddy and Max came out of hospital, and Tom lived with them and his stepson, John Clayton, in the Ladbroke Road house, but it was not a happy household. If John Clayton (then twelve years old) has remembered accurately, not only did Tom and Biddy get on worse than ever, but Tom was physically abusive to her.

Friends recall that Biddy knew how to get under Tom's skin and enrage him, but it was not just home life that repelled this reluctantly returned Englishman. As Tom wrote in the September 28, 1946, issue of the *New Statesman*, he felt lonely among undemonstrative, coolly polite Englishmen:

> After Australia, . . . a Sarawak long house or the easy friendship of soldiers, it is horrid to stand solitary in a city pub, or face your fellows in the train speechless, almost ashamed. One longs to reach out and talk a little to the elderly gentleman with the checked waistcoat reading Kafka, to strike up an unambitious, inter-station intimacy with the nice, dumb-looking blonde. . . .

Resuming contact with friends, especially those now wielding power in a Britain governed by Labour, claimed much of Tom's attention during his first months back. Tom had done remarkable things, but the war was over and no one in London seemed to care as much about his extraordinary past year and a half in Borneo as about things going on in England now. Tom, whose need to be the center of attention had been fully met in the Far East, found himself being upstaged when he most wanted to impress.

His companion during his 1932 climb of Mount Dulit, Eddie Shackleton, born the same year as Tom, looked up to him as a great and positive influence on his life. Eddie had ended the war a wing commander, not a mere major, and was now a Labour M.P. Tom Driberg, a fellow journalist and a favorite prewar companion of Tom's for drinking and gossiping, was also a new Labour M.P., even though a notoriously indiscreet homosexual. Woodrow Wyatt was a Labour M.P. as well; as an Oxford undergraduate he had been an M-O volunteer in Bolton, winding up the gramophone while Tom composed his newspaper articles and M-O reports.

In Tom's search to reestablish himself among the movers and shakers of Britain, he even renewed his uneasy "friendship" with Solly Zuckerman. Addressing the future "Mr. British Science" at his office at the University Museum in Oxford, Tom wrote:

> Dear Solly,
> I have just got back from the Far East and am trying to pick up the threads to date. Could we possibly meet some time for a short talk?
>
> Yours ever,
> Tom Harrisson
>
> P.S. I flew back in a plane with a monocled Colonel Welch, who claimed he had been organising you and [Desmond] Bernal. I shouldn't have thought anybody could have done that at less than a Field Marshal.

To which Solly replied cordially, adding as a postscript: "Only Field Marshals did. It was the other way round."

In Tom's search for a role for himself in postwar Britain, Mass-Observation was the obvious choice, but two major obstacles stood in the way. One was the growth in the popularity in Britain of public opinion polls, partly thanks to M-O. In 1985, Angus Calder pointed out that "it may be that [M-O's] greatest significance in the history of social science in Britain is that its reputation accustomed people to the idea that such surveys should be taken seriously." The other surveys, such as Gallup's, were not quite like M-O's; they depended primarily on posing relatively simple yes-no questions to large samples of people. As Tom stated repeatedly in the press and in scholarly journals, such techniques can sometimes give false information. Events sometimes bolstered his arguments, as when he correctly predicted more than a year ahead the Labour victory in the first postwar British general election, while virtually everyone else guessed wrong, even up to the last minute, although the 1945 Labour victory was overwhelming.

The other major obstacle to M-O continuing to command serious attention was the mushroomlike growth of sociology as a social science heavily dependent on statistics. Tom still questioned the scientificness of sociologists' assumptions and results, especially their obsession with quantitative methods, but nobody wanted to hear such arguments. It was fairly obvious by mid-1946 that Tom had little hope of convincing the large corporations and government bodies that were the main consumers of Gallup's and similar mass polls to use M-O instead. Small, quirky, and ideological in its approach, M-O had too much of a thirties flavor.

If his future did not lie with M-O, where then? Postwar England was proving less hospitable to people with verve but no formal credentials than it had formerly been. As a friend from Tom's New Hebrides days commented in a letter to Jock Marshall:

> It is a pity the colonial times are over, when a well-bronzed man could still excite the glands of a well fed Parliament or the femininity of a romantic country. . . . Men like Tom will have to sacrifice half of their personality to please the actual times. The shame is that the dullest of all engineers or any technician is welcome to make love with our time; the whore now likes to be fucked by spectacles. Poor Tom must become a specialist (or rot) and, I hope, he will never like it, although he might achieve something great through it.

Jock was back at Oxford, embarked on a doctoral program under John Baker, and Tom stayed with the Australian in Oxford for a few days in February. Jock, who turned thirty-six on February 17, recorded in his diary that day that Tom

> has changed in only one way: he now realizes what power prominent people have to damage him; and he becomes ingratiating, especially in 'phone conversations where the mind, voice and vocabulary are the only tools, in his dealings with some of them. The whole sum of all his relations is a desire for Power—and he goes about it in different ways with different people. . . .

Tom's quest for a new career ended when he was nominated by the colonial office to be curator of the Sarawak Museum and government ethnologist. This was the post held by his 1932 Sarawak enemy, E. Banks, who, before leaving Sarawak in 1945 after years in a Japanese prison camp near Kuching, had said that he would not return. The job was thus vacant. Years later, Tom told a BBC audience:

> There was this lovely museum that the Second Rajah had started largely under the influence of Alfred Russel Wallace, who worked in Sarawak for two years. And they *weren't* at that time intending to appoint a curator and so I said I'll [be] curator pretty well for nothing and I'll spend part of my time doing this and part of my time helping the people in the interior.

That he was willing to accept a position where (he said) he would be working "pretty well for nothing" tells us how much he wanted to get back to Sarawak and how much he wanted to get out of England. It is not clear how long he intended to stay in Sarawak, probably not more than a year or two. It is, however, clear that he intended to make a name for himself out of his research on the Kelabits.

In May, he asked Solly Zuckerman for "POINTERS FOR FURTHER RESEARCH BY ME [Tom's capitals]" into aspects of Kelabit life. Solly promised to ". . . send you any suggestions which I may have about enquiries which it might be worth your while to pursue," but he appears never to have done so. Tom genuinely wanted guidance on how to conduct a social scientific study in a way acceptable to British scientists and academicians. A major obstacle to obtaining or absorbing such guidance was that he thought that there must be some trick to it that he could pick up from people like Solly who were successful in science and/or academia.

In addition to trying to get help from Zuckerman, Tom, during the time he was in Britain, worked tenaciously at renewing and strengthening contacts with people and organizations that had proved useful in the past or might be in future. He was determined that, once back in Borneo, he would not again be forgotten by his friends in England's political, governmental, academic, and media milieus.

Meanwhile, drawing on the presence in England of Jock Marshall, Eddie Shackleton, and Paul Bartram, he concocted an amusing BBC script entitled "Borneo Jungle" for the four men to act out on the *BBC Light* program of February 22, 1947. The first half brought him almost to blows with Jock when their light banter started to ignite old rivalries. The second half of the broadcast was devoted to SEMUT 1, with Paul Bartram reading from his diary entries of the stirring days of October 1945 when he and Tom had been on either side of the belligerent Fujino Tai.

The timing of the BBC show added to the impact of the announcement within the fortnight of the granting of military honors to large numbers of SEMUT veterans, beginning with the DSO for Tom, Toby Carter, and Bill Sochon. SEMUT 1 did conspicuously better than the other SEMUT, or "Z" Special, parties in Borneo: while SEMUT 2 and 3 (active elsewhere in Sarawak) and AGAS (active in British North Borneo) had less than a dozen honors to divide among them, half of SEMUT 1's forty-two veterans received them. Tom was especially pleased that Sergeant Sanderson was awarded the DCM (Distinguished Conduct Medal) and that Driver Henry "whom 9 Div. tried to try for murder" was Mentioned In Dispatches. Finally, after half a year of feeling unappreciated by his countrymen, Tom could write to his SEMUT 1 colleagues on March 10, 1947:

> Those who have felt that higher command simply scrubbed SEMUT can now feel happier. . . . We can forget the mean and petty jealousies of some elements of the Australian regular forces on the spot and among some of the prewar local officials. HM [His Majesty] The King is above this sort of thing, and I think it is fair to say that the recognition with which he has honoured the ["Z" Special Unit] in

Borneo will be seen to be fully merited when the whole war in that theatre can be seen in perspective. . . .

It is impossible to exaggerate the sense of gratification that receiving the DSO gave Tom. It was the medal his father had received that Tom most admired and envied. Getting the DSO symbolized equaling his father's heroic record.

In late May 1947, therefore, Tom left for Borneo not as someone escaping a bad marriage, not as someone who found he could not be a decent parent to a sick child whose mental illness might have been inherited from him, not as someone accepting an obscure job in the colonies rather than stay and watch the swifter rise of his contemporaries at home, but as a decorated hero returning to the scene of his triumph. He reached Kuching in June.

# Chapter 27

## Government Ethnologist

As Tom's plane descended over Sarawak on a day in June 1947, he saw again, after nine months' absence, the low coastal area of mangrove and nipa palm unfolding into a vast plain with a series of pyramidal mountains in the background. The familiar blanket of dark green jungle was still there, broken only by the coffee-brown rivers snaking their way to the sea.

Since Kuching was the capital of Sarawak, Tom's first official act was to cross the river by the little ferry to "sign the Governor's book." Sir Charles Arden-Clarke, the newly installed colonial governor, lived in the Victorian Gothic *Astana* (palace) of the Brooke Rajahs.

The Astana was set on a hill above the Sarawak River, across the water from the main part of Kuching. With its Gothic Revival tower, it was a nice compromise between mid-nineteenth century grandeur and tropical comfort. Aside from the tower, it was chiefly the dining room that distinguished the Brooke palace from other westerners' houses. Palatial in its dimensions, it was furnished in gleaming mahogany, with long tables that could hold all the crested silverware, china, and crystal for state dinners for dozens of guests. A dashing oil portrait of the youthful and romantic founder of the Brooke Raj, Sir James Brooke, looked down from the wall, as if to assure that governor and guests were still maintaining the Brookes' idiosyncratic style of dealing with their subjects, now that the last Rajah had passed the reins of government to the British Crown.

The Crown's senior representative, Malcolm MacDonald, commissioner general for South East Asia and governor-general of Malaya and British Borneo, recognized that

> The Rajah's government in Sarawak was personal. His word was law. Problems in his small kingdom were so few and simple that he could virtually cope with them all himself. . . . On the Rajah's journeys he was accessible to everyone. Penghulus consulted him about tribal affairs, Chinese leaders told him of their community

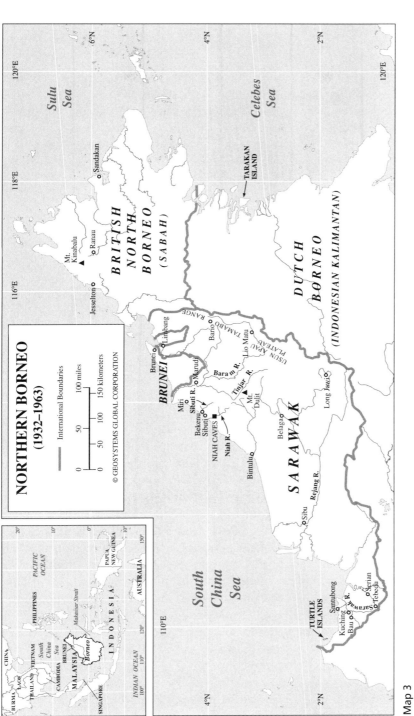

## NORTHERN BORNEO
## (1932–1963)

—— International Boundaries

© GEOSYSTEMS GLOBAL CORPORATION

0        50        100        150 kilometers
0        50        100 miles

*Sulu Sea*

120°E

118°E

116°E

6°N

4°N

Sandakan

Mt. Kinabalu ▲    Ranau ○

**BRITISH NORTH BORNEO**
**(SABAH)**

Jesselton ○

*Celebes Sea*

TARAKAN ISLAND

**DUTCH BORNEO**
**(INDONESIAN KALIMANTAN)**

120°E

2°N

Limbang

Brunei ○
**BRUNEI**

Bario ○    Lio Matu ○
TAMABU RANGE
USUN PLATEAU
Bara m R.

Marudi ○

Miri ○
Sibuti R. ○
Bekenu ○
Sibuti ○
**NIAH CAVES** ■
Niah R.

Mt. Dulit ▲
Tinjar R.

Long Jawi ○

Belaga ○

Bintulu ○

**SARAWAK**

Sibu ○
Rejang R.

*South China Sea*

110°E

4°N

2°N

TURTLE ISLANDS

Santubong ○
Kuching ○
Bau ○
SARAWAK R.
Serian ○
Tebedu

Map 3

### (inset map)

CHINA
BURMA
LAOS
THAILAND    VIETNAM
CAMBODIA    *South China Sea*
MALAYSIA    BRUNEI
SINGAPORE    *Makassar Strait*
*Borneo*
**INDONESIA**

*PACIFIC OCEAN*

PHILIPPINES

PAPUA NEW GUINEA

AUSTRALIA

*INDIAN OCEAN*

20°

10°

0°

10°

100°    110°    120°    130°    150°

problems, petitioners sought his aid in the settlement of grievances. . . . A pleasant, friendly informality graced these occasions. . . .

The Rajah had expected his small hand-picked expatriate administrative staff to establish similar personal contacts with the people they administered. They had done so. MacDonald, (resident in Singapore), coming to Sarawak in 1946, saw this personal contact as "combining the best features of autocracy and democracy" and was determined "as Governor-General . . . that this tradition of personal rule must be preserved. . . ." This habitual dialogue between leaders and the led had won Tom's heart during his 1932 visit to Sarawak. He was delighted that MacDonald meant to continue it.

He and MacDonald liked and respected one another on sight and remained friends ever after, although Tom, perhaps recognizing his own and MacDonald's need to be the center of attention, prudently kept his distance from MacDonald when the latter was on his imperial tours of the hinterlands. Rarely accompanying the governor-general on these trips, Tom essentially left to MacDonald the southern two-thirds of Sarawak as his special area. There lived the bulk of Sarawak's people: most of the state's Malays, Chinese, and Dayaks. Conversely, perhaps because of the absence of roads and airstrips, MacDonald rarely, if ever, ventured onto Tom's turf: the sparsely populated upper reaches of the Baram, Trusan, and Limbang Rivers and the high tableland beyond, the home of the *orang ulu*—the Kelabits and Muruts, Kenyahs, and some of the Kayans and Punans. Tom would, however, sometimes go to Singapore to see MacDonald and to pass on snippets of information to the intelligence people on the governor-general's staff.

Tom's new job had two parts: "Government Ethnologist" and "Sarawak Museum Curator." Although he had announced in a letter to the *Sarawak Gazette* his intention to put "the Museum back into shape after . . . years of neglect," he was more interested in the ethnologist part of his job. He was anxious to get back to "continue my Kelabit studies after nine months blessed relief from sliding down hillsides and picking off leeches."

While still in Kuching doing the minimum to get the museum up and running, however, Tom relied for his off-duty social life almost entirely on his fellow white colonial officers. These were the men in whom all political and administrative power resided. The Rajah had made it a rule that his officers could not marry until they had been in Sarawak for at least ten years. While the new colonial administration did not forbid marriage, it maintained Brooke Raj conditions—virtually no appropriate schools and little medicine—that discouraged the presence of wives and children. Thus, the expatriate community was composed primarily of men on their own, and the usual social arena was the bar of the Aurora Hotel, the only hotel in town patronized by Europeans. It was just down the road from the museum, and

Tom could be found there most weekday afternoons at the end of the day, unwinding over drinks alongside many of Sarawak's senior colonial officers. At the Aurora Bar, or on Saturday noon after the offices closed for the week and the same people assembled at the Resthouse Bar, or among those same people drinking Tiger beer to wash down their curry tiffin on Sunday afternoons at the Sarawak Club, Tom was already famous, not as a World War II hero or as the founder of Mass-Observation but as the notorious leader of the rampaging youths of the Oxford expedition of 1932. Since Tom, as in the past, tended to get surly and pugnacious when he drank too much, Kuching's expatriates soon had new scandalous stories to spread about him, lending credibility to the mostly untrue earlier tales.

Tom, however, took pains to keep on good terms with Governor Arden-Clarke and those immediately under him. They, knowing Governor-General MacDonald's regard for Tom and being aware that he had well-placed friends in the British media and in Parliament, were wary of disciplining him as they might have another neophyte colonial servant.

The social ambience of expatriate life in colonial Kuching was a bit claustrophobic for someone of Tom's originality and rambunctiousness. He was anxious to get back to his free and easy Kelabits. The Colonial Office had assigned him the job of making a census of the *orang ulu* as part of an overall census of Sarawak, to be completed before the end of December 1947. But perhaps the main reason why Tom wanted to move back to the Kelabit highlands as soon as possible was the arrival, within weeks of his own return to Sarawak, of Dr. E. R. (later Sir Edmund) Leach, a social anthropologist and protégé of Professor (later Sir) Raymond Firth.

Dr. Leach had come to Borneo because Arden-Clarke, whose expertise and previous colonial experience lay in Africa, as one of his first acts as governor of Sarawak, had asked the Colonial Office to arrange for a "socio-economic survey" of this new colony in order to help him choose appropriate social and economic policies. The survey was to be in two parts: an initial quick assessment by a qualified social anthropologist to find a few topics for detailed research that would have both practical and scientific value, followed by sending out three or four young scholars to carry out the proposed research. The Colonial Office had asked Professor Raymond Firth, secretary of the Colonial Social Science Research Council (CSSRC), which would be supervising the project, to recommend a social anthropologist for the initial survey. Firth had proposed Leach.

Firth, the heir to Malinowski's famous social anthropology seminar at the London School of Economics, was all too familiar to Tom as the man who in 1939 had launched the most devastating attack ever made on Mass-Observation techniques and procedures. For someone to come out to do a social survey of Sarawak on the recommendation of Firth was enough to bring out Tom's paranoid tendencies. And, justifying Tom's paranoiac reaction in his own mind, Firth, when recommending Leach to the Sarawak government as "a trained social anthropologist with experience of 'slash-and-burn' cultures," had remarked that Tom, in spite of his local experience, was not qualified to conduct the social survey.

This was an extremely prejudicial statement to appear in Tom's personnel file so early in his Sarawak colonial career. If correct, Tom was not qualified to be Sarawak's "government ethnologist" either. When, inevitably, Tom got to see Firth's comment in his file, Tom's generalized dislike for academic social science and scientists became focused on social anthropology. He looked upon its practitioners as sworn enemies.

Tom and Leach had first met in late 1946 or early 1947, when Tom attended a few of the Firth seminars and had emerged bloodied after crossing swords with the promising young Dr. Leach. Tom would no doubt eventually have picked a quarrel with Leach after the social anthropologist reached Kuching, but it appears it was Leach who commenced hostilities. He chose to do so in the pages of the staid official monthly *Sarawak Gazette*.

Months before he returned to Sarawak, Tom had been filling many pages of the *Gazette* with six long installments of his report on "The Kelabit Peoples of Upland Borneo." By June, having arrived in Kuching, he used the *Gazette* to introduce himself as the new museum curator and government ethnologist and to describe how he envisioned carrying out his job.

Within a month of Leach's arrival, the anthropologist used a letter to the editor in the September *Gazette* as a way to attack Tom—with seemingly little cause. In the August issue of the *Gazette*, Tom had given a description of a ceremony of a Land Dayak community involving the ritual "feeding" of old heads left over from the headhunting days. He had witnessed the rite in the company of the governor during a short visit to the Bau District in late June. Tom's account of the ceremony is appropriately brief and, typical of Tom, vivid and informal. Both he and the shaman had been blind drunk at the time (which had caused Arden-Clarke to vow never to include the government ethnologist on future gubernatorial trips).

In the September *Gazette*, Leach deplored Tom's description of the rite and blamed Tom's "keen sense of the dramatic" for having led him to "draw rather hasty inferences from a single and incompletely observed instance of a very interesting ritual." Leach claimed to be "at a complete loss to understand what Mr. Harrisson means" by the terms he used and ended his letter with his own opinion that Dayak festivals involving the use of heads may merely be occasions for "individual and group boasting and it is quite possible that there is not much more to it than that."

Such a statement was as a red flag to a bull. For Leach, who had spent only a month in Sarawak—much of it in Kuching, where he would not have witnessed any head ceremonies—to dismiss some of the most important rituals of pagan Sarawak as mere "occasions for individual and group boasting" was an act of arrogance, of ignorance, of which even Tom had never suspected trained social anthropologists to be capable. It was also untypically cavalier and simplistic of Leach to make such a bald statement in writing. Leach must have been deliberately out to provoke Tom. He did not have to wait long to see the bull charge.

Invited to reply in the same issue, Tom went on at length to make the case for the fact that "head-hunting and head-feasts played, and in some ways still do subtly play, a deep and vital part in the pagan ideology of Dayak and other groups." He asked Leach for the evidence on which he had chosen to contradict so much of what had been written on head ceremonies. He sought the "privilege of publishing his evidence in the *Sarawak Museum Journal*," which Tom was starting to revive.

The duel then moved to a private arena, with letters exchanged between Tom and Leach (see Chapter 28). This correspondence would eventually goad Tom into trying to find answers to the various questions raised by social anthropology, questions he had been dodging for years. These were: could the discipline of social anthropology—which he had disparaged along with its related discipline, sociology—prove useful to him and, if so, could he master it?

He knew that what he had written on primitive peoples thus far would not pass muster among scholars. Much as his *Savage Civilisation* had been admired for its many useful insights and had had a more enthusiastic popular reception than Firth's classic work, *We the Tikopia* (published at almost the same time), it had never been taken seriously by anthropologists. It was more than a mere travel book but less than a serious study of a Melanesian society. Similarly, his six-part report on "The Kelabit Peoples of Upland Borneo," though ideal for the *Gazette*'s readers, telling them more than they could ever learn themselves about their isolated neighbors, was, he knew, not proper anthropology. He ended the last installment: "I am returning to the Kelabit country shortly. These notes are provisional, and very incomplete. I have tried to sketch, very roughly, the outlines of a unique people. The detail, the body, I hope to fill in fully, after I have been back to my friends far away in the Ulu [upriver] Baram."

He left Kuching for the interior in early September, bringing with him four museum staffers, and collected en route a SEMUT 1 veteran whose chief contribution now was his good knowledge of upland dialects, including "Murut" and Kelabit. Tom brought with him bolts of cloth and other trade goods, since, in addition to conducting a census of the *orang ulu* and studying Kelabit society, he planned to use this trip to enrich the museum's already creditable collection of bird skins, stuffed mammals, native art and artifacts, and imported ceramics and beads as well as anything else that struck him as interesting.

To conduct the census, Tom first revisited the areas that he had come to know well during the 1932 Oxford expedition and the days of SEMUT 1: the valleys of the Limbang, Trusan and Tinjar. He had a tiny portion of Sarawak's people to count but a hard one to find. Of Sarawak's half-million inhabitants, one-quarter lived along the coastal plains (Malays, Melanaus, and related groups) and another quarter (the Chinese) lived in or near towns along the main rivers as far up as they were navigable to craft with outboard motors. Most of the remaining 250,000 inhabitants were Dayaks—primarily Ibans but also Bidayuhs (then called Land Dayaks)—who lived along rivers and tributaries in the broad region between the coast and the central highlands. Fewer than 30,000, about 5 percent of Sarawak's total population, consisting of Muruts (Lun Bawang and Lun Dayeh), Kelabits, Tagals, Kenyahs, Kayans, Tabuns, Sabans, Punans, and similar *orang ulu*, lay in Tom's census district, but Tom was determined to find them and count them all. By the end of the census, Tom could take pride in having located 1,833 Punans, mostly nomads living in the inmost recesses of the primary jungle. (Tom's figure for Punans is more than double the figure in the 1939 census. Since the nomadic Punans' habitat had shrunk in those years, the new figure is more likely the result of Tom's thoroughness than that the Punans had doubled their numbers in less than a decade.)

Eager though he was to get up to the Kelabit plain to complete his census and begin to conduct his "Kelabit Studies," he went briefly along the Niah River, to the south of the lower Baram, to see the Great Cave of Niah, where the naturalist Alfred Russel Wallace had thought there might be evidence of the missing link between earlier and modern man.

He had no time to do any digging but was fascinated by the special breed of swiftlets (*Collocalia*) in the cave whose edible nests were made from their own hardened saliva. These nests were prized by the Chinese for their bird's nest soup and had formed an important part of the Sino-Bornean trade for centuries. He watched native collectors harvest the nests. They shinned up their slim poles to the dizzyingly high cave ceiling and brought down the nests, which the tireless swiftlets would then set about replacing. Tom determined that someday he would examine these caves carefully to see if Wallace's hunch had been correct.

He reached Bario in early October. His return there, after fourteen months away, meant far more to him than a chance to complete his census or carry out his ethnological studies. It meant coming back to the only place that had ever felt like home. At Bario, Penghulu Lawai Besara, sporting the British Empire Medal for which Tom had nominated him, and many other Kelabits who had worked with Tom in the SEMUT days were present to welcome him back. Bongan was there and resumed her role as Tom's Kelabit wife.

*Chapter 28*

# Tom Responds to Leach's Challenge

At Bario was a letter from Dr. Edmund Leach, replying to Tom's riposte in the September *Gazette*. It is one of a handful of letters Tom kept all his life. It began:

Miri, 16 September 1947

Dear Tom,

    I have just seen your long letter in the September *Gazette*. I must say you seem to fly off the handle a bit easily. I assure you I had no intention of riling you to that extent or indeed of doing anything beyond throwing a large question mark into the argument. But seriously this question of "heads" interests me and I'd like to thrash the thing out further.

Leach went on to explain that "every myth-based ritual has two forms of 'purpose' behind it," a practical purpose and an ideological purpose that may or may not be demonstrable. While such nondemonstrable purposes, such as driving away evil spirits, might be the ones for which the head-rite feasts were supposedly done, in fact they had the practical purpose of enhancing the prestige and even the wealth of the feast-giver. Leach continued: "Now such a feast, as I would have it, is in its primary essentials 'an occasion for individual and group boasting' similar to feasts he had seen for like purposes in upland Burma. He also mentioned having been to an Iban head feast on the upper Rejang and, using an interpreter,

I got what seemed to me a pretty coherent ideological explanation of the whole process. That purpose boiled down to wealth and prosperity for [the host] himself. If that is what you mean by "cleansing, fecundity, placatory and regenerative processes" well and good; it is certainly what I mean by "an occasion for individual and group boasting". . . .

But please don't misunderstand me. Frankly I would like to be convinced that headhunting *has* some connection with "fertility" however you choose to define it; but the evidence isn't there yet.* Perhaps your Kelabit will produce it.

You know you needn't belabour me quite so much for my local ignorance. After all I have already seen quite a few corners of Sarawak which you haven't, and I can speak as much (or as little) Grogo Land Dayak as you can! And outside Borneo, despite your Melanesian experiences, I have seen far more diverse forms of primitive life than you have. Granted an interpreter is never ideal. I'll still back my opinions against yours!

There was enough in this letter of interest to Tom for him to consider it less dismissively than Leach's remarks in the *Gazette*. He replied (in a letter that has not yet surfaced), and Leach wrote him again from Kuching before leaving Sarawak.

This second letter from Leach, which Tom also kept, provides the kind of detailed guidance from a recognized expert or "scientist" that Tom had vainly sought from Solly Zuckerman a few months earlier:

> As you know my job has been in the nature of reconnaissance. I was required to make an appreciation which might justify three or more potential schemes of detailed research which would have both a practical and a scientific value. . . .
>
> Your present work of course falls right outside this scheme and I am naturally not expecting to exercise any control over it. On the other hand with a view to economy of effort I am leaving the Murut-Kelabit area out of the scheme of projects to be proposed by me on the assumption that your work will meet the bill for that particular area.
>
> . . . The notes given below are therefore a skeleton of the type of data which will be common to all the schemes to be organised by me on behalf of the CSSRC, and if you include this type of data in your work it will obviously greatly assist in making comparisons between the different areas.

Leach then gave a paragraph each to a number of subjects he would want Tom to cover if his work were to fit in with the overall socioeconomic survey: physical distribution of ethnic groups; formal rules of marriage, divorce, adoption, inheritance, succession; "an . . . analysis of household expenditure and income of a selected group of households . . . [and] sources, scale and uses of cash income if any"; and the like.

He concluded:

---

*Years later, Prof. Derek Freeman did produce such evidence. See his "Severed Heads that Germinate" in R. H. Hook, ed., *Fantasy and Symbol: Studies in Anthropological Interpretation* (London: Academic Press, 1979), 233–246.

I don't know whether this rates as "cooperation" or not, and I care less, and the last thing I want you to think is that I am trying to tell you how to do your job. It is merely that if you do collect concrete well documented data under the above heads it will be of great value to the overall research plan.

Yours,

E. R. Leach

[P.S.] Finally, if you are going to enlarge upon depopulation, for God's sake be detailed and statistical.

If Leach's exasperation jumps off the page, it is still greatly to his credit that he took such pains to try to set Tom on the right road. During the next half-year, Tom appears to have tried hard to follow Leach's guidelines.

Leach, in this letter, expresses his desire to avoid being accused of not "cooperating." This must have been in response to a complaint by Tom—one he repeated regularly during his Sarawak years—that visiting scholars came to Borneo for their own career reasons and were unwilling to give anything back to those who helped make their research possible. But Tom's problem with visiting anthropologists went well beyond that. Fundamentally, and increasingly as Tom's relationship with the Kelabits grew more personal, his approach was at odds with that of the typical academic anthropologist. He was not interested in helping to develop what Leach in his letter called "valid comparative generalisations" through the study of different ethnic groups in order to learn something about "man" or "primitive man" or even "hill tribes." His interest was in learning about a group primarily to benefit that particular group. This had also been his approach to fieldwork in the New Hebrides and in Bolton. In that sense, though he was less "scientific," he was more idealistic and less personally ambitious than most professional anthropologists. He may once have toyed with the idea of going back to Oxford and drawing on his research to win a degree or diploma, but the real motive behind his research was to help him in his role as protector of, and advocate for, the people he loved, the hill people of Borneo, particularly the Kelabits.

Nonetheless, he was prepared to try to follow Leach's guidelines to see if they would lead him to better understand, and more successfully record the features of, Kelabit society. Over the next six months, along with his usual notebooks on other subjects, he kept a notebook entitled "General Considerations" in which he jotted down thoughts on how to write up what he observed, with reference to the Leach guidelines.

These jottings are Tom's most eloquent statement of his problems with social anthropology as then practiced. He commented:

One is constantly making British-judgement or whatever you like (footnote: state in full my biases—cf. education, politics, experience, sex;) judgement, even when feeling most fully *in* the thing. This matters, because—in my view—the investigator, though bound to affect the situation (even if he was, in this case, a Kelabit, and no one knew he was investigating anything, his presence would or could affect this) should do so outside their pattern as little as possible. For, at one end of the scale, is the ethnologist, who simply sits in a house eating tons and paying people to "tell him their stories" or who tears round with an interpreter to record all he can as widely as possible—Dr. W. Rivers in Melanesia 1912 or Dr. E. R. Leach in Borneo 1947. He affects everything. On the other, is the one who lives long and sees deep, such as Malinowski. But one always wonders how deep. . . . All must have prejudices and none can ever alter colour of skin or accent or knowledge of the world, to put it at extreme.

Such a comment could have been penned by an anthropologist of the 1980s or 1990s. Tom continued:

The ideal I sought was to be as unobtrusive as possible and *not* normally to take notes openly. In ten years M-O, I have learned many ways of disguised note taking and they were invaluable. Much of what I have seen and heard I would not have seen and heard (1) if I had *not* been there a long time; (2) if I had *not also* won and rewon the confidence of most of the people in a special way, shortening that time by say 50% (or rather, increasing the value of each time period by two). (3) If I had *not* shown a positive sympathy with their culture and an *active* participation in a large part of it; (4) If I *had* been visibly interested in all I saw and heard; (5) If I had displayed any prejudices antipathetic to their culture and race. I claim to have got a long way in, and that on many occasions I recorded much, of which they had no idea.

These were mostly tiny occasions, which to my way of approach—and contrary to that of nearly all social scientists—are vital material, and to be recorded in detail, without fear of "being swamped in trivial data"; indeed that fear can only show that the investigator either: (a) had a preconceived theory (in which case of course all his fieldwork is dead anyway, and his arrogant attitude can be as he pleases); [or] (b) has a mediocre intellectual equipment and no confidence in his power to investigate.

For an investigator to be afraid of being "overwhelmed by fact" is about as idiotic as for a Kelabit cutting down a tree to fear being crushed by his own work; he would be no fit Kelabit and occasionally one does fail in this, as in other ways, to live his standard. . . .

Tom's desire to first collect detailed data and then follow wherever it led was his single biggest obstacle in going along with social anthropology and getting along with its practitioners. They faulted him for "failing" to begin his research with a theoretical framework. It is a failing shared by Professor Firth in his first book. Adam Kuper, in *Anthropology and Anthropologists* (1978), commented: "*We, the Tikopia* runs to almost 600 pages, and because there is not a theoretical framework of any substance, one wonders almost why the author stopped when he did. . . ."

In Tom's case, the absence of a theoretical framework was deliberate. As he stated in these "General Considerations" notes:

> I believe in the bombardment of fact and that in our present state of knowledge in the sociological field, we need especially much and especially intense bombardment. For our theories are seldom based on facts, but on the subjective theorisings of armchair sociologists (though there are, of course, plenty of exceptions). But sociology [by which Tom also meant social anthropology] is still in the explorer stage. We are still finding out the names of the main mountains; supposed contour sketches of the little valleys may appear imposing, but be absurd. . . . One function of this bombardment is corrective, constantly imposed upon the investigator. Only by living right *in* the community, can he learn his "mistakes"— mistakes which if uncorrected can mislead his whole work and conclusions, a fact that has yet barely been realized because so little anthropological work has been repeated nor can it normally be read and corrected (as yet) by its subject matter.

Tom asserted:

> The process of anthropology is, like any, selective. In order to direct and control the selection, investigators have generally tended to follow one of two plans: (1) to take certain conspicuous elements of the culture and develop from these; this way is the method of early ethnologists and has been given a new boost in recent years by Margaret Mead, Gregory Bateson and others or (2) to take a structural plan of imposed approach and limit observation within that framework. The so-called "functional" school of anthropology, established by Prof. B. Malinowski, has increasingly tended in this formal and largely economic direction, best expressed in R. Firth's *Malay Fishermen*, which is barely sociological any more, concentrating on "economic facts." Both tendencies are natural reactions to the *difficulties* of getting into the culture pattern oneself and sorting out the elements in it anyway.

Instead, Tom asserted:

> As far as possible, I have *tried* to use a slightly different approach, insofar as I have built up largely from the trivial, the overheard, and the stray incident, I have sought in my years to seek out the theme and stresses of the culture as they operate on the people themselves.

Once again, as with Mass-Observation, Tom wanted to collect more and more data rather than try prematurely to draw out underlying principles and patterns.

It would have been easier, for instance, to have taken the death-feast, funerary and stonework complex, the most dramatic, remarkable and extensive expression of Kelabit activities, and built my whole study round that thesis, perhaps as an extension of the approach in John Layard's brilliant *Stone Men of Malekula*. There would not have been anything *wrong* in doing that. It is a legitimate approach and generally reflects the ethos from one angle and all my cards would have been on the table. But the trouble is that though they were on the table and in theory anyone else can check and confirm and even contradict, in the essential interchange of ideas, in fact, the Kelabit plateau is so far away that probably no one would ever do so and the culture itself is changing so rapidly that exact checking would be difficult too. The temptation to mould an elaborate synthesis is that much increased, and I cannot help feeling that some of the Meadian style of anthropologists have considerably succumbed to it.

Tom had a point, in noting that, during his lifetime, few major works of anthropology were subjected to reexamination of the field data relatively soon after the first study. One could cite anthropologist Derek Freeman's findings, when he reinvestigated the sex life of Samoan adolescent girls fifteen years after Margaret Mead had done the fieldwork that resulted in her world-famous book, *Coming of Age in Samoa*. Freeman wondered why he and Mead found such different data. Girls he observed and interviewed did not appear to have anything like the sexual freedom Mead had described. Decades later, in 1983, Freeman published a formal refutation of Mead's conclusions. Then, in 1987, a Samoan woman who had spent much time with Mead when they were both twenty-four years old in Samoa, confessed in a sworn statement, that she and a friend had, as a typical Samoan prank, deliberately misinformed Mead about the sexual mores of Samoans. If Freeman's information is correct, it would appear that Mead, having come to Samoa for a few months, with a thesis to prove about sexual freedom in primitive societies, fell into just the kind of trap Tom was warning against. It is easy to wonder, as Tom did, how many of the findings of those early studies would have stood up to a second look. Today, modern communications have broken the isolation of virtually every society. Even those untouched by the outside world thirty years ago are, for the most part, so changed that a second examination of the phenomena those early anthropologist saw is no longer possible.

Tom's notes show how seemingly straightforward facts, such as Leach had asked him to obtain, are hard for a short-time visitor to ascertain. For example, Tom devoted several pages to telling different versions of how a sum of money borrowed from him by a Kelabit had been spent. In the first version, Tom drew on the accounting made by the debtor to him afterward. This, Tom asserted, was the kind of information Leach had requested, with a ledger showing precisely what was claimed to have been purchased for each outlay of cash. But, as he tried to verify what actually happened, by talking to more and more people involved in the various transactions, the figures in the neat ledger came hilariously unstuck. Eventually, drawing on partially correct versions from a dozen sources, he learned what really happened to the cash. The implicit moral is that even such a seemingly simple matter as determining how a sum of money is spent cannot be done without a deep familiarity with the people involved and lots of time. This example also showed how a trivial situation can be as revealing of the principles governing social behavior as a spectacular ceremony might be.

Tom gave, as another example of the danger of drawing conclusions from brief visits, the fact that Banks, when he wrote of "argumentless" and "molestingless" drunken evenings among the Kelabits, and when he claimed that "even in his cups the Kelabit remains a sportsman, not only individually but as a tribe," had got it wrong. Tom asserted that, after eight months of thinking Banks was correct, he learned that boasts and fights and exhibitions of vanity had "been hidden from every visiting white, . . . by a deliberate agreement, an armistice of all the senior men, who feel that the concomitant uproars are unsuitable before such a visitor."

The implicit moral that Tom drew here is that sixteen years of occasional short visits are no substitute for a long period of uninterrupted participation in a community's life to avoid major mistakes describing it. In this example, as elsewhere in his "General Considerations," Tom made statements that underline his point that "primitive" societies are not simple and that a visiting anthropologist cannot expect to master one in a series of short trips or in a year or two of fieldwork, any more than he/she could master an alien developed society in the same amount of time.

Announcing his last example of this point, Tom warned that it is "a final (rude) sound, perhaps, and not undirected."

It was not until November 26, 1947, that I heard a Kelabit emit wind from the anus. It was in a jungle shelter, when Ulit Ratu, Vasen Kilu, Jumen and I were on a hunting trip. (We got four deer and a monkey in three days, some 50 lbs. of dried meat to take home.) Sitting drying the meat in the evening, Vasen Kilu made a small noise. The others laughed and looked at me. Then Ulit (always bold) asked me if white men do this in the presence of women and all the men laugh at him. I say, not exactly, normally, but he would be very embarrassed and most present probably would. They said this was exactly how it was among Kelabits. I told of the very different ethic for this activity among exclusively male groups of certain types and how at my public school contests were held and champions declared. They said they too had games of this sort.

Tom concluded triumphantly:

> In over two and a half years, this common and quite normal activity . . . had been
> carefully hidden from me as from all whites, as one of many things "not to do
> before a *tuan*" and only the accident of Vasen Kilu's really excessive meal on
> deer's entrails opened yet one more window onto the Kelabit soul!

Tom's doubts about the accuracy and validity of the approved academic
approach to anthropology—what one 1990s anthropologist describes as
"the assemblage of hard facts unearthed in distant fields and carefully
reassembled at home"—sound modern today. Clifford Geertz, the leading
English-speaking anthropologist of the generation that did fieldwork in the
1950s, has led the way in rethinking what social anthropology has accomplished and can hope to achieve. In his view, social anthropology can no
longer be seen as the means for unearthing and reassembling "hard facts" to
reveal basic cultural patterns. Geertz sees its current aims as much less ambitious, perhaps merely limited to attempts to describe odd bits and pieces of
life in the society under study, what he describes as "mini-narratives with the
narrator in them."

As for "sociology"—that is, social anthropology for developed societies—its claims to "scientific" accuracy are now being questioned, and
Tom's objections to sociologists' overreliance on statistics are being shared by
some distinguished scientists. A 1995 leader in the *Economist,* under the
heading "74.6% of sociology is bunk," cites approvingly a respected biologist (Richard Lewontin) and a prominent social scientist (Richard Sennett),
who both condemn modern sociology for its "fixation on numbers and the
resulting neglect of those topics (which tend to be the interesting ones) that
cannot be quantified." This was Tom's view from early Mass-Observation
days onward. His little experiment with trying to find out what happened to
a small sum of money borrowed from him by a Kelabit reconfirmed his belief
that, unless handled with extreme care, figures disguise facts at least as often
as they reveal them.

In his notes, Tom lamely referred to the most glaring weakness in his own
fieldwork: "I had one serious disadvantage. In 1932 I had learned Malay as
necessary on the Oxford Expedition to the Baram. I started in with this. So
difficult to learn after. . . . " That Tom never advanced linguistically beyond
a rudimentary "Bazaar Malay" is one reason establishment anthropologists
dismiss him. (It is a good reason, although one wonders how good Mead's
Samoan was.) His inability to learn local languages was certainly a serious
handicap in his fieldwork but, in his view, "When all is said and done, my
greatest difficulty—or at least trial—has been to keep up with myself. . . . "
There is much truth in this. In Tom's literally insatiable desire to know more,

he rarely took time to sit down and properly organize the rich material he had already obtained. His nanny noticed when Tom was still a young child that he always wanted "to get onto the next thing before he had finished that one." His obituary in *The Times* hints tactfully at the same problem: "At no time did it appear that he was lost for a hundred worth-while things to do; and although they were mostly done, nothing was ever 'final'—each one led on to something new."

He was not, of course, devoting anything like full time to his ethnographic study of the Kelabits. He was collecting specimens, buying old jars and new mats, finding Kelabit stone megaliths, and carrying out his duties as a colonial officer in the far interior. Once again, he was both "Tuan Mayor" and local magistrate handling all accusations of theft or other unresolved disputes. He devoted pages of his notebooks to recording how and why he came to a decision regarding determination of guilt and punishment for some minor infraction or a major crime such as the theft of an axe, a crime that in the old days would doubtless have led to bloodshed. In the course of these duties, Tom learned a lot about Kelabit customary law, knowledge he would use later on the Kelabits' behalf.

He also helped the Bario longhouse welcome visitors, including the Reverend Mr. and Mrs. Hudson Southwell, evangelical missionaries. The Plain of Bah's Kelabits had been instructed before the war in the basics of American-style fundamentalism by Christianized teachers from the Dutch East Indies. Unlike their strictly Christian teetotal cousins on the Bawang Plain over the border, the Sarawak Kelabits of the Plain of Bah had taken from the new religion only what had suited them and still engaged in heavy drinking, premarital promiscuity, and many rites (such as those involving megaliths) left over from their pagan past.

By now, the Kelabits of the Plain of Bah were not averse to being taught more about Christianity. They had seen their more orthodox evangelical Christian neighbors across the border on the Bawang Plain living longer, healthier lives and growing better crops. So the people of Bario were happy to meet the Southwells, who had arrived in Sarawak many years earlier to found the Borneo Evangelical Mission and had spent most of the war as prisoners in the Batu Lintang internment camp on the outskirts of Kuching, to see if they were people they would want to have living among them and teaching them. The Kelabits were also eager to meet the first white woman most of them had ever seen. During the Southwells' visit, Tom and the missionaries regarded each other warily. Not only were they very different—the Southwells were teetotal and relatively humorless—but they were, in a sense, rivals in a battle for the Kelabit soul. Nonetheless, no doubt recalling his New Hebrides experience, Tom respected the Southwells' knowledge of the uplands and its people and their fluency in several upland languages. He and the missionary couple also recognized the other's good intentions toward the Kelabits. Soon after this late 1947 visit, the people of Bario sent for the Southwells to come to teach them. The Southwells accepted the invitation and, in time, utterly changed the style of life in the Plain of Bah longhouses.

# Chapter 29

## A Kelabit Wedding

All this time in the uplands, busy as he was, Tom doggedly gathered material to meet the requirements laid out by Leach. With Bongan as his chief informant, by March 1948 he thought he had "90 percent" figured out the "complete kinship network" of the Kelabit families in Bario. Oddly, though, he was having trouble getting the facts about the kinship ties of Bongan herself. He had always known that she was related by marriage to Penghulu Lawai Besara, a member of the highest class of Kelabits. But when he asked to what class she belonged, his informants displayed a curious vagueness. Bongan would not answer, and her friends and neighbors claimed to have forgotten.

By May, Tom had unraveled the mystery: Bongan belonged to the lowest of the three main classes of Kelabit society, below which were only those who in former times would have been slaves. As some Kelabits remembered fifty years later, nobody had wanted to tell the Tuan Mayor that his wife was not of noble birth. Tom was angry at Penghulu Lawai for having foisted a lower class woman on him and asked the *penghulu* to find him one of a higher status. Tom thought anyone wanting to interact successfully with people of a foreign society should take pains to be on close terms with the highest class, a belief he shared with Captain Cook. He may also have used this excuse to get rid of a "wife" who had never pleased him.

When the *penghulu* proposed that Tom take a recent widow named Sigang, whom Tom had always admired for her wit and intelligence, Tom asked around as to who were Sigang's relatives. This time he found no vagueness or forgetful hesitation. Sigang was of the highest class.

On May 29, 1948, Tom's notebook has the brief entry: "Bongan move." By late June, Sigang was living with Tom and acting as his main informant. It is clear in Tom's notes over the next several months that he liked and respected her.

In her youth, Sigang had been much sought after by the young men. Her skin was freckled but very fair, a mark of beauty among the Kelabits, and she was not retiring like most Kelabit women but was brave and self-confident. Although past her first youth, she was still admired for being hardworking, a quality prized by Kelabits of both sexes. The Kelabits appear to have been pleased by Tom taking Sigang as his "wife." They began planning a traditional Kelabit wedding for the couple, something they had not done for Bongan. The wedding would require much preparation. Many jars of *borak* would have to be brewed for the friends and relatives coming from all over the Plain of Bah and beyond. The ceremony was scheduled for early October.

Before that, in July, Tom started off for Kuching, to take down to the museum the things that he and his team had collected over the previous ten months. It was a colossal hoard. There were 900 bird skins, a few live birds (including a parrot), 200 mammals (all dead, to be stuffed as museum specimens); many pots and jars, plates and bowls, "Ming, Ch'ing, Birmingham and all," representing a sampling of the imported china kept and used by the inland peoples; stone axes and adzes (about 150 stone implements in all), hats and mats and beads and blankets; and much film to be developed. Seventy-six men carried the bulk of the collection for fourteen days down the Trusan to Lawas to load on a coastal ship bound for Kuching. Tom and another party of men walked eleven days and then paddled four big canoes for weeks, manhandling with care at every rapid, to bring the more fragile things down the Baram, via Lio Matu and Marudi to Miri, and take them on a Kuching-bound ship. Tom later boasted that only one piece of china was damaged (not seriously) and a bit of a bear's skin was chewed by a dog.

This was Tom's first return to "civilization" since he had left Kuching the previous September. While Sigang stayed up-country to prepare for the wedding, he took with him nine Kelabits. Among these were Lian and David Labang, two brothers who had been teenagers when Tom first dropped out of the skies at Bario; they had been among the first to join SEMUT 1's guerrilla forces. Since shortly after the end of the war, the Labang brothers had attended the school at Pa Main. Tom had started the Pa Main school—the first on the Plain of Bah—in mid-1945. It was nonsectarian and was taught in Malay by a Timorese Christian who had been one of Tom's SEMUT 1 agents. By the time Tom returned to Kuching in mid-1948, he had already arranged for five Kelabits from the earliest group of Pa Main students to get more academic training at the new Batu Lintang Teacher Training College just outside Kuching, housed in the barracks in which Banks, the Southwells, and the other British and Commonwealth civilians had been interned during the war. While the older brother, Lian Labang, was to go straight to work for the museum, the younger brother, David, was to be in the second group of

Kelabits to receive further education at Batu Lintang Teacher Training College so he could go back to the highlands to teach more Kelabits. For the rest of Tom's years in Sarawak, Lian Labang always and David often would work for the museum in many capacities, chiefly as collectors and taxidermists.

By the time Tom reached Kuching in August, he was thin and run-down and promptly caught hepatitis, very likely from the ice in the cool drinks for which he had longed while up-country. Sick enough to be hospitalized, he quickly recovered. Within the month, he was back in Bario. The "wedding" took place on schedule, on October 4. It had no legal standing—Tom was, after all, still married to Biddy—but Kelabits saw it as a genuine marriage and celebrated it in proper Kelabit style with plenty of *borak*.

There was no bride price or dowry among the Kelabits. The marriage service was simple. A bowl was filled with *borak* and Tom drank from it and passed it to Sigang, who drank from the other side of the bowl. With that act, the couple became man and wife. Tom then drank again and passed the bowl to all of Sigang's relatives to drink from and then back to the bride. She drank and passed the bowl on to all of Tom's ascribed relations. The couple next visited the various "doors" of the longhouse. Everywhere, they were given presents, in some cases quite generous gifts, such as a whole chicken. The size of these gifts showed that the people were happy that Sigang had married Tom. They would not have handed out chickens for Bongan, because she was of a lower class.

Tom and Sigang traveled around the Kelabit uplands on a combination honeymoon and ethnographic research trip. Sigang was both Tom's bride and best informant; his notebooks are full of their conversations. In the first week of December, the two of them were at Pa Main, the longhouse village where Tom had established the first school for Kelabits; Sigang heard the school's bamboo pipe band playing in front of the longhouse near the veranda. "It is *senang* (pleasant, comfortable) to hear the bamboo. It is good," she said. And Tom agreed, "It is as if they said, 'We are here, all well.'"

All was not well, however, for Bongan back at Bario. Probably unbeknownst to Tom, she had become pregnant by him. While he and Sigang were away, she had a miscarriage. The Kelabits say the baby looked Caucasian, and no one doubted that it was Tom's. When Tom heard about its death, he was said to have tears in his eyes. To the best of anyone's knowledge, he never again fathered a child.

On December 21, Tom and Sigang are back at Bario. Tom records in his notebook that Sigang asks to look at Tom's watch. And then, "she for the first time(!) seeks to learn to tell time." Tom records her "terrific concentration as she gazes at the figures on the face for 20 minutes." She listens to the soft sound the watch makes and is pleased by it. She makes Tom take the watch off and hand it to her. "She looks at the face, at the second hand, and says she supposes that's what makes the big noise." She hands the watch back. The next day, she tells Tom what time it is the first time he asks. He writes in his notebook: "She has learned properly and accurately within 1/4 hour! Only one lesson was necessary for all numbers and system."

This honeymoon period was a happy time. Years later, Sigang recalled to her nieces and nephews that Tom (whom she referred to as *Tuan Tauh*, "our Tuan") was very kind to her always and that they had been happy together. Sigang, fortunately, was capable of standing her ground and not allowing Tom to be rude to her. Once when he and Sigang were talking of some doubtful point, he got up to go somewhere but she held him back. "Never *lari* [run away]," she told Tom, "if the talk is not yet finished. If like that, *tidak senang* [not happy, not comfortable]."

He was delighted by Sigang's quickness to grasp new ideas, but he also took some pleasure in her ignorance of certain things. One day in February 1949, he asked her to pass Firth's book, *We the Tikopia*, to him.

> She thinks this, as all my books, are written by me, a delightful idea, which I can never bring myself to disabuse her of. (After all, I have written as many as I have here.) She gives me the book and comments, "Your work is certainly *mahal* [costly, valuable]." I ask why she thinks so and she says, "Even this book is something, *banyak kerja* [a lot of work]."

Tom was certainly working hard at writing during this time in Bario. He was making notes about the Kelabits and also drafting articles for the revived *Sarawak Museum Journal*, the first issue of the magazine to appear since before the war. He wanted this publication, over which he had total control, to have a good mix of scholarly material that would bring the admiration of his British scientist friends (to whom he planned to send copies) as well as items that would amuse and interest a local audience. He had already begun scouring the community for amateurs and experts who might be persuaded to draft something suitable for a journal whose only criterion was that the article should be about, or of special interest to, the people of Sarawak.

The resulting publication was just such a mix of the scholarly and the gossipy, serious and amusing, expatriate and native, as Tom wished. On receiving this first postwar issue, Solly Zuckerman wrote to Tom to thank him for putting him on the *Journal*'s mailing list and to say that "While I don't suppose I'll be interested in every article you publish, I am quite certain that I shall be in many." This prediction proved correct. Three years later, he would write to Tom to correct his mailing address for the *Journal*, to congratulate him on the "magnificent work you are doing" in editing the *Journal*, and to note "You are setting a high standard for scientists in outlying parts of the world." Throughout his years as editor, Tom had dozens of his senior scientist friends on the list to get the *Journal*. It proved to be an inspired public relations gesture for the benefit of Sarawak and, of course, of Tom.

Although the *Journal* became his special mouthpiece, Tom was also still producing items for the *Sarawak Gazette*. In addition, he was writing on a variety of Bornean subjects—zoological, ornithological, conservationist, archaeological, anthropological, linguistic, historical, or simply reportorial—for the *Journal of the Malayan Branch of the Royal Asiatic Society*, for the British colonial service journal *Corona*, for the prestigious British scientific magazine *Nature*, for *Man* (the journal of the Royal Anthropological Institute), the *Bulletin of the Raffles Museum* (Singapore), the *Malayan Nature Journal*, the *Journal of the Polynesian Society*, *International Affairs*, and *Eastern World*, among others. He wrote for all these journals during his first year and a half back in Borneo, and the pieces were published in 1948 and 1949.

He kept up at least this rhythm of writing and publication for the rest of his Sarawak career, jotting in his notebooks, or dictating whenever he had secretarial help. Seated at a desk with his papers spread out around him, ensconced on a mat on a longhouse veranda with a cup of *borak* next to him, jiggling along a bumpy road in a Land Rover, in a longboat with his knees braced to the sides while the paddlers negotiated the rapids, or walking along a beach path with a museum secretary at his side, Tom was always drafting letters, articles, chapters, or simply notes for possible use. At his peak, in the mid-1950s, he wrote 8,000 words a day. Much of what he wrote was published, and by no means all of it in his own *Museum Journal*.

By the time the first issue of the revived *Sarawak Museum Journal* came out in 1949, Tom was back in England on his first home leave since he had taken up the job of government ethnologist and museum curator. He arrived in London during Easter Week 1949; he had been gone nearly two years during which little had changed. Biddy was still drinking heavily and taking "purple hearts," heart-shaped amphetamine tablets that her psychoanalyst Dr. Carl Lambert liked to recommend to his alcoholic and depressed patients, such as Biddy; her best friend, Sheila Hill; and Tom's mother, Doll Harrisson. Tom and Biddy's son, Max, having had a mental breakdown three years earlier, seemed to be normal, although nervous and quirky, an "odd" little eight-and-a-half-year-old.

Tom entertained Max and his stepson, John, by taking them to the theater and to films, to the London Zoo and to museums, but he did not spend time with them at "home." It was not Tom's "home"; his home was in Sarawak. His "home away from home" was the Reform Club in Pall Mall. (In the mid-1950s, though, he would leave it for the Travellers' Club next door.) Starting from this home leave, Tom would use his London club to read, write letters, and meet his friends and business contacts, never Ladbroke Road, where Biddy had reclaimed her house from Mass-Observation.

By 1949, the M-O files had been moved to a basement on the Cromwell Road, London. While Tom was home on leave, plans were made to turn M-O into Mass-Observation Ltd., with Tom as one of the shareholders. Tom would not be involved in the day-to-day running of the company, which was essentially engaged in market research—a field that M-O techniques had pioneered. Mass-Observation Ltd., a private company (that is, one whose shares were not sold on the stock market), duly came into being on November 21, 1949. Tom remained a shareholder in this and its successor company, Palmdec, but never took charge of its activities.

He returned to Sarawak in May 1949 after six weeks rather than the six months normally granted by the Colonial Service to its Sarawak expatriates who have been abroad for two years. He was soon on his way up to Bario. In Limbang, en route back up-country, Tom learned of the newest developments resulting from a tragic event that had occurred in early 1947 while he had been in England. At that time, one of Tom's Kelabit friends, a man called Lawan Aran, had run amok while traveling with two other Kelabits through the Murut country in the middle Trusan. Lawan had suddenly taken his parang and attacked a number of his Murut hosts. In the few minutes before the three Kelabits were seized, three Muruts had been killed and four others seriously injured. Lawan, who had a history of mental instability, had broken away from his captors and run off, committing suicide a few days later. Lawan's two Kelabit companions had been left to face murder charges. By the time Tom got back to Sarawak in May 1949, they both had been tried, convicted, and condemned to hanging. Awaiting execution, they appealed to Tom from the Limbang jail, claiming their innocence. Tom insisted that the case be reopened.

> The Appeal Judge and the Government Lawyers had to make the long sea trip back to Limbang, convinced that it was unnecessary. The convicted Kelabits maintained that the attack was made only by their companion, now dead. The prosecution case rested in part on the impossibility of one man having inflicted so many terrible wounds in the short time before the three were seized. In a dramatic court-room demonstration, Tom, without warning, drew a wooden parang from his coat and "slashed" a dozen persons in the court in a few seconds, while a colleague timed him with a stop watch. The two Kelabits were acquitted.

Soon Tom was back with Sigang in Bario, but not for long. It was time for him to complete his current uplands research and start performing his duties as museum curator. That meant going down to Kuching. This time, Sigang would go with him. On their last trip together through the plains of

Bah and Bawang before leaving for Kuching, Sigang began to be anxious. On June 4, Tom wrote:

> As we pass on the way to Pa Main, Sigang says "*Ah Kua*" [an expression of nostalgia or sorrow] because she remembers me shooting pig here. *Sakit hati* [sad; literally, heartsick] to remember. I probe, not being clear why SAD (?) to remember. She says everyone thus. As we come to the *sulap* [Tom's old lean-to shelter], Sigang says "Your house." Again she says *sakit hati* to *ingat* [remember] these things associated with us.

Later, Sigang had bad dreams. One of them was about a cat ("Kuching" is the Malay word for "cat") that had eaten her lower body; she cried out for Tom and he was not there. Then she awoke, lying beside him.

An underlying tension had begun to affect even what had once been some of their best times together. For example, Tom taught Sigang to write her name and later, jokingly, he asked her to write it again for him. She said that she wanted to do it alone. She went into another room, and he found her there trying to copy her name from the previous time. Unlike her triumph about learning to tell the time, this time she was "*malu*" [embarrassed].

A few days later, Tom gazed at Sigang and, just to see what would happen, he did not smile. Her reaction was immediate. She asked him, "*Kenapa kita tidak ketawa?* [literally, 'Why aren't you laughing?'] She thinks I must be *marah* [angry]. Laughter is the Number One Kelabit [re]assurance way, and is very near, even in full sex." But there was continually less for Sigang to laugh about as she thought of accompanying her English "husband" down to the coast where he would be the well-versed informant and she the ignorant outsider. She was right in thinking that nothing would ever be the same again. Although they returned to the uplands together on other occasions during the next few years, Tom's center of gravity was shifting to the museum at Kuching.

# Chapter 30

## Museum Curator

Kuching, with fewer than 35,000 inhabitants in 1947, was the biggest town in Sarawak. The expatriates lived in white bungalows set in well-kept lawns, away from the Chinese-dominated dun-colored town center and from the Malay *kampongs* (villages, neighborhoods), with their pastel wooden houses on stilts.

Aside from a stretch of road where Pakistanis and other South Asians sold their cloth and spices, almost all of Kuching's shops were owned and staffed by Chinese. These shops, sheltering in their semigloom behind the arcades, carried a motley mix of merchandise, from outboard motors to china bowls to cotton shirts. Sugar, rice, flour, dried fish, and beans stood in open sacks on the floor alongside pretty Süchow earthen tubs with preserved duck eggs from China. "The shelves groaned with bottles of beer, Chinese wine and foreign liquor, and a bewildering choice of tinned goods from all parts of the world." The shop assistants, and even the proprietor, usually dressed in singlets and undershorts. They would bargain briskly in any of several Chinese dialects, Bazaar Malay, or pidgin English, weigh the items on a hand-held brass scale, and write up the sale in Chinese characters on an old scrap of paper.

Nearby, a block-long fresh food market came to life in the early morning with stands displaying every tropical fruit, from the prickly pungent durian to the fragile fragrant mangosteen as well as many imported temperate fruits and vegetables. Laid out on mats under a layer of flies were boneless hunks of water buffalo, pork, and goat. Live chickens and ducks stood tethered inside woven baskets, fresh fish lay expiring on trestle tables, and live eels swirled in tin buckets.

Kuching must have seemed very foreign to Sigang. There were few Dayaks, almost no *orang ulu*, and no Kelabits but the handful that Tom had brought down to go to school or to work at the museum. Like most *orang ulu*, the Kelabits had extremely long earlobes, with all sorts of ornaments stuck in them or hanging from them, which made them look "savage" to people unfamiliar with them. Stories circulated at the Batu Lintang Teacher Training College that these long-eared tribesmen would kill you with their blowpipes.

Faced with this social pressure, one of the Kelabit youths in the first group to study there had his earlobes cut and sewn, so that he no longer had loops of flesh hanging down to his chin. When David Labang told Tom that he and his elder brother Lian wanted to do the same, Tom raised strong objections. Nonetheless, the next day David and Lian both had their ears cut. When Tom next saw David he shouted, "David, where are your ears? Gone already? Why? I told you people before that I wanted you to be 'original', the way you were before I came to Bario." But David answered:

> Tuan, when I was in the womb of my mother, and when she gave birth to me, I had short ears. And I think that is the "original" state of my ears. When we put in holes, that was something new. Now I have put them back to their original state.

Tom made a face and let him go.

The British doctor who cut their earlobes asked the brothers if Tom had given them permission. When Lian said, "No," the doctor said, "You tell Harrisson that if he wants long ears, to come here and I'll make a hole in his for him." "So then," Lian recalls, "I went back to Harrisson and he said, 'Why did you cut your ears?' And I said, 'They are my ears, not yours. If you want, the doctor says he will make *your* ears any length you want,' and then Tom laughed and walked away."

The Labang brothers had learned, as eventually did everyone who worked successfully with Tom, that he only liked people who stood up to him. Once when Lian and David were following Tom about the museum, Tom complained, "You are like dogs, following me." And one of the brothers answered, "You are like a pig and that is why we follow you like dogs," a riposte to which Tom hooted with laughter.

One wonders if Sigang, living in Kuching where little she knew how to do was valued, had the self-confidence to stand up to Tom the way she had in the Kelabit uplands. We know only that she also had her long earlobes cut—the more-than-shoulder-length loops prized as a sign of beauty among women of the uplands—and abandoned her traditional Kelabit style of dress in favor of Malay apparel. When she wore a tight-fitting, long-sleeved Malay blouse above a batik sarong wrapped tightly over the hips and extending from her waist to her ankles, no one could tell that she was a Kelabit. Replacing the proud semi-nudity with which she had grown up with hot constricting clothing was probably the least difficult adjustment the move to Kuching demanded of her.

Tom, on returning with Sigang to Kuching, had also been obliged to make adjustments in his own life-style. His first priority had been to find a place to live. He could not have Sigang with him at the Government Resthouse. Entertaining a native lady in one's rooms there was simply unacceptable in the expatriate world. He looked for a house and found one with a glamorous, scandalous history. This was a small wooden bungalow on the Serian road, the only drivable road leading out of Kuching, built as a place of assignation for the last Brooke Rajah, who had been a great womanizer. After the war, the house had been a police barracks. Tom got permission to have it moved and set up on a small empty parcel of land in Pig Lane, not far from the museum. Sigang lived in the house in Pig Lane, but there were so many visitors from the interior who came for brief or longer periods that her presence was not conspicuous. In the great tradition of British colonies in the East, her relationship to Tom could be ignored.

An early expatriate visitor to Pig Lane was Roman Catholic Bishop A. D. Galvin. Galvin's putative job was to convert to Catholicism the pagan peoples living along the Baram River valley, but he became interested in—and respectful of—the culture of the upland peoples, especially the Kenyah, whose language he learned and whose epic literature he collected and wrote down. The bishop and Tom had liked each other immediately, after meeting over dinner in Lawas at the house of Ah Chong, the "dresser" who had run SEMUT 1's "hospital" on the Bawang Plain. Bishop Galvin had quickly recognized Tom's fertile and creative mind. He was favorably struck by the fact that Tom was completely at ease at Chong's modest home "and took delight in amusing the children." Tom found once again that, although he objected in principle to foisting western religions on people whose own beliefs were so interesting, he had to admire missionaries of Galvin's breadth of knowledge, knowledge he would cull for the *Sarawak Museum Journal*. He also appreciated the bishop's fine brain and warm heart. Galvin later recalled:

> To be invited to dinner in the house in Pig Lane . . . was a unique experience. Tom would have forgotten the invitation and when one arrived he would be dressed in a pair of shorts and a singlet. The living room was a riot of colour and design, with books, papers, and *objets d'art* scattered all over the room. He would flit from one subject to another, suddenly scribble down some notes whilst handing you a glass of beer. Kenyahs and Punans who were staying with him would wander in and out. He would fly into a rage if one dared to mention certain names but it was all a storm in a tea cup and he would be laughing and joking about his experiences in the jungle. The dinner meanwhile was completely forgotten and we generally ended up [dining] in the open market! . . .

At such a meal, out under the stars with cheap, good Chinese food eaten off trestle tables, Tom's up-country houseguests would come along, and probably Sigang as well.

Now that Tom had made Kuching his base of operations, he added to the excellent local multiethnic museum staff that he had begun hiring two years earlier. He was pleased with the staff but did not tell them so. Instead, as he had done in his SEMUT days, he would shout and go into towering rages in front of them, shaking and turning red in the face.

He was, however, also full of stimulating ideas and would push his staff to do new things. He was particularly good at getting his subordinates, many of whose written English was poor, to note down what they knew about birds or animals or people or customs or legends; he would then edit or rewrite or get translated what they had written and have it published in the *Journal* with the staff member named as author or co-author. In that sense he was encouraging and productive. Almost all of the permanent staff Tom hired for the museum stayed with him the next two decades. They learned to discount his loud threats and rages and enjoy the excitement of participating in new and ambitious projects.

Benedict Sandin, the Iban who would succeed Tom as museum curator—and one of the men who worked closest with Tom and received more than his share of Tom's scoldings—later noted that although Tom bullied his staff and "frequently demanded the work to be done with unreasonable speed," he would do everything to rescue any of his staff from danger and was helpful with personal problems. Sandin conceded that Tom "could be extremely harsh" to his subordinates, but if he found their work satisfactory "they could be certain that this would be rewarded by an increase in salary." Because of Tom's close personal ties with the appropriate higher-ups in the Sarawak government, Tom's "promise for promotion," Sandin averred, "was virtually a certainty." Tom also saw to it that almost all of his professional staff, however modest or nonexistent their educational backgrounds, received fully funded training abroad—a year or two in England, New Zealand, Australia, or Hawaii—to equip them to do their jobs better.

The museum was housed in one of Kuching's grandest buildings. The second Rajah's architect had modeled it on a nineteenth-century neorenaissance French town hall. Elegantly wide, it crowned a hill above the well-tended lawns of the museum gardens. The gardens, with their flower beds and wrought-iron bandstand, could have graced the park of any pretty provincial town in Europe. On Sunday afternoons, young Malays conducted a promenade there similar to what one finds in Latin countries. The girls in long bright-colored tunics and sarongs of artificial silk would saunter together along the paths and by the bandstand, tittering behind their hands, pretending not to see the freshly combed white-shirted young men watching them for signs of encouragement.

Tom wanted these Malay young people and all the other people of Sarawak to come inside the museum—the only one on the island of Borneo at that time—and look at its collections of the animal, plant, and insect life of Sarawak on the ground floor and the native art and artifacts displayed upstairs. He wrote in the *Gazette* that he was anxious to make the museum a place that "every visitor wants to see at once, and every old hand to visit regularly." He arranged for it to be open eight hours a day and kept the atmosphere informal "so that even people from the far interior in loin cloths can feel relaxed and stay in the place all day if they like." He wanted scientists and scholars from all over the world to use the tens of thousands of items in the reference collection crowded into two smaller buildings at the foot of Museum Hill. He was determined that the museum would be a "two-way, in and out breathing affair—not just a dump of dead corpses, dusty china and sleepy attendants."

He liked the fact that many requests for information came to the museum from outside the country: "a planter in Papua asking about flowers; a linguist in London wanting local vocabularies; an archaeologist [asking] about Stone-Age finds." He was equally determined to keep up a productive dialogue with the people of Sarawak:

> Inside Sarawak during a typical recent period [mid 1947] we answered queries about guano in bird caves; the *maias* (orang-utan) population; the long-term effects of *tuba* [native vegetal poison] fishing; animals suitable for designs on stamps; how long it takes a termite to travel a foot; . . . flying* and spitting snakes; construction pattern of a Murut longhouse; difference between a Penan and a Punan (Answer: Nil?); does a crocodile have a tongue? (Answer: Yes, always, or it couldn't be); how many eggs a turtle lays (average, Sarawak, about 109); . . . the identification of a stone for a Chinese trader (antimony); and how to feed a *wah-wah* [gibbon] in six easy lessons! All part of the Museum's job—and a pleasure.

As he began, so he continued. Over the next twenty years, Tom would move heaven and earth to make this museum the best of its kind: a local Asian museum responsive to local people's interests, "so arranged that even illiterate people can enjoy the museum," and yet a resource for the world of art and science as well. That he achieved his goal is something agreed on by virtually everyone who knows the Sarawak Museum. He developed it, as one knowledgeable witness confirms, "into an institution of world standing."

He had display cases showing stuffed animals in natural poses and settings and live animals in a miniature zoo behind the museum. One of the first animals he obtained for his zoo was a spectacularly fierce six-foot king

---

*Tom dropped a "flying,"that is, gliding, snake from the museum's upstairs window to see how far it could "fly." Answer: 50 yards.

cobra, a gift from a local donor. Feeding time attracted a crowd because the snake was so fast and furious in attacking its prey, but keeping the cobra fed—it would only eat live snakes—eventually proved to be impossible, and the animal died. The zoo had better luck keeping orangutans. It was, even then, illegal for Sarawakians to have these rare, friendly, herbivore hominoid apes as pets or to capture them without specific permission from the game warden. Confiscated orangutans were given to the curator to care for.

Other jobs that went with being museum curator and editor of the *Sarawak Museum Journal* were the administration and regular inspection of the green sea turtle egg industry of Sarawak, which was conducted on three so-called Turtle Islands off the southwest coast. Ex officio, Tom was also one of the colony's officers responsible for natural conservation, and for protecting natural parks, game reserves, and ancient monuments. He was keeper of the state archives and in charge of setting rules to control the collection and trade in edible birds' nests (one of the most expensive delicacies in Chinese cuisine) and, later, to control the cave guano industry. Any archaeological dig required his permission, as did the export of items of historical value, such as ancient porcelain or old carvings or textiles. Finally, as the acknowledged specialist on the Kelabits and their *orang ulu* neighbors in the central uplands, he also could expect to be consulted on any governmental contact with those groups. All these roles (except those to do with the *orang ulu* and guano) had been part of Tom's predecessors' responsibilities. But, in Tom's hands, the job of museum curator and government ethnographer grew to be more activist. This was a result of his great energy, imagination, and breadth of interest. He also knew how to present a proposal for a project in a way that would attract funds from the Colonial Office and other donors both within Sarawak and abroad.

Always on the lookout for good Museum staff, he rarely missed a chance to enlist volunteers to help the museum carry out its many old and new activities. For example, Neville Haile, a new officer in Sarawak's Geological Survey Department, was encouraged by Tom to continue his hobby of collecting frogs and lizards and to donate them to the museum. Haile remembers:

> Tom made me Honorary Curator of Reptiles and Amphibians. He got anybody who showed an interest made an Honorary Curator and their picture, drawn by a local artist, would be displayed in the Museum—a good piece of Public Relations. . . . He was always very positive when it came to Natural History and he was interested in everything. If anyone brought along any sort of specimen to show him, he would not say, "Oh this is the commonest beetle, there are millions of them." No, he would always say, "Oh, this is very interesting. Where did you get it?," and he would encourage people to write [chiefly for the *Sarawak Museum Journal*] and to do research and to do all sorts of things, amateurs or not.

They were not all amateurs. In 1950, for example, Robert Inger, curator of reptiles at Chicago's Field Museum of Natural History, came out for six months at Tom's encouragement to collect and study reptiles and amphibians and to make observations on their ecological distribution. Inger was delighted with the breadth of Tom's interests and recalls that "I could talk to Tom about frogs and he would be just as interested as if he were a herpetologist or I could talk to him about lizards and he would have the same acute kind of interest," although on such matters he found Tom to be more interested than knowledgeable.

In his never-ending search for funds for the museum and for material for study or display, Tom sought out members of Kuching's biggest and richest ethnic group, the Chinese. The Ong family, descendants of an enterprising Hokkien who came to Sarawak in the 1840s, was socially one of the leading Chinese families of Kuching. Since the Ongs (almost to a man—or woman) were charming, well educated, intelligent, scientifically curious, and tolerant, they got on well with Tom. Tom had already met Ong Kee Hui in 1946, when Tom had come breezing into the Land Survey, Agriculture and Forest Department, where Ong was head of the agriculture section, to complain to Ong's boss, David Leach, the head of the combined department, that the Sarawak map was all wrong on its inner border. (In the 1990s, it still was.) Tom became acquainted with other members of the Ong family via the Kuching Turf Club, which Henry Ong—Ong Kee Hui's younger brother—had helped to found after the war. Henry, a man of wide interests and a serious amateur collector and breeder of "everything that lives in the water," from wild plants to uncultivated fish, liked Tom's omnivorous curiosity.

Henry recalls:

> There was a time when every day, instead of going home, I used to call in at the Museum (my father's house being down the hill) and Tom used to stop me and ask me to share his lunch. All he had for his lunch was two boiled eggs and coffee and a bit of toast. (And he expected me to thrive on that!) He was so engrossed in things that he paid no attention to what he ate. . . . He would be writing away and he always had something outrageous to say—either angry or upset or impatient. . . . But he would then always end up by getting me interested in what he was doing. He was good at cajoling you into being used in his scheme, on his team.

Gradually, via the Turf Club and via the newly established Kuching branch of the Rotary Club, which Tom joined expressly for the purpose of cultivating the Chinese and other local business and professional leaders, Tom rounded up Henry's elder brother Ong Kee Hui; his father, Ong Kwan Hin; a close family friend, C. P. Law; and others knowledgeable about Chinese culture and made them all "Honorary Curators." These men developed the habit of donating to the Museum money, expertise, and interesting Chinese artifacts, such as an ancestor's wedding dress and bridal furniture.

Henry Ong was inveigled into converting one of his aquaria into a turtle-breeding tub, part of an experiment Tom was conducting in connection with conservation of the green sea turtle. Tom had other Chinese friends do the same. "Tom made us write little reports and he would call up and discuss turtles," recalls Henry. "He would say, 'Come over and discuss turtles over lunch.' And I would say, 'Not on your ruddy life. I need more than an egg for lunch.'"

Henry and Tom got to be friends, after a fashion. Henry remembers:

I would quarrel with Tom and we would use foul language with each other. We would fight about the way he did things. He could be quite crude, quite nerve-wracking. Pushing his hair straight back, like Leopold Stokowski, or a magician, and those wild eyes, and the way he would speak to you. And then I would wonder why I had got mixed up with him.

But, as Henry discovered,

If you fought back—or talked back—to Tom, you might think the next time he would be angry or ignore you. But no, you would be a bigger man to him next time. He would not leave you alone, but would come straight for you next time. Meanwhile, you have told everybody what a shit Tom is. And then here he would come around like an old friend. And then you are ashamed and your wife thinks you are the one who was wrong.

Tom had even the youngest generation of Ongs donating items to the museum. Little Bobby Ong, Henry's nephew, once went up to Tom saying, "I have a little python for you," whereupon he opened up his schoolbag. The snake he had put in his bag, however, was not a harmless python but a young king cobra. Tom's reaction to this particular gift is not documented, but he was usually very gracious about donations from children. John Young, the five-year-old son of Robert Young, an Englishman in the Colonial Service then posted in Kuching, noticed that a museum display of a Sarawak bauxite mine lacked an excavator. This bothered young John because he had himself been to the mine at Sematang, opposite the Turtle Islands, and had seen an excavator there. His mother remembers that "John took one of his Dinky toy excavators along to Pig Lane and said to Tom, 'You don't have an excavator in the model in the Museum.' And lo and behold, the next time we went to the Museum, there was John's excavator with a little label on it saying 'presented by John Young.'"

Tom took pains to be on good terms with the members of Sarawak's Malay nobility resident in Kuching, especially those titled Malays who had a hereditary claim on the profits from the sale of turtle eggs laid on the beaches of the Turtle Islands. These men were represented on the "Turtle Board of Management," of which Tom was the "Executive Officer" as part of his job as museum curator. He did not, however, seek out the young western-educated Malays the way he did their Chinese counterparts. This would turn out to be a mistake. Two decades later, he would find himself lacking the friends and patrons he needed in this group in order to continue working in Sarawak after retirement.

# Chapter 31

# Looking for a Friend

Tom's main problem as a colonial servant in Sarawak was his inability to get along with most of the expatriates, even though he spent much of his free time with them when he was in Kuching. He detested many of them, and they reciprocated his feelings. Women tended to like him better, but he preferred socializing with men. G. E. Wilford, an expatriate friend of Tom's with the Geological Survey Department, still has a book about climbing inside caves that Tom gave him for a wedding present. On the flyleaf Tom wrote:

> Wilf,
>
> I hear you are to be married. Well, everyone does it at least once, I suppose, poor chaps.
>
> This is a pre-marital gift, in the Kelabit tradition. It begs you continue to climb about in caves without considering your wife or (no doubt) the little Wilfs to come.
>
> Your affectionately,
> T. H.
>
> PS. If you are NOT getting married so much the better.

Tom himself was not behaving like a married man, either to Biddy or Sigang. Returning to Kuching from the uplands in mid-1949, his attention turned away from a near-exclusive focus on the Kelabits and their neighbors to an interest in all the different things being curator had brought within his range. About these things Sigang had almost nothing to offer. Adrift in Kuching, Sigang quietly suffered from Tom's frequent absences and, even when he was present, from his inattention to her. He seems to have all but given up making love to her soon after settling down in Pig Lane. He certainly never made her pregnant, although she had a child by another Kelabit during one of her trips back to Bario in 1950 or thereabout.

He was not seeking other sex partners in Sarawak. Instead, he would wait until he left the colony for Singapore or Bangkok, where he had bachelor friends from the wartime cloak-and-dagger network who were now working in Southeast Asia and who always had attractive women around. While staying with his bachelor friends, Tom would "tomcat" as much as he wanted before returning to a near-celibate life in Pig Lane. This rhythm of long periods of self-imposed continence interrupted by occasional sexual sprees would continue for most of the rest of Tom's life. In addition to prostitutes, any attractive woman was fair game while Tom was away from Sarawak. A small, slender, blonde Australian diplomat's wife once met Tom at a cocktail party at the high commissioner's residence in Singapore. "And," she recalled, as her big blue eyes grew bigger still, "he tweaked me, there!" pointing downward.

In Sarawak, Tom was still searching for a male friend with the brains and guts to match his own, with whom he could enjoy his leisure moments, another Jock Marshall, if possible. He tried to court the social anthropologists that Leach had sent out—Freeman, Geddes, Morris, and T'ien—but they had been warned by Leach and Firth to avoid him. He began a friendship with a highly intelligent old China hand and bird-watcher, Alastair Morrison, a contemporary in the Colonial Service in Sarawak but, by allowing his pugnacious side too much free rein in this gentle man's company, and especially by criticizing Morrison's wife once when he was drunk, he turned Morrison into a lifelong enemy. In this case, as with Corlette, offending a highly regarded man would have long-term damaging effects on Tom's reputation, this time as a scientist, scholar, and colonial officer.

Then, in early 1950, he found a friend in the new governor of Sarawak, Sir Anthony Abell, KCMG. Tony Abell was charming and original. He had started his colonial career in Nigeria. His genuine liking for people of all ages, races, and classes and his loathing of pomposity had made him seem odd there but would serve him wonderfully well in Sarawak. He was the ideal friend and patron for Tom Harrisson. The two had much in common. Like Tom, Abell had a powerful intellect and great physical stamina. He loved bird-watching. He had been a commando in one of the more disreputable "special operations," the surreptitious sinking in neutral waters of a German merchant vessel en route home with a strategic mineral. Like Tom, in spite of his many talents, he was the less admired of a pair of boys from an upper-middle-class family. He had left Oxford without a degree, while his brother had won a double First and a double Blue.

Abell was a bachelor, though he liked women and had had a succession of girlfriends before Sarawak. For Tom, the crucial consequence of Abell's bachelorhood was that the Victorian Gothic Astana, the governor's residence, lacked the presence of a censorious female to interfere with the high jinks that Abell and Tom enjoyed. These were the product equally of alcohol and an irrepressible sense of fun, the chief trait that drew the two men together. Because Sir Abell was five years older than Tom and, even more, because he was Tom's hierarchical superior, Tom was careful not to allow the uglier side of his personality to have free rein in the governor's company.

Abell thought of Tom as the only person who really knew anything about Sarawak worth knowing. He admired how Tom had made the museum the best in Southeast Asia. He liked the way, when Tom took on a project, such as the green sea turtles, that he would get everybody interested. "Tom got into everything," Abell recalled. For example, "when they renovated the Council Negri building [Sarawak's parliament], Tom was responsible for its decoration and saw to it that the Kayans decorated the ceiling panels, which are very beautiful." "But," admitted Abell ruefully, "Tom used to get people into boiling rages by his manner of using money." For example, Abell recalled:

> In his annual budget to Andrews, then Sarawak Financial Secretary, Tom put in a request for better office equipment for the Museum, more typewriters, etc., and this was granted. But the next year the same request went in. Andrews said, "Hold on, now, I already gave you the money for that last year." And Tom answered, "Come and see what I *did* buy with that money." It was something else for the Museum that was in itself acceptable but had not been requested. So Andrews came to me about it and I said, "Well, Tom still does need those typewriters," so he got the money a second time. But Tom was always doing that sort of thing.

Sir Anthony, in his attitude toward the local people, was a man whom the first White Rajah, His Highness Rajah Sir James Brooke, looking down from his portrait on the dining room wall, must surely have smiled upon. A typical story about his accessibility to Sarawakians comes from Margaret Young:

> It was my husband Bob's first day as private secretary to Abell. Abell had a VIP dinner he was giving that evening—the High Commissioner was in town—and that day Mr. Yap (a Chinese from some bazaar up country) rang up and spoke to Bob, who told Abell that Yap had called to say he was in town today and that Abell had said he wanted him to dine at the Astana when next he came to town. Efforts to make it the next night failed; Yap was going back in the morning. So Abell said that it had to be tonight, then.
>
> So Yap came, with his wife and his nine year-old daughter. I was sat next to the little girl to help her sort her way through the ranks of cutlery and she never put a foot wrong. But the fun really began when Yap had had a fair amount to drink. There were two bottles of port circulating, and when one of the bottles got to Mr. Yap, he leapt from his chair and started filling everyone's glass and shouting "Yam Sing" [Chinese for "bottoms up"].
>
> First everyone was a bit shocked. [Short of digging up a cricket pitch, it is hard to imagine anything in those days that would have been more upsetting to a

colonial Englishman's sense of propriety.] But then everybody started to enjoy themselves as Yap danced around the table. For some of those stuffy people, I think it made their evening.

There are countless stories of parties at the Astana in Abell's day, from 1950 to 1959, and Tom was present at some of the wilder ones, often bringing with him his *orang ulu* retinue, including Sigang. After one particularly liquid lunch, Kuching residents remember Tom swimming the river from below Astana Hill back to the town side, followed by an interested iguana.

Tom never gave lunch or dinner parties but would often have people come to stay. There were sometimes a dozen *orang ulu* guests sleeping in the back of the house, but he would invite expatriates to stay with him as well. He would also offer visitors the use of his house when he planned to be away. An expatriate couple from an outstation remember that in 1951 they were booked into the Resthouse, which seemed a dreary uncomfortable place, when "suddenly like a rush of wind Tom arrived and said, 'You can't possibly stay here. You can have my house as I'm off to the Kelabit country,' and rushed out. (He was always in a fearful hurry.) As he did so, he called over his shoulder, 'Don't put soap in the turtles' eyes.' With this mystifying statement . . . he was gone." Soon someone from the museum came to take the visitors to the house in Pig Lane.

> It was a wooden bungalow on low stilts. Beneath it was a honey bear [a benign-looking but dangerous animal] and near the house was a tethered Rhinoceros Hornbill. With its red eye and huge bill it was a formidable-looking bird.
>
> Inside, the house was fascinating. . . . On the window ledge in a cage was a Pen-tailed Shrew, with a foxy smell very strong for such a tiny animal to emit.
>
> The inside door of the bathroom opened off the bedroom and was in darkness until I opened the outer door off the garden. There was a terribly strong fishy smell and as the outer door opened I found the reason not only for the smell but for Tom's parting remark. All the walls had shelves with enamel basins filled with tiny turtles, each with a number painted on the carapace. Almost daily, someone arrived from the Museum to measure their growth. (Sometime later they were taken back to the sea near their islands and released.) I left the outside door open, a mistake which became evident the next time I went there. On the wooden water tub meant for our use was a grey heron sitting on the edge, hissing and making dives at me with its very sharp bill. I retreated into the garden.

The houseguests felt that "It was nonetheless a delightful stay and we learned to avoid the hazards. If we left the inner door to the bathroom open, we would find ourselves pinioned in the passage by the heron. . . . We learned to listen for the little bell on one of its legs to warn of its presence." They did wonder, though, what Tom was doing with those turtles in his bath.

# Chapter 32

## Turtles

What *was* Tom doing with all those turtles in his bathroom?

The so-called Turtle Islands off the southwest coast of Borneo did and still do provide among the world's richest sources of green turtle eggs. Control of the industry was vested in a Turtle Board of Management, with the museum curator as executive officer. In line with strongly held local traditions, the board did not permit the killing of turtles, only the collection of eggs. The turtle board's executive officer oversaw proper collection of the eggs to assure their continued supply and made sure that the proceeds went to appropriate Malay charities and religious institutions after reimbursement to the museum for administrative costs.

The edible green turtle (*Chelonia mydas*), found in all warm oceans, was and still is a mysterious reptile. It lives in saltwater all of its adult life except for a few hours during breeding season, when the female lays her eggs in a hole that she has dug in the sandy beach of a particular coral island to which she returns whenever she lays eggs. The eggs take fifty or more days to hatch in their nest a foot deep in the clean coral sand just above the high-water mark. The hatchlings scramble toward the water and are never seen again until they are adults. By 1995, some evidence had emerged that the newly hatched green turtles swim out quickly and within forty-eight hours are in the main ocean.

Adult males and females appear in the shallow water off the beach from time to time all year long, most often in the middle of the year. There they mate in a remarkably clumsy exercise in which the female keeps turning the wrong way and other males try to push the winning male off his slippery perch atop the female's shell. The fertilized female lumbers onto the shore after dark about four weeks later to lay her eggs. At that point in her breeding cycle, any light or noise, large object, or almost anything else will frighten the skittish female back to sea. But once she has arrived above the high-water mark and has dug a hole in the sand with her front flippers and begun depositing eggs, nothing can distract her from her duties until she has laid her eggs, covered the nest with sand, and headed back to sea before dawn.

Tom ensured that a turtle-watcher waited on the beach during the laying process. As soon as the female turtle finished and started off, he would mark the nesting area with a flagged stick. In the morning, the watcher and his helpers would dig up all the eggs, take some for sale, and—a Tom Harrisson innovation—redeposit others in temperature-controlled fenced-off hatchery areas, safe from other females accidentally digging them up.

When Tom took over responsibility for the Turtle Islands in 1947, it was known that there were many fewer eggs being laid in the Turtle Islands (and in all known green turtle egg sites throughout the world) than there had been before World War II. Experts everywhere feared that the green turtle, like so many other reptiles hunted for food, was in danger of extinction. Before the war, the three little Turtle Islands had produced two to three million eggs a year. At a price of between six and ten cents Straits per egg (about one-third the cost of a hen's egg), turtle eggs were an inexpensive and much appreciated seasonal protein source for Chinese, Malays, and Dayaks alike.

One of the "perks" of being curator was control over visitation of the Turtle Islands, veritable tropical paradises. Consonant with the turtles' needs, the water was crystal clear, the sand clean and white, and the number of people around very, very few. Tom banned all visits to the islands except with his permission, to prevent people disturbing the females arriving to lay eggs. Tom's little bungalow on the main Turtle Island of Talang-Talang Besar was, as described by a VIP visitor, "a dream, a tiny hut of wood and thatched with palm leaves." Knowing precisely how to impress important guests, Tom stocked the museum launch with champagne and served picnic meals on the old Rajah's crested china dinner service, to the mild annoyance of Governor Abell, who had given the china to Tom for the museum.

The Turtle Islands also provided a locale and an occasion for an annual wild party of just the sort Tom enjoyed. This was the so-called *Semah* ceremony, a Malayo-Dayak rite that took place a few weeks after the end of the Muslim fasting month. The *Semah* rite goes back to pre-Muslim ceremonies, combining singing, dancing, and uninterrupted playing of drums, gongs, and other musical instruments all through the night.

It ended with a big egg battle the next morning, in which sides were chosen and one side stayed on shore as defenders, representing the old year's turtles, while the other arrived as invaders from the sea, representing the new year's turtles. Each side was armed with turtle eggs. As the invaders approached the shore, both sides fired their ping-pong-like missiles. The game was rigged to assure victory for the invaders, since otherwise—or so the local people believed—the turtles might not return the following year. During the battle no one was spared, and everybody ended up covered with raw egg. It was a messy, rowdy game, involving only men. The combatants—especially Tom's guests—were encouraged to shrug off their inhibitions by the generous provision of alcohol. Ong Kee Hui, a guest one year during the 1950s, remembers that "It was fun throwing turtle eggs at the Governor." One year Tom brought along a wastepaper basket to wear on his head like a helmet. The next year, several government offices were denuded of wastepaper baskets for a few days in May.

In spite of the amusement Tom obtained from his turtle stewardship, he was in deadly earnest about wanting to find out why the number of eggs kept dropping. Nothing was known about how and where the turtles lived when not mating or laying eggs, what they ate, how long they lived, whether and how often they returned to the same beach, how many eggs a female laid each year, or how many clutches she laid in a year. In 1951, Tom decided that nothing could be learned about egg production variation without knowing more about the adult females. The next year he invited a thirty-one-year-old American zoologist at the University of Malaya in Singapore, John R. Hendrickson, to come and collaborate with him in studing the turtles.

Hendrickson seemed a good choice. He was certainly enthusiastic. He tried to label about 250 of the laying females but had difficulty drilling holes in their shells to attach the tags; furthermore, the copper tags he used tended to disintegrate in the ocean. He then had an idea that became a major contribution to the the study of turtles worldwide. He used tags such as those that were used in the United States to clip to a cow's ear, and he arranged for the tags to be made out of monel metal (a nickel-copper alloy). Making a slit on the inner edge of a female turtle's front flipper and inserting the nonrusting tag could be done quickly and painlessly while she was absorbed in egg-laying. From this point on, turtle tagging everywhere in the world has been done this way. Tom was duly impressed. He left Hendrickson in charge of this tagging effort while he went up-country for a trip expected to last six weeks. Hendrickson and his helpers set about tagging every female turtle they felt they could without unacceptable disturbance to them. They had tagged about 1,500 females on Talang-Talang Besar (the biggest turtle island) by the time Tom got back in April 1953, two months later than he had planned.

Tom was by then not only sick from scrub typhus, contracted in the uplands, but also exhausted from walking down to the coast after the Auster sent to bring him home had turned upside down and crashed on take-off with him inside it. This accident, in February 1953, was almost an exact replay of the crash when he had taken off in the first Auster to try to fly out of the Bawang Plain in 1945. Once again, it was the first flight from a new airstrip, this time at Bario, built thanks to Tom's lobbying on behalf of the insistent Penghulu Lawai Besara. But this time Tom was forty-one years old.

While Tom was delayed up-country, Hendrickson, in addition to tagging females, had tried to learn more about the turtles' lives. He had tried to follow the hatchlings into the sea, but all he had learned was that young turtles once at sea are very good at avoiding large objects, such as a man or a canoe. Undaunted, Hendrickson tried to learn more about how the adults mated. To do this, he floated by them on an air mattress, using his hands as paddles. Twice, a tiger shark, the adult turtle's most dangerous predator aside from man, approached and Hendrickson had scurried back to shore. One night, Hendrickson waded out waist deep. His back bent over the water, he got very close to a mating couple when another male tried to mount *him*. The zoologist limped back to shore and told the story to someone, who told it to Tom.

Later, after a row in which Hendrickson accused Tom of "stealing" his field notes to publish them in the *Sarawak Museum Journal* as his own, (publishing without alerting the younger man and "scooping" him in the process), Tom told a friend that he had had to send Hendrickson back to Singapore after the man had become so besotted with the sea turtles that he had tried to participate in their sex life. This is a typical Tom throwaway line, a telescoped, funny, and scurrilous story that has elements of truth but gives a totally false impression. As to the rights and wrongs of Tom's use of Hendrickson's turtle field notes, it is likely that Tom incorporated the zoologist's notes in his own reports without attribution. Since his M-O days, Tom had never been overly conscientious about giving others written credit for work done on a project that he had organized or arranged.

Yet undoubtedly the most important factor gradually creating bad feeling between Tom and Hendrickson ultimately culminating in this row was that Tom, from 1953 onward, became increasingly unhappy with the whole tagging project, especially Hendrickson's zeal in carrying it out. In the three years that followed the 1953 tagging season, not a single turtle tagged in 1953 or later returned to the Turtle Islands. In 1954, Tom cut back on tagging, and in early 1955, he suspended the program altogether, by which time about 4,000 turtles had been tagged in all.

Thanks to the continued tagging of females in 1954 and early 1955, Tom had more information, but it only served to increase his dismay. A check of the tags on incoming females confirmed a tentative finding from the 1952 copper tagging season: females laid eggs not once a year, as had been supposed, but from two to seven times a laying season. Since they produced about a hundred eggs in each clutch, the number of adult females involved in laying a million eggs, the total annual output of the three Turtle Islands at this time, was much smaller (1,400 to 5,000 females) than the 10,000 previously estimated. If the 4,000 tagged females of 1953–1955 never returned, Tom and Hendrickson, by scaring them off, would have precipitated a much greater catastrophe in three years than many years of gradual decline. (Had Tom known that evidence now suggests that the green turtle can live 40 or more years, he would have been still more upset.)

Fortunately, on July 4, 1956, after three years' absence, the first of the 1953 monel tags turned up on a healthy female's flipper as she lumbered up the beach at Talang-Talang Besar. Over the next two weeks, a dozen more appeared from that group and still more came over the next several years. One question about the green turtle now appeared answered: green turtles lay several times a laying year but breed only one year in three, four, or five years. Information from other sources on the basis of the Hendrickson tags showed that the turtles migrate hundreds, perhaps thousands, of miles during the nonlaying years.

Tom also made some significant discoveries about the juvenile green turtle, not in the wild but using the large numbers of baby turtles raised in tubs by himself and his friends. He learned what these young turtles eat (fish and shrimp, not vegetal matter as had been thought); what water they like (very clean, very salty); what kinds of swimming they are able to do soon and what kinds they do later; and many other new facts about them. Into the mid-1960s, Tom continued his studies of seasonality, clutch size, individual fecundity, diet, fertility, growth, location of breeding areas, and learning skills of green turtles raised in aquaria and looked into different modes of protecting the next generation.

Ultimately, the problem of turtle population decline remained unsolved. Although conservation publicity led to turtle soup no longer being on the menu in most of the places where it had been served, accidental capture of turtles in fine-mesh fishing and shrimping nets and the destruction of the turtles' habitat continued—and still continues—to threaten their survival. Tom's work on the green turtle, however, added to his international reputation as a conservationist and would gain him a position on the turtle survival committee of the International Union for the Conservation of Nature (IUCN), the world's leading conservationist organization, then based in Morges, near Lausanne, Switzerland. Until the green turtle's habitat is improved and protected, little can be done to ease its plight, but Tom added significantly to the small amount known about it.

# Chapter 33

## Explorations and Excavations

During the early 1950s, Tom devoted much effort to shrinking the gaps in knowledge about northern Borneo's geography, history, and prehistory. He made a number of trips to explore Sarawak's central uplands. One of the most ambitious trips was to the Usun Apau plateau, up-country from the upper Rejang, where, as Tom boasted, "The effort was rewarded by adding 1,600 miles to the map."

He also undertook archaeological digs to learn something of the island's history and prehistory. There had been no previous digs in Borneo, apart from an attempt in the 1870s to examine caves near Bau and along the Niah River, at the behest of Darwin and Wallace, in search of the "missing link" in the land of the orangutan. When these excavations failed to reveal anything worthwhile, interest in efforts to find traces of early man in Borneo evaporated.

Tom had a hunch that Wallace and Darwin had been right and that one of the Borneo caves might provide evidence of early Stone Age habitation. In 1949, Tom had taken a quick look at the Bau cave. He had then invited M. W. F. Tweedie, director of the Raffles Museum to come across from Singapore to "help start us on the right foot." Tweedie, not an archaeologist, had a strong scientific background in geology. In 1950, he and Tom excavated one Bau cave and examined twenty-six others, but found nothing earlier than Neolithic.

Tom kept looking all over Sarawak on foot, by boat, and from the air and decided that the Sarawak River delta near Santubong and the giant Niah caves, on the Niah River south of the lower Baram, might be fruitful places to investigate. Because the Sarawak River delta was more accessible than the caves at Niah, he would excavate the delta first.

In 1951, Tom sent a young Sarawak Chinese, Chen Boon Kong, to Britain for archaeological training and then put him in charge of a dig over an enormous two-mile-long area at Santubong. The dig produced a great deal of interesting material, but none of it was older than Early Iron Age. A more serious disappointment was that Chen soon decided to quit Sarawak, leaving Tom without a trained archaeological helper.

In 1952–1953 Tom resumed digging at Santubong and found examples of a new-to-Borneo twelfth- to fourteenth-century type of Chinese pottery. While digging here, he spent more time than ever before among the dominant ethnic group of Sarawak's southwest coast, the Malays. From what he learned about them then, he was able to convince the Colonial Office that these Malays were not like those across the South China Sea in Malaya. Tom argued that one could not merely rely on Firth's work on Malays of the Malayan peninsula to understand a group of people constituting nearly one-fifth of Sarawak's population and who would be certain to play an important role in Sarawak's political future. Thus, in 1952, he was given a colonial development research grant to conduct a socioeconomic survey of Sarawak's Malays, similar to those done on the Ibans, Land Dayaks, Melanaus, and Chinese by Leach's nominees. He worked on this project on and off for years, but of course never full time. The completion date for his report was postponed repeatedly during the next two decades, and it was not until 1970 that the full text was published.

Sad news came to him while he was digging at Santubong in August 1952: Zita had died suddenly at age fifty-two of a brain hemorrhage. As he confessed to Jock, "It takes a lot to shake me deeply . . . but for days I felt silly. Oddly, she'd written me a long letter which I was halfway answering. She and you are the only two people I still keep in touch with in England. . . . Ah Jock, she was a great girl." He nonetheless kept up his near incredible work pace and, by the end of the next year, the digs he had initiated had unearthed approximately ten tons of Sarawak material that needed to be sorted and studied.

In July 1953, he flew off in a Comet from Singapore for "home leave" in England, his second since taking up his curatorship in 1947. He was granted three months extra leave due to ill health, the combined effects of the scrub typhus six months earlier, the plane crash at Bario's new airstrip, and the long trek back to the coast. These events had taken a permanent toll on his health.

As with his previous trips back "home" to England, it brought him little pleasure. Biddy was suing for divorce, and Tom was anxious about his son. Thirteen year-old Max was a high-strung but very intelligent boy with his father's voice but Biddy's whine in it. Biddy was now in a permanent daze of drink and drugs, but Tom could not seem to find the strength to deal effectively with her and her solicitors over the custody of Max. The divorce went through in 1954, and Tom lost the custody battle. Given his virtual abandonment of Max for almost all the boy's life up to then, Tom could not have been surprised at the judgment of the court, and he resigned himself to it. On the eve of his departure for Sarawak, he apologized by note to a friend for his evident preoccupation during this home leave, explaining that "I was being driven nearly nuts by my wife (the detective stage) and Max troubles. Now I am free and I have just CUT. Nothing else to do. I intend to adopt children— 1 Chinese, 1 Malay, 1 Kelabit, 1 turtle, etc." By the time of this note, Max had passed the entrance exam for Bryanston, perhaps the best "progressive" public school of its day, and Tom could take some comfort from the hope that his son was now en route to liberation from his "infernal" (Tom's word) mother.

When Tom got back to Kuching in mid-June 1954, after nearly a year away, he was noticeably fatter and puffy with drink and lack of exercise but was recovered from his illness and exhaustion. He was also in an even more combative mood than usual and soon found many things to fight about. One was the decision by the diocesan authorities to destroy the fine old ironwood Anglican cathedral in Kuching, sell the land for construction of a new hotel, and build a new big concrete neo-Gothic cathedral on a different site. Tom, invited to give a weekly unscripted seven-minute talk called "Off the Record" for the newly established government-run Radio Sarawak, devoted one of his first broadcasts to an attack on this cathedral project on the grounds that it would rob Sarawak of one of the few handsome architectural remnants of its past. After giving his talk, he wrote to a friend:

> Boy, I've buggered the Bishop. I . . . went all out against the new cathedral, ending: "Do NOT—I say do NOT—give a cent to the new cathedral." Uproar. Bishop sees Governor, etc. etc. No good. Damage done. So next time you come, the nice wood one may still be there.

In fact, Tom's stature among the local Church of England parishioners was such that his tirade had the opposite effect: contributions for the new church building came rolling in. Two years later, an anonymous letter writer to the *Gazette* would point to the presence of the new cement cathedral and gloat that rumor had it that the diocesan council planned to put up an ostentatious marble plaque that would read:

IN MEMORIAM T. H. H.

"GOD MOVES IN A MYSTERIOUS WAY HIS WONDERS TO PERFORM."

Tom was more successful with another radio appeal made during the mid-1950s, this time on behalf of the Sarawak Mental Hospital. According to a reliable witness:

> In the fifties, mental patients were still housed in one wing of the old General Hospital in Kuching. The place was rather like the eighteenth-century Bedlam. Tom made a powerful appeal over Radio Sarawak pointing out that the condi-

tions were a disgrace and that it was high time something better was provided. It was this appeal which really stirred the whole country, and led to the building of the new mental hospital and the training of special staff.

In the year and a half following Tom's return from home leave in 1954, he was often involved in rows and often drunk and disorderly. There were barroom brawls in some of which Tom was knocked down. When Tom would stay in Singapore with one of his expatriate bachelor friends, a former commando, he would also drink heavily and become pugnacious. His wild behavior led, on three occasions, to physical fights in which the friend "could tell from the look Tom had that he would have killed me if he could."

It is only by luck that Tom did not kill anyone while driving. His dark green Ford Prefect, overpainted with bold red and white dragon designs by Kenyah houseguests, would career drunkenly around Kuching's few streets with, occasionally, the hairy arm of an orangutan reaching out the passenger's window.

There is also a claim that one time during this period, Tom was hosting a drinks party at his Pig Lane house and got completely sozzled and went off to his bedroom. "When the party was well-advanced, a cry from Harrisson summoned some of the guests to his room; there they found Harrisson copulating with a native woman," presumably Sigang. A disgusted colonial officer was present but did not stay to watch.

Tom had always relied on drink to help him through long or difficult social evenings. Now, it was no longer helping him. Still, he was glad to be back "home" in Borneo. As he wrote a friend from the early M-O days, Sidney Bernstein, in late 1954, "I must have been crazy to stay a year over that side. Here I have it all. . . ."

Tom was writing to congratulate Bernstein (later Lord Bernstein) on having received governmental permission to launch the Granada private television channel in the North of England and to suggest six programs about Borneo. Some of the programs that Tom had in mind were: "Ma Turtle"; "Edible Birds' Nests—Are they?"; "Nomads of the Mountains"; and "Equatorial Excavation—Niah Caves," about which Tom commented "incredible—just been digging there, fantastic."

The "fantastic" results at Niah had occurred in October 1954, when Tom, Michael Tweedie, and an English filmmaker friend, Hugh Gibb, did a preliminary dig there with a local team of thirty diggers, funded by the Sarawak government and the Shell group of companies.

The Niah Great Cave, with its twenty-three-acre floor and great high ceilings covered with bird nests, was intimidating in scope. Still, as Tweedie later wrote me, "we located an area near the cave mouth which proved to be a habitation site dating back between 30,000 and 40,000 years, and so well into Pleistocene or 'Ice-Age' times." The site was a *pousse-café* of strata, each layer showing human habitation, at the bottom of which were signs of dense occupation, with masses of charred animal bones and flake and blade tools. Their existence so deep down indicated that man had been making fires there during the Early Stone Age.

To Tom it was "at once evident that to tackle this cave properly, we were going to need personnel by the score, financial resources by the tens of thousands, and a long-term program of continuing work both in the field and with excavated material back in the Museum." It would take three years to assemble the wherewithal for a major excavation of the Great Cave at Niah, a project that now climbed to the top of Tom's list of things to be done. At nearly the same time, a new site of the protohistorical period was found by Tom's diggers on the Sarawak River delta, near Santubong. The delta site contained artifacts suggesting iron smelting and other evidence of a trading post for Indian and Chinese merchant fleets, existing for six centuries—now believed to be only three centuries—up to the 1300s. With two such splendid finds coming at once, for the next dozen years archaeology would be Tom's primary Bornean interest.

The question is often asked: Why did Tom not get qualified archaeologists to help him? Tweedie was a sound scientist but not a trained archaeologist, and Gibb was merely a part-time journalist and freelance filmmaker. A partial answer is that Tom, after losing his Chinese archaeological assistant, began in 1952 to urge one appropriately trained archaeologist, the American Wilhelm Solheim II, to come out, but was not able to get Solheim there until 1958.

In fairness to Tom's detractors, it must also be conceded that Tom hesitated to have ambitious experts come and steal his thunder, and he often found means to keep visiting archaeologists away from Niah. He was soon, though, to have a very intelligent, meticulous, hardworking, and utterly loyal amateur collaborator for his archaeological work: a young German woman named Barbara Güttler Brünig, wife of a German forestry officer who had come to work for the British Colonial Service in Sarawak in 1953.

Barbara Brünig, although her undergraduate studies, which had been interrupted by the war, were in art history, did not start out at the museum working on archaeological material. She was first hired to do secretarial and other odd jobs. She was one of a string of low-paid or unpaid expatriate women helpers that Tom or his deputy had taken on from time to time, women with time on their hands in a town where the housework and childrearing were done chiefly by Asian servants, leaving many educated and intelligent expatriate wives ready to scream from boredom. Tom never flirted with these women; he barely spoke to them. But he knew how to give them work that interested them, much as he had done with his women "observers" in the M-O days in London.

Mrs. Brünig, having no children, was particularly eager to find something interesting to occupy her time and had begun work at the museum while Tom was still in England. She met him only after he returned to Sarawak in June 1954. She would come back home from the museum office with the same kind of stories the other working wives told about Tom's tardiness in the morning; his drinking; his shouting at the staff; his careless way of bringing artifacts home to Pig Lane to study so that it was hard to know what was the museum's and what was his; his "creative" accounting procedures that allowed him to fund one project with money set aside for another; and the like.

Gradually, some of her friends began to notice that she was not telling stories about Tom any more, and she was arriving late for dinner. People working at the museum knew more: occasionally when walking unannounced into Tom's office, they might find the dark head of the willowy Mrs. Brünig close to that of the curator. They knew that Mrs. Brünig had gone alone with Tom to Santubong, and Tom's secretary, coming to Pig Lane to take dictation, found Mrs. Brünig there with him. Finally, after repulsing Tom's attempt to see her at her house when her husband was away—which would have caused the scandal to spread beyond the museum—she realized the situation had become intolerable. In October 1955, she left for Germany to file for divorce, taking all the blame on herself. In December, Tom went on home leave, and on March 14, 1956, in London, he and Barbara married, with the surprising consequence that Tom finally had the loyal, intelligent, and courageous friend and companion he had for years been trying to find in a man.

**Figure 27** Sigang, Tom's second Kelabit "wife," in 1978. (James Barclay)

▼ **Figure 28** Tom's house at Pig Lane, Kuching, Sarawak, circa 1957. (Barbara Harrisson)

▲ Figure 29 The Sarawak
Museum, built in 1891 by
Rajah Charles Brooke on the
recommendation of naturalist
Alfred Russel Wallace.
(©Albert Teo)

Figure 30 Tom on the phone at
Pig Lane, circa 1950.

**Figure 31** The Great Cave of Niah, showing the area where the archaeological staff slept in the late 1950s and early 1960s.

**Figure 32** Plankwalk to the Niah cave, over the swamp, in 1966. (Robert Pringle)

**Figure 33** Barbara Harrisson, behind the Deep Skull from "Hell," December 27, 1958.

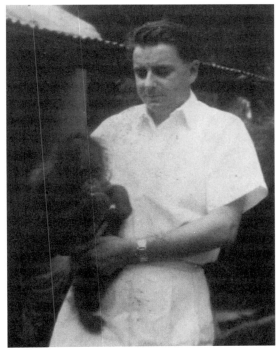

**Figure 34** Tom with an orangutan orphan in Kuching, circa 1956.

**Figure 35** Tom's son, Maxwell Barr Harrisson, age 20, in 1960, on a day away from the sanitarium.

**Figure 36** Barbara Harrisson in Sarawak, circa 1960.

**Figure 37** Lord Medway in Sarawak, 1958.

▼ **Figure 38** Pengiran Shariffuddin in Niah Great Cave, 1958.

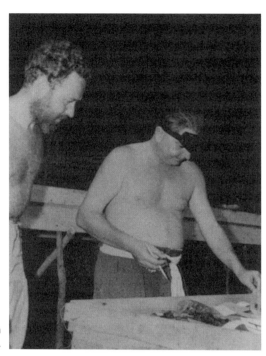

**Figure 39** Bill Solheim and Tom at Niah, 1958.

**Figure 40** Derek Freeman, in 1951, after completing two years of fieldwork among the Iban of Sarawak.

**Figure 41** Tom showing a mysterious life-size carving near Santubong to senior Sarawak officials while Stan O'Connor looks on, 1966.

**Figure 42** Tom calling on Tan Sri Taib bin Mahmud and Puan Sri Laila in 1966 to celebrate the Muslim holiday, Hari Raya Idul Fitri. Tan Sri Taib later became Sarawak's chief minister. (©Hedda Morrison)

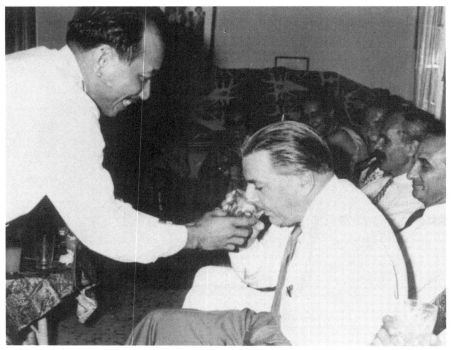

**Figure 43** Lian Labang, Tom's Kelabit long-time aide and friend, pours a drink down Tom's throat one last time, at the Kuching airport on October 1, 1966.

**Figure 44** Tom and Christine in 1970. (Ludmilla Forani-Rhein)

▲ **Figure 45** Tom on a whirligig with Christine's granddaughters, circa 1970. (Ludmilla Forani-Rhein)

**Figure 46** Tom with unsorted files at the Mass-Observation Archive, University of Sussex, 1971.

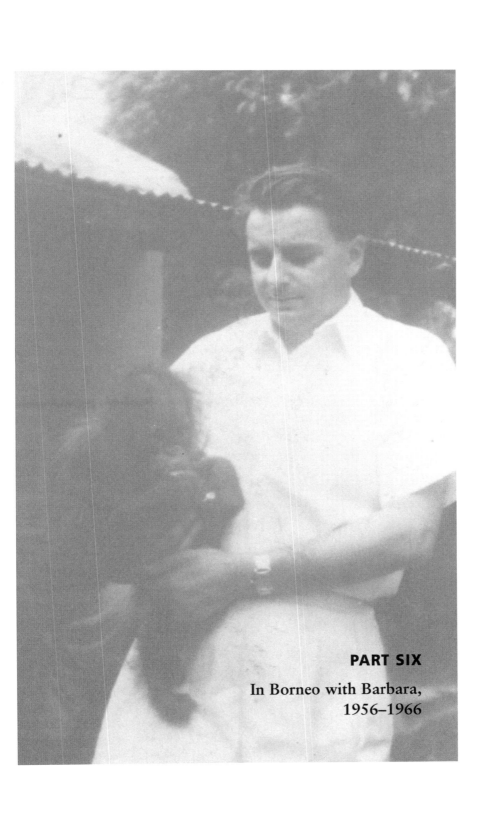

**PART SIX**

In Borneo with Barbara,
1956–1966

# Chapter 34

## The Best Year

Barbara at thirty-three was eleven years younger than Tom and quietly good looking. She wore no makeup and needed none on her smooth olive skin. Tall and long limbed, though not quite so thin and far less fragile than Biddy, she more closely resembled Biddy than she did Zita or any of the other small blonde women Tom had found sexually appealing in the past. With thick chestnut hair usually worn in a single braid and lustrous brown eyes under well-shaped brows, she was at the height of her looks. She moved well and had the calm self-confidence that comes from having survived hardships with dignity.

Born Barbara Güttler in 1922, she came from a wealthy and cultivated German family from Reichenstein, Silesia (then in Prussia, now in Poland). The only daughter, with three brothers, in 1927 she moved with her family to a house on the Königstrasse in Berlin so that the children could attend a good school. In 1941, she began Berlin University, studying art history and languages. After a year there, she was drafted into war service as a typist for the armed forces. By then the two older of her brothers were off to war. Every day, she remembers, she had had to deliver ten pages typed flawlessly. "If you made a mistake, you had to redo it until it was perfect. It sometimes took 12 hours a day." Toward the end of the war, she worked for Admiral Canaris' military intelligence organization in Berlin, a posting that allowed her secretly to fish out the forms to make fake travel documents for her youngest brother to prevent his conscription into a "youth force" being called up to die for the honor of Germany in the last months of the Third Reich. The two older brothers had already died in battle, providing, she thought, honor enough for one family. After the war, Barbara's parents, who had belonged to Germany's lighthearted wealthy playboy set in the twenties and thirties, found themselves deprived not only of two sons but also of the various industrial investments (including gold mines) that had been the source of their fortune, since the investments were in territory by then part of Communist Poland.

Unsentimental and self-disciplined, Barbara had learned not to expect too much of life. She would probably have stayed on in a not terribly happy marriage to Forestry Officer Eberhardt Brünig if Tom had not focused his attentions on her. But once he had done so, she was ready to give him her love. She had a good mind, a refined sense of beauty, and an adventurous spirit. She had no illusions about Tom's weaknesses, but his strengths—the powerful brain, the wildly active imagination, the inexhaustible productivity, the verve and energy—were enough to captivate her. She was ready to give him whatever she could to fuel the engine that drove him.

In England waiting for her divorce to become final in Germany, Barbara went with Tom once to see his mother, who was essentially bedridden, the result of drink and depression. Tom told Barbara that his mother was "just bloody lazy."

While in England, Tom arranged for Hugh Gibb to come again to Niah in February 1957 to help him, Barbara, and Tweedie excavate the Niah caves. Gibb and Tom would also make a film about the dig, one of six films on which they would collaborate. These were to be roughly along the lines of those Tom had suggested in 1954 to Sidney Bernstein. Instead of doing them for Bernstein's Granada company, they decided to do them for the BBC.

Tom took advantage of being in England to renew his ties with the media. He appeared on television and radio and published articles in various popular and professional newspapers and magazines. One of his big themes was how to prevent the extinction of rare animals. Of these, closest to Tom's heart was the legendary "man of the forest," the orangutan. As he pointed out in articles written at this time, these lovable red-haired humanoid apes were near extinction not because of their use in Chinese medicine—there was none, unlike the many uses of the nearly extinct Borneo rhinoceros—or because the local people chose to kill them—they did not—but quite simply because nice animal-loving people around the world wanted to see orangutans when they went to the zoo. For each young orangutan delivered live to a zoo, dozens died or were killed. Worse still, once the animals arrived at zoos or circuses, most promptly died. Tom publicized the fact that, even at such a prestigious institution as the London Zoo in Regent's Park, the orangutans usually died within their first months of incarceration. As Julian Huxley, one-time secretary of the London Zoo, noted in his *Memories* (1970):

> I think the London Zoo was at fault, especially in regard to . . . most mammals. The cages were too small, there were not enough opportunities for play and exercise, and visitors were encouraged to feed their favourite animals, often with serious effects on their digestion. . . .

During this home leave, Tom was also thinking about what to do about Max, who had had a nervous breakdown in mid-November while Tom was still in Sarawak. The crisis had been precipitated by a visit that the boy's mother had made to Bryanston. Biddy arrived in a highly inebriated state and, when paying a call on the headmaster, had started to undress in his office. This incident, or rather the way Max's schoolmates ragged him about it, was thought at the time to have caused the already high-strung fifteen-year-old to snap. With Biddy clearly incapable and Tom out of the country, Max's godfather, Admiral Sir Charles Lambe, now second sea lord, had been rung up and asked to take the boy out of school. Lambe placed Max in the Bethlem Royal Hospital in Kent, which was in those days just such a place as its corrupted name, Bedlam, would conjure up.

Tom was at a loss about what to do. He did not have custody of the boy and, having put in train so many projects for 1956 and the first half of 1957 involving big sums of money and many other people, he appears to have felt he had to wait until at least May 1957—after the Niah digging season and the completion of the television films—before he could return once more to England to try again to gain custody of his only child.

Tom and Barbara returned to Sarawak on March 21, 1956, a week after their wedding, and set up housekeeping in Pig Lane. Sigang had already gone back to Bario. Next, Barbara removed a pair of doves that had previously inhabited the bedroom. Without touching any of Tom's papers, which she knew would throw him into a frenzy, she started to make the house more attractive. Staying with them in Pig Lane were some very fine *orang ulu* carvers and painters (Berawans and Kenyahs). They decorated the walls and ceilings of the house and the museum with murals in bold red, black, green, white, and yellow, often with graceful black tendrils curling out from a central tree or dragon figure. The carvings were also in bold colors but were chunkier. Many of them—the Berawan pieces especially—looked like a cross between European gargoyles and Indian temple carvings, with humans and animals engaged in various kinds of sexual congress.

Everywhere one looked there were fascinating things. There were finely woven Bornean straw hats and mats and blankets as well as daggers and swords in intricately carved bamboo holders. There were lacy Kenyah carvings, given to Tom when he had visited the Bahau-Kayan River valley toward the end of the war. There was also Tom's vast collection (mostly bought abroad) of intricately carved amber-colored hornbill ivory and rhino horn, and his smaller collection of ancient blue and white Chinese and Thai porcelain, much of it bought in Thailand and Singapore, as well as things Tom had bought in Sarawak for the museum and had brought home to study.

Barbara displayed all of these objects to their best advantage, while respecting the ensemble as having long surrounded Tom and having become part of him. She later wrote: "This house and its contents have grown over the years. . . . It has grown to fit its master, his ideas and fancy, his work. It is a living thing. . . . You either love it or hate it." Because it was Tom's, she loved it.

She next began a campaign to get Tom's drinking under control. She placed the gin, whisky, and brandy bottles out of sight, and came to an agreement with Tom that he would ask her to get the bottle and serve him when he wanted a drink. She would give him a drink whenever he asked, but the bottle would not simply sit by his side until it was empty. The program worked and gave his life a real renewal.

Tom assessed his first year of marriage to Barbara, 1956, as the "hardest (but I think the most useful) year since the War. Being married to a nice girl makes such a difference. . . ." This remark, written in a letter to a happily married man he knew, is the warmest tribute to Barbara that I found in Tom's personal writings. At no time did he say either to her or to anyone else that he had married her for love. To her he would say, in a joking manner, "I married you because I needed a secretary." In a letter to the anthropologist Derek Freeman, he announced that he was now married to "a German girl, archaeologist, stenographer, etc. This makes it easier to keep the moth out of the old suits."

This cold-blooded comment may be a fairly accurate gauge of his feelings at the time. As with Biddy, the sexual spark began to flicker even before they married. Whatever his reason for marrying, it was clear to all of Tom's friends that Barbara was doing him a lot of good. He was now sober most of the time and able to focus for longer periods on his big projects rather than flitting restlessly from one subject to another.

One of the reasons, perhaps, why Tom was now willing to reduce his consumption of alcohol was that he was ambitious to accomplish an enormous amount during what he expected to be the second half of his life. In his youth, he had had a premonition that he would die at age thirty-six. Having passed that hurdle, he now expected to live into his eighties. A year earlier, 1955, at age forty-four, he had written:

> As I have a satisfactory secured job and as I [still have half my life] in front of me, I am not hurrying. Except only in things which may vanish if I do not hurry. For this reason, I have rather concentrated on folklore and archaeology with several major sites. . . . I [also] hope to complete a report on the Malay community next year and I think it may be an interesting one which will both fit in and contrast with the Leach series.

Later in the same letter, Tom wrote, "Of course, I try to do too much but I will not stop myself." Thanks to a dictating machine, he was "writing 8000 words a day."

In addition to all his writing in 1956, Tom had another cause for satisfaction (and relief!) when he and Barbara, on a combined honeymoon-and-research trip to the Turtle Islands, were present on July 4 when the first of the 1953 monel-tagged turtles lumbered up the beach to lay her eggs again after a three-year absence, to be followed soon thereafter by other female turtles of that cohort.

Tom's efforts to preserve Borneo's fauna took another step forward that year, partly thanks to Barbara. She felt sorry for the captive orangutan juveniles in their cages behind the museum and worried about all the dreadful things that the zoo's visitors gave them to eat. When Tom suggested that she take the next orangutan baby that was confiscated to Pig Lane and look after it in their bathroom, Barbara agreed enthusiastically.

They named their first orangutan baby "Bob," after Dr. Robert Inger, curator of reptiles at the Chicago Field Museum of Natural History, who was returning to Sarawak in December to continue his observations and study the reptile collection of the Sarawak Museum—"countless bottles packed full with snakes, lizards, frogs, turtles."

Inger was only one of a string of foreign scientists who came to Sarawak during the 1950s, many of them at Tom's behest. One who arrived in August 1956 was Gathorne Gathorne-Hardy, Viscount Medway, the eldest son of the Fourth Earl of Cranbrook and the nephew of Max's godmother Ruth Gathorne-Hardy. Lord Medway, just down from Cambridge, came to Kuching as a very low-paid technical assistant at the museum. He stayed in a new guesthouse Tom had had built that year at the bottom of the garden in Pig Lane for visiting scientists and *orang ulu* guests.

Tom was delighted to have Medway working for him. This tall, slender, quiet young man of twenty-two with a quick mind and imagination was seriously interested in zoology (his father was an expert on prehistoric fauna). He had the inbred self-confidence needed to get along with Tom without confronting him or suffering tongue lashings by him. Tom had encouraged him to come to Sarawak to collect material for a doctoral dissertation in zoology, perhaps on the swiftlets that made the edible bird nests.

Quite aside from Medway's talents and tact, Tom enjoyed having a lord working for him and loved to brag about it—not always to great effect. In writing to encourage Inger's second visit, Tom noted that "we are very lucky to have Lord Medway working with us," to which the American replied, "I look forward to meeting Mr. Medway when I come." Tom wrote again to Inger saying something about "Lord Medway, (who incidentally is a peer of the realm)," only to get another note from Inger in which "Mr. Medway" is mentioned.

In late 1956, however, Tom heard of another "expert" visitor who would be coming to do research the following spring and objected violently. The "expert" was the noted historian Sir Steven Runciman. He was coming, at the behest of the Colonial Office, to write a history of the Crown Colony as part of a series of histories of British colonies. Sir Steven, whose specialty was the Middle Ages and who had never before attempted to write a modern history or anything about the Far East, had been chosen because a friend of his was the public relations officer in Sarawak and had suggested him.

Sir Steven mildly recalls that Tom "had made it clear that he did not approve of me being invited to write the history of the Rajahs, on the reasonable grounds that I knew nothing about their country." What Tom actually said, or rather shouted, to the denizens of the Aurora Bar as part of a long diatribe was, "Why, of all people, they should have chosen that mincing little queen!" Tom's real objection to Runciman was not the historian's alleged sexual orientation but that he would be presenting Sarawak to the world without any commitment to the people or the place.

Despite his annoyance about Runciman, Tom, looking back over the past year as he sat at his dining table with Barbara, Medway, and Bob Inger at Christmas 1956, had much cause for satisfaction. His new wife had made his house a charming place to live and entertain; she was also helping transform the immense flow of his writings from tape to typescript while entering fully into his professional interests, especially archaeology and saving orangutans. He had two affectionate orangutan babies. The second one, the tiny Eve, arrived just in time for Christmas. Lord Medway, almost a nephew, was proving an excellent assistant. The BBC was prepared to underwrite, help produce, and air the series of six films that Tom and Hugh Gibb planned to make the following February through May. The Sarawak and Brunei governments, and the Shell companies of both places, were ready to provide the money, logistics, and some of the personnel to make an extensive dig at the Niah caves.

Fitter than he had been in years, Tom also felt more in control of his job than ever before. He had written Derek Freeman in October, "I am getting gradually more organized. The stage seems to be passing when I have to fight. Now I have to argue." All in all, 1956 had been a great year, so long as one ignored the fate of Tom's son, still incarcerated at Bethlem Hospital, a fact Tom did not share with anyone in Sarawak except Barbara.

In late February 1957 the Niah dig advance party moved up the Niah River to Pangkalan Lobang, the nearest landing place by shallow-draft boat to the caves, bringing literally tons of equipment and provisions needed for a two-month stay, a few skilled technicians, and a handful of experienced Malay diggers from the Sarawak River delta.

The caves were a mile and a half inland from Pangkalan Lobang through swampy and often flooded jungle scattered with sharp limestone rocks. A plankwalk, starting at Pangkalan Lobang and ending at the Great Cave, had been put there years earlier to help the guano diggers bring their heavy gunny sacks from the cave to the launches for shipment to Miri. The plankwalk was less than a foot wide, and each hardwood plank was balanced, without being nailed down, on trestles some three or four feet above the rock-strewn swampy jungle. Having walked the length of the slippery plankwalk, best done barefoot or in thin-soled tennis shoes, one then had to climb a long, steep ladder up into the west mouth of the Great Cave.

Inside, it looked just as it had when the British Consul Everett had gone there in 1873 in a vain search at Wallace's and Darwin's behest for signs of early man:

> [It was] a large arched cavern, several hundred feet broad, and over two hundred feet high; huge stalactites were pending from the ceiling and a fringe of vegetation drooping from its outer edge. . . . We were met by thousands of bats and swallows [swiftlets, in fact]; the latter are the manufacturers of the edible nests. . . . Now descending a gentle declivity, we found ourselves in an immense amphitheatre; the roof of the cave assuming a circular shape, high in the centre resembling the interior of a dome.

The only changes since Everett's day had been the construction of the plankwalk and the guano-collecting industry for which the plankwalk was built. Guano collection, begun in the 1920s, threatened to carry away as fertilizer the very cave floor that Tom's party had come to dig in hopes of finding a fossil of "Borneo man of a million or so years ago," increasing Tom's impatience to start digging.

Given the difficulty of getting to the caves, when Tom invited the newly arrived Sir Steven Runciman to visit him there, the historian rightly regarded the invitation as a challenge. Tom admitted to him that he had invited him "largely . . . in the hope that I would find the discomfort there too much for me and would be deterred from continuing my commission."

Before Runciman arrived, Tom's team of diggers had been "going down and down and down," digging out "huge great trenches," as Medway, then only an onlooker to the digging at Niah, recalls, "desperately looking for human artifacts" and not finding any. But the day of Runciman's arrival, a few stones were found showing signs of having been made into tools in the Early Stone Age, the first of that age uncovered in Borneo. Runciman recalls that "Tom at once regarded me as a *porte-bonheur*, and thenceforward our relations were of the most cordial."

After finding these Palaeolithic artifacts, a gleeful Tom wrote in *Man*, the journal of the Royal Anthropological Institute, "Even at this stage of excavation at the Great Cave of Niah, it is possible to learn . . . more about the past than had hitherto been deducible from any cave in this part of the world. . . ." He was particularly pleased to have found proof of man's early residence in a cave in the tropics because it contradicted the conventional wisdom of the time. Such authorities as the German Dr. Ralph von Koenigswald, one of the discoverers of *Homo erectus* (Java Man), had written the year before that, whereas in Europe men went into caves to find shelter, in the tropics this was not the case. Tom ends his *Man* article characteristically, "Fortunately (for me) for once von Koenigswald is wrong!"

Tom, Barbara, and Gibb did the last two of their six BBC films in the Great Cave. One was entitled "Birds' Nest Soup" and showed the centuries-old and spectacularly dangerous collection of edible bird nests by local tribesmen who shinned up slender poles to detach the nests from the high cave roof. The other documentary was called "Borneo from the Beginning" and told the story of the ongoing excavations. The films would need to be cropped and edited with the help of the BBC's David Attenborough when Tom and Gibb got back to England, but Tom (who determined what to film) and Gibb (who had a good grasp of how to film it) were pleased with the footage they had shot.

Once back in England that summer (1957), in addition to continuing to try gain custody of Max (who had been discharged from Bethlem Hospital in early June), Tom spent days with Hugh Gibb at the BBC studios working with David Attenborough on the films. This involved many arguments that occasionally led to Tom flouncing out of the studio to sit in his car with the windows up. Eventually, after Gibb and Attenborough had come to an agreement on a solution they thought might also meet Tom's demands, young Attenborough would run downstairs and out to the car. Tom would roll down his window an inch and Attenborough would pass through a note from Gibb describing the compromise. Tom would come back upstairs and the editing would continue. The resulting films were good, and the last two, shot in the Niah caves, were even better than the first four. Looking back thirty-six years later, Sir David Attenborough described "Birds' Nest Soup" as "epoch-making really, much the best [such] film that had come" to the BBC by then. In 1958, the judges at the Cannes Eurovision Film Festival gave it their top prize for documentaries.

During this period in London, Tom rented a small flat and began pouring out to a stenographer a long tale, without benefit of his notes (all of which were back in Kuching) that drew on his memories of the Kelabits on the Plain of Bah in 1945. He seems to have deliberately kept his mountains of data out of reach, perhaps seeking to circumvent his habitual urge to let detail drown his narrative. Some Kelabits, who lived in the Plain of Bah then, have pointed out the inaccuracy of some details, such as occasional statements in which Tom seems to have confused living people with mythic figures. Some Kelabits, born since the Southwells' arrival, contest his assertion that unmarried women in 1945 were promiscuous. On the whole, though, Kelabits today agree that this picture of Kelabit life in those days is accurately drawn. It thus passes a test to which few anthropological texts were put in Tom's day: a review by the people under study.

Tom's description of Kelabit life in 1945 takes up the first half of the book. After a brief interlude to introduce himself and how he had arrived in Kelabit country, he devotes the rest to a disjointed but essentially accurate account of Operation SEMUT. The result is at least as interesting and fun to read, if not quite so ground-breaking, as *Savage Civilisation*. Tom sold the manuscript in September 1957, before leaving England. The book would be released in March 1959 as *World Within: A Borneo Story*, published by Cresset in London and Ambassador in Toronto.

He and Barbara also found time to visit a Dutch laboratory to give samples from that year's Niah dig for carbon-14 testing. The tests confirmed, to Tom's great satisfaction, that the stone tools he thought were Palaeolithic were indeed 30,000 to 40,000 years old.

He was equally successful with the main purpose of this trip to England, obtaining custody of Max. Tom had never been a proper father to his son, but Biddy's unsuitability as a parent was now well documented. With Barbara along to show the judge that Tom had a proper wife to help him care for the boy, the court consented. When Tom and Barbara returned to Sarawak in mid-September 1957, Max was with them.

# Chapter 35

## Tom, Max, and Young People

Tom had a fondness for young children and a gift for dealing with them, but nothing in his experience—or Barbara's—had prepared them for the job of caring for an English teenage boy. And this boy, having spent eighteen months in an insane asylum, required special handling. The diagnosis was "paranoiac schizophrenia," for which a predisposition is thought to be inherited. It is a heartbreaking illness in which the patient can give the appearance of being more or less normal much of the time, with the result that the family expects that if only they tried hard—and if only the sufferer tried harder—all could be well.

Max, interviewed thirty years later, recalled much of his time in Sarawak as happy, with his father playing badminton with him and taking him to the Rex Cinema and to see the Turtle Islands and various sites in and around the capital. He remembers Barbara giving him exotic gifts—a statue of Kwan Yin (the Chinese Buddhist goddess of mercy) and a Chinese black silk dressing gown—possibly for his seventeenth birthday, a few days after he reached Borneo.

But Tom and Barbara were often away. Tom went to international conferences and supervised conservation work on the Turtle Islands and digs in the Sarawak River delta, while Barbara was often in the jungle observing wild orangutans to try to figure out how to prepare her charges for adulthood.

When Tom and Barbara were in Kuching, they still had little room in their lives for Max. They were now foster parents to a growing family of orangutans who vociferously demanded cuddling and playtime. As Tom noted in *The Straits Times Annual 1958*, one-year-old Eve "still needs hours of affection every day." She insisted on being held and, if put down, "there is an outbreak of hysterical tantrums which would make most delinquent infants jolly jealous. . . ." There was little time or energy left for Max unless he wanted to participate in what Barbara and Tom did.

Tom, not having had loving or caring parents himself, had no idea how to be a father to Max. Max, for his part, wanted to be the focus of his parents' attention. He did not see the orangutans as adorable playmates but as rivals. Attempts to amuse him by sending him off on adventures—such as a trip upriver in a longboat in the company of a museum guide—only frightened him, and so he spent much of his time sitting in the museum library, bored.

Tom and Barbara never just sat. They were used to dealing with others by giving them assignments and not expecting to see them again until their tasks were completed. Tom raised his voice at subordinates when they made mistakes and rarely praised them. The way an assistant would know Tom was pleased was if he assigned a more challenging job with reduced supervision the next time. That was the way he had dealt with his Mass-Observer teams in London and Bolton and with his SEMUT subordinates. He dealt that way with Barbara much of the time, and with Lord Medway, who was only five years older than Max.

It was also the way he handled Pengiran Shariffuddin, a Brunei Malay aristocrat, who at nineteen was midway in age between Max and Medway. (*Pengiran* is a Brunei title of nobility.) "Sharif," as his friends call him, had been sent by the Brunei government in April 1957 to spend three years learning about museum work in Kuching in preparation for Brunei's first museum. His headmaster in Brunei had chosen him for this training. Sharif recalls:

> I first met Harrisson when I was introduced to him by the College Principal, prior to an interview with him, at the Sultan Omar Ali Saifuddin College. When I arrived at Santubong one month later, he straight away asked me to work, to do marking on the ceramic sherds. . . . There was a mountain of sherds on the floor and I wondered how one could ever finish the job. I had to write the word "surface" for "surface find" in ink on each sherd. There was a big hole near the rest house full of sherds from Santubong. And half of those things have labels in my handwriting.

Tom would take Sharif with him on boat trips along the Sarawak River. Sharif remembers:

> When I was travelling with Harrisson, we would be for hours in a boat and I would get tired and start to read a book. . . . He would get very angry and say, "Look, don't waste your time. You can read a book in the house. But what you can do, you can watch every part of the river, how the river flows, how the tree grows, how the tree behaves, how the birds are, and observe and make a note of it. You seldom are on this part of the river"—which was true—"and you can read your books in the house. Look at the fish and the people paddling the boats, and the houses we pass." And if you think about it, he was right.

Here was a boy who would have been a perfect son for Tom, a happy choice by the Brunei headmaster. Not that Tom was gentle with Sharif. He used to blow up at him regularly: "When Tom was angry, he would be really angry for two minutes or five minutes or ten minutes. But after that he would cool down and talk to you normally as if nothing had happened."

As Sharif says,

> If it had been other boys from Brunei, I think they would have run away, the way Harrisson treated me. But I learned a lot from him. He made me a better man.
>
> One day, Harrisson asked me to follow the people to catch green frogs. The Chicago Natural History Museum wanted so many frogs to be sent them. So one night I followed Lian and the other collectors to catch frogs. And I think to myself, "It is a good training." I don't mind.
>
> And I try, but I cannot catch a frog. It is night time and it is in a muddy area and we have to walk in the swamp and with a torch-light in my hand. I caught only one frog. And next morning in the Museum at about 11:30 a.m., Tom . . . asked how many I caught. And I said, "I got one."
>
> So, my God! he really scolded me: "You are useless, you'll never do anything right! . . . "
>
> But the next night, we did it again and I started thinking how to catch frogs. I asked the taxidermist, the old man, the one we called the *ketua kampong* [village headman]. I asked him, "Can you make me a net, like for catching butterflies—a long one, about four feet long?" And that night I caught about 50 frogs, using the net. From far away, it jumps in your net and then you put it in spirit and in the formaldehyde.
>
> Next day, Harrisson came over and looked at my jars, full of frogs, and he said, "How did you do it?" and I just looked at him and tapped my forehead with my finger and he just walked off. And he smiled.

Sharif did not mind working hard under difficult conditions. All he needed was an occasional smile of approval from Tom and the knowledge that he had earned it.

Max, two years younger than Sharif, was emotionally far younger. His history of mental illness was known in Kuching only to Tom, Barbara, the governor, and the chief secretary. With everybody either ignorant of Max's problem or trying to ignore it, Max's frequent demands for attention and his refusal to amuse himself made him seem thoroughly spoilt. He was clearly not up to the standard set by Sharif or Medway, or even Bidai, a sixteen-year-old Land Dayak who lived in Pig Lane and was Barbara's highly competent assistant in caring for the orangutan babies.

Tom was also making use then of some forty overage Land Dayak Primary School boys and girls, a few years younger than Max, as "trainees" at the Santubong dig during school holidays. These children worked so well that Tom took a great liking to them and laid on seaside outings to the Turtle Islands and special tours around government departments in Kuching and provided other treats for them. It would not have required "paranoiac schizophrenia" for an inexperienced teenage English boy to feel unloved and unwanted in such a situation.

One day around New Year's Day 1958, while at the beach at Santubong where he had been brought by a friend of Tom's, Max walked out into the sea carrying his suitcase, having expressed the intention of walking home to England. If no one had noticed him, he would have drowned. After a night in the Kuching hospital, he was on a plane, accompanied by the male nurse who was responsible for mental patients and whose instructions were to put Max in a Singapore mental institution.

Max's crisis and his reincarceration proved devastating to Tom and Barbara as well. Tom could no longer pretend to himself that Max was normal or that he, the father and legal guardian, was competent to care for him. He told Barbara that if she wanted children (which she did), they must adopt because, between his genes and hers (she also had an insane relative), he would not risk producing a child together, at least not until Max got well. Tom suggested that they start with a Kenyah leper's son whom Barbara was caring for, but Barbara was reluctant to formally adopt a child of another race. Also, raised a Catholic, though she had long given up going to church, she still felt a certain repugnance about making love with no hope of becoming pregnant. From the day they sent Max off to Singapore, their already tenuous sexual relationship came to an end, although they continued to share a bed.

Tom had difficulties with other young people besides Max. He worked well with Geoffrey Barnes, a young colonial officer who had included anthropology and archaeology in his degree studies at Cambridge and was on loan from the Sarawak government to the museum to handle the Niah dig's logistics. But Mary Adams' daughter, Sally—taking a break from university—and a couple of other university students who were children of Sarawak-resident expatriates and who came to Niah to give a hand, all thought of Tom as an "ogre." While it was chiefly to the young women that he was gratuitously coarse and insulting, he was certainly a hard taskmaster to all the young people. Shariffuddin, who was at Niah that season, recalls what it was like to be a student-helper on the dig:

> We lived in the cave. It took from 45 minutes to one hour by foot to reach Pangkalan Lobang from the caves where we were. . . . At that time there were not many outboard boats going down to Miri. All our stores were in Pangkalan Lobang. . . . Once a month we were allowed to go shopping [at Batu Niah village], buy a shirt, but we had to be back by 6 o'clock.

And after 8 o'clock we were not allowed to make noise. We were supposed to go to sleep. If Harrisson heard a noise, just the noise of somebody talking, he would shout, "Nyandoh, [an archeology supervisor from the Museum] (or whoever) what a noise! Keep quiet!" No light at all, whatsoever. We lived in an area with no roof, except the roof of the cave. At night we put a mosquito net to keep the guano off us. And we kept healthy on tinned food, sardines, and sometimes fresh fish from the town of Niah. The water supply was strictly rationed. Tom and Barbara slept in the same cave but at the other end of the camp.

. . . At 6 a.m. we would wake up, clean up, eat breakfast. We had to walk fifteen minutes from the settlement area of the cave to the excavation area, in another cave from where we slept. We had to be on the site by 7 a.m. . . .

[At the excavation cave], at first there was a small trench in the middle of the cave and then we started opening around it, until the whole area was open. In this part of the Great Cave, the ground was so poor, so porous, you touch it and it collapses and then Harrisson gets so mad at you that we called it "Hell".

It was in "Hell" that Tom and Barbara had found their first Palaeolithic tools the previous year, the day of Runciman's visit. And it was there that they now hoped to find something of that age or older, something that would repay all of the time and effort and discomfort that they and their helpers were undergoing.

# Chapter 36

# The Deep Skull from Hell

On February 7, 1958, the diggers in "Hell" called Barbara over to look at something unusual that they had uncovered with their brushes. Having found some Old Stone Age tools during the previous year's dig, they were no longer shoveling out the cave floor. Tom did not know how to follow the natural stratigraphy of the cave, and Michael Tweedie, who was Tom's guide on archaeology, was equally unfamiliar with this technique. It was a technique that was new to archaeologists in the 1920s and was still relatively little known in the tropics in the decade after the war. Instead, they dug down six inches at a time in areas where they had few expectations and in areas such as Hell, where they hoped to find important remains, two inches at a time, with brushes.

Peering down at what the diggers' brushes had uncovered, Barbara agreed that it was, indeed, really special. She suspended digging at the site and hurriedly sent a messenger with a note down the plankwalk to Pangkalan Lobang. The note asked Geoff Barnes to send a telegram to Tom in Kuching telling him "that the top of a probable human skull" had been unearthed this afternoon, "on top of 40,000 BP C14 layer, at the 106 inch depth level." The next morning, Barnes went by plankwalk to the cave to see the new find and wrote in his diary that he "saw the probable skull cap which had been discovered yesterday. Shellac had been put on it to harden it and it has been covered with cotton wool and left for Tom."

Tom arrived on February 12, bringing with him the world authority on *Homo erectus*, Professor R. von Koenigswald. This visit had been planned months before, but Tom had feared that all he would be able to show his guest would be a Stone Age tool or two and indications of fires in the cave made by man close to 40,000 years ago. Now there was something much more likely to interest his distinguished visitor.

Von Koenigswald, arriving with Tom, was at first dismissive of the "Deep Skull," saying that it was merely *Homo sapiens sapiens*, "modern man." During his week at Niah, however, the professor began to realize its significance. According to Barnes' diary, "Von Koenigswald thinks that this Niah excavation is very important, since its discoveries are filling a gap in the prehistory of South East Asia, the important late Palaeolithic and Mesolithic era. . . ."

Nonetheless, from the moment word reached the outside world that a skull of fully modern man, *Homo sapiens sapiens*, had been found in the Niah caves at a layer dating from about 40,000 years ago, doubts about its authenticity began to be raised. This was despite what Cornell human paleontologist Kenneth Kennedy, in 1977, described as "the extreme caution exercised by Tom Harrisson and his staff in their treatment of the Deep Skull and other materials recovered from Niah [which] has not been appreciated sufficiently by many of his critics, few of whom are familiar with the primary published sources. . . ."

Tom realized immediately the great importance of this find. If the skull tested out to be as old as he thought, it would dethrone Cro-Magnon man (only 33,000 years old) as the first dated example of fully modern man. It would also move the throne eastward. As Kennedy later remarked to me, "If Niah was genuine, then Europe no longer had the oldest modern man." Furthermore, it meant that Neanderthal man (also European) was not the direct predecessor of modern man, since he, too, was younger than 40,000 years. (Since the discovery of the Niah Skull, remains of much older fully modern men have been found in the Near East and Africa, thus dethroning Europe's Cro-Magnon man and moving Neanderthal man out of the direct line, regardless of the Niah Skull.)

Aware that the Niah Skull could be the greatest achievement of his many-sided career, instead of rushing into print, Tom first wanted to be sure of the skull's date and to have the experts' backing on it. On the advice of von Koenigswald, the cranium was forwarded to the British Museum of Natural History—Barbara flew with it on her lap—where it was examined by a highly qualified physical anthropologist, D. R. Brothwell, after being shown to his famous boss, Kenneth Oakley.

The fact, however, that there was no stratigraphic record—or at least none that outside professional archaeologists got to see—of what had lain above the skull proved to be a serious handicap in getting recognition for it. There was no way for those not present when the skull was unearthed to know whether it belonged to the layer that Tom and Barbara claimed or had been put there later.

In 1957, Tweedie had taken samples from a "continuous stratum between one and two metres thick." Carbon-14 testing of these samples had established that humans had been making fires in the cave 40,000 years ago. Thus, when Tweedie heard in 1958 (after he had left Singapore for retirement in England) that Tom's team had found what he called "Palaeolithic-type stone tools . . . and a human skull" and that "charcoal samples from its vicinity indicated a date of nearly 40,000 years ago," this seemed to him "interesting and reasonable." He later wrote that "the sampling and dating of the quartzite flake stratum [the layer just below the layer where the skull was found] was done carefully and methodically and establishes an early date for [its maker] *Homo sapiens* in S.E. Asia. I see no obvious reason for doubting the correct association of the carbon sample with the skull." He concluded that "Tom Harrisson's excavation at Niah was an important piece of research and he should be given the credit for it."

This is an impressive endorsement, given Tweedie's widespread reputation as a first-rate scientist, but doubts about the skull have continued. Scholars unfamiliar with soil conditions prevailing in the Niah caves have been suspicious of the fact that the skull was not fossilized. Not being fossilized, the skull looks like a modern skull. How could one tell that it was not of much more recent date and had somehow turned up in that ancient layer, having been put there or having fallen there from high above? Carbon-14 testing of the skull itself was not a real option at that time. Given the state of technology then, an unacceptably large piece of the skull would have had to be tested and would have been destroyed in the process. Tom's amateur status as a scientist—much less an archaeologist—and his reputation for not always being straightforward were factors in the minds of the early doubters.

Archaeologist Professor Solheim, one of the few experts to see Tom working at Niah, acknowledges both Tom's amateur status and his sometimes devious ways, but in 1992, he stated, "I don't think [the Deep Skull] is a fake. I think he treated it more or less properly. I don't think he jiggered it. I don't think he knew enough to jigger it." Others with less knowledge of Tom and Barbara's fieldwork are more ready to believe otherwise.

A crucial element in the early suspicions of the Niah Skull's age was that it was the wrong skull in the wrong place at the wrong time. Dr. Chris Stringer, head of the Human Origins Group at the Natural History Museum, London, explains:

> The Niah Skull, when first found, elicited many doubts and beliefs that it must be an intrusive find because the general belief at that time was that modern man did not reach Asia until much later. We know now that Modern Man *did* reach Asia much earlier than first thought and thus people have much more of an open mind about the Niah Skull. . . .

In Cornell Professor Kenneth Kennedy's view, "The burden of proof rests with those critics who assume that the Deep Skull was an intrusion in the part of the site where it was first observed," but some of the leading experts insist that the Deep Skull must prove its own date. Dr. Peter Bellwood of the Australian National University, the leading specialist today on Insular Southeast Asian prehistory, doubts that the Niah Skull is really 40,000 years old, since "no other bone survived the soil conditions in Niah Cave for as long as this." Bellwood believes that only atomic mass spectrometry (AMS) testing of a bit of the skull can determine the Niah Skull's date. At long last, in 1998, new AMS testing was begun in the United States on bone fragments from the skull.

For those who believe the skull is genuinely 40,000 years old, it seems a great pity that Tom's reputation robbed him of credit for what ought to be his greatest scientific achievement. (That it was found when Barbara was in charge does not make the skull Barbara's discovery, as she would be the first to say. The credit belongs to Tom for the decision to dig at Niah and his flair in choosing where in a twenty-three-acre site to dig deep trenches.)

At the time the Niah Skull was found, if it had been more widely acknowledged as being the age Tom claimed for it, it would have caused a sensation as the oldest dated anatomically modern human in the world. Even now, if its alleged date were to be confirmed, it would be the oldest in the Far East.

Aside from Tom's personal reputation, his chief "problem" vis-à-vis the archaeological establishment was his ignorance of what is now a basic tool of the archaeologist's trade: stratigraphy. This was a failing common among American archaeologists in to the 1950s, who, like Tom, excavated by arbitrary levels rather than by the stratigraphically ordered layers that made up the deposit at the site. Another problem was that Tom, with his lifelong fascination with connections among data, would not confine himself to a narrow investigation of what was uncovered, any more than he was willing to narrow the area being dug. In the breadth of his interests he was truly in advance of his time. He wanted to know what the ancient people of Niah had eaten, how had they obtained it, how had they prepared it, what they had used for tools, what animals and plants had coexisted with them, how high the Niah River had then risen, what the weather had been like, what minerals had been present or absent, and how all this correlated with how people on the Niah River lived today.

These are questions archaeologists and palaeontologists ask now, but though the best scientists were asking them in 1958, many were not. What made it a "problem" for Tom was that each question led to another question. He could never reach the stage where he felt ready to write a synthesis of what the finds at Niah meant, as opposed to the periodic summaries he wrote of what his people were uncovering.

Solheim has said of Tom that "he was neither a trained archaeologist nor a particularly good one but he had many extremely good ideas that he applied at Niah." He has concluded that "In some ways his overall program at Niah was probably more successful than even a first-class archaeologist would have managed, as much more was involved in the program at Niah than dirt archaeology." By "much more" being involved, Solheim means the many nonarchaeological aspects of the work that only someone of Tom's gifts and temperament could have handled. First, there was the need to organize funding for the work, for which Tom was uniquely equipped. By this time, he was "Mr. Sarawak" as far as Britain and the western world were concerned, thanks to his television films and his many other media appearances. Next, there was need to protect the site from vandalism, treasure seekers, or other agents of destruction. Tom convinced the Sarawak government and the Chinese company that bought the Niah guano that all guano collecting should be under Tom's control, so he could prevent guano collectors from removing all the cave floor, and that the cave should be out of bounds to anyone who did not have Tom's permission.

Finally, there was the need to assemble a team of outside experts to help. In archaeology after Tweedie retired, Tom trusted only Barbara not to try to steal his thunder. He limited even Solheim's access to Niah and kept other archaeologists well away. In other fields, though, such as geology, soil analysis, and pottery, Tom recruited very good people. In zoology, as Solheim notes, "Not only has the Niah zoological work been large in quantity but the collaborators have all been first class scientists. . . ." In sum, as Jonathan Kress (another archaeologist) wrote in 1977, Tom was "ill-prepared" and "untrained" to be an archaeologist. "Yet, however we might cavil, nothing can detract from the man's status as a pioneer of boundless energy and vision."

# Chapter 37

# Going Back for Another Look

The late 1950s were a trying time for Tom, as social anthropologists with whom he had sparred earlier returned to Sarawak for another look at "their" people. Two anthropologists were especially annoying. One was Derek Freeman from The Australian National University, a Leach socioeconomic survey nominee, who was back in Sarawak from December 1957 to March 1958 to revisit the Iban upcountry. The other was Rodney Needham of Oxford University, who from 1951 to 1952 had studied the "Penan" and was back in 1958 to see them again.

Tom's disputes with these scholars were conducted on technical grounds. Tom argued that the Kajang were not (as Freeman and other professional anthropologists claimed) an ethnic group, believing that "Kajang" was a term, like "Dayak," that subsumed a number of ethnic groups. (It is now known that Freeman was right and Tom was wrong about this; see Notes and Sources.) As for Needham, he had learned to speak "Penan" during fourteen months of fieldwork among a group of nomads he called "Penan," as distinct from other nomads he called "Punan." He alleged that this was the nomads' own nomenclature. Tom, however, airily called them all "Punan" or "Penan" as the mood seized him. Tom claimed, after having met all the Punan/Penan during his census, and after asking his best informants throughout the *ulu*, that the difference in nomenclature depended on whom one asked and did not provide a reliable way to distinguish among different bands of these jungle nomads. To insist otherwise, as Needham did, seemed to Tom mere pedantry by a literate foreigner dealing with a preliterate society. (Current usage seems to support Tom's view.)

These disputes, however, were only skirmishes in the long war Tom fought against social anthropology. Both Freeman and Needham had—at the very least—doubts about Tom's motives and methods in doing "ethnology." Tom, whose self-described "paranoia" made him abnormally prickly at all times, felt under siege with these academically accredited scholars on "his" turf, challenging his claims to expertise.

By January 1959, fresh from home leave, Tom should have felt less paranoid and more cheerful. He had received the OBE on the New Year's list, thanks to the efforts of Sir Anthony Abell, who felt that Tom's many accomplishments on behalf of Sarawak deserved recognition, especially the work at Niah and the highly successful BBC films that were earning Sarawak a good name around the world. (The films were shown on television everywhere except the United States, where, allegedly, the fact they were not in thirteen installments made them unsalable.) Tom told Geoff Barnes that "At least I feel I am on a level with my father now," but he was very conscious that friends his age or only a few years older had much higher honors. Solly Zuckerman had been knighted in 1956, as had one of the painters from the M-O days, William Coldstream, while Max's godfather, Charles Lambe, had received the accolade in 1953. Eddie Shackleton had been made a peer in 1958, the same year that Tom Driberg (later to be a peer) had spent as Labour Party chairman. Thus, Tom's pleasure at having more or less caught up with his father must have been dampened by the faster rise of his contemporaries. This, of course, was part of the crisis all men of his stripe must go through when they realize that they are no longer the youngest anything any more. But in Tom, the sense of rivalry with his contemporaries, connected as it was to his unsuccessful competition with his younger brother for his father's approval and affection, went far beyond what seems reasonable for a man of his age and accomplishments. Another event that soon came along and should have cheered Tom was, in late March 1959, the very friendly reception given his new book, *World Within*. The *Sunday Times* made *World Within* its book of the week, with a long review article by Raymond Mortimer, who wrote that Tom "As guerrilla leader and as anthropologist . . . pours out fascinating facts with delightfully sensible comments," and he promised that the book "will delight the general reader."

The splendid writer and critic V. S. Pritchett remarked in the *New Statesman* of Tom's writing style that "His prose is sometimes as difficult as his personality, but it is the writing of an eager, vivid, voracious mind, the mind of a non stop talker of unending curiosity. He is rather disorganised as a narrator, but his book is searching and dramatic." Tom must have been especially pleased with Pritchett's comment that, while Tom recorded "all the things we expect from anthropological writing," he did not do so dryly. "He is able to generalise the sights and sounds of real days and nights, so that we catch that respect for human life so missing in scientific studies, where the anthropologist stops at his own specialised interest. . . ." While not a bestseller like *Savage Civilisation*, the book sold several thousand copies within three months and sold steadily for years. In the mid-1990s it was still in print in an Oxford paperback edition.

Tom was also pleased to have obtained a contract from his friend Sidney Bernstein to do three television films for Granada, on the Sarawak rain forest, the swamp, and the caves. Even more pleasant was the prospect of returning to the Plain of Bah. In October 1959, leaving Barbara to complete the films for Granada, he set off for Bario.

This was his first trip back since his 1953 scrub typhus and plane crash. In a Borneo Airways Twin Pioneer, from 10,000 feet, he saw the uplands and remembered his first look at the region in 1945. This time, as before, he saw at first

> not a trace of human life anywhere below, just endless . . . jungle, mountain, and torrent, ineffably dark green. . . . For thirty or forty miles, run range after range after range of sandstone ridges, cut with waterways, aged and in feeling infinitely ancient. This way, quite lost in the air-world, one realises the tremendous scale of Borneo's interior and the almost insignificant effect man has had upon it.
>
> . . .12.25 through nowhere there is Bario and my heart glistens. . . . And at 12.35 we are down on it at last, slithering a little but a lovely clear landing—and oh to be back in the Kelabit slime.

Tom found "the atmosphere is as ever, but there is less swilling and—great new thing—no dogs *in the house*. Lots of war medals and the almost immediate revival of jokes I had for years forgotten. . . ." Sigang was there, still growing the potatoes that Tom had introduced to Bario years before, but all that was left of their "marriage" was a lingering mutual respect.

After six years away, Tom's attention was drawn to the changes in the interval. The reduced liquor consumption was one change, dogs being kept out of doors was another, fencing-in of the pigs that had lived under the house was a third. Thanks to an antimalaria program by the World Health Organization, there were now almost no mosquitoes or cockroaches. But, as Tom discovered, there were now also no cats; they had been poisoned by eating spray-killed cockroaches. With the cats gone, there was an explosion in the number of rats. Without cockroaches, bed bugs, which had never been a serious problem before, proliferated. One conclusion Tom drew was that although "the benefits of malarial spraying so far are tremendous, . . . there are anxious nights ahead" from the possible danger of typhus, cholera, and plague from rats, bed bugs, and their parasites. Tom's moral was that "All who wish the *ulu* well should daily repeat this motto: "DO GOOD CAREFULLY."

Meanwhile, he came up with his own method for righting the ecological imbalance. In a wireless message of November 23, 1959, to Borneo Airways, Tom asked the pilot to "bring some hungry cats to tackle plague of rats. I guarantee immediate payment all." The plea went out to all Kuching. Ong Kee Hui and many other old friends contributed kittens for Bario. Barbara had the thankless job of caring for them until a plane could fly to Bario and deliver the cats and, she hoped, collect Tom. She wrote to Tom that the kittens were very naughty and she worried they might prove to be too much for Lawai to handle. According to an account* that Tom published later, "in all the coast towns . . . the WHO opened special centres" for donations of "surplus cats."

The project hit a snag when no plane could be made available that could land on Bario's short strip, but, as Tom wrote, with the help of the RAF from Singapore "special containers were devised" in which to pack the cats. One clear day, an RAF aircraft from Singapore collected the cats in Kuching and flew inland. Then, "into the interior uplands suddenly cascaded parachute-borne containers bulging with cats of every degree of age and race." This may have solved the problem of the rats, if not the bed bugs.

Tom had hoped to get back to the coast by plane to Kuching but, with no plane to collect him, he took the opportunity to walk over the Tamabo mountain range with a handful of his good Kelabit friends, including some who had been in the hunters' hut when one of them had emitted his famous fart.

As with all trips in those days in Borneo's jungly interior, there were days of negotiating the rapids by dugout canoe and evenings spent sitting soaking wet while being bitten by insects. Tom's delight at being back with his old Kelabit cronies, however, was unquenchable. And then an ornithological "first" occurred to bless the trip for him:

> At night we collect the noisy frogs (but keep moving, the sandflies are really venomous here . . . ) or talking, mostly listening or asking about this country and its inhabitants, now and before, with the intimacy one best gets when out with a group of Kelabit men all from one village and interlinked by years of shared intricate experience. . . .
>
> One evening we were interrupted after full dark by a sudden melodic almost bull-like "Tewo-tow-tow." I asked what on earth it was, quite near out there in forest dark. "That's *Suit Rudap* [the frogmouth], it always calls like that." At very long last I had *heard* the call of a Frogmouth—probably the first white *knowingly* to do so in Borneo. . . .
>
> What a thrill to hear one. From now on, I am armed with an extra bird-eye into the Borneo night. Before, I—and other ornithologists—had literally *no idea* what size or shape of a noise any Frogmouth here made. And my Bario friends are surely right. No owl or nightjar could make such sound, and no daybird does.

---

*For an alternate version of the story, see the Notes and Sources.

As often before, the presence of a special bird crowned what was already a wonderful moment in Tom's life, in this case the delight of climbing mountains and being "one of the boys" among a group of Kelabit men. Such a combination of events gave Tom his most undiluted moments of happiness.

Having left Bario on December 1, he got back to Kuching in time to broadcast on Radio Sarawak on Boxing Day. Early in the new year, however, a new development demanded Tom's return to England. This was word from Bethlem Royal Hospital that Max was now believed to be well enough to be released if there were someone to release him to. Tom flew back to England in May while Barbara sailed back on a cargo ship with four frolicsome young male orangutans destined for zoos in Europe.

Tom's job of wrestling with Max's fate was more complicated—and much less amusing—than Barbara's job with her orangutan charges. Max was clearly not normal and thus not able to return to Sarawak with Tom. Max's godfather, Admiral Sir Charles Lambe, was ill; he died in August 1960 in the middle of Tom's home leave. Tom's mother and Biddy were both hopeless. Both would die the next year, Biddy from an overdose of sleeping pills. This left Tom with only his brother to help him with Max, a duty Bill reluctantly took on almost entirely due to the strenuous conscience of his Quaker wife, Nancy. Tom, who dreaded visiting Max in the hospital, could not handle him outside of an institution for more than a few days at a time. He pushed off the care of his son onto Bill and Nancy to the extent possible, so he could attend to other projects, such as doing the voice-over for his three films for Granada. There were also arrangements to be made with various museums to give appropriate training to Tom's Brunei trainee, Shariffuddin. (Meeting Sharif at London airport, Tom brought him to town by taxi and Sharif remembers that Tom slipped him £6 in pocket money, after paying the cabby.)

There were also mid-summer conferences in Vienna and Paris, where Tom had been invited to give papers. There were trips with Barbara to see their orangutan babies at two different zoos in Germany, and there was a trip to Japan for the month of September while Barbara visited her family in Germany.

While still in England, Tom found something else to do: temporarily revive Mass-Observation in order to research a book that would take a brief second look at the people of Bolton the way that Freeman and Needham and others were taking another look at "their" people in Borneo. Having decided to reexamine "Worktown" (Bolton), he contacted his old M-O observers.

Julian Trevelyan was no longer married to Ursula, and Julian's new wife, the painter Mary Fedden, not knowing Tom's habitual effect on her husband, was amazed that when Tom rang up Julian and asked him to drop everything and come up to Bolton again, he went. Humphrey Spender, similarly summoned, went, too. Michael Wickham and Sir William Coldstream, from the original group of M-O painters answered the call. Woodrow Wyatt, by then an M.P. and a television personality, came. So did two other former denizens of 85 Davenport Street, the proletarian novelist John Sommerfield and the former coal lorry driver Bill Naughton, who by 1960 was beginning to have his plays performed on television and radio. Celia Fremlin, Tom's best Mass-Observer during the war, was now a published writer of crime thrillers, and she, too, responded to Tom's call for help. M-O veteran Leonard England, assisted by old M-O observer Mollie Tarrant, had been running M-O Ltd. since it had become a market research company. They were both ready to go to Bolton. Richard Fitter, at one time on the staff of M-O, and Stanley Cramp and Humphrey Pease, all three of them distinguished ornithologists and naturalists by now, were co-opted into a revival of Mass-Observation's original activity. They all were to observe the "mass" of ordinary people and record what they saw and heard, thus providing data for Tom to compare with M-O's records from two decades earlier.

A petite but curvaceous blonde who had been one of Tom's Mass-Observers in the old days was at loose ends after having just divorced her husband. For the research on "Sex at Blackpool," she was asked to befriend the prostitutes "who would be standing in Woolworth's doorway at half past twelve at night." After chatting with them and obtaining all the information Tom wanted, her next job was emptying bedpans in a hospital for a few days. Over the course of a week or two, she also worked in pubs and in a factory. She and Tom had an amiable little affair during the research for the book.

> I remember meeting him in a pub. I had not met him for 15 years. I remember what I was wearing. [Her hair at the time was still very blonde and she was well dressed.] I remember he was at the bar and turning and looking at me and there was another chap with him. He ignored this other fellow and we were off. He poked me in the diaphragm and said something like "You little bit of gristle." His intentions were clear and I wasn't being difficult. But we worked, my God, we worked, and it wasn't for money.

Even Charles Madge, unable to participate more fully because he was about to leave for Southeast Asia, was induced to write a postscript to the finished work. Tom seemingly had not lost his mysterious gift for getting people to do what he wanted. The help was not all one way. For example, in July, without telling Bill Naughton, Tom wrote Sidney Bernstein that the ex-lorry driver was "an absolute original. . . . I think you ought to see him yourself rather than leave it to a subordinate." Naughton had just had a play on BBC television, but was not yet well known, having yet to write his finest work, *Alfie*.

The result of this temporary revival of M-O, entitled *Britain Revisited* (Gollancz, 1961), had all the vices of the earlier M-O books, as *The Times* (March 30, 1961) reviewer pointed out. Nonetheless, the reviewer commented that "It remains so good that anyone curious about what is really going on today among one wide cross-section of his fellow citizens will find it rewarding." He recommends that it be made "compulsory reading for all embryo novelists. They should see from it how much richer workaday life is in human drama than are the case histories of queer folk." By October 1960 the typescript of *Britain Revisited* was at Gollancz', the three films for Granada were done, and plans for more films for Granada were under consideration. Max, having proved incapable of coping with life outside an asylum, was back in Bethlem. Tom left England and soon reached Kuching, where Barbara rejoined him.

Within weeks of returning to Borneo, Tom was more deeply embroiled than ever in rows with academics, one of which became so bizarre that it is still widely remembered. Tom's adversary was one of the Leach nominees, the brilliant but intellectually combative New Zealander Derek Freeman, tall, rangy, handsome, by then holder of a Cambridge Ph.D. and a senior research fellow at the Research School of Pacific Studies of the Australian National University in Canberra.

In the early 1950s, during Freeman's first fieldwork among the Iban of Sarawak, relations between Tom and Freeman had been guarded but outwardly friendly, but the two men were unlikely to have remained friends in any case. Freeman likes to make moral judgments about people and things, while Tom loved to shock his interlocutors. Relations between them worsened when in 1957, without consulting Tom, Freeman arranged to have a graduate student installed in an area Tom had written Freeman of as a place where he wanted to do research himself some day. The student, however, proved—in Tom's view (and not only Tom's)—to have "brains" but "no guts." Instead of plucking a fruit from Tom's garden, Freeman's student left Sarawak without completing his research but also without causing problems while he was there.

Subsequent letters and meetings between Freeman and Tom aggravated suspicion and irritation on both sides. Tom offered and then rescinded an invitation to Freeman to visit Niah. Finally, later that year, Tom, after smoldering with resentment for what he perceived as Freeman's contempt for his anthropological efforts, blew up at the New Zealander. It happened in Tom's car, in the presence of a young colonial officer, on the way to take Freeman to the Kuching airport en route home. Tom, Freeman recalls, "ranted and raved and abused me in every conceivable way."

Two years later, the next student Freeman sent to Sarawak, again without going through Tom, seemed much more impressive, a highly articulate Belgian with an aristocratic handle to his name. His curriculum vitae included a Ph.D. from a German university and fieldwork in Mexico under a renowned French anthropologist. He was to work in the upper Rejang, among the Kajang, a people even more interesting to Tom than the subjects of the American's research.

In reply to a letter from Tom telling Freeman he had heard of the Belgian's planned arrival and wished him well (a statement that would elicit scepticism from anyone acquainted with Tom's territoriality), the New Zealander underlined the new man's remarkable credentials and encouraged Tom to meet him. Tom met the Belgian within days of his arrival and wrote Freeman that the man "has the makings of a deep 'seer' into Sarawak. There is room for one of these, especially around Belaga."

But Freeman wrote again a few months later, upping the ante, to say the Belgian had expanded his research project to include a comparative study of the mythology of Borneo, or at the very least, "the Kajang, Kenyah, Kayan, Iban, Land Dayak and Melanau." Tom's politely negative response undoubtedly masked much stronger feelings: "I will think about this carefully. But are you SURE [the Belgian] is the man to do all this great job—and in what time, and with what reciprocal advantages to those of us who have spent *years* collecting raw material. . . ." Freeman wrote back citing the man's many qualifications and added that "Very few anthropologists indeed have the experience and training of Dr. [X]; in fact I cannot think of anyone better fitted to do the job proposed." It was not until at least a year later that Freeman would begin to look into the Belgian's credentials and discover, to his embarrassment, that the Belgian was a total fraud, without any degrees or fieldwork and with no claim to his noble-sounding name. "He was an imposter," Freeman now recalls, "of consummate effrontery."

Though Tom, too, was taken in by the Belgian, he was also puzzled by something odd about him. In late November 1960, Tom spent three days in Belaga to try to get a better fix on him. He found the Belgian had been obliged to move out of the longhouse, having unwittingly become involved in a political battle among local tribal factions. Tom, in the course of trying to remedy the situation, privately accused the Belgian of various acts of misconduct and also made clear to the local chief that his loyalties were with him, not with the foreign interloper, a circumstance that further damaged the Belgian's effectiveness.

Nonetheless, Tom agreed to the elaborate myth-collecting project and offered what the Museum had in the way of research materials, manpower, and equipment for what Tom now christened "Operation Belagalore." If this were a game of poker, one might say that Freeman had pushed all his chips forward in making the proposal for the Belgian to take on such a big project. And, if this were poker, Tom had just called Freeman's bet.

In early 1961, after the Belgian—whom local people recall as "delusional"—got into trouble again, Tom wrote Freeman:

> Soon now . . . social anthropology must have to face up fully to the question of the
> extent to which it is responsible for the sorts of persons sent into the field. . . . This
> is my 14th year in the ring-side seat observing the process—and BOY *is* it begin-
> ning to add up. . . .

When he went up the Rejang to oust the Belgian, he got drunk before doing
so and administered the coup de grâce publicly, in an especially humiliating
way. He delivered a virulent verbal attack on the man in the presence of the
local chiefs, ending his peroration with the announcement that the Belagalore
project was over.

In Canberra, Freeman, not yet aware that the Belgian was an imposter, on
the basis of dramatic accounts from the field by the Belgian, persuaded the
vice chancellor of the Australian National University (ANU) to write a letter
of complaint to the Sarawak authorities about Tom's treatment of the student
before he came out himself on March 3, 1961, to rescue his protégé and try
to rid Borneo of Tom Harrisson.

In Kuching, Tom was away. Freeman, after successful demarches on
senior Sarawak government authorities to set in motion having his man rein-
stated up-country, was encouraged to press on with his efforts to rid Sarawak
of Tom Harrisson by several of Tom's enemies, including the Anglican bishop
whom Tom had vainly tried to deprive of a concrete Gothic cathedral. This
prelate's plea was one that Freeman, who travels with a small portrait of St.
George, could not ignore. He decided to stay a bit longer to see what he
could do.

The next day, Freeman took a walk through the museum and began to
notice things that he had never noticed before. He noticed especially the ithy-
phallic and copulatory carvings. Thinking about what he had seen afterward
at night at the Government Resthouse, where he was sharing a room with the
Belgian, he became convinced that Tom had turned the museum into a palace
of pornography, Kraft-Ebbing in wood. Tom had *orang ulu* carvers living at
Pig Lane, and Freeman felt that the work they made, not having been created
in a longhouse for longhouse purposes, was "fake" and had no place in a
museum (a view with which others disagree; see Notes and Sources). In trying to figure out why Tom would pervert his museum in this way, he came to
the conclusion that Tom was a madman. He spent the next few days announcing his finding to various people in Kuching. He then returned to the museum
to take photographs of offending displays. Emerging into the gardens, in order
to call attention to Tom's having displayed this "fake" and "pornographic" art,
he smashed one of the Berawan statues on the lawn—one showing a man and
woman about to come together sexually, a common Berawan artistic theme—
and saw that word of his action reached the authorities.

When nothing happened as the result of his gesture, on the last day of his week in Kuching, he went to Pig Lane. Tom and Barbara were both out of town and the house was empty, except for a servant. Freeman walked in, found it full of what he regarded as pornographic carvings and similar things, and took pictures to use as evidence in his campaign to have Tom removed from his job. He pried open a locked drawer, in search of more such evidence, but it contained nothing but trinkets. Tom's servant called the police, who came and met Freeman at the door.

The police were Iban, whose language Freeman spoke well, with an impressive display of classical verbiage. Even more impressive was the camera, hanging from a strap around the tall, fair foreigner's neck, which was recharging and flashing. Freeman walked between the two amazed Ibans and out the door. Back at the Resthouse, he rang up the Sarawak authorities to inform them that he would be leaving that afternoon by plane for Singapore.

Taken by police escort to the airport that afternoon, Freeman flew to Singapore, hand-carrying his film. In Singapore, he decided that rather than continue with his planned itinerary, he should go on to the United Kingdom, where he could consult the professor of psychological medicine at the University of Edinburgh, and then they could go to London and make a submission about Tom to the House of Commons. Sometime after Bangkok, however, he decided it would be better to go back to Canberra. He asked the pilot to send a signal to the Australian High Commission in Karachi, since he would be debarking there. The high commissioner, when he saw Freeman, insisted he see a psychiatrist. While Freeman was telling the Pakistani doctor about Tom and how Tom's behavior was contributing to the rot that could lead to a communist insurrection in Borneo, the High Commissioner sent a wire to the ANU vice chancellor to report on Freeman's condition. Freeman's department head, Professor of Anthropology John Barnes, was sent out to bring him home.

Tom remarked to friends later: "It is the only time in my life when I was able to drive someone round the bend without even seeing him." (Professor Freeman's version of this story is in Notes and Sources.)

# Chapter 38

# The British Sun Sets on Borneo

In 1961, while Tom and Freeman concluded their epic battle, the British Crown was preparing to release its remaining territories in Southeast Asia. The prime minister of the Federation of Malaya proposed the formation of the Federation of Malaysia, to consist of Malaya, Singapore, Brunei, British North Borneo (to be known as Sabah), and Sarawak. The Federation of Malaysia was born on August 31, 1963; Sarawak and Sabah, the two British colonies on Borneo, became member states of it.* It seemed the best way to safeguard Sarawak's security. Sarawak's big neighbor, Sukarno's Indonesia, looked ready to swallow Sarawak and the other two mini states above Indonesia's thousand-mile unmarked inner Bornean border unless Britain or Malaya protected them. Sarawak's colonial legislature, the Council Negri, in mid-1962 gave its grudging consent to joining Malaysia.

Meanwhile, concern about communism had spread from the Southeast Asian mainland to all of Borneo. In Sarawak, the small Clandestine Communist Organization (CCO) was active, chiefly among Chinese in the area between Kuching and the Indonesian border. Many of these rural Chinese, mostly gold miners and pepper farmers, were eventually assigned to protected "new villages" so that the comings and goings of potential CCO guerrillas and their supporters could be controlled by the police. Such measures had been taken earlier to deal with an analogous problem among Chinese in Malaya.

Once the idea of Malaysia was bruited, it was obvious that there would be no place for loud, bossy, hard-drinking Englishmen, no matter how talented, well meaning, or knowledgeable. It took Tom a long time to realize this, if he ever did. So many of the projects that he was directing in the early

---

*Within a few years Singapore withdrew from the Federation. Brunei, by 1963 rich enough from oil to stand on its own, never joined.

1960s, although admired by most Sarawak officials up until then, were out of tune with the themes emanating from Kuala Lumpur. Much of what Tom did in the museum and wrote about in the *Sarawak Museum Journal* and *Sarawak Gazette* or publicized all over the world via his BBC and Granada films had an emphasis on wonderful pagan activities and how it would be a pity for them to disappear, while Kuala Lumpur was trying to make one Malay-led nation out of its disparate parts.

Tom was aware that some of his wishes for Sarawak ran counter to those of Kuala Lumpur but felt he was adroit enough to help work out a decent relationship between Sarawak and the metropole regarding the concerns of non-Muslim indigenous peoples. To do this, he might need to stay on (perhaps part-time) beyond 1966, when he would face obligatory retirement at age fifty-five. On one level, he knew no white man would be welcome in a "boss" role under the new government, but, on another level, he thought somehow an exception would be made for him, because he was irreplaceable.

Certainly the digs that he and Barbara were supervising in the Niah caves and the Sarawak River delta were welcomed by the Malaysian government. The discoveries that Tom and Barbara were making were replacing Sarawak's, and thus Malaysia's, nearly blank early history with a Hinduised/Sinicized one consonant with those of her neighbors, Indonesia and Thailand. Even better, Tom's and Barbara's work on behalf of protecting the orangutan led the world. It must have been particularly satisfying to the new federal government that it put Malaysia way ahead of Indonesia, the only other country with native orangutans.

In November 1961, Tom and Barbara began their first attempt to provide sheltered jungle conditions for three of their home-reared orangutans at Bako, a Sarawak national forest reserve near Kuching. This pioneer plan for releasing the apes into a sheltered bit of jungle was Barbara's. All the later ones in Sabah, Sumatra, and Indonesian Borneo (Kalimantan) followed her example. New animals were put in quarantine for a month or more at the sheltered jungle camp. Later, they were uncaged and encouraged to go into the trees but given extra food by the guardians at the camp. Their cages were left open to serve as temporary housing for animals not yet ready for life in the wild.

The results of such procedures were mixed. Some of the female orangutans were able to breed with wild males and adjust more or less to life in the jungle. The home-reared males, however, continued coming back to camp for food and friendship. Without meaning to, a big strong young male could be a killer. Tourists and game wardens, faced with an enormous playful uncaged ape, were understandably frightened. One of the saddest moments in Barbara's life came when she learned the fate of Arthur, one of her home-reared orangutans. While being transferred from Bako to a bigger and better camp in Sabah, Arthur ran away. When he came back to the Sabah camp, a man working there who did not know him felt threatened, took his gun, and shot him dead.

More scholarly work might have been done on the Sarawak orangutan had it not been for Tom's bouts of bad temper. George Schaller, an American primatologist famous for his work on the gorilla, came to Sarawak briefly in late 1960 and ran afoul of Tom, then in the midst of his row with Freeman. Although Schaller received help from Barbara and people in the Sarawak Forestry Department, he was so offended by Tom's behavior that he suggested to other researchers of the orangutan that it might be easier to work in Sumatra or Indonesian Borneo instead. Still, Barbara's book, *Orang-utan*, though not regarded as scientifically serious when it was released in the summer of 1962, sold quite well and, most important to Barbara, widely publicized the threat to the survival of the orangutan.

Perhaps the Harrissons' most enduring contribution to the protection of these apes was Tom's setting up the Orang-utan Recovery Service (OURS) in May 1964. At a meeting in Malaysia of zoo directors, conservationists, and government officials from all over the world, it was agreed that the worldwide Zoo Directors' Union would pay the costs of OURS's sheltered jungle areas— in Bako and eventually in Sabah—and fund efforts to convince the various governments to curb the illegal market in wild orangutans. Tom and Barbara would arrange for the zoos that contributed to OURS, and which had adequate facilities, to receive orphaned orangutan infants. In April 1965, Sir Solly Zuckerman wrote to Barbara that "as a result of your propaganda, we have doubled the height of our present Orang Quarters. I say 'present Orang Quarters' since we are now starting on the design of our new Primate House." The Harrissons' complaints about the London Zoo were getting results.

Eventually, however, the Harrissons' conservation efforts for these apes foundered on the same rock as did their turtle conservation: destruction of habitat. Although capturing orangutans for the export market declined, orangutan orphans kept being delivered to the Harrissons and to the sheltered jungle camps as their forests were felled by the growing Bornean timber industry. Yet, as Schaller's colleague, a research scientist with Wildlife Conservation International's office at the Bronx Zoo, said in 1992, when he was running a training and conservation program in Sabah, "although it is hard to treat Tom seriously as a scientist, . . . if I were to eliminate what he did, it would be hard to do my job now."

Drawing on stories such as Schaller's, Tom's detractors often accuse him of having kept trained scholars and scientists away from Borneo, but the facts are otherwise. In a letter to an acquaintance in August 1961, Tom notes in passing that

Right now I have four outside experts working in association with the Museum. One is a vertebrate biologist, one a leading expert in Hindu-Buddhist art and pre-history, one the director of the marine-biological station at the University of Tokyo and personal adviser to the Emperor of Japan (a marine biologist). The fourth is the emeritus Professor of Zoology at the University of Kansas, a world authority on reptiles. Two of these occupy the annex, one is in the Talang-Talang bungalow and the fourth in the Aurora Hotel.

There were few periods in the 1950s and early 1960s without several scholars or scientists visiting Sarawak, often the result of Tom's efforts to recruit them and with funding he had arranged. He did, however, continue to be skittish about anthropologists and about letting archaeologists, palaeontologists, or prehistorians see the excavations at Niah. He was frank about his reasons, writing Lord Medway in late 1961, "I simply don't want arrivistes cashing in and being a bore here."

One outsider Tom was always glad to see at Niah or anywhere else in Sarawak was Medway. He was living next door, so to speak, having obtained a lectureship in zoology at the University of Malaya in Kuala Lumpur. For much of the period between 1960 and 1965, Tom counted on Medway to be almost an assistant curator and would ask his help to handle occasional problems with the museum staff.

In June 1962, for example, Tom wrote to Medway that his best collector, Gaun, had been working in Sarawak for the Cambridge botanist Corner and would be working for Bob Inger in September up in the *ulu* Baleh, but that meanwhile Gaun was being moody and would benefit from going to Kuala Lumpur to work with Medway: "He takes a lot of notice of you, so please cope gently. (I just have not the time and patience left for such matters at present.)" He added that he would pay Gaun's official expenses and had recently lent him "a tidy sum . . . in personal cash also." A few months later, Tom wrote Medway that "Gaun . . . is in far better shape than when he left. I am most grateful to you. The trouble is that people like him *need* personal attention and leadership and fussing etc., etc., etc. It's only at Niah that I ever begin to get time to spend that way. . . . Most grateful to you, dear boy. . . ."

Tom was paying little attention to his family "at home" in England. Biddy died in November 1961, at age fifty-three, of an overdose of sleeping pills; it was never determined whether it was suicide or accident. Tom's contact with Max remained minimal. He would go to see him at the asylum whenever he went to England and would occasionally take him out for the day, but he seldom wrote to him. Similarly, Tom seems to have shown no emotion when, less than a month after Biddy's death, his mother died at age seventy-five.

While the remnants of his family ties to England fell to bits, his home life in Sarawak gradually turned into something both less and more than a marriage. At his request or on his behalf, Barbara was often away filming on-site for Granada, or at Niah supervising the digging, or in the jungle observing orangutans. When Tom went away, she would usually stay behind at the museum organizing the display and study of the ceramic collection and the reassembling of ancient ceramic sherds into pots, becoming in the process an expert on Chinese export ware.

Barbara's relationship with Tom, in spite of the absence of sex, remained affectionate and loving on her side, but Tom's attitude toward her was gradually evolving into one of trust in a reliable, loyal, professional colleague. She had never been his closest confidante or a companion with whom to have fun. For that role, he continued to prefer men, while for sex he confined himself to short-term encounters with various women outside Sarawak.

By the early 1960s, Barbara was spending roughly three months a year at Niah, while Tom would come up for a few days or weeks at a time. Amenities at the cave and the resthouse at Pangkalan Lobang, on the Niah River opposite the plankwalk to the caves, were better than they had been. In 1962, even the plankwalk was improved slightly. This would make it easier to run down to the river and on down to the *kubu* at Kampong Niah. (*Kubu*, literally "fort," in Sarawak means an up-country government station with its district officer, police constabulary, small armory, and gaol.) At the *kubu*, there was now not only a wireless but a telephone, a valuable link to Kuching, given the worsening situation inside Sarawak due to increased tensions along the border with Indonesia.

# Chapter 39

## Guerrilla Again

On December 9, 1962, Barbara went from the Niah Great Cave downriver to the *kubu* to call in her weekly report to Tom in Kuching. She found the phone line dead. The native officer in charge of the *kubu* told her that there was an armed rebellion taking place in Brunei and the coastal area south of there. He said that Kampong Niah was threatened and that she and her team should stay in the caves and lie low. Instead, she decided to go upriver to the nearest Iban longhouse, a large one, with some 250 inhabitants.

Barbara had enough stores, food, and water to have stayed in the cave with her staff from the museum, but she was worried about how to defend the store of petrol at Pangkalan Lobang, on the dock next to the Resthouse. The cave workers depended on that fuel for cooking, electricity for lighting, and other purposes. She also felt that "you couldn't make plans with no intelligence" and thought she could hope to get information and help at the nearby Iban longhouse. With her went Michael Chong, a museum trainee from Sabah, and a few others from the dig. They motored up the Niah River in their little boat, past Malay and Kedayan villages that had become ghost towns overnight.

The Ibans at the longhouse immediately invited Barbara and her people to stay with them. They also agreed to conduct a river watch, day and night. They said that they had heard that an Indonesia-backed group of Malays and Kedayans (a small Muslim ethnic group living along the coastal plain from Brunei to Bintulu) were calling themselves the National Army of Northern Borneo (TNKU) and were killing people at Bekenu, between Miri and Niah, very near. On December 10, a pair of Australian surveyors arrived at the longhouse from upriver, where they had been working unaware of any problem. At Barbara's request and with Iban help, they spent the night felling trees to build a bar over the river so boats could not pass quickly or undetected in either direction.

By five o'clock the next morning, Barbara and others, armed with shot-guns filled with bird shot, were on their way with the Australians to the *kubu* at Kampong Niah. They found the rebel flag hoisted, the native officer gone, the office closed, and the whole fort empty. The Australians took down the rebel flag and accompanied Barbara and the others back upriver. This time, Barbara decided to stay at the Resthouse at Pangkalan Lobang, where the petrol supply was kept.

Members of the museum staff and Michael Chong stayed with her. Chong was not as quick or confident as Shariffuddin. At one point during the pre-vious digging season, Tom had shouted at him, "Bloody fool, I don't know what the North Borneo Government is going to do with you." Some of the Malays who owned the Niah cave's bird nests came upriver to be with Barbara and helped the museum staffers keep watch day and night on the petrol tanks and the traffic along the Niah River. Altogether, they were not a very experienced crew for such a job.

Once, in the middle of the night, Barbara was awakened by Michael Chong crying, "Shots, shots!" Chong, one of the youngest, had been given the job of providing coffee for the watch and was walking in the dark with the coffee pot. (The Resthouse was being kept dark to improve the sentries' abil-ity to see along the river and avoid notice by the rebel army.) Chong recalls:

> I ran along in the dark with the coffee pot and stumbled and spilled all the cof-fee. I was young and afraid to die and I stumbled. Then I ran back to the Resthouse and cooked another pot of coffee and while I was boiling the water for the second pot, I heard a shot!

It was then that he had cried out and awakened Barbara. The "shot," in fact, was merely the noise of a cat running into a row of glasses that had been left on the Resthouse veranda.

But, as Chong recalls, "the Malays heard the noise and thought it was the beginning of a fire fight and one of them had an automatic or semi-automatic weapon and it went off, just like that. When the gun went off, the man who had fired it left the gun on the floating platform along the river and jumped into the water. (He was later found half a mile away.) He had nearly killed one of his friends!"

On December 12, Barbara and the Australians revisited the *kubu* to see if it was flying the rebel flag again. It was not. At half past seven that evening, "C" Company of the First Battalion Royal Green Jackets arrived with a note from Tom. By eight o'clock Barbara was in bed and asleep.

Early the same morning, the Forty-second Royal Marine Commando had reached Limbang town and had rescued (at the cost of five marine lives) eight expatriates, including the Resident for the Limbang valley and his wife, whom the TNKU had held hostage and had planned to execute that day.

John Fisher, the first man in the Bornean colonial administration to warn of a TNKU-led rebellion, had already on December 9 drawn on his experience as an old Rajah's servant to send a red feather, a traditional call to arms, up the Baram River. Tom's friend and SEMUT veteran, the paramount chief of the Kayan and Kenyah tribes of Sarawak, Temenggong Oyong Lawai Jau, and all of the other chiefs of the Baram (some of whom had also seen action in the SEMUT days) responded with enthusiasm, coming downriver with hundreds of armed Kenyahs, Kayans, and Ibans eager to man patrols or to fight. Expatriates from the Public Works Department, the Rubber Development Office, the Police, Land and Survey, Education, and Agriculture Departments all got into the Dunkirk spirit and took charge of these impromptu volunteer forces.

Meanwhile Tom, flying about in helicopters and Single and Twin Pioneers with the Royal Air Force, helped the newly arrived British forces (1/2nd Gurkha Rifles and the First Battalion, Queen's Own Highlanders, chiefly) reconnoiter the Bornean interior. Wherever they landed, Tom would rally up-country volunteers to cordon off the interior along the rivers and the jungle tracks to prevent the escape of rebels inland. Tom insisted on dressing in the style in which he would be most recognizable to the *orang ulu*, in a dirty Aertex shirt, shorts, and sandals. As Major-General Walter C. Walker, Director of Operations, Borneo, later recalled, the people of the uplands "certainly recognised [Tom]. As soon as he landed and stepped out they all came rushing up to him. It was as if Jesus Christ had arrived."

Flying over the Sibuti River, Tom saw that the rebels appeared to be holding the *kubu* at Bekenu. On December 15, he helped plan the successful recapture of the fort by a combined attack of native irregulars from the rear and troops of the British army's First Battalion Royal Green Jackets from the front. More important in defeating the rebels than winning back this pocket from the TNKU were Tom's recommendations that the British forces provide radios, radio batteries, and a little ammunition to subcoastal villages, where the people were ignorant, bewildered, and unnerved. Ever alert to the morale aspects of guerrilla warfare, he convinced the British forces that the impact of their officers arriving by helicopter in the village square, "dishing out some ammunition and a spot of leadership" would make those villagers more firmly loyal to the government and less easy prey to TNKU threats or blandishments. According to two historians of the "undeclared war": "It was decided to place the [native] irregulars under one command. The obvious choice was Tom Harrisson."

General Walker, who took command of Borneo operations on December 19, had much experience in this kind of fighting from the "Emergency," a civil war that ran from 1948 to 1960 on the Malay Peninsula in which the still British-run government of the Federation of Malaya successfully defended itself against local Chinese guerrillas, who had, at the least, moral support from the People's Republic of China. Walker recalled that "What came to be known as Harrisson's Force grew to a strength of nearly two thousand and played a major part in containing the rebellion and, later, in cutting the escape routes of fugitive rebels." Tom was playing the role that he liked best, that of guerrilla warfare leader. For the next six months, he devoted himself to being one of the British army's and military intelligence's closest advisers in Borneo.

General Walker, nearly as unconventional an army general as Tom was a museum curator, confessed:

> I liked Harrisson's zest and imagination. We would spend the day up-country, flying between longhouses collecting intelligence, and be back in Brunei for the evening conference. . . . During this first week, both of us flew together the full length of the Indonesian frontier, nearly one thousand miles from the sandy beaches of West Sarawak to the mangrove swamps of eastern North Borneo. . . . Between stops, the two of us looked down on to the jungle-covered hills and mountains while Harrisson pointed out the routes across the frontier which he had already marked on my map.

During this time in the air, most days for three months starting on December 11, 1962, Tom could not help noticing the birds as well as the features of the terrain of military interest. He later wrote about what birds he had seen, in what numbers and densities per mile, and at what heights, for the *Sarawak Gazette*.

In pointing out features of the inner Sarawak landscape to the general, Tom drew on what he had learned during his many long treks of exploration in central Borneo over the last thirty years, which in 1962 culminated in being awarded the Royal Geographical Society's Founder's Medal, a royal medal given to such explorers as David Livingstone and Richard Burton. General Walker recognized Tom as a "rogue elephant." He noticed that after Tom stayed behind overnight with some local tribe, when the helicopter came to pick him up, Tom usually showed the effects of heavy drinking and (Walker believed) womanizing. The general was willing to tolerate these failings in a man who was a walking, talking encyclopedia of things his soldiers needed to know.

The more astute British authorities, military and civil, and especially General Walker, rightly recognized that the "Brunei Rebellion" was merely a curtain raiser to a larger effort by Sukarno's Indonesia to prevent the formation of the Federation of Malaysia. And, as Walker's biographer has explained, "If the Indonesian threat did develop, the problem [of protecting British Borneo] would be, on the face of it, almost insuperable. With enemy raiding parties able to strike across a thousand miles of frontier from secure bases, how could the defenders hope to stop them . . . ? But, flying along the frontier with Harrisson, the task *did* seem possible. Good intelligence was the answer." Tom's role would be crucial to obtaining that intelligence.

In January 1963, the long-anticipated *Konfrontasi,* "Confrontation" by Indonesia against Malaysia, began. General Walker, a Gurkha officer, promptly brought into northern Borneo a squadron of the Twenty-second Special Air Service (SAS) and the Gurkha Independent Parachute Company, which was formed January 1, 1963, for this purpose.

As Walker recalled, "The SAS liked Tom Harrisson, with whom they formed so close a relationship that . . . they set up their headquarters in his garden" in Pig Lane. In early February, Walker asked Tom to produce a pamphlet on the *Background to a Revolt: Brunei and the Surrounding Territory,* for "all those officers and men who serve in Borneo." Succinct and distinctly unmilitary, it gave practical advice on how to avoid offending the local people, especially those living along the inner border, and is remembered by military intelligence as having helped the newly arrived British troops adapt smoothly to Borneo.

Having announced their "Confrontation" early in the year, the Indonesians did not move against Sarawak militarily until April 12, when a platoon of Indonesians attacked the police station at Tebedu, near Kuching. A Sarawak policeman (an Iban) was killed, two others were wounded, and the armory was ransacked. As Peter Dickens states in his authoritative account of the SAS in Borneo, *SAS: Secret War in South-East Asia,* the raid was "clearly intended to test British reactions. If we were to vacillate, morale throughout the territories would surely plummet, the CCO would be encouraged to rise, and Malaysia would be still-born. . . ."

Five days later, the Sarawak Defence Committee met and a working group was set up, with Tom as its chairman and notetaker, to prepare an outline plan for establishing the "Border Scouts," Tom's idea. As the working group minutes state: "The role of the Border Scouts . . . will be to serve as an auxiliary, with expert local knowledge—aggressive within Sarawak's own territory and opposing any intrusion by outsiders thereon. . . ." Tom's minutes continue: "Recruitment is open to any keen able-bodied male of good character between the ages of 17 and 45. . . . The essence of this force is the use of native skills, local knowledge and natural mobility." They warn:

> Elaborate equipment and technique are not required. On the other hand, firepower must be sufficiently strong and well-handled to give confidence and to counter trained intruders with automatic weapons. . . . The advantage will always be with the Border Scouts on their own ground, if kept highly mobile and properly led—and this potential superiority must not be sacrificed needlessly to elaboration, organization, or unification (all of which cost money, too).

The Border Scouts soon came into being and were put under the command of Major Tom Leask, Commander of "D" Squadron, 22d SAS, for training.

Tom quickly moved to the next stage: preparing secretly to move the war into the enemy's camp. Beginning in mid-1963, groups of indigenous "Cross-Border Scouts" were sent in units of at most seventy men, but often many fewer, into Indonesian Borneo to carry out specific aggressive tasks assigned to them by British military intelligence. At first they were all indigenous and thus more easily deniable by the British and Malaysian governments, since they belonged to the identical ethnic groups as their neighbors across the unmarked border. Later, they were combined into teams with SAS personnel.

Tom, in the initial period of the Cross-Border Scouts, provided advice on which communities and which individuals to use. The man who ran the program recalled that "Tom's advice paid off. He was good." Tom's judgment would go astray occasionally, as when he would give preference to an aristocrat over a Mission-educated social climber, on that basis alone, "but his knowledge of the hierarchical structure among the Kayan and Kenyah was very valuable."

In early 1964, Indonesian uniformed paratroopers began crossing into Malaysian Borneo, not as hit-and-run terrorists, as before, but as "proper military forces which if intercepted would make a fight of it and only withdraw after setting ambushes." Once this happened, the British and Malaysians were a bit less nervous about having their cross-border operations unmasked. It was at this point that the Gurkhas were brought in. After that, Tom no longer had an important role to play in the war, except for the occasional briefing and debriefing of itinerant cross-border native traders and artisans accustomed to turning up in Pig Lane to see Tom or stay in the annex, now conveniently located next to SAS headquarters. Thus, when Solly Zuckerman arrived in Sarawak, as chief scientific adviser to the minister of defense, "to see if the weapons being used by the Gurkhas and others were as good as they needed to be (they weren't)," he found that Tom was not involved in any of the briefings he was given. He assumed that Tom's home-leave stories about his cloak-and-dagger activities the previous year had been empty boasts.

Tom missed the excitement of being at the center of all this glamorous activity. But by then he was already embroiled in a new project, one that might lead to a new career for himself after he was forced to retire from the Sarawak Museum in just two years.

# Chapter 40

## Cornell Connections

In 1958, Tom began exchanging letters with Professor George McT. Kahin of Cornell University, a noted American political scientist specializing in modern Indonesia. In April 1963, when they met in Kuching, Tom suggested to Kahin that the museum might work with Cornell in a mutually useful arrangement by which a few graduate students would come to Sarawak. These Cornell students, during their one- or two-year stays, would spend three to six months working at the museum to help process, edit, and write up data gathered by museum staff members with poor written English. Tom would reciprocate by supplying guides, interpreters, transportation, and introductions for these young scholars to carry out the research they had come to Borneo to do.

This arrangement was promptly put into effect and produced useful publications by both sides in several fields. For example, in exchange for helping Cornell historian Robert Pringle with the research for his history of the Ibans during the Rajah Brooke period, Benedict Sandin, Tom's long-suffering Iban deputy and heir to the curatorship, received substantial help from Pringle in readying his own book about the Ibans in the pre-Brooke days for publication. This happy partnership between the museum and Cornell led, in 1965, to an agreement that Tom would go to Cornell as a senior research associate—not, to Tom's regret, as a visiting professor—with a three-year contract to begin in the autumn of 1967.

Despite his new tie to the United States, Tom had a tendency to look down on Americans. This disdain was strengthened by the fact that, during the period when Britain was preparing to hand over Sarawak to the Malaysian federation, a new group of expatriates was being scattered all over Tom's beloved up-country: American Peace Corps volunteers.

The volunteers started arriving in Sarawak in 1962. Soon there were 200, most of them there to teach English. By the mid-1960s, 20 percent of the Sarawak secondary schoolchildren had American teachers. The volunteers fell in love with Sarawak and with "their" people: Iban, Kayan, and other native tribespeople. But most of them were also young and self-righteous, harboring a visceral dislike of anything that they thought smacked of British colonialism. Tom's attitude toward this Yank invasion was ambivalent at best.

Shortly after the Americans, came volunteers from Colombo Plan countries, including Australia. One of these was a SEMUT 1 veteran, Herbert Reuben Hirst, who, having written repeatedly to Tom without receiving a reply, after nearly two years in Sarawak, suddenly stormed into Tom's office one day to demand the return of the war diaries he had sent Tom, at Tom's request. These diaries had been sent to Tom sometime in the 1950s when Tom had been gathering material for his book about Operation SEMUT. Tom, who had met Hirst at most twice during the war, at first denied having the missing diaries, but eventually he located them among a pile of documents. Tom gave them back, but not before Hirst had engaged counsel. By then, a totally false rumor had spread that Tom had written *World Within* by making unacknowledged use of Hirst's diaries (see Notes and Sources).

Hirst was not the only SEMUT veteran to reappear about this time. In 1965, Tom arranged for his favorite Australian sergeant, Fred "Sandy" Sanderson, to come back to Sarawak to help the Queen's Own Gurkhas, then garrisoned at Bario. Tom flew to Bario to see his old mate and found to his disgust that the longhouse at Bario, the place nearest to being "home" for him, had become completely teetotal since his last visit. When Tom asked Penghulu Lawai Besara, his oldest friend there, to give him a drink, the old man answered, "We don't drink now." This reply so enraged Tom that, in front of Sandy, he ripped the British Empire Medal off the *penghulu's* shirt and threw it out of the longhouse, saying: "I got this for you and I can take it away."

Although Bario had changed, Sandy had not. Before long, he got into an argument with a British officer of the Gurkhas garrisoned there. The cause of the argument, Sandy claimed, was that the officer "was molesting a 15 year-old Kelabit girl. So they got rid of the officer and they got rid of me too."

Tom was rather fed up with all the changes taking place in what had been British Borneo, including efforts by the new Malaysian government to unify its diverse realm. In the *Sarawak Gazette's* March 31, 1965, issue, he complained of the excessive playing of the Malaysian national anthem on the radio, "treating radio as a bludgeon, which (I fear) may cause people to turn to alternative stations, not out of disloyalty but sheer boredom." Malaysia's government and its new governor of Sarawak, a courtly Sarawak Malay to whom Tom years earlier had been rude, were not amused by such offhand insulting remarks made by a British colonial officer.

Partly, perhaps, to keep out of trouble during his remaining time as a British colonial officer in a country no longer British nor a colony, and partly to complete as much as he could of the excavations at Niah before his retirement the following September, Tom spent his longest time ever at the Niah caves, from August to November 1965. He wrote a friend that he was now "practically a piece of guano. . . . I am now a dapper 174 lbs. but, Gosh, do I smell."

Tom may have kept away from Kuching to avoid friction with the new administration, but he could not seem to keep his pen from offending Sarawak's new political leadership. In the *Sarawak Gazette* issue of December 31, 1965, Tom reminisced about getting drunk during a visit to Bau with Governor Arden-Clarke in 1947 and claimed that drunkenness was why Arden-Clarke had never again invited the government ethnologist along on a gubernatorial trip. In the next issue, Tom persisted in this vein, recording a comically drunken conversation between a resident and a chief secretary some years earlier. Most of the readers who would have chuckled at the dialogue had already accepted their "golden handshake" and left for Cheltenham or Bath.

More important, it was the kind of story that is unfunny to a Malay. Malays are by definition Muslim and are enjoined from drinking alcohol. Tom knew better. He had just published 170 pages of his "The Malays of South-West Sarawak Before Malaysia" in the *Sarawak Museum Journal*. These pages demonstrate Tom's awareness of Malay sensitivities. He may have been testing the friendship of Sarawak, a land to which he had devoted twenty years, in the same way he had often tested his friends, by doing something unpardonable to see if they would still like him.

Tom had good reason to expect Sarawak to like him. He had put this obscure place on the world map, not only popularly through his television films, radio broadcasts, and newspaper and magazine articles but internationally within intellectual and scientific circles. His and Barbara's pioneering work on turtles and orangutans and the finding of the Deep Skull at Niah had been reported in the world's major scientific publications.

Tom's best tool for spreading good publicity about Sarawak was the *Sarawak Museum Journal*, of which Tom was rightly proud. Selected people all over the world had received free copies of the *Journal* once or twice a year for nearly two decades. Tom had chosen those recipients with care. Almost every one of them was in a position to do Sarawak or the museum a good turn at some point. Most were happy to do so, thanks to the goodwill built up by years of receiving this scientifically stimulating but nonetheless likeably parochial and unpretentious publication. The pages of the *Journal* presented the image of a land where scholars, scientists, Sunday hobbyists, and untutored but knowledgeable tribesmen respected one another. Insofar as this image was accurate, Tom had played a significant role in making it so.

The *Sarawak Museum Journal* was the incarnation in print of the Sarawak Museum, which—probably unique for lands where hunter-gatherer nomads, Iron Age farmers, and twentieth-century urbanites all lived—was a place where all the local people, from whatever background or level of culture, liked to go. The tone of the museum was set before one walked in the door. On the grounds near the front steps stood a big rock with a replica carving of a nearly full-size human spread-eagled on it, wearing a weird headdress. On the plaque next to it, Tom had had inscribed, "How old is this carving? We think it dates back to about 950 A.D. What do you feel?" As one visitor recalls, "Everything was laid out to interest not daze the visitor." At the end of each gallery stood "a chair, a small desk and a neat sign saying 'Please sit down, read and relax.' On each desk [was] a stack of pamphlets, many of them by Tom Harrisson, on such varied subjects as *Borneo Birds*, *Borneo Fauna Anxieties*, *Borneo Writing* or *Maloh Coffin Designs*."

Tom's interest in having everything about Sarawak represented at the museum went far beyond collecting merely what was natural or traditional. He had on display Sarawak's first telephone switchboard, an early steam fire engine, and the wheel from the first White Rajah's yacht. He encouraged local artists to give samples of their works to the museum.

As Tom's days as museum curator grew short, he completed arrangements with George Kahin to go to Cornell. His attitude toward his future relations with Borneo was positive. In an August 1966 letter to Medway, Tom wrote that "Rather surprisingly, the new politicians are being even nicer to me than the old ones and, for the first time ever, we had not only one Minister but three visiting the excavations in the past month, including the boss." The dig that these ministers visited was in the Santubong delta, where that month, Tom and Cornell art historian Stanley J. O'Connor, "found a proper stone structure with a beautiful silver box and lots of gold pieces," as Tom wrote to Medway. This stone structure, found at Bongkissam in the Sarawak River delta, was the first ancient stone edifice discovered in the lowlands of Borneo. Its silver box held a solid gold emblem of the Hindu god Shiva, and in association with it were found 140 small gold objects and a number of semiprecious stones. The structure and its contents are believed to be from a Tantric Buddhist shrine of the twelfth or thirteenth century A.D. While such structures containing similar funerary boxes and ornaments had been found in a few places elsewhere in Southeast Asia, this was the first, and may still be the only, found in Borneo. The find gave Borneo its first, however small, historical connection with the rich ancient Hindu-Buddhist world of its neighbors.

On September 16, Tom announced in a letter to Medway: "I actually retire at midnight on the 26th of this month, my 55th birthday presumably coming to an end then. The Governor insists on throwing a farewell party at the Astana." A change in Sarawak's chief ministers took place at about this time, but Tom was unperturbed by this and wrote Medway:

. . . As I am fundamentally only interested in Sarawak and primarily in Sarawak's past, I think I have sufficiently managed to steer clear of the factions. Anyway, both factions in recent months have suggested that I should continue to work in Sarawak more or less on my own terms, for part of the year, with special reference to Niah and other archaeology.

The Brunei Government have also been very nice indeed [agreeing to provide annual round-the-world first class air tickets for Tom and Barbara], and I am now negotiating a contract with them which should cover other expenses in this part of the world. And also provide a back-stop if there is a difficult period in Sarawak. Sabah relations are also cordial and we are going to do a dig for them next month with funds they have earmarked for us. In these jet days, I think it is possible to work in America and Asia simultaneously, though of course much depends on health and, in the ultimate analysis, everything on politics. I am now in the somewhat invidious position of being the senior expatriate officer as regards length of service, and in fact nearly all the "old hands" of the immediate post-war period have now been eliminated.

Adding undoubtedly to Tom's sense of satisfaction as he tidied things up was the fact that Indonesia's Confrontation of Malaysia had been declared at an end on August 11, 1966.

After his official retirement, Tom stayed in Sarawak for an additional eight months, mostly working on a long administrative report on the Niah digs. But he also saw to it that materials from a Brunei dig, which had been stored or displayed in Kuching pending the completion of the Brunei Museum building, were returned to Brunei. There were also items that he had bought for the new Brunei Museum using the sultan's money. When the sultan sent his ship to collect his property, the denizens of the Sarawak Club and the Aurora Bar spread the story that Tom was giving away Sarawak's heritage in order to sweeten his relations with the oil-rich sultanate so he would be retained as an adviser there. The facts are otherwise, according to senior people at the two museums, but the rumors were accepted and repeated by the great army of Tom's detractors in Borneo, enemies he had made—often seemingly deliberately—in nearly twenty years of rambunctious activity.

During his final days there, Tom was also working on Sarawak's ancient ceramics, trying to create a time line, drawing on the experience of two capable expatriate women helpers working at the museum on the thousands of pottery sherds dug up over two decades. One helper was Eine Moore, who had long been involved with the museum's ceramics (chiefly sorting and attempting to reconstruct sherds into pots). The other was an energetic and ambitious Peace Corps volunteer assigned to the museum named Carla Maness Zainie, who had an undergraduate background in Chinese ceramics.

With the assistance of Mrs. Charmian Woodfield in Miri, a trained British archaeologist whom Barbara had invited to examine and report on a collection of previously excavated cave ceramics, it seemed possible that the groundwork for a good paper on ancient ceramics in Sarawak could be laid. At this time, Tom was having disagreements on technical points about these ceramics with all three of these women. Such differences of view were normal, he must have thought, and would be resolved eventually.

All in all, things were looking good for the museum and for Tom's and Barbara's work connected with it. Benedict Sandin, the Iban who had been Tom's nominee to replace himself as curator, had been given the job. The rest of the staff was staying on. Tom had sent to Ithaca the notes for his delta excavations and the nearly completed manuscript for the Malay survey, work he could finish at Cornell. The Niah unpublished research records were to be left at the museum to be consulted by Tom's former colleagues and be ready to hand when Tom and Barbara came back to complete their work. Everything seemed in order. The only serious annoyance, as Tom spent his final days in Pig Lane, was the presence of stones in Tom's salivary glands. These were very painful, made talking difficult, and prevented him from being able to eat any food with salt or spice in it, but they did not noticeably slow him down.

On the morning of May 12, 1967, various Sarawak notables and the entire museum staff came out to the airport to see him off. Barbara would be staying for a few more weeks, primarily to clear up work from various Neolithic cave burials and to resolve some questions about ceramic materials with Mrs. Woodfield of Miri. In Kuching's modest airport waiting room, while Tom's friends and colleagues sat and drank to Tom's good health, Lian Labang, Tom's Kelabit friend from the early days of SEMUT and a long-time museum subordinate, forced liquor down Tom's throat one more time. Tom then boarded the plane for Singapore en route to England.

In three months, he and Barbara would go to America. The pay would be low, but Tom's obligations to Cornell would be minimal, leaving him free to return to Niah and to engage in other Southeast Asian projects. He was not worried about money for these other projects. In addition to the annual round-the-world air tickets Brunei had agreed to provide, he felt sure that funds would be available from private sources in America to help sponsor the various schemes he had in mind. He wrote Medway that "I have never found any difficulty in getting adequate money to do anything I want wherever I want in the last 30 years, and I shall be surprised if this is more difficult based in the States." So confident was he that he offered to "take on a specific fund raising operation for you in this area. . . ." At age fifty-five, with an anticipated thirty years left to him, Tom was looking forward to conquering a new world.

**PART SEVEN**

A New World, 1967–1976

# Chapter 41

## Dark Days

Tom's plane had barely disappeared from the sky over Kuching on its way to Singapore when his reputation came under the fiercest attack it had yet known and from a source he must have found surprising. The source was one of those well-educated, unpaid women who had long provided skilled and highly motivated help at the museum or on museum projects elsewhere in Sarawak. Largely due to her efforts, Tom entered a long period of dark days.

All his working life, Tom had drawn on the labor and talents of such women. Mass-Observation would never have functioned without them. In the days before, during, and just after World War II, his female assistants had been so happy to be using their brains doing something interesting, or something seen to be a part of a worthwhile project, that they had not objected (at least not strenuously) when their written work was severely edited by Tom to see that it made his points. They had not fought back even when their work was simply folded into publications bearing Tom's name, with a polite mention in the footnotes or foreword of the woman or women who had done most of the spade work. In the 1960s, however, educated women were no longer so self-effacing.

Charmian Woodfield, the archaeologist wife of an architect who was the new Public Works Department deputy divisional engineer in Miri, was one of these "new" women. Tom and Barbara had given her thousands of pottery sherds found, before Woodfield's arrival in Sarawak, by Tom's diggers in a side cave. As a new resident expert, she was invited to write a description of this cave's pottery, to be edited by Tom and published in the *Sarawak Museum Journal*. Tom had warned her in writing that "We must NOT [Tom's capitals] get off into long "evolutionary" stylistic discussions in a discussion of the limited . . . material. . . . To go into generalisations for the whole area and period is out of place and likely to be embarrassing if not very much more widely based." Woodfield had confirmed that her report

would contain "no long evolutionary stylistic discussions," but after studying the material and having with her husband laboriously reconstructed a
number of the pots, she felt she must at least include her ideas about the
chronological sequence of the pottery. Immediately upon receiving her
report, just before leaving Kuching definitively, Tom wrote her that he
thought "we agreed to stick to the VISIBLE DATA you studied," and he
made it clear that he would omit her points about the dating of the pottery.

An offended Woodfield replied by wire:

WOODFIELDS NOT HACKS TO DO MR HARRISSONS LABORIOUS
WORK FOR HIM AND TAMELY CONCUR WITH HIS FIXED IDEAS STOP
REQUEST IMMEDIATE RETURN OF . . . TEXT AND ALL DRAWINGS
WHICH ARE WOODFIELD PROPERTY AND COPYRIGHT. WOODFIELD

Over the next several months, she wrote to various archaeologists to enlist
their aid in keeping Tom out of Sarawak and, preferably, all of Borneo. She
then wrote Malaysian and Bornean government departments, the Malaysian
prime minister, the Malaysian Anti-Corruption Board, Pengiran Shariffuddin
(by then curator of the Brunei Museum), and many others. In these letters,
she claimed that, as far as the Harrissons' archaeology was concerned, "the
ghastly incompetence behind the very slick publicity has become clearer
every month." She warned that "In December this year, about Christmas,
we understand, Harrisson is due to return and proceed to Niah, where he
is due to dig for some lengthy period. This should successfully destroy most
of the evidence [of Stone Age man, etc.] that is left. . . ." She accused Tom
of selling Sarawak's patrimony to the Brunei Museum and keeping the
money, stealing the museum's Chinese ceramics for his personal collection,
neglecting proper accessioning of most of the material in the Sarawak
Museum (thus allowing him and others to help themselves), plagiarizing
the written work of Bishop Galvin and others, and so on. She presented no
evidence in support of these allegations but argued that, "Even if you discount 50% of [these stories], the residue is frightening enough." She asked
that her readers bring pressure to bear on the government "to keep Harrisson
out of the country."

The Woodfield allegations were a hodge-podge of half-truths, truths out
of context, and unsubstantiated rumors mixed with a few genuine facts, but
her allegations were very plausible, especially to the expatriates and educated
Sarawakians whom Tom had offended over the years. She was most credible,
being a trained archaeologist, when complaining of the Harrissons' incompetence in that field, and, in criticizing the Harrissons' work, she had the
enthusiastic backing of museum insiders Eine Moore and Carla Zainie. Yet
Wilhelm Solheim, one of the few professional archaeologists who, unlike

Woodfield, had actually seen Tom and Barbara at work, responded to Woodfield, saying that he himself had not known how to do stratigraphic excavation when he had been in Sarawak and that "Harrisson's early excavation was on a par with much of the rest of archaeology done in Southeast Asia." Solheim insisted that "When you are used to the 0-6 inch method, this does present some good information," though he conceded that "it is certainly not as trustworthy as following natural stratigraphy." (See Notes and Sources for a further statement of Professor Solheim's views.)

As for Woodfield's other charges, most were partly or wholly false. For example, Woodfield claimed that the museum lacked proper accessions procedures. In fact, new acquisitions were entered into the latest volume of a series of leather-bound accessions books that now goes back more than a hundred years. Each item was indelibly marked to show that it was museum property. It is true, though, that aside from ceramics and the museum library's books and documents, no systematic inventories were conducted during Tom's curatorship. Thus, it was not always possible to show where an accessioned item was located, making it theoretically possible for pilfering to have occurred unnoticed. That is not to say, however, that pilfering occurred. Eine Moore did an inventory of the museum's ceramics and recalls there were "a lot of things missing" but not especially items of value. She remembers concluding at the time that there were "no signs of thievery."

The most serious of Woodfield's accusations, that Tom stole items from the museum and took for himself things intended for the museum, were accepted as fact by Tom's enemies within the Sarawak government, but no evidence ever surfaced in support of these allegations. Certainly some museum items are missing, but not a single item that Tom is alleged to have stolen has been reported being seen anywhere. Rumors still circulate that Tom smuggled various items to Cornell, either as quid pro quo for his job there or for his personal collection. Professor Kahin, however, and others at Cornell point out that Cornell in those days lacked a museum or other place to display ceramics, statues, or other Borneo items. Nor did anyone, including such knowledgeable visitors as Professor O'Connor or Dr. Bedlington, who often went to Tom's and Barbara's small Ithaca apartment, see anything there that made them suspect that Tom had taken things of value from the museum. More relevant to refuting this charge of thievery is the fact that Tom never had much money and that no hoard of valuable oriental treasures other than his rhino and hornbill ivory and his Chinese and Thai pots, worth a few thousand pounds in total, showed up in his or Barbara's possession or in Tom's estate after his sudden death, at which time he owned no car, house, or other valuable property.

As to Woodfield's assertions that Tom "stole" the work of other people, one could say that Tom absorbed other people's ideas and used them, sometimes without giving credit. But he also ghostwrote many *Sarawak Museum Journal* and *Sarawak Gazette* articles that the named authors could never have produced in English on their own. It is not known if Tom used Bishop Galvin's work without acknowledgement. If he did, it was not a big issue between them. The bishop in a letter written after Tom's death states that "whatever others may say of him, Malaysia will always remain in his debt." He and Tom corresponded and collaborated closely to the very end of Tom's time in Sarawak.

One of Tom's chief aims in life was to get facts down on paper and into print fast. A "checklist"* giving the titles and brief bibliographic information of his published writings was done after his death and totals fifty-six pages; it fails to include perhaps twenty more pages' worth of Tom's publications, not to mention his many unpublished manuscripts. He wrote in bed and complained that the ink in the Biro, held business end upward, would dry out. He wrote while riding in a Land Rover bumping along a dirt road, his fingers high on the pen with the words dribbling onto one of the exercise books without which he never went anywhere. When he traveled, he would take a bundle of these notebooks. When he returned to the museum, he would put a pile of them in front of Sonia, his favorite local secretary, to type. In a typical week, he filled fifteen notebooks. He wrote while walking along the beach at Santubong, dictating to a secretary, interspersing perhaps three or four letters a day to far-flung correspondents, each on a different subject. At the office, he could write in an exercise book while holding the phone to his ear with one shoulder, talking to the person seated across from him on a different subject, and signaling someone waiting in the hall to come in. People marveled at the way he could keep all these different strands from tangling. He wrote every day of his whole adult life, mostly with an eye to publication. His extraordinary productivity does not excuse his periodic failure to acknowledge sources adequately, but the size, speed, and variety of his output help explain how it happened.

We do not know how people in general inside Sarawak felt about the charges made by Woodfield and her supporters, but they were probably neither shocked nor surprised. Most of these allegations were not new. Those who were prepared to believe them had already done so, while others probably ignored them as they had in the past. Speaking for museum staff, the new curator, Benedict Sandin, replied to one of Mrs. Woodfield's letters: "We are beginning to get fed-up with your remarks about the Harrissons and we do not wish to hear any further on this." Barbara was thoroughly fed up,

---

*A Checklist of the Works of Tom Harrisson (1911–1976)*, prepared by David Alan Miller, (Williamsburg, Virginia: Special Publication of the Borneo Research Council), June 1978.

too, when she finally left Kuching on June 3, having failed to heal the rift with her former friend, Charmian Woodfield.

Tom by then was in England, in considerable physical discomfort because of his salivary glands, and miserable with guilt and regret about his son Max, who was no longer at Bethlem but at another institution some distance out of London. Tom, who dreaded visits to his son, waited a month before going to see him, in mid-June 1967. Max was no longer a boy. He was twenty-seven and looked much older; his hair was already partly gray. For Tom, it must have been deeply upsetting to see his only son living in this grim, shabby place inhabited by sad, maimed souls and to listen to this young-old man with his own face talking one part sense to three parts paranoiac non-sense in the timbre and cadences of his own voice. All in all, Tom described himself that summer as "marking time." He was eager to leave England to once more put an ocean between himself and Max.

# Chapter 42

## Tom the Teacher

Tom and Barbara flew to New York City on August 18, 1967. With them were twenty-three suitcases containing, among other things, Tom's collection of Thai ceramics. Emerging from the ordeal of customs and immigration into a driving rainstorm, they took a taxi from the airport to the train. The cabby would not turn on the meter and demanded the then outrageous sum of $50.00; otherwise, he would dump them and their luggage in the rain. When they reached Ithaca, long hours north from New York City, their extraordinary amount of baggage must have caused a sensation. They had to find room for it in their modest university-owned apartment, without any of the household help to which they had long been accustomed.

Still, Tom found the campus and the hilly lake-dotted landscape rather pretty. He was also invigorated by the presence of so many young people. On September 17, he gave the first lecture of his course. His boastfulness was the chief complaint of those who did not like his lectures, but most of his audience sat enthralled. His iconoclastic and quirky oral presentation delighted them. On that and subsequent occasions, they found his films brilliant, and at other sessions he would have something of almost equal interest to show them. On the last day of class, he brought in bird's nest soup for them to taste.

A student recalled that "On occasion, he would suddenly duck beneath the lectern . . . and reappear wearing a hornbill mask to make the point that many people in Borneo believe the hornbill sometimes takes on human form." The students loved the show but were also impressed by the extent of Tom's first-hand experience, the range of his interests, the breadth of his views.

When he was talking about the archaeology of Borneo, for example, he was very different from the usual run of academic lecturers. As Carl Trocki, a young historian who took Tom's seminar, remarked:

> The average archaeologist is interested in the formula of the particular thermal luminescence from that pot and the exact stratigraphy. But if you asked him,

"What does it mean?" he would say "Oh, Jesus, I don't know. You'd have to ask somebody else," whereas Tom would give the big picture. He would step back and say, "This is what the world around Niah looked like in 3,000 BC."

All in all, Trocki stated, "It was an experience to sit in the same room with him for a while. He knew an enormous amount."

Another student who remembers the seminar vividly is Stanley Bedlington, who was an older doctoral candidate, having already had a career as a policeman for the colonial government of British North Borneo (Sabah). Bedlington had not known Tom in Borneo, and when he came to ask Tom's permission to sit in on the seminar, he introduced himself as "an ex-North Borneo copper." Tom had rudely replied, "I hate bloody coppers," to which Bedlington responded, "You are the first museum curator I've ever met, so I am reserving my opinion." Tom "sort of laughed" and a warm friendship began that would last the rest of Tom's life. Bedlington describes Tom's lecturing style as ". . . almost stream of consciousness, but Tom's stream of consciousness was extraordinarily well worth listening to." There were many others who shared this view. Unusual for university courses, Tom's audience grew instead of shrinking as the semester advanced. An Australian woman who had lived in Sarawak traveled to Cornell during this time and wrote a letter in which she reported to Carla Maness Zainie, who was sorry to get the news, that Tom was "the most popular lecturer" on the Cornell campus.

In mid-September, however, two days after his first lecture, he and Barbara had a most distressing evening at the home of Professor George Kahin, the man who had hired Tom as a senior research associate of the Southeast Asia Program. Kahin, having received word of rumors circulating in Southeast Asianist circles, undoubtedly thanks to Woodfield's letters to various people and lent credence by the twenty-three suitcases, hinted over dinner in his diffident way that he had heard that Tom had taken things with him that should have been left in Sarawak. A few days later, on Tom's fifty-sixth birthday, Tom had Barbara drive him—he had failed his New York driver's test—along Lake Cayuga while they had "harrowing discussions," according to Barbara's diary, about Kahin's veiled accusations.

Tom was greatly upset by these hints of misbehavior coming from the man on whom he now depended to earn a living. What would happen if he lost this job? The Cornell job paid poorly, but added to Tom's tiny Sarawak pension and odd sums from other sources, it was enough for them to live on. More important, it gave him an academic connection and thus provided him more access than he would otherwise have had to invitations to give paid lectures and to take paid trips to world conferences on a variety of subjects. He and Barbara did not care about clothes or food but, for Tom at least, access to travel was a basic need. While in Sarawak, he had used helicopters, small planes, river launches, and Land Rovers to go wherever he wanted within Borneo and had often been granted trips to Bangkok, Hong Kong, and elsewhere, plus he received several months of home leave in England every few years. Now all of that was gone, except for the sultan of Brunei's once-a-year round-the-world first-class air tickets for each of them. They made their tickets stretch as far as possible.

Tom and Barbara were planning to go back to Sarawak just before Christmas to resume work at Niah. On November 18, however, Charmian Woodfield succeeded in getting the Kuala Lumpur *Straits Times* to publish a letter drafted by her with help from Carla Zainie and signed "CONCERNED, Miri," that reiterated most of her allegations. She had tried to publish such a letter in a Borneo paper, but the publisher had refused to print it. Two weeks later, she had a second letter published in the *Straits Times*, under her own name, giving more details.

On the morning of Christmas Eve, 1967, undoubtedly aware that these letters had been published, Tom and Barbara boarded a plane in Singapore for Kuching. When they landed, however, the immigration authorities told Tom that their names were on a list of people not permitted entry into Sarawak. When Tom realized that he and Barbara were going to have to stay in the waiting room and reboard a plane that afternoon for Brunei, he must have been amazed, but he made it appear to others as a mere bureaucratic hitch that would be resolved, if not now, then before his next trip to Borneo.

It never was resolved. That the barrier stayed in place the rest of Tom's life can be taken as a monument to the power of a scorned woman's anger. Yet Woodfield could never have been so successful in her efforts to rid Sarawak forever of Tom if his behavior over two decades had not provided her with a cheering throng of supporters among the remaining expatriates and western-educated Sarawakians. Under the British regime, Tom's position as a Sarawak fixture had been unassailable, as Freeman had found, to his chagrin. Now, the new Sarawak Malay leadership, whom Tom had systematically snubbed and offended over the years, had a handle with which to close the door on Tom, and they used it.

On that Christmas Eve, as Tom waited at Kuching's airport, he did not bluster or throw a tantrum. Instead, he tried to be discreet, to keep others from learning of his banishment. Tom would have realized that, sooner or later Cornell would find out that instead of having an especially good network of contacts in Sarawak, he was not even allowed to cross the immigration line at the Kuching airport, but later was better than sooner. He appears to have succeeded in keeping news of his banishment from spreading. He managed to keep the news even from Barbara, who only learned of it years later.

On their way home from Brunei, Barbara was allowed to enter Sarawak. Tom went on to England and thence back to Cornell while Barbara stayed in Borneo to complete some research. Tom took advantage of her absence from Cornell to engage in "rutting," as one of his friends described it. He boasted to his close men friends about sleeping with Cornell secretaries and picking up women in the elevator on the way up to his flat.

When Barbara returned and there were once again two people in one small apartment, Tom felt cramped. Fortunately, they had a temporary respite from overcrowding when they were offered the use of a colleague's house for the summer. For three months, they enjoyed this charming house and garden. In July, they both went to a fauna conservationist conference on the East Coast, where they met Charles Lindbergh, the famous aviator, who was active in conservation matters.

Tom and Barbara had to give back the borrowed house at the end of the summer but found a slightly bigger apartment in their old building. They were in the process of moving into it in early September when Benedict Sandin came for a month's visit to the United States, a trip that Tom had arranged so that he could take Sandin to the founding meeting of a new association to bring together social scientists interested in Borneo. The result of an idea of Tom's, it was called the Borneo Research Council and is still active.

Leaving Barbara to complete the move to the new apartment, Tom, Benedict Sandin, and Stan Bedlington went to New York, Connecticut, and Maine to see people connected with the new Borneo Research Council. During this trip, the three men stopped at the home of a Wall Street millionaire, who had a large house in Connecticut. The tycoon, an elderly man, having given his three guests an excellent elegantly served dinner, went to bed early and left them to help themselves to nightcaps. The three men spent the next few hours availing themselves generously of their host's brandy. The main purpose of the trip was a visit to an island just off the coast of Maine owned by one of the prime movers of the Borneo Research Council, the young anthropologist George Appell. The meeting was successful and, in this Borneo context, Tom was a star again. But at the Appell home, as at the tycoon's, and at the homes of most of his colleagues in Cornell, Tom could see that many people—some younger, some older, but all having done less that was memorable than he—were living in far greater comfort and security than he could hope for. Despite his earlier boast to Lord Medway that he could easily raise money in America for Southeast Asian projects, he now saw that America's dislike for the Vietnam War would soon dry up the sources of money for such studies, making it improbable that his contract would be renewed on more favorable terms. Furthermore, if Kahin learned that Tom was persona non grata in Sarawak, he might not renew the con-

tract on any terms. A visit to Ithaca in October by Bill Solheim, by then professor at the University of Hawai'i's East-West Center and famous in his field,
must have added to Tom's sense that once again he was being left behind
while younger men moved ahead.

Soon winter came to Ithaca. In late November, Tom and Barbara invited
two couples to their apartment for dinner, one being the Bedlingtons. Stan
Bedlington remembers:

> It started to snow, one of the biggest snowstorms in years. So we started
> drinking and we went through every single bottle of wine in the house. And it was
> so bad that the other guests could not drive home. At one stage the evening got
> very bawdy and the men started talking about male underpants and we started
> dropping our trousers and showing what sort of underpants we wore and Tom
> was wearing a pair with a Union Jack.

As always in convivial male company, Tom's language was full of slangy sexual and bathroom words, like a Harrow schoolboy's.

Tom hated the cold and, when the fall term came to an end, he and
Barbara were able (thanks to the sultan of Brunei) to escape from Ithaca's
infamous winter weather and fly off to the tropics. They stayed a month at
the Brunei Resthouse as guests of the sultan and were treated as distinguished
visitors. It must have been a great pleasure for Tom to be back in a world he
understood and which valued him. Even more soothing to his ego, he was
being interviewed and followed about almost everywhere he went during the
winter and spring of 1968–1969 by a British writer named Timothy Green,
who was doing Tom's "profile" for a book about four living "adventurers" of
renown. In addition to the section on Tom, the book, which was published in
1970 under the title *The Adventurers*, included the life stories of Jane Goodall
(the chimpanzee expert), Wilfred Thesiger (the explorer of Arabia), and Col.
Sir Hugh Boustead, a soldier and colonial administrator in the Sudan and
Arabia. Tom must have been pleased to be in such distinguished company.

Shortly after New Year's Day 1969, Tom left Barbara in Borneo and flew
to Manila to work on conservation business on behalf of the International
Union for the Conservation of Nature (IUCN) and the World Wildlife Fund.
For six weeks, he wandered through Philippine jungles to survey the situation of the tamaraw, a small water buffalo that in historic times had been
confined to the island of Mindoro where its numbers had now shrunk to a
total of perhaps a hundred animals. He did a similar survey of the monkey-
eating eagle (now more often called the Philippine eagle), which is the
Philippine national bird and an even more endangered species than the tamaraw. A deputation led by Charles Lindbergh and Tom paid a call in February
on Philippine President Ferdinand Marcos to persuade him to enforce the

Philippine law that theoretically protected these endangered fauna. Marcos endorsed the plan that Tom and Lindbergh proposed for the protection of these animals. In addition, largely thanks to Tom's efforts, a Philippine Wildlife Conservation Association was established with adequate capital from private Philippine sources; it made saving the tamaraw its first project.*

Barbara and Tom met again in mid-March in Morges, Switzerland, the headquarters of the IUCN. They attended meetings for several days on endangered species, and Tom worked with the great American turtle conservationist Archie Carr on strategies to protect the green turtle. One afternoon, there was a cocktail reception and a presentation to the IUCN of a statue, attended by its sculptor. She was a middle-aged Belgian widow, the Baroness Forani. Small, wiry, blonde, and vivacious, with a lined, expressive face, she looked somewhat like Zita might have, had she still been alive. Tom spoke to her and found her charming. She also appeared to find him interesting and, as a joke, gave him a stuffed toy turtle in recognition of his connection with turtle conservation. She also gave him her address in case he ever came to Brussels, where she lived, or to Cannes, where she spent summers in an apartment that she owned in a chateau overlooking the beach.

By early May, Tom and Barbara were back in Ithaca. The previous summer, Tom had failed his driver's test again, from a seeming inability to make himself follow the examiner's instructions; he never drove again. And so, on lovely spring days, he had Barbara drive him around the Finger Lakes, some of New York state's loveliest countryside. He enjoyed these rides, but he was becoming restless and bored. The publications he was preparing show it. Never a painstaking editor, he seemed more careless and impatient than ever. His long book, *The Malays of South-West Sarawak Before Malaysia* (published in 1970 by Macmillan in London and by Michigan State University in Lansing), shows that, at the end, he had no patience left. One of his reviewers, Gale Dixon, noted that "This big, heavy volume is packed with good information important to professional anthropologists, historians, economists, geographers and sociologists and of interest to a wide readership of informed people who make the social sciences their avocation." But this reviewer, and nearly everybody else who tried to find a path through the dense jungle of prose that continues for 650 pages, became filled with rage and sorrow at Tom's "bad grammar, awkward sentences and utter lack of organization."

There were similar problems with his next two publications. These were two "data papers" written in collaboration with Dr. Stanley O'Connor, a

---

*The Philippine eagle is still approaching extinction as its forest habitat disappears, but Tom's work was effective in helping save the tamaraw. By 1987, the conservation program he started had led to a three-fold increase in the number of these animals.

Cornell art historian who had come to Sarawak to participate in the Sarawak River delta digs. One of these "data papers" is on their excavations of the prehistoric iron industry at Santubong, the other on the gold and megalithic activity found at the site. The data paper on the iron industry was truly pioneering, one of his reviewers remarked, but also "maddening in presentation . . . ," and "so inflated and colloquial" that it "threatens to bring the craft of prehistoric archaeology into disrepute." (See Notes and Sources for recent views on this work.)

The other data paper, *Gold and megalithic activity in prehistoric and recent west Borneo*, was applauded by a reviewer (Dales, in *Man*) for the fact that "Lengthy and fascinating discussions are presented on the history and uses of gold in South-east Asia in both ancient and modern times. Equally interesting material is presented on the . . . widespread use of both megalithic monuments and arrangements of small stones [associated with the gold and iron, which has] prompted the authors to introduce the term 'micro-megalithic'. . . . (See Notes and Sources for recent work drawing upon this data paper.) Yet this same reviewer, while finding the book "literally a gold-mine of information," also complained of its "disjointed presentation." Could one blame Tom's co-author, Stan O'Connor, for its faults? Only in that O'Connor found Tom's convoluted, involuted way of connecting things so interesting he did not mind that Tom's sentences gave the reader the sense of riding on a roller-coaster. For O'Connor, Tom's idiosyncratic daring was an exhilarating change from the often narrow-focused and conventional prose of archaeological and art historical writing.

Others were more censorious. An archaeologist at the University of London, I. C. Glover, reviewing the second book, gave a contemptuous rendering of its ideas before coming to a crashing conclusion: "A reviewer of the authors' previous publication . . . noted that it 'threatens to bring the craft of prehistoric archaeology into disrepute'; one fears that this has now been achieved and the next casualty can only be Cornell University if the Southeast Asia Program continues to lend its name to such work."

Fortunately for Tom, by the time of this appallingly harsh review, he was no longer associated with Cornell University. Long before this review appeared, Tom was no longer living in the Untites States, or with Barbara. His entire life had changed.

# Chapter 43

## Escape from the New World

Almost from the day he and Barbara arrived in Ithaca in driving rain with twenty-three suitcases, Tom had been looking for a way out. He had never much liked Americans or America. As did many Englishmen of his class and generation, he resented that the United States had become the premier world power and thought of it as a crude gigantic Rome overshadowing England's small but civilized Greece.

After a year at Cornell, something happened across the Atlantic that made him hope that he might be able to rekindle a career in England out of the ashes of his 1930s British invention, Mass-Observation. A doctoral candidate in history, writing a thesis on British politics during World War II, came across the hoard of old Mass-Observation materials stored in the West London basement of Mass-Observation Ltd., the market survey firm that had evolved out of Tom's old organization. The doctoral candidate was a young Scot, Angus Calder, son of Lord Ritchie-Calder, the science reporter who had unwittingly started the 1940 "Cooper's Snoopers" uproar.

A friend of young Calder named Paul Addison, also a budding historian working on the 1940s, had discovered this collection of Mass-Observation material from the war years and told Calder about it. Calder recalls that "Paul and I were like kids with a lucky dip. I remember reaching up to get a box down from a shelf in the cellar where everything was stored higgledy piggledy, and great cascades of the raw material from which M-O had compiled their reports fell down. Paul and I scrabbled around for hours finding all kinds of fascinating things." Calder spoke to his thesis supervisor, Asa Briggs (now Lord Briggs), professor of history in the School of Social Science at Sussex University. As Calder explains, "Briggs is a great fixer and within a very short time Briggs had fixed up a giant pantechnicon to come to West London and pick up the entire contents of the cellar and take them to the University of Sussex."

Briggs, looking for source materials on the twentieth century's social and cultural history for use by his students, arranged that, in exchange for bequeathing these papers to the University, Tom would have a contract with Sussex to work with some of Briggs's students to research and bring out new studies, mining this rich lode of modern British historical material. Briggs had known Tom as a founder of Mass-Observation and respected his accomplishments there. As the historian of British broadcasting, Briggs also admired Tom as "a keen student of broadcasting." Funding for the establishment and operation of a "Tom Harrisson Mass-Observation Archive" was provided for an initial three years by the Leverhulme Foundation. Tom, having always claimed that he had first gone to Bolton because of the Lever connection, must have been pleased to have the name of Lever associated with his latest Mass-Observation activity. In 1969, a personal chair (without pay) was promised to Tom with which went the title of visiting professor at Sussex University. Short of a knighthood, it is hard to imagine a title that Tom would have liked more.

Although the pleasure of being a professor would almost make up for the absence of any payment except for expenses, it would not provide for his own needs, much less Barbara's. If he were still at Cornell, he and Barbara could just manage on the basis of his Cornell salary, his M-O expenses, and his Sarawak pension. On the other hand, if he came back to live in Britain, he could more easily reactivate his ties to the media and earn money that way.

He found it a daunting prospect to have to keep on hustling, trying to find new projects, simply to pay the household bills. He was approaching sixty. What would happen when he could no longer work so hard? During the second year in Ithaca, the problem was at the front of his mind. There seemed to be no solution.

Then in late May 1969, he told Barbara that he wanted to go to Switzerland in July for a special animal conservation meeting in Morges. Barbara protested they did not have the money to go to that meeting and to Europe again in the autumn, as planned, on their way to their annual month in Brunei. Tom said he wanted to attend the meeting in Morges and he really needed to see Briggs in England to make final arrangements about his visiting professorship. Barbara agreed that he should go alone.

In early July, Tom flew off to Europe, to the meeting in Morges and to see Briggs in England. But he also visited the glamorous Baroness Forani in Cannes.

He had sent her a note saying, "I'm coming through Brussels in July and I want to see you." The baroness had replied that she was not going to be in Brussels then and suggested he come to Cannes. Thus it was that in late July she told her elder daughter Ludmilla, who, accompanied by the grandchildren, was on her annual visit to her mother, that "I'm going to go to Cologne to see a man I've met."

When Ludmilla asked more about him, her mother said merely that she had met him in Morges and liked him but was not altogether sure she would be able to recognize him. She said that they had agreed he should wear something by which she could pick him out of the crowd at the train station in Cologne, whence they would fly to Cannes.

Tom had no trouble recognizing her, "a wiry, tanned blonde with high cheekbones, a bowl haircut and a husky voice." Although she was fifty-three years old and her tanned face was very lined, she was small and slender and this combined with her energy and sheer physicality to make her seem younger.

They reached her apartment in the upper portions of a Scottish tycoon's Victorian Gothic crenelated castle overlooking the Mediterranean and went immediately upstairs to a little room. There she and Tom spent the next few days, barely emerging for meals. Ludmilla waited discreetly below with her young daughters. After about three days, Tom said to Ludmilla, "You know what I'm doing with your mother, don't you?" Ludmilla answered, "Well, I guess you are getting to know her." And he said, "I am saving her life."

It is safe to say that one of the things they were doing upstairs in that little room was making love. Sex was a big part of their relationship from then on. It had always been an important part of the baroness' life. She had been widowed for three years and was currently without a man, a rare occurrence. Her last love affair, with a respectable Belgian businessman, had ended badly. After the lover had left the house, following an interview with Christine in which it became clear he did not intend to marry her, her father found her toying with a pistol that she had kept from the war. It was not clear who had been the intended target, her faithless lover or herself. Fortunately, hot-headed and impulsive though she was, she had not pulled the trigger.

Before that, Salvador Dalí had been a close admirer, and she had worked as a collaborating sculptor with him in 1964 and 1965. That relationship had already begun to cool when, in 1965, she erupted into hot anger when she saw a bronze head of the poet Dante that she had made, in collaboration with the surrealist artist, for sale at the Wildenstein Gallery in New York and credited to Dalí alone. She immediately returned to Europe to sue him; the eventual judgment was in her favor.

If one can safely assume that Tom and the baroness spent part of their time in the upstairs room making love, it is also probable that Tom had never had such a satisfying sexual partner. She was not only experienced but remarkably agile and had great physical stamina. Tom would later tell his men friends that he found her incredibly sexually attractive.

During their time alone in the little room upstairs, they also did a lot of talking. She later told her daughter, "Well, I had to know who he was. I did not have much time. So I asked him, 'Who are you? Are you an adventurer?

Are you an explorer? Are you a Jew? What are you?'" Ludmilla recalls that
Tom had had no money, "And we had to go to Juan les Pins to buy him a
nice shirt and a pair of pants so that he could be presentable. And he was a
little chubby. And my mother said, 'You have to eat well. You have to be
healthy.' And she started mothering him." She bathed him and scrubbed his
back with a brush. She washed and trimmed his hair and clipped his nails.
She put him on a diet and made him eat yogurt and mashed cloves of garlic.
"And after a week, they were a couple. It was just like that."

During those days and nights of discovery, it must have emerged how
much they had in common. Baroness Christine Forani was also a war hero
and a parachutist. Tom surely would not have let ten minutes elapse before
he told her about being "the first white man to drop into Borneo." As for
Christine, who almost never spoke of her wartime activities, the one accomplishment from the war that she boasted about was being the first Belgian
woman military parachutist.

Christine's late husband, an Italian baron, Antonio Forani, had had to keep
a low profile in Belgium during the war to avoid having to collaborate with the
Axis side. Christine's parents had asked him to do this and, being wealthy, had
promised to take care of him after the war. So Baron Forani had stayed at home
with Christine's parents and his and Christine's little daughters (born in 1937
and 1939). To keep occupied, he joined Christine in giving tennis lessons at the
tennis club while clandestinely helping the family to hide Jewish refugees from
the east on their way to havens off the European continent.

By 1942, Christine had become too restless to stay home. She wanted to
do something actively against the Nazis, so she joined the Belgian Resistance.
It was during this time that she acquired the name "Christine" as a nom de
guerre. She had been christened Madeleine Lucie Antoinette, only child of
Nestor and Lucie Bonnecompagnie in Arlon, in Wallonia, the French-speaking
part of Belgium, in 1916.

Through the Belgian Resistance, she was sent to England in 1944 for
parachute training. According to Belgian military records, she became an
"auxiliary, 1st class" of the Belgian military underground, the *"Services de
Renseignements et d'Action."* In 1944, something she never talked of won
her the Belgian Croix de Guerre (*lion en bronze*) and the Belgian Resistance
Medal. Then, as the Allies made their final push into Germany in early 1945,
Christine found a new outfit to join. This was the Special Allied Airborne
Reconnaissance Force (SAARF), a unit created after victory by the Allies was
merely a matter of months or weeks. SAARF teams were supposed to jump
into areas near the German prisoner of war camps, ahead of Allied troops.
The SAARF operatives' main mission was to prevent the mass murder of
prisoners in advance of their liberation, by discreetly contacting the prison

commandants and warning that they would be held personally accountable for whatever happened to their charges. The mission was enlarged to include the Nazi concentration camps when news of these camps reached Supreme Allied European headquarters. SAARF operatives were also supposed to collect information about conditions in the prisons and camps, make contact with the inmates, and in every way try to protect the prisoners from their keepers and from the local population during the interval between SAARF's arrival on the scene and liberation by the Allied armies.

Christine was in the squad that went into Dachau ahead of the U.S. Sixth Army. Before she reached Dachau, however, the camp was liberated on April 29 by an American major of the Forty-second "Rainbow" Division. By the time Christine got there, the leader of the clandestine inmates' organization had been evacuated, leaving his deputy, Belgian underground fighter, Arthur Haulot.

Although Dachau was now "liberated," it was still a horrifying place, stinking of death and decay. Corpses lay everywhere and what seemed to be walking corpses stood about. On May 1 or 2, 1945, into this hellish scene walked a Belgian army parachute colonel, leading a half-dozen Belgian army parachutists, including, incredibly, a young woman. She was dressed in trousers like the rest. "They all called her Blondie," Haulot remembers. "She was beautiful, joyous, charming." She was Christine.

Christine's job was to report on conditions at the camp, and she stayed on, near Dachau, for a week or so to do this. Arthur Haulot, a tall handsome man of imposing presence who was then in his thirties (later made a baron by King Baudouin for his services on behalf of Dachau survivors), recalls that, a week after Christine had first appeared, she turned up in a small red convertible: "Who knows how she came by it!" She suggested to him that they take a drive. As they were driving, Christine switched on the radio and they heard the announcement of the German surrender. They fell into each other's arms and celebrated the victory by making love. "Making love to her was '*L'amour contre la mort*,'" Haulot remembers. They remained lovers for a time and stayed friends ever afterward.

Besides having a "good war" in common, Tom and Christine had a bad conscience about their children. Christine had more or less abandoned her daughters when they were five and three, to the care of their father. After the war, Forani went off to the United States to try to earn a living rather than remain dependent on his parents-in-law, while Christine developed a serious career as a sculptor. The girls were given over to the care of their grandmother and sent to various boarding schools in Belgium and Switzerland.

In spite of her earlier neglect of them, Christine managed to retain a strong relationship with her children and enjoyed having them and her grandchildren with her. This was yet another attraction for Tom. For the first time in his life, he was part of a big, rowdy, quarrelsome, demonstrative, loving family.

Christine also shared with Tom a love of "primitive" art and people. In 1954 at age thirty-eight, she won a fellowship from the Belgian Ministry of Colonies to go to the Belgian Congo on behalf of the (Belgian) Royal Central African Museum in Tervuren, to take impressions and make casts of the ornamental scars still being worn by some of the tribal peoples of central and eastern Belgian Congo. She made portrait busts of five tribal leaders, which were later displayed at the Tervuren Museum, and had become their friend in the process. She had collected many masks and other Congolese sculptures, which crowded her tables and hung all over her walls, no doubt reminding Tom of Pig Lane. Her Congo adventures had given her a taste for ethnology. Since then, she had visited many other "primitive" places and had experimented with peyote and psychedelic mushrooms in Mexico. She was a good photographer and liked to take photos of ethnographic subjects.

Christine grew up as the only child of rich parents of farming stock who had made a fortune after the First World War teaching the bourgeois of Brussels deportment, how to dance, and how to keep fit, in a school they had established. She had been a sickly baby, and her parents had indulged her. They had not sent her to school but had arranged for private tutors. When it became clear that she was not an intellectual but had an artistic bent, they sent her to Paris to study art, and she became a sculptor. Her work was exhibited in perhaps fifty shows over twenty-five years beginning in the late 1940s, including a number of prestigious ones, but she never earned a living as an artist. Fortunately, she never had to. After the war, her parents gave her husband an air conditioning and plumbing supplies import company to run. She inherited the company upon his death in 1966. She also owned a handsome art deco house her parents had bought in the prettiest part of the outskirts of Brussels. She owned the tower apartment in a nineteenth-century Scottish-Gothic chateau in Cannes to which belonged a small private beach opposite the chateau, across a little bridge over the railway that skirted the coast. She still had her husband's beautiful old Jaguar sports car and an enormous saloon car for everyday use. While not terribly rich, she had the freedom that money can buy. She traveled wherever she liked and paid little attention to what she spent.

That she was independently wealthy had been a major reason why Tom had kept her address and come to see her. However attractive he had found her when he met her at the reception in Morges in April, he would never have contemplated leaving Barbara if Christine had not had enough money to be able to keep him. Here was Tom's solution to the problem that had been worrying him for the previous two years.

Tom was quite frank to friends, telling them that the thought of leaving Barbara had saddened him but that he had realized that he could not live himself, nor offer her a decent life, on the income he could obtain by his own efforts. Having long ceased thinking of Barbara as a wife, much as he loved her in a platonic way, he presumed she must feel the same. After all, she willingly spent months away from him. They had not made love in many years. She was always affectionate toward him but never possessive.

Could she manage alone? She was now a more competent scholar in a number of fields—orangutans, ceramics, even archaeology—than he was. She was happy at Cornell, and everybody liked her. If she wanted, she might find a job there without a degree. Or, possibly, Cornell might support her to obtain a doctorate. Furthermore, if Tom were to be supported by Christine, he could give Barbara his small monthly Sarawak pension.

Spelled out at its baldest, leaving a loving and loyal wife to be kept by a rich woman he had just met seemed a bit shameful, even to Tom. But bathing in the warm waters of the Mediterranean with this amazingly attractive woman and her charming daughters and grandchildren, he saw how wonderful life could still be for him. He cabled Barbara on August 13 that he was having a lovely holiday near Nice with friends and could he stay another week? Barbara cabled back saying, "It's perfectly OK. Enjoy yourself." He did.

Tom returned to Ithaca on August 22 to find Barbara tranquilly working on her papers on the orangutan. He had been away a month. After waiting nearly a week, Tom finally spoke to her about what he had done during his holiday with friends in the south of France. Barbara's diary for August 27, 1969, described it as a "black night." The agony continued for the next several months and, to some extent, remains with her. Tom always claimed to friends to have been astonished at how hard Barbara had taken the news that he had fallen in love with another woman. Because Barbara had turned a blind eye to Tom's need to "break out" sexually from time to time when away from her, because she had learned not to hang on Tom's sleeve, nor to allow herself to be thrown off balance by his moods or the way he could shout at her when he wanted something done, he had thought she did not care. In fact, her love for him was the most important thing in her life. She never stopped loving him, however angry she was at him for leaving her, nor did she ever allow her love for him to turn sour or bitter, even decades later.

In October, Tom left for England. A few weeks later, at Tom's request, Barbara went to London to see his solicitor to discuss a divorce. Tom never went back to Cornell to live. He and Christine soon left for the Far East and the Pacific, beginning with a pleasant visit in Japan to spend time with Christine's daughter Isabelle and her family. Then Tom and Christine went to Singapore. While Tom stayed there, Christine flew to Sarawak to take some photographs for him before joining him in Brunei, where they stayed the month of February. The couple then traveled together to Singapore, Bali, Tahiti, Noumea, and the New Hebrides. The trip to the New Hebrides was Tom's first since the 1930s. It was "a shattering experience," he later wrote to Mary Adams, to find out what was happening to the "splendid people" he had known. "Several of the sons of the chiefs I knew are in prison for nothing more than loving their own patch of yam or taro. . . ." Christine then took photographs in the Solomon Islands for a chapter Tom was writing on erotic art in the Pacific while Tom went to Fiji.

Returning to Brussels with Christine in early March, Tom went to England to look for a home for the "Mass-Observation Archive" in or near the campus of Sussex University. He saw Barbara again in London in late March. She had started divorce procedures, but Tom did not let most of his friends know about the breakup. Even Max wrote to "Dear Tom and Barbara" on December 17, although the divorce would become final the next day. Those people who knew Barbara expressed shock and dismay, making Tom feel like even more of a heel. That is probably the reason why he did not tell Mary Adams until more than a week after the final decree, and then only in response to a letter in which she reported she had heard that he and Barbara had separated.

In this letter to Mary, one of his oldest and best friends, he described the whole mixture of thoughts, feelings, and hopes he had at this time:

> You are right. Barbara and I split up. My "fault" really, and some of it goes back to deep inner failure via Max (yes grief, grief indeed, the hardest thing to bear in aging). Next week I hope to marry a clever, rich, tough grandmother (of four) Belgian Baroness, sculptor, and successful business woman. Barbara is hurt more than we thought and I remain very concerned about her. But I just felt life was slipping away and that before I die I must take one more cruel chance to see if, before it is too late, I cannot somehow achieve that youthful promise of semi-genius and come up with one at last lasting book or something . . or other . . or something.
>
> I do know a lot now, some of it not shared by others in the same strange melange of experience. I am now trying to work out a new way to reexpress this. Thus a return to M-O, in part. Also a lot of study of alchemy, Flemish 15th and 16th century art plus Durer and Cranach, the megalithic and my new term MICRO-MEGALITHIC. . . . And so on.
>
> I suppose it reads crazy put like that. What I seek is to bridge, in a fresh way, that old savage civilisational gulf, but now linking the prehistory of savciv to the Renaissance, Iron technology, Magellan, Niah Caves, Worktown 1971, etc., mixed in—messed up with—war, spying, student unrest, cannibalism, coloured television and all the rest. Maybe I've left it too late, though . . . I do not really think-feel so. . . .

# Chapter 44

## Second Youth

In the spring of 1970, *The Times* reported that "Tom Harrisson, the celebrated anthropologist, who over 30 years ago founded Mass-Observation—the first of the now prolific organizations for discovering and tabulating public opinion—is to spend three years at the University of Sussex sorting through the material he collected during the 12 years he ran the organization. . . ."

Over the next few years, Tom had all the major dailies and weeklies write about the new Mass-Observation Archive. Drawing on his experience with the media, when some television photographers were coming to film the archive at its new home at the University of Sussex, he asked the M-O archivist, Dorothy Sheridan, to take a felt-tip pen and quickly write out big legible labels, such as "Sex," "Money," and "War," and tape them onto the file cabinets without regard to the files' actual contents, which no one yet had had time to sort through. He explained to Sheridan, whose first day of work this was, that file cabinets were not photogenic in themselves and the photographers would need something to take pictures of.

In April 1970, Tom went to Brussels and collected Christine and Ludmilla and Christine's car to go back to England to see his mother's sister, Aunt Violet, and retrace the steps of his childhood. When they reached the corner of the road where seven-year-old Tom had stood waving goodbye to the car that was carrying his parents away, he burst into tears. He told them how his parents had stayed away for years; how his father had not cared for him but only for his brother; and how he, Tom, had done everything in his power, even scandalous things, to get his father's attention, if not his respect.

Much of the time that Tom and Christine were together was spent not in tears but in laughter. Christine loved to play the monkey and do clownish things, such as fart and make rude noises, and Tom enjoyed it, too. He called her "Monkey" or "Connie" (from *con*, a French term of abuse with roughly the same connotations as "asshole"). She called him "Baby."

Christine bought a minivan that she called the "Tom bus." They would go around in it with the grandchildren, who found Christine's and Tom's outrageous manners delightful. Once, Tom and Christine and her four little granddaughters went to the beaches of Zeeland, in the Netherlands, where they all behaved riotously and were thrown out of restaurants. Christine would organize birthday parties and frequent unbirthday parties that were gay and full of silly behavior. She would make everybody wear clown makeup while she, with a pair of underpants on her head as a hat, directed them in an improvised pantomime.

One of the things this odd couple had in common was a horror of being bored. They went to great lengths to avoid it. One day Ludmilla found a cheap package trip for a week's skiing at St. Moritz. Christine and Tom said, "What a good idea! We will go there too." But instead of flying with Ludmilla and staying at her bargain pension, they reserved a room at a famous hotel and drove there in Baron Forani's splendid ancient Jaguar sports car. In order to do honor to the old car, they decided to dress appropriately to the period. They found some old parachutist uniforms from the war in the basement. Tom and Christine put these on and wrapped themselves in old parachutes. They wore old Lindbergh-type aviator's goggles, and Christine had her hair curled in a 1940s style. In this getup, they drove all the way from Brussels to the door of their chic St. Moritz hotel. Tom had not had so much fun since the days when he was courting Biddy, and on a whim she had hired out the floor of a hotel and ordered up magnums of champagne.

As with many wealthy people, Christine had a miserly side. She hated wasting the free hotel breakfast. She would pack up the uneaten croissants and the brioches, the little pats of butter and the little pots of jam and, to Tom's great amusement, sneak them out of the hotel in her bag so that they could have them to snack on at a picnic lunch.

This was Tom's first experience of living as a European on the continent, and he was intrigued. After Tom introduced Christine to his family, she—after some hesitation—let him meet her relatives in Wallonia, rich farmers who lacked Christine's international sophistication. She was worried that he, being such a snob, might not like her Arlon family, but, once again, his genuine interest in people and love of novelty made him a good guest in new surroundings.

He admired Christine's handsome Brussels house and promptly took over one of the nicer rooms for his office. To commemorate the toy turtle that Christine had given him in Morges, he began with Christine's enthusiastic complicity to fill all the house's empty surfaces, including the window sills, with a growing collection of "turtles," everything they could find in the shape of a turtle, from valuable T'ang pottery tomb statues to cheap plastic shapes meant to float in the bath. Members of Christine's family saw the encroachment of this turtle collection on her house as indicative of Tom's territoriality.

Both Christine and Tom had a very aggressive side that needed to find periodic expression, and they enjoyed venting it together and would often involve the grandchildren. Tom and Christine would tell the children to go pick fruit from the trees belonging to the farmer whose property ran alongside the chateau in Cannes where she had her apartment. One day, on their way home to Brussels, driving with the grandchildren in Christine's big car, they stopped once again by the side of the farmer's fields and told the girls to go and steal figs from his trees and tomatoes from his vines. But this time, the farmer came out with his old shotgun and aimed it at the children, who ran shrieking back to the car, thrilled by their brush with danger. They were still talking of it when they reached Brussels, along with Tom, Christine, her maid Rosa, and Rosa's lover, all tanned from the sun and covered with food crumbs and dust from the road, looking like a band of happy gypsies.

Another time in Cannes, Tom and Christine became seriously annoyed that the little bridge over the railway line that led to their bit of beach was habitually being used by a bunch of exhibitionist homosexuals to "flash" at passers by and at passengers on trains. Complaints to the police failed to dislodge the nuisance. After the flashers had invaded their beach in revenge for the call to the police, exposing themselves and making obscene gestures, Tom and Christine went on the attack. Tom slashed the tires of the trespassers' illegally parked cars. When that did not succeed in ridding the beach and the bridge of the enemy, they prepared to take stronger measures.

They donned their bathing suits and some crazy hats. Then, with Tom carrying an instrument for underwater spearfishing, he and Christine proceeded onto the beach at the head of a small column made up of the four granddaughters, Ludmilla, and a couple of Ludmilla's friends. Tom and Christine shouted at the first flasher they saw, and the agitated flasher, in trying to escape, threw himself headlong into a nettle bush. The other trespassers ran away, and Tom said to the little girls, "You see, that's how you should behave to people like that."

On January 9, 1971, soon after Tom's divorce became final, and after nearly a year and a half of "living in sin," as he gaily described it to his future stepdaughters, he and Christine were married. Rather than maneuver their way around the bureaucratic hurdles to marriage in Brussels, they had a quiet wedding at St. Pancras Town Hall in London. Two of Tom's old expatriate friends from Southeast Asia were there, as was Mary Adams, this being the third Tom Harrisson wedding she had attended.

Although Tom had forewarned few of his friends about his divorce and remarriage, afterward he and Christine sent almost everyone they knew a wedding announcement. Nobody who received one ever forgot it.

Christine's Belgian friends, cheated of a wedding, rallied with parties afterward in the couple's honor. Arthur Haulot gave a reception at his house, to

TOM HARRISON   D.S.O.  O.B.E.

BARONNE FORANI   CROIX DE GUERRE

Married in London 9th January 1971

LONDON                                                    BRUXELLES 1180
TRAVELLERS' CLUB – PALL MALL                45, AVENUE LANCASTER

which he invited many of Christine's old friends, including a number of her old flames. He later said: "I can still remember seeing [Christine] seated on a chair in my reception room with, on their knees before her, five of the men who had been her lovers at various times in her life, during and since the war. In the next room stood Tom, all by himself, consoling himself with whisky."

Christine was accustomed to having her own way and to being the center of attention. Her first husband, Baron Forani, had loved her enough to tolerate her affairs and her "difficult" character. Tom was the first man Christine had ever known who was able and willing to "tell her off, to tell her that she was foolish, to say that she was exaggerating, that she was paranoid, that she was difficult, who would tell her to 'fuck off.'"

Much of the time, Christine liked having Tom stand up to her. She recognized in him someone worth subordinating her own interests to. She gave up her sculpting to assist him in his work. She provided secretarial help from her family firm, served as his photographer, and managed the house to make it a pleasant place for him to live and work. Sometimes, though, she would feel ill-used and grow angry and resentful. And, sometimes, merely the rubbing together of their two "difficult" characters made sparks that ignited into rage. They would scream and call each other filthy names. Occasionally it would go beyond that. Once, Christine rang up Arthur Haulot to ask him to come over right away, Haulot recalls, "because Tom wanted to beat her up." Haulot came and order was temporarily restored. Another time, Tom said to Ludmilla, "See my nose? Your mother just bit my nose."

One day while Tom was in London getting an award, Ludmilla called on her mother at her Brussels home and found her in a strange mood. They had tea, and Ludmilla asked, "Where is Tom?" And her mother answered, "Oh, he is in England for a ceremony. He will be home soon." Ludmilla asked, "Why did you not go with him?" And Christine answered, "Oh, I was busy; I did not have time." But Ludmilla could see she was angry.

> Then Tom arrived. And you could see he was angry because she had not gone with him. And he said, "Here, I got you some chocolates." And Christine said, "I don't eat English chocolates. This is ridiculous. Where are these chocolates?" And she took them. They were in a room with a white rug and she stamped the chocolates into the rug. The rug was all brown, disgusting, and I was horrified to see this happen.
>
> And Tom said, "Well, dear, you don't like the chocolates. Perhaps you would like to see the decoration they gave me." He took it out to show to her and she said, "I don't want to see the decoration," and snatched it and threw it out the window into the garden.

After this incident, Tom got drunk. He would sometimes drink heavily, usually cognac. And when he got drunk, he could become violent and abusive. Usually, though, quarrelling with Christine just seemed to stimulate him, and this was true for her as well. Tom once told Ludmilla, "You know when I and your mother have a big quarrel, a big outburst. That's just another kind of orgasm. She can have orgasmic fury." Friends agree, one of them commenting that Tom and Christine were two monstres sacrés who were either throwing themselves into each other's arms or attacking one another with physical violence.

Different from Tom's previous marriages, where the act of signing the register seemed to put an end to Tom's interest in making love, sex remained a major feature in his marriage to Christine. A little notebook of Tom's survives from 1972 in which Tom recorded page after page of what the Belgian dentist was doing to his teeth and salivary glands. But when the notebook is turned upside down and started from the other cover, one finds that the other half of the notebook's pages are devoted to recording Tom's sex life with Christine. Five times in one night appears to be the record during the period of this notebook, but the number of occasions and the variety of positions during an average month would be the envy of lovers one-third their age.

In order to keep up this pace of lovemaking Tom lost weight and became more fit. By November 1972, under Christine's careful regime, he was able to boast to Medway that he weighed only 157 pounds, his lowest weight in 20 years, and that he was swimming a mile a day in the neighborhood's Olympic-size pool. "[I] never drink alcohol," he wrote Medway, "only wine."

"Never" would be too strong a word to describe his hard liquor consumption during this period, but it had ceased being part of his daily diet.

Now that they were married, Tom felt able to invite his relatives to stay with him and Christine, either in Brussels or, better still, in Cannes. His favorite relative, Aunt Violet's daughter Jill Webster, found Christine a gracious hostess, glad to entertain her English family-in-law.

Peter and Betsan Harrisson (cousins on Tom's father's side and good friends of Hugh Gibb) had a summer house not too far from Cannes. They stayed the night at Christine's apartment in the nineteenth-century Scottish chateau in September 1971 and were given a sumptuous dinner. It was Tom's sixtieth birthday, and everyone was enjoying a pleasant evening until Tom, feeling the group's attention wander away from its focus on him, became sulky and complained of being neglected. He might have been six years old instead of ten times older. For better and for worse, marriage to Christine had made him feel young again.

Among the members of Tom's family that sometimes came to visit after Tom married Christine was Max. This was undoubtedly at Christine's urging. Though Tom might dread reunions with Max, Christine with her strong sense of family found it unnatural for Tom not to see his son, regardless of the son's condition. Max came to stay in Cannes on several occasions, each time for a week or two. He would follow along to the beach and elsewhere, trailing behind the four little granddaughters like a big harmless dog. Christine accepted Max as one of the family, setting the tone for others to do the same.

Christine was not always so gracious to Tom's family, especially if her instinctive and elemental jealousy was aroused. Once, at Tom's cousin Jill's instigation, a reunion was arranged between Tom and his very attractive Australian cousin. He had enjoyed a flirtation, if not more, with her in Melbourne in 1944–1945, while waiting to drop into Borneo. The cousin invited Tom, Christine, Jill, and Aunt Violet to lunch at her rented villa near Grasse in the south of France.

Tom, perhaps recognizing trouble in Christine's expression the moment the two women met, retreated up into a tree, whence he looked out into space until he was called to lunch. Christine, in an agitated and overly animated way, dominated luncheon conversation and kept getting up to go over to the grass to pluck out what she described as edible herbs. The Australian cousin was amused by the bizarre behavior of her guests, but all the way home to Cannes in the car, Christine fulminated against their luncheon hostess.

Christine was equally ungenerous in her attitude toward her defeated rival, Barbara, undoubtedly because she could see that Barbara still had a hold on Tom's affections. Barbara continued to write Tom letters, addressing him as "Darling," letters Christine doubtless read without asking permission.

What really excited Christine's jealousy was Tom's continued admiration and respect for Barbara, feelings different from those he had for her and, in their own way, just as strong. Christine, whose money was supporting Tom almost totally, was also annoyed that Tom was still helping Barbara financially by allotting her his Sarawak pension and was still worrying about her future.

Tom's concern for Barbara appears to have been genuine. He was glad to see her in Brunei and at conservationist meetings in Switzerland, where they discussed many subjects of mutual interest. At one point, he told a Cornell friend he could not accept an invitation to go to Cornell right then because Barbara was taking her doctoral examinations, and he did not want to upset her at this important moment in her career. He was awed by her achievements, especially earning a Ph.D at her age and after only a year as an undergraduate half a lifetime earlier. When he heard that she had received the degree and a proper university job, he commented wistfully to another friend, "I shall never do that."

# Chapter 45

## Professor At Last

Tom, unlike Barbara, never earned a doctoral degree, but he did get his professorship. When the Sussex University visiting professor title was approved in June 1974, he charged the M-O archivist with letting his friends know, saying that this was "one in the eye for the academics."

By then, Tom had been appearing often in the British press, usually in connection with the revival of the M-O Archive. In 1972, he had been invited to the BBC's *Desert Island Discs* program a second time. He had been restored to his rightful place as a fully fledged member of Britain's chattering class. A typical comment about him during the early 1970s comes from *The Times* "Diary" for April 10, 1973:

> Tom Harrisson can fairly be counted among the last of the great British polymaths. An ornithologist, explorer, anthropologist, archaeologist, and pioneer of social observation; he now spends most of his time in Brussels, with the occasional trip to his favourite stamping ground in Borneo. . . .

By 1973, he was spending more time in Britain, making use of the M-O Archive for a major project: a study of how Britons had actually behaved under the Blitz and what their thoughts and fears had been, as recorded in their diaries and in eyewitness accounts at the time of their "finest hour," and to compare this with what was later written about that period, including what the M-O diarists thought they "remembered." Tom saw this project as the "first exercise in the orderly use of this social documentation of the late Thirties and Forties."

When Mass-Observation began in the late 1930s as a "pioneer of social observation," it had been, as one later critic described it, "a slightly dotty enterprise." But by the 1970s, when Tom revived M-O, he knew what was valuable about it: its enormous archive of unedited diaries, letters, filled-in questionnaires, and eyewitness and earwitness accounts of ordinary people of an earlier era.

What would an historian today not give to have everyday records of the activities, preoccupations, thoughts, and feelings of ordinary people in ancient times? Or in the Middle Ages? Or even during the First World War? Such records do not exist because, almost up to the time of M-O, most ordinary people could not write. What we know about history before the 1930s comes almost entirely from people who were part of, or close to, the ruling elite.

There have always been writers, from Chaucer and Shakespeare to Dickens, Jack London, and Orwell, who have attempted to observe, describe, and empathize with the poor and the working class. But that is not the same—nor is sociology or market surveying—as a systematic effort to let them speak for themselves. Thanks largely to Tom and Madge, such an effort began in the late 1930s. And thanks not only to increased literacy but also in large part to Tom's example of focusing attention in an organized way on the British man-in-the-street, such information will be available to researchers in the future when they want to know what ordinary people in Britain were doing and thinking today.

There are undoubtedly similar repositories of such material elsewhere, but one of the best is the Mass-Observation Archive of Sussex University. This archive still enlists diarists and stores their anonymous but frank personal accounts of their lives and their reactions to the world around them for use by serious scholars. In sociological and historical terms, the Mass-Observation Archive is a gold mine, but one constantly being replenished rather than exhausted. It is one of Tom's most valuable legacies.

Tom took a proprietary interest in the Mass-Observation Archive. No longer having a museum and Sarawak's interior to defend, he transferred his paranoiac protectiveness to it. After the archive opened officially on October 1, 1975, Tom worried about students breaking in and damaging it. "Not just that," recalls M-O archivist Dorothy Sheridan, "he said he was worried about students breaking in and making love between the shelves. He had this particular fantasy."

In dealing with subordinates at the M-O Archive, Tom, as in the past, could be both unreasonably demanding and surprisingly generous, often to the same person. For example, he continually pestered Sheridan to drive him places, since he no longer had a driver's permit. She did not then know how to drive, which made him cross because he wanted her to be able to collect him at the train station and ferry him around. Sheridan recalls:

> He'd say, "Look. All those Mass-Observers are getting a bit doddery. They really need you to be able to drive them." And I wasn't sure that this was part of my job. And one day he said, "Here is a hundred pounds. Buy yourself an old car."

He had always behaved that way to his staff, shouting at young Shariffuddin and asking nearly impossible things of him and then giving him £6 when he arrived as a student in England in the 1950s so that Sharif would have some cash to hand. Similarly, Tom became enraged at the moodiness of his excellent Iban collector and taxidermist, Gaun, but then lent him enough money of his own to free Gaun from moneylenders and arrange for him to go to Malaya for a change of scene and a chance to work under a man he liked, Lord Medway.

Everybody who knew Tom conceded that he could be a "total bastard," but "encouraging" was also a word many used to describe him. It is the term applied to Tom by a number of graduate students and young faculty members at Cornell and Sussex, who say that he gave them the self-confidence to find their own road, to develop their own gifts. "Encouraging" is the chief word used by such successful men as Lords Wyatt and Shackleton to describe Tom's influence on them. Humphrey Spender credits Tom with encouraging him to go back over his photographs from the Bolton and Blackpool days to produce an album that could be turned into a book. The result was *Britain in the 30s*, an attractive slender volume published in 1975 with Spender's photographs and Tom's foreword. This led to Spender finally getting acclaim as one of Britain's best thirties photographers.

Tom, however, also continued to make nearly unacknowledged use of the help of his subordinates and collaborators. From 1973 to 1975, he worked harder than he had ever before worked on a book. He wanted to make *Living Through the Blitz* a worthy testament to the wealth of material lodged in the Mass-Observation Archive and a real contribution to modern European history. He drew heavily on the talents and hard work of M-O observers and staffers, especially Celia Fremlin, Mollie Tarrant, and Bob Willcock. And as before, he stole the limelight, appearing on the title page as sole author.

Still, although much research and some of the writing was others', most of the reviewers agreed that only Tom could have conceived of and produced it. The reviewer in *The Observer* described Tom as "admirably, perhaps uniquely, equipped to separate fact from legend, private attitudes from public postures" on this subject that politicians "have tended to recall . . . with nostalgia and self-glorification." In contrast to these politicians, the reviewer contended, Tom had "written with insight and candour about deficiencies in leadership" while recording the capacity to endure, which was "the greatest contribution to national victory . . . by the preponderance of ordinary citizens."

Stephen Spender, writing in *The Guardian*, complained that Tom had become "somewhat submerged under his information," and therefore the book was "not quite the masterpiece by a man of immensely independent mind—Churchillian, Lawrentian*—which one hoped it would be" but that, nonetheless, "After reading this book one feels that something important has

---

*The reference is to T. E. Lawrence, "Lawrence of Arabia."

been told us about human nature." The novelist C. P. Snow, in the *Financial Times,* described the book as "the best account of the 1940–41 Blitz that has been written."

Tom's sloppy drafting and slipshod editing were still a problem. The *New Statesman* reviewer wrote of Tom's prose style that it "would bring into disrepute even a parliamentary sub-committee on an off-day" but went on to state that, "Despite a lot of really frightful writing, his book emerges, bloodied, mutilated, but still indisputably a triumph. . . ."

As had been the case when M-O worked for the Ministry of Information and the Director of Naval Intelligence, this book exposed flaws in government planning for the Blitz, such as no facilities provided for tens of thousands of people who, to the planners' astonishment, used the London underground as a bomb shelter or who "trekked" to the country every evening to escape the bombs. The book pointed out the near total lack of coordination during the Blitz by such organizations as neighboring fire brigades. It told of failure to pass on what had been learned by communities already hit to those likely to be next. It spoke of poor and patronizing propaganda. It described widespread failure in Whitehall to anticipate what would bother ordinary people or to gauge how much they could take and still go back to work.

In exposing these flaws, Tom trod on some sensitive toes, including those of his old "friend" Lord (Solly) Zuckerman, who had been involved in organizing and directing the Hull and Birmingham inquiries about the effects of bombing on civilian populations. Lord Zuckerman wrote to protest Tom's remarks in a letter to the *Times Literary Supplement.* Zuckerman's fury at dismissive comments about studies done under his direction would last to the end of "Mr. Science's" days.

Although Tom's book showed that the British government's preparation and response to the Blitz did not support nostalgic and self-glorifying recollections by the nation's leaders, it also gave exact quotations from the time of the Blitz that lent some credence to the wartime image of the phlegmatic English working man. There was the fifty-year-old button maker who had been bombed out twice and was asked if he wanted to be evacuated. He answered: "And miss all this? . . . There's never been nothing like it! Never! And never will be again." Or the way, under such conditions, literary metaphor came naturally to ordinary people, as in this dialogue overheard in a pub after a raid on Plymouth:

1st Man: Where's the gents?
2nd Man: Everywhere's the gents now.

While Tom was working on *Living Through the Blitz,* he was also engaged in many other activities. He was thinking of reviving his work on the New Hebrides, producing a "then and now" work. He was active in world efforts to protect endangered species. When in Brunei, he spent time on ornithology, having neglected his first scientific love for decades. He was trying to narrow down the date of the Niah Deep Skull by having more tests done on animal bone found near it. He was reading about and going to see pebbles and other stones all over the world for a "Micro-Megalithic" project, following up on what he and Stan O'Connor had found in the Sarawak River delta. He was looking into alchemy and early Renaissance painting to see the connections between them.

In June 1975, he began to make notes and interview relatives and others who had known him in his youth for use in his autobiography, tentatively titled *Was I That Man?* He was also starting work on his next big project for M-O, the subject of which was provoked by the 1936 event that had led Jennings and Madge to try to conduct an "anthropology of ourselves": the abdication of Edward VIII. The new study that Tom had in mind—one that seems timely today—involved investigating how ordinary subjects really felt about their monarch. It would focus especially on the British monarchy but would include glimpses of other kingdoms where there had been a twentieth-century abdication, such as Belgium and Brunei.

One of the few activities not in his plans was to go back to work in the United States. On April 26, 1974, the date of his official but erroneous birthday, he gave up his American work and residence permit.

Tom was also trying to help Christine with the plumbing supplies business that her parents had given the late Baron Forani to run. Although Tom often described Christine as a "successful businesswoman," she was not. She had inherited a healthy enterprise, but her lack of a business instinct was killing the milk cow on which she and Tom and, to some extent, her children and grandchildren depended. By the time Tom took an interest in the matter, the cow was very sick. His efforts probably did not help much. He had had no experience in how to obtain money other than to threaten or cajole government departments or rich patrons, and he was also distressingly good at finding new ways for Christine to spend it. By 1975, for example, he was considering endowing a Kelabit education fund for schooling Kelabit orphans. The fund papers were being drawn up by a lawyer friend of Tom's in Brunei, but the money would be Christine's.

Anxiety about Christine's business became a dark cloud over Tom and Christine. Rows over what to do about it were the most serious and least amusing of the quarrels between them, quarrels that grew more frequent as the firm's situation worsened. As Tom's morale deteriorated, he reverted to old bad habits. He had a late-onset diabetic condition and, for that reason, as well as to keep his weight down, Christine had urged him not to eat sweets. But she, who could eat them without gaining an ounce, used to buy large amounts of chocolates and other sweets for the grandchildren. Tom took to sneaking some from the grandchildren's supplies. Worse still for his health, his weight, and his temper, he went back to drinking cognac in ever-increasing quantities. Some of their rows resulted from Christine nagging Tom to stop eating sweets and drinking, while Tom's aggressiveness and bad moods would increase with every swig of liquor.

Life was still mostly pleasant, however, in 1975 as Tom finished his work on *Living Through the Blitz*. He and Christine, her daughter Isabelle, her son-in-law, and three grandchildren all had a splendid summer holiday together in North Africa. Tom looked forward to December in Brunei. After Brunei, he planned to take another trip through Southeast Asia. This time Christine would not go to Brunei but would go first to Japan and join him either in Sabah for Christmas or in Bangkok for the new year after he visited Singapore and Kuala Lumpur. Then Tom and Christine would visit Burma together and return to Thailand. It was a good way to escape winter in Brighton and Brussels, where Tom could no longer tolerate the cold.

In September, months before he left for Brunei, while he was at Sussex attending to his duties as a "visiting professor," Tom received what was perhaps his most pleasurable honor of the year. This was finding his name in *The Times* list of "Birthdays Today" on September 26, 1975, the day he turned sixty-four. His name had appeared there yearly since 1963, but he had not known and thought that this was only the second time. He took the mention in *The Times* as confirmation that he was back in the swim of things in England. To his delight, he was the only mere "Mr." on the list. He wrote a note to himself about it:

> Second birthday—in *The Times*!! "Mr. Tom Harrisson" (all others Sir, Adm., etc.). Seven Sirs, (including A. Blunt), one Dr., one Lord. Phone Christine again— good news for THH.

This undoubtedly helped to make up for some bad news he had received a couple of months earlier in a "private and confidential" letter from someone at the Sarawak Museum telling him that all of the Museum's employees were "duty-bound not to communicate with you. . . . We all feel it is indeed stupid that we are not even allowed to accept any contribution from you for the *SMJ*. . . . I know how painful this is to you but believe me, such a situation did not develop on our account. We are still totally in the dark as to why you are given this treatment. . . ." Tom wrote to Medway in 1972:

> The loss of access to Sarawak is <u>heartbreak</u> for me. . . . I have not much time left now, of fitness.

If Tom had still been hoping to return to Sarawak, this 1975 letter from a museum colleague must have dashed those hopes.

In early December, when the Sussex academic term ended, Tom headed for Brunei. Once there, he wrote to his old trainee, Michael Chong, now deputy curator of the new Sabah Museum, to ask if it would be all right if he and Christine spent Christmas there. This would be instead of Tom staying on in Brunei alone until Boxing Day, while Christine stayed in Japan.

Chong, a timid man aware that the Sabah state government was in a period of extreme nervousness about visits by foreign scholars and was banning them from any but the biggest towns, did not dare reply. He put the letter on the desk of his boss, who was away on holiday. Not having heard from Chong, Tom spent Christmas in Brunei alone. He would meet Christine in Bangkok in time for New Year's Eve.

The nostalgia brought on by being alone in Borneo during a season so charged with memories impelled Tom to write Barbara:

> This is perhaps the first Christmas I have ever spent alone. It is not bad. The odd thing is that I've got used to the two Chinese "Associations" opposite. From dusk the noise of *Mahjong* counters is like the washing of shingles on a beach. Sunday it starts at seven in the morning. Tonight the waves are still. I suddenly *miss* something. I look across the street . . . nothing. Lights on, but no one there.
>
> So deep is Christmas, even to the Unchristian. They must be paying lip service at home, with the kids.
>
> 8:30 p.m.: I am saved. They are back! The ivory waves wash on the tight shingles of their restless minds. . . . It is very, very re-assuring, don't you think?
>
> All this writing is not—as they say in Bolton—"for regular." I am in limbo and think of our previous Borneo Christmases.

He left Brunei on December 27, 1975, for Singapore, where he stayed with one of his bachelor friends with whom he had spent wild evenings in the past. He did not do so this time; Christine was his favorite companion for high jinks now. He went on to see friends in Kuala Lumpur and then to Bangkok to rejoin Christine on New Year's Eve. From there they went to Burma and back to Thailand.

At the end of their stay, they hired a minibus to drive them from a game reserve in the north back to Bangkok, whence they planned to fly home to Brussels. As was the custom, other paying passengers were also allowed on the bus, although the best seats for viewing and photographing went to Tom and Christine, up front, to the left of the driver.

It was January 16, 1976, one of Europe's shortest days. In Thailand, the sun did not go down until six o'clock, but sunsets are short in the tropics, and soon the unlighted road was pitch dark. There was a timber truck parked—with typical Thai insouciance—in the middle of the road, without any lights and with a great teak log jutting far out from the rear. By the time the bus driver saw it in the beam of his headlights, it was too late to avoid it. The log stove in the left windshield and impaled the passengers in the first two rows.

It was the kind of accident that occasionally happens on Thai roads. As often in such circumstances, the driver ran away, abandoning the damaged bus and its passengers, four of whom were dead. These four were Tom, Christine, and two Thais.

# Epilogue

One afternoon in January 1976, the same British consul who had phoned months earlier to ask if I knew a man named Tom Harrisson rang up again, sounding equally harassed, to ask if I knew Tom's next of kin.

> The man has got himself killed in a road accident way off in Thailand somewhere and nobody knows how to get in touch with his family—or with his Belgian wife's for that matter.

It seemed incredible that such a powerful force had been extinguished by a mere accident. As one of his M-O colleagues wrote of Tom, "It is still bewildering to contemplate this brutal halt to his energy, creativity and panache."

Arrangements were made for Tom and Christine to be cremated at a Buddhist *wat* in a fashionable Bangkok suburb. The cremation was to be done by the *wat's* Buddhist monks, but the little ceremony that preceded it was led by an Anglican clergyman. One of Tom's American Cornell students was living in Bangkok and came to the service. He recalls that there was just a handful of people. The Belgian and British embassies each sent someone. The clergyman, who knew nothing about the dead couple, mouthed a few platitudes and opened the Book of Common Prayer, and Tom's Singapore friend read the lesson. The florid British embassy official, who appeared to have drunk his lunch, looked about him and commented aloud on how he loathed "all this superstition."

The "superstition" the diplomat loathed was not the pallid little Anglican service but the more colorful Buddhist cremation ceremonies that were going on about the *wat*. During the ceremony for Tom and Christine, a half-dozen ovens were in use, with crowds of people moving in and out, going to this or that cremation.

Thai Buddhist funerals often last four or five days. Much prestige is attached to having the *wat* full of friends, relatives, and business contacts during those days. The Cornell student, married to a Thai, explained:

> If it is an important person who has died or is the chief mourner, the place will be packed and everybody will be coming in and loading the place up with flowers and it is just like a long wake. And the monks will be sitting around chanting and there will be incense burning and maybe you will have people bringing in a traditional Thai orchestra that will play music and sing and chant.

While Tom and Christine would have enjoyed all this hubbub, most of the Europeans there for Tom's and Christine's cremation "looked extremely uncomfortable and did not know what to do." The two coffins were closed because of the damage caused by the accident. Tom's coffin was big and difficult to maneuver. It took some twenty minutes to get it into the furnace.

Peter Harrisson, who happened to be visiting Bangkok a few days after the cremation, collected Tom's and Christine's effects and handed them over, along with the ashes, to Tom's solicitor in London, who forwarded them to Brussels. There, some weeks later, a small group huddled under umbrellas on a cold wet day to watch a Belgian veterans' association pay homage to Christine's Croix de Guerre before her ashes and Tom's were placed in the grave dug ten years earlier for Baron Forani. No mark on the baron's tombstone was made then or later to indicate that the grave also harbors Christine's and Tom's remains. Tom, who in his marriages had been like a cuckoo, habitually taking over nests built by others, undoubtedly would not have minded. It was not in a cemetery that he wished to be remembered.

Mary Adams, to whom word came in London three days after Tom's death, knew precisely how Tom would want his death commemorated. She saw that the press was informed and that timely obituaries appeared on the BBC and in *The Times*. *The Times* had a draft obituary of Tom on file in its "morgue," written by Sir. W. Le Gros Clark, a polymath and a great scientist, who had predeceased Tom. Mary Adams undoubtedly helped bring the obituary up to date. It is, in the opinion of most people who knew and liked Tom, the best statement to appear in the press, giving the real flavor of the man and his gifts. She asked Professor Asa Briggs to chair a memorial meeting in Tom's honor, to be held in London on the premises of the Royal Society of Arts. Briggs was already vice chancellor of Sussex University and about to become a Life Peer that year. With his consent, Adams set about finding the right people to speak.

The meeting took place on March 17, 1976, and many people who knew Tom attended, to listen to recollections of him by the speakers Mary Adams had chosen. She almost forgot that Tom had a brother but remembered in time to write to ask him if he wanted to be part of the program. Bill answered, "I would like to come along to listen."

Max Nicholson, the speaker who had known Tom earliest, was first. His subject was not only Tom's work in ornithology but the "amazing intricacy of his interests and life pattern." Nicholson claimed that this pattern, which resembled "a patchwork of conventionally unrelated elements" had been put in place right at the start of Tom's career and had been assembled "with consummate skill to compose the total Tom harmony." He cited the extraordinary number and variety of things Tom had done in ornithology between the ages of seventeen and twenty: several major bird censuses, the scientific soundness of which had been confirmed many times since; two Arctic expeditions; a paper on bird flight in *Nature* and numerous articles in other learned journals.

Nicholson pointed out that all during the time that Tom was busily pioneering in ornithology, he was also interested in many other things, each part of the patchwork. After the expeditions to Sarawak and the New Hebrides, Nicholson asserts, Tom was ready to transmute what he knew about birds and was learning about people into "a new kind of organised effort to understand what makes people tick in society"—Mass-Observation. Before he was twenty-six, the major pieces of the patchwork were already basted together.

Nicholson reminded his audience what Tom had written as his credo, in his *Letter to Oxford*, early in 1933, when he was twenty-one:

> Be mob-conscious, it is one of the grandest feelings[. . . . ] Argue for arguing's sake occasionally—just to make people see there are two sides, to make them *aware*. . . . Never swallow anything or anyone whole before you know exactly what it is you are swallowing[. . . . ] Do not be content to see something wrong; do something about it, put it right[. . . . ] Don't be afraid all the time. Attack as well as defend. Put some guts into things. . . . There is no excuse for anyone to be miserable for more than one day a month, unless he is hungry or ill. . . .
>
> This all sounds like a sermon. And so it bloody is. Things are wrong, you will agree. They have got to be made alright. I mean to try, and a lot of little shots like you might have a crack at it too. . . .

Asa Briggs spoke along the lines of a letter he wrote to *The Times* a week after the accident, in which he stated that "During what proved, alas, to be his last years, Tom Harrisson was as vigorous and as inquisitive as he was during the early years of Mass-Observation." Eschewing nostalgia, Briggs added, Tom had remained "as curious about [students' and colleagues'] attitudes and ways in Brighton as he was about those of the people of Bolton."

Lord Shackleton, having used alcohol to try to anaesthetize the pain of losing one of his oldest friends, could not recall later what he had said at the memorial meeting. He could only comment afterward that he would, "without hesitation, describe Tom as the most remarkable man of my generation."

Richard Fitter, a vice president of Fauna and Flora International and a longtime officer of IUCN, focused chiefly on Tom as "one of the buccaneers of wildlife conservation." Tom's buccaneering, in Fitter's view, was as much in evidence around a conference table at Morges as in the jungles of Southeast Asia:

> There was nobody like Tom Harrisson for blowing away cobwebs, sweeping away outworn rules, and penetrating behind bureaucratic verbiage and obstructions. . . . Indeed, perhaps his greatest value to the conservation movement was his readiness to speak his mind, however unpalatable his views might be.

Charles Madge, prevented by sudden illness from attending the meeting, had planned to speak about his days with Tom as co-founder of Mass-Observation. Although he acknowledged having "had some difficulty in reconciling myself to Tom's showmanship and to the excessive claims that he tended to make for his work," he had found Tom's "energy and magnetism . . . irresistible."

Michael Tweedie spoke of Tom's contributions to archaeology, especially the Deep Skull, and Malcolm MacDonald told of Tom in Borneo, his work for the Sarawak Museum, and his guerrilla operations during the war. Mary Adams spoke about Tom during M-O in wartime, his many appearances on BBC television and radio from 1936 onward, and his insightful critical reviews of wartime BBC broadcasting that he wrote for *The Observer*. Hugh Gibb described making award-winning films with Tom.

Tom would probably have wanted most to be remembered for his anthropological work, which was never taken seriously by the professionals. His books *Savage Civilisation* and *World Within* and his Mass-Observation publications were admired by the reading public for their insights about "primitive" peoples abroad and "the man on the street" at home. The information in them was far deeper than one would find in a travel book about the former or a market survey on the latter. Yet even his best works lacked the theoretical underpinning and methodological discipline that would have helped them cross the threshold into serious anthropology or sociology.

On the other hand, his anthropological and sociological writings were filled with insights and connections between things that in many ways were more enlightening than a standard anthropological work and without some of its failings. Lauriston Sharp, a Cornell anthropology professor who had long worked on Southeast Asia, made his students read Tom's *Savage Civilisation* description of Big Nambas initiation rites to teach them how it felt to be a traditional Melanesian teenager. Professor Sharp complained that one could read Sir Edmund Leach's classic, *Political Systems of Highland Burma*, and come away with the wholly false impression that the modern world's value systems had not impinged on the people that Leach had studied. Leach, like most social anthropologists of the "British School" writing at that time, had limited the discussion in this early work of his to traditional systems. Tom's writings were never so narrowly focused or narrow-minded. Moreover, their purpose was less to inform and impress establishment scholars than to enlighten the general public and, especially, to help the group being studied.

An archaeologist seeking to assess Tom's contributions to his field gave one of the best descriptions of the problem that exists in trying to define Tom's intellectual and scientific legacy:

We live and work in an age of extreme academic specialization. The proper course for the proper scholar is to claim for himself a precisely defined area of interest and to remain strictly within those boundaries. Woe be unto him who steps beyond—intellectually or geographically. He is regarded with suspicion and mistrust by his colleagues. He has lost his label. One difficulty we experience in understanding Tom Harrisson's career is that he never had a label. We cannot define him by discipline. . . . It was in ornithology that he began his scientific career and he maintained a keen interest in it throughout his life. But his paramount interest was in Borneo. Every aspect of it fascinated him—its land, its people, its plants, its wildlife, its history. As an ethnographer he understood better than most that the lives of no people could be fully appreciated without some knowledge of their past. It was inevitable that his catholic interests would eventually engross him in Borneo's prehistory. . . .

This man, being an archaeologist, does not realize that some of the accomplishments Tom is best known for have nothing to do with Borneo. In England, Tom is best known for Mass-Observation; in international circles, for fauna conservation; in the South Pacific, for his early work on the New Hebrides; in Australia, for his wartime guerrilla operations. This is without mentioning his stellar work on radio, television, and in documentary films, some about Borneo, but some on entirely different subjects.

The archaeologist rightly points out Tom's first and most enduring area of interest: birds. Lord Medway (now Lord Cranbrook), trying after Tom's death to conjure up a picture of him, describes him

> clad in singlet and checked sarong, seated commandingly at his desk in that unique house in Pig Lane, or at a table in the cave mouth at Niah, or on a veranda at Santubong . . . or Talang-talang, talking or writing, and suddenly dropping everything to snatch up the ever-handy pair of binoculars, observe the behaviour of some particular bird, scribble a note in his illegible handwriting on a fresh page of a school exercise-book, and then resume his former business.

It is certainly as a "bird man" that Tom was first brought to the frontiers of science. His interest in birds never ended. Medway is undoubtedly correct in stating that "I have often heard it said that in Mass-Observation, Tom Harrisson applied to people the techniques of bird-watching. On the other hand, I am certain that whenever observing humans, he also invariably had an eye and part of his mind on the surrounding birds."

Nonetheless, the connecting thread that ran through Tom's main interests was not birds or Borneo but, simply, people. The most important insights he brought to ornithology were on the links between bird and man. For example, his best-known work on birds in the New Hebrides is on their use as auguries and, in Borneo, on the use of their migrations to determine the farming calendar. Similarly, although Tom's work about turtles covered many aspects, his interest in them was aroused by people in Sarawak wanting and needing turtle eggs. His interest in the orangutan was in large part because it is a near relative of man. His efforts in archaeology were in order to learn more about the past of people he cared about.

His primordial interest in people is most evident in his Mass-Observation research and in his studies of native groups in Sarawak and the New Hebrides. All the knowledge he obtained by this research was meant to be passed back to the people themselves or to be used on their behalf. Because of a commitment to the people of Borneo's interior, he had stayed at war against the Japanese for months after "peace" had been officially declared. Tom's and SEMUT 1's stubborn refusal to abandon a commitment to the people who had risked their lives for them may help explain why Borneo, unlike other Japanese-occupied areas of Southeast Asia, did not get caught up in postwar anticolonialist belligerence.

To Tom, omnivorously curious though he was, knowledge for its own sake was sterile. It had to be part of a dialogue with the affected people, helping them to change or to adapt to changes thrust upon them. This was what had led him not only to strengthen the Sarawak Museum but also to play a key role in creating museums in Brunei and Sabah. If knowledge was power, it was uncivil and immoral not to share it with the mass of people. He insisted on getting things into print, on the air, or in the museum as quickly as possible in a form that ordinary people could grasp and use. That is one reason why Tom was seen as "unscientific" and would have remained an unwanted outsider to the academic world even if he had had dozens of degrees or diplomas. It is no wonder that Mary Adams was one of the few to understand him. Like her, Tom cared desperately about educating the general public.

What is Tom's legacy? To answer the question literally first, Tom's will, dated January 9, 1971, left everything to Christine. If she did not survive him, it all went to "my son Maxwell Barr Harrisson but in that event I give to such charity as my executors think best £1000, my collection of objects, my personal chattels and unpublished writings (except Mass-Observation archives which I give to Sussex University)." There was little money in Tom's estate for Max to inherit. Probated in February 1976, it had a net value of well under £5000. According to Christine's daughter Ludmilla, Tom's "collection of objects" was given, along with Christine's, to various French museums.

Of more permanent value than his "collection of objects" were Tom's papers. These were divided by his trustees according to subject. All the M-O material and everything that did not belong elsewhere went to the M-O Archive at Sussex University. The Borneo peacetime material was given to the

Malaysian National Archive in Kuala Lumpur. The SEMUT papers were donated to the Australian War Memorial Library's archives in Canberra. One of Tom's detractors claims that "much of his writing was too hasty and careless to endure," which is true, although, thanks to Tom's immense production, that still leaves a handful of books in print decades after his death. The same critic predicted that Tom's voluminous notes "would probably be unintelligible to anyone else." They have proved intelligible, though barely.

But what Tom would have found to be the most valuable part of his legacy is what remains in people's memories. In the Kelabit highlands, Tom is still remembered as their principal benefactor. Asked by a visitor to name the person who had helped them the most, Kelabit leaders in the late 1970s, by then very devout Christians, nonetheless rated Tom as having done more for them than anyone else, even the Reverend Hudson Southwell.

Dorothy Sheridan, whose job as M-O archivist makes her a sort of official keeper of the Harrisson flame, had a personal problem to resolve upon hearing of Tom's death: what to do with the £100 he had given her to buy a used car. She knew that she could not buy that car. The cash he had given her was not nearly enough and she could not make up the difference. So, in an effort to be true to the spirit of the gift, she bought a motorbike with the money:

> I taught myself to ride this motorbike and I used to whip round and, when I got on it, I would think that "If it hadn't been for Tom Harrisson, I wouldn't be on this motorbike." I did eventually get a car and learn to drive—in order to go up to Scotland to see an old M-O diarist, Naomi Mitchison.

For Sheridan, Tom—though dead—was still a liberating and encouraging force.

For Michael Chong in Sabah, word of Tom's death brought a different reaction. Chong's feelings toward Tom had always been mixed. He could still hear the famous voice echoing through the Great Cave at Niah, shouting: "Bloody fool, I don't know what the North Borneo Government is going to do with you!" But he also could not forget that, without Tom's efforts, he would not have had a career at the Sabah Museum.

> When I was applying for museum training in the UK, I did not have the educational background for it. I had only passed Form I in 1952. But, when Tom went to the UK in 1967, he worked to patch things up for me and I went to the UK in 1968. First I went to the Commonwealth Institute in London, then Glasgow for three months, then Leicester for three months. Then it was display, conservation and cataloguing at Liverpool and finally back to London where I was with the Horniman Museum for fifteen months while attending lectures at the University of London as an unenrolled student. That too was Tom Harrisson. He helped me a lot.

With all this training, Chong was offered the curatorship of the Sabah Museum, but timidity caused him to give back the top job after only a month in office. A similar diffidence caused him to pass on to his boss Tom's request in December 1975 to come to Sabah for Christmas. As Chong recalled in 1991, "The Director was away and the letter was never attended to. And today, I must say that I feel a bit guilty. His trip might have been to Sabah instead of to Thailand. Much as I wanted to help, I was not the head. But, sometimes, I feel guilty about it, still today."

Shariffuddin, Tom's first Brunei Museum trainee, upon hearing of Tom's death, went to Brussels as on a pilgrimage, to see Tom's turtle collection. Sharif had once been asked by Tom: "What is your hobby?"

And I said I did not have a hobby. And Tom got very angry with me. "You have to have a hobby," he said. "Otherwise you are wasting your time." I went to Tom and Christine's house with Tom's lawyer from London. Harrisson, when I was in Brunei, had asked me to collect for him turtles and anything about turtles. And he said he had a nice collection of turtles and I wanted to see it, simply to see how it was. But it was not there. . . . So when I came back home I said "OK, I'll take up collecting turtles." So now I collect turtles, like Harrisson did.

"I could never decide if he was a goody or a baddie," reflected Nic Hill, Tom's English godson's brother, unconsciously reverting to the vocabulary he would have used in the days when he had known Tom best, when Tom had taken him for an unforgettable ride with a giant panda. It is a question that deserves examination.

If one listened only to the gossip of old Sarawak hands, one could easily conclude that Tom was a "baddie." As one of his friends remarked to me in 1995, all of Tom's admirers acknowledge his faults, but few of his detractors concede that he had virtues. One of the few who does is a Malay, Datuk Amar Abang Yusuf Puteh. Yusuf Puteh, who held high office in Sarawak after Tom retired, remembers and still resents that Tom had "little to do with the local intellectuals," aside from those on his own staff or those working in his research areas. He blames the snub on a mixture of arrogance and jealousy on Tom's part. "As a person, there were a lot of minuses about Tom. And with the expats, that was where he [most] showed his arrogance. He would even chase a Head of Department from Talang-Talang." Nonetheless, Yusef Puteh says that "As regards Tom's contribution to Sarawak, I would without hesitation see him as a big plus. Nobody else would have done what he did in his day, in a singlet and shorts and no shoes. He was a pioneer, without all the facilities and amenities that they have now. . . ."

Alastair Morrison, whose great dislike of Tom somewhat distorts his otherwise gentle memoir of Sarawak's colonial era (*Fair Land Sarawak*), is like

Yusuf Puteh, nonetheless willing to admit that Tom did some things of value. Because of this, many people regard his assessment of Tom in that memoir as the best and the fairest to appear in print. Morrison describes Tom as "an extraordinarily gifted, imaginative, wayward egocentric who seemed to take perverse pleasure in misusing or failing to use to the full his great endowment of talent. His life seemed to be devoted very largely to flouting the elementary disciplines and restraints which form the basis of civilized life and good scholarship." He goes on at some length, conscientiously trying to weigh Tom's worth, and ends with the statement that "Not all his deeds, however, were evil. He did some good in his own way and despite the many unpleasant episodes with which he was associated, Sarawak would have been a duller and poorer place without him."

Drawing on many of the same facts but on others as well, I have come to a rather different assessment than has Morrison. My main conclusion is that Tom was a strong force for good in an almost countless variety of fields. Certainly he would have been a stronger force for good if he had been better able to control his temper. Had he not made the enemies that blocked his return to Sarawak, does anyone seriously believe we would still be waiting to learn how old the Niah Deep Skull is? And almost certainly, if he had been better trained for some of his work, archaeology and anthropology, especially, his achievements might have been more readily accepted by the world of science. But most of the work would never have been done at all without his curiosity, energy, and drive, not to mention his skill as a publicist and fund raiser. The guano diggers would have carried away Sarawak's prehistory, and the missionaries and the transistor radios would have wiped out the traces of the upland cultures he so lovingly recorded before they all but disappeared.

Tom is accused of having kept out experts who would have done the work better. But look around Southeast Asia, in places where he was not present and thus was unable to prevent good work being done by others, and compare it with what was done while Tom ruled the roost in Sarawak. I think the facts show that Sarawak's contributions to anthropology and archaeology (to name merely the two most deprecated of Tom's areas of interest) stand up well. Indonesia might have had better anthropologists and Thailand better archaeologists, but nowhere was so much good work done in both of those fields simultaneously as in little Sarawak before 1968. The reason is simple: Sarawak had Tom.

Bishop Galvin, whom Tom encouraged to write up what he learned about the people of the Baram River valley, was asked to assess Tom in 1976, shortly after Tom's death. Galvin asserted that Tom's "place is shoulder to shoulder with Wallace" and the other great naturalists of Borneo's heroic age. The bishop, who had spent many years in Sarawak, claimed that "To the ordinary people of Sarawak [Tom] was a giant, not a goblin; someone from outer space but not an ogre."

Tom's character was extremely complex with many dark sides. He was, for example, an appalling husband and father. Yet he also often showed a genuinely caring interest in people individually and in society at large and a high courage and enthusiasm many people, including the author, found life-enhancing.

Professor Stanley O'Connor, a colleague and a close friend during Tom's last ten years, captures the excitement of being in Tom's presence. He recalls traveling with him in 1966, during the time the two of them were doing research on the iron industry in the Sarawak River delta:

> On one of those trips [in the delta] Tom insisted that we go ashore at a charcoal burner's post several miles above Santubong. By then it was evident that charcoal was the fuel for the ancient iron hearths at Santubong, and it was typical of his approach to recovering archaeological material that he should interpolate it into the lived world of the present. As we stood in the cool domed oven in a clearing on the river bank, Tom's conversation turned through the growth pattern of mangrove trees, the price of charcoal, the movements and values of Malay wood gatherers, the pig and coconut raising of the Chinese owners, the fragrance of food cooking over charcoal in Kuching, the use of palm fronds for sails over the firewood boats. And, then shifting slightly but without perceptible break, back down into the deep trenches where the charcoal mixed with iron slag and Chinese stoneware sherds from the Sung dynasty. It was rather like taking up residence in the shifting, transparent planes and interpenetrating space of a cubist painting.

Having had a word on Tom from so many people, let us give him a last word of his own. Three months before he died, preparing notes for his autobiography, Tom scribbled on a card a short list of "Words I Hate." Two of the words he hated were "*Obvious*—nothing is" and "*Vulgar*—everything should be". He did not leave a card to show what words he loved the most, but one of them surely must have been "*Alive.*"

# Persons Interviewed and/or Corresponded With

Many of the people in the following list helped me in many ways, providing me with material I would never have found otherwise, introducing me to other informants, and encouraging me during the long struggle to write the book and find a publisher:

the late Sir Anthony Abell, KCMG

Haji Abdul Rahim bin Haji Ahmad

Mr. and Mrs. Freddie Abun Tadam

Sally Adams

Dr. Paul Addison

Prof. Michael R. Allen

Dr. George Appell

The Honorable David Astor

Sir David Attenborough, CH, FRS

Gilbert Baker

James Barclay

Mr. and Mrs. Geoffrey T. Barnes, CBE

Prof. Emeritus J. A. Barnes

Keith Barrie

Venice Barry

Mrs. Paul Bartram

Josephine Batterham

Dr. Stanley Bedlington

Grace Bell

Kenneth Bell

Dr. Peter Bellwood

Sgt. Ray Bennett, AIF

A. Bertheux-Graatsma

Roland Bewsher

R. J. Blair

Pamela Faulkner Boler

Lord (Asa) Briggs

Dr. Richard and Dr. Shelagh Brooks

Prof. Eberhard F. Brünig

Dr. Ron Brunton

the late John Buchan, the second Lord Tweedsmuir

Dr. Angus Calder

Tom Capin

Lucas Chin

Michael Chong

John D. Clayton

Prof. Georges Condominas

Margaret Corlette-Theuil

Ronald Corlette-Theuil

Prof. Emeritus E. J. H. Corner, FRS

Lt. Col. G. B. Courtney, MBE, MC, AIF

Gervase Cowell

The Earl of Cranbrook

Barbara I. Crewe

Prof. Bernard Crick

Lt. Col. J. P. Cross, OBE

Jonathan Darrah

Madeleine Daubeny

Natalie Davenport

Roger Davenport

Lord Deedes

the late Michael Denison

Reece Discombe

Ronald Dunn

Susi Dunsmore

H. H. Edmeades

Major Jon Edwardes, GM, MBE

Lady William Empson

Leonard England

Mary Fedden Trevelyan

Prof. Sir Raymond Firth

Ruth Fisher

Richard Fitter

Baroness Ludmilla Forani-Rhein

Gordon Forbes

Diana Forrest

Tessa Fowler

Prof. Emeritus Derek Freeman

the late S. James Fulton

B. C. Gane, CMG, OBE

Margaret Gardiner, MBE

Peter Gathercole, Fellow of Darwin
     College, Emeritus

Isobel Gidley

Dr. Ian Glover

Robert Goh

Prof. Jack Golson

R. John Graham

Dulcie Gray, CBE

Capt. G. R. Gribble

Dr. Colin Grove

Prof. Jean Guiart

Neville S. Haile, M.A., D.Phil., D.Sc.,
     FGA, FGS, and Mrs. Haile

Prof. Terry Harrison

Dr. Barbara Harrisson

Celia Harrisson

Maxwell Barr Harrisson

Mr. and Mrs. Peter Harrisson

Ralph Harrisson

the late William D. Harrisson

the late Air Marshal Sir Christopher
     Hartley, (Ret.), KCB

Baron Arthur Haulot

the late Sgt. John D. "Stroke" Hayes,
     MM AIF

O. G. Haydock-Wilson

Prof. Emeritus John R. Hendrickson

Driver Philip Henry, MID AIF

Prof. R. H. Hickling

Lady Anne Hill

Heywood Hill

Nicolas Hill

Prof. Sir Harry Hinsley

P. A. D. Hollom

the late Dr. Dirk Albert Hooijer

John Hope

the late Donald Horsnell and Mrs.
     Horsnell

Anthony Howard

The Right Reverend Peter Howes

Kirk Huffman

Col. Daniel Illerich, BEM, C of G (VN),
     USAF (Ret.)

Dr. Robert F. Inger

Dr. Tom Jeffery

Dr. Margaret A. Jolly

Tuton Kaboy

Prof. and Mrs. George McT. Kahin

Pengiran Karim Pg. Osman

Dr. Peter Kedit

Prof. Kenneth A.R. Kennedy

Suzie Kitto

Dr. Daniel Kok

John Krigbaum

Mr. and Mrs. David Labang

the late Lian Labang

Prof. and Mrs. Michael Leigh

Robert Lian

The Honorable Dato Paduka LIM
  Jock Seng

WO II Bob Long, MID AIF

Dr. Jeremy MacClancy

T. H. Manning

the late Jane Marshall

the late F. W. Marten, CMG, MC, and
  Mrs. Marten

Yang Mulia Awang Haji Matussin bin
  Omar

David McClintock

Col. Neil McIntosh

WO I Colin McPherson, MM psc AIF

Marjorie Merchant de Collingwood

The Reverend Dr. J. Graham Miller

Celia Richardson Milne

Celia Fremlin Goller Minchin

the late Naomi Mitchison

Ursula Darwin Trevelyan Mommens

Eine Moore

Desmond John Morris

Mr. and Mrs. Richard Morris

the late Dr. Stephen Morris

Datuk Alastair Morrison

Mr. and Mrs. Sidi Munan-Oettli

Dr. Rodney Needham, Fellow of All
  Souls, Emeritus

John Nelson

E. M. Nicholson, CB, CVO

The Reverend Basil R. C. Nottage

Prof. Stanley J. O'Connor

Betty O'Dwyer

Carew O'Dwyer

Dr. OEY Giok Po

Tan Sri Datuk ONG Kee Hui

Henry Ong

Ramsay Ong

Dr. Mary Patterson

Dr. Michael Pietrusewsky

Dato' John Pike, CBE, PNBS,
  and Datin Pike

Prof. Nicholas Polunin, CBE, M.A.
  D.Sc., D.Phil.

Ambassador Robert Pringle

Dr. Julian J. Putkowski

Dr. Allen Rabinowitz

Patricia Regis

Sallie Rée

A. J. N. Richards

Prof. Emeritus Paul Richards

David Richardson

The Honorable Datuk Robert Jacob
  and Datin Garnette Ridu

Dr. César A. Rios

Prof. Margaret Rodman

Prof. William Rodman

Prof. Jérôme Rousseau

The Honorable Sir Steven Runciman

Joyce Rushen

Dr. G. H. W. Rylands, CH, CBE, M.A.

the late Sgt. Fred Sanderson, DCM AIF

Mr. and Mrs. Peter Scanlon

Dr. George B. Schaller

the late Lord (Eddie) Shackleton

P. M. Dato Paduka Pengiran Shariffuddin

the late Prof. Lauristan Sharp

the late Dato' D. A. T. Shaw and Datin Shaw

the late Tan Sri Dato' Mubin Sheppard

Dorothy Sheridan

Dr. Gale Sieveking

Patrick Slocock

Col. I. F. "Tankie" Smith

the late B. E. Smythies

P. L. D. Sochon

Prof. Emeritus Wilhelm G. Solheim II

The Reverend Hudson Southwell

Humphrey Spender

Prof. Nick Stanley

Mr. and Mrs. Geoffrey Stephens

Prof. Brian Street

Prof. Guy Stresser-Péan

Dr. Chris Stringer

Mrs. P. M. Synge

Datuk Amar Laila Taib

Mollie Tarrant

The Reverend Ian Taylor, BD

Pierre Theuil

Dato' Peter Tinggom

Prof. Robert Tonkinson

R. C. Trebilcock, M.A.

WO II Jack Tredrea, MM AIF

Dr. Carl Trocki

Dr. Darrell Tryon

the late Michael Tweedie

M. le Comte William Ugeux

Mr. and Mrs. Ian Urquhart

Prof. B. Vandermeersch

Sir Alexander Waddell

Lt. Rowan E. Waddy, AIF

Dr. Karl Waldebäck

Gen. Sir Walter Walker, KCB, CBE, DSO++

Lindsay Wall

Dr. David Walsh

Gillian Webster

Jeff Westley

Dr. and Mrs. G. E. Wilford

Darvall K. Wilkins, OBE

Charmian Woodfield

Col. John Woodhouse

Keith Woodward, OBE

Brian Wormald

the late Lord (Woodrow) Wyatt

Margaret Young

Dr. Michael Young

Datuk Amar Abang Yusuf Puteh and Datin Rugayah

Philip Ziegler, CVO

the late Lord (Solly) Zuckerman

Prof. Zuraina Majid

# Notes and Sources

To avoid interrupting the main text with references, and to keep the references at the end of the book manageable, I have used a simplified system of citation. The following paragraph describes the most important sources, published and unpublished, for the biography as a whole. Additional key sources are included by part or chapter, as appropriate. Full bibliographical information is given the first time a source is cited; thereafter, I refer to it in a shortened form. Individual notes are keyed to phrases and pages in the main text. In general, if no note is given, the person or work mentioned in the text is my source and the information is taken directly from that person's correspondence with me, from an interview I had with that person, or from the work mentioned. Almost all of the interviews were taped and transcribed by me. Unless otherwise noted, all letters and interviews date between 1986 and 1996.

My main sources were hundreds of scribbled, miscellaneous notes (at the Mass-Observation Archive, University of Sussex Library, Brighton, used with the kind permission of the Trustees of the Mass-Observation Archive) that Tom wrote in the mid 1970s for his projected autobiography, tentatively titled *Was I That Man?* These notes provide a very rough schema and, more important, his opinions on many things and people, including himself. Next in usefulness were the Harrisson papers at the Australian War Memorial Library in Canberra (AWM 3 DRL 6502, AWM File No. 419/35/25). The most important published source is Tom's book, *World Within* (London: Cresset, 1959, and Toronto: Ambassador, 1959; Singapore: Oxford in Asia paperback, Oxford University Press, 1990); followed by Timothy Green's profile of Tom in *The Adventurers: Four Profiles of Contemporary Travellers* (London: Michael Joseph, 1970), published also as *The Restless Spirit* (New York: Walker, 1970); and Lionel Birch's interview of Tom in "Mass-Observer, Observed," *Daily Telegraph Magazine* 493 (April 19, 1974): 22–25. Also helpful were an interview Tom gave Stewart Wavell, August 17, 1960, on the BBC's *People Today*; the Harrisson papers at the Malaysian National Archive in Kuala Lumpur (SP.8) and Tom's letters, memoranda, and a diary included among the Jock Marshall papers (MS 7132) in the National Library of Australia (located at the Australian Science Archive Project at the University of Melbourne's Department of the History and Philosophy of Science); and a manuscript by Angus Calder, given to me by the author, entitled "The Mass-Observers 1937–1949." Tom's lifelong correspondence with the former Lord Medway, now Lord Cranbrook (in his possession), Mary Adams (at the M-O Archive), Mr. Hinks of the Royal Geographical Society (RGS)(quoted by permission of the Royal Geographical Society with The Institute of British Geographers), Lord Bernstein (Granada Headquarters, London), and Lord Zuckerman (Zuckerman Archive, University of East Anglia) have been used, and almost everything Tom wrote has autobiographical content. David Alan Miller's *A Checklist of the Works of Tom Harrisson (1911–1976)* (Williamsburg, Virginia: Borneo Research Council Special Publication, June 1978), includes most of Tom's publications. Data from Barbara Harrisson, Gillian Webster, and the late Bill Harrisson were essential for Tom's family history and many other matters.

Throughout the following notes, Tom as author is listed as THH, Mass-Observation is abbreviated as M-O, and *The Times*, unless otherwise indicated, is the London newspaper.

## Prologue

PAGE

1    *Who's Who 1975* (London: A. and C. Black, 1975).

1    Tom's birth certificate: It shows "Tom [not Thomas] Harnett Harrisson," born *April* 26, 1911, in Buenos Aires, but a telegram of *September* 27, 1911, sent to his maternal grandfather reports Tom's birth as having taken place the day before, leading to a Hampshire newspaper's birth announcement that week.

2    "a self-pitiless account": THH notes, M-O Archive.

2    BBC: British Broadcasting Company.

2    DSO: Distinguished Service Order.

3    "sent down from Oxford": In conversation with me.

4    "the most remarkable man": Lord Shackleton's letter to me, July 14, 1992.

### PART ONE: Early Days, 1911–1933

#### 1. The View from Mount Dulit

7    "two of the conscious impulses": THH, *World Within*, p. 154.

7    "intellectual" and "tough": Birch, "Mass Observer, Observed," p. 24.

7–8   "saw a party going on . . .": Birch, "Mass Observer, Observed," p. 24.

8    Davenport: Quotations come from Constantine FitzGibbon's introduction in Dylan Thomas and John Davenport, *The Death of the King's Canary* (London: Penguin Books, 1978); Julian Trevelyan, *Indigo Days* (London: Macgibbon and Kee, 1957), p. 17; Davenport's obituary in *The Times* (June 28, 1966); and Ian Parsons' letter in *The Times* (July 2, 1966).

| | |
|---|---|
| 8 | "very unimpressive young man": Paul Richards, recalling to me meeting Tom for the first time in 1930. |
| 8 | Lowry: Gordon Bowker, *Pursued by Furies* (London: HarperCollins, 1993). |
| 8 | "pseudo-hyper male" and "sort of rough": Letter from THH to Dr. Muriel Bradbrook, 1974, shown to me by Gordon Bowker. |
| 8–9 | Tom's mother: Quotations regarding her come from THH notes, M-O Archive. |
| 9 | CMG: Commander of the Order of St. Michael and St. George. |
| 9–18 | Tom's childhood: Information comes from Tom's notes, M-O Archive, including Tom's interview of and correspondence with his nanny, "Kitty" Asbury; and my interviews of Bill Harrisson and Gillian Webster. His father's military record comes from the (British) Ministry of Defense. |
| 10 | "These holidays, among assorted Danes": Green, *The Adventurers*, p. 103. |
| 10 | A young Englishman aboard: (Later the Reverend) R. G. Heawood, whose letters home and memoir, "An Argentine Interlude" (M-O Archive) are also the source of the description of the sea and rail trip to Concordia. |
| 11 | "their shocking accent" and "the native Spanish tongue": A. Graham-Yooll, *The Forgotten Colony* (London: Hutchinson, 1981), pp. 20–28. |
| 11 | "companion then": THH in Green, *The Adventurers*, p. 103. |
| 12 | The account of the owl: THH, "Tameness in Birds," *The Listener* (October 7, 1936): 679–680. |
| 12 | "I think being born": Green, *The Adventurers*, p. 104. |
| 13 | "Kitter's criminals": My interview of the late Lord "Eddie" Shackleton. |
| 13 | "Kitter was a splendid man": Green, *The Adventurers*, p. 104. |
| 13 | "The speed at which": THH, "Notes on Class Consciousness and Class Unconsciousness," *The Sociological Review* XXXIV, 3–4 (July–Oct. 1942): 152. |
| 13 | "who was rather thin": Interview of Tom Manning, a Harrow friend of Tom's. |
| 13–14 | "When you say Harrow" and "I have never been able": THH, *Letter to Oxford* (Wyck, Gloucestershire: Reynold Bray, The Hate Press, 1933), pp. 27–29. |
| 14 | "I loved him a bit": Interview of a Harrow schoolmate I choose to keep anonymous. |
| 14 | "blond, acne,": Green, *The Adventurers*, p. 104. |
| 14 | "He was allowed": Green, *The Adventurers*, p. 104. |
| 14–15 | "hideous murderous place": Green, *The Adventurers*, p. 104. |
| 15 | "a sort of a cross": Letter from Ronald Dunn, March 14, 1993. |
| 15 | "partially-arrested development": Alastair Morrison, *Fair Land Sarawak* (Ithaca: Cornell Southeast Asia Program, 1993), p. 98. |

15    "What is most telling": Jeremy Paxman's review of P. Craig, ed., *The Oxford Book of Schooldays*, *Sunday Times* (January 23, 1994).

16    "a somewhat strange-looking": Max Nicholson's notes for the memorial meeting for Tom at the Royal Society for the Arts, March 17, 1976, in Nicholson's possession.

16    "encouraging adventurous": "Founding of the Argonauts Travel Club at Harrow School," *The Times* (November 26, 1929): 21.

16–17  great crested grebe census: THH and P. A. D. Hollom, "The Great Crested Grebe Enquiry, 1931," *British Birds* XXVI, 3–6 (Aug.–Nov. 1932) and my interview of Mr. Hollom.

18    "Had lunch with Weatherby": THH notebook at the Edward Grey Institute, Oxford.

## 2. Arctic Adventures

19    Lapland Expedition: Oxford University Exploration Club, *Third Annual Report 1930–1931*.

19    "greatly helped me": THH, *World Within*, p. 156.

20    "a great contempt" and "one-fiftieth": THH, ed., *Borneo Jungle* (London: Lindsay Drummond, 1938; Singapore: Oxford University Press, 1988), p. 14.

20    "hearties": Interview of Bill Harrisson.

20    "richest time": C. P. Snow, "Chemistry," in H. D. Wright, ed., *Cambridge University Studies 1933* (London: Nicholson and Watson, 1933). In the natural sciences, however, the teaching was pedestrian, according to famous ornithologist David Lack and Oxford Professor of Tropical Botany, J. H. Corner.

21    "tough," "intellectual," and "were two different things": Birch, "Mass-Observer, Observed," p. 24.

21–22  St. Kilda expedition: John Buchan, Second Lord Tweedsmuir, *Always a Countryman* (London: Robt. Hale, 1953), pp. 135–142; and 1993 letters to me from the late Lord Tweedsmuir.

22    "used to go stunting": Green, *The Adventurers*, p. 106.

22    "I once reached" and "Everybody ought to get drunk": THH, *Letter to Oxford*, pp. 70–71.

23    "set upon by a gang": Bowker, *Pursued by Furies*, p. 116.

23    "What's Wrong with Our Colleges: Pembroke, the Public School" by a Pembroke man, *Varsity* (Cambridge) (October 31, 1931).

23    "After a while Forman": Green, *The Adventurers*, p. 106.

23–24  Tom and the General: Interviews of brother Bill Harrisson and cousin Gillian Webster.

| | |
|---|---|
| 24 | Reynold Bray: Letters from Lord Tweedsmuir and Prof. N. Polunin. |
| 25 | "beginning to rebel": Naomi Mitchison, *You May Well Ask* (London: Gollancz, 1979), p. 201. |
| 25 | "It's the cheapest way": Quoted by Lord Zuckerman in my interview of him. |
| 25–26 | Financing the Borneo expedition: THH, *Borneo Jungle*, p. 19, and *Oxford University Exploration Club, Fifth Annual Report, 1932–1933*. Stories still circulate that Tom and Eddie's drinking brought the expedition heavily into debt, but the OUEC report (not written by Tom) attests otherwise. |
| 26 | "head boy of Eton": THH, *Borneo Jungle*, p. 19. Eton, however, has no single head boy. The small group of "scholars" have their own head, but the thousand other students, called Oppidans, have as their "captain" the one among them with the highest academic record. Cub Hartley was captain of the Oppidans. |
| 26 | KCB: Knight Commander of the Order of the Bath. |
| 27 | "Despite the speed": Nicholson, at Royal Society for the Arts memorial meeting for Tom, March 17, 1976. |
| 27 | "I have to advertise": Quoted in a letter to me from Ronald Dunn, March 14, 1993. |
| 27 | Lowry regarding Tom: A. Ackerley and L. Clipper, *A Companion to "Under the Volcano"* (Vancouver: University of British Columbia, 1984). |

## 3. Borneo, 1932

The chief unpublished sources for this chapter are the expedition diary, June 17, 1932, to January 13, 1933, kept by Paul W. Richards, who later became professor of botany at The University of Wales, Bangor, and interviews of the late Lord Shackleton, the late Sir Charles Hartley, the late Professor Paul Richards, Madeleine Daubeny, Dulcie Gray, and the late Michael Denison. The published sources are THH, *World Within*; various writers' contributions to *Borneo Jungle*; THH, "The Oxford University Expedition to Sarawak, 1932," *Geographical Journal (GJ)* LXXXII, 5 (November 1933); *Sarawak Papers: Scientific Results of the Oxford University Expedition to Sarawak (Borneo) in 1932* (Oxford: Oxford University Press, 1952); and THH, *Letter to Oxford*.

| | |
|---|---|
| 29 | "Mr. Banks and I": THH, *World Within*, p. 153. |
| 29 | "If you don't want a lot": THH, *Borneo Jungle*, p. 1. |
| 30 | "I found in these people": THH, *World Within*, p. 154. |
| 31 | "Bringing back your head": THH, *Borneo Jungle*, p. 27. |
| 31 | "It is generally said": THH, *Borneo Jungle*, p. 40. |
| 32 | "Winding slowly up": THH, quoting from his notes, *Borneo Jungle*, p. 41. |
| 33 | "broad noses": John Ford, "Borak and Belles, "in THH, *Borneo Jungle*, p. 68. |

| | |
|---|---|
| 33 | "apart from whatever passes": Ford, "Borak and Belles," p. 68. |
| 33 | "the European is . . . treated": THH, "The Oxford University Expedition to Sarawak, 1932: A paper read at the Evening Meeting of the Society on 12 June 1933," *GJ*, LXXXII, 5 (November 1933): 388. |
| 33 | "quietly budgeted:" THH, *Borneo Jungle*, p. 43. |
| 33 | "shows signs of wilting": Ford, "Borak and Belles," p. 71. |
| 33 | "No sooner had we arrived" and "for all these": Ford, "Borak and Belles," p. 65. |
| 34 | "nucleus of fire": THH, *Borneo Jungle*, p. 43. |
| 34 | "wanted us to sit down": THH, *Borneo Jungle*, pp. 45–46. |
| 35 | "three-day celebration": THH, "The Oxford University Expedition to Sarawak, 1932": 396. |
| 35 | "my first heterosexual experience": THH, *Letter to Oxford*, p. 25. |
| 35–36 | "absolutely no manners": Interview of Madeleine Daubeny. |
| 36 | "Every bit as important": Quoted in THH, *World Within*, p. 153. |
| 36 | "People like me": THH, *World Within*, p. 153. |
| 36 | "I fell for Sarawak": THH, *World Within*, p. 154. |
| 37 | "anglo-snobs": THH, *Letter to Oxford*, p. 85. |
| 37 | Dulcie was struck: Interview of Dulcie Gray. |

### 4. Letter to Oxford

The main published source is THH, *Letter to Oxford*.

| | |
|---|---|
| 38 | *The Times* (October 4, 1932). |
| 39 | "rather liked the Liberal Party's": THH letter to E. M. Nicholson in 1930, quoted by Nicholson in his remarks at the Royal Society of Arts meeting, March 17, 1976. |
| 40–41 | Zita: Anthony Howard, *Crossman: The Pursuit of Power* (London: Pimlico, 1991). |
| 41 | "the love of his life": Interview of Gillian Webster. |
| 41 | "it raised a considerable storm,": Naomi Mitchison, *You May Well Ask* (London: Gollancz, 1979), p. 201. |
| 41 | "The principle involved": THH letter to Hinks, June 17, 1933 (RGS, Corr. Block, 1931–1940, Harrisson, T.). (Others of Tom's letters to Hinks quoted in this book come from this same collection at the RGS Library in London.) |
| 41 | This talk: THH, "The Oxford University Expedition to Sarawak, 1932," *GJ* LXXXII, 5 (November 1933): 1, 1a, 388–410. |
| 41 | paint his toenails: Mitchison, *You May Well Ask*, p. 202. The event was also witnessed by a horrified relative of Dr. Stephen Morris, who mentioned it to me. |

**PART TWO: In the South Pacific, 1933–1935**

In addition to interviews and/or letters of people mentioned in the list of Persons Interviewed and/or Corresponded With and in earlier notes, I used documents from the Western Pacific Archive, Records Branch of the Foreign and Commonwealth Office, Hanslope Park, England. The main published sources are Tom's books, *Savage Civilisation* (London: Gollancz and Left Book Club, 1937) and, as *Savage Civilization* (New York: Knopf, 1937), and *Living Among Cannibals* (London: Harrap, 1943 and New York: AMS Press, 1989); Baker's talks (with Zita's comments) before the RGS, published in the *Geographical Journal* (*GJ*) LXXIII, 4 (April 1929) and LXXXV, 3 (March 1935); Tom's three articles on the New Hebrides for the *GJ* LXXXVIII (Aug., Sept., and Oct. 1936); and A. J. Marshall, *The Black Musketeers* (London: Heinemann, 1937). John Baker's manuscript diary is used with Gilbert Baker's permission. All letters cited from Tom to Naomi were lent by Naomi Mitchison, while all those from Zita to Naomi are thanks to Venice Barry.

### 5. Zita and Santo

The main published sources are THH, *Savage Civilisation*; Tom's and Baker's articles on the New Hebrides in the *GJ*; B. and S. Fahnestock, *Stars to Windward* (London: Hale, 1939); and Templeton Crocker, *The Cruise of the Zaca* (New York: Harper, 1933)

48    "For several days": THH, *Savage Civilisation*, p. 372.

48    "had sworn": THH, *Savage Civilisation*, p. 372.

48    "It would take them": THH, *Savage Civilisation*, p. 373.

48    "daughter and wife and pigs": THH, *Savage Civilisation*, p. 373.

49    "wildest, blackest": B. and S. Fahnestock, *Stars to Windward*, p. 203.

49    "nature's gentlemen" and "ugly, ill-developed": J. R. Baker, "Espiritu Santo," *GJ* LXXXV, 3 (March 1935): 211.

49    "Cook had a genius": THH, *Savage Civilisation*, p. 116.

49    "I saw by the path": THH, *Savage Civilisation*, p. 373.

49    Mountain starling: See E. M. Nicholson and Lord Medway, "Tom Harrisson," *The Ibis: Journal of the British Ornithologists' Union* CXVIII (1976): 597.

50    "had blown": Baker, "Espiritu Santo," p. 216.

50–51    "there was nothing else": THH, *Savage Civilisation*, p. 374.

53    "continual danger of being swept away": Baker, "Espiritu Santo," p. 219.

55    When I first arrived: Zita Baker's comments are published in J. R. Baker, "Espiritu Santo," pp. 230–232.

## 6. Gaua

Unless otherwise indicated in the text, Zita's comments come from her "Marooned on an Island," *The Listener* (March 1936): 486–487, and her statements to the RGS included in J. R. Baker: "Espiritu Santo," *GJ* LXXXV, 3 (March 1935): 230–232. John Baker's comments come from his "Espiritu Santo," pp. 14–16, 219–220.

## 7. Jock Comes to Santo

The chief published source, aside from *Savage Civilisation* and Tom's articles for the *GJ* (1936), is Jock's book, *The Black Musketeers*. Unless otherwise indicated, all quotes from Jock come from this book. Unpublished sources are interviews of Jock's late widow, Jane Marshall; letters from Tom to Jock; and Tom's diary for March 1–23, 1934, labelled "Diary No. II." (Diary No. I has not surfaced and may be one he wrote at age fourteen.) Unless otherwise noted, all quotations from Tom in this chapter come from this diary. The diary and all letters between Tom and Jock and to Jock from Zita, John Baker, and others are in the Marshall papers (MS 7132) in the National Library of Australia.

62     The quoted remarks about Jock come from his obituary in Peter Bowers, ed., *DATA* (July 21, 1967), in the Marshall papers at the National Library of Australia.

65     "grew to love the old gramophone": Marshall, *Black Musketeers*, p. 264.

67     "not statistically serious" and "the most important property": THH, "Living in Espiritu Santo," *GJ* LXXXVIII, 3 (September 1936): 258.

69     "Watch out": Interview of Kirk Huffman.

71     "to pick a fight": Interview of Professor Wilhelm G. Solheim II.

71–72   "a few days of hurricane": THH, *Savage Civilisation*, p. 375.

72     "would never do to give offence": THH, *Savage Civilisation*, p. 384.

72     "The great chief": THH, *Savage Civilisation*, p. 385.

75     "I do not plan to leave": THH letter to Hinks, July 25, 1934 (RGS, Corr. Block 1931–1940, Harrisson, T.).

## 8. Living among Cannibals

Main sources are memos and letters that Tom wrote to Jock, which are now among the Jock Marshall papers, National Library of Australia; THH, *Living Among Cannibals*; THH, *Savage Civilisation*; Colin Simpson, *Islands of Men* (Sydney: Angus and Robertson, 1955); A. B. Deacon, *Malekula: A Vanishing People* (London: Routledge, 1934); THH, "Living with the People of Malekula," *GJ* LXXXVIII, 2 (August 1936): 7, 98–127; and Evelyn Cheesman, *Things Worth While* (London: Readers Union, 1958).

76    "I was wearing": THH, *Living Among Cannibals*, p. 21.

76    "had no gun": THH, *Living Among Cannibals*, p. 21.

77    "might be a Bolshevik": Letter to me from Margaret Corlette Theuil, February 21, 1993.

79    "to behold this man": Letter from Margaret Corlette Theuil, February 21, 1993.

79    "White and thin": Colin Simpson, *Islands of Men* (Sydney: Angus & Robertson, 1955), p. 114.

79    "famously" and "they had both": Letter from Margaret Corlette Theuil, February 21, 1993.

80    cannibalism and Arens' theory: Since completing my research, I have learned of a serious book by a careful researcher who interviewed Big Nambas informants that would appear to contradict Arens: Michael Krieger, *Conversations with Cannibals: The End of the Old South Pacific* (Hopewell, New Jersey: Ecco Press, 1994), ISBN 0-88001-360-5.

80–81    "When a native's face goes sort of grey": THH, *Savage Civilisation*, pp. 405–406.

81    "the technique of war": THH, *Savage Civilisation*, p. 403.

81–82    "When they saw a white leg": THH, *Savage Civilisation*, p. 417.

82    "These little folk": THH, *Savage Civilisation*, p. 417.

82    "a trial of character": THH, *Savage Civilisation*, p. 409.

82    "acting on people": W. H. R. Rivers, writing in 1921, quoted in THH, *Savage Civilization*, p. 270.

82–83    Tom's views on depopulation: THH, *Savage Civilization*, pp. 269–274. John Baker's 1927 census had led Baker to doubt the Rivers thesis, but Tom's censuses, being later and covering a larger portion of the New Hebrides, greatly strengthened the body of anti-Rivers evidence.

83    Tenmaru moved to the coast in the 1940s, according to a personal communication from Kirk Huffman.

83    Ringapat's name is properly Arnhapat, according to Kirk Huffman.

84    "Most of the time" and "until the conditions": THH, "Living with the People of Malekula," *GJ* LXXXVIII, 2 (August 1936): 112–113.

84    Layard's comments appear after Tom's talk published as "Living with the People of Malekula," *GJ* LXXXVIII, 2 (August 1936): 125–127.

84–85    kava: THH, *Savage Civilization*, pp. 275–277.

85    no hangover: But long-time kava drinkers are given to bouts of depression, according to my interview of anthropologist Dr. Michael Young.

85    He did not do it for a year: Tom was not the only researcher to exaggerate the length of his fieldwork. Malinowski, the inventor of modern fieldwork methods, allowed people to think that he had spent four years in the

Trobriand Islands, when in fact he had spent under twenty months there, less than half the time claimed. See Michael Young, "A Myth Exposed," *The Asia-Pacific Magazine* (Canberra) (June 1996): 44–48.

86     "After some hours": THH, *Savage Civilization*, pp. 403–404.

86–87     sex with Big Nambas women: See Corlette's letters in the *Pacific Island Monthly*, June 23, 1937 and February 21, 1938. Corlette's comments on this point are confirmed by Kirk Huffman.

## 9. On His Majesty's Service

The chief unpublished sources are papers located by Will Stober at the Western Pacific Archive, Records Branch, Foreign and Commonwealth Office, Hanslope Park, England (especially WPHC 1643/1935 and, for the Siller story, file MP 52/1935); Tom's and Zita's correspondence with Jock Marshall (Jock Marshall papers, National Library of Australia); the February 21, 1993, letter to me from Margaret Corlette Theuil; and interviews of Dr. Margaret Jolly, Dr. Mary Patterson, Dr. Michael Young, Kirk Huffman, and Darvall Wilkins, British Agent for Malekula for nineteen years. The main published sources are THH, *Savage Civilisation*; THH, *World Within*; and A. J. Marshall, *The Black Musketeers*.

88     He had written harriedly: Letter from E. Corlette to Mr. Adams, January 10, 1935, now at the Western Pacific Archive, Hanslope Park.

89–90     a "Tom" document: the report is in the Western Pacific High Commission's files, No. 1643, 1935, Western Pacific Archive, with a note from the secretary of state for the colonies.

90     "started by scorning": THH's preface to A. J. Marshall, *The Black Musketeers*, p. xii.

91–93     Antonio Bruno Siller: THH, *Savage Civilisation*, pp. 290–297.

## 10. A Hollywood Interlude

The main published source is *Savage Civilisation*, chiefly pp. 424–432.

98     Tenmaru wedding: The version in *Savage Civilisation* (pp. 413–414) is supported in almost every detail by French eyewitness Charles Van den Broek d'Obrenan in his *Voyage de la Korrigane* (Paris: Payot, 1939), of which I have translated some parts. Nonetheless, the eminent French scholar Jean Guiart wrote to me on February 27, 1992, that Tom and Chuck Lewis had instead filmed a fake pig-killing ceremony using natives as actors and the Countess de Ganay, a *Korrigane* passenger, dancing in a grass skirt. No evidence has emerged to support Guiart's story.

101     "no fans, lights," "else the Pacific," "when that glorious place," and "I stopped there for three months": THH, *Savage Civilisation*, p. 430.

102     Tom's return from Tahiti: That the General wired Tom the fare comes from my interviews of Bill Harrisson and Gillian Webster. Tom in a letter from

Papeete to the British resident commission in Vila, November 1, 1935 (Western Pacific Archive file R6/12, 52/35) notes that he has been "ordered home" on the S.S. *Céphée*. A letter from the acting British consul, Papeete, to the British resident commissioner, Vila, November 12, 1935 (Western Pacific Archive file 52/35) confirms that Tom sailed with the *Céphée* on November 4, 1935.

102    Peregrine falcon: THH, *Savage Civilisation*, p. 431.

## PART THREE: People-Watching in Britain, 1936–1942

The main resource is the Mass-Observation Archive at the University of Sussex, its collection of Tom's personal papers, its books and files of M-O materials, and its knowledgeable archivist Dorothy Sheridan.

### 11. Tom and the Thirties

113    "If you are not born": Green, *The Adventurers*, p. 102.

114    "Dear Doug": A handwritten copy of this message by THH is in the M-O Archive.

114–115  Zita's affair with Richard Crossman: In addition to previously mentioned sources, such as Zita's and Tom's letters to Naomi Mitchison and Anthony Howard's *Crossman: The Pursuit of Power* (London: Pimlico, 1991), there are letters between Zita and Crossman (seen with the kind permission of Anne Crossman) in the Crossman Archive at the Modern Records Centre of the University of Warwick.

115    "one of the most colourful": Bookseller's blurb for Anthony Howard's *Crossman*, circa 1994.

115    Naomi, who had sympathized: Her views regarding Zita, Tom, and Crossman come from my interview of her.

116–117  Layard: His obituary by Ian Langham in *Oceania* XLV, 3 (1975): 237–239; J. W. Layard, *Stone Men of Malekula*, (London: Chatto and Windus, 1942); Margaret Gardiner, *A Scatter of Memories* (London: Free Association Books, 1988), pp. 135–144; interviews of Margaret Gardiner (in London), Kirk Huffman (in Ibiza), and Dr. Margaret Jolly (at the Australian National University, Canberra). Information on Layard's relations with Tom comes from Huffman's recollections of conversations with Layard.

117    "a physical and mental wreck": Interview of Margaret Gardiner.

117    *Christopher and his Kind* (London: Eyre Methuen, 1977).

118    "an invention in the sphere": Words of W. A. Robson (1935), cited in Asa Briggs, *The BBC: The First Fifty Years* (Oxford: Oxford University Press, 1985), p. 151.

118–119  Royal Geographical Society lecture and comments: THH, "Living with the People of Malekula," *Geographical Journal* LXXXVIII, 2 (August 1936): 7, 98–127.

119      FRS: Fellow of the Royal Society, a high honor for scholars and scientists.

119–120  Gollancz: See R. D. Edwards, *Victor Gollancz* (London: Gollancz, 1987).

120      "You are one of the few people": Quoted in S. Hodges, *Gollancz* (London: Gollancz, 1978), pp. 113–114.

## 12. Bolton

Criticisms of *Savage Civilisation* include those definitely or probably based on fact, those based on a mixture of fact and falsehood, and total fabrications, all from highly regarded sources. Probably factual are Layard's complaints of unacknowledged use of his notes by Tom; Layard noted those thefts on the endpapers of his own copy of Tom's book (now owned by Sir David Attenborough). Part fact/part falsehood are Corlette's letters published in the *Pacific Islands Monthly* (*PIM*) (June 23, 1937, and February 21, 1938). The old planter almost certainly was right in objecting to Tom's hints that he witnessed cannibal feasts, and he pointed out correctly that Tom did not spend a year living with the Big Nambas. But he also had Tom's Malekula dates wrong by an entire year and deliberately gave the false impression that Tom was not an official member of the Oxford expedition. Worst of all, he claimed that Tom never visited any Big Nambas village but the oft-visited Tenmaru, except in the company of the district agent. Corlette, judging by a January 10, 1935, letter he sent to Blandy (now in the Western Pacific Archive), knew better. Evelyn Cheesman, the British lepidopterist who had traveled throughout Malekula in the late 1920s, published a letter in the *PIM*, October 22, 1937, to state that Tom's book was a brilliant piece of work and to say it was clear from Corlette's criticisms that he was animated by "some private grudge which needs sating." Western Pacific Archive documents show District Agent Adams writing of visiting the Big Nambas area for the first time with Tom on Tom's second trip there. Tom wrote of other visits to less accessible Big Nambas villages in his letters to Jock. Current scholars (William Rodman, Kirk Huffman, Michael Young, Margaret Jolly, etc.) believe that Tom could not have described these villages so well without having spent time in them. Yet Corlette's allegations have had a long life. For example, Jean Guiart, writing to me on July 27, 1992, persisted in claiming to have learned that Tom, out of fear, never went inland to the Big Nambas area. Guiart also claimed that Tom wrote in *Savage Civilisation* about a (nonexistent) sixteen-class marriage system, but Tom never did so, in that book or elsewhere.

Recently, English anthropologist Gareth Stanton published two articles that make many points about Tom's work in the 1930s that are so close to my views that it is as if we had read each other's work, which is not the case. I learned of his articles only after completing my research and writing. The articles are "In Defense of *Savage Civilisation*: Tom Harrisson, Cultural Studies and Anthropology," in Stephen Nugent and Chris Shore, eds., *Anthropology and Cultural Studies* (London: Pluto Press, 1997), pp. 11–33, and a fuller version of the same discussion, "Ethnography, Anthropology and Cultural Studies: Links and Connections," in James Curran, David Morley, and Valerie Walkerdine, eds., *Cultural Studies and Communications* (London: Arnold Press, 1996), pp. 334–358.

121    *News Chronicle*: The following month it reviewed Raymond Firth's *We, The Tikopia*, which would become a classic of social anthropology.

121    "poor ignorant": *Times Literary Supplement* staffer E. E. Mavrogordato, reviewing *Living Among Cannibals* on July 31, 1943, p. 364.

121–122  J. Layard review of *Savage Civilisation*: *Man* II, 165–166 (August 1937): 134–135.

122    RGS critic: O. W. F. F., "*Savage Civilisation*: Book Review, *Geographical Journal* LXXXIX, 4 (April 1937).

122    Crossman letter to Zita: Early 1937, in the personal section of the Crossman Archive, Modern Records Centre, University of Warwick.

122    Dr. Michael Young's comments come from my 1992 interview of him.

122–123  "One does not know quite how": P. O'Reilly, *Hébridais* (Paris: Société des Océanistes, Musée de l'Homme, 1957), pp. 248–249, my translation.

123    Tom's letters to Jock are in the Jock Marshall papers at the National Library of Australia.

123    going to see Zita and Crossman: Their letters in the personal section of the Crossman Archive.

124    "I am working in a cotton mill": THH letter to Hinks, November 1, 1936 (RGS, Corr. Block 1931–1940, Harrisson, T.).

124    "with the shock": THH, *World Within*, p. 158.

124    Orwell: Bernard Crick, *George Orwell* (New York: Penguin Books, 1982).

125    Spain: In a note at the M-O Archive, Tom calls himself "a mugwump" about Spain.

125    suggestion of Bolton: E. Nixon, *John Hilton* (London: Allen and Unwin, 1946), pp. 258–259.

125    1937 statistics on Bolton: Jeremy Mulford's preface to Humphrey Spender's book of photographs, *Worktown People* (Bristol: Falling Wall Press, 1982), p. 10.

125    "What excited me most": THH, *World Within*, pp. 159–160.

126    "discourteous," "working physically," and "dreadful drab": THH letter to Hinks, undated, received December 12, 1936 (RGS, Corr. Block 1931–1940, Harrisson, T.).

127    "necessarily sprinkled": THH, *World Within*, p. 159.

127    "For the first discovery": THH, *World Within*, p. 159.

127    "Please do not bother": THH letter to Hinks received December 12, 1936.

### 13. Mass-Observation

Sources not listed below that were consulted for this chapter include the best book on the thirties, Julian Symons, *The Thirties: A Dream Revolved* (London: Faber and Faber, 1976); Tom Jeffery, *Mass-Observation: A Short History* (Birmingham: Centre for Contemporary Cultural Studies, stencilled occasional paper, December 1978); and Charles Madge interview transcripts by Angus Calder (March 1979) and Nick Stanley (March 23, 1978, and May 26, 1978), in the M-O Archive.

128　　　"coincidences": Jeremy MacClancy, "Brief Encounter: The Meeting, in Mass-observation, of British Surrealism and Popular Anthropology," *Journal of the Royal Anthropological Institute* (n.s.) I, 3 (1995): 456–474.

129　　　"Humphrey Jennings, who": David Gascoyne, *Journal 1936–37: Death of an Explorer* (London: Enitharmon Press, 1980), p. 10.

130　　　"*See* what people are doing": Birch, "Mass Observer, Observed," pp. 22–25.

130–131　"a sounding of the English collective unconscious": Gascoyne, *Journal 1936–37*, p. 11.

131　　　"many observed details": Neil Mercer, *Mass-Observation 1937–40*, Faculty of Economics and Social Studies Working Papers in Applied Social Research No. 16 (Manchester: University of Manchester, November 1989), p. 4.

131　　　"Even *Punch*": Bronislaw Malinowski, "A Nation-wide Intelligence Survey," p. 84, in Charles Madge and Tom Harrisson, eds., *Mass-Observation: First Year's Work* (London: Lindsay Drummond, 1938), pp. 83–121.

132　　　"Oh don't imagine": G. W. Stonier, "A Thousand Mass-Observers," *New Statesman* (October 9, 1937): 533.

132　　　"crazy idea": Letter from THH to Geoffrey Gorer cited by D. Pocock in his afterword to the 1987 paperback edition of *May the Twelfth: Mass-Observation Day-Surveys 1937 by over two hundred observers*, C. Madge and H. Jennings, eds., (London: Faber and Faber, 1987).

132　　　"what was wrong with that title": THH quoted in A. W. Hodgkinson, "Humphrey Jennings and *Mass-Observation*: A Conversation with Tom Harrisson," *Journal of the University Film Association* (Philadelphia) XXVII, 4 (Fall 1975): 31–35. See also Nick Stanley's Ph. D. thesis, "'The Extra Dimension': A Study and Assessment of the Methods Employed by Mass-Observation in its First Period 1937–40," Birmingham Polytechnic, 1981.

133　　　"no intellectual": Dorothy Sheridan and Angus Calder, eds., *Speak for Yourself: Mass-Observation Anthology 1937–1949*, paperback edition (Oxford: Oxford University Press, 1985), p. 23.

## 14. Thrice Betrayed

Chief sources for this chapter were Jock's diary, in the Jock Marshall papers at the National Library of Australia; Tom's preface to Jock's book, *The Black Musketeers* (London: Heinemann, 1937); Tom's book, *World Within*; and minutes of a 1937 meeting of the Royal Geographical Society (at the RGS Library, London).

135   "children when Tom spoke": Interview of Margaret Young, among others.

135   "alarming fervour": Anthony Howard, *Crossman: The Pursuit of Power* (London: Pimlico, 1991), pp. 62–63.

135   "huddled among mills": Jeremy Mulford's preface to Humphrey Spender, *Worktown People: Photographs from Northern England 1937–38* (Bristol: Falling Wall Press, 1982), p. 10.

136–137   He wrote Naomi: THH letter to Naomi Mitchison, undated, courtesy the late Naomi Mitchison.

## 15. M-O in Bolton

The chief published source is Tom Jeffery, *Mass-Observation: A Short History* (Birmingham: Centre for Contemporary Cultural Studies, stencilled occasional paper, University of Birmingham, December 1978). The chief unpublished source is my interview of Humphrey Spender.

138   "it was his job": Calder and Sheridan, *Speak for Yourself*, p. 39.

138   "The ugliness is so complete": J. B. Priestley, *English Journey* (London: Heinemann, 1934), p. 262.

139   "instead of being an ordinary": Woodrow Wyatt, *Into the Dangerous World* (London: Weidenfeld and Nicholson, 1952), pp. 33–35.

139   "every single feature": Interview of Humphrey Spender.

140   "for their single week's industrial holiday": THH, "The Fifty-Second Week: Impressions of Blackpool," *Geographical Magazine* (April 1938): 388.

140   "You might as well list": 1937 letter from J. R. Baker to THH, M-O Archive.

140–141   "The effect Tom had on me": Interview of H. Spender.

141   "was lean" and "Tom went out": Julian Trevelyan, *Indigo Days* (London: Macgibbon and Kee, 1957), pp. 81–102.

141   "had this peculiar gift": Letter from Henry Novy to Richard Fitter, February 3, 1976, in the M-O Archive.

142   "You needn't talk": Calder and Sheridan, *Speak for Yourself*, pp. 21–22.

142   for the first eighteen months: Jeffery, *Mass-Observation*, p. 26.

142   Zita at Blackpool: Calder and Sheridan, *Speak for Yourself*, p. 54.

143     Ursula Darwin's comments: Interview.

143     "a turmoil of activity": Angus Calder's typescript of an interview with Charles Madge in March 1979, pp. 16–17, in the M-O Archive.

143–144  Painters at Bolton: Trevelyan, *Indigo Days*; Bruce Laughton, *The Euston Road School: A Study in Objective Painting* (Aldershot: Scolar Press, 1986), pp. 113, 183–187; Julian Symons, *The Thirties: A Dream Revolved* (London: Faber and Faber, 1975), pp. 90–91.

144     "operate quite differently": T. H. Marshall, "Is Mass-Observation Moonshine?" *The Highway* (published by the Workers Education Association) XXX (December 1937): 48–50. THH's reply is on pp. 46–48 of the same issue.

145     It is a sign of how uncomfortable: Liz Stanley, *The archeology of a 1930s Mass-Observation project*, University of Manchester, Department of Sociology, Occasional Paper 27 (May 1990), p. 11.

145     *First Year's Work:* Charles Madge and Tom Harrisson, eds., *Mass-Observation: First Year's Work* (London: Lindsay Drummond, 1938) with essay by Dr. Bronislaw Malinowski, "A Nation-wide Intelligence Survey," pp. 83–121.

145–146  ambivalence: L. Stanley, *The archeology of a 1930s Mass-Observation project*, p. 40, note 1; and interviews of Madge by Nick Stanley (1978) and Angus Calder (1979), transcripts of which are in the M-O Archive.

146     "Make a parody": Malinowski, "A Nation-wide Intelligence Survey," p. 88.

146     several M-O books: Gollancz first gave advances for four books: *The Pub and the People*, by John Sommerfield and Bruce Watkin; *Politics and the Non-Voter*, by Walter Hood and Frank Cawson; *How Religion Works*, by J. L. Willcock et al.; and *Blackpool: One Week a Year*, by Herbert Howarth and Richard Glew. Though promised in various M-O books and articles for the autumn of 1938, the book on pubs was the only one to be completed and published by Gollancz, and then not until 1943. A fifth volume for which Gollancz gave an advance was suggested by Tom to Madge; the subject was to be the "Economic Life of Worktown," with the research to be carried out chiefly by Madge.

146–147  "a sharply accurate survey" and "put the finger on": Valentine Cunningham, *British Writers of the Thirties* (Oxford: Oxford University Press, 1989) p. 79.

146–147  THH, "Mass-Opposition and Literature," *Light and Dark* II, 3, Special Tom Harrisson Issue (February 1938): 9–15.

147     "The earth is an oyster": W. H. Auden, in W. H. Auden and Louis MacNeice, *Letters from Iceland* (London: Faber, 1937), as quoted by THH in "Mass-Opposition and Literature," p. 14.

147     "Buchmanites, Rotarians and Nudists": G. W. Stonier, "Mass-Observation and Literature," *New Statesman* (26 February 1938): 326–327.

147 "Everyone has now heard": Editor's introduction to THH, "The Fifty-Second Week: Impression of Blackpool," *Geographical Magazine* (April 1938): 36.

## 16. M-O and Munich

148–149 Munich crisis: Angus Calder, *The People's War* (London: Jonathan Cape, 1969), pp. 21–34; and THH and Charles Madge, *Britain by Mass-Observation* (London: Cresset, 1986) with introduction by Angus Calder.

149 "what people do want": THH and Madge, *Britain by Mass-Observation*, p. 231.

149 100,000 copies in ten days: Rod Varley, *Mass-Observation 1937–1987* (Brentford, Middlesex: Watermans Arts Centre, 1987), p. 17.

149 "provide the first comprehensive": p. xi of Angus Calder's excellent introduction to the 1986 Cresset edition of *Britain by Mass-Observation*, pp. vii–xv.

149 Yet M-O did have something: Penny Summerfield, "Mass-Observation: social research or social movement?" *Journal of Contemporary History* XX, 3 (July 1985): 239–452.

150 "You know how it is": Graham Greene, *The Confidential Agent* (London: Penguin, 1971) pp. 119–120.

150–151 Raymond Firth: "An Anthropologist's View of Mass-Observation," *Sociological Review* XXXI, 2 (April 1939): 166–193.

152 "to analyse popular opinion": See Jeffery, *Mass-Observation*, pp. 35ff.

152–153 Biddy: Interviews of John Clayton and members of the Hill and Gathorne-Hardy families and Will Stober's interview of George H. W. Rylands, Fellow of King's College, Cambridge, Biddy's cousin and best friend to Biddy's sister, Hester.

153 "really was somebody": Interview of George Rylands by Will Stober.

## 17. M-O Goes to War

Important sources for this chapter are Ian McLaine's *Ministry of Morale* (London: Allen and Unwin, 1979) and THH and Madge, eds., *War Begins At Home by Mass-Observation* (London: Chatto and Windus, 1940).

154 "Everything is blowing": Letter from THH to Madge, September 20, 1939, in the M-O Archive.

154 "The war which started out slowly": THH, *World Within*, pp. 162–163.

154 "The civilian's job" and "Defeat might not flow": McLaine, *Ministry of Morale, p. 2.*

155 "to obtain information": MoI memorandum to Treasury, June 10, 1939, cited in McLaine, *Ministry of Morale*, footnote 47, p. 287.

155    "a good deal of nervousness": McLaine, *Ministry of Morale*, p. 23.

155    cup of tea: McLaine, *Ministry of Morale*, p. 27.

156    "Very good work": THH and Madge, eds., *War Begins At Home by Mass-Observation*, p. 11.

156    "The results of this": Madge interview by Angus Calder in March 1979, a transcript of which is in the M-O Archive.

156    "barometer that politicians": THH and Madge, eds., *War Begins At Home by Mass-Observation*, p. 10.

156    "exceptionally out of touch": THH, *Picture Post* (July 30, 1940).

157    "For me, M-O has become practically an obsession": THH letter to Charles Madge, January 18, 1940, in the M-O Archive.

157    "I see grave danger": Letter from Madge to THH, January 21, 1940, cited in Jeffery, *Mass-Observation*, p. 39.

157    "It is useless": Letter from THH to Madge, January 1937, in the M-O Archive.

157–158  "How *could* you," "basically false," and "those purple choirboys": Tom recalls these in a letter to Mary Adams, December 28, 1970, in the M-O Archive.

158    Cooper's Snoopers debate: Hansard, Commons, Social Survey, August 1, 1940, pp. 1514–1556, and press clippings in the M-O Archive.

158    allegedly rode away: T. Jeffery, interviewed in 1994, said that Tom had told him this.

158    "Oh are you one of Cooper's Snoopers?": Interview of Celia Fremlin Minchin.

159    "People want questions asked": Dorothy L. Sayers, *Unnatural Death* (London: Gollancz, 1927), p. 32.

159    "I remember my first meeting": Interview of Leonard England.

## 18. Living through the Blitz

161–162  giant panda: Interviews of the children involved, Nicolas Hill, Josephine Hill Batterham, and John Clayton, with confirmation from the St. John Cooper column, "I must say" in the *Manchester Daily Express* of May 27, 1939.

162    RN: Royal Navy.

162    Max's "Log" is now the property of his cousin, Peter Harrisson.

162    "filled with bric-a-brac" and "Biddy took": Letter from Margaret Payne to Elaine Dudley-Smith, January 23, 1993, which Mrs. Dudley-Smith allowed me to copy.

163    "not one pub is permitted": THH, "Wowsers," *New Statesman* (November 23, 1946): 375.

163     "The war saved M-O's methodological bacon": Angus Calder, "Mass-Observation 1937–1949," in *Essays in the History of British Sociological Research*, M. Bulmer, ed., (Cambridge: Cambridge University Press, 1985), p. 130.

163–164     "Every single morning" and "One of the most enjoyable,": Interview of Celia Fremlin Minchin.

164, 166     "Art, sport, cinema" and "field day for M-O," respectively: H. D. Willcock, "Mass-Observation," *The American Journal of Sociology* XLVIII, 4 (January 1943): 450.

164–165     "Take the case of a sailor's wife": in the John Godfrey files (ADM223) at the Public Records Office (PRO), Kew, and also quoted in THH, *Living Through the Blitz* (Collins, 1976; Penguin, 1978; reprinted with new intro. by A. Bullock, 1990; first U.S. edition, Schocken Books, 1989), pp. 224–225.

166     "so he rang up all kinds of people": Interview of Humphrey Spender.

166–168     Working for Godfrey, DNI: PRO records, especially ADM223/476/XC/18749 and ADM223/47b/XL/18749. A letter from DNI introducing Tom to the commanders of the ports of Plymouth and Portsmouth, dated May 1, 1941, is in the M-O Archive.

167     "Tom Harrisson and I": Interview of the Honorable David Astor.

168     Advertising Service Guild: Calder, "Mass-Observation 1937–1949," p. 122.

168     "sicked up his breakfast": Interview of Mollie Tarrant.

168     Tom's induction and early days in the Army: THH, *World Within*, pp. 166–178; THH personnel records from the Ministry of Defense; THH, "The British Soldier Today," *Infantry Journal* (Washington, D.C.) LIV, 1 (January 1944): 54–57; and letters from Biddy to Lady Anne Hill (in Lady Anne's possession); and Green, *The Adventurers*.

168     He missed most meals: Humphrey Brooke, quoted in Green, *The Adventurers*, p. 126.

169     Tom's "Radio" columns: Interview of David Astor, and *The Observer* (March 1942–June 1944).

169     top of his class: No record of rank in class for Tom's Officer Cadet Training Unit class has been kept by the archivists at Sandhurst, but at the time, Tom claimed the honor of being top of his Sandhurst class to friends such as Humphrey Spender and repeated this in *World Within*.

169     "views and extra-territorial": Dick Horton, *Ring of Fire* (London: Leo Cooper/Secker and Warburg, 1983), p. 74.

169–170     SOE and Tom's place in it: Interview of SOE Advisor Gervase Cowell, and Gabrielle McDonald, *New Zealand's Secret Heroes* (Auckland, New Zealand: Reed Books, 1991).

170     "a few men": THH, *World Within*, p. 173.

170   "the acquisition of so much": THH, *World Within*, p. 173.

170   "The party was full" and "We left him": Woodrow Wyatt, *Confessions of an Optimist* (London: Collins, 1985), pp. 95–96.

## PART FOUR: King of the Mountain, 1942–1946

The main published sources, aside from THH, *World Within*, are G. B. Courtney, *Silent Feet: The History of "Z" Special Operations 1942–1945* (Melbourne: McPherson's Printing Group, 1993); Bob Long, ed., *"Z" Special Unit's Secret War: Operation SEMUT 1: Soldiering with the head-hunters of Borneo* (Hornsby, New South Wales: Australian Print Group, Maryborough Vic./Transpareon Press, 1989); Gabrielle McDonald, *New Zealand's Secret Heroes* (Auckland, New Zealand: Reed Books, 1991); Gavin Long, *The Final Campaigns*, Australia in the War of 1939–1945, Series One: Army VII (Canberra: Australian War Memorial, 1963); and Roland Griffiths-Marsh, *Sixpenny Soldier* (North Ryde, New South Wales: Collins/Angus and Robertson, 1990). For the main unpublished sources, see notes and sources for Chapter 20.

## 19. Waiting for Dawn on Mindoro

The chief unpublished source for this chapter is Keith Barrie's manuscript "Borneo Story." The main published source is THH, *World Within*.

173   "What I adored in myself": THH, *World Within*, p. 187.

175   "This led to the execution": G. Long, *Final Campaigns*, p. 454.

175   "How could it fail," "These strong energetic" and "through the good will": THH, *World Within*, p. 179.

176   "My ego could hardly": THH, *World Within*, p. 180.

177   "living right in the very centre" and "these Kelabits," respectively: R. S. Douglas, "An Expedition to the Bah Country of Central Borneo," *Sarawak Museum Journal* I, 2 (1912): 17–30.

177   "flat as a board": E. Banks, "Some Megalithic Remains from the Kelabit Country in Sarawak with some Notes on the Kelabits Themselves," *SMJ* IV, 15 (1937): 411–437.

177   "Lt. Col. I. M. English": "An Englishman in Australia" (series of 21 articles), *Argus* (Melbourne) (March 10–May 11, 1945).

178   "We did rather uncertainly": THH, *World Within*, p. 150.

179   Schneeberger's trip: Letters from Schneeberger to Keith Barrie, given to me by Mr. Barrie.

179   "I must not": THH, *World Within*, p. 187.

## 20. SEMUT 1: Impact of Ants

Tom produced at least three written accounts of his role as special operations leader in World War II Borneo: "The Army of the Jungle Hole" on page 2 of four issues of the *Sunday Express* (January 19 and 26, and February 2 and 9, 1947); a half-hour scenario for the *BBC Light* program, a transcript of which is in the THH file at the Australian War Memorial Library in Canberra; and *World Within* (1959). *World Within* is a much fuller account but was written much later than the early pieces and without reference to his own notes or other documents. I have gone straight to the contemporary record whenever possible: the entries that Tom made in his diary every day from March 25, 1945, until well past the end of the war and the signals, situation reports, orders, notebooks on particular subjects, and letters to and from Tom from this period that are in the Harrisson papers at the Australian War Memorial Library (AWM 3 DRL 6502) in Canberra. Unless otherwise noted, all references to Tom's wartime diaries, notebooks, and SEMUT 1 documents are from these files in Canberra.

Other than Tom's published works, my main published sources are eyewitness accounts in Bob Long, ed., *"Z" Special Unit's Secret War* and the official Australian history in Gavin Long, *The Final Campaigns*. Smaller books by or about people closely involved in SEMUT 1 have also been consulted: G. B. Courtney, *Silent Feet*; Dick Horton, *Ring of Fire* (London: Leo Cooper/Secker and Warburg, 1983); Gabrielle McDonald, *New Zealand's Secret Heroes*; Sheila Ross, *And Tomorrow Freedom* (Sydney: Allen and Unwin, 1989); and Roland Griffiths-Marsh, *The Sixpenny Soldier*. I interviewed two Kelabits (David and Lian Labang) who recalled the day SEMUT 1 fell from the sky, and on June 16, 1990, James Barclay interviewed a third, who had been the *tuai rumah* (longhouse headman) of Bario in 1945. Other sources are interviews and/or correspondence with SEMUT 1 survivors and their families (see Persons Interviewed and/or Corresponded With); with four of the surviving American airmen (see notes for Chapter 21), with Lt. Col. G. B. "Jumbo" Courtney, MBE, MC, and with survivors of other SEMUT parties such as Keith Barrie, MM; the late Don Horsnell, MID (who gave me snapshots); and Rowan Waddy (who gave me maps). Unpublished diaries and memoirs of Barrie and Waddy have also been used.

180 "Drifting nervously": THH, "The Army of the Jungle Hole," *Sunday Express* (January 19, 1947): 2.

181 "there appeared three": THH, "The Army of the Jungle Hole" (January 19, 1947): 2.

184 "hung their backsides": Sanderson in B. Long, *"Z" Special Unit's Secret War*, p. 49.

187   Guns: The Bren gun is a caliber .303 inch, magazine-fed, light machine gun, while the Austin, Sten and Owen guns, also used by SEMUT operatives and their guerrillas, are all caliber 9 mm magazine-fed submachine guns. The Owen gun was an Australian invention; the SEMUT men liked it in spite of its tendency to fire if mishandled because, unlike the Sten, it did not jam when covered with mud. Gun information comes from WO II Jack Tredrea, MM AIF.

187   "Fuck 'em all": Various later memoirs by SEMUT personnel date the big Bario party March 25, the first evening, but Tom's contemporary diary places it on March 26.

187   "What a wonderful way": Edmeades in B. Long, *"Z" Special Unit's Secret War*, p.30.

188   "If a man is shot": Bob Long citing an unnamed native guerrilla in B. Long, *"Z" Special Unit's Secret War*, pp. 133–134.

188–189   No Japanese were left: Tom claims in "The Army of the Jungle Hole," *Sunday Express* (January 19, 1947): 2, that the Japanese on the coast never learned about SEMUT's presence until after the Allies invaded Brunei Bay. This is confirmed by Col. Courtney (then Tom's "Z" Special commanding officer) in *Silent Feet* and is supported by Robert Goh, the step-son of one of SEMUT 1's best agents who was assistant district officer in the district where SEMUT 1's territory lay (see R. Goh in B. Long, pp. 24–25). Tom's diary entry for June 23, 1945, records that Japanese documents captured earlier that month revealed that two spies had separately reported SEMUT 1's presence to the Chief Police Officer (CPO) in Lawas but neither had been believed. Surely, if the Japanese had known about SEMUT 1's presence, they would have sent punitive patrols to the Kelabit highlands.

189   the amazed corporal: Roland Griffiths-Marsh, MM, in his *The Sixpenny Soldier*, p. 267.

190   Corrin's letter: Located among the THH papers in the Australian War Memorial Library (AWM 3 DRL 6502) in Canberra, this letter is used with permission of Corrin's widow, Jean Corrin Morris.

## 21. Moving Out

The story of the eleven American survivors of two shot-up B-24s, one air force and one navy, deserves a book of its own, which I hope to write. *World Within*'s account of the Yanks' story has a number of minor errors. Mine is drawn from documents in the THH papers in Canberra, various people's accounts in Bob Long's book, *"Z" Special Unit's Secret War*, and documents and interviews given by survivors Tom Capin, Dan Illerich, John Nelson (U.S. Air Force), and Robert Graham (U.S. Navy).

Other sources used in this chapter include excerpts from 2d Lt. Philip R. Corrin's diary, which were provided me by John Nelson; THH's

Operational Report of SEMUT 1, covering events up to June 10, 1945, provided by the SOE adviser, London; the unpublished memoir of Phil Henry's war service that he showed me; interviews of Phil Henry, the late Fred Sanderson and Lt. Col. G. B. Courtney; and letters or documents given to me by Courtney or sent me by Sanderson for use in this book.

191    Halfway down the Trusan: E. Edmeades in B. Long, *"Z" Special Unit's Secret War*, p. 32.

192    Captain McCallum: His disagreement with Tom is recounted by Bob Long in B. Long *"Z" Special Unit's Secret War*, p. 133.

193    murdering Tom: Cpl. C. McP. Hardy threatened Tom with an automatic (C. Hardy in B. Long, *"Z" Special Unit's Secret War*, p. 452) and Cpl. R. Griffiths-Marsh promised himself to kill Tom "at the first chance" (R. Griffiths-Marsh in B. Long, *"Z" Special Unit's Secret War*, p. 396).

194    "real brains," "rather opinionated," "intelligent and tough," and "No brains": THH, report to "Z" Special headquarters, June 20, 1945 (Australian War Memorial Library).

195    "I have given": THH, Operational Report to SOE of SEMUT 1, covering events up to June 10, 1945. Copies of these SOE files given to me by SOE Adviser Cowell.

195    "type of mental exercise": THH, *World Within*, p. 212.

195    "only one phrase": B. Long in B. Long, *"Z" Special Unit's Secret War*, p. 127.

195    "if anyone thought": B. Long in B. Long, p. 127.

198    "There was something about the tension": THH, *World Within*, pp. 232–233.

198    "within a few minutes" and "our party was split up": Trooper R. C. Griffiths in B. Long, *"Z" Special Unit's Secret War*, p. 432.

198    "report on Jap dispositions": Phil Henry's memoir.

198–199 airstrip: Tom's diary in the THH papers in the Australian War Memorial Library; Westley's account in B. Long, *"Z" Special Unit's Secret War*, pp. 287–288; and Trooper R. C. Griffiths in B. Long, *"Z" Special Unit's Secret War*, pp. 432–434.

200    KBE: Knight of the British Empire.

200    First landings and take-offs: Chaney's account in B. Long, pp. 538–541, and see also p. 546 for the record of his logbook, which is more accurate on dates than are his recollections.

## 22. The Ants Take Heads

The main sources, in addition to the Harrisson papers at the Australian War Memorial Library, are Phil Henry's unpublished memoir and Sanderson's remarks in correspondence to me and in Bob Long's book, *"Z" Special Unit's Secret War*.

201    "to think—or any way to talk" and "appeared to be too concerned": THH, *World Within*, p. 243.

202    "lopped two Japanese heads off": Phil Henry's memoir.

202    "The Ibans then took the four heads": F. Sanderson in B. Long, p. 64.

203    "The civil authorities": F. Sanderson in B. Long, p. 65.

203    "Again there was a confrontation": Phil Henry's memoir.

203    real numbers of enemy: The estimated strength of the Japanese on Borneo in 1945 was generally agreed upon (by the Americans, the Australians, and SEMUT) to be between 25,000 and 30,000. After the war, it was confirmed that there had been some 28,500 Japanese on Borneo just prior to the Labuan landings. During the war, SEMUT reported that more than half the Japanese in Borneo were in the north, and these figures were proved correct when, at war's end, 17,000 Japanese army and 3,500 Japanese civilians working for the military surrendered to Allied forces there. The AIF, however, or at least Ninth Division, persisted in thinking, in spite of reports they were getting from SEMUT, that there were well under 10,000 Japanese in the north. See *Reports of General MacArthur: The Campaigns of MacArthur in the Pacific* (Washington, D.C.: Government Printing Office, 1966), p. 372. For Ninth Division estimates of enemy forces in the area, see G. Long, *Final Campaigns*, pp. 456, 470, 494–495.

203–204    "The 10th of June 1945 was the day": Dick Horton, *Ring of Fire* (London: Leo Cooper/Secker and Warburg, 1983), p. 96.

204    "caused massive disruption": Horton, *Ring of Fire*, p. 96.

204    Australia's casualty rate on Tarakan: G. Long, *Final Campaigns*, p. 451.

204    "The Dyaks offered" and "Permission granted": G. Long, *Final Campaigns*, p. 490

206    "Prior to the invasion": Australian Archives, File CRS A 3270, Vol. ii, Pt. 3, p. 70, as cited in G. B. Courtney, *Silent Feet*, p. 55.

206–209    The story of confrontations between Ninth Division and Sanderson and Henry comes from official records quoted in G. Long, *Final Campaigns*, Tom's diary, interviews of Courtney, Sanderson, and Henry, and written recollections given to me by Fred Sanderson and Phil Henry.

208    Kamamura: probably Captain Kamimura, who, after the war, was tried as a war criminal by the British in Hong Kong for killing POWs. The story of Japanese treatment of 100 Indian POWs is in G. Long, *Final Campaigns*, pp. 484, 488.

## 23. End Game

The main source is Tom's papers at the Australian War Memorial Library in Canberra. Unless specifically noted, all quotes come from these. Also important is the official Australian history in Gavin Long, *Final Campaigns*.

Regarding Tom's headquarters, Tom kept a transcript of a BBC program broadcast on February 22, 1947, on the *BBC Light* program, including the extracts from Bartram's diary quoted in this chapter. Besides Bartram's, another description of Tom's Belawit headquarters exists, in Gabrielle McDonald, *New Zealand's Secret Heroes*, p. 119, with SEMUT 1 veteran Frank Wigzell the implied source. It has Tom living in a "palatial private [lean-to]. . . ." In fact, Tom took over a part of a Celebes-born Netherlands Indies local administrator's home and his quarters were "very basic," according to Bob Long, who wrote me that he stayed there frequently when Tom was away. The Wigzell-based description continues: "Six attractive young Kelabit girls, aged between 12–14, attended to his every need. . . ." Wigzell spent little or no time in Belawit. Sgt. Bob Long and others who had been long in Belawit told Jumbo Courtney that this story about Tom and the girls was "absolute nonsense," and Bob Long confirmed to me that "there was never any evidence of Kelabit girls."

210    "Wingate complex": Orde Wingate was a heroic headline-grabbing British officer who used guerrillas on a massive scale in Burma and died there during World War II.

210    "the 9th Division had reached": G. Long, *Final Campaigns*, p. 494.

211    SEMUT 1's "score": Tom recorded in his diary any SEMUT 1 unit reported killing or capture, with the responsible SEMUT 1 person indicated. Some entries are dated March, May, or early June, but most are after the June 10 Allied landings. For most engagements, the entry is only one or two Japanese killed. The only questionable figures, both because of the large number of enemy alleged killed and because they were not strictly SEMUT 1 kills, are fourteen killed at Long Berang at the behest of William Makahanap to safeguard his U.S. airmen fugitives, and thirty-five Japanese and five auxiliaries killed on May 4 at Malinau (in Dutch Borneo) by air strikes requested by SEMUT 1 operative Tredrea, who was then in charge of SEMUT 1 activity near Malinau.

211–212  "For the 9th Division": G. Long, *Final Campaigns*, p. 491

212    "sometimes . . . the ["Z" Special] guerillas": G. Long, *Final Campaigns*, p. 491.

212    no intention of surrendering: The Japanese at the Sapong Estate were among those showing no signs of wanting to surrender, according to SEMUT 1 operative, the late John "Stroke" Hayes, who had them watched until September 12, 1945, when he was sent to hospital and discharged.

214–215  NICA fuss: Unless otherwise noted, quotes on this subject come from THH, *World Within*, pp. 310–312.

## 24. SEMUT 1 and the Fujino Tai

Aside from Tom's papers at the Australian War Memorial Library (the source of all quotes not specifically noted), Bartram's diary, as transcribed in Bob Long's book and in the BBC transcript Tom kept, is the main source for the story of the Fujino Tai and is vouched for as accurate by Lt. Col. G. B. Courtney, to whom SEMUT 1 had been reporting at this time.

216      "all known areas": G. Long, *Final Campaigns*, p. 562.

217      "As soon as the Japs": Carter quoted in G. B. Courtney, *Silent Feet*, p. 71. Bill Sochon's manuscript account of the easy surrender in his SEMUT 3 district is in the THH file in Canberra.

217      "a superb letter pro me": The letter is from CIC AIF Blamey to Lt. General van Oyen, September 8, 1945, in the Public Records Office, Kew, England (PRO file HS1/253).

217      impertinent signal: Sandy denied having sent such a signal. Other veterans suggest that an operative working under Sandy on the Limbang who shared Sandy's impatience with Ninth Division might have sent the signal in the name of the head of his unit, "Sanderson."

218      "The expected forces": THH, *World Within*, pp. 319–320. The Japanese had gone up to Long Nawang early in their stay on Borneo, where they tracked down and murdered white missionaries who had fled there rather than surrender and be taken to Japanese prison camps. After that, the Japanese never came back to that part of the Bahau-Kayan.

221      stores of food: Courtney in *Silent Feet* wondered if Tom had kept food from SEMUT operatives so that he could amass these supplies. While it is conceivable that Tom came to see this stock as worth accumulating for such a purpose, it is hard to believe that when he instituted his live-off-the-land policy, back in March, he had had such a plan in mind.

221      "I was quite used": Interview of Lt. Col. G. B. Courtney.

222      "If Tom Harrisson had expected": Sheila Ross, *And Tomorrow Freedom* (Sydney: Allen and Unwin, 1989), p. 158.

223      "It was a bloody journey": Sheila Ross, *And Tomorrow Freedom*, p. 161.

224      "rather a dirty . . . piece of paper": a photograph of the actual note appears in B. Long, p. 502.

224      "read Rex's bullshit": Sheila Ross's book about Rex Blow, *And Tomorrow Freedom*, overemphasizes Blow's role and nearly eliminates Tom's, no doubt drawing on Blow's account, to which Tom here refers. Tom's daily diary entries and the dispatches he sent and received (in the Harrisson papers at the Australian War Memorial Library in Canberra), plus recollections of Jumbo Courtney (who researched this matter for his own book, *Silent Feet*), are my sources.

## 25. Officer Administering the Interior

The main sources are the THH papers at the Malaysian National Archives, Kuala Lumpur, and interviews of Alastair Morrison; the Reverend Hudson

Southwell; Lian, David, and Lucy Labang and Garnette Ridu, (Kelabits from the Plain of Bah); and Tan Sri ONG Kee Hui.

225    Bongan: Interviews of Alastair Morrison and the Reverend Hudson Southwell.

228    "When a hill tribesman dies,": THH, "The Army of the Jungle Hole," *Sunday Express* (February 9, 1947): 2.

228–229  A 1988 guidebook: John Briggs, *Mountains of Malaysia* (Petaling Jaya, Malaysia: Longman, 1988) shows the Batu Lawi wooden board (p. 48). Texts of the wooden boards Tom put up come from Tom's diary for March 15–May 10, 1946 (Malaysian National Archive file SP8/10 in Kuala Lumpur). See Briggs' book for how to climb Batu Lawi and for the statement that Tom and his six Kelabit companions were the first to climb it. Briggs mentions the view and the sighting of a peregrine falcon. Tom described the view in a letter to Jumpmaster Ellis' brother, February 27, 1947 (copy in THH papers, National Library of Australia) and mentioned, in another document (which I have now mislaid) that, on the occasion of climbing Batu Lawi, he saw the only peregrine falcon he ever saw in Borneo.

229–230  Letter from a friend about Biddy: This was copied by THH into his diary March 16–May 10, 1946 (Malaysian National Archive file SP8/10 in Kuala Lumpur).

230    A woman friend: Interview of the woman, who prefers not to be named.

230    At least one had gone to bed: Interview of one man who did and who asked me not to divulge his name.

230    Sally Adams: Interview.

231    A signal came: Dick Morris, a Sarawak colonial officer, saw the message when it came in and told me that Tom later confirmed to him having received it.

## PART FIVE: Sarawak Museum, 1947–1956

The chief unpublished sources are Tom's diaries, correspondence, and notes now among his papers (file SP8) at the Malaysian National Archive, Kuala Lumpur.

### 26. Back "Home" Again

241    John Clayton: Interview.

241    "After Australia": THH, "Demob. Diary," *New Statesman* (September 28, 1946): 221.

242    "Dear Solly": THH letter to Dr. Solly Zuckerman, September 16, 1946. Zuckerman's reply is dated September 30, 1946. Tom's letter and a copy of Zuckerman's reply are in the Zuckerman Archive, University of East

Anglia library, and (as with all my quotations from Lord Zuckerman) are used with the kind permission of his widow.

242 "it may be that [M-O's] greatest": Angus Calder, "Mass-Observation 1937–1949," *Essays in the History of British Sociological Research*, M. Bulmer, ed., (Cambridge: Cambridge University Press, 1985), chapter 7.

242 correctly predicted: THH, "Who'll Win," *Political Quarterly* XV (January–March 1944): 21–32.

243 "It is a pity": Letter from Alfred Guthmann to Jock (undated, probably 1946) in the Jock Marshall papers, National Library of Australia.

243 "There was this lovely": THH on the BBC's *People Today*, August 17, 1960.

244 Correspondence with Zuckerman: Zuckerman Archive, University of East Anglia.

244 "Borneo Jungle": The transcript is among the Harrisson papers at the Australian War Memorial Library.

## 27. Government Ethnologist

Chief sources are Tom's diaries, correspondence, and notes now among his papers at the Malaysian National Archive.

246–249 Kuching in 1947: Malcolm MacDonald, *Borneo People* (London: Jonathan Cape, 1956); various issues of the *Sarawak Gazette* (*SG*) (Kuching) for 1947, and interviews of the late Sir Anthony Abell and Dick and Dorothy Morris.

246, 248 MacDonald: Quotations from him come from his *Borneo People*, pp. 49–50.

248 "years of neglect" and "picking off leaches": THH, "London Letter," *SG* (June 2, 1947): 101.

250 Firth . . . had remarked: Recalled by Prof. Firth in a letter to me dated August 27, 1992, and confirmed by Gillian Webster, who heard of it from Prof. Firth. For THH's reaction: interview of Margaret Young and a note by THH in the Malaysian National Archive (file SP.8).

250–251 *Sarawak Gazette*: THH, "The Kelabit Peoples of Upland Borneo," was serialized in the *SG* (September 2, 1946): 6–5; (October 1, 1946): 21–22; (November 1, 1946): 39–40; (December 2, 1946): 56; (January 2, 1947): 11–12; and (February 1, 1947): 28–29. Tom's description of the Land Dayak ceremony that he had attended with the governor was published in the *SG* as part of the unsigned article "Governor at Grogo," (August 1, 1947): 138–139. The letter to the editor from Leach objecting to this description of Land Dayak rites, dated August 9, 1947, appeared in the *SG* (September 1, 1947): 175, with Tom's lengthy reply on pages 175–178.

252    Census: 1947 census results are in the *Sarawak Annual Report* (Kuching: Sarawak Government Printing Office, 1954), p. 11. For Tom's census efforts: THH, "Inland Peoples of Sarawak," *Corona* (August 1949): 18–19.

252    "Kelabit studies": THH, "London Letter," *SG* (June 2, 1947): 103.

252    Tom at Niah: "The Caves of Niah: A History of Prehistory," *Sarawak Museum Journal* VIII, 12 (1958): 564–567.

## 28. Tom Responds to Leach's Challenge

253–255    The letters from Leach (used with the kind permission of his daughter, Louisa Brown) and Tom's draft replies and "General Considerations" notebook are in file SP.8/42 in the Malaysian National Archive, Kuala Lumpur.

255    more idealist and less personally ambitious: This idea comes from an "un-Ph.Ded" scholar with similar motives, Kirk Huffman, curator emeritus of the Vanuatu Cultural Centre.

256    Such a comment: Compare James Clifford and George Marcus, eds., *Writing Culture: The Poetics and Politics of Ethnography* (Berkeley: University of California Press, 1986) and the following statement from Paul A. Erickson, *A History of Anthropological Theory* (Ontario: Broadview Press, 1998), pp. 145–146: "Recognizing the impossibility of pure objectivity, a recent generation of ethnographers has attempted to cir-cum[vent] the ethical and methodological dilemmas raised by postmodern theory. They have done so by looking for ways in which to describe different cultures and societies *without* denying the subjectivity of the people being analyzed, and *without* laying claim to absolute, or authoritative knowledge about them."

258    Freeman vs. Mead: See Derek Freeman, *The Fateful Hoaxing of Margaret Mead* (Boulder, Colorado, USA: Westview Press, 1999).

260    Clifford Geertz: His mature view of the limits of social anthropology, expressed in *After the Fact: Two Countries, Four Decades, One Anthropologist* (Cambridge: Harvard University Press, 1995), are discussed by anthropologist Scheper-Hughes in a May 7, 1995 *New York Times* book review.

260    "74.6% of sociology is bunk": Title of a leader in *The Economist* (May 13, 1995).

261    Obituary: "Tom Harrisson: Exploring life under cannibals and bombers," *The Times* (January 21, 1976).

261–262    The Southwells, and Tom's attitude toward them: Interview of Southwell; of the Labang brothers, David and Lian; letter from THH to the *Sarawak Gazette* (February 2, 1948): 40–41; and THH, "Outside Influences on the Upland Culture," *Sarawak Museum Journal* VI, 4 (1954): 115.

## 29. A Kelabit Wedding

263 Bongan's class: THH notebook "Kelabit character" (file SP.8/33 in the Malaysian National Archive), and interviews of David and Lian Labang, Lucy Labang, and Garnette Ridu.

263–266 Sigang: Interviews of the Labangs and Garnette Ridu and Tom's diaries and notebooks in the Malaysian National Archive.

264 started off for Kuching: THH, "A Trip to the Uplands," *Sarawak Gazette* (*SG*) (September 1, 1948): 171.

264 first school at Pa Main: THH, "Postscript: Two Views of Kelabits," *SG* (March 1, 1947): 42; interviews of David and Lian Labang.

265 "wedding": Interview of Lian Labang (who was present).

265 Bongan's miscarriage and Tom's reaction: Letter from Robert Lian, October 8, 1992.

265 never again fathered: Two stories of Tom's putative parenting persist in Sarawak today. One is that he is the father of a Kayan who calls himself Harrison Ngau, but he is pure Kayan. Tom is also rumored to have a Kelabit son, Peter Iboh, but, as Peter has said himself, he is Sigang's son by another Kelabit.

266 the revived *Sarawak Museum Journal* (*SMJ*): Some old Sarawak hands claim that Tom did nothing for the first postwar issue but publish pieces E. Banks had assembled before war broke out. A glance at the index of that issue disproves this assertion.

266–267 Zuckerman: His letters to Tom of October 15, 1947, and August 9, 1952, copies of which are in the Zuckerman Archive at the University of East Anglia.

267 Max and Biddy: Interviews of the Gathorne-Hardy and Hill families.

268 Mass-Observation: Interview of Leonard England, M-O's managing director, 1950–1970.

268 amok: THH, "Adventure Story," *Sunday Pictorial* (London) (April 24,1949), confirmed by interviews of Lian and David Labang.

268 "The Appeal Judge": Dr. N. S. Haile, M.A., D.Phil., D.Sc., FGA, FGS, "Personal Glimpses," *Journal of the Malaysian Branch of the Royal Asiatic Society* XLIX, Pt. 1 (1976): 145. These facts were confirmed by Lian and David Labang. Tom also gave evidence in two cases to commute Kelabits' death sentences for murder to imprisonment for manslaughter. He was successful once, drawing on his knowledge of Kelabit culture to show that the victim had provoked the attack by pulling off the other's bead necklace, a deadly insult.

268–269 Sigang and Tom: THH notebooks in the Malaysian National Archive.

## 30. Museum Curator

270    Kuching: My memories of living there, 1966–1968, and P. Goullart, *River of the White Lily: Life in Sarawak* (Kuala Lumpur: S. Abdul Majeed & Co., uncopyrighted 1991 reprint).

271    earlobes: Interviews of David and Lian Labang.

271–272    The house in Pig Lane: Interview of Ramsay Ong.

272    Bishop Galvin's description of Tom as a guest and host is from a letter he wrote to Stan Bedlington, March 18, 1976, which he gave to me.

273    Tom as a boss: Benedict Sandin in "Tom as I Knew Him," *Journal of the Malaysian Branch of the Royal Asiatic Society* XLIV, Pt. 1 (1976): 147–148, and my interview of Datuk Lucas Chin.

273–274    Tom's views on how to run the museum: THH, "An All-round Museum in a Small Country," *Sarawak Museum Journal* IX, 13–14 (1959): 249–250, and "The Two Way Job of Our Museum," *Sarawak Gazette* (October 1, 1947): 188–190.

274    "into an institution of world standing": Alastair Morrison, *Fair Land Sarawak* (Ithaca: Cornell Southeast Asia Program, 1993), p. 97.

275–277    Haile's, Inger's, and Henry Ong's comments come from my interviews of them.

277    John Young's excavator: Interview of Margaret Young.

## 31. Looking for a Friend

279    Sigang: Interview of the late Dr. Stephen Morris (an occasional houseguest at Pig Lane during this time), and of some of Sigang's Kelabit friends and relatives.

280    Tom and the Morrisons: Interviews of Neville Haile and Alastair Morrison, letters from Morrison, and Morrison's *Fair Land Sarawak*.

280    Tom's sex life: Interviews of a bachelor friend from Singapore who asks not to be named, various former Sarawak expatriates, and the Australian diplomat's wife.

280    KCMG: Knight Commander of the Order of St. Michael and St. George.

280–281    Abell: His obituary in *The Times* (October 14, 1994); filled out by my interview of him and Malcolm MacDonald's in *Borneo People* (London: Jonathan Cape, 1956), p. 214.

282    High jinks at the Abell Astana: Interviews of Heidi and Sidi Munan, Ramsay Ong, Suzie Kitto, Sir Anthony Abell, and Tony Shaw.

282    "suddenly like a rush": Mr. and Mrs. Geoffrey Allen's notes left at the M-O Archive.

## 32. Turtles

The main source is John R. Hendrickson, Professor Emeritus of Biology at the University of Arizona, in "The Green Sea Turtle in Malaya and Sarawak," *Proceedings of the Zoological Society of London* CXXX (1958): 456–535, and his generous replies to repeated phone queries. Also Tom's many "Notes on the Edible Green Turtle" in the *Sarawak Museum Journal (SMJ)*. Information on the green turtles' breeding also comes from a letter from Professor Dave Owens of the Department of Biology, Texas A&M University, July 30, 1996.

284    "a dream": Peta Lambe, quoted in Oliver Warner, *Admiral of the Fleet: The Life of Sir Charles Lambe* (London: Sidgwick and Jackson, 1969), pp. 166–168.

284    *Semah*: THH, "Notes on the Edible Green Turtle," *SMJ* (1958), note 5; facts confirmed by interviews of several participants.

## 33. Explorations and Excavations

288    Tom's explorations: THH, "Inside Borneo," *Corona* (May 1954): 172–174; THH and D. Leach, "Towards the Usun Apau," *Sarawak Museum Journal (SMJ)* VI, 4 (1954): 65–95; and THH notes while on these trips (now at the Malaysian National Archive).

288–289 Tom's early efforts at archaeology: THH, "Alfred Russel Wallace," off-print dated July 1963, perhaps from R. D. Purchon, ed., *Proceedings of the Centenary and Bicentenary Congress of Biology*, Singapore, December 2–9, 1958 (Singapore: University of Malaya Press, 1960), pp. 25–38; THH, "Borneo Archeology to 1955," *SMJ* (1954): 188–192; THH and M. F. W. Tweedie, "Excavation of Gua Bungoh," *Journal of the Polynesian Society* (Wellington, New Zealand) LX, 2–3 (June–Sept. 1951); and letters to me from Tweedie.

289    "Ah Jock": Letter from THH to Jock in the Jock Marshall papers, National Library of Australia.

289    Max and Biddy: Interviews of the Hill family.

290    "I was being driven": THH, June 1954 letter to Sidney Bernstein, in Lord Bernstein's archive at Granada Headquarters, London.

290    "infernal" and "buggered the bishop": THH letters to Sidney Bernstein of late 1953 and June 1954, respectively, in Lord Bernstein's archive, Granada Headquarters.

290    noticeably fatter: According to a comment in a 1954 letter written by G. E. Wilford, which he kindly quoted to me.

290    The old Anglican church: Tom's vain efforts to save it are described in Alastair Morrison, *Fair Land Sarawak*, p. 93; letters from Tom to Sidney Bernstein (Granada Headquarters); and in an anonymous article, "Mr. Harrisson in a New Light," *Sarawak Gazette* (June 1956): 161.

290–291    "In the fifties": The surprise witness is the former Anglican Assistant Bishop of Kuching Peter H. H. Howes, in a letter to me dated February 25, 1993.

291    "killed me if he could": The friend wishes to remain anonymous.

291    "When the party": This story comes from John Matthews, a young man that Tom treated badly, who recounted it to Derek Freeman in a letter Freeman has kept, dated April 27, 1961. Matthews claims to have heard it in 1958 from a fairly senior government official who had been at the party in Pig Lane. Secondhand from a man with a grudge, this story would be easy to dismiss, but it fits with other descriptions of Tom's behavior during this period.

291–292    Digging at Niah: Interviews of Barbara Harrisson, retired Shell engineer Freek Van Veen, Professor Wilhelm G. Solheim II, and Alastair Morrison; a letter to me from Michael Tweedie; M. F. W. Tweedie, "Tom Harrisson, Archeologist" *Journal of the Malaysian Branch of the Royal Asiatic Society* XLIX, Pt. 1 (1976): 149–150; and THH, "The Prehistory of Borneo," *Asian Perspectives* XIII (June 1972): 18–45.

292–293    Barbara Brünig: Information about her comes from my interviews of her, documents she lent me, and interviews of Alastair Morrison and staff of the Sarawak Museum.

## PART SIX: In Borneo with Barbara, 1956–1967

My interviews of Barbara Harrisson are the main unpublished sources for this part of the book. Also important are letters from Tom to Lord Medway (now Lord Cranbrook) in the latter's possession. All letters from Tom to Medway in this part of the book come from that source. In 1974, a collection of Tom's unpublished papers for this period were given (at Tom's request) by Barbara to Jérôme Rousseau, Professor of Anthropology at McGill University, Montreal, Canada. These consist chiefly of transcripts of interviews with central Borneo informants; they are listed in Rousseau's *Central Borneo: A Bibliography,* Special Monograph no. 5 (Kuching: Sarawak Museum, 1988). Copies of nearly all these documents are in the archives at the Sarawak Museum. I did not consult these papers except for thirty-two letters to and from THH that were not included in Rousseau's 1988 bibliography, which he kindly arranged to have photocopied for me.

## 34. The Best Year

308    Tom publicized the fact that: THH, "Orang-utans in the London Zoo," *Sarawak Museum Journal* VII, 7 (1956): 226–228. The points were then taken up in some London papers.

308    "I think the London Zoo": Julian Huxley, *Memories* (London: Allen and Unwin, 1970), p. 232.

308–309    Max: Interviews of Max Harrisson, Gillian Webster, Heywood Hill, and the late William Harrisson.

309–310   "This house and its contents": Barbara Harrisson, *Orang-utan* (London: Collins, 1962), pp. 32–33.

310   Tom's drinking under control: Undated memo by Mrs. G. Allen in M-O Archive.

310   "hardest (but I think": Letter from THH to Derek Freeman (DF), May 25, 1957. All correspondence cited between THH and DF was copied with DF's permission.

310   "a German girl": Letter from THH to DF, March 23, 1956.

310   "As I have a satisfactory": Letter from THH to DF, March 21, 1955.

311   "countless bottles": Barbara Harrisson, *Orang-utan*, p. 30.

311   "we are very lucky": Interview of Dr. Neville S. Haile.

311–313   Runciman: Tom's changing attitude comes from an anonymous witness at the Aurora Bar; a letter to me from Runciman; and Sir Steven Runciman, *Traveller's Alphabet* (London: Thames and Hudson, 1991), pp. 140, 146–147.

312–314   1957 Niah dig: THH, "The Great Cave of Niah," *Man* (November 1957), 161–166.

313   ". . . a large arched cavern": A. H. Everett, *Sarawak Gazette* (July 17, 1873): 59–60.

313   "Borneo man of a million years": THH, "First Man in Borneo," *Salam* (Seria, Brunei: Borneo Shell) (December 15, 1956).

313   Medway: My interview of Lord Cranbrook (formerly Lord Medway).

313   Early Stone Age tools: THH, "Carbon-14 Dated Paleoliths from Borneo," *Nature* CLXXXI (March 15, 1958): 792.

313   "*porte-bonheur*": S. Runciman, *Traveller's Alphabet*, p. 147.

313   "Even at this stage": THH, "The Great Cave of Niah: A Preliminary Report on Bornean Prehistory," *Man* LVII, 21 (November 1957): 161–166.

314   Attenborough: Interview of Sir David Attenborough.

### 35. Tom, Max, and Young People

317–318   Sharif: Interviews of Pengiran Shariffuddin.

318–319   Land Dayak Primary School: Letter from Assistant Bishop Peter H. H. Howes, February 25, 1993. Howes had been seconded by the Sarawak government to run a community development scheme for Land Dayaks from 1957 to 1960.

319   Max's walk into the sea and his removal to Singapore: Interviews of Max and Barbara Harrisson, Sally Adams, and Maureen Haile (a nurse at the Sarawak Hospital at the time this happened).

319   Tom vs. Sally Adams and other young people: A collection of letters and memos that Tom had left in Kuching and were eventually given to me;

interviews of Sally Adams, Geoff Barnes, Margaret Young, Prof. W. G. Solheim, Lois Mitchison, Heidi Munan, and Prof. Michael Leigh.

## 36. The Deep Skull from Hell

This chapter draws heavily on interviews of Barbara Harrisson and Professor Wilhelm G. Solheim II and on Solheim, "The Niah Research Program," *Journal of the Malaysian Branch of the Royal Asiatic Society* (*JMBRAS*) L, Pt. 1 (1977): 28–40.

321      two inches at a time: One of Lord Medway's diary entries for 1958 describes the procedure being used in Hell as "minute search (with brushes only) in deep trial pits (72"–144")," as quoted in THH, "The Caves of Niah: A History of Prehistory," *Sarawak Museum Journal* (*SMJ*) VIII, 12 (1958): 515, and confirmed by Lord Cranbrook to me in 1998.

321      Discovery of the Deep Skull: Geoff Barnes's diary entries for the week the Deep Skull was found, interviews of Barnes, Barbara Harrisson, and Shariffuddin. The official announcement of the find is by D. R. Brothwell of the British Museum in "Upper Pleistocene Human Skull from Niah Caves," *SMJ*, IX, 15–16 (1961): 323–349.

321–325      In favor of the skull's authenticity: In favor is Kenneth Kennedy, in an interview and in "The Deep Skull of Niah: An Assessment of Twenty Years of Speculation Concerning its Evolutionary Significance," *Asian Perspectives* XX, 1 (1977): 32–50. Tweedie, in letters to me and in "Tom Harrisson, Archeologist," *JMBRAS* XLIX, 1 (1976): 149–150, regarded the discovery as "reasonable," as does Solheim, in an interview (1992) and in "The Niah Research Program," *JMBRAS* L, 1, (1977): 39. Chris Stringer, in an interview, found it reasonable, and Bordeaux University's Professor B. Vandermeersch (who found the oldest *Homo sapiens sapiens* yet known, nearly 100,000 years old, in Israel) claimed to me in 1991 that the Niah Skull was the first of its age to be linked to a modern population. Physical anthropologist Professor Terry Harrison of New York University confirmed in a 1995 interview that the C14 dates of Niah are numerous and internally consistent, "providing one of the best sampled sites in the world," with the "sampling going down to that specimen." Dato' Dr. Zuraina Majid, who reported the results of her 1977 reexcavation of the west mouth of the Niah cave in "The West Mouth of Niah, in the Prehistory of Southeast Asia," *SMJ* Special Monograph 3, XXXI, 52 (December 1982), confirms some of Tom's datings, but, though she wrote to me that she believes the skull is "genuine," she is not convinced that it is as old as Tom claimed.

323      Tweedie heard in 1958: Letter to me from Tweedie, October 6, 1994.

323      first-rate scientist: Dr. Gale Sieveking, Professor W. G. Solheim, and John Krigbaum, a New York University physical anthropologist studying the Niah Cave human remains.

324     new AMS testing: Interview of John Krigbaum, May 2, 1998.

324     Against the skull's authenticity: Dr. Peter Bellwood, the Australian National University, the acknowledged expert on early man in Southeast Asia and Australasia, is the most important doubter of the Niah Skull's authenticity, both in letters to me and in his chapter, "Southeast Asia Before History," in Nicholas Tarling, ed., *Cambridge History of Southeast Asia* I (Cambridge: Cambridge University Press, 1992), chapter 2. Bellwood, however, is eager for AMS testing results from the skull to resolve the matter. For more nuanced doubts, see P. Hapgood, "The Origin of Anatomically Modern Humans in Australasia," in P. Mellars and C. Stringer, eds., *The Human Revolution: Behavioural and Biological Perspectives on the Origin of Modern Humans* (Edinburgh: Edinburgh University Press, 1989) and K. L. Hutterer, "Reinterpreting the Southeast Asian Paleolithic," in J. Allen, J. Golson, and R. Jones, eds., *Sunda and Sahul: Prehistoric Studies in Southeast Asia, Melanesia and Australia* (London: Academic Press, 1977).

324     Tom's problems vis-à-vis the archaeological establishment: Jonathan Kress, "Tom Harrisson, North Borneo, and Palawan: A Preliminary Assessment," *Asian Perspectives* XX, 1 (1977): 75–86; interviews of Professor W. G. Solheim (University of Hawai'i) and Professors Jack Golson and Colin Groves (Australian National University). But Kress and Solheim also point out that Tom's breadth of vision in conducting archaeology was unusual for the time, a fact also mentioned by Zuraina Majid (1977) and in interviews of Dr. Ian Glover (University of London) and Professor Terry Harrison (New York University).

325     In zoology: Professor Wilhelm G. Solheim II, "The Niah Research Program," *JMBRAS*, 29.

## 37. Going Back for Another Look

326     disputes about terminology: For the terms Kajang, Punan, and Penan, Tom wired various district officers up-country and the replies he received (confirming his views) form part of the packet of papers he left in Kuching that were given to me. While Tom appears to be wrong in denying the Kajang's status as an ethnic group (see S. Strickland's contribution to the *Sarawak Museum Journal* Special Monograph No. 8 [December 1995]), the equation Punan = Penan is accepted by many recent anthropological writers, such as John B. Avé and Victor T. King, in their *Borneo: The People of the Weeping Forest* (Leiden, Netherlands: National Museum of Ethnology, 1986). Nowadays, in official reports, such as census summaries, these nomads and ex-nomads are usually all called Penan, whereas in Tom's day in such reports they were all called Punan.

327     OBE: Order of the British Empire.

327     *World Within* reviews: The citations here come from a round-up article on

the book in the *Sarawak Tribune*, April 17, 1959, which does not include the dates of the reviews.

328 "not a trace": THH, "An Inward Journey," *Sarawak Gazette (SG)* (November 30, 1959).

328 "benefits of malarial spraying" and "DO GOOD CAREFULLY": THH, "A Kelabit Diary," Part IV, *SG* (March 31, 1960): 44–45.

328–329 cats: Various Ongs remember donating cats at Tom's request. Tom's draft wireless message asking to have cats collected is in the SP.8/43 file of the Malaysian National Archive alongside a letter from Barbara, saying that the cats may turn out to be more of a handful than Penghulu Lawai had bargained for. Tom later wrote up the "Operation Cat-drop" for *Animals* (London) V (February 19, 1965): 513ff. Malcolm McSporran, however, who was in Bario rebuilding the airstrip that Tom had had built in the early 1950s, remembers the story differently. He says that he had not heard of Tom's efforts but decided himself in late 1959 or early 1960 (that is, a month or more after the date of Tom's November wireless message) that cats were needed in Bario and made arrangements via the late John Seal, the Sarawak civil affairs operations officer, who collected stray cats from Kuching via the Fire Department and arranged for the RAF to drop them in by parachute along with airfield building materials. He recalls that he was there when these cats dropped. It is this version, with some minor errors of detail, that Morrison recounts in *Fair Land Sarawak* (Ithaca: Cornell Southeast Asia Program, 1993), pp. 135–136. Tom, in his *Animals* version, does not say he himself arranged the parachutes, so it is likely that the idea of importing cats to Bario occurred independently twice, first to Tom and later to McSporran, but that the parachute cat drop only happened once, after McSporran's and John Seal's efforts. That still leaves a discrepancy about the cats Barbara collected for the project, but *nous avons d'autres chats à fouetter.*

329 Frogmouth's voice: Tom's notebook, entitled "Kelabit 1959," in which he recorded hearing the frogmouth is in file SP.8./64A at the Malaysian National Archive. There is no recognition of this event in Smythies's *Birds of Borneo* (1960) which states that frogmouths "seem to be incapable of making any sound." In 1998, Smythies explained to me that Tom had never mentioned hearing a frogmouth to him but assured me that a forthcoming edition of *Birds of Borneo* will correct that error. G. N. Appell, in his "Errors in Borneo Ethnography: Part I," *Borneo Research Bulletin* XXIII (1991): 87, writes that, since the Smythies book came out, "voices of three of the six species of Borneo Frogmouths have been recorded" and ends by saying that "Frogmouths do indeed have voices." This suggests that Tom may have been right in late 1959 to speculate that he was the first white man *knowingly* to hear the call of the frogmouth.

330 word from Bethlem: Letter from Dr. Kenneth Cameron to THH, dated March 10, 1960, now in the packet of Tom's Kuching papers given to me.

330–331 Reviving M-O: Tom's BBC interview on *People Today* (1960), and interviews of Humphrey Spender, Mollie Tarrant, Celia Fremlin Minchin, Ursula Trevelyan Mommens, Mary Fedden Trevelyan, and a woman whose anonymity I choose to preserve. These interviews also tell of Tom's pied piper techniques when researching *Britain Revisited* (London: Gollancz, 1961).

331 Naughton: THH letter to Sidney Bernstein, dated July 22, 1960, in Lord Bernstein's archive at Granada Headquarters.

332–335 The Freeman affair: Sources are (mostly taped) interviews of Professor Freeman and of his colleagues and friends at the Australian National University and elsewhere as well as members of the then Sarawak Museum staff; correspondence between Tom and Freeman, much of it provided me by Professor Freeman; and letters from Freeman to me.

333 total fraud: The Belgian's real name is on his birth and death certificates. Dr. G. Condominas, a famous French anthropologist, says that the Belgian presented one brilliant chapter toward a doctoral thesis to be done under his supervision but nothing more. Another famous French anthropologist, resident in Mexico, Prof. Guy Stresser-Péan, denies the Belgian's claims to have done fieldwork in Mexico or under him. Freeman states the man never presented proof of his German doctoral degree, (which, given the Belgian's scenario, would have had to have been obtained after a total of only two years of post-secondary school study). The Belgian claimed that records had been destroyed in a wartime fire. An account by someone who believed him states that the Belgian claimed to have been in the Resistance and in Nazi concentration camps; official records, however, only show that he was arrested for robbery as a teenager in Liege during the German occupation and was treated as a common offender: allowed visitors, mail, and packages, and soon released. The Belgian also claimed five years' fieldwork in Sarawak but actually was there for only eighteen months.

334 palace of pornography: My other informants who knew the Sarawak Museum and the art and life of the Baram, though some of them disliked or disapproved of Tom, never expressed to me, or in any other forum that I know of, any doubts or complaints about the art that Tom displayed in the museum. Nor did any of them see anything wrong with Tom displaying at the museum work that had been carved at Pig Lane. Indeed, except from Freeman, the display aspects of Tom's curatorship have received nothing but praise.

335 "It is the only time": Interview of the friend (whom I choose not to name) to whom Tom made this comment. Yet, although this episode did affect Freeman's *personal* reputation, nobody would deny (not even Tom) that Freeman was one of the best social anthropologists ever to do fieldwork in Sarawak; after Tom's departure from Sarawak, Freeman was soon again supervising young scholars there.

335 Professor Freeman's version: In 1998 I sent him a draft version of the 1960–1961 events, essentially the same as that appearing in this chapter, and asked if he wished to add his own version. He chose instead to edit my text to read as follows, and I agreed to add it to the book, properly labelled as to source:

> Within weeks of returning to Borneo, Tom was more deeply embroiled than ever in rows with various professional anthropologists. One of Tom's adversaries was Derek Freeman who, having completed at Cambridge a Ph.D., based on his two and a half years of field work among the Iban of Sarawak, had been appointed to a senior fellowship in the Research School of Pacific Studies at the Australian National University in Canberra.
>
> During the early 1950s, relations between Harrisson and Freeman had been guarded, for the two men had radically different values. Freeman insisted on the highest professional standards, while Tom loved to shock his interlocutors. Relations between them worsened when, in 1957, Freeman arranged to have an American student (who had been recommended to him by Margaret Mead) to do fieldwork among the Bisaya of the Limbang, a people in whom Harrisson was also interested. When Freeman visited the American student in the field in 1958, his researches were going well, but, for personal reasons, he returned to the United States, and they were never satisfactorily completed.
>
> Subsequent letters and meetings between Freeman and Tom aggravated suspicion and irritation on both sides. Tom offered and then rescinded an invitation for Freeman to visit Niah. Then, in March 1958, smoldering with resentment at what he perceived as Freeman's contempt for his anthropological efforts, Tom launched an outright attack on the profession of anthropology in general and on Derek Freeman in particular. It happened in Tom's car when he was driving Freeman and a government official to the Kuching airport. Tom, Freeman recalls, "ranted and raved and abused me in every conceivable way."
>
> Two years later, the next student Freeman sent to Sarawak was (to all appearances) much more impressive, a highly articulate Belgian with a Ph.D. from a German university, fieldwork in Mexico under a renowned French anthropologist, and an aristocratic handle to his name. He was to work in the upper Rejang among the Kajang, a people even more interesting to Tom than the Bisaya.
>
> In reply to a letter from Tom telling Freeman he has heard of the Belgian's planned arrival and wished him well, Freeman dwelt on the new man's credentials. Tom met the Belgian within days of his arrival and wrote Freeman that he had "the makings of a deep 'seer' into Sarawak," adding that there was "room for one of these, especially around Belaga." But then Freeman wrote again, a few months later, to announce that the Belgian was proposing to expand his research project. He was proposing to make a comparative study of mythology, including, as well as the Kajang, the Kenyah, Kayan, Iban, Land Dayaks, and Melanau.
>
> Tom's negative response undoubtedly masked stronger feelings: ". . . I will think about this carefully. But are you SURE [the Belgian] is the man to do all this great job—and in what time, and with what reciprocal advantages to those of us who have spent years collecting raw material? . . ."

Freeman wrote back citing the man's many qualifications, adding that "very few anthropologists indeed have the experience and training of Dr. [X]; in fact, I cannot think of anyone better fitted to do the job proposed." It was not until 1961, after observing [the Belgian] at close quarters in Kuching, that Freeman instigated a full inquiry into his past history. It was then revealed that [the Belgian]'s credentials had been fabricated. "He was an imposter," Freeman recalls "of consummate effrontery" who had taken in all of the authorities at the Australian National University.

Although Tom, too, was taken in by [the Belgian], he was puzzled by something odd about him, and in late November 1960, Tom spent three days in Belaga trying to get a better fix on him. He found that the Belgian had had to move out of the long-house where he was living after having become involved in a political dispute among local factions. Tom, in the course of trying to straighten things out, accused [Dr. X] of various acts of misconduct, while making it clear to the local chief that his loyalties were with him and not with the foreign interloper. Nonetheless, Tom agreed to the elaborate myth-collecting project and offered what the museum had in the way of research materials, manpower, and equipment for what he now called "Operation Belagalore."

Early in 1961, after the Belgian had got into trouble again, Tom wrote to Freeman: "Soon now . . . social anthropology must have to face up fully to the question of the extent to which it is responsible for the sorts of persons sent to the field. . . . This is my 14th year in the ring-side seat observing the process— and BOY is it beginning to add up. . . ."

Tom then returned to Belaga, and having become drunk launched an unrestrained verbal attack on [Dr. X] in the presence of the local chiefs. So humiliating and traumatic was this attack that the Belgian suffered a breakdown. He then sent to the Australian National University a graphic account of what had happened.

In Canberra, Freeman was about to set out on a protracted tour of Southeast Asia during the course of which he would be continuing fieldwork among the Iban and visiting students in Sumatra and Sabah. He was asked to travel to Kuching to investigate what had happened and to discuss with the government of Sarawak Harrisson's attack on [Dr. X.].

The accounts of his behavior by senior government officers and others confirmed Freeman's view that Harrisson ought not to be holding the position in Sarawak of government ethnologist. In the Sarawak Museum, of which Harrisson was the curator, Freeman found objects, some of them pornographic, that had not been collected in the field but were being manufactured at Harrisson's bidding in the grounds of his house at Pig Lane. This, in Freeman's judgment, was a flagrant departure from professional curatorial practice, and, to draw attention to what Harrisson was up to, he smashed one of these inauthentic carvings that was on display in a building occupied by the British Council.

In Freeman's eyes, Harrisson, who lacked any formal training in anthropology, was not only a charlatan, but also, given the nature of his attack on [Dr. X], a psychopath, and in an attempt to collect further evidence for these conclusions he decided to call, as he had been invited to do, at Harrisson's house at Pig Lane.

The house was unoccupied, and Freeman, who had a camera with him, grasped the opportunity to photograph various of the pornographic carvings it contained. Then, having obtained the evidence he was seeking, he informed the government of Sarawak that he would be leaving for Singapore that afternoon.

In Singapore, he decided to fly to Great Britain to discuss the evidence he had gathered with a colleague, the professor of psychological medicine at the University of Edinburgh. But, on reflection, he elected instead to disembark in Karachi and return to the Australian National University. While in Kuching, in the throes of trying to comprehend the actions of Harrisson and [the Belgian], Freeman had experienced a cognitive abreaction: a sudden and deep realization of the inadequacy of the assumptions of contemporary anthropology. It had become his guiding passion in life to radically reexamine these assumptions and to work toward a more scientific anthropological paradigm.

Tom remarked to his friends later: "It is the only time in my life when I was able to drive someone round the bend without even seeing him." Freeman had indeed been driven around the bend in the sense that his vision of anthropology had been transformed and, since 1961, his energies have been given to the development of an evolutionary aproach to the study of human behavior.

Regarding Freeman's evolutionary approach: For a further statement of Freeman's views on the direction he thinks anthropology should be taking, see the Afterword to his book, *The Fateful Hoaxing of Margaret Mead* (Boulder, Colorado, USA: Westview, 1999).

## 38. The British Sun Sets on Borneo

337–338    sheltered jungle conditions: Barbara Harrisson, *Orang-utan* (London: Collins, 1962) and George Schaller, "The Orang-utan in Sarawak," *Zoologica* (NY) XLVI, 6 (1961): 73–82.

338    Schaller: Interviews of Barbara Harrisson and George Schaller.

338    *Orang-Utan*: See Desmond Morris' (unsigned) critical review, *Times Literary Supplement* (August 13, 1962).

338    Zuckerman: A copy of his letter to Barbara, dated April 19, 1965, is in the Zuckerman Archive, University of East Anglia.

338    "although it is hard": Interview of Dr. Schaller's colleague, Dr. Allan Rabinowitz, now director of science in Asia at the Wildlife Conservation Society.

339    "Right now I have four": August 6, 1961, letter to Professor W. R. Geddes, at the University of Sydney. Tom's carbon copy of this letter was in a packet of his Kuching papers that was eventually passed to me.

340    Tom and Barbara: Interviews of Barbara Harrisson and various people who saw them frequently at that time.

## 39. Guerrilla Again

My main published sources on the Brunei Rebellion are Harold James and Denis Sheil-Small, *The Undeclared War: The Story of the Indonesian Confrontation 1962–1966* (London: Leo Cooper, 1971); THH's account of the first days of the Brunei Rebellion in "Chronicle," *Sarawak Gazette* (January 31, 1963): 3–6; and Michael Carver, *War Since 1945* (London: Weidenfeld and Nicholson, 1980). Barbara read to me from her diary for the period, and I interviewed Michael Chong and Richard and Dorothy Morris; corresponded with General Sir Walter Walker and Colonel J. P. Cross; and read Cross' *Jungle Warfare: Experiences and Encounters* (London: Guild Publishing, 1989).

My main source on *Konfrontasi* is Peter Dickens, *SAS: Secret War in South-East Asia* (London: Greenhill Books, 1991). Also published in paperback as *SAS: The Jungle Frontier: 22 Special Air Service Regiment in the Borneo Campaign 1963–1966* (Kuala Lumpur: S. Abdul Majeed and Co., 1991), its information is confirmed and expanded by the minutes of the first subcommittee meeting Tom chaired (included in the packet of Tom's Kuching papers given to me); an interview of the military intelligence man who liaised with Tom during *Konfrontasi*; a letter from Col. John Woodhouse (commanding the 22 SAS regiment in 1962–1963); and interviews of Major Jon Edwardes (commanding "A" Squadron of the 22 SAS in 1963 and commanding groups of "Cross-Border Scouts" in 1964–1965), the late G. A. T. "Tony" Shaw, (chief secretary of Sarawak in 1962–1963), Peter Tinggom (a district officer in 1963), and Lord Zuckerman.

344    nearly as unconventional: Other sources on Walker are Timothy Green, *The Adventurers*, p. 147; and Tom Pocock, *Fighting General—The Public and Private Campaigns of General Sir Walter Walker* (London: Collins, 1973).

344–345    "If the Indonesian threat" and "The SAS liked Tom": Pocock, *Fighting General*, portions of which were transcribed and sent to me by General Walker.

345    Dickens: *SAS*, p. 54.

345    "elaborate equipment": Major Jon Edwardes, who had commanded "A" Squadron of the 22 SAS in 1963, recalled to me in 1993 that Roy Henry (later Sir Roy Henry), then heading the Sarawak constabulary, insisted that the Border Scouts, who were to be attached to the police as an auxiliary force, be given uniforms, which turned out to be a mistake, since it led others to treat them as if they were a regular force. Eventually, this requirement was rescinded and they reverted, much of the time, to being barefoot guerrillas again. Sir Roy declined to be interviewed or to answer questions by letter.

346    "proper military forces": Philip Warner, *The Special Air Service* (London: Wm. Kimber, 1971), p. 226.

346    Zuckerman: Interview of Lord Zuckerman, July 14, 1992.

## 40. Cornell Connections

347 Cornell: Interviews of Professor and Mrs. George McT. Kahin and Professor Stanley J. O'Connor of Cornell University, Professor Michael Leigh of the University of Sydney and the University of Malaysia, Sarawak, and Dr. Robert Pringle.

347–348 Peace Corps volunteers: Their strengths and weaknesses were described to me by Jonathan Darrah, an ex-Peace Corps volunteer in Sarawak and subsequently Peace Corps director in the Philippines. For Tom's attitude toward them, I draw on my own recollections.

348 Hirst affair: Hirst claimed that he had written repeatedly, without result, to ask Tom to return the diaries, before he stormed into Tom's office. The Hirst diaries cannot have covered much of what Tom wrote about. They start with Hirst's arrival, two months after Tom jumped into Bario, end well before Tom's move against the Fujino Tai, and are devoted chiefly to the easternmost part of SEMUT l's territory, an area only briefly mentioned in *World Within*. Unable to locate Hirst, I pieced together my account of the row about the diaries from documents contained in Tom's papers from Kuching and those in the Australian War Memorial Library.

348 "We don't drink now" and "I got this for you": Interview of Fred Sanderson.

348 a courtly Sarawak Malay to whom Tom . . . had been rude: An informant who shall remain nameless recalled to me Tom's having been discourteous years earlier to Haji OPENG bin Abang Sapi'ee, who by now was Sarawak's governor.

349 "practically a piece of guano": Letter to "B. G.," November 16, 1965. Tom's carbon copy of the letter was left in Kuching and later passed to me.

349 170 pages of his "The Malays of South-West Sarawak": See *Sarawak Museum Journal (SMJ)* XI, 23–24 (1964): 341–511.

350 "How old is this carving": Green, *The Adventurers*, p. 140; this is my source for most of this description of the museum.

350 Bongkissam: Lucas Chin, "Summary of Archeological Work in Sarawak," *Sarawak Museum Occasional Paper No. 1* (Kuching: Sarawak Museum, 1977), p. III, and Tom Harrisson and Stanley J. O'Connor, Jr., "The 'Tantric Shrine' Excavated at Santubong," *SMJ*, XV, 30–31 (1967): 201–222.

351 "we are going to do a dig": The results of this dig, together with intermittent study of Sabah materials from previous years, resulted in a book by Tom and Barbara (written mostly by Barbara), *The Prehistory of Sabah* (Kota Kinabalu: Sabah Society, 1971).

351 The facts are otherwise: Interviews of Datuk Lucas Chin and Pengiran Shariffuddin, former curators of the Sarawak and Brunei Museums, respectively, as well as Barbara Harrisson.

351   expatriate women and ceramics: Interviews of Eine Moore, Charmian
      Woodfield, and Barbara Harrisson and Tom's correspondence with Carla
      Zainie in the packet of his Kuching papers that were passed to me.

## PART SEVEN: A New World, 1967–1976

### 41. Dark Days

The main source is the collection of letters and other documents compiled
by Charmian Woodfield (who made copies for me), filled out by interviews
of Barbara Harrisson, the Woodfields, Prof. Wilhelm G. Solheim II, Datuk
Lucas Chin, Prof. Michael Leigh, Eine Moore, Lindsay Wall, and Pengiran
Shariffuddin.

357   Solheim on stratigraphy: Looking back on the Niah dig from a 1998 van-
      tage point, Solheim believes the Harrissons would have had a better
      response from the archaeological community if they had published a final
      report, with (ideally) stratigraphy shown in photographs and artifacts
      reported and dates correlated with the stratigraphy. In their defense, one
      may note they had planned to return and complete their work and were
      unable to do so (though it is by no means certain that they would have
      used stratigraphy in any event).

357   proper accessions procedures: Interview of Barbara Harrisson, with con-
      firmation in interviews of Eine Moore and Lindsay Wall (both of whom
      worked on ceramics at the Sarawak Museum) on how things were acces-
      sioned and labeled.

358   Bishop Galvin: Letters from Bishop Galvin to THH during the 1960s in
      the possession of Prof. Jérôme Rousseau of McGill University and a March
      18, 1976, letter from Galvin to Dr. Bedlington (given to me).

358   "We are beginning to get fed-up": Letter from Benedict Sandin to
      Charmian Woodfield, in her possession.

359   Max: Interviews of Max and his doctor in 1987.

359   "marking time": THH letter to Lord Bernstein, May 22, 1967, in the
      Bernstein archive, Granada Headquarters.

### 42. Tom the Teacher

Most of the material for this chapter comes from interviews of and diary
readings by Barbara Harrisson.

360   "On occasion he would suddenly duck": Green, *The Adventurers*, pp. 151–
      152.

360–361  Trocki: Interview.

361   Bedlington: My interview is the source of all quotations of him.

361   An Australian woman: Elaine McKay, in a letter to Mrs. Zainie, who sent
      it with her comments to Charmian Woodfield, who kindly photocopied it
      for me.

361  hinted over dinner: The Kahins, interviewed in 1993, did not recall this conversation or hearing these rumors at the time, but Barbara Harrisson's diary for September 17, 1967, mentions a "disastrous evening with the Kahins" in which "Kahin goes off the deep end on TH transports from Sarawak."

361  tiny Sarawak pension: According to Barbara Harrisson, Tom had taken half of his pension (then worth about U.S. $30,000) in cash in 1967, when he left Sarawak, and had banked it in London. By the time he died, it appears that virtually all that money had been spent. The pension referred to here is the other half, which he had arranged to receive in monthly payments of about U.S. $200.

362  Woodfield's two letters to the editor of *The Straits Times* (Kuala Lumpur) are in the November 18 and 30, 1967, issues, respectively.

362  Tom at Kuching's airport: Interviews of several people who came to see him there.

362  He managed somehow to keep the news even from Barbara: Her diary for that day confirms this. She learned of the banning eventually from Sarawak officials.

363  rutting: Interview of a male friend at Cornell.

363  Sandin's visit: Barbara Harrisson's diary and interview of Dr. Stanley Bedlington.

364–365  Saving the tamaraw (*Anoa mindorensis*, also known as *Bubalus mindorensis*): Interview of Richard Fitter and his articles in *Oryx* (1973–1974) and (1975–1976); and THH, "The Tamaraw and Philippine Conservation" in *Biological Conservation*, Volume III, 1 (Essex: Elsevier Publishing Co., October 1970), pp. 45–46. The most recent tamaraw figures come from Charles Santipillai, "The Status, Distribution and Conservation of Tamaraw (*Bubalus mindorensis*) in the Philippines," (Bogor, Indonesia: WWF/IUCN Project, April 1990).

364–365  Trying to save the Philippine (monkey-eating) eagle: See Les Line, "Giants of the Eagle Kind," *International Wildlife* (Vienna, Virginia) (July/Aug 1996): cover and 29–37.

365  Baroness Forani: Interview of her daugher, Ludmilla Forani-Rhein.

365  "This big heavy volume": Gale Dixon, Book review in the *Sarawak Museum Journal* (*SMJ*) (1970): 420–422.

365–366  two "data papers": THH and Stanley J. O'Connor, *Excavations of the Prehistoric Iron Industry in West Borneo*: I, "Raw Materials and Industrial Waste"; II, "Associated Artifacts and Ideas," Southeast Asia Program, Department of Asia Studies, Data Paper 72 (Ithaca: Cornell University, April 1969); and THH and Stanley J. O'Connor, *Gold and Megalithic Activity in Prehistoric and Recent West Borneo*, Southeast Asia Program, Department of Asia Studies, Data Paper 77 (Ithaca: Cornell University, 1970).

366    "maddening" and "so inflated": William Watson, *Bulletin of the School of Oriental and African Studies* XXXIV, 1 (1971): 187–188.

366    Recent views on THH and O'Connor's work on the iron industry of Santubong: Recent discoveries and reexamination of earlier data have led O'Connor and others to discard some of this work's conclusions: that the Santubong earliest remains were T'ang rather than Sung, and that Santubong's iron was made for a foreign market and was produced by a method using crucibles. But the sheer amount of ancient pottery uncovered by Tom's delta excavations has led one scholar to conclude that the site was even more important than Tom thought it was, i.e., that Santubong was the famed "Po-Ni," the 10th to 13th century Borneo port mentioned in Sung dynasty chronicles. See three articles by Jan Wisseman Christie: (1) "On Po-Ni: The Santubong Sites of Sarawak," *SMJ* XXIV, 55 (December 1985): 77–89; (2) "Trade and the Santubong Iron Industry," in Ian and Emily Glover, eds., *Southeast Asian Archaeology 1986: Proceedings of the First Conference of the Association of Southeast Asian Archaeologists in Western Europe, Institute of Archaeology, University College London, 8–10th September 1986* (Oxford: BAR International Series 561, 1990), pp. 231–239; and (3) "Ironworking in Sarawak," in J. W. Christie and V. T. King, eds., *Metal-working in Borneo: Essays on Iron- and Silver-working in Sarawak*, Occasional Papers No. 15 (University of Hull, Centre for South-East Asian Studies, 1988), pp. 1–27. For O'Connor's reply, see his "Tuyères and the Scale of the Santubong Iron Industry," in R. Brown and N. Eilenberg, eds., *Leading a Buddhist Life: Essays in Honor of Jean Boisselier* (Bangkok, Silpakon, 1997).

366    "Lengthy and fascinating": George F. Dales, *Man* IV, 4 (Dec. 1971).

366    More recent works drawing upon THH and O'Connor's data paper on ancient gold and megaliths in Southeast Asia: Susan Rodgers, *Power and Gold: Jewelry from Indonesia, Malaysia and the Philippines* (Barbier-Muller Museum, Asia Society, and Smithsonian Institute, January 1985); Michel Jacq-Hergoualc'h, *La Civilisation de Ports-Entrepôts du Sud Kedah (Malaysia) Ve-XIVe siècle* (Paris: Editions l'Harmattan, 1992); John Miksic, *Old Javanese Gold* (Singapore: Ideation, 1989); and Christophe Munier, *Sacred Rocks and Buddhist Caves in Thailand* (Bangkok: White Lotus Press, 1998).

366    "A reviewer of the authors' previous": I. C. Glover, *Bulletin of the School of Oriental and African Studies* XXXV, Pt. 2 (1972): 413–415.

### 43. Escape from the New World

How the M-O Archive came into existence comes from an interview of Dr. Angus Calder and is confirmed by correspondence with Lord Briggs.

368    "a keen student of broadcasting": Asa Briggs, *The BBC: The First Fifty Years* (Oxford: Oxford University Press, 1985), p. 151.

368–372  Christine: I knew her slightly, but almost all the information on her and her relationship with Tom comes from interviews of her daughter, Baroness Ludmilla Forani-Rhein, with Tom's feelings toward her reported by several of his friends in my interviews of them. Facts of her war career come from the Belgian *Sûreté d'Etat;* from interviews of Baron Arthur Haulot and Count William Ugeux, who was a parachutist with the Belgian Resistance; the chapter on SAARF in Len Whittaker, *Some Talk of Private Armies* (Harpenden, Hertfordshire: Albanium Publishing, 1984), pp. 80–83; and from Leroy Thompson, "*SAARF: L'Unité Ultra-sécrète du Supreme Headquarters Allied Expeditionary Force, AMilitaria* 6 (Sept.–Oct. 1968): 16–20.

369  "a wiry, tanned blonde:" Carlton Lake, *In Quest of Dalí* (New York: Paragon House, 1990), p. 95.

374  Letter to Mary Adams: THH to Mary Adams, December 28, 1970, Mary Adams file in the M-O Archive.

## 44. Second Youth

The chief sources are interviews of Dorothy Sheridan, Ludmilla Forani-Rhein, Gillian Webster, Peter and Betsan Harrisson, Tom's pretty Australian cousin (who recalls Tom in the tree and Christine plucking herbs) whose name I prefer not to give, Barbara Crewe, and Dr. Stanley Bedlington.

375  "Tom Harrisson, the celebrated": *The Times* (April 24, 1970).

379  award: On October 30, 1972, he received the Queen's permission to wear the insignia of Darjah Dato Seri Laila Jasa, (somewhat like a knighthood, with no stipend) conferred on him by His Highness, the Sultan of Brunei. This may have been the decoration mentioned here.

379  The little "Sex-Teeth" notebook is in the M-O Archive.

379  "never drink alcohol": Letter from THH to Lord Medway, November 7, 1972, in Lord Cranbrook's possession.

381  "I shall never do that": THH to Neville Haile, who told me.

## 45. Professor At Last

382  "one in the eye": Interview of Dorothy Sheridan.

382  "first exercise": THH and H. D. Willcock, "A Mass-Observation Appeal," *New Statesman* (April 6, 1973).

382  "a slightly dotty enterprise": Jonathan Raban, "Night Out at the Blitz," *New Statesman* (July 30, 1976): 147.

384  "admirably, perhaps uniquely,": Stephen Koss, *The Observer* (August 1, 1976).

384–385  Stephen Spender, "People's War," *The Guardian* (July 29, 1976): 14.

385   "the best account": C. P. Snow, "When bombs fell," *Financial Times* (August 5, 1976).

385   "would bring into disrepute": Jonathan Raban, "Night Out at the Blitz," p. 147.

385   Lord Zuckerman's letter of protest: "Living Through the Blitz," *Times Literary Supplement* (November 26, 1976). In my 1992 interview of him, he repeated the sense of this letter.

385   "And miss all this?" and "Where's the gents": THH, *Living Through the Blitz* (London: Collins, 1976), pp. 128 and 222, respectively.

386   The new study Tom had in mind: Interview of Philip Ziegler, who took on the project later himself, publishing *Crown and People* (London: Collins, 1978); and of Diana Forrest, who worked for Tom in Brussels on it.

387   "Second birthday": Tom's personal papers in the M-O Archive.

387   "duty-bound not to communicate": I choose not to name the letter writer. The letter, dated July 14, 1975, is in Barbara Harrisson's possession.

387   "The loss of access to Sarawak": THH letter to Medway, in Lord Cranbrook's possession.

388   "This is perhaps the first Christmas": THH letter to Barbara published in "Tom Harrisson: Living and Working in Borneo," *Borneo Research Bulletin* VIII, 1 (April 1976): 25–30.

388–389   Tom's death: "Tourists Die in Crash," *Bangkok Post* (January 20, 1976).

## Epilogue

For the memorial meeting at the Royal Society of Arts, the sources include notes written by Mary Adams to Tom's literary executor James Fulton (shown to me by Barbara Crewe) and memos of phone messages from Mary Adams to Lord Bernstein (Granada Headquarters); an article in *The Times* of March 18, 1976, reporting on the memorial meeting; and notes and comments by Max Nicholson and Richard Fitter of their remarks at, and recollections of, the meeting.

390   "It is still bewildering": David Pocock, "Obituary: Tom Harrisson, OBE, DSO," *Royal Anthropological Institute News* 13 (March–April 1976).

390   Cremation in Wat That Thong: Interviews of Carl Trocki and of an anonymous bachelor friend of Tom's.

392   Asa Briggs: "Mr. Tom Harrisson," letter to *The Times* (January 23, 1976): 16.

392   "the most remarkable man": Letter from Lord Shackleton to me, July 14, 1992.

392   "one of the buccaneers": Richard Fitter, "Tom Harrisson DSO OBE," *Oryx* XIII (1975–1976): 423–425.

393      Charles Madge: Quotes come from his "The Birth of Mass-Observation," *Times Literary Supplement* (November 5, 1976): 1395. Madge declined to be interviewed, but I assume what he would have said would have been along these lines.

394      "We live and work in an age": Jonathan H. Kress, "Tom Harrisson, North Borneo, and Palawan: A Preliminary Assessment," *Asian Perspectives* XX, 1 (1977): 75–76.

394      "clad in singlet" and "I have often heard it said": Lord Medway, "Tom Harrisson, Ornithologist," *Journal of the Malaysian Branch of the Royal Asiatic Society* XLIX, 1 (1976): 143 and 144, respectively.

396      "much of his writing" and "would probably be unintelligible": Alastair Morrison, *Fair Land Sarawak* (Ithaca: Southeast Asia Program, 1993), p. 98.

396      Tom is still remembered: James Barclay asked the Bario longhouse elders in 1979. Their view has remained the same, according to younger Kelabits to whom I posed the question in 1991 and 1997.

396      Dorothy Sheridan: Interview.

396–397 Michael Chong: Interview.

397      Nic Hill: Interview.

397      Yusuf Puteh: Interview.

398      "an extraordinarily gifted" and "Not all his deeds": Morrison, *Fair Land Sarawak*, pp. 96 and 99, respectively.

398–399 "shoulder to shoulder with Wallace" and "To the ordinary people of Sarawak": Letter from Bishop Galvin to Dr. Bedlington, March 18, 1976, given to me.

399      "On one of those trips": Professor Stanley J. O'Connor, "Tom Harrisson and the Literature of Place," *Borneo Research Bulletin* VIII, 2 (September 1976): 78.

# Index

THH stands for Tom Harnett Harrisson. Italic page numbers refer to photographs and maps. Footnotes are followed by the letters "fn."

## About the Author

Born in New York City into a family of writers, Judith M. Heimann has spent much of her life in Western Europe and Southeast Asia, as a diplomat's wife and a diplomat herself. She first met Tom Harrisson while living in Borneo. Heimann spent a decade researching Harrisson's life, sifting through countless stories and rumors and traveling to four continents in the process. She has coauthored numerous country studies—on China, the South Pacific, and various Southeast Asian nations—published by the U.S. government, but this is her first biography.